Biofeedback and the Modification of Behavior

Aubrey J. Yates

The University of Western Australia
Nedlands, Western Australia

PLENUM PRESS · NEW YORK AND LONDON

Library of Congress Cataloging in Publication Data

Yates, Aubrey J
  Biofeedback and the modification of behavior.

  Includes bibliographical references and index.
  1. Biofeedback training. 2. Medicine, Psychosomatic. 3. Psychology, Pathological. I. Title.
BF319.5.B5Y37   152.1'88   79-400
ISBN 0-306-40226-2

© 1980 Plenum Press, New York
A Division of Plenum Publishing Corporation
227 West 17th Street, New York, N.Y. 10011

Printed in the United States of America

Preface

In this book, I have attempted to evaluate critically the very large literature which has accumulated in the area of biofeedback over the past 10–15 years. As might be expected in any area of psychology with clinical possibilities, the literature divides itself into two main categories—fundamental research studies and therapeutic studies. It is now apparent that the clinical applications of biofeedback have far outstripped their fundamental research bases, with the inevitable result that the initial wave of enthusiasm may be replaced with an unnecessarily severe skepticism. Either extreme position is unjustified. Biofeedback does represent an important new approach to the elucidation of the role played by internal systems in the adjustment of the organism to its environment. But its potential will only be revealed if its use in practice is soundly based on fundamental research. There are promising signs that this is being realized so that there is cause for optimism.

Aubrey J. Yates

Perth, Australia

A Note on the References

With the exception of no more than two or three papers, all the references in this book have been obtained and read. However, many of them were published in journals which will not be readily accessible to the reader who may be interested in consulting more directly particular articles which attract his attention. However, the volumes entitled *Biofeedback and Self-Control,* published annually since 1971 by Aldine/Atherton have reprinted a significant proportion of the references listed in this book, thus making them more generally accessible. A *Reader* was published simultaneously with the first volume of *Biofeedback and Self-Control* which collected together many of the historically important articles relevant to biofeedback.

In the references at the end of each chapter, the location of each article, if it has been reprinted, is indicated in parentheses at the end of the reference. The nomenclature should be understood to avoid confusion. *Biofeedback and Self-Control, 1973,* for example, reprints many articles published in 1973 (together with some earlier ones) but the volume itself was published in *1974.* The location of an article is indicated by reference to the year appearing on the *outside cover* of the volume, not to the year of publication (shown inside). Thus, the reference: 1973:6 refers to *Biofeedback and Self-Control, 1973* (which was published in 1974). As each article is clearly numbered in each volume, the number of the article is given, not the page numbers (which can easily be confused with the page numbers of the original paper). The nomenclature R:6 refers to the sixth article in the *Reader* (only one *Reader* volume was published).

It should be noted that a new journal, *Biofeedback and Self-Regulation,* commenced publication in 1976. At the time of writing this note, it is not known whether any articles published in this journal will be reprinted in the *Biofeedback and Self-Control* annuals.

Contents

CHAPTER 1

Some Antecedents of Biofeedback

Introduction

Biofeedback refers to the display of some aspect of the physiological functioning of the individual with the expectation that observation of the characteristics of the display will enable the individual to attain increased voluntary control over the physiological function being displayed. The means by which the increased voluntary control is attained is currently a matter of much controversy which will be considered in detail in a later chapter.

The wide public interest aroused by the development of biofeedback techniques over the past 10 years derived, in part at least, from the apparent exotic possibilities inherent in its use. The early experiments on the enhancement of alpha activity in the brain attracted the attention of those for whom the attainment of higher states of consciousness is a main aim in life, since alpha enhancement appeared to offer a new and exciting way of inducing such states. Not unnaturally, this interpretation of the "meaning" of biofeedback produced an adverse reaction among the more hard-headed research scientists and therapists who had become interested in the possibility that biofeedback offered on the one hand of investigating the control of internal physiological processes not readily accessible to observation, and on the other hand of applying these techniques to the amelioration of certain disorders of physiological functioning. The situation has now been reached where the earlier claims relating to biofeedback have been toned down and a considerable scientific literature has accumulated which enables a sober appraisal of the status of biofeedback to be attempted. In this book, the technical and methodological aspects of biofeedback will be considered in some detail (Chapter 2); a thorough review of the empirical literature on the voluntary control of muscle activities (Chapter 3), autonomic activities (Chapter 4), and the electrical activity of the brain (Chapter 5), as well as

1

the use of biofeedback training in various other disorders (Chapter 6), will be provided. Following this, a detailed account of the various interpretations of how voluntary control with biofeedback is achieved will be given (Chapter 7) and an assessment will be made (Chapter 8) as to whether biofeedback has gone beyond the stage of being "a promise as yet unfulfilled" (Blanchard & Young, 1973).

New approaches in psychology rarely if ever appear unheralded; more usually, the attachment of an exotic name focuses attention dramatically on work which has been proceeding quietly for a long time. Biofeedback is no exception. No doubt at some future date a learned paper will be published tracing the antecedents of biofeedback into the mists of time, with appropriate quotations from Greek and Roman (or even earlier) writers.[1] In this chapter, the aim is more modest: namely, to outline some of the antecedents of biofeedback, as a result of which the work of the past 10 years will be placed in a historical context. No claim whatever in respect of completeness is made; the examples chosen represent either particular interests of the author, or serendipitous observations made in the course of reading the literature.

Bell and Visible Speech for the Deaf

Alexander Bell (1790–1865),[2] the grandfather of Alexander Graham Bell, was a Scotsman who became interested in speech and elocution as a result of his brief flirtation with the stage. He also developed a lifelong interest in the treatment of stuttering and produced a minor classic in the history of this problem, *Stammering and Other Impediments of Speech* (1836). These interests he communicated to his son Alexander Melville Bell (1810–1905), who employed the methods developed by his father to treat stuttering. Following a brief emigration to Newfoundland from 1838 to 1842, Melville Bell returned to London where he spent the next 25 years in research into the characteristics of the vocal organs. After writing books on *The Art of Reading* (1845) and *A New Elucidation of the Principles of Speech and Elocution* (1849), he worked on phonetics and the symbolic representation of speech which culminated in the invention of visible speech, the representation of sounds in the form of a phonetic script in which shapes stood for particular parts of the tongue employed (for consonants) and the breath aperture (for vowels). The system, developed after many trials and tribulations, was eventually described in his famous book *Visible Speech: The Science of Universal Alphabetics*. In 1847, his son Alexander Graham Bell (1847–1922) was born. In demonstrating the validity of his system for visible speech, Melville Bell made remarkable use of his talented but erratic son. He would invite learned philologists and other language experts to utter unusual and

---

[1]McMahon (1974) has already drawn an analogy between the aims of biofeedback and the approach to life of the Stoics.

[2]The material in this section is drawn from the recent biography of Bell by Bruce (1973).

outlandish sounds from equally unusual and outlandish languages (or from no language at all) which he would transcribe phonetically in terms of his system. His son, who would be waiting in another room, would then enter and, using only the phonetic transcription, would reproduce the sound with an uncanny accuracy that amazed the expert who had produced the sound.

It is interesting to note that Alexander Graham Bell's mother (Eliza Grace Symonds) was almost totally deaf, so deaf in fact that she played the piano with the mouthpiece of her ear tube resting on the sounding board which enabled her to hear every note and play expressively. In 1868, Alexander made the first use of his father's visible speech alphabet in the teaching of deaf children, showing them how to place their vocal organs in the correct position so as to produce the sounds represented by the phonetic script. Following the emigration of the family to Canada in 1870, Alexander spent many years (especially in Boston) teaching the principles of visible speech and its application to the training of profoundly deaf people in competition with the two other main approaches, the teaching of sign language and lip-reading, as advocated by another Scotsman, Braidwood, and by Howe (who taught the famous blind and deaf Laura Bridgman). He described his work in a celebrated article published in 1872 in the *American Annals of the Deaf and Dumb*. While the use of the visible-speech technique is not strictly a biofeedback approach, Alexander subsequently developed approaches which did indeed involve genuine feedback. After considering the possibility of transmitting vibrations which would enable lip-readers to distinguish /p/ from /b/ in words spoken by other people, he became interested in two inventions made by other scientists of the period. One was the phonautograph, invented by a Frenchman, Léon Scott. The subject spoke or sang into the larger opening of a cone, across the narrow end of which was a diaphragm which vibrated. The vibrations were detected by a cork attached to a small rod, fixed at one end of the cone but free to oscillate at the other. To the free end of the rod was attached a brush which produced a trace of the vibrations on a smoked glass moving past the brush, thus producing a trace of the wave form (this was, of course, the precursor of the smoked-drum kymograph, used extensively by early psychologists). The other invention was the "manometric flame" of Rudolph Koenig. In this invention, a membrane was stretched across a hole in a gas pipe and vibrations produced by sounds resulted in variations in the shape of the gas flame by making the gas pressure vary. These variations were reflected from four mirrors mounted on the circumference of a revolving wheel, producing broad bands of light which had a characteristic pattern of light for each sound. As Bruce has reported:

> "If we can find the definite shape due to each sound," Bell wrote home, "what an assistance in teaching the deaf and dumb!!" The teacher could show them what a sound looked like in the manometric flame and then help them experiment until they reproduced it. "In any future publication concerning Visible Speech, pictures of the vibrations due to each sound could be given, and thus the sounds be identified through all eternity." (1973, p. 111)

This visible display of the speech sound was, of course, the precursor of the sonagram which enables interpretation of the various characteristics of speech. Thus, although Alexander Graham Bell is remembered primarily for the invention of the telephone, his work on the teaching of speech to the deaf can be regarded as a genuine antecedent to biofeedback.[3]

Bell's techniques have exercised a profound influence on the teaching of the deaf down to the present day, with persistent attempts being made to improve his system or develop new approaches.[4] The work to be reported in Chapter 6 on modern methods of biofeedback training of the deaf merely uses more sophisticated instrumentation (specifically, computer-generated displays of visible speech) to achieve what Bell did with the crude apparatus available to him 100 years ago.

Tarchanoff and the Voluntary Control of Heart Rate

Tarchanoff was one of the most distinguished physiologists of the second half of the nineteenth century. In 1885, he published a classical paper on voluntary acceleration of the heartbeat, a paper in which he reports investigating practically every aspect of the voluntary control of heart rate to be found in modern research. Instead of following the current tendency of group design studies, he utilized the experimental methods developed by his great predecessor Claude Bernard (1865/1957), who stressed the hypothetico-deductive approach applicable to the study of the single case. Tarchanoff was not the first to observe apparent voluntary control of the heartbeat,[5] but he was suspicious as to whether genuine voluntary control by the "will" had been obtained or whether muscular mediation was involved, particularly mediation via respiratory changes. Consequently, when a suitable patient became available, he instigated a long series of careful observations under conditions which were as controlled as he could make them. The subject, who appeared able to accelerate his heart rate at will, denied that he used "pleasant images" or muscle activity and maintained that he accelerated his heart rate by an "act of will" and by "concentrating his attention," but as he showed exceptional overall voluntary control of muscle activity, Tarchanoff carried out a series of studies in an attempt to rule out (or, conversely, to implicate) mediating processes. In his first experiments, Tarchanoff satisfied himself that the accelerated heart rate could not be a function of changes in respiration rate, and confirmed this by manipulating respiration rate and showing that there was no reliable relationship between changes in the two variables.

---

[3]For Bell's continuing involvement in the training of the deaf and particularly his long relationship with Helen Keller, see Bruce (1973), especially Chapters 29 and 30.

[4]See, for example, reviews of modern work by Platt (1947), Provonost (1947), Martony (1968), and Pickett (1968).

[5]He provides a summary of earlier observations.

Next, he showed that acceleration of heart rate was followed (not preceded or accompanied immediately) by vasoconstriction at the extremities, and that a rise in blood pressure occurred some time after the acceleration of heart rate, remaining at this higher level for some time after heart rate had returned to normal. That is, it appeared that increased heart rate produced increased blood pressure. But the diminution in peripheral circumference (vasoconstriction) lasted only as long as heart rate was elevated. He concluded that the elevated heart rate was therefore produced directly via peripheral blood vessel constriction and not indirectly via increased blood pressure. He further observed that as heart rate increased, peripheral temperature decreased by 1–2°C in the hands, but increased in the face, forehead, and cheek. Overall, therefore, he concluded that heart-rate increases resulted from voluntary effects on the regulatory nerve centers and nerve pathways of the heart, effects which were directly, not indirectly, innervated. With respect to the regulatory mechanisms which might be involved, Tarchanoff considered two possibilities: acceleration might result from depression of the heart-slowing centers believed to be located in the medulla oblongata, or from arousal of the heart-speeding centers believed to be located in the upper part of the spinal cord in the region of the neck. He reasoned that if the first mode of control were operative, heart acceleration should be accompanied by rapid pulse changes, whereas the second mode of control should lead to slow pulse changes. Since he found empirically that voluntary acceleration of the heart was accompanied by slow pulse changes, he concluded that heart-rate acceleration is mediated via voluntary alteration of the spinal centers which result in accelerated heart rate. At this point, Tarchanoff ran out of steam as it were, for, in probing further, he could only conclude that the control of the spinal speeding centers was itself mediated via activity in some unknown "higher" (cortical) center of the brain. Nonetheless, however, Tarchanoff's systematic approach allowed him to rule out fairly conclusively some possible low-level mediating variables (such as respiration) and remains an object lesson in controlled research which appears to have been lost on modern researchers who remain slaves to the group approach.

Interest in Tarchanoff's demonstrations was renewed intermittently during the next 80 years. Thus, West and Savage (1918) reported the case of a young medical student with normal heart function and no other abnormalities who was able to increase his heart rate by 27 bpm from a rather low resting level of 69 bpm. In the same year, Carter and Wedd (1918) examined a 29-year-old male who could voluntarily initiate tachycardia (rapid heartbeat) by "various slight abrupt muscular efforts" but who could not reduce his thus elevated heart rate via muscular relaxation. However, the subject apparently could reduce his self-induced tachycardia by "some conscious subjective effort." King (1920) studied the ability of a young man of 26 with tachycardia to increase and decrease his heart rate. However, the variability of his resting level heart rate made it difficult to interpret the results obtained by King using various procedures. Perhaps

King's most important finding was that pressure on the left or right vagus nerve failed to produce any marked changes in heart rate. In spite of the variability of his results, King concluded that voluntary control of heart rate could be achieved by a primary decrease in vagus inhibition, augmented by accelerator influences. Nearly 20 years later, Ogden and Shock (1939)[6] reported on results obtained with two subjects who voluntarily accelerated their heart rate while measurements were made of systolic and diastolic blood pressure, respiration rate, ventilation volume, oxygen uptake, and carbon dioxide output to determine whether changes in general metabolic functioning were associated with heart-rate acceleration. The possible role played by muscle tensing in the arm and leg was also investigated. Their results suggested that voluntary acceleration of heart rate was invariably accompanied by hyperventilation with excess elimination of carbon dioxide and a true increase of metabolism with oxygen utilization in excess of metabolic requirement. McClure (1959) described the case of a 44-year-old male who, it was claimed, induced complete heart stoppage voluntarily, sinus arrest occurring for 5 sec, followed by several atrioventricular nodal beats and the resumption of a slow heart rate at 55 bpm.

Although all of these studies constitute barely more than uncontrolled, anecdotal accounts of the alleged voluntary control of heart rate, they undoubtedly provided a background of persistent reports of such control against which the large-scale investigations of the voluntary control of heart rate, blood pressure, and other autonomic functions were instituted some years later, utilizing biofeedback displays and reinforcers for success.

Bair and Woodworth and the Voluntary Control of Muscle Function

One year after the publication of Tarchanoff's studies of the voluntary control of heart rate, Schäfer, Canney, and Tunstall (1886) succeeded in making the first reliable measurements of the rate of muscle contraction in man in response to "volitional impulses." Some years later, Bair (1901) produced a major study of the voluntary control of the retrahens muscle of the ear. He chose to work with this muscle because it is completely isolated from all other muscles, it is not normally under voluntary control (but is supplied with motor nerves, indicating it should be possible to control it), and it contracts clearly and immediately. The methodology used by Bair is of great interest. First, he produced reflex contraction in the muscle by electrical stimulation, with the subject remaining passive but attending to the contraction so as (in the terminology then in vogue) to obtain an "idea" of the contraction which could then be used to obtain voluntary control. Then the subject was instructed to try to increase voluntarily the amount of movement produced by electrical stimulation at the time the reflex

---

[6]This paper contains a list of all known studies on voluntary heart acceleration from the time of Tarchanoff's observations to the publication of the paper.

was involuntarily produced, or to diminish the effect of the reflex stimulation by inhibiting movement. Finally, in the absence of electrical stimulation the subject was required to try to produce movement in the muscle voluntarily. These experiments were a failure; in the absence of electrical stimulation, voluntary control was not achieved, nor did Bair believe that any of his subjects had been able to increase or diminish the reflex produced by stimulation, even though some of his subjects felt that they could. He concluded that either he had not succeeded in giving his subjects an "idea" of the movement by reflex stimulation or that they were unable to utilize the "idea" to achieve voluntary control. He proceeded to associate involuntary retrahens movement with the movement of associated muscles which *were* under voluntary control by getting his subjects to bite their jaws together or vigorously raise their brows, both of which movements are associated with retrahens contraction. Under these conditions, a considerable degree of voluntary control of the retrahens muscle was achieved. Bair then required his subjects to inhibit activity in the associated muscles and contract only the retrahens. Not only were his subjects now able to do this, but they were subsequently able to achieve differential control, that is, contract the retrahens muscle in one ear while simultaneously inhibiting contraction of the muscle in the other ear. He stressed the importance, in achieving differential control, of not trying initially to contract one muscle while keeping the other at rest. Rather, the trick was to withdraw attention from the muscle to be inhibited and concentrate only on the muscle to be contracted. The degree of differential control obtained by one of Bair's subjects is clearly shown in Figure 1. In studying the "uncoupling" of the retrahens muscle response from the complex into which it was initially locked, Bair had continued to use electrical stimulation to increase the

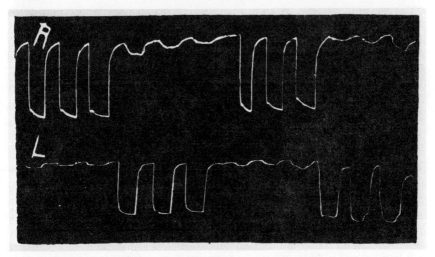

Figure 1. Differential bilateral control of the retrahens muscle of the left and right ears. (From Bair, 1901, Curve X.)

magnitude of the response (again, presumably to allow the subject to "observe" what was happening more closely). Subsequently, however, he repeated these experiments without the use of electrical stimulation and found that voluntary control over the retrahens muscle could be achieved, provided use was made of associated muscles which were already under voluntary control. From all of these studies Bair drew three important conclusions:

1. Before voluntary control over a muscle is acquired it takes more than the idea of the movement of that muscle, in order to be able to reproduce the movement.
2. We first get control over a muscle in a group, and then only can we single it out and get independent control over it.
3. The more closely the attention can be directed to a movement to be made and the more nearly the part of the movement desired not to be made can, for the time being, be forgotten, the more likely is the desired movement to be accomplished. (1901, p. 487)

Bair's achievement was a truly remarkable one, anticipating not only most of the important methodological aspects of modern research in biofeedback (many of which are, however, still ignored) but stressing the importance of taking into account the role of integrated muscle activity in relation to the specific muscle under investigation, a point of great importance in therapeutic applications of biofeedback but one which also has been largely ignored in modern research and therapy.[7]

In the same year that Bair published the results of his brilliant experiments, Woodworth (1901) reported his studies on the voluntary control of the force of movement. His subjects were required to "deliver a blow" and the extent of the upward movement prior to delivery of the blow was correlated with the force of the blow. Several variations (such as making the extent of the upward movement identical on each occasion, but with a different force involved) on this basic condition were studied. Woodworth provided his subjects with feedback by letting them view a record of the upward movement. He found that the feedback display did not help to increase the accuracy of the force with which the blow was delivered when blows of equal force were required and concluded that direct feedback from the muscle sense is necessary and is the critical factor in improving performance to a set criterion.

The role of muscle tension in the voluntary control of many of the functions of the body remained high over the succeeding years with particular emphasis being directed toward the maladaptive effects of abnormally high levels of tension and the beneficial effects of reducing such high levels. Perhaps the most important work during this period was that of Jacobson, the pioneer of progressive relaxation training. Jacobson (1925) reported that three subjects with excessive esophageal spasms which made it difficult to swallow food were able to overcome their problems with minimal training in relaxation of the relevant muscles. Later (Jacobson, 1939) he investigated the role of muscle tension in

[7]The significance of Bair's research will be appreciated if the reader manages to persist as far as Chapters 7 and 8 of this book.

blood pressure. He inserted electrodes into the arm flexor muscles below the nervous equator of Piper (occasionally elsewhere) and trained subjects with normal blood pressure and patients with chronic vascular hypertension to relax the forearm muscle. Normal subjects in the resting state manifested no relationship between forearm muscle activity and either systolic or diastolic blood pressure, and similar findings were reported for the patients trying to relax before they had been trained. He claimed that following training in muscle relaxation there was a tendency for both systolic and diastolic blood pressure to fall (although in fact the results were not very clear-cut). He concluded:

> Both diastolic and systolic phases have tended to fall with advancing relaxation. In general, the findings suggest that blood pressure tends to vary to a certain extent with the tension in the total mass of skeletal musculature; but the possibility remains that certain muscle groups are of particular moment, specifically the abdominal muscles. (1939, p. 1210)

Thus, at a very early stage Jacobson raised the specificity/generality issue which will be given extensive attention later in this book (see Chapter 7). Jacobson (1940) later reported evidence suggesting that muscle relaxation is accompanied by a reduction in heart rate. Jacobson (1955, 1973) must also be given credit as one of the pioneers in the use of feedback in muscle-relaxation training.[8]

It will have been noted that Jacobson (1939) used implanted electrodes which enable the detection of the activity of specific muscles without interference from surrounding muscles. Later developments have shown that the use of implanted electrodes enables the detection and voluntary control of single motor units and this development must be regarded as an important antecedent of biofeedback, insofar as the precision of the results obtained served as a definite encouragement to the wider use of biofeedback. Priorities are difficult to assign here, but three investigators should perhaps be singled out for mention. Hefferline (1958) and Hefferline, Keenan, and Harford (1959), actually using surface electrodes, demonstrated remarkable ability in normal subjects to control voluntarily very small muscular movements. Hefferline displayed activity of the masseter muscle in the form of visual feedback and required the subject to control the display by very small jaw movements. With practice, some of his subjects were able to discriminate muscle changes that were of the order of 10 nV. Some years later, Basmajian (1963) and Carlsöö and Edfeldt (1963), using implanted electrodes, reported equally astonishing control of precisely located single motor units with feedback, although Basmajian had undoubtedly been working on the problem for many years before his influential paper was published.[9]

All of this work culminated in two studies which opened the way to the application of these techniques to the treatment of abnormalities of function with biofeedback. Marinacci and Horandi (1960) described nine areas in which bio-

---

[8] Jacobson (1938, 1970) has reported his experimental and clinical work in detail in these two books.
[9] The work of Hefferline, Basmajian, and Carlsöö and Edfeldt is described in more detail in Chapter 3.

feedback might be useful: inability to initiate nerve impulses, as in auditory aphasia; where some nerve cells have escaped destruction but are not transmitting impulses; in cases of reversible physiological block due to local edema (for example, cellulitis in one extremity); inability of the patient to reactivate a muscle after prolonged nonuse (for example, inhibition due to pain); regeneration of nerve following a lesion; where substitute muscles have taken over the tasks of a nonfunctioning muscle which has recovered but is not being used; following complete paralysis with considerable destruction of lower motor neurones; as a result of functional paralysis leading to atrophy of muscle; and in cases of excessive muscle tension. Essentially, they were arguing that, provided some residual muscle function remained, and provided it could be detected and displayed, then it might well be a base from which to build. And indeed it has been shown that there are instances in which it is possible, particularly with the use of implanted electrodes, to detect residual muscle function where standard neurological and clinical tests reveal nothing and the patient himself believes the muscle to be totally paralyzed. Marinacci and Horandi (1960), using implanted electrodes and auditory feedback in the form of a musical tone or a click,[10] provided case histories in the use of biofeedback training, including patients with left hemiplegia, reversible physiological block, left upper extremity disuse following severe pain, right upper extremity disuse following severe nerve injury, substitute muscle activity in place of a recovered but nonused muscle, Bell's palsy, and 20 cases of residual paralysis as a result of poliomyelitis. Training, using standard techniques, had been attempted with many of these patients, but without success. In the absence of quantitative data, the case histories can be regarded only as demonstrational in nature but this report, in spite of its publication in a little-known journal, did exercise a great influence on the development of biofeedback training techniques in the rehabilitation of physical function. The publication of this paper also drew attention to the importance of using unimpaired contralateral function as a model for training the impaired function.

It is extraordinary that nearly 10 years were to pass after the publication of this work before Budzynski and Stoyva (1969) were able to draw attention to the possibility (using surface electrodes) of a much wider application of biofeedback training for the control of muscle function and the appropriate apparatus setup with which to pursue it. Their study was carried out with normal subjects and involved training in frontalis muscle reduction, using auditory feedback and employing appropriate control groups (see Chapter 3). With the publication of this study, the slow buildup to research and clinical application in the area of biofeedback suddenly became a torrent of activity, and the explosion of empirical research which is the subject of this book became a reality.

Several other historical developments of interest to biofeedback may be mentioned briefly. The "Alexander technique" was developed in the late 19th

---

[10]It is unclear whether the feedback was continuous and proportional or not (see Chapter 2).

century by an Australian actor who became convinced of the importance of the proper coordination of bodily function for mental health and who developed procedures for correcting defects in body posture and teaching correct integration of the body's muscular system. Alexander's teachings have continued to exercise much influence down to the present time, although never presented in systematic form. His teachings have recently been presented in detail by Barlow (1973) and critically assessed by Weinstock (1976). The "dysponesis" factor described by Whatmore and Kohli (1968) closely resembles the formulations of Alexander. Dysponesis is defined as "a psychopathologic state made up of errors in energy expenditure within the nervous system" (Whatmore & Kohli, 1968, p. 103). The role of "effort" (*ponesis*) in normal behavior involves very small muscular movements, often not detectable by ordinary means, in performing and bracing activities (as well as higher activities, such as thinking). Dysponesis consists of covert errors in energy expenditure via motor and premotor cortical nervous and pyramidal and extrapyramidal tracts and their feedback pathways in attempting to cope with input stimulation. The errors are physiological errors. The action potentials constituting effort, when misdirected, interfere with adjustment because they feed signals into the reticular activating system, the hypothalamus, the limbic system, and the neocortex, producing excitatory and inhibitory influences inappropriate to the immediate objectives of the organism. Dysponetic responses are intermittent at first, but can become a "way of life." Whatmore and Kohli (1968) provide examples of the effects of effort and dysponesis on emotional behavior, ideation, autonomic function, primary sensation, and so on, and outline the role they believe dysponesis can play in anxiety, disturbances of the digestive and circulatory systems, impotence and frigidity, headaches and backache, insomnia and fatigue states, depression, hyperventilation, eczema and neurodermatitis, obsessions, compulsions, hypochondriasis, schizophrenia, and myocardial infarction. Treatment (ponesiatrics) involves training in the recognition and regulation of energy expenditures, and the application of the skills achieved in the course of daily activities so as to produce a measured response in the face of stress. They provide case histories to illustrate dysponetic analysis and therapy.

Another pioneer whose work deserves a mention is Alfred P. Rogers, who developed the techniques in dentistry known as myofunctional therapy. His contributions have recently been described by Cottingham (1976). Rogers developed his approach in the first third of the present century and was particularly concerned with devising appropriate exercises for the pterygoid and masseter-temporal muscles, and the tongue, as an aid to overcoming difficulties arising from malocclusion. Malocclusion difficulties are usually treated in dentistry by physical means (the use of appliances), but Rogers stressed the importance of muscular balance and the elimination of weaknesses in muscle activity which produce strain and consequent tension and discomfort associated with, for example, the temporomandibular joint dysfunction syndrome (see Chapter 3).

Kubie and Margolin (1944) described instrumentation for transmitting the sounds associated with breathing into earphones, thus effectively providing feedback of breathing rate to their subjects, although their intention was to use the breathing sounds as a hypnagogic stimulus. It will be evident that there is a long and interesting history of research into the control of muscle function and its importance in general bodily adjustment; no doubt, innumerable other examples could be tracked down to illustrate the point.

Schultz and Autogenic Training

So great was the influence of Freud outside Europe in the first half of this century that other important developments which occurred in Europe during this period tended to be ignored. The work of Schultz, a psychiatrist and neurologist in Berlin, achieved immense popularity in Europe, his book, *Das Autogene Training* (1932) reaching its tenth edition in 1961 and being translated into many European languages. Yet not until 1969 was an English translation published, in six volumes (Schultz & Luthe, 1969). The interested reader must be referred to these volumes for a detailed exposition of the work of Schultz, but a brief account may be found in a paper by Luthe (1963). Basically, autogenic training consists of a set of six standard exercises focusing on the neuromuscular system (involving sensations of heaviness) and the vasomotor system (involving sensations of warmth), and seven meditative exercises focusing on mental functions. When the standard and meditative exercises have been mastered, a series of special exercises is introduced involving the reduction of exteroceptive and proprioceptive afferent stimuli, the mental repetition of verbal formulas, and the ability to engage in passive concentration. Details of the specific procedures used will be found in Luthe (1963, pp. 176–178) but it will be obvious that the approach has features in common with work of Jacobson (previously described) on relaxation, and with the technique known as transcendental meditation (TM) and techniques used by yogis and in Zen Buddhism. Since it is not intended in this book to provide a detailed review of the literature on autogenic training, TM, yoga, or Zen Buddhism, a brief comment may appropriately be made here on these systems since they all undoubtedly exercised some degree of influence on the development of biofeedback.

In all these systems, very large claims (exceeding even those made in some quarters on behalf of biofeedback) have been made on behalf of the benefits to be obtained by the regular practice of the exercises taught. It is claimed that emotional stability, more effective thinking and decision making, and even the attainment of ''higher states of consciousness'' may be achieved by the use of these techniques, which are also claimed to be effective in the treatment of a wide range of disorders of behavior and even, when practiced in group form on a large scale, to result in significant reductions in crime rates (this latter claim has been made particularly by the advocates of TM). No satisfactory evidence whatever exists in support of any of these claims. Autogenic training has frequently been used in conjunction with biofeedback training, thus effectively confounding both, and it appears that no scientific studies of autogenic training as such have ever been carried out. The situation is somewhat different with respect to yoga, Zen Buddhism, and TM. The alleged extraordinary feats of bodily control (such as total suppression of heart rate and control of sensitivity to extremely painful stimuli) have long excited interest in the Western world, accompanied by little understanding of the techniques themselves or of the philosophy underlying the techniques, a deficiency which has been repaired to some extent by careful accounts of the meanings of terms (Dalal & Barber, 1969) and the philosophy underlying yoga practices (Bagchi, 1969) in recent years. Studies conducted "on the spot" (and, hence, not under controlled laboratory conditions) have, however, generally failed to confirm many of the claims made. Bagchi and Wenger (1957) reported that four yoga practitioners were not able to stop their hearts from beating as they claimed to be able to do (what they apparently did was to use the Valsalva maneuver to make the heartbeat nonperceptible). In an investigation of 45 Hathayoga practitioners in India, Wenger and Bagchi (1961) found only one subject who could achieve voluntary control over visceral functions, while in another study, Wenger, Bagchi, and Anand (1961) found only one of four yoga practitioners could markedly slow the heart rate, which was achieved indirectly by the use of breath control on the one hand, and control of muscle tension in the abdomen and thorax with closed glottis, producing retardation in venous return to the heart, on the other hand. Green (1972), however, reported that Swami Rama could voluntarily produce a difference of 10°F within 3 min between adjacent areas of the hand, could speed and slow his heart rate, could produce heart stoppage by means of atrial fibrillation, and could induce high levels of alpha and theta. Anand, Chhina, and Singh (1961) also reported an increase in alpha abundance during meditation in six yogis. Kasamutsu and Hirai (1966) studied 48 Zen Buddhist practitioners with widely varying degrees of experience (16 were priests, the remainder disciples). They found that changes in alpha and theta abundance paralleled the four stages involved in Zen meditation. Datey, Deshmukh, Dalvi, and Vinekar (1969) trained 47 patients suffering from hypertension (mostly "essential," but some with renal or arteriosclerotic hypertension) in yoga exercises (breathing while relaxing in the supine position) for 3 weeks, followed by further practice for an unspecified period. Successful reduction of hypertension was claimed in 52% of the patients (in some cases, lowered blood pressure which had been achieved by the use of drugs was maintained when the drug usage was reduced). Similar results were achieved for the essential and renal hypertension patients, but no success was obtained with the arteriosclerotic patients. More recently, Elson, Hauri, and Cunis (1977) compared a group of yoga meditators with a group of nonmeditators in a condition where the meditators practiced their skills and the nonmeditators practiced relaxation. A large number of physiological measures were recorded. The meditators tended to increase and remain in alpha while the nonmeditators tended to pass through alpha to theta very quickly and then fall asleep. The meditators showed a significant increase in basal skin resistance (recorded from the palm and dorsum of the right hand), indicating increased relaxation, whereas the nonmeditators showed a decrease. The meditators also showed an increase in heart rate and a significant drop in respiration rate as compared with the nonmeditators, but no differences were found in forehead or finger temperature during the practice of meditation or relaxation. Thus, the evidence overall, both in respect of very experienced yoga practitioners and persons trained in yoga exercises, regarding increase in voluntary control remains conflicting.[11]

Transcendental meditation, which might be called the poor man's yoga, has received a good deal more experimental attention. Although a great amount of mystique has surrounded the technique, its basic features are of an unnerving simplicity, given the complexity of the disorders for which it has been claimed to be beneficial. It amounts, in fact, to no more than a set of instructions to relax, coupled with the repetition of and concentration on a magical word or mantra, which by some mysterious means is supposed to be able to be specified uniquely for the individual. Practice of the relaxation, together with the use of the mantra, in a quiet environment, constitutes the essence of the technique. The method has been more accurately described, perhaps, by Benson, Beary, and Carol (1974) as the "relaxation response." As was the case with yoga, early studies suggested that induction and maintenance of the TM state produced physiological changes. Wallace (1970) measured these changes in 15 normal subjects who had been trained in TM and practiced it for periods varying from 6 months to 3 years. As compared with simple rest periods, he found that oxygen consumption decreased by 20% during the period of meditation; heart rate decreased in one-third of the subjects; the galvanic skin reflex (GSR) increased markedly at the onset of meditation, then tended to decrease; there was an increase in alpha abundance, leading in some cases to an increase in theta activity. It was claimed that the physiological changes observed were different from those seen in sleep, hypnotic, or autosuggestive states. These findings were replicated and extended on a larger sample by Wallace and Benson (1972)[12]. In addition to the variables measured in the study by Wallace (1970), they examined the effects of meditation on blood pressure, rectal temperature, respiration rate, carbon dioxide elimination, and lactate concentration. A typical result is shown in Figure 2, indicating the drop in oxygen consumption and carbon dioxide elimination during meditation, as compared with pre- and postmeditation periods of rest. The

---

[11]Green, Green, and Walters (1970) have comprehensively reviewed the area of yoga meditation and related areas (such as the effects of hypnagogic imagery); the book by Barber (1970) should also be consulted.

[12]The report by Wallace, Benson, and Wilson (1971) is scientific account of the study; that by Wallace and Benson (1972), a more "popular" account of the same study.

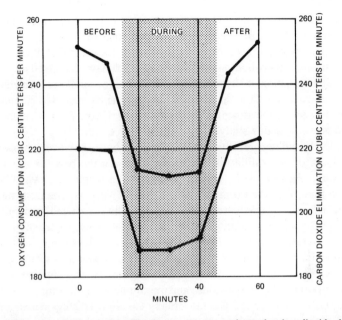

Figure 2. Effect of meditation on the subject's oxygen consumption and carbon dioxide elimination was recorded in 20 and 15 cases, respectively. After the subjects were invited to meditate, both rates decreased markedly. Consumption and elimination returned to the premeditation level soon after the subjects stopped meditating. (From Wallace, R. K., and Benson, H. The physiology of meditation. *Scientific American*, 1972, *226*, 86. Reprinted by permission of the author and the publisher.)

correlation between the changes in O_2 uptake and CO_2 elimination suggested metabolic changes which were confirmed by the demonstration that lactate concentration (which indicates a state of anaerobic metabolism, that is, metabolism occurring in the absence of free oxygen) in the blood declined four times faster during meditation than happens in the normal resting state. Respiration rate declined during meditation by an average of two breaths per minute and the volume of air was correspondingly 1 liter less per minute. The findings of Wallace (1970) in respect of GSR changes were confirmed while alpha activity increased in intensity in the frontal and central regions. However, no changes were recorded in blood pressure. The claim was repeated that these changes were different from those found during sleep and in hypnotic states. Similar findings were reported by Beary, Benson, and Klemchuk (1974). In all of these studies, the subjects were used as their own controls in an A–B–A design, and a control group of subjects simply instructed to relax for the entire period involved was not examined. Orme-Johnson (1973), however, compared trained and untrained meditators with a control group of nonmeditators on GSR and found that level and rate of habituation of the GSR response was lower and faster, respectively, in the meditators, a result not necessarily conflicting with the findings for GSR of

Wallace and his colleagues. These kinds of results led to the large claims made for meditation. Thus, Benson (1974) claimed positive effects in relation to alcoholism as a result of a retrospective, uncontrolled survey of 1862 alcoholics, while Benson, Greenwood, and Klemchuk (1975) have discussed clinical applications of meditation to hypertension, drug usage, smoking, and headaches. Wilson, Honsberger, Chiu, and Novey (1975) have claimed that meditation may be a useful aid in the treatment of asthma (see Chapter 6, "Asthma," for a detailed account of this study).

Recently, more carefully controlled studies have, however, thrown considerable doubt on the validity of the claims made for the benefits of meditation. Cauthen and Prymak (1977) measured changes in respiration rate, GSR, heart rate, and thumb skin temperature in five groups: very experienced, moderately experienced, and inexperienced meditators who had practiced meditation for an average of 5 years, 14 months, and 7 days, respectively; a control group which had been trained in and used relaxation only for 5 days; and a control group which practiced "simulated" meditation (thinking about a specified word). The meditation groups practiced meditation during the experimental period, the relaxation group practiced relaxation, and the simulation group simply repeated the mantra. The very experienced, moderately experienced, and relaxation groups showed greater but equal decreases in heart rate, whereas the inexperienced meditators and the relaxation groups showed increases in skin temperature. However, no changes were found in either GSR or respiration rate, contradicting the findings of Wallace and his colleagues. Curtis and Wessberg (1976) found no differential changes in GSR, heart rate, or respiration rate in groups of experienced meditators, experienced relaxers, and subjects inexperienced in either meditation or relaxation when they were required to meditate, relax, or sit quietly with eyes closed, respectively. Nor did any significant change in these variables occur within the groups. However, subjective reports indicated that meditators believed that beneficial changes occurred while they were meditating whereas the control subjects found the experience unpleasant. Pagano, Rose, Stivers, and Warrensburg (1976) asked five experienced meditators to meditate or to nap over a series of 10 sessions while occipital, frontal, and central EEG responses, eye movements, chin muscle activity, and skin resistance were measured. They reported that these meditators were physiologically asleep (as indicated by various criteria) during 40% of the time supposedly spent in meditation. The amount of sleep indicated physiologically did not differ during the meditation and nap sessions. Travis, Kondo, and Knott (1976) compared changes in EEG, frontalis muscle activity, heart rate, and eye movements in experienced meditators and control relaxers while meditating and relaxing. They found no change in the alpha output, heart rate, or frontalis muscle activity in the meditators while meditating as compared with baseline levels at rest or while relaxing; the relaxation controls showed a significant decrease in alpha activity (the change being characteristic of sleep), a reduction in heart rate, and a decrease in frontalis muscle activity, while relaxing as compared with baseline resting levels. It should be noted, however, that very significant effects of meditation on physiological function have been demonstrated under tightly controlled conditions. Hebert and Lehmann (1977), for example, have recently demonstrated very marked changes in levels of theta activity in very experienced meditators as compared wth control subjects (see Chapter 5 for a detailed account of this study). The effect of TM on physiological functions therefore remains a controversial matter. However, equally careful recent investigations seem to have demonstrated conclusively that whatever physiological changes may be produced by TM can be produced equally well by progressive relaxation training or even simpler techniques which produce relaxation (Fenwick, Donaldson, Gillis, Bushman, Fenton, Perry, Tilsley, & Serafinowicz, 1977; Michaels, Huber, & McCann, 1976; Morse, Martin, Furst, & Dubin, 1977).

It has been claimed that TM produces beneficial effects on cognitive and intellectual performance. However, recent studies by Williams and Herbert (1976) and by Williams and Vickerman (1976) cast doubt on this claim. They required moderately experienced meditators to meditate, and nonmeditators to sit quietly, for a period of time before practicing the pursuit rotor task (both groups not having had prior exposure to this learning task). Not only did they not find a facilitating effect of prior meditation on pursuit rotor learning, there was a suggestion that meditation impaired performance on the task. These results have been confirmed by Williams, Lodge, and Reddish (1977), using more experienced meditators and extended to mirror drawing with the same results by Williams (1978). Zuroff and Schwarz (1978) found that TM and muscle-relaxation training had equal effects in reducing anxiety, although the TM subjects believed they had reduced their anxiety more than did the relaxation subjects.

As indicated earlier, TM essentially involves relaxation combined with concentration on an individual mantra. Only recently have attempts been made to determine whether the mantra does in fact play the vital role assigned to it in TM. However, J. C. Smith (1976) has recently completed two large-scale studies which bear on this question. In the first, TM was taught to one group by TM instructors (including the mantra) while another group was taught TM by specially trained instructors, but omitting the mantra component. In the second study, TM training with the mantra included was compared with training which included a mantra but the subjects were instructed to indulge in as much cognitive activity as possible. In the first study, equally significant reductions were found in measures of A-trait anxiety, indicators of striated muscle tension, and indicators of autonomic arousal (as compared with an untrained control group), while in the second study, no differences were found on these variables between the two experimental groups. It should be stressed that this study by Smith was exceptionally well designed, even to the extent of deceiving the non-TM instructors that the technique they were trained to administer was a genuine one (by the production, for example, of a detailed manual of instructions which paralleled closely the manual used by the TM instructors). Smith concluded that the alleged vital components of TM are not essential to the production of the results alleged to flow from TM training, and that the results obtained with both techniques could be accounted for in terms of the way in which TM is conducted (use of authority figures, induction of positive expectations, and so on).

No attempt has been made here to survey the entire literature on TM,[14] but it will be clear from what has been presented that the validity of TM (that is, the necessity to use the specific components of TM) has not been demonstrated. Nevertheless, movements such as TM did exercise an influénce on the development of biofeedback in its early stages and may properly be regarded as one of the antecedents of biofeedback.

Miller and Operant Control in Curarized Rats

No one has ever doubted, of course, that voluntary control of skeletal muscle activity is possible. The astonishing feats of circus acrobats and jugglers suggest that the normal person may be much less skilled in such control as compared with the possibilities of control with appropriate training, and the notion that biofeedback might be used to enhance such control has never seemed other than reasonable. Within experimental psychology, however, the clear distinction made in the first half of this century between classical and instrumental conditioning bore witness to the very strong belief among experimental psychologists that autonomic functions such as heart rate, blood pressure, and temperature could not be controlled voluntarily in the way that skeletal functions could be.[15] During this period, there were one or two reports which threw some doubt on the validity of this belief. Hudgins (1933), for example, successfully established voluntary control of the pupillary light reflex. First, he classically conditioned the reflex to sound (bell as conditioned stimulus, with light as the unconditioned stimulus). On command from the experimenter, the subject then contracted his hand to close the bell and light circuits. The bell hand responses were then gradually eliminated, leaving only verbal commands from the subject as conditioned stimuli. Finally, the verbal command from the subject was subvocalized. Successful control of the pupillary response to subvocal verbal commands was thus established, even though most of the subjects were unaware that the pupillary response was being trained. The conditioned pupillary response to the bell and hand response (as conditioned stimuli) extinguished (as would be expected in classical conditioning when the unconditioned response is omitted) but extinction to the subvocal verbal commands did not occur over a period of 15 days during which the primary reinforcer was never presented. Lindsley and

[14]See J. C. Smith (1975), Swinyard, Chaube, and Sutton (1974), and Woolfolk (1975) for reviews of the literature on TM and its present status.
[15]Kimmel (1974) has reviewed the situation as it existed between 1928 and 1961.

Sassaman (1938) reported the case of a middle-aged male who could voluntarily make the hairs on the dorsal surface of his forearm, the lateral surface of his thigh, and the anterior surface of his leg just below the knee, become erect from their normal resting position on command. These changes were accompanied by dilation of the pupils and increase in heart rate and respiration rate (but not blood pressure) together with significant EEG changes, suggesting a general innervation of the sympathetic division of the autonomic nervous system, characteristic of the natural response to a danger signal. The subject denied that he used imagery or muscle activity to produce these changes which he could apparently control while simultaneously engaging in other activities. However, these occasional demonstrations of apparently voluntary control of functions mediated via the autonomic nervous system failed to disturb the consensus that such voluntary control was impossible and that, consequently, the apparent control must be mediated indirectly by way of functions which could be brought under voluntary control and which would, as a consequence, produce concomitant changes in autonomic activities. Much the same explanation was, of course, believed to explain the occasional reports of voluntary control of heart rate which were described earlier in this chapter. It is not surprising, therefore, that Miller's apparent demonstration of the voluntary control of autonomic functions in the rat in a curarized state (that is, with the musculature system totally paralyzed) caused a sensation.[16] In a long series of studies carried out with DiCara, Miller apparently demonstrated that heart rate could be instrumentally conditioned, using direct electrical stimulation of the brain reward centers (DiCara & Miller, 1968a; Miller & DiCara, 1967). Similar results were claimed for blood pressure (DiCara & Miller, 1968b) and renal blood flow (Miller & DiCara, 1968), rate of saliva secretion in dogs (Miller & Carmona, 1967), and contraction of the intestines (Miller & Banuazizi, 1968). It was believed that transfer of an autonomic response (heart rate) acquired under curarization to the noncurarized state (DiCara & Miller, 1969) and differential control of the temperature in the ears of the rat (DiCara & Miller, 1968c) had been obtained. Similar results obtained by other workers (e.g., Hothersall & Brener, 1969; Slaughter, Hahn, & Rinaldi, 1970; Trowill, 1967) encouraged belief in the validity of these results. Unfortunately, Miller found that he had less and less success in replicating these results and he was finally forced to admit that he did not know whether or not he had ever genuinely demonstrated instrumental conditioning of autonomic function in the rat (Miller & Dworkin, 1974). The whole episode is strikingly reminiscent of the celebrated ''discovery'' of N-rays by the eminent French physicist Blondlot at the turn of the century. The discovery led to intensive research both in Europe and the United States to determine the properties of N-rays and many papers on the properties discovered were published in the most distinguished

---

[16]Miller has described these experiments and their implications in many review papers. Perhaps the most comprehensive and useful of these are Miller (1969a, b), and Miller, DiCara, Solomon, Weiss, and Dworkin (1970).

physics journals. When doubts set in as to whether N-rays really existed, a visit by a leading American physicist to Blondlot's laboratory established that Blondlot had convinced himself that he could observe events which it was conclusively demonstrated he could not possibly have observed. Within a very short time, investigations of N-rays ceased to appear in journals of physics.[17] It is unnecessary to describe these experiments by Miller and his colleagues on the instrumental conditioning of autonomic responding in rats. There can be no doubt, however, that they had a profound effect in encouraging attempts to demonstrate voluntary control over autonomic functions in humans (see Chapter 4).

In the course of carrying out these studies, Miller drew attention to the existence of a remarkable paper to which little attention had been paid up to that time. Lapides, Sweet, and Lewis (1957) used succinylcholine or D-tubocurarine to totally paralyze all striate musculature in normal subjects and reported that the paralysis did not lead to incontinence (the urethral sphincters are mediated entirely by the autonomic nervous system). Furthermore, the paralyzed subjects were able to initiate urination on command as fast as they could do so when not paralyzed, although their ability to inhibit urine flow, once started, was significantly affected (although not rendered impossible).

All of this evidence helped to produce the breakdown of the rigid distinction between classical and instrumental conditioning (or voluntary control of the skeletal nervous system but involuntary action of the autonomic nervous system) that had persisted for so long in experimental psychology, and encouraged belief that voluntary control of autonomic functions in normal subjects might be demonstrable.

Razran and Interoceptive Conditioning in the Soviet Union

In 1961, Razran published a long review of Russian work on interoceptive conditioning which had been carried out over the previous 50 years, and 8 years later he described some possible applications of this work in the classical area (Razran, 1969). Interoceptive conditioning had been largely neglected in American experimental psychology because of the influence of behaviorism, first under Watson and later Skinner, while the technical difficulties involved in transducing internal responses deterred those who would willingly have carried out such research had the facilities been available to them. Razran's monumental reviews were important for several reasons. In the first place, they demonstrated that the technical problems could be solved, certainly in animals, and very probably in humans also. Second, they demonstrated that classical conditioning of internal visceral responses was definitely possible, while some results obtained in Russia indicated that instrumental responding was also possible. Third, they demon-

---

[17]A brief account of this episode (by no means an isolated instance) will be found in Gardner (1957, p. 345).

strated that the techniques had potentially powerful clinical applications. The timing of Razran's reviews could scarcely have been better, given that the slowly increasing interest in biofeedback was directed in considerable degree toward the control of autonomic functions. Earlier accounts of Russian work by Bykov (1957) and a later review by Adam (1967) also exercised a considerable influence at this time.

Razran pointed out that:

> interoceptive conditioning may best be defined as classical conditioning in which either the conditioned stimulus (CS) or the unconditioned stimulus (US) or both are delivered directly to the mucosa of some specific viscus. (1961, pp. 81–82)

Three basic forms of conditioning situation may be distinguished: intero-interoceptive conditioning, in which both the CS and the US are internal; intero-exteroceptive, in which the CS is internal but the US is external; and extero-interoceptive, in which the CS is external but the US is internal. In Razran's view, only the first two forms constituted genuine examples of interoceptive conditioning, representing as they do situations in which the conditioned information is transmitted by the viscera, whereas this is not so in the third situation. He regarded the second kind (intero-exteroceptive conditioning) as being the most significant, although the first kind (intero-interoceptive conditioning) may well be the most significant from the point of view of relevance to biofeedback.

Razran (1961) distinguished five kinds of reaction that may be studied in interoceptive conditioning (visceral, skeletal, sensory-verbal, and the special cases of exteroceptive verbal stimuli in extero-interoceptive and intero-extero-ceptive conditioning), resulting in a total of 15 classes of interoceptive conditioning, examples of each of which he provides in his review, using studies from both animal and human conditioning.

A distinction made by Mowrer (1960) provides an interesting link with the work reviewed by Razran. Mowrer distinguished between non-response-correlated and response-correlated avoidance behavior. The former may be illustrated by the example of an animal that escapes, then subsequently avoids, a threatened shock (e.g., a tone) by moving from one compartment to another. In this case, the conditioned stimulus (tone) occurs independently of any response the animal makes (hence the terms ''non-response-correlated'' or ''active avoidance behavior''—the animal waits for the conditioned stimulus to occur and then actively seeks to avoid the occurrence of the threatened unconditioned stimulus). The latter may be illustrated by the example of an animal traversing a straight runway, in the course of which it receives an aversive stimulus (e.g., shock). On subsequent occasions, as the animal traverses the runway and reaches the region of shock, its own movements (which will tend to be similar on each trial in the confines of the runway) will produce feedback which will serve as conditioned anxiety-arousing stimuli (hence the terms ''response-correlated'' or ''passive avoidance behavior''—the animal itself produces the conditioned stimulus and responds to it by passive avoidance). In the latter case, the animal carries around with it its own anxiety-arousing stimuli, whereas in the former case the animal responds when a stimulus external to it arouses anxiety.[18] Thus, in passive avoidance learning, interoceptive conditioning is involved which poses a problem for the animal (how to avoid the threatened unconditioned stimulus) and motivates it to trial-and-error learning until it discovers the "correct" response.

A paper published by Lisina (1965) also exercised a considerable influence about this time because it appeared to demonstrate instrumental conditioning or voluntary control over vasoconstriction. It has since been shown that muscular mediation was almost certainly operative in Lisina's study but, as with Miller's work, the impact of the paper was far greater than the actual validity of the results. Mention should also be made of an influential study by Jones (1956) based on the work by Bykov (1957) in which excessive frequency of urination was alleviated by conditioning the degree of "urgency" to a reading on a manometer which was then surreptitiously changed so as to associate a lower level of "urgency" with a higher reading in the manometer. The treatment reduced the intense urge to urinate at low levels of bladder volume and pressure which had characterized the patient when she first presented for treatment.

Of course, nearly all of this work was carried out within a classical conditioning framework, but as has been seen, the possibility that such responses could be instrumentally conditioned or that voluntary control over these functions could be obtained was implicit in the techniques used, as indicated, for example, by the studies of Uno (1970) on interoceptive and exteroceptive conditioning of the GSR, who specifically pointed out that interoceptive conditioning could be either classical or instrumental, at least in principle.

Smith and the Disruption of Behavior

Both in fundamental research and as a therapeutic tool, biofeedback has almost invariably been used to determine the extent to which voluntary control of behavior can be increased. Nevertheless, any system (particularly if it is under computer control) which is set up for biofeedback purposes may also be used to disrupt ongoing behavior and to measure the consequences of that disruption. The importance of such work does not seem to have been generally appreciated by those working in the biofeedback area. In attempting to explain and ameliorate disorders of behavior, it is often extremely helpful if the disorder can be simulated in normal subjects and then removed by the development of appropriate techniques. Thus, if it is believed that brain damage leads to an increase in inhibitory potentials in the brain, the induction of inhibitory brain states in

---

[18] In actual fact, the runway situation is confounded because the runway itself may become a conditioned stimulus for anxiety.

normal subjects (for example, by massed practice) may lead to valuable insights into the growth of abnormal modes of responding as compared with merely being able to examine the end product as it is manifested in a presenting patient.

A classic example of the usefulness of biofeedback-induced abnormal behavior in normal subjects is the well-known phenomenon of delayed auditory feedback (Yates, 1963a). Normal speech output is monitored by way of feedback from the airborne and bone-conducted channels as well as feedback arising from the movements of the organs (lips, tongue, larynx, etc.) involved in speech. Under normal speech conditions the feedback from each of these channels provides the same information as to the progress of emitted speech; by comparing this feedback information with the expected feedback (based on knowledge of the conditions in which the speech is being emitted and expectations based on past experience) adjustments are made from time to time so that the characteristics of the speech output are appropriate to the circumstances. Of course, errors in the speech output are corrected as well. In the delayed auditory feedback condition, however, information transmitted along one of the channels (usually the airborne) is delayed so that instead of hearing the speech feedback with the normal delay of about 1 msec a delay of about 200 msec is experienced. Under these conditions many normal speakers manifest a profound disturbance in speech output, sometimes to the extent of becoming incoherent. A kind of artificial stutter occurs. The detailed investigation of what happens under conditions of delayed auditory feedback is highly relevant to the explanation of stuttering which may be conceptualized as being due to the effects of a faulty feedback mechanism in a servocontrol system, and this conceptualization of stuttering has led to the use of various techniques designed to override or correct the faulty feedback system (Yates, 1963b).

There is, of course, a very long history of research into the effects of disrupting the feedback control systems of normal subjects, particularly the relationships between movement and perception in the visual field.[19] In recent years, the most striking contributions to this area have been made by Karl U. Smith, but the relevance of his contributions to biofeedback has been largely overlooked. It is beyond the scope of this book to provide a comprehensive account of the contributions made by Smith to the use of biofeedback in examining the disruption of control in normal human subjects and the reader must be referred to the many excellent reviews of his work given by Smith himself,[20] as well as the dozens of empirical studies referenced in these reviews. In his early studies, Smith ingeniously utilized the flexible properties of TV cameras to invert, reverse, or both invert and reverse the visual representation of reproductions (drawing triangles or squares, writing letters of the alphabet) made by the subject so as to produce a conflict of feedback information arising from what the

[19]K. U. Smith and Smith (1962) have provided an excellent historical review of much of this work.
[20]See, for example, K. U. Smith (1961a, b); K. U. Smith, Ansel, and Smith (1963); K. U. Smith and Henry (1967).

subject was seeing and what feedback from the muscles producing the representation was telling him. Later, he was among the first to introduce real-time computer control to produce the distorted feedback, and in particular to introduce delayed visual feedback. Under these conditions, he was able to produce effects paralleling those found with delayed auditory feedback. This work is particularly relevant to biofeedback research since delay is inevitable in any biofeedback situation and it does not seem to have been generally realized that such delays may act as a disrupting influence. As will be shown later, it has only been by accident that the disruptive effects of delayed visual feedback have generally been avoided in biofeedback research and therapy.

This historical review of the antecedents of biofeedback makes no claim to completeness and should be regarded only as a sampling of the available relevant literature. Many other examples could be considered in detail, such as Carr's (1907, 1908) early demonstrations of apparent voluntary control of the visual field. Enough has been provided, however, to demonstrate beyond doubt that biofeedback did not arise *de novo* and that it may be firmly anchored within an historical context. The trigger point for the upsurge of interest in biofeedback, however, apart from the general background influences described in this chapter, was undoubtedly the development of technical means for investigating biofeedback effects and presenting appropriate feedback displays to the subject or patient, as illustrated particularly by the relatively unacknowledged work of K. U. Smith.

References

Adam, G. *Interoception and behavior*. Budapest: Akademiai Kiado, 1967.

Anand, B. K., Chhina, G. S., & Singh, B. Some aspects of electroencephalographic studies in yogis. *EEG and Clinical Neurophysiology*, 1961, *13*, 452–456. (R:63)

Bagchi, B. K. Mysticism and mist in India. *Journal of the American Society of Psychosomatic Dentistry and Medicine*, 1969, *16*, 1–32. (R:60)

Bagchi, B. K., & Wenger, M. A. Electrophysiological correlates of some yogi exercizes. *EEG and Clinical Neurophysiology*. Suppl. 7, 1957. (R:62)

Bair, J. H. Development of voluntary control. *Psychological Review*, 1901, *8*, 474–510.

Barber, T. X. *LSD, marihuana, yoga, and hypnosis*. Chicago: Aldine, 1970.

Barlow, W. *The Alexander technique*. New York: Alfred A. Knopf, 1973.

Basmajian, J. V. Control and training of individual motor units. *Science*, 1963, *141*, 440–441. (R:45)

Beary, J. F., Benson, H., & Klemchuk, H. P. A simple psychophysiologic technique which elicits the hypometabolic changes of the relaxation response. *Psychosomatic Medicine*, 1974, *36*, 115–120.

Benson, H. Decreased alcohol intake associated with the practice of meditation: A retrospective investigation. *Annals of the New York Academy of Sciences*, 1974, *233*, 174–177.

Benson, H., Beary, J. F., & Carol, M. P. The relaxation response. *Psychiatry*, 1974, *37*, 37–46.

Benson, H., Greenwood, M. M., & Klemchuk, H. P. The relaxation response: Psychophysiologic aspects and clinical applications. *International Journal of Psychiatry in Medicine*, 1975, *6*, 87–98.

Bernard, C. *An introduction to the study of experimental medicine.* New York: Dover, 1957. (Originally published, 1865.)

Blanchard, E. B., & Young L. D. Self-control of cardiac functioning: A promise as yet unfulfilled. *Psychological Bulletin,* 1973, *79,* 145–163. (1973: 30)

Bruce, R. V. *Bell: Alexander Graham Bell and the conquest of solitude.* London: Gollancz, 1973.

Budzynski, T. H., & Stoyva, J. M. An instrument for producing deep muscle relaxation by means of analog information feedback. *Journal of Applied Behavior Analysis,* 1969, *2,* 231–237.

Bykov, K. M. *The cerebral cortex and the internal organs.* New York: Chemical Publishing Company, 1957.

Carlsöö, S., & Edfeldt, A. W. Attempts at muscle control with visual and auditory impulses as auxiliary stimuli. *Scandinavian Journal of Psychology,* 1963, *4,* 231–235.

Carr, H. Apparent control of the position of the visual field. *Psychological Review,* 1907, *14,* 357–382. (R:58, abstract only)

Carr, H. Voluntary control of the visual field. *Psychological Review,* 1908, *15,* 139–149. (R:59, abstract only)

Carter, E. P., & Wedd, A. M. Report of a case of paroxysmal tachycardia characterized by unusual control of the fast rhythm. *Archives of Internal Medicine,* 1918, *22,* 571–580.

Cauthen, N. R., & Prymak, C. A. Meditation versus relaxation: An examination of the physiological effects of relaxation training and of different levels of experience with transcendental meditation. *Journal of Consulting and Clinical Psychology,* 1977, *45,* 496–497. (+ extended report)

Cottingham, L. L. Myofunctional therapy: Orthodontics–tongue thrusting–speech therapy. *American Journal of Orthodontics,* 1976, *69,* 679–687.

Curtis, W. D., & Wessberg, H. W. A comparison of heart rate, respiration, and galvanic skin response among meditators, relaxers, and controls. *Journal of Altered States of Consciousness,* 1976, *2,* 319–324.

Dalal, A. S., & Barber, T. X. Yoga, "yogic feats," and hypnosis in the light of empirical research. *American Journal of Clinical Hypnosis,* 1969, *11,* 155–166. (R:70)

Datey, K. K., Deshmukh, S. N., Dalvi, C. P., & Vinekar, S. L. "Shavasan": A yogic exercise in management of hypertension. *Angiology,* 1969, *20,* 325–333. (R:67)

DiCara, L. V., & Miller, N. E. Changes in heart rate instrumentally learned by curarized rats as avoidance responses. *Journal of Comparative and Physiological Psychology,* 1968, *65,* 8–12. (a)

DiCara, L. V., & Miller, N. E. Instrumental learning of systolic blood pressure responses by curarized rats: Dissociation of cardiac and vascular changes. *Psychosomatic Medicine,* 1968, *30,* 489–494. (b)

DiCara, L. V., & Miller, N. E. Instrumental learning of vasomotor responses by rats: Learning to respond differentially in the two ears. *Science,* 1968, *159,* 1485–1486. (c)

DiCara, L. V., & Miller, N. E. Transfer of instrumentally learned heart-rate changes from curarized to noncurarized state: Implications for a mediational hypothesis. *Journal of Comparative and Physiological Psychology,* 1969, *68,* 159–162.

Elson, B. D., Hauri, P., & Cunis, D. Physiological changes in yoga meditation. *Psychophysiology,,* 1977, *14,* 52–57.

Fenwick, P.B.C., Donaldson, S., Gillis, L., Bushman, J., Fenton, G. W., Perry, I., Tilsley, C., & Serafinowicz, H. Metabolic and EEG changes during transcendental meditation: An explanation. *Biological Psychology,* 1977, *5,* 101–118.

Gardner, M. *Fads and fallacies in the name of science.* New York: Dover, 1957.

Green, E. Biofeedback for mind–body self-regulation: Healing and creativity. In *The varieties of healing experience: Exploring psychic phenomena in healing. A transcript from the interdisciplinary symposium of October 30, 1971.* Academy of Parapsychology and Medicine, 1972. (1972:11)

Green, E. E., Green, A. M., & Walters, E. D. Voluntary control of internal states: Psychological and physiological. *Journal of Transpersonal Psychology,* 1970, *2,* 1–26. (1970:1)

Hebert, R., & Lehmann, D. Theta bursts: An EEG pattern in normal subjects practising the transcendental meditation technique. *EEG and Clinical Neurophysiology*, 1977, *42*, 397–405.

Hefferline, R. F. The role of proprioception in the control of behavior. *Transactions of the New York Academy of Science*, 1958, *20*, 739–764.

Hefferline, R. F., Keenan, B., & Harford, R. A. Escape and avoidance conditioning in human subjects without their observation of the response. *Science*, 1959, *130*, 1338–1339. (R:43)

Hothersall, D., & Brener, J. Operant conditioning of changes in heart rate in curarized rats. *Journal of Comparative and Physiological Psychology*, 1969, *68*, 338–342.

Hudgins, C. V. Conditioning and voluntary control of the pupillary light reflex. *Journal of General Psychology*, 1933, *8*, 3–51. (R:53, abstract only)

Jacobson, E. Voluntary relaxation of the esophagus. *American Journal of Physiology*, 1925, *72*, 387–394.

Jacobson, E. *Progressive relaxation*. Chicago: University of Chicago Press, 1938.

Jacobson, E. Variation of blood pressure with skeletal muscle tension and relaxation. *Annals of Internal Medicine*, 1939, *12*, 1194-1212.

Jacobson, E. Variation of blood pressure with skeletal muscle tension and relaxation: II. The heart beat. *Annals of Internal Medicine*, 1940, *13*, 1619–1625.

Jacobson, E. Neuromuscular controls in man: Methods of self-direction in health and in disease. *American Journal of Psychology*, 1955, *68*, 549–561.

Jacobson, E. *Modern treatment of tense patients*. Springfield, Ill.: Charles C Thomas, 1970.

Jacobson, E. Electrophysiology of mental activities and introduction to the psychological process of thinking. In F. J. McGuigan & R. A. Schoonover (Eds.), *The psychophysiology of thinking*. New York: Academic, 1973.

Jones, H. G. The application of conditioning and learning techniques in the treatment of a psychiatric patient. *Journal of Abnormal and Social Psychology*, 1956, *52*, 414–420.

Kasamatsu, A., & Hirai, T. An electroencephalographic study of the Zen meditation (Zazen). *Folio Psychiatrica et Neurologica Japonica*, 1966, *20*, 315–336. (R:64)

Kimmel, H. D. Instrumental conditioning of autonomically mediated responses in human beings. *American Psychologist*, 1974, *29*, 325–335. (1974:2)

King, J. T. An instance of voluntary acceleration of the pulse. *Johns Hopkins Bulletin*, 1920, 303–305. (1972:2)

Kubie, L., & Margolin, S. An apparatus for the use of breath sounds as a hypnagogic stimulus. *American Journal of Psychiatry*, 1944, *100*, 610.

Lapides, J., Sweet, R. B., & Lewis, L. W. Role of striated muscle in urination. *Journal of Urology*, 1957, *77*, 247–250. (R:30)

Lindsley, D. B., & Sassaman, W. H. Autonomic activity and brain potentials associated with "voluntary" control of the pilomotors. *Journal of Neurophysiology*, 1938, *1*, 342–349. (1972:3)

Lisina, M. I. The role of orientation in the transformation of involuntary reactions into voluntary ones. In I. G. Voronin, A. N. Leontiev, A. R. Luria, E. N. Sokolov, & O. B. Vinogradova (Eds.), *Orienting reflex and exploratory behavior*. Washington, D.C.: American Institute of Biological Sciences, 1965, pp. 450–456.

Luthe, W. Autogenic training: Method, research and application in medicine. *American Journal of Psychotherapy*, 1963, *17*, 174–195. (R:66)

McClure, C. M. Cardiac arrest through volition. *California Medicine*, 1959, *90*, 440. (1972:5)

McMahon, C. E. Voluntary control of "involuntary" functions: The approach of the Stoics. *Psychophysiology*, 1974, *11*, 710–714.

Marinacci, A. A., & Horande, M. Electromyogram in neuromuscular re-education. *Bulletin of the Los Angeles Neurological Society*, 1960, *25*, 57–71.

Martony, J. On the correction of the voice pitch level for severely hard of hearing subjects. *American Annals of the Deaf*, 1968, *113*, 195–202.

Michaels, R. R., Huber, M. J., & McCann, D. S. Evaluation of transcendental meditation as a method of reducing stress. *Science,* 1976, *192,* 1242–1244. (1976/77:9)

Miller, N. E. Learning of visceral and glandular responses. *Science,* 1969, *163,* 434–445. (a) (R:1)

Miller, N. E. Learning of glandular and visceral responses. In D. Singh and C. T. Morgan (Eds.), *Current status of physiological psychology.* San Francisco: Wadsworth, 1972. (b) (1972:8)

Miller, N. E., & Banuazizi, A. Instrumental learning by curarized rats of a specific visceral response, intestinal or cardiac. *Journal of Comparative and Physiological Psychology,* 1968, *65,* 1–7.

Miller, N. E., & Carmona, A. Modification of a visceral response, salivation in thirsty dogs, by instrumental training with water reward. *Journal of Comparative and Physiological Psychology,* 1967, *63,* 1–6.

Miller, N. E., & DiCara, L. V. Instrumental learning of heart-rate changes in curarized rats: Shaping and specificity to discriminative stimulus. *Journal of Comparative and Physiological Psychology,* 1967, *63,* 12–19.

Miller, N. E., & DiCara, L. V. Instrumental learning of urine formation by rats: Changes in renal blood flow. *American Journal of Physiology,* 1968, *215,* 677–683.

Miller, N. E., & Dworkin, B. Visceral learning: Recent difficulties with curarized rats and significant problems for human research. In P. A. Obrist (Ed.), *Cardiovascular psychophysiology.* Chicago: Aldine, 1974, pp. 312–331.

Miller, N. E., DiCara, L. V., Solomon, H., Weiss, J. M., & Dworkin, B. Learned modifications of autonomic functions: A review and some new data. *Circulation Research,* 1970, *27,* Supp. 1–3 to 1–11. (1970:20)

Morse, D. R., Martin, J. S., Furst, M. L., & Dubin, L. L. A physiological and subjective evaluation of meditation, hypnosis, and relaxation. *Psychosomatic Medicine,* 1977, *39,* 304–324.

Mowrer, O. H. *Learning theory and behavior.* New York: Wiley, 1960.

Ogden, E., & Shock, N. W. Voluntary hypercirculation. *American Journal of the Medical Sciences,* 1939, *198,* 329–342. (1972:4)

Orme-Johnson, D. W. Autonomic stability and transcendental meditation. *Psychosomatic Medicine,* 1973, *35,* 341–349. (1973:42)

Pagano, R. R., Rose, R. M., Stivers, R. M., & Warrenburg, S. Sleep during transcendental meditation. *Science,* 1976, *191,* 308–310. (1975–6:6)

Pickett, J. M. Recent research on speech-analysing aids for the deaf. *IEEE Transactions on Audio and Electroacoustics,* 1968, *AU-16,* 227–234.

Platt, J. H. The Bell reduced visible symbol method for teaching speech to the deaf. *Journal of Speech Disorders,* 1947, *12,* 381–386.

Provonost, W. Visual aids to speech improvement. *Journal of Speech Disorders,* 1947, *12,* 387–391.

Razran, G. The observable unconscious and the inferable conscious in current Soviet psychophysiology. *Psychological Review,* 1961, *68,* 81–147. (R:56)

Razran, G. The observable unconscious in current Soviet psychophysiology: Survey and interpretation of experiments in interoceptive conditioning. *Progress in Clinical Psychology,* 1969, *4,* 1–31.

Schäfer, E. A., Canney, H. E. L., & Tunstall, J. O. On the rhythm of muscular response to volitional impulses in man. *Journal of Physiology,* 1886, *7,* 111–119.

Schultz, J. H., & Luthe, W. *Autogenic therapy.* New York: Grune & Stratton, 1969.

Slaughter, J., Hahn, W., & Rinaldi, P. Instrumental conditioning of heart in the curarized rat with varied amounts of pretraining. *Journal of Comparative and Physiological Psychology,* 1970, *72,* 356–360. (1970:24)

Smith, J. C. Meditation as psychotherapy: A review of the literature. *Psychological Bulletin,* 1975, *82,* 558–564.

Smith, J. C. Psychotherapeutic effects of transcendental meditation with controls for expectations of relief and daily sitting. *Journal of Consulting and Clinical Psychology*, 1976, *44*, 630–637.

Smith, K. U. The geometry of human motion and its neural foundations: I. Perceptual and motor adaptation to displaced vision. *American Journal of Physical Medicine*, 1961, *40*, 71–87. (a)

Smith, K. U. The geometry of human motion and its neural foundations: II. Neurogeometric theory and its experimental basis. *American Journal of Physical Medicine*, 1961, *40*, 109–129. (b)

Smith, K. U., & Henry, J. P. Cybernetic foundations for rehabilitation. *American Journal of Physical Medicine*, 1967, *46*, 379–467.

Smith, K. U., & Smith, W. M. *Perception and motion*. Philadelphia: Saunders, 1962.

Smith, K. U., Ansell, S., & Smith, W. M. Sensory feedback in medical research: I. Delayed sensory feedback in behavior and neural function. *American Journal of Physical Medicine*, 1963, *42*, 228–262.

Swinyard, C. A., Chaube, S., & Sutton, D. B. Neurological and behavioral aspects of transcendental meditation relevant to alcoholism: A review. *Annals of the New York Academy of Sciences*, 1974, *233*, 162–173.

Tarchanoff, J. R. Über die Willkürliche Acceleration der Herzschläge beim Menschen [Voluntary acceleration of the heart beat in man]. *Pflüger's Archive der gesamten Physiologie*, 1885, *35*, 109–135. (1972:1)

Travis, T. A., Kondo, C. Y., & Knott, J. R. Heart rate, muscle tension, and alpha production of transcendental meditators and relaxation controls. *Biofeedback and Self-Regulation*, 1976, *1*, 387–394.

Trowill, J. A. Instrumental conditioning of the heart rate in the curarized rat. *Journal of Comparative and Physiological Psychology*, 1967, *63*, 7–11.

Uno, T. The effects of awareness and successive inhibition on interoceptive and exteroceptive conditioning of the galvanic skin response. *Psychophysiology*, 1970, *7*, 27–43.

Wallace, R. K. Physiological effects of transcendental meditation. *Science*, 1970, *167*, 1751–1754. (1970:6)

Wallace, R. K., & Benson, H. The physiology of meditation. *Scientific American*, 1972, *226*, 84–90. (1972:28)

Wallace, R. K., Benson, H., & Wilson, A. F. A wakeful hypometabolic physiologic state. *American Journal of Physiology*, 1971, *221*, 795–799. (1971:7)

Weinstock, S. A. "Mens sana . . ." once more: A review of *the Alexander technique*. *Biofeedback and Self-Regulation*, 1976, *1*, 241–246.

Wenger, M. A., & Bagchi, B. K. Studies of autonomic functions in practitioners of yoga in India. *Behavioral Science*, 1961, *6*, 312–323.

Wenger, M. A., Bagchi, B. K., & Anand, B. K. Experiments in India on "voluntary" control of the heart and pulse. *Circulation*, 1961, *24*, 1319–1325.

West, H. F., & Savage, W. F. Voluntary acceleration of the heart beat. *Archives of Internal Medicine*, 1918, *22*, 290–295.

Whatmore, G. B., & Kohli, D. R. Dysponesis: A neurophysiologic factor in functional disorders. *Behavioral Science*, 1968, *13*, 102–124.

Williams, L. R. T. Transcendental meditation and mirror-tracing skill. *Perceptual and Motor Skills*, 1978, *46*, 371–378.

Williams, L. R. T., & Herbert, P. G. Transcendental meditation and fine perceptual-motor skill. *Perceptual and Motor Skills*, 1976, *43*, 303–309.

Williams, L. R. T., & Vickerman, B. L. Effects of transcendental meditation on fine motor skill. *Perceptual and Motor Skills*, 1976, *43*, 607–613.

Williams L. R. T., Lodge, B., & Reddish, P. S. Effects of transcendental meditation on rotary pursuit skill. *Research Quarterly*, 1977, *48*, 196–201.

Wilson, A. F., Honsberger, R., Chiu, J. T., & Novey, H. S. Transcendental meditation and asthma. *Respiration*, 1975, *32*, 74–80. (1975–6:7)

Woodworth, R. S. On the voluntary control of the force of movement. *Psychological Review,* 1901, *8,* 350–359.

Woolfolk, R. L. Psychophysiological correlates of meditation. *Archives of General Psychiatry,* 1975, *32,* 1326–1333. (1975–6:4)

Yates, A. J. Delayed auditory feedback. *Psychological Bulletin,* 1963, *60,* 213–232. (a)

Yates, A. J. Recent empirical and theoretical approaches to the experimental manipulation of speech in normal subjects and in stammerers. *Behavior Research and Therapy,* 1963, *1,* 95–119. (b)

Zuroff, D. C., & Schwarz, J. C. Effects of transcendental meditation and muscle relaxation on trait anxiety, maladjustment, locus of control, and drug use. *Journal of Consulting and Clinical Psychology,* 1978, *46,* 264–271.

CHAPTER 2

Instrumentation and Methodology

Introduction

However simple or sophisticated it may be, a biofeedback system must be capable of performing four functions: detection and transduction of the response under investigation, amplification (including, where necessary, rectification, smoothing, and integration) of the response, generation of a suitable display of the response, and on-line analysis, or storage for future analysis, of data representing characteristics of the response over time. In some instances the satisfaction of these requirements does not pose serious problems (the detection, transduction, amplification, and display of peripheral temperature is a good example); in other cases, however, there are major problems to be overcome in obtaining signals from the subject that are artifact-free with high-quality equipment needed for satisfactory results (examples would be the measurement of muscle activity, blood volume and flow, and the electrical activity of the brain, in spite of a tendency for these problems to be glossed over or even ignored in published reports). It would be impossible here to provide a detailed review of the technical aspects of transducing and amplifying each and every function that has been investigated in the biofeedback situation. Whole volumes have been devoted both to the problems of measurement of a wide range of physiological functions[1] and to detailed accounts of, for example, the kind of transducers necessary to detect the functions in question (see, e.g., Thompson & Patterson, 1974). Instead, a different approach will be adopted here in which the methodology of biofeedback research and clinical application will be the main object of discussion, with instrumentation being introduced as necessary.

---

[1]The manual by Venables and Martin (1967) represents an admirable example, covering most of the physiological functions studied in biofeedback experiments so far.

The methodology of research in any area of psychology may be most simply and effectively approached by recognizing that in any projected or published study four aspects need careful consideration: the specification of the dependent variable or variables, the specification of the independent variable or variables, the specification and control of possible relevant confounding variables (where a confounding variable is defined as an independent variable which is not under experimenter control and may account for significant results which are thereby incorrectly assigned to the variations in an independent variable which is under experimenter control), and what for want of a better term will be referred to as procedural matters—such as the instructions given to the subject, whether he is fully informed or not, the specification of technical aspects of the experimentation, such as lighting conditions, and so on. (It is recognized that these aspects may also become confounding independent variables if they are not uniform across experimental and control groups.) Each of these aspects will be considered in turn, with reference to relevant studies where appropriate. Some account will also be given of the kinds of experimental designs which have been utilized in biofeedback research. The treatment of these matters is not intended to be exhaustive; rather, the intention is to provide an overview of the methodology of research in the area of biofeedback so that the reader is alerted to careful analysis and comparison of individual studies with respect to the methodology used. As pointed out by Yates (1972) in another connection, in a very real sense empirical knowledge is a function of the methodology involved in generating that knowledge, and significant changes in empirical knowledge result very often from important changes in methodology.

The Dependent Variable in Biofeedback

The dependent variable in biofeedback research or clinical treatment may be any function whatsoever which a subject or patient may possess, limitations being set only by the ability of the experimenter or clinician to detect, transduce, and quantify the response in question. As already pointed out, the difficulty of reliably and validly measuring a response and changes which may occur as a result of biofeedback training varies enormously. In many areas of potential importance to biofeedback, successful investigation still awaits the development of adequate detection and transducing instrumentation. Examples will be given here of the problems of detecting and transducing some commonly investigated responses, as well as some unusual techniques for detecting and transducing responses which have only rarely been investigated.

The detection of muscle activity is accomplished by the use of bipolar electrodes that reflect the difference in electrical potential between the two active electrodes which are placed over the muscle in which the activity is being recorded. Standard lead placements developed by Davis (1952) are used by most research workers, and the most common are conveniently illustrated in Lippold (1967, pp. 284–292). Thus, it is recommended that the following procedures be followed when frontalis muscle activity is being recorded:

> First electrode: Using as a guide the nasion and the inion . . . draw a line through the center of the forehead, from nasion to hairline. Draw a horizontal on the right side of this central dividing line 2 in. in length and approximately 1 in. above the eyebrow. Center of the first electrode should be placed over this point. Second electrode: Repeat above procedure on the left side of central dividing line for the second electrode. (Lippold, 1967, p. 284)

The procedure is illustrated in Figure 1. The relative subjectivity of the procedure will be apparent since it is not stated what should be done in the case of a bald subject; but, of course, the frontalis muscle is sufficiently large that small variations in positioning across subjects are relatively unimportant; it is of greater

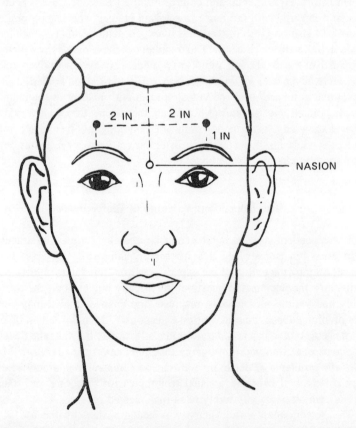

Figure 1. Standard forehead lead. (From Lippold, O. C. J. Electromyography. In P. H. Venables & I. Martin (Eds.), *A manual of psychophysical methods*. Amsterdam: North-Holland Publishing, 1967, p. 285, Figue 8.21. Reprinted by permission of the author and the publisher.

importance to follow the same rules on different occasions in the same subject. The precision with which recording from surface electrodes reflects the underlying activity of the muscle in question and the degree to which activity from other muscles (including some far distant from the forehead) is picked up by the surface electrodes have been a matter of some dispute. It has been maintained that only the use of inserted or needle electrodes which penetrate the muscle itself can guarantee relatively uncontaminated recording and certainly the measurement of single motor unit activity requires the use of inserted electrodes. However, for many purposes the correlation between recordings made by needle and surface electrodes used simultaneously is sufficiently high to justify the use of surface electrodes for most purposes (see Chapter 3). It is necessary to prepare the skin below the electrode placements carefully so as to reduce electrical resistance to the flow of current at least below 10,000 Ω and a good contact is essential if reliable recordings are to be made (see Lippold, 1967, for a detailed account of techniques).

Movements by the subject are, of course, often a source of interference and artifact in electromyography, but it should be noted that movement and its control are of great interest in biofeedback research and treatment. In cerebral palsy, for example, a great deal of ingenuity has been demonstrated in attempts to measure movement in order to display its characteristics to the subject. For example, Harris, Spelman, Hymer, and Chase (1973) have described several devices intended to measure movement in different planes of various bodily parts in cerebral-palsied subjects. The Head Control Device consists of a helmet in which mechanoelectrical transducers are mounted which respond to vertical and lateral head movements away from the neutral ("normal") head position. These movements can be translated into auditory or visual feedback which indicates to the subject when his head position deviates from the neutral position. Similar devices for use in cerebral palsy training have been described by Halpern, Kottke, Burrill, Fiterman, Popp, and Palmer (1970)[2] and by Wooldridge and Russell (1976). Harris *et al.* (1973) have also described the use of a Limb Position Monitor to measure the angle of rotation about the axis of individual joints, and a Multiple Axis Limb and Head Position Monitor which provides the subject with visual indications of the positions of five body parts simultaneously so that training in the maintenance of coordinated (rather than single) body parts may be undertaken (especially of the head, elbows, wrist, and fingers to facilitate, for example, self-feeding).[3]

Considerable ingenuity has been shown in overcoming problems associated with the detection of malfunctioning in the organs associated with speech disabilities. Nasalization in the speech of deaf and retarded children has been

---

[2]Their device, however, appears to have an aversive consequence (constriction) for failure to maintain the upright position built into it.

[3]A more readily accessible description of the Head Control and Limb Position Monitors will be found in Harris, Spelman, and Hymer (1974).

detected by the use of an accelerometer which detects vibrations in the nasal cavity (Stevens, Nickerson, Boothroyd, & Rollins, 1976), while the system called TONAR developed by Daly (1974) separates and utilizes sound levels from the oral and nasal channels involved in the production of sounds to detect, quantify, and display the degree of nasalization in connected speech. Even more ingeniously, Moller, Path, Werth, and Christiansen (1973) have described how to use displacement transducers to monitor directly the activity of the soft palate in producing velopharyngeal closure (the contact of the soft palate with the posterior pharyngeal wall). Finger-spring sensor wire is attached to the free end of a cantilever strain-gauge transducer which is rigidly attached to an orthodontic band and cemented to a maxillary molar tooth. A sensor contact point is positioned on the middle third of the soft palate at the midline and follows the movement of the palate. Since the degree of nasality in speech is a function of the position of the soft palate relative to the posterior pharyngeal wall, direct training of the soft palate position during speech may be undertaken if it is desirable to reduce nasalization. Ingenuity has also been shown in the development of sensing devices to detect bruxing (teeth-grinding) activity during sleep, the requirements, of course, being a system which can be worn during sleep and which will not easily be disturbed by movements during sleep. Such a device has recently been described by Dowdell, Clarke, and Kardachi (1976). Essentially, the system detects activity in the masseter and temporalis muscles and transduces it into a feedback signal of an auditory kind, presumably serving either as an aversive signal or to wake the subject. Similar systems used by other workers have capitalized on the sound produced by bruxing to determine when the activity is taking place.

The detection and transduction of autonomic functions varies very greatly in respect of the difficulties involved. The detection of heart rate, for example, is relatively uncomplicated, with the interval between successive R waves[4] usually being taken as the interbeat interval or heart rate. Other aspects of heart activity are also of great interest, although relatively neglected in biofeedback research. Similarly, the measurement of peripheral temperature poses few problems, extremely sensitive and reliable sensors now being available for this purpose. However, the measurement of other autonomic functions has posed considerable problems, toward the solution of which a great deal of energy has been expended. Of these functions, the detection of changes in systolic and diastolic blood pressure has perhaps attracted the most attention. Until relatively recently, only two techniques were in use, representing the extremes of clinical and research procedures. For clinical purposes, the use of the sphygmomanometer (using an inflated cuff) was considered adequate, whereas for research purposes the use of a catheter directly inserted into the blood stream was considered essential for accurate recording. The latter procedure, however, was not lightly

[4]See Chapter 4 for a description of the major features of the heart cycle.

to be used and was certainly not considered appropriate for use in biofeedback experiments. Hence, a search was instituted in an attempt to discover ways of obtaining continuous monitoring of blood pressure changes, either by means of modifications of the inflated-cuff technique or in other ways which would not necessitate the use of invasive procedures. These procedures are described in some detail in Chapter 4 and need not be repeated here. Similar difficulties are involved in the measurement of blood flow and volume by techniques known as plethysmography. While the difficulties can mostly be overcome fairly readily in the case of the measurement of blood volume and flow in the fingers (where either photoplethysmography or strain-gauge techniques[5] may be used), the measurement of blood volume in the cranial arteries (of importance in biofeed-back studies of migraine) is a very much more difficult matter since strain-gauge measurement clearly is inappropriate and the placing of a transducer directly over the artery is a delicate matter with respect to successive placements, as well as the need to avoid pressure on the cranial artery itself. Strain-gauge measurements are obviously applicable to the measurement of penile circumference (and hence blood volume) but only recently has success attended attempts to measure vaginal blood volume as an indicator of sexual arousal. Similar technical problems are encountered in the measurement of electrodermal responding, salivation, and, of course, internal functions such as gastrointestinal activity. All of these problems will be considered in some detail at the appropriate places in this book.

Finally, the detection and measurement of the electrical activity of the brain has attracted a great deal of attention. As will be described in Chapter 5, international agreement was reached some 20 years ago in respect of a nomenclature for some 20 or so standard electrode placements for recording the electrical activity of the brain and it is now mandatory to use this nomenclature when describing electrode placement. However, as will be seen in Chapter 5, no such agreement has been reached in any other aspect of research in this area and the variations in methodology are largely responsible for the disagreements which have occurred on such a large scale (Hardt & Kamiya, 1976).

The range of difficulties (from small to great) experienced in detecting and transducing the signals emanating from the organism are almost exactly paralleled in the subsequent stages of amplification and treatment of the signals so that they may be displayed to the subject on the one hand, and analyzed on the other. Thus, an electrically shielded room may be unnecessary even for research purposes in relation to electromyography provided it is possible to eliminate mains interference (using a notch filter, for example). To eliminate artifacts such as heart rate and gross movements from the EMG record it is essential to pass the signal from the electrodes through a filter which only accepts information in the frequency range 80–1000 Hz. On the other hand, the complexity of the EMG

---

[5]The strain gauge fits around the finger and measures directly increases in finger volume as a function of increased engorgement of the capillaries with blood.

information requires that the signal be smoothed and integrated before it is analyzed and presented in a display. It is not generally appreciated that integration, by definition, introduces a delay into the feedback display, and as was seen in Chapter 1, such delays may interfere with obtaining and maintaining control over the activity. The amplification of temperature signals, on the other hand, involves few problems since the changes which occur are relatively slow and uncomplicated. Likewise, it is not difficult to amplify heart rate, although the accurate detection of the occurrence of successive R waves may present problems.

Thus, the accurate detection and transduction of the dependent variable of interest may present insuperable difficulties unless adequate instrumentation is available for the purpose.

The Independent Variable in Biofeedback

The most important independent variable in biofeedback research is of course the display to the subject of the function under investigation. The types of feedback displays which have been used have varied greatly; broadly speaking, however, they fall into three categories: visual, auditory, and digital, with occasional excursions into other modalities such as the tactual. Within the visual modality, the possibilities for displaying feedback are almost unlimited. One of the most common types of visual display involves the use of a scale (usually, but not necessarily, in the shape of a curve rather like the speedometer of a car) with the midpoint representing average baseline level and deviations to the left and right representing decreases and increases in performance, respectively (e.g., Blanchard, Scott, Young, & Haynes, 1974). Brener and Kleinman (1970) used a manometer gauge which provided a continuous vertical display of absolute systolic blood pressure values. The use of an oscilloscope enables a continuous display to be provided of functions such as muscle activity, with the added advantage that the display remains visible until the oscilloscope resets at the end of a sweep (the sweep time being, of course, adjustable) so that the subject can follow the changing course of his performance. Even without an oscilloscope, it is possible with a little ingenuity to arrange displays of this kind. Blanchard, Young, and Haynes (1975), for example, focused a TV camera on graph paper on which the experimenter plotted a point representing systolic blood pressure changes minute by minute and displayed the resultant graph continuously to the subject via a videomonitor.

Another type of visual display is illustrated in the study by Lubar and Bahler (1976), who used a bank of lights which were illuminated progressively each time 12- to 14-Hz cortical activity reached a specified criterion (based on amplitude and duration of the activity). A similar feedback display was used by Manuck, Levenson, Hinrichsen, and Gryll (1975) to represent changes in heart rate. One type of visual display worthy of special mention is that used by Lang, Troyer, Twentyman, and Gatchel (1975) which has been quite widely adopted.[6] They provided a vertical line as the ''target'' at the right-hand side of an oscilloscope display. A horizontal line which moved from left to right across the screen toward the target varied in its length on a beat-by-beat basis as a function of changes in heart rate. The target could, for example, indicate baseline heart rate. If heart rate increased during training, the horizontal line would go beyond the target line, whereas if heart rate decreased the horizontal line would fall short of the target line.

It might be thought that digital displays (in which numbers represent the level of activity) would be very popular, but this has not proved to be the case. Manuck *et al.* (1975) represented heart-rate changes by a changing display of the numbers 2 through 8, although, of course, it would be possible simply to present a changing digital display of the actual heart rate on a one-to-one basis (e.g., 75, 76, 77, and so on, corresponding to rates of 75 bpm, etc.). A similar (7-point) digital scale was used by Levenson (1976) to represent changes in heart rate, while Brener and Kleinman (1970) used an electromagnetic counter operating at a rate directly proportional to systolic blood pressure. There is no difficulty in presenting digital displays of level of activity and the use of such displays under computer control appears very attractive. The availability of a TEC terminal, for example, would enable a display of peripheral temperature such that moment-by-moment changes could be followed by the subject while at the same time other values (such as baseline level, previous trial means, and so on) could also be provided. However, such numerical displays are in fact much harder to track than nonnumerical graphical displays and tend to confuse the subject.[7]

Auditory feedback has been even more commonly used than visual feedback. It usually takes the form of either a change in pitch as a function of change in activity, or a change in click rate. Thus, Kinsman, O'Banion, Robinson, and Staudenmayer (1975) presented feedback in the form of two clicks per second when frontalis muscle activity was absent, while one click, corresponding to one EMG count, was given whenever the half-wave rectified EMG signal reached an integrated value of 0.169μV-sec. If feedback is being provided for more than one activity (for example, left and right finger temperature changes), stereo headphones may be used, with auditory feedback provided separately in each headphone, or if differential control is involved, a single auditory feedback signal may be provided, with the sound moving from left to right to represent differential changes in finger temperature.

So far, little attention has been paid to other possible feedback modalities although these could be of great importance, particularly in the clinical area (for

---

[6]This type of display appears to have been used first by Jacobs and Felton (1969).

[7]This assertion is based on observations made in the author's laboratory, using digital displays of peripheral finger temperature. Empirical evidence of the relative value of digital and graphical displays is lacking.

example, in blindness where, of course, visual feedback cannot be utilized). Schandler and Grings (1974) have described a voltage-controlled pulse generator and tactile transducer which enables pulses to be presented to the skin at rates varying from zero to 30 pulses per second.

A satisfactory taxonomy of feedback displays has not yet been achieved. As a result, the description of the parameters of feedback display (other than the simple division into modalities just described) has been very variable, with a resultant degree of confusion in the literature. Several attempts have been made in recent years to compare the effectiveness of different kinds of feedback in promoting control of function. Before considering these studies, however, an attempt will be made to clarify the taxonomic situation. Broadly speaking, three "dimensions" of feedback display (which cut across the categories of visual, digital, auditory, and tactile) may be discerned:

> within trial versus end of trial (W/E)
> proportional versus binary (P/B)
> continuous versus noncontinuous (C/NC)[8]

If all possible combinations of these dimensions were relevant, a total of eight types of feedback situation could be defined. In fact, a careful examination of the eight combinations reveals that not all of them make experimental sense. The most relevant ones are described below. It should be noted carefully that the terminology used is sometimes different from that used in some of the studies to be mentioned; hence, in reviewing the comparative studies some of the experimental conditions will be reinterpreted in the light of the schema suggested here.

Four main categories of feedback may be distinguished when the feedback is presented *within* a trial. The first is *within trial, proportional and continuous feedback* (W/P/C). Examples would be the display of muscle activity on an oscilloscope screen in continuous graphical form or on a visual meter, or the presentation of a continuously varying tone. Providing the sampling rate is fast enough and the integration is over a sufficiently small time the display changes will appear continuous to the subject. Another example of the W/P/C type would be the continuous proportional change in the intensity of a single light source as a function of change in activity of the function being measured.

The next category which may be distinguished is the *within-trial, proportional but noncontinuous* (W/P/NC) presentation of feedback. It should be noted that several examples in the literature which are usually regarded as examples of a continuous (W/P/C) display are in fact examples of the W/P/NC category. Thus, displays which represent heart rate on a beat-by-beat (R–R interval) basis fall into the latter category because the R–R interval represents only part of the heart cycle (see Chapter 4) which itself is, of course, continuous. A display of heart rate which would fall into the W/P/C category would be an oscilloscope

---

[8]The question of whether the feedback is relevant ("true") or irrelevant ("false") is a separate issue.

display of the continuous total heart cycle (which would then be equivalent to a continuous display of muscle activity). The oscillographic display of beat-by-beat changes (Lang *et al.*, 1975) described earlier also falls within the W/P/NC category, although usually described as continuous feedback. The intermittent information presented in the W/P/NC category can, of course, take a wide variety of forms. Thus, it can consist of a single proportional reading presented every so often within a trial, representing the state of activity at that moment proportionally; or it can consist of a single reading presented every so often within a trial but representing the average level of activity since the last reading.

The third category is the *within-trial, binary, continuous* (W/B/C) presentation of feedback. Here again, a difference from the common terminology used in the literature needs to be noted. Thus, Blanchard, Young, Scott, and Haynes (1974) used two running time clocks. When the left-hand clock was running, the subject knew he was succeeding at his task of controlling heart rate; when the right-hand one was running, he knew he was not succeeding. This is a clear example of the W/B/C category. However, in other studies (e.g., Blanchard, Scott, Young, & Haynes, 1974), the feedback stimulus (e.g., a light) is illuminated only when a specified criterion level of performance is met. A feedback display of this kind is correctly described as binary but it would be incorrect to describe it as noncontinuous because information is, in fact, being presented when the light is off as well as when it is on (on the other hand, in the example given earlier, true discontinuity is achieved where a single reading is presented intermittently but no information whatever is given between presentations). A rare and special case of the W/B/C category which also involves proportional feedback is found in a study by Young and Blanchard (1974). They presented auditory feedback (1000-Hz tone) whenever a specified criterion was met but, additionally, as long as the criterion was met the tone varied as a function of changes in level of activity.

The fourth category is the *within-trial, binary, noncontinuous* (W/B/NC) presentation of feedback. This procedure is not common but was used by Blanchard, Young, Haynes, and Kallman (1974, experiment 2) who informed the subject each 1 min within a trial whether or not his level of responding over the previous minute was "correct" or "incorrect" (where "correct" was defined as a systolic blood pressure at least 5 mm Hg below baseline). However, no information was provided about the magnitude of the change. Another example comes from a study by Brener, Kleinman, and Goesling (1969), who provided auditory feedback for heart-rate changes whenever a specified criterion was achieved. However, within a trial feedback was given either on every occasion the criterion was exceeded (100% feedback), on half of the occasions (50% feedback) or not at all (0% feedback).

These four categories appear to exhaust the *within-trial* possibilities, although many other variations within the four categories could be described. Where feedback is given at the *end of a trial* (but not during a trial) two main categories may be discerned. The first is *end-of-trial proportional* (E/P) presentation of feedback in which information is provided as to how performance on that trial compared with performances on some previous trial or baseline performance, the difference being specified in quantitative form. The second is *end-of-trial binary* (E/B) presentation of feedback in which comparative information is likewise provided but the difference is not quantified. Several points need to be noted about end-of-trial-only feedback which also apply to intermittent within-trial feedback. Any feedback which is not continuous inevitably introduces a delay into the presentation of the feedback. The importance of this fact does not appear to have been appreciated by most biofeedback research or clinical workers. The introduction of delay of feedback may have quite catastrophic effects on the integrity of performance, as was illustrated in Chapter 1 by the effects of delayed auditory feedback on speech and delayed visual feedback on visual tracking performance. The injudicious use of feedback in biofeedback training could certainly interfere with the acquisition of control rather than enhance it, and the inadvertent introduction of such delays might well account for some of the failures to obtain positive results in biofeedback training. One reason such delays may not have had severe effects in biofeedback training may have been simply a matter of good fortune. In delayed auditory feedback, the effects of the delay diminish as the delay increases (for reasons which are quite clear but need not be specified here) so that when the delay exceeds 1 sec speech is hardly affected. Most biofeedback studies in which delay is built into the design of the experiment may have avoided adverse effects simply because the delay was accidentally a very long one. However, it should also be pointed out that the longer the delay before feedback is presented, the less representative the feedback will be of the changes which have taken place between two successive instances of feedback. The relationship between delay of feedback and the acquisition of control has hardly been investigated at all as yet, a situation which is in urgent need of rectification.

Two other aspects of feedback categories should be mentioned here. First, feedback gain or amplification is an important parameter which has so far received insufficient attention. Chase, Cullen, Openshaw, and Sullivan (1965), for example, showed that errors in tracking of finger movement with a visual feedback display proportional to performance were progressively reduced as amplitude of movement feedback was magnified up to four times (but not beyond this point). Studies such as this one are of considerable importance in relation to the control of muscle activity and tremor. Second, the relevance or irrelevance of the feedback presented has clearly been shown to be important in feedback control. In an early study, Budzynski and Stoyva (1969) showed that control of frontalis muscle activity was facilitated by the presentation of relevant feedback (an auditory tone) but that control was not achieved if a continuous noncontingent low tone was presented—indeed, the latter may have interfered with the establishment of control since, as will be demonstrated elsewhere, there is now convincing evidence that control may be established in the absence of feedback. A control group used by Budzynski and Stoyva (1969) which received no feedback did in fact show more reduction in muscle activity than did the group provided with irrelevant feedback.

It may readily be concluded that the display aspect of biofeedback raises difficult and complex questions, the resolution of which are important if the alleged advantages of biofeedback training are to be maximized. Yet surprisingly little fundamental research into these questions has as yet been completed. The studies which have attempted to investigate these problems will now be considered and placed within the framework described above.

There are several studies which have directly compared within-trial, proportional, continuous (W/P/C) or discontinuous (W/P/NC) feedback with within-trial, binary, continuous feedback (W/B/C) using the same modality (visual or auditory) of feedback. Blanchard, Scott, Young, and Haynes (1974) compared the effects of proportional (visual meter) and binary (a red light activated whenever a criterion level was reached or exceeded) feedback when the task was to increase or decrease heart rate. For heart-rate increase proportional feedback was superior to binary, but for heart-rate decrease there was no difference and neither kind of feedback display was in fact helpful. Using a cross-over design, they also reported that when the group trained to increase heart rate with the aid of proportional feedback was switched to binary feedback, there was a significant decline in control, whereas the reverse occurred with the group switched from binary to proportional feedback. Similar results for initial training in heart-rate control were reported by Colgan (1977) who, however, found the same advantage for proportional over binary feedback in the case of heart-rate decrease as well. When feedback was withdrawn, Colgan (1977) found that control was maintained better in the proportional feedback group. Manuck et al. (1975) compared two kinds of within-trial, proportional but noncontinuous (W/P/NC) feedback (a string of 16 lights, and a display of the numbers 2–8) with within-trial, binary, continuous (W/B/C) feedback and could find no differences between the three groups in control of heart-rate increases and decreases. There was, of course, confounding between the two W/P/NC conditions and the W/B/C condition since the former involved discontinuous and the latter continuous display of feedback. Lang and Twentyman (1974) compared the effectiveness of W/P/NC type feedback with W/B/C type feedback and could find no difference between proportional and binary feedback in the control of heart-rate increases and decreases. However, their study was doubly confounded: continuous feedback in the W/B/C condition with discontinuous feedback in the W/P/NC condition, and the moving horizontal line in the W/P/NC condition with the printed word "good" in the W/B/C condition.

The superiority of proportional over binary feedback in control of heart-rate increases (but not decreases) in initial training was also reported in the auditory feedback modality by Young and Blanchard (1974). Likewise, Travis, Kondo, and Knott (1974) showed that proportional feedback was superior to binary feedback in eyes-closed alpha-enhancement training, although there was a suggestion that the reverse might be the case for eyes-open training.

On the whole, therefore, this group of studies tends to suggest that within-trial, proportional, continuous (W/P/C) or discontinuous (W/P/NC) visual or auditory feedback is superior to within-trial, binary, continuous (W/B/C) feedback. The control of heart rate, however, is not a particularly good function to use in comparing proportional and binary feedback because of certain peculiarities of heart-rate control. In particular, a failure to find differences in the control of heart-rate decrease may be due primarily to difficulties in producing heart-rate decreases under any feedback conditions because baseline (resting) heart-rate levels may be close to the lowest levels obtainable under the usual feedback training conditions.

Several studies have examined the relative effectiveness of different feedback modalities (such as visual versus auditory). Blanchard and Young (1972) compared within-trial, proportional, continuous (W/P/C) feedback in the auditory (varying tone) and visual (meter reading) modalities in the control of increases and decreases of heart rate and found no difference in their effectiveness in the control of increases, both being superior to a no-feedback condition. However, neither mode of feedback proved helpful in the control of heart-rate decreases. Blanchard, Young, Haynes, and Kallmann (1974) found that proportional (W/P/NC) feedback (visual graphical, plotted every 1 min) was superior to binary (W/B/NC) feedback (the subject told every minute whether his performance was correct or not) in the control of systolic blood pressure, but the result is confounded since the visual feedback was proportional whereas the auditory feedback was binary. The remaining comparative studies in this category deal with the control of muscle activity. Alexander, French, and Goodman (1975) presented within-trial, proportional, continuous (W/P/C) feedback in the auditory modality (with eyes open or closed) and the visual modality while the subject attempted to relax the frontalis muscle. Auditory feedback (eyes closed) produced a significant drop in frontalis muscle activity but auditory feedback (eyes-open) and visual feedback did not. This result, however, must be treated with considerable reservation because it is contrary to the results obtained in many studies using visual proportional or auditory (eyes-open) feedback. Furthermore, and unusually, the experimenter was in the same room as the subject, peering over his shoulder to read off the frontalis activity levels, a procedure which could have had quite unpredictable effects on the subjects' performance. Budzynski and Stoyva (1973) trained subjects to reduce activity in the masseter muscle under conditions of auditory (W/P/C) feedback or visual (W/B/C) feedback, no difference in effectiveness being apparent between the two modalities. This study is also confounded, however, since the auditory feedback was proportional and the visual feedback binary. Even more confounded was the study by Kinsman *et al.* (1975) dealing with reduction of frontalis muscle activity, in which auditory (W/P/C) feedback was compared with verbal (E/B) feedback. The auditory feedback consisted of continuous clicks whereas in the verbal feedback condition the subject was told at the end of each trial whether his level of activity had increased or decreased (but not by how much). Auditory feedback was found to be superior to verbal feedback, but of course double confounding was present (within- versus end-of-trial information, and continuous versus binary feedback). An interesting study was conducted by Schandler and Grings (1976). In their first experiment, the subjects were required to reduce forearm muscle activity when provided with either visual meter or tactile feedback (both involving the W/P/C type of feedback), while in the second experiment tactile feedback was compared with auditory. While tactile feedback was found to be superior to visual, no difference was apparent between tactile and auditory feedback. The results of all of these studies leave open the question of whether auditory feedback is superior to visual feedback, and of course, it may well be that the relative effectiveness of these modalities (as well as tactile feedback) will vary as a function of the response being controlled. The degree of confounding in many of the studies carried out so far renders interpretation of the results very difficult.

Some attention has also been paid to the question of whether there is any advantage to be gained by providing multiple-modality feedback. Clearly, a fine line exists here between providing the maximum amount of feedback information and the limited processing capacity of the human organism. Carlsöö and Edfeldt (1963) required their subjects to press the thumb and forefinger together to produce single motor unit activity (recorded from an electrode implanted in the first dorsal interosseus muscle) and measured the time to achieve a stable level of single motor unit activity and the ability of the subject to maintain the stable level once achieved. In one experimental condition the subject was required to rely on internal proprioceptive feedback only, and the effects of adding visual alone, auditory alone, and combined visual and auditory feedback to the proprioceptive feedback were examined. The "search time" to achieve stable single motor unit responding was dramatically reduced over three trials when proprioceptive feedback was augmented by visual and auditory feedback, maintenance time of stable responding was significantly reduced when the subject had to rely on proprioceptive feedback alone, and the addition of auditory feedback produced better results than the addition of visual feedback. Colgan (1977), in the study described earlier, found that the positive effects of proportional feedback were not further enhanced by the addition of binary feedback in the control of increases in heart rate, both being superior to binary feedback alone. However, the combination of proportional and binary feedback was more effective in the control of heart-rate decrease than either proportional or binary feedback presented alone. Kinsman *et al.* (1975), whose study has also been described earlier, found that proportional auditory feedback was superior to a combination of that feedback and binary, end-of-trial verbal feedback and to the verbal feedback alone. The confounding involved in this study has already been described. Shapiro, Tursky, and Schwartz (1970) provided visual feedback (a 100 msec red light flash) each time an increase in heart rate occurred. For half the subjects, simultaneous similar auditory feedback (a 100 msec 2000-Hz tone) was also provided; the remaining subjects were provided, in addition to the visual feedback, with continuous auditory feedback (a 70-Hz frequency change being equated with a change of 2 bpm in heart rate). Another group of subjects was treated similarly with respect to heart-rate decreases. Control of increased heart rate was not obtained,[9] whereas control of decreased heart rate was, the difference between the increase/decrease groups being significant. However, no differential effect of combined over single feedback modality was found in this study. Surwit (1977), in a study of peripheral finger temperature control, compared the effects of providing visual proportional meter feedback with the effects of combining the proportional feedback with a four-light display designed to indicate decreases in temperature, negatively accelerating decreases in temperature, and positively accelerating increases in temperature. No differential effect of the combined over the single feedback modality was found. However, this study was also confounded in that the combined feedback also included auditory feedback for increases and decreases in temperature.

Finally, mention should be made of the study by Gatchel (1974) in which subjects were given informational feedback after every heartbeat, after every five heartbeats, or after every ten heartbeats, the feedback being of the kind developed by Lang, described earlier (the results of this study are more fully described in Chapter 4). Suffice it to say here that the more frequently feedback was presented, the better the control of heart-rate increases (but not decreases) that was obtained.

The only clear conclusion that can be drawn from all of this work is that it has been too unsystematic to enable clear-cut results to be obtained. In particular, the possible interaction between the type of feedback provided and the response over which control is to be obtained has not yet been adequately investigated. It is not impossible that visual feedback may be preferable for some kinds of function but that auditory feedback will be preferable for other kinds of function. Individual subject preferences may be also important. What is needed here is large-scale research carried out systematically, as the question is clearly of fundamental significance.

The number of other independent variables which could be manipulated in the biofeedback situation is, of course, almost unlimited. Since, however, the display modality as an independent variable is of primary interest, it will be convenient to consider these other variables as potential confounding variables.

---

[9]But see the discussion of the "drift effect" later in this chapter for an analysis of such "failures" of control.

Confounding Variables and the Design of Experiments in Biofeedback

Leaving aside for the moment single-subject experiments (usually, but not exclusively, found in clinical biofeedback studies) the experimental strategies most favored in biofeedback research have involved between-group and within-group designs. Two general points may be noted first. Since biofeedback studies almost invariably involve the assessment of change in performance over time, between-group designs almost always involve within-group factors as well, so that interactions between the two kinds of factors are important. Second, the designs are primarily intended to control for, or evaluate the effect of, possible confounding variables so that it is appropriate to consider the problem of confounding variables within the context of experimental designs in general.

Between-group designs usually (and should always) involve the measurement of the function in question under three basic sequential conditions: baseline, training, and transfer. Thus, in the case of frontalis muscle training the baseline level of frontalis muscle activity should first be assessed over a number of trials in which the subject is instructed simply to rest quietly with no feedback being presented. The training trials are then instituted in which feedback is presented to the subject who is usually instructed that the feedback will vary as a function of the level of frontalis muscle activity and that his task is to reduce that level as much as possible, with changes in the feedback signal indexing decreases (and increases). In the case of frontalis (or other) muscle activity a decrease in level is usually what is required; but, of course, in the case of many functions (such as heart rate the task may be to increase or decrease heart rate (or to reduce the level of variability in heart rate). When training in voluntary control has been completed, a second baseline set of trials without feedback may be given (in which the subject is instructed to rest quietly again) or a transfer set of trials without feedback may be presented (in which the subject is instructed to maintain his level of activity as low or as high as possible, that is, to transfer whatever control he has achieved with feedback to the no-feedback situation).

Such a simple design is, of course, inadequate to demonstrate either voluntary control or transfer of control since the changes which may occur during the training and transfer periods may, in the absence of appropriate controls, be the result of uncontrolled confounding variables such as the effects of naturally occurring changes over the passage of time. As a bare minimum, a control group which is treated in exactly the same way, except that it is never given feedback, is essential. With the incorporation of a control group of this kind, quite elaborate between-group designs may be utilized. A simple example would be an experiment in which the effects of between-group variables are examined. Thus, the effects of feedback/no-feedback, instructions to use imagery versus no instructions about using imagery, and sex (male versus female subjects) may be examined. With three stages involved (baseline–training–transfer) such an experiment would involve three between-group factors and at least two within-group factors (stages, and number of trials within stages), requiring eight independent groups of subjects to carry out the study. Such designs have serious disadvantages which are often not recognized. In the first place, many subjects are required to provide reasonable numbers of subjects in the higher order interaction cells (in the above design, 80 subjects would be required to obtain 10 subjects, for example, in the feedback/imagery/female and other triple interaction cells). In the second place, the addition of another (and any subsequent) factor immediately doubles the number of subjects required. Given the very high degree of intersubject variability in functions of interest in biofeedback research, such designs are uneconomical and it may be very difficult to detect significant interactions between factors, even though such interactions may be present and important. Many biofeedback researchers have turned to within-group designs in an effort to overcome these difficulties. In these designs, of course, the subjects are used as their own controls, thus reducing the effects of within-subject variability.

There is no difficulty in providing examples of each of these two main designs. It should be remembered, however, that both designs are extremely flexible. A good example of a combination of a combined between- and within-group design is provided by a study carried out by McCanne and Sandman (1975). They utilized a $2 \times 2 \times 3 \times 4 \times 2$ factorial design with only one of the factors being treated as a between-groups factor (no doubt because they only used a total of ten subjects in all). Half the subjects were required to accelerate heart rate and half to decelerate heart rate (between-groups factor). However, the subjects within each group were provided with two kinds of "reinforcement" (monetary reward and feedback), three sessions were run with each "reinforcer," four blocks of five trials were given in each session, and the effect of "response sample" (pretrial versus trial responses) was assessed. Each of these last four variables was treated as a within-groups variable, although it would be more customary to treat the "reinforcement" variables as a between-groups factor (clearly the use of only ten subjects made this impossible in this instance). A simple example of a between-groups design is found in the study by Schwartz (1972) in which 40 normotensive males were allocated to four groups which were provided with the same feedback for, respectively, simultaneously increasing systolic blood pressure and heart rate, decreasing systolic blood pressure and heart rate, increasing systolic blood pressure while decreasing heart rate, and decreasing systolic blood pressure while increasing heart rate. All subjects received 5 baseline, 5 random "reinforcement," and 35 training (feedback) trials where each trial was 50 heartbeats in length. Schwartz, Shapiro, and Tursky (1971) had earlier carried out a similar study utilizing only two groups. Schandler and Grings (1976), in the study previously mentioned, allocated 100 normal subjects to one of four training conditions: progressive relaxation training, visual (meter) feedback, tactile (trains of pulses) feedback, and no-feedback control. The feedback was given for forearm extensor muscle activity and the subject's task was to reduce the activity in that muscle. Baseline, training, and posttraining baseline measures were obtained so that the design was a 4 (between) × 3 (within) factorial design.

These between-group designs are, of course, quite conventional, involving analysis of variance. The within-group designs using a single group of subjects serving as their own controls are of considerably more interest. Two examples may be provided. Lang *et al.* (1975) used the basic design shown in Table 1 in a study of voluntary control of increases and decreases in heart rate in college students, older males, and patients with ischemic heart disease. It will be seen that each experimental session consisted of six timed phases, with phases 3–5

Table 1. Standard Format across Experimental Sessions and Tasks Associated with Each Time Phase[a]

	Session	
Time phase	Heart rate control	Tracking
1. 3 min	Initial baseline period	Initial baseline period
2. 1 min	Try period *For the next few minutes try to increase (decrease) your heart rate as much as possible.*	Time estimation period *Time estimation—Please press the button every ten seconds.*
3. 3 min	Feedback period *The feedback display will now be presented to help increase (decrease) your heart rate.*	Tracking period *The visual display will now be presented. Press the button each time the moving line falls short of (exceeds) the target.*
4. 1 min	Transfer period *For this period continue to increase (decrease) your heart rate as much as possible.*	Time estimation period *Time estimation—Please press the button every ten seconds.*
5. 1 min	Time-out period *Stop working on the heart rate task but continue to sit quietly. You will receive further instructions shortly.*	Time-out period *Stop working for a while but continue to sit quietly. You will receive further instructions shortly.*
6. 3 min	Final baseline period *Instructions same as time-out period above.*	Final baseline period *Instructions same as time-out period above.*

SOURCE: Lang, P. J., Troyer, W. G., Twentyman, C. T., & Gatchel, R. J. Differential effects of heart rate modification training on college students, older males, and patients with ischemic heart disease. *Psychosomatic Medicine*, 1975, *37*, Table 1. Reprinted by permission of the author and the publisher.
[a]Periods 3–5 (feedback or tracking, transfer or time estimation, and time-out) were repeated five times in sequence prior to the final baseline period. The feedback and tracking instructions displayed on the oscilloscope screen (shown here in italic) were presented for 6 sec prior to the 3 min feedback or tracking work period. Instructions for other experimental periods were on continuously during the entire interval.

replicated immediately five times. An initial 3-min baseline period was followed by a 1-min period in which the subject attempted to raise (or lower) his heart rate in the absence of feedback. Then followed a 3-min period during which feedback was provided while the subject tried also to raise (lower) heart rate, a 1-min transfer period in which control was attempted in the absence of feedback, and a 1-min time-out period in which the subject did not try to increase (decrease) heart rate, but rested quietly. After five replications of the feedback, transfer, and time-out periods, a final baseline period was run during which the subject also did not try to control heart rate but rested quietly.

As is evident from Table 1, Lang *et al.* (1975) used control (tracking) groups, but the basic control was exercised by within-group manipulations. Bell and Schwartz (1975), however, utilized a rather similar within-group design without any between-group controls, as shown in Table 2. Following adaptation and baseline periods, the effects of engaging in active (recite alphabet or perform mental arithmetic) or passive (listen to tones or lights) forms of mental activity on heart rate were assessed (phase 3, reactivity) after which the subjects attempted voluntary control of heart-rate increases and decreases in the absence of feedback (phase 4). Voluntary control was then attempted in the presence of feedback (phase 5) following which the degree of transfer of the control to a no-feedback situation was assessed (phase 6). Only one group of subjects was used, with all of whom the above procedures were followed.

These two designs have many features in common; taken together they illustrate many of the methodological problems which arise in biofeedback re-

Table 2. Within-Group Control Design in the Study of the Voluntary Control of Heart Rate[a]

Phase	Procedure	Duration
1.	Adaptation period	15 min
2.	Baseline (prestimulus rest period)	4 min
3.	Reactivity period—elicited heart rate (HR) a. Up HR trials—recite alphabet backward —backward arithmetic subtraction b. Down HR trials—listen to tones —watch lights	6 min
4.	Prefeedback instructional voluntary control (increase/decrease HR without feedback)	6 min
5.	Feedback voluntary control (increase/decrease HR with feedback)	6 min
6.	Postfeedback voluntary control (transfer) (increase/decrease HR without feedback)	6 min

[a]SOURCE: Bell and Schwartz, 1975 (table constructed from text description)

search, particularly with respect to confounding variables. In both studies it is considered essential to adapt the subject to the experimental situation in all sessions (not just the first). A baseline period during which the subject rests quietly while the function in question is measured is intended to demonstrate that the function is stable (and in some instances, although not all as will be shortly apparent, to provide a level from which changes in performance with feedback can be assessed). The important question of whether the changes produced with feedback could have been produced merely by instructing the subject to increase or decrease heart rate in the absence of feedback (in these two studies) is approached by incorporating such trials into the design. Following the feedback training, an attempt is made to determine whether the control achieved can be maintained voluntarily when the feedback is withdrawn (the transfer period) and to determine what happens if the subject in addition, or alternatively, is asked to rest quietly (and by implication or direct instructions, not to try to exercise voluntary control). In addition, Bell and Schwartz (1975), in their study, attempted to determine whether indulging in active mental activity would produce increases, and indulging in passive mental activity would produce decreases, in heart rate—an important consideration since in most studies no attempt is made to control the cognitive activity of the subject during either baseline, feedback, or transfer (rest) phases of the experiment. Bell and Schwartz (1975) in fact found that during the "reactivity" period, large increases, averaging 12 bpm, were found during active cognitive behavior, while passive mental activity produced much smaller decreases, averaging 1.5 bpm.

It is not intended here to attempt a comprehensive review of the methodology of biofeedback research even though this would undoubtedly prove to be of considerable interest. Attention should, however, be drawn to a number of particularly important methodological issues involving experimental controls which are surprisingly often neglected in biofeedback studies. Indeed, it is apparent that even some of the most distinguished workers in the field are unaware of the importance of these matters since they persistently neglect them in their work. Three particular issues will be highlighted: the "drift" effect and the "law of initial values," the importance of veridical feedback, and instructional control.

It is intended to illustrate the importance of both the drift effect and the law of initial values mainly by reference to the study of the voluntary control of peripheral finger temperature. However, it will be helpful to demonstrate first the apparent universality of the drift effect, in particular in relation to a large range of autonomic functions commonly studied in biofeedback research.[10] The effect first showed up clearly (although not recognized fully at the time) in operant studies of the control of electrodermal functions. Crider, Shapiro, and Tursky (1966) recorded the skin-potential response from the thenar eminence of the right

[10]It seems unlikely that a significant drift effect would be found in muscle activity, but recent work suggests that this assumption may be false (Kinsman & Staudenmayer, 1978; Malec, Phillips, & Sipprelle, 1977).

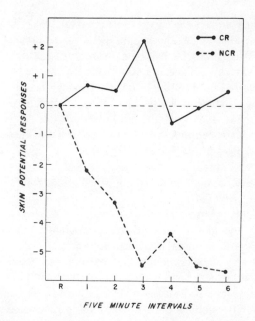

FIVE MINUTE INTERVALS

Figure 2. Mean spontaneous skin potential responses per 5-min interval for nine CR subjects and nine NCR subjects, adjusted for resting rate. (From Crider, A., Shapiro, D., & Tursky, B. Reinforcement of spontaneous electrodermal activity. *Journal of Comparative and Physiological Psychology,* 1966, *61,* 22, Figure 2. Copyright 1966 by the American Psychological Association. Reprinted by permission of the author and the publisher.

palm and the dorsal aspect of the right forearm. In the first experiment (the only one which will be considered here[11]), groups of subjects matched on baseline levels of responding were given either contingent reinforcement (a 70-db tone of 1.5 sec duration) for producing an unelicited criterion electrodermal response, or were given noncontingent reinforcement (that is, the tone occurred in the absence of an unelicited electrodermal response). The tone was regarded as a secondary reinforcer since its occurrence accumulated primary monetary reinforcement. A total of 30 min of training was given, with results as shown in Figure 2. It was claimed by Crider *et al.* (1966) that the results illustrated in Figure 2 indicated

> that contingent reinforcement of electrodermal responses increases the probability of
> their occurrence when evaluated against a noncontingent reinforcement control.
> (p. 23)

An inspection of Figure 2 confirms that the claim is based on the significant *difference* in the number of spontaneous responses in the reinforced and non-reinforced groups during the training period, and *not* on an increase in responses

[11]See Chapter 4 for a more detailed account of all of the studies briefly mentioned here in relation to the drift effect.

in the reinforced group and a decrease in responses in the nonreinforced group. Indeed, the reinforced group shows no tendency whatever to increase the number of unelicited responses over the rate manifested during the baseline period. The nonreinforced group, of course, would have been expected to show the performance curve actually shown by the reinforced group (that is, no change in performance level during training) *in the absence of uncontrolled (confounding) factors*. Instead, it manifested what it is proposed should be called the *drift effect*. Had it not been for the existence of the drift effect in the control (nonreinforced) group in the experiment by Crider *et al.* (1966), no significant results would have been obtained at all.[12]

This study was by no means the first in which the drift effect had clearly manifested itself. Fowler and Kimmel (1962, Figure 1), also working with the electrodermal response, had obtained almost identical results some years earlier, while similar findings have been reported in many subsequent studies of this response (e.g., Gavalas, 1967; Shapiro & Crider, 1967; Shnidman, 1970; Shnidman & Shapiro, 1970). A clue to the correct theoretical interpretation of the empirical findings was first clearly provided by Gavalas (1967):

> The modification of autonomic responses may be described as the prevention of adaptation. Overall increases in absolute frequency of responses of the kind usually seen in skeletal learning curves are not found. Instead, the experimental group appears to maintain a level of responding higher than that of a matched control group. The control group, under the conditions of these experiments, shows decreasing reactivity from beginning to end. (pp. 129–130)

The existence of the drift effect has clearly been apparent in studies of the voluntary control of systolic and diastolic blood pressure. Glickstein (1960) long ago pointed out the presence of a gradual decline in blood pressure in experimental situations, onto which he could superimpose temporary elevations of pressure when a stressful stimulus was introduced. Results almost exactly paralleling those obtained with the electrodermal response were reported by Shapiro, Tursky, Gershon, and Stern (1969, Figure 2) for increases and decreases in systolic blood pressure, and by Schwarz *et al.* (1971, Figure 2) for simultaneous increases or decreases in systolic blood pressure and heart rate. Schwartz (1972, Figure 2) replicated this latter result and found similar, although less striking, results when one group was required to raise blood pressure while decreasing heart rate and another group was required to do the reverse. The drift effect does not always, however, involve the "increase function" group in apparently showing no change while the "decrease function" group shows a steep decline (or drift downward). The reverse effect was found in a study of the control of diastolic blood pressure by Shapiro, Schwartz, and Tursky (1972, Figure 1), thus introducing the further confounding problem of ceiling and bottoming effects, to be considered in more detail later in this chapter. All of these results have been

---

[12]Similar drift effects are apparent in the second and third experiments reported by Crider *et al.* (1966).

fully confirmed in more recent studies (e.g., Elder, Leftwich, & Wilkerson, 1974; Fey & Lindholm, 1975).

Similar results have also be found in studies of the voluntary control of increases and decreases in heart rate. Engel and Chism (1967), in a study of heart-rate speeding, found that both the experimental and control groups increased heart rate, but differentially so that a significant effect of training was found. In an investigation of heart-rate slowing, on the other hand, Engel and Hansen (1966) had earlier found that a group of subjects given feedback for slowing showed a mean change of only -0.5 bpm, whereas a control group not given feedback showed an increase of $+5.6$ bpm, the difference between the groups being interpreted as evidence that control of slowing had been obtained (in neither experiment were the subjects informed about the task).[13] Evidence for a drift effect may also be gleaned quite readily from the reports of Brener et al. (1969, Figure 1) in which a general drift downward in heart rate was found for both increase and decrease groups; of Schwartz (1972) and Schwartz et al. (1971), previously discussed in connection with blood pressure; and of Shapiro et al. (1970). In the latter study, separate groups were required to increase or decrease heart rate and the results showed that a large drift downward occurred in the decrease group with no change in the increase group, the difference between the groups at the end of the training being taken as evidence that differential control had in fact been achieved. This, of course, is the "usual" interpretation that was applied also in the areas of electrodermal responding and blood pressure. However, exactly the opposite result was found by Headrick, Feather, and Wells (1971), who found large increases in heart rate in the increase group but no change at all in the decrease group. This kind of discrepancy could, under the appropriate conditions, undoubtedly occur in the other areas of autonomic functioning discussed here as well. The nature of the discrepancy in these findings will become clear later when the methodology of the drift effect is examined more closely. The drift effect in heart-rate control studies has been fully confirmed in more recent and carefully controlled investigations (e.g., Bouchard & Granger, 1977, Figure 1; Lang & Twentyman, 1974, Table 2; Sirota, Schwartz, & Shapiro, 1974, Figure 1).

One other area in which the drift effect has assumed considerable importance—the voluntary control of electrical activity of the brain—needs only brief mention at this point since, for a number of reasons peculiar to this area, it is dealt with in some detail in Chapter 5. The drift effect in alpha-enhancement training was in fact identified very early on by Kamiya (1969) and was later implicated in the eyes-open/eyes-closed baseline controversy in the course of which it was maintained that the voluntary enhancement of alpha apparently demonstrated in many studies was artifactual and never exceeded the levels of

---

[13]Both studies were criticized by Murray and Katkin (1968), essentially for failure to take proper account of the drift effect.

alpha achieved in the resting state with eyes closed (see Chapter 5 for a detailed documentation). The drift effect has proved to be a serious problem in the area of alpha control (e.g., Crosson, Meinz, Laur, Williams, & Andreychuk, 1977; Kuhlman & Klieger, 1975; Nowlis & Wortz, 1973; Peper & Mulholland, 1970) as well as in related areas such as sensorimotor rhythm training for epilepsy (e.g., Lubar & Shouse, 1976), but these matters need not be pursued here.

The empirical findings outlined above in relation to electrodermal responding, blood pressure, heart rate, and the electrical activity of the brain have all been described as involving the drift effect. The authors of most of these papers, however, have tended to describe the results in terms of "experimental" versus "control" conditions and in relation to assumed underlying theoretical constructs such as the provision of "feedback" or "no feedback" on the one hand, or "contingent reinforcement" or "noncontingent reinforcement" on the other. It is necessary now to look more carefully at the nature of the drift effect as well as two closely related matters (the "initial law of values" effect, and the reliability and stability of baseline performance) in order to grasp more clearly why the drift effect is of such great importance in biofeedback research and treatment. This can best be done by reference to research on the voluntary control of peripheral finger temperature.

As pointed out earlier in this chapter, biofeedback experiments usually involve three stages, often carried out within a single session lasting 60–90 min. A baseline period (in which the function under examination is recorded while the subject rests quietly and no feedback is provided) is followed by a training period (in which an experimental group is trained with feedback to gain voluntary control over the function) and a return to the initial baseline condition or the introduction of a transfer period during which the experimental group attempts to maintain, in the absence of feedback, whatever control has been achieved during the training period (in this event, the transfer period may be succeeded by a final baseline period). The use of control groups will be ignored for the moment.

Consider now the data illustrated in Figure 3, which shows peripheral finger temperature of small groups of males and females over a period of 90 min in a room temperature of either 20°C or 25°C. If no other information were provided it might be reasonable to interpret the results shown as demonstrating a stable baseline, followed by successful control of reduction of finger temperature in males and females when the room temperature was 20°C but not when it was 25°. In fact, however, the data shown in Figure 3 represent the results obtained with normal males and females in a 90-min, no-feedback, baseline period in which the subjects simply rested quietly while their peripheral finger temperature was recorded from both index fingers. The results are shown for only one finger but were virtually identical for the other, and have been replicated on numerous occasions under highly and less well-controlled baseline conditions.

When the temperature in the room in which the subjects reclined was 20°C, it will be noted that after an initial period of about 10 min during which finger

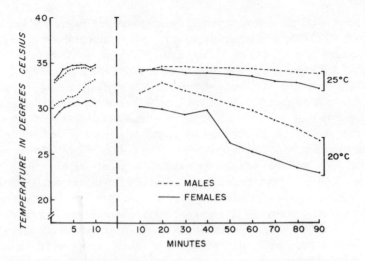

Figure 3. Baseline changes in peripheral finger temperature in males and females at two room temperatures.

temperature remained stable, or even increased somewhat,[14] there was a steady drift downward toward the room temperature, which would be reached by many subjects given a sufficiently long baseline; that females drift downward faster than males (the drift is almost universal in females but is not shown by all males, although this is not apparent in Figure 3); and that females tend to have lower starting temperatures than males (both of these sex differences have been confirmed on many occasions in the author's laboratory). Figure 3 also shows that the drift effect is very markedly attenuated when the room temperature is raised to 25°C although it will certainly manifest itself clearly if the baseline period is made long enough.

The importance of the drift effect in distorting the effects of biofeedback training will be readily apparent. A simple illustration is shown in Figure 4. Let us suppose that group A is required to increase finger temperature while group B is required to decrease finger temperature, both groups being provided with feedback. Further, let us suppose that at the end of the first 18 min of training group A subjects have, on average, "increased" finger temperature by 2°C and that group B subjects have, on average, "decreased" finger temperature by 2°C. If after 18 min a drift effect downward of 3°C has occurred in *both* groups, then the "increase" group will appear not to have succeeded while the "decrease" group will appear to have succeeded very well. The change in group A will appear to be a decrease of 1°C in 18 min (failure), and in group B a decrease of

---

[14]This initial rise, which is quite commonly found, may not be observed if only the mean of the first 10 min is reported.

5°C (success), although in actual fact *both* groups have been equally successful. This is bad enough, but a further important consequence has apparently been neither noticed nor remarked upon in studies of the voluntary control of peripheral finger temperature. Feedback which is being provided to the subjects in both groups will indicate to the subjects in the "decrease" group that they are doing very well (and in fact will exaggerate their success), but the feedback to the "increase" subjects will indicate that they are failing miserably since the display shows that their peripheral finger temperature is dropping steadily. A likely result of this, of course, is that the "increase" subjects will abandon whatever strategies they have been using (and which have in fact been successful) and hence become even less successful than they (wrongly) think they have been so far.

Now, as will be seen shortly, there are various ways in which the drift effect can be overcome. However, some further clarification of the drift effect is necessary first. It will be recalled that the drift effect is much attenuated if the room temperature is maintained at 25° instead of 20°. It would seem, therefore, that the simplest way of avoiding the problem of the drift effect would be to maintain the room temperature at 25°C or even higher. Unfortunately, this turns out to be no solution at all, for at this room temperature a new confounding variable rears its head—the law of initial values. Provided certain variables, to be mentioned shortly, are controlled, the peripheral finger temperature of males at the start of the baseline period will be around 31–33°C and that of females around 29–31°C. It is true that if the room temperature is maintained at 25°C or higher the drift downward will be much attenuated or even (particularly in

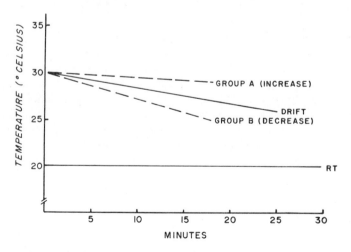

Figure 4. Differential influence of drift effect on voluntary control of increases and decreases in peripheral finger temperature.

males) not occur at all. But such a high initial temperature will make it very difficult if not impossible for males (and probably females as well) to demonstrate voluntary control of *increases* in temperature since a ceiling effect will be present (that is, it is probably impossible for males to increase finger temperature above 32–33°C). One is forced, therefore, to work at lower room temperatures if voluntary control of increases in peripheral temperature is to be demonstrated. Similarly, voluntary control of decreases in finger temperature may be difficult to demonstrate because if the room temperature is set at 25°C, it is impossible for peripheral finger temperature to fall below this value. Since many females have starting levels of peripheral finger temperature of only 27–28°C, the demonstration of voluntary control of decreases may be extremely difficult, at least in female subjects. Some females also manifest "cold hands," that is, their starting baseline temperature will be exactly the same as the room temperature. It is impossible to use such subjects, of course, in studies of the voluntary control of decreases in peripheral finger temperature.

One final point needs to be made with respect to the drift effect before turning to ways of dealing with it. The purpose of taking baseline measurements is often said to be the establishment of a "stable level of responding" prior to the introduction of the experimental period, and it is often implicitly assumed that the "stable level" achieved during the baseline period will thereafter be maintained during the voluntary control and transfer periods so that any changes which occur during these periods may properly be attributed to the experimental manipulations and not to uncontrolled variables. What is actually required, however, is reliable and valid knowledge of what would have happened during the experimental periods if the baseline had been continued during that time. For this purpose, a changing level of performance may be fully as acceptable as a baseline as an unchanging level of performance. Thus, the performance curves shown in Figure 3 are perfectly acceptable as baselines provided (1) the changes are predictable from one minute to the next within a session, and (2) the changes within one session predict the changes in subsequent sessions. That is to say, both within- and between-session reliability is necessary. This, in fact, is readily obtainable in peripheral finger temperature studies provided three factors are controlled: (1) the room temperature, (2) the effects of outside variations in temperature, and (3) the effects of activity indulged in by the subject immediately prior to entering the baseline situation. The latter two variables are frequently neglected in research in this area but can readily be controlled to an adequate degree by placing the subject in another room held at a controlled temperature of about 25°C for about 30 min prior to entering the experimental chamber. It may be added here that biofeedback researchers working in the area of the voluntary control of temperature seem remarkably unaware of the very carefully controlled and detailed studies which have been carried out on the adaptation of human subjects to various levels of ambient temperature and which confirm in detail the points made above about the drift effect (e.g., Montgomery

& Williams, 1976, 1977; Raven & Horvath, 1970). In other areas, of course, it is much more difficult to obtain a stable baseline. Tursky, Shapiro, and Schwartz (1972), for example, found fluctuations in blood pressure which exceeded 25 mm Hg over periods as short as 1 min. Furthermore, the effects of the law of initial values can be troublesome. Gatchel (1974), for example, reported a correlation of -0.47 between baseline heart-rate levels and success in speeding heart rate with feedback, whereas for slowing heart rate the correlation with baseline heart rate was $+0.48$. That is, success in speeding heart rate with feedback was asssociated with low resting levels of heart rate, whereas success in slowing heart rate was associated with high resting levels of heart rate.

The drift effect may not only obscure what is actually going on during biofeedback training but may produce results which may be misinterpreted. A striking example of this has been provided in a study by Blankstein, Zimmerman, and Egner (1976). They trained a small group of normal males to raise and lower heart rate with visual (meter) feedback. An initial baseline without feedback was run before the training trials, and each training trial with feedback was preceded by a pretrial baseline period. The changes occurring in heart rate under increase and decrease instructions with feedback were calculated in two ways *from the same data*. One score was the difference between trial heart rate and the heart-rate level during the last minute of the initial baseline period; the other score was the difference between trial heart rate and the heart rate recorded in the immediately preceding pretrial period (that is, one score was derived from a *fixed* preexperimental baseline, the other from a *running* or changing pretrial baseline). The extraordinary difference in results obtained from these two different ways of analyzing the same data is shown in Figure 5. It will be seen that when the fixed preexperimental baseline was used as the reference point, large decreases in heart rate with feedback were obtained, but not increases,[15] whereas the reverse was the case when a running pretrial baseline was used. The results are readily explainable in terms of a steady shift downward in heart rate throughout the experiment. If a preexperimental baseline is used as the reference point, the decrease control achieved will be exaggerated and the increase control will be masked. On the other hand, if the running pretrial baseline is used, the exaggerated effect of drift on decrease control data appears to be overcome but it remains unclear whether the problem is solved by this technique since, as Figure 5B shows, a reverse effect appears to occur. However, significant bidirectional control of heart-rate responding was obtained when the pretrial baseline was used in this study. Furthermore, if the initial law of values is invoked, it makes more sense to suppose that voluntary control of heart-rate increases should be greater than voluntary control of heart-rate decreases.

It will be evident that the running pretrial baseline involves a within-subject design of the kind illustrated earlier in Table 1, and indeed this kind of design is

---

[15]These results, of course, parallel exactly those discussed earlier and illustrated in Figure 2.

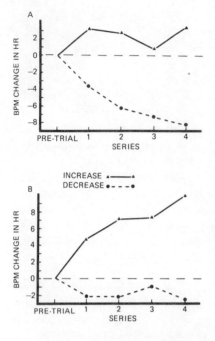

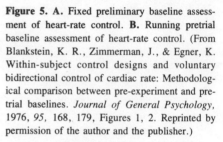

Figure 5. A. Fixed preliminary baseline assessment of heart-rate control. **B.** Running pretrial baseline assessment of heart-rate control. (From Blankstein, K. R., Zimmerman, J., & Egner, K. Within-subject control designs and voluntary bidirectional control of cardiac rate: Methodological comparison between pre-experiment and pretrial baselines. *Journal of General Psychology,* 1976, *95,* 168, 179, Figures 1, 2. Reprinted by permission of the author and the publisher.)

now very commonly used, particularly in studies of heart rate (e.g., Headrick *et al.,* 1971) and blood pressure (e.g., Steptoe & Johnston, 1976). It may be noted also that the differential results obtained by Blankstein *et al.* (1976) have not always been found in other studies which have compared both methods of analysis. Thus, Johnston (1976, 1977), in studies of the voluntary control of heart rate and of digital pulse amplitude, respectively, found similar results whichever of the two analytic methods he used. On the other hand, Steptoe (1976), in a study of blood pressure control, found feedback superior to instructions without feedback for increases but not decreases when preexperimental baseline scores formed the reference point, whereas feedback was superior for both increases and decreases when pretrial baseline scores formed the reference point. Blankstein *et al.* (1976) have also pointed out some of the difficulties inherent in using pretrial scores as a baseline measure, such as carryover effects from an experimental trial into the next pretrial baseline, inability (except by instructions) to prevent the subject from continuing to exercise control during the pretrial baselines, and the fact that the subject may spend the pretrial period not in resting but in actively planning strategy for the next training trial. An additional important criticism has been raised by Peper (1976), who has pointed out that poor control may be a consequence of experimental designs which involve rapid switches over very short periods of time from "control" to "rest" conditions, particularly in the early stages of training. Peper's criticisms are directed particularly at alpha training but his remarks are applicable to all areas of bio-feedback. As Peper points out, the fact that an individual is temporarily unable to initiate urination in the presence of others (whereas he is able to initiate it rapidly when alone) does not mean that this individual is unable to control urination voluntarily. Similarly, rigid experimental conditions, particularly where the subject is required to control a function he has never tried to control before, may produce poor performance and an underestimate of the degree of voluntary control attainable. Peper suggests as an alternative that subjects be allowed to pace themselves, that is, initiate a control period when they feel ready to do so.

The use of the within-subject, pretrial baseline design may be regarded as an alternative to the contingent/noncontingent feedback (reinforcement) between-groups design described earlier in this chapter as used, for example, by Crider *et al.* (1966), Fey and Lindholm (1975), and Fowler and Kimmel (1962), among others. There are, however, other possibilities which should be mentioned briefly before leaving this topic.[16] If a preexperimental baseline is run on an occasion prior to the training session and is of a length equal to the training session, and if it is known that this baseline is replicable on separate occasions, then using a within-subjects design it would be possible to use the baseline curve of performance to correct for the drift effect at any point in the training session for each individual subject. Thus, in the case of temperature control, if it is reliably known that in a room temperature of 20°C a subject will start at 27°C and drift 2°C in the first 10 min, this empirical knowledge may be used to correct for the observed change after 10 min training to increase or decrease temperature. It is likely that such a technique would have only limited applicability, however, since within-subject variability is usually too great for the correction to be applied reliably. A variation of this procedure has been suggested by Jones, Vaught, and Weinrott (1977), who have described the use of the autocorrelation technique as a form of time-series analysis in operant research. The technique involves the correlation of scores which are progressively further removed from one another and indicates the degree to which scores in a time series are serially dependent. Six main types of obtainable dependencies are illustrated in the paper.

It cannot be said that the difficulties associated with the drift effect have been either fully overcome or even completely understood as a methodological and theoretical problem. However, the importance of the drift effect in distorting data is gradually being fully appreciated, and it may be anticipated that specific research on the drift effect will be carried out in the future. What is perhaps most urgently required are careful studies of the changes which take place in various functions (particularly autonomic) over significant periods of time on repeated occasions in the resting state. Until data of this kind are available, the results of

---

[16]The general problem of measuring change reliably has been discussed in detail by Benjamin (1967), Cronbach and Furby (1970), and Tucker, Damarin, and Messick (1966).

biofeedback studies will continue to be difficult to interpret and will often be interpreted wrongly.

The assumption that veridical feedback of performance will produce a greater increase in control over a function than nonveridical feedback has been investigated in several ways. Thus, Brener and Kleinman (1970) used a control group which was instructed only to "pay special attention" to the (feedback) stimulus in a study of the voluntary control of blood pressure. This group showed a smaller drop in blood pressure compared with the experimental group which was fully informed about the feedback stimulus. Because the Lang feedback system effectively requires the subject to track the feedback stimulus as it moves across the screen, Gatchel (1974) used a "tracking" control group, the subjects simply being required to press a microswitch when the moving line terminated. In some studies where proportional feedback is presented to the experimental group, the control group may receive a continuous tone (e.g., Budzynski & Stoyva, 1973) or a steady click rate (e.g., Kinsman *et al.*, 1975). In both cases the feedback provided no useful information about changing performance and served as a control for the properties of the stimulus *per se*. Control subjects may be provided with feedback from another (yoked) subject such that changes in the feedback stimulus which appear to be reflecting expected changes in performance do occur—but, of course, the changes do not reflect precisely what may be happening in the subject (e.g., Budzynski & Stoyva, 1973). Control subjects may be deliberately misled by being given false feedback (e.g., they may be told that a tone will increase in pitch as muscle activity increases, but in fact the reverse is programmed to occur). This procedure (which is ethically objectionable) should not be confused with the provision of an increasing tone for decreasing muscle activity and vice versa, and where the subject has been fully informed of the relationship. Such feedback may confuse the subject, but it should not be regarded as "false" feedback.

The question of whether the provision of feedback is necessary at all for increases in voluntary control reduces essentially to the question of whether instructional control can be achieved—that is, will subjects who are simply verbally instructed to increase heart rate, for example, succeed as well as subjects who are both instructed to increase heart rate and are provided with feedback of changes in heart rate as they attempt to do so?[17] The results of the empirical research carried out thus far on this important question present a confusing picture. Most of the research has dealt with the control of heart rate and most, but not all, of it has been reviewed briefly by Bouchard and Granger (1977). Where the effects of instructions plus feedback have been compared with the effects of instructions alone, several studies have shown an advantage for feedback over

[17]This methodological question should not be confused with the question of whether biofeedback training as a therapeutic technique is superior to alternative therapeutic techniques, such as progressive relaxation training without feedback, or to no treatment at all. This matter is considered in Chapter 8.

instructions in the case of heart-rate *increases* (Blanchard & Young, 1972; Blanchard, Scott, Young, & Edmundson, 1974; Colgan, 1977; Davidson & Schwartz, 1976; Lang & Twentyman, 1974; Stephens, Harris, Brady, & Shaffer, 1975; Young & Blanchard, 1974). Other studies, however, have failed to find such an advantage (Bergman & Johnson, 1972; Johnston, 1976, Experiment 2; Lang *et al.*, 1975; Levenson, 1976; Manuck *et al.*, 1975). Stephens, Harris, and Brady (1972) found feedback superior to instructions alone but, rather surprisingly, discounted their own result. Blanchard, Young, Haynes, and Scott (1975) reported that a group of subjects instructed to increase heart rate (without feedback) were able to do so whereas a control group merely instructed to "pay attention to" their own heart rate showed no comparable increase (however, a feedback group was not included in this study). Thus, the results for heart-rate increase are equivocal.

Many of the studies considered above also reported comparative data relating to heart-rate *decreases,* and here the results are more clear-cut in that nearly all of the studies found no difference between instructions alone and instructions plus feedback. However, Colgan (1977), Lang *et al.* (1975), and Lang and Twentyman (1974) did find feedback superior to instructions alone, as did Blanchard, Scott, Young, and Edmundson (1974) in one of their two experiments.

Similar discrepancies have been found in those few studies where a difference score between heart-rate increases and decreases was the dependent variable. Thus, Brener *et al.* (1969) and Ray (1974) found feedback superior to instructions alone, whereas Bergman and Johnson (1971) and Ray and Lamb (1974) found no difference.

Much less work has been carried out comparing instructions alone with instructions plus feedback in relation to other functions. Steptoe and Johnston (1976) found no superiority of feedback in a study of blood pressure control. On the other hand, Steptoe (1976) found feedback superior to instructions for both increases and decreases in blood pressure if pretrial scores were used as the baseline measure, whereas if preexperimental scores were used as the baseline, feedback was advantageous for increases but not decreases. Blanchard, Young, Haynes, and Kallmann (1974, Experiment 2) obtained significant reductions in systolic blood pressure in subjects simply instructed to decrease the pressure; the instructions were as effective as instructions plus binary feedback, but less effective than instructions plus proportional feedback. Redmond, Galor, McDonald, and Shapiro (1974) showed that significant increases and decreases in systolic and diastolic blood pressure could be obtained through instructions alone, the subjects being three males and three females who manifested moderate levels of hypertension.

Three other areas in which the effects of instructions alone have been examined may be briefly mentioned. Instructional and voluntary control of penile erection without feedback has been clearly demonstrated in a number of studies (e.g., Laws & Rubin, 1969; Rubin & Henson, 1975). No advantage for feedback over instructions alone, on the other hand, was demonstrated in a study by Johnston (1977) of digital pulse amplitude. Finally, Beatty (1972), in a well-controlled study, showed that alpha activity could be equally well increased under instructional as under feedback conditions.

The instructional control of behavior is a matter closely related to an issue which arose (for a number of reasons) early in the development of biofeedback research: the question of whether subjects should be fully, partially, or not at all informed about the task. There can be no doubt that the failure to inform subjects, for example, that their task was to increase heart rate was dictated by the operant framework within which many of the early studies were conducted, allied to a fear of induced expectancy effects. The tendency not to inform subjects received some support from a study which appeared to show that informed subjects achieved less control than did subjects who were not informed (Engel & Hansen, 1966). However, this finding, and the suggestion emanating from it, have received no support whatever from subsequent research and may safely be discarded. Studies which have investigated the role of information in biofeedback have demonstrated the point clearly. Bergman and Johnson (1972), for example, provided their subjects with one of three kinds of information in a study of heart-rate control: no specific information that the study was concerned with heart rate (the subjects were told only to try and control an internal response), specific information (the subjects were told to try and control their heart rate), and augmented specific information (the subjects were told to try and control their heart rate and were given feedback of their own heart rate). The specific and augmented specific information groups demonstrated better control of heart rate than did the nonspecific information group. Similar findings were reported by Blanchard, Scott, Young, and Edmundson (1974).

The demonstration that voluntary control of functions may be increased as much in the absence of feedback as in its presence must, of course, be regarded as somewhat disturbing since it raises the possibility that the elaborate apparatus used by biofeedback researchers (and often clinicians) may not be necessary. Such a conclusion would be unwarranted. The aim of biofeedback is to increase the fineness and precision of voluntary control—it has never been suggested that voluntary control could not be increased in the absence of biofeedback. The fact that biofeedback not infrequently does not appear to offer an advantage over instructional control may represent only the relatively crude state of the art and science of biofeedback training to this point in time. A much more important matter relates to the difficulty of training subjects with biofeedback to exercise simultaneous control over more than two (at the most) functions simultaneously, even though in the normal circumstances of life a much greater degree of integration of the control of bodily functions is achieved continuously. This point will be taken up again later (see Chapter 8).

The design of experiments (particularly those relating to the clinical treatment of individual patients) in biofeedback calls for a good deal of ingenuity on the part of the experimenter or clinician, an ingenuity which has not so far been shown very often. One or two instances should, however, be mentioned. Turin and Johnson (1976) argued that if migraine headaches could be alleviated by training the patients to warm their fingers, then it should follow that training migraine patients to cool their hands should have no beneficial effects and might, indeed, be expected to increase the frequency and severity of the headaches. This procedure, of course, also represents a control for expectancy effects, since the patients trained to cool their hands were given the same expectancy instructions as those trained to warm their hands. It was found that the subjects trained to cool their hands showed no clinical improvement until they were switched to warming their hands. The small numbers of patients used precludes reaching any definitive conclusions about the benefits of handwarming to migraine patients, but the methodological control exercised is of considerable interest.

Another methodological procedure which is potentially of great importance in biofeedback, but has rarely been used as yet, would capitalize on the fact that most body functions are bilaterally represented, and that dysfunctions often affect only one side of the body, leaving the other side unaffected. Thus, the performance of the unaffected muscle system or whatever may be displayed to the patient as a model or template against which the degree of deficiency in the impaired function may be measured, and will provide a target to achieve in respect of increased voluntary control of the impaired function. The only area in which bilateral representation of function has been used in biofeedback is the rehabilitation of physical function following physical trauma. Strangely, the importance of bilaterality of function in training in voluntary control was recognized long before biofeedback was thought of (see the study by Bair, 1901, described in detail in Chapter 1); and was used on several occasions in clinical studies of rehabilitation in patients suffering from hemiplegia (Andrews, 1964) and a patient with left facial paralysis following an accident (Booker, Rubow, & Coleman, 1969), only to be neglected almost completely since then, although the advantages of being able to show a patient normal function in the same muscle contralateral to the one that is not under complete voluntary control would seem to be too obvious to need emphasis (see Chapter 3 for a detailed account of these studies).

The more formal aspects of clinical work with patients using biofeedback need not be dealt with in detail here. The use of single-case designs has been admirably explicated quite recently by Barlow, Blanchard, Hayes, and Epstein (1977), together with clinical examples from the literature. Several specific examples may be mentioned, however, to illustrate the payoff from carefully designed clinical studies in terms of interpreting the results obtained, and the superiority of an experimental approach to one in which a standard technique is blindly applied. Reeves (1976), for example, treated a 20-year-old female with tension headaches of 5 years duration. He was able to show that discussion and recording of the frequency and duration of the headaches had no effect, nor did frontalis muscle activity change during this time. The introduction of cognitive-skills training led to a reduction in headache activity but had no effect on frontalis muscle activity. The introduction of biofeedback training in reduction of frontalis muscle activity (while the cognitive-skills training was continued) led to a further reduction in headache activity but also produced a reduction in frontalis muscle activity. Apart from the general improvement in relation to headache activity which was obtained (and which in such a study could not, of course, be un-equivocally related to the treatment operations), the way in which the study was conducted threw up important findings. For example, the fact that a reduction in headache activity was obtained via cognitive-skills training but without any concomitant reduction in frontalis muscle activity (which was, however, reduced when feedback was introduced) has important implications for the alleged relationship between tension headaches and levels of frontalis muscle activity. Other good recent examples of single-subject replication designs have been provided by Blanchard, Haynes, Young, and Scott (1977) in relation to the control of heart rate; Feuerstein and Adams (1977) in relation to migraine and tension headaches; and Peck (1977) in relation to blepharospasm.

This concludes this selective review of some aspects of the methodology of biofeedback research. It will be clear that a multitude of complex methodological issues make biofeedback a trap for the unwary—a trap into which many research workers have fallen. Most if not all of the contentious issues in biofeedback are largely the result of important, and sometimes unrecognized, differences in methodology. Until a great deal more work is done on the resolution of these issues, the results of research will continue to be a matter of often-unnecessary controversy.

References

Alexander, A. B., French, C. A., & Goodman, N. J. A comparison of auditory and visual feedback assisted muscular relaxation training. *Psychophysiology*, 1975, *12*, 119–123.

Andrews, J. M. Neuromuscular reeducation of the hemiplegic with the aid of the electromyograph. *Archives of Physical Medicine and Rehabilitation*, 1964, *45*, 530–532.

Blair, J. H. Development of voluntary control. *Psychological Review*, 1901, *8*, 474–510.

Barlow, D. H., Blanchard, E. B., Hayes, S. C., & Epstein, L. H. Single-case designs and clinical biofeedback experimentation. *Biofeedback and Self-Regulation*, 1977, *2*, 221–239.

Beatty, J. Similar effects of feedback signals and instructional information on EEG activity. *Physiology and Behavior*, 1972, *9*, 151–154. (1972:19)

Bell, I. R., & Schwartz, G. E. Voluntary control and reactivity of human heart rate. *Psychophysiology*, 1975, *12*, 339–348. (1975/76: 34)

Benjamin, L. S. Facts and artifacts in using analysis of covariance to "undo" the law of initial values. *Psychophysiology*, 1967, *4*, 187–206.

Bergman, J. S., & Johnson, H. J. The effects of instructional set and autonomic perception on cardiac control. *Psychophysiology*, 1971, *8*, 180–190. (1971:17)

Bergman, J. S., & Johnson, H. J. Sources of information which affect training and raising of heart rate. *Psychophysiology*, 1972, *9*, 30–39. (1972:16)

Blanchard, E. B., & Young, L. D. The relative efficacy of visual and auditory feedback for self-control of heart-rate. *Journal of General Psychology*, 1972, *87*, 195–202.

Blanchard, E. B., Scott, R. W., Young, L. D., & Edmundson, E. D. Effect of knowledge of response on the self-control of heart rate. *Psychophysiology*, 1974, *11*, 251–264. (1974:13)

Blanchard, E. B., Scott, R. W., Young, L. D., & Haynes, M. R. The effects of feedback signal information content on the long-term self-control of heart rate. *Journal of General Psychology*, 1974, *91*, 175–187.

Blanchard, E. B., Young, L. D., Haynes, M. R., & Kallmann, M. D. A simple feedback system for self-control of blood pressure. *Perceptual and Motor Skills*, 1974, *39*, 891–898.

Blanchard, E. B., Young, L. D., Scott, R. W., & Haynes, M. R. Differential effects of feedback and reinforcement in voluntary acceleration of human heart rate. *Perceptual and Motor Skills*, 1974, *38*, 683–691.

Blanchard, E. B., Young, L. D., & Haynes, M. R. A simple feedback system for the treatment of elevated blood pressure. *Behavior Therapy*, 1975, *6*, 241–245. (1975/76:47)

Blanchard, E. B., Young, L. D., Haynes, M. R., & Scott, R. W. Long term instructional control of heart rate without exteroceptive feedback. *Journal of General Psychology*, 1975, *92*, 291–292.

Blanchard, E. B., Haynes, M. R., Young, L. D., & Scott, R. W. The use of feedback training and a stimulus control procedure to obtain large magnitude increases in heart rate outside of the laboratory. *Biofeedback and Self-Regulation*, 1977, *2*, 81–91.

Blankstein, K. R., Zimmerman, J., & Egner, K. Within-subject control designs and voluntary bidirectional control of cardiac rate: Methodological comparison between pre-experiment and pretrial baselines. *Journal of General Psychology*, 1976, *95*, 161–175.

Booker, H. E., Rubow, R. T., & Coleman, P. J. Simplified feedback in neuromuscular retraining: An automated approach using electromyographic signals. *Archives of Physical Medicine and Rehabilitation*, 1969, *50*, 621–625.

Bouchard, M. A., & Granger, L. The role of instructions versus instructions plus feedback in voluntary heart rate slowing. *Psychophysiology*, 1977, *14*, 475–482.

Brener, J., & Kleinman, R. A. Learned control of decreases in systolic blood pressure. *Nature*, 1970, *226*, 1063–1064. (1970:22)

Brener, J. P., Kleinman, R. A., & Goesling, W. J. The effects of different exposures to augmented sensory feedback on the control of heart rate. *Psychophysiology*, 1969, *5*, 510–516.

Budzynski, T. H., & Stoyva, J. M. An instrument for producing deep muscle relaxation by means of analog information feedback. *Journal of Applied Behavior Analysis*, 1969, *2*, 231–237.

Budzynski, T. H., & Stoyva, J. An electromyographic feedback technique for teaching voluntary relaxation of the masseter. *Journal of Dental Research*, 1973, *52*, 116–119.

Carslsöö, S., & Edfeldt, A. W. Attempts at muscle control with visual and auditory impulses as auxiliary stimuli. *Scandinavian Journal of Psychology*, 1963, *4*, 231–235.

Chase, R. A., Cullen, J. K., Openshaw, J. W., & Sullivan, S. A. Studies on sensory feedback. III. The effects of display gain on tracking performance. *Quarterly Journal of Experimental Psychology*, 1965, *17*, 193–208.

Colgan, M. Effects of binary and proportional feedback on bidirectional control of heart rate. *Psychophysiology*, 1977, *14*, 187–191.

Crider, A., Shapiro, D., & Tursky, B. Reinforcement of spontaneous electrodermal activity. *Journal of Comparative and Physiological Psychology*, 1966, *61*, 20–27. (R:22)

Cronbach, L. J., & Furby, L. How should we measure "change"—or should we? *Psychological Bulletin*, 1970, *74*, 68–80.

Crosson, B., Meinz, R., Laur, E., Williams, D., & Andreychuk, T. EEG alpha training, hypnotic susceptibility, and baseline techniques. *International Journal of Clinical and Experimental Hypnosis*, 1977, *25*, 348–360.

Daly, D. A. Quantitative measurement of nasality in EMR children. *Journal of Communication Disorders*, 1974, *7*, 287–293.

Davidson, R. J., & Schwartz, G. E. Patterns of cerebral lateralization during cardiac biofeedback versus the self-regulation of emotion: Sex differences. *Psychophysiology*, 1976, *13*, 62–68.

Davis, J. F. *Manual of surface electromyography*. Montreal: Laboratory for Psychological Studies, Allan Memorial Institute of Psychiatry, 1952.

Dowdell, L. R., Clarke, N. F., & Kardachi, B. J. Biofeedback: Control of masticatory muscle spasm. *Medical and Biological Engineering*, 1976, *14*, 295–298.

Elder, S. T., Leftwich, D. A., & Wilkerson, L. A. The role of systolic- versus diastolic-contingent feedback in blood pressure conditioning. *Psychological Record*, 1974, *24*, 171–176.

Engel, B. T., & Chism, R. A. Operant conditioning of heart rate speeding. *Psychophysiology*, 1967, *3*, 418–426.

Engel, B. T., & Hansen, S. P. Operant conditioning of heart rate slowing. *Psychophysiology*, 1966, *3*, 176–187. (R:3)

Feuerstein, M., & Adams, H. E. Cephalic vasomotor feedback in the modification of migraine headache. *Biofeedback and Self-Regulation*, 1977, *2*, 241–254.

Fey, S. G., & Lindholm, E. Systolic blood pressure and heart rate changes during three sessions involving biofeedback or no feedback. *Psychophysiology*, 1975, *12*, 513–519. (1975/76:40)

Fowler, R. L., & Kimmel, H. D. Operant conditioning of the GSR. *Journal of Experimental Psychology*, 1962, *63*, 573–577.

Gatchel, R. J. Frequency of feedback and learned heart rate control. *Journal of Experimental Psychology*, 1974, *103*, 274–283. (1975/76:39)

Gavalas, R. J. Operant reinforcement of an autonomic response: Two studies. *Journal of the Experimental Analysis of Behavior*, 1967, *10*, 119–130.

Glickstein, M. Temporal patterns of cardiovascular response. *Archives of General Psychiatry*, 1960, *2*, 12–21.

Halpern, D., Kottke, F. J., Burrill, C., Fiterman, C., Popp, J., & Palmer, S. Training of control of head posture in children with cerebral palsy. *Developmental Medicine and Child Neurology*, 1970, *12*, 290–305.

Hardt, J. V., & Kamiya, J. Conflicting results in EEG alpha feedback studies: Why amplitude integration should replace percent time. *Biofeedback and Self-Regulation*, 1976, *1*, 63–75.

Harris, F. A., Spelman, F. A., Hymer, J. W., & Chase, C. E. Application of electronic prostheses in rehabilitation and education of multiply handicapped children. *Proceedings of the 1973 Carnahan Conference on Electronic Prostheses*. Lexington: University of Kentucky College of Engineering, 1973, pp. 33–42.

Harris, F. A., Spelman, F. A., & Hymer, J. W. Electronic sensory aids as treatment for cerebral-palsied children: Inapproprioception. Part II. *Physical Therapy*, 1974, *54*, 354–365.

Headrick, M. W., Feather, B. W., & Wells, D. T. Unidirectional and large magnitude heart rate changes with augmented sensory feedback. *Psychophysiology*, 1971, *8*, 132–142. (1971:16)

Jacobs, A., & Felton, G. S. Visual feedback of myoelectric output to facilitate muscle relaxation in normal persons and patients with neck injuries. *Archives of Physical Medicine and Rehabilitation*, 1969, *50*, 34–39.

Johnston, D. Criterion level and instructional effects in the voluntary control of heart rate. *Biological Psychology*, 1976, *4*, 1–17. (1976/77:22)

Johnston, D. Feedback and instructional effects in the voluntary control of digital pulse amplitude. *Biological Psychology*, 1977, *5*, 159–171.

Jones, R. R., Vaught, R. S., & Weinrott, M. Time-series analysis in operant research. *Journal of Applied Behavior Analysis*, 1977, *10*, 151–166.

Kamiya, J. Operant control of the EEG alpha rhythm and some of its reported effects on consciousness. In C. Tart (Ed.), *Altered states of consciousness*. New York: Wiley, 1969, pp. 507–517. (R:36)

Kinsman, R. A., & Staudenmayer, H. Baseline levels in muscle relaxation training. *Biofeedback and Self-Regulation*, 1978, *3*, 97–104.

Turin, A., & Johnson, W. G. Biofeedback therapy for migraine headaches. *Archives of General Psychiatry,* 1976, *33,* 517–519. (1976/77:15)

Tursky, B., Shapiro, D., & Schwartz, G. E. Automated constant cuff-pressure system to measure average systolic and diastolic blood pressure in man. *IEEE Transactions on Biomedical Engineering,* 1972, *19,* 271–276.

Venables, P. H., & Martin, I. (Eds.). *A manual of psychophysiological methods.* Amsterdam: North-Holland, 1967.

Wooldridge, C. P., & Russell, G. Head position training with the cerebral palsied child: An application of biofeedback techniques. *Archives of Physical Medicine and Rehabilitation,* 1976, *57,* 404–414. (1976/77:42)

Yates, A. J. Technical, methodological and theoretical problems in dichotic stimulation research. *Australian Psychologist,* 1972, *7,* 2–19.

Young, L. D., & Blanchard, E. B. Effects of auditory feedback of varying information content on the self/control of heart rate. *Journal of General Psychology,* 1974, *91,* 61–68. (1974:15)

CHAPTER 3

Voluntary Control of Muscle Activity

Introduction

It is not generally appreciated by the nonphysiologist that the body contains an extraordinarily large number of muscles, large and small, short and long, fat and thin, rarely acting in isolation and often sitting, as it were, cheek by jowl. For example, in performing the simple act of opening the mouth, at least nine different groups of muscles must be innervated in an appropriate pattern of relative tension (the zygomaticus major and minor, the levator labii superioris and superioris alaeque nasi, the levator anguli oris, the risorius, the depressor anguli oris and labii inferioris, and the mentalis); and, of course, a different pattern is required for closing the mouth. Similar complexities apply in the apparently equally simple action of flexing or extending the fingers, severally or jointly, while in the calf various muscles are tightly packed but with each performing a special function. It is partly for this reason that some physiologists have considered that surface electromyography is inadequate as a technique for detecting specific muscle activity as compared with the use of implanted needle electrodes. Although this viewpoint has been expressed quite strongly by some physiologists and while the point may be conceded in principle, there is empirical evidence that results obtained with the use of the two techniques, at least where absolute precision is not vital, are quite comparable (Bouisset & Maton, 1972). Nevertheless, it should be borne in mind that recordings made with surface electrodes will usually reflect the activity of a group of muscles rather than a single muscle (to a greater or lesser degree depending on the site from which the recording is made) and that uncontrolled action at a distance from the muscle site may momentarily activate a muscle which is otherwise in a resting state (for example, a low level of frontalis muscle activity may be disrupted by swallowing or eye movements). To some extent, the unwanted activity may be eliminated by appropriate filtering at the amplification stage but careful instructional control will usually also be necessary.

It is neither necessary nor desirable here to provide an account of the muscular system in general nor of the structure of the voluntary muscles and their innervation via the nervous system. However, in relation to the material to be considered in this chapter a number of specific points may usefully be made.

Only voluntary, skeletal (striated) muscle activity will be considered in this chapter. Striated muscle (so called because of the striped appearance of the myofibrils—complicated linkages of protein molecules possessing the property of contractility—under the microscope) is made up of bundles of fibers, varying in length up to a maximum of about 30 cm and in width up to less than 0.1 mm, which can contract (shorten) in length by up to 55% of their resting length. When they contract within a particular muscle, the muscle fibers do not all shorten simultaneously but rather do so successively, depending on the momentary requirements of the organism. Nevertheless, because of the successive recruitment of very large numbers of fiber bundles, the muscle appears in normal circumstances to contract smoothly as a whole. An individual group of fibers which can contract together is innervated by an electrical pulse traveling along the axon (or nerve fiber) emanating at the spinal cord level from the cell body of a neuron. The rate of impulse along the axon varies but is usually less than 50 impulses per second. The neuron, its axon with terminal branches, and the muscle fibers innervated by the branches together constitute the fundamental building block of muscle activity, the *single motor unit* (SMU). Figure 1 shows schematically the structure of an SMU. The number of fibers innervated by a single axon varies considerably. Where the muscle subserves fairly gross functions one axon may innervate a large number of fibers, but in the case of very fine movements one

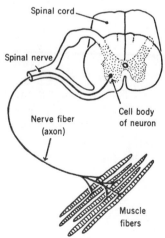

Figure 1. Diagram of a single unit, the functional unit of contraction. (From Basmajian, J. V. Electromyography comes of age. *Science,* 1972, *176,* 604, Figure 2. Reprinted by permission of the author and the publisher.)

axon may activate only a small number of fibers. As a rule, the smaller motor units are recruited first, with the larger ones becoming active as the intensity of stimulation increases. At the same time that the number of active units increases, the frequency with which individual units fire will increase, at least up to the point at which a refractory period intervenes to protect the system from exhaustion. From the point of view of recording the level of muscle activity, the most interesting consequence of the innervation of muscle activity is that the contraction of the muscle fibers generates an electrical potential of brief duration (around 10 msec) and exceedingly small amplitude of the order of only several millionths of a volt. Direct recordings of the muscle potentials via implanted electrodes show that the potentials are characterized by triphasic or biphasic spikes.

As has been pointed out, the electrical potential may be detected by the use of surface or implanted electrodes. The tiny signal thus detected must then be amplified and distinguished from surrounding noise, both from the body and that generated in the detection system itself. The amplification should be sensitive to the range 10–1000 Hz with appropriate filters to eliminate unwanted artifacts such as 60 Hz mains hum or low-frequency bodily responses such as heart rate (a range of 90–1000 Hz will accomplish this without eliminating important information from the muscle potential). Because of the minute amplitude of the original signal, very high amplification (up to $\times$ 100,000) may be required, although for biofeedback studies smaller amplification may be adequate. If the amplified signal is displayed in some form to the subject without further adjustment (i.e., in its raw form) it is unlikely that it will make such sense to him so it is usual to rectify (make the negative values positive), smooth, and integrate the detected signal first. These adjustments (especially the smoothing and integrating) involve a good deal of subjective judgment on the part of the experimenter but the important thing is that the experimenter detail precisely how the signal was smoothed and integrated.

Two other points should be noted. Although it is true to say that a muscle is never completely inactive, it is apparently the case that the electrical activity of the muscle can effectively be reduced to zero (i.e., no activity is detectable even with the most sensitive instruments) when the muscle is completely relaxed. This, however, does not mean that the muscle is without tonus. It should also be noted that coordination of muscle function does not necessarily imply reciprocal inhibition of flexor and extensor muscles at the gross level of activity with which biofeedback studies are usually concerned. Thus, in relation to flexion of the biceps muscle, the triceps muscle (which controls extension) need not necessarily be extended (i.e., relaxed), and vice versa.

Voluntary Control of Normal Muscle Activity

In this section, studies of the voluntary control of SMU activity will first be considered, followed by studies of gross muscle activities. In the former case, implanted needle electrodes have invariably been used to achieve the required precision of location; in the latter case, surface electrodes have customarily been used. Finally, studies of tremor in normal subjects will be considered.

Voluntary Control of SMU Activity

Credit for the discovery of the extraordinarily fine degree of control which can be obtained over SMU activity must undoubtedly be given to Hefferline (1958), whose work was described in Chapter 1. It will be recalled that Hefferline recorded from the ·masseter muscle, using surface electrodes with visual (meter) feedback, and that he included a test of the continuation of acquired control when feedback was withdrawn. Although Hefferline did not specifically refer to the control of SMUs and although most subsequent work has been carried out with implanted electrodes, there can be no question, given the degree of control achieved by Hefferline's subjects, that he was demonstrating the establishment of SMU control.

The use of electromyography to record and measure SMUs in human subjects preceded the work of Hefferline by many years.[1] However, V. F. Harrison and Mortensen (1962) seem to have been the first to provide feedback to the subject from implanted electrodes (they also used surface electrodes and examined carefully the characteristics of the SMU obtained with each technique). At roughly the same time, Basmajian (1963, 1967, 1972; Basmajian, Baeza, & Fabrigar, 1965; Simard & Basmajian, 1966) was beginning to report his studies, while in Scandinavia the little-known work of Carlsöö and Edfeldt (1963) was published.

A very substantial measure of agreement is apparent in all of these studies as to the main findings, which may be summarized as follows:

1. If feedback (usually visual or auditory is *not* provided when training commences, the subject will experience great difficulty in isolating an SMU (Carlsöö & Edfeldt, 1963).

2. With the provision of feedback, however, an SMU may, by trial-and-error flexing and relaxation of the muscle, rapidly be isolated by most subjects. The time taken may vary from only a few minutes to up to an hour or more.

3. After identifying and bringing under voluntary control an SMU, the subject will be able to isolate and produce independently of each other several SMUs.

4. Eventually the subject may be able to produce any one of the SMUs in his repertoire on command in any specified order.

5. The characteristics ot an SMU may be varied by the subject once control has been established. Thus, he may vary the frequency of firing of the SMU so that it fires once every second or every 10 sec. The number of times the SMU fires in a single burst may also be varied, resulting in what Basmajian

---

[1]The main references to this work will be found in V. F. Harrison and Mortensen (1962).

called "special effects" such as a "drumroll." This control, of course, may be demonstrated in a peculiarly vivid manner to an audience by playing the auditory representation of, for example, a drumroll through loudspeakers. Not all subjects are able to achieve this level of sophistication.

6. If SMU control is regarded as a skill, no relationship with skills which might be thought relevant (e.g., manual dexterity) has been demonstrated. Nor has any relationship with personality variables been shown. Athletes are no better than the man in the street at controlling SMUs (Scully & Basmajian, 1969).

7. Auditory feedback has usually been found to be more helpful in achieving SMU control than visual feedback, although the results of V.F. Harrison and Mortenson (1962) suggested that combined visual/auditory feedback might be superior to either alone.

8. Once control has been gained with feedback, the skill may be retained when feedback is withdrawn. Hefferline (1958) originally found this to be the case and retention has repeatedly been demonstrated since.

9. Hefferline (1958) maintained that a genuine curve of learning was not found in SMU control. While there may be an initial period of confusion and error (e.g., under-/overshooting of the target in the display), near-perfect performance will be demonstrated once these initial perturbations are eliminated. More recent studies, to be discussed below, require qualification of this early conclusion.

10. SMU control has been shown with implanted electrodes in many muscle sites: abductor pollicis brevis (e.g., Basmajian, 1963; Clamann, 1970), tibialis anterior (e.g., Basmajian & Simard, 1967; V. F. Harrison & Mortensen, 1962), first dorsal interosseus (Carlsöö & Edfeldt, 1963), abductor digiti minimi (e.g., Gray, 1971; Scully & Basmajian, 1969), biceps belly (e.g., Johnson, 1976; Maton, 1976), and trapezius (Simard & Ladd, 1969a).

Many of the early studies on the control of SMUs were essentially demonstrations rather than carefully controlled studies. More recently, some painstaking investigations have been carried out in an attempt to elucidate some of the factors involved in SMU control and to specify the characteristics and limitations of the control achieved. The first set of investigations relates to the degree of control which can be maintained under varying circumstances. H. M. Smith, Basmajian, and Vanderstoep (1974) recorded simultaneously from electrodes implanted at three different sites in the left biceps muscle, but provided feedback (auditory and visual) from only one site at any one time. They found that it was possible to isolate and control individual SMUs from one site with feedback, and that as control increased SMU activity from the neighboring sites (from which no feedback was being given) became progressively less and less. Some qualification of this finding is indicated from the results obtained by Kato and Tanji (1972), who demonstrated that the individual fibers of an SMU are distributed over a significant spatial area. It has also been shown, however, that recruitment of SMUs tends to occur in a fixed, orderly sequence (Sussman, MacNeilage, &

Powers, 1977; Yemm, 1977), which may well be an important factor in the high degree of control that can be achieved.

Gray (1971) examined voluntary control of SMU activity in the left external anal sphincter muscle which has the unusual characteristic of demonstrating continuous tonic activity even when completely at rest. Although his subjects were able to isolate and control SMUs with large potentials in the usual way, they were not able to control SMUs with small potentials unless they could suppress the continuous tonic activity of the muscle to a significant degree. The most detailed and comprehensive study of the parameters of SMU control is that by Lloyd and Leibrecht (1971). Recording from the belly of the right tibialis anterior muscle, a trial commenced with the activation of a white light which signaled the subject to isolate and produce an SMU. If the subject was successful during the first 5 sec of the trial, the white light remained on as long as the SMU was present and the trial was extended to a maximum of 10 sec. If, however, an incorrect response was made during the first 5 sec (e.g., activation of two SMUs), an amber light came on for 0.8 secs and that trial was terminated. Each trial was separated by a rest interval of 15 sec and subjects were run to a performance criterion of five successive trials in which continuous activation of an SMU occurred for a minimum period of 5 sec. Each training session consisted of 100 trials with a maximum of five sessions each day, and retesting (an exact duplication of the initial training) was carried out 15 days later. The results obtained by Lloyd and Leibrecht (1971) are depicted in Figure 2, which shows

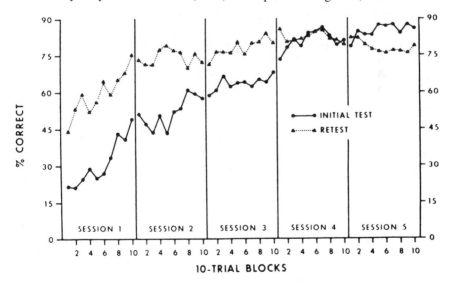

Figure 2. Mean percent correct response of successive ten trial blocks for initial and retest series. (From Lloyd, A. J., & Leibrecht, B. C. Conditioning of a single motor unit. *Journal of Experimental Psychology,* 1971, *88*, 393, Figure 1. Copyright 1971 by the American Psychological Association. Reprinted by permission of the publisher.

that the mean percentage of correct responses in successive 10-trial blocks increased from a starting level of 45% to a final level of around 90%. On retest, both the starting and final levels were somewhat lower than in the initial training sessions. The length of time for which an isolated SMU could be maintained increased progressively over the training period. In the initial training series, 13 of 17 subjects achieved the criterion set in 26–325 trials with a mean of 182 trials, whereas in the repeat series 12 of 17 subjects reached the criterion set in 6–245 trials, with a mean of 66 trials. The same subjects failed in both training sessions. The latency of correct responses varied between 1.5 sec and 2.0 sec, subjects tended to alternate between different SMUs rather than always producing the same SMU, and a definite learning curve (Figure 2) was evident, with an asymptotic level of approximately 85% correct performance and duration of 6.5 sec in each 10-sec trial.

In the study by Lloyd and Leibrecht (1971), the only feedback available consisted of the white light (indicating successful performance while it was on) and the amber light (indicating failure). In a replication study, Leibrecht, Lloyd, and Pounder (1973) provided continuous auditory feedback in the initial training session but omitted it from the retraining session 2 weeks later. They found that the addition of auditory feedback enabled their subjects to surpass the performance level of those in the earlier study, 100% correct response level being achieved by the third session and maintained thereafter. However, the omission of auditory feedback in the retraining session resulted in a performance which was no better than that obtained in the retraining session of the earlier study. The role played by auditory feedback appeared to these authors to be that of reducing, or even eliminating, the initial search process for SMUs; once this process was completed, however, the importance of continuing to provide auditory feedback diminished considerably (according to the authors; this conclusion would not seem to be supported by the retraining results and was not specifically tested in this study).

The criteria used by Lloyd and her colleagues represent a significant advance in sophistication of measurement of SMU control. C. P. Johnson (1976) has developed an SMU "test battery" in which five criteria are examined as measures of degree of SMU control achieved. These tests are as follows:

1. Maintenance of electrical silence
2. Maintenance of "picket-fence" pattern
3. Demonstration of frequency control
4. Demonstration of on-off control (activate SMU on cue, then stop and maintain silence)
5. Demonstration of control of rhythm (fire SMU at specified rate, maintaining silence between individual firings)

The tests enable performance to be scored on a continuum rather than in a binary (control achieved or not) fashion. The face validity of the test battery was examined by C. P. Johnson (1976) in a study involving control of SMU activity from the dominant biceps muscle belly (implanted electrodes) with visual (oscilloscope trace) feedback. Multiple regression analysis was used to determine which of the test variables contributed most to total test score. Johnson found that on–off control, rhythm control, and SMU isolation control (maintenance of "picket-fence" pattern) were the best predictors of overall performance.

As pointed out earlier, Lloyd and Leibrecht (1971) stated that the latency of an SMU varied between 1.5 sec and 2.0 sec. However, Thysell (1969) claimed that the latency of fully mastered SMUs was much shorter but bimodal (either between 150 msec and 174 msec or between 200 msec and 224 msec with occasional excursions up to 274 msec). Thysell had expected to find that the reaction time (RT) of SMUs would be significantly shorter than the RT for whole muscle movement on the assumption that preparatory EMG activity occurs prior to a response's being made in the usual RT situation but that this would not occur in SMU recruitment. His expectation was not, however, confirmed as can be seen from the RTs he obtained. The discrepancy between the results of Lloyd and Leibrecht (1971) and of Thysell (1969) is more apparent than real since the former were dealing with the acquisition of SMU control whereas Thysell was measuring the latency of SMU activation in subjects who had fully acquired the skill.

Thus far, the studies examined have dealt with SMU control in isolation, as it were, and in highly controlled and artificial situations. From the point of view of the reinstatement of muscle control in real-life situations where that control is defective, it might be important to determine the extent to which SMU control can be maintained in the presence of distracting movements from other muscles, or in a situation in which movements are being made by the very muscle in which control is being exercised over SMUs. Several studies have addressed themselves to this area of research.

In an early study, Simard and Basmajian (1966) first established voluntary control of SMU activity in the right tibialis anterior (isolation of SMU, maintaining its action, controlling frequency), using visual and auditory feedback. The control achieved was then tested by requiring the subject to produce three spike potentials under varying conditions:

1. While counting 1, 2, 3, silently
2. Matching a galloping horse's rhythm
3. Matching musical notes played by the experimenter
4. Matching the same note repeated three times
5. Repeating a set of three taps

Success in these tasks was reported, but it can only be regarded as an interesting "special effects" demonstration. More important was the study of Basmajian and Simard (1967), again using the tibialis anterior muscle but also (in one-quarter of the subjects) placing surface electrodes over five neighboring sites to study synergistic effects. This time, after acquiring control of SMU activity, the task of maintaining it in the face of distraction was made significantly more complex. Continued control was required:

1. While contralateral movements of the left hip joint and left ankle joint were made;
2. While segmental body movements (e.g., of head and shoulder) were made and maintained;
3. While movements were made of the ipsilateral proximal joints (e.g., hip), crossed joints (e.g., ankle), and distal points (e.g., toes); and
4. While inhibiting the synergistic muscles.

In general, control of SMU activity was found to be feasible in the presence of gross activity in other muscles, involving proximal and distal joints.

An even more dramatic example, involving continued control of SMU activity from a muscle which itself was being used to perform a complex activity, was provided by Simard and Ladd (1969a). They first trained normal subjects to control SMUs from three sites in the large right trapezius muscle. The electrodes were implanted in: (1) the inferior fibers, located 2 cm lateral to the 7th spinous process of the dorsal vertebra; (2) the middle fibers, located 1 cm above the medial third of the spine of the scapula; and (3) the superior fibers, located 4 cm above the precedent in a frontal plane passing by the shoulder articulation. After their subjects had been trained to activate and inhibit SMUs in these three areas alone and in various combinations with auditory and visual feedback, and then to maintain that control without feedback, they were required to perform a complex, mechanically assisted movement involving drinking from a glass while maintaining control over SMUs. Of the 13 subjects studied, all were able to learn differential control of superior and inferior SMUs and 4 of the subjects were able to maintain this control while making the movements involved in drinking. That is, it was possible to activate the trapezius muscle as a whole while simultaneously suppressing activity of SMUs in parts of the muscle. Similar results have recently been reported by Simard (1977).

Basmajian and Newton (1974) reported that skilled musicians (clarinet players), with electrodes implanted in the buccinator muscle, learned within minutes to suppress activity in that muscle while continuing to play their instrument in what appeared to be exactly the same manner (and this in spite of the fact that each player manifested a specific pattern of muscle activity while playing). It was also found that these players could simultaneously increase activity in the upper buccinator muscle while decreasing activity in the lower buccinator muscle, and vice versa. Basmajian and White (1973) had previously reported that trumpet players showed differential patterns of activity in the muscles innervating the lips according to their experience and skill.

The voluntary control of SMU activity represents perhaps the most unequivocal example of the importance of feedback in the biofeedback literature. It illustrates the specificity of control that can be achieved. Until feedback training is provided, control (relying on proprioceptive feedback alone) is weak and unstable, whereas following training control can be maintained when the feedback display is not longer present.

Basmajian believed that:

> the experiments . . . suggest that pathways from the cerebral cortex can be made to stimulate single anterior horn cells while neighboring anterior horn cells remain dormant or are depressed. (1963, p. 441)

In other words, there is a direct, uninterrupted link between the motor command system in the cortex and the neuron at the spinal cord level, with no significant role played by intermediate levels nor by what is happening in the muscle involved as a whole nor by activity in other muscles.

A study of Fukushima, Taniguchi, Kamishima, and Kato (1976) has thrown some light on the differential control mechanism involved in direct SMU control. Electrodes were inserted into the abductor pollicis brevis and/or opponens pollicis and subjects were trained, using auditory and visual feedback, to discharge an SMU at both 10-Hz and 1-Hz frequency after a visual demonstration of the required rates. Then a 1% xylocaine solution was applied to the median nerve at the wrist and the subject was asked to discharge the SMU at these rates alternately at intervals of 1 min. The ability to discharge the SMU at a rate of 10 Hz was seriously impaired 5 min after the injection (full recovery occurring about 50 min later) whereas the ability to discharge the SMU at a rate of 1 Hz was unaffected. Since xylocaine blocks the γ fibers before blocking the α fibers, Fukushima et al. (1976) had predicted that if the tonic frequency (i.e., 10 Hz) was mediated by the γ-loop (activated by pyramidal input to the γ-motoneurones) control of this frequency pattern would be lost before the low-frequency discharge control which they hypothesized is mediated by the α-loop (activated by pyramidal input to the α-motoneurones); and this was exactly the result which they found.

This conclusion of Basmajian, however, has not gone unchallenged. Wagman, Pierce, and Burger (1965), for example, reported that in the early stages of SMU training the relative position of the muscle systems is very important, providing differential feedback which is essential if the subject is successfully to activate an SMU. In switching from one SMU to another, very slight changes in limb position may be required. What this means is that in the early stages of training a significant amount of activation of SMUs may be required to produce both significant changes in the concomitant proprioceptive stimulation and the visual/auditory feedback displays for the subject to acquire knowledge of the "language" of the internal system. As this knowledge is acquired, the importance of the external feedback will diminish and true internal control be established, as Leibrecht et al. (1973) pointed out. This interpretation has been expanded by Lloyd and Shurley (1976), who point out:

> The biofeedback approach, viewed from a simple cybernetic analysis of a signal to noise ratio, is a technique which amplified a weak proprioceptive signal generated by the motor unit contraction in a relatively noisy system and which is presented through an exteroceptive input channel. (pp. 340–341).

An alternative approach to amplifying the weak signal in a noisy system would be to reduce the noise in the system. Lloyd and Shurley (1976) attempted

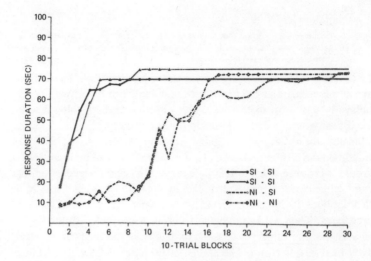

Figure 3. Total response durations for ten-trial blocks of initial learning session under the four conditions. In the initial learning session, there were only two conditions, sensory isolation (SI) and nonisolation (NI). (From Lloyd, A. J., & Shurley, J. T. The effects of sensory perceptual isolation on single motor unit conditioning. *Psychophysiology,* 1976, *13,* Figure 1. Reprinted by permission of the publisher.)

to do just this. Using the same training procedures as in their earlier studies, they examined the effects of sensory isolation and nonisolation on SMU acquisition (the muscle involved was the belly of the tibialis anterior in the right leg). After a 2-week interval, the half of the group initially trained in a sensory isolation condition was switched to the nonisolation condition and vice versa, while the remainder were retrained as before. In the initial training, the isolation group required only 27 trials on average to reach the criterion set, whereas the nonisolation group required an average of 129 trials. On retraining, the isolation subgroup which continued in isolation required fewer trials (13.4) to reach criterion, whereas the isolation subgroup switched to nonisolation training now required an average of 51 trials. On the other hand, the nonisolation subgroup switched to isolation needed now only 42 trials to achieve criterion. The striking nature of the results obtained in the initial training session is shown in Figure 3 (where SI means "sensory isolation" and NI means "nonisolation"). The criterion SMU appeared much earlier in the sensory isolation group as compared with the nonisolation group, while at the retraining stage the isolation subgroup which continued in isolation immediately activated a single SMU. Thus, the results clearly supported the interpretation of SMU training advanced by Lloyd and Shurley (1976). In summary, SMU training requires the subject to reduce the signal-to-noise ratio and this is normally achieved by increasing the signal but could be achieved by reducing the noise.

Voluntary Control of Gross Muscle Activity in Normal Subjects

As we saw in Chapter 1, interest in the voluntary control of striate muscle activity has a long history in psychology (e.g., Bair, 1901; Woodworth, 1901). No doubt the work on voluntary control of SMU activity played a part in the upsurge of renewed interest which started in the late 1960s with the publication of studies by Budzynski and Stoyva (1969) on the frontalis muscle; Green, Walters, Green, and Murphy (1969) on the forearm muscles; and Jacobs and Felton (1969) on the trapezius muscle. Actually, however, the number of different muscles investigated, and indeed the number of studies specifically attempting to demonstrate voluntary control of muscle function, has not been as great as might be expected. The frontalis muscle has been the most popular, even though it is repeatedly alleged that it is a difficult muscle to work with (in some cases, control of forearm muscle activity is attempted before moving on to the frontalis muscle). The three other muscles with which significant work has been done have been the masseter (Budzynski & Stoyva, 1973), the trapezius (Jacobs & Felton, 1969), and the forearm (Green *et al.,* 1969).

There is no need to review in detail each study which has demonstrated that voluntary control of striated muscle activity is possible when the subject is presented with feedback of the activity of the muscle in one or another form (usually visual and/or auditory of various kinds). Such control has clearly been demonstrated in the case of the frontalis, trapezius, masseter, and forearm muscles. Almost all such demonstrations have involved establishing the resting level of muscle activity in the absence of feedback and any attempt to manipulate the level of activity by the subject, followed by an attempt to *reduce* the level of activity with feedback. Reduction of activity has, of course, been of interest because of the possibility of using feedback to help people reduce abnormally high resting levels of muscle activity, assumed to be associated with (and perhaps a cause of) various disabilities such as tension headache and general anxiety. Several studies require specific mention, however. While most of the investigators have contented themselves with obtaining a significant reduction in muscle activity, Green *et al.* (1969) claimed that zero firing or SMU firing in large forearm muscle bundles was achieved by one-third of their subjects in less than 20 min of training with visual or auditory feedback. Unfortunately, they did not in this study provide any quantitative data to back up the claim (although, as will be seen later, similar results were achieved with patients suffering from severe anxiety neurosis).

The work of Alexander should also be mentioned at this point. Alexander (1975) found a reduction in frontalis muscle activity when feedback in the form of auditory clicks was presented. In a subsequent study, however, Alexander, French, and Goodman (1975) found results which have not been reported by any other investigator. After one baseline session without feedback (the subjects were instructed to relax with eyes closed) and a second session in which the subjects were instructed to relax the left forearm extensor muscles, a further four training sessions on the frontalis muscle were given. The subjects were divided into four matched groups:

I (AFC)	Auditory feedback with eyes closed
II (AFO)	Auditory feedback with eyes open
III (VF)	Visual feedback
IV (NFC)	No feedback, eyes closed

The surprising results reported by Alexander *et al.* (1975) were that group III did not significantly reduce frontalis muscle activity with visual feedback, nor did group II, given auditory feedback with eyes open. Both of these findings represent a unique contradiction of the findings of other workers, even though it is generally agreed that auditory feedback is more helpful than visual (at least the kind of visual feedback that has commonly been used in studies of frontalis muscle control). Alexander *et al.* (1975) did find a significant reduction in group I (given auditory feedback with eyes closed). Their results with visual feedback cannot be accepted as valid in the face of the overwhelming evidence from other studies that visual feedback does lead to a reduction in frontalis activity and the explanation must be sought in the methodology of Alexander *et al.* (1975). In this connection, it should be noted that in this study the experimenter was in the same room as the subject and was trying to record from the visual display at the same time as he was monitoring the subject to check that he was complying with the experimental condition (e.g., keeping eyes open or closed)—a situation hardly conducive to accurate recording, apart altogether from the possible effects on the subject of having the experimenter literally breathing down his neck.

It was mentioned earlier that nearly all the studies in this area involved a reduction in muscle activity. Lloyd (1972), however, demonstrated that with auditory feedback subjects were able to sustain a constant force with the expenditure of less muscle activity than if not provided with any feedback. The possible importance of *maintaining* a given level of muscle activity (and presumably reducing the variance of the average level) in relation to training patients with impaired muscle activity does not seem to have been realized and little work in this area has so far been reported.

Is it justifiable to infer from these results that biofeedback training represents a significant new approach to the reduction of undesirably high levels of muscle tension? The question can be broken down into several subsidiary questions. First, there seems no doubt that the provision of *relevant* feedback (auditory or visual) leads to a greater reduction in muscle activity than the provision of *irrelevant* feedback or no feedback (Budzynski & Stoyva, 1969, 1973; Jacobs & Felton, 1969; Wickramasekera, 1971). The position is more complex, however, with respect to the question of whether, *in respect of specific muscles,* training with feedback provided from the specific muscle is superior to training in general relaxation, although there seems no doubt that simply instructing the subject to relax (without actually training him in relaxation) does not lead to a significant reduction. Thus, Coursey (1975) told one group of subjects to relax, and another group how to relax, without giving any actual training in relaxation. Both of these groups showed inferior performance in relaxing the frontalis muscle as compared with a third group given proportional auditory feedback. However, when subjects were trained to relax, conflicting results have been obtained. Haynes, Moseley, and McGowan (1975), in a large-scale study, allocated their subjects to one of five conditions:

I.   Auditory feedback (proportional)
II. Passive relaxation training
III. Active relaxation training
IV. Noninformative (false) auditory feedback
V.   Instructed relaxation group (no training)

The passive relaxation training group is somewhat misleadingly described, as Wolpe's relaxation training techniques were used. In the active relaxation training group, the Jacobson technique was used, involving alternate tensing and relaxation of muscles. The results of this study are shown in Figure 4. Passive-relaxation training (Relaxation A in the figure) was as effective as biofeedback training in reducing frontalis activity. Reinking and Kohl (1975) also used five groups but a different design compared with Haynes, Moseley, and McGowan (1975). One group was provided with visual or auditory feedback, a second with feedback and relaxation training, a third with feedback and monetary reinforce-

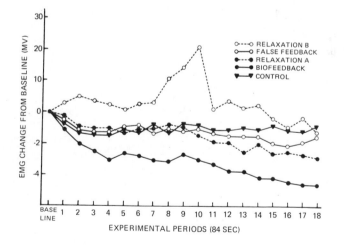

Figure 4. Average EMG changes during the experimental phase for each group. (From Haynes, S. N., Moseley, D., & McGowan, W. T. Relaxation training and biofeedback in the reduction of frontalis muscle tension. *Psychophysiology*, 1975, *12*, 549, Figure 1. Reprinted by permission of the author and the publisher.)

ment whenever a criterion level was achieved, a fourth with Wolpe-type relaxation training (equivalent to the passive relaxation training group of Haynes, Moseley, and McGowan, 1975), and a fifth group was simply instructed to relax. The results of this study are shown in Figure 5. Of particular interest is the finding that the auditory/visual feedback training group was superior to the passive relaxation training group, which directly contradicts the conclusion of Haynes, Moseley, and McGowan (1975). Reinking and Kohl (1975) also found that there was no difference in performance among the three groups given feedback, which they interpreted to mean that the addition of relaxation training or reinforcement did not enhance the effects of feedback training alone.

Two other studies may be considered here briefly. Kinsman, O'Banion, Robinson, and Staudenmayer (1975) compared the effects of two kinds of feedback training alone and in combination. Auditory feedback in the form of clicks proportional to frontalis muscle activity was used, as was binary verbal feedback, the subject being told at the end of each trial whether his EMG activity was up or down. The results indicated that biofeedback alone was superior to the other

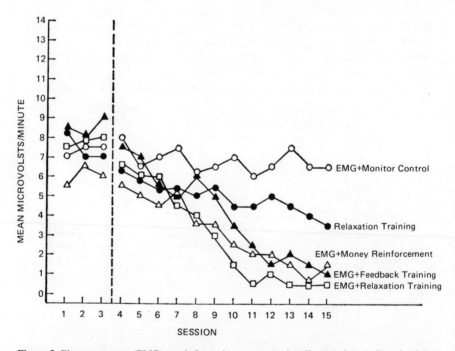

Figure 5. Electromyogram (EMG) trends for each group across baseline (sessions 1–3) and training (sessions 4–15) periods. (From Reinking, R. H., & Kohl, M. L. Effects of various forms of relaxation training on physiological and self-report measures of relaxation. *Journal of Consulting and Clinical Psychology,* 1975, *43,* 597, Figure 1. Copyright 1975 by the American Psychological Association. Reprinted by permission of the author and the publisher.)

three conditions (verbal feedback alone, biofeedback plus verbal feedback, neither verbal nor biofeedback). A combination of biofeedback and verbal feedback was superior to verbal feedback alone, the latter producing better results than no feedback. Finally, Epstein and Webster (1975) claimed that control of respiration rate could be achieved if the subject was given external stimulation setting a pacing rate and that pacing was superior to merely instructing the subject to achieve a specified rate. It is likely that this is indeed so, but Epstein and Webster's (1975) demonstration was not unequivocal, since the effect of pacing was not clearly separated out from the effects of instructions and verbal feedback. In this connection, it should be noted that Frankstein, Sergeeva, Sergeeva, and Ivanova (1975) have provided evidence indicating that feedback from the respiratory muscles does not play a significant role in the regulation of normal breathing.

It is interesting that the role of feedback in the voluntary control of gross muscle movement is not as clear as in the case of SMU activity. Certainly, the results obtained in the studies just described cannot be said to resolve the issue. The matter is not unimportant, given the implications of a clear demonstration that simple training in muscle relaxation without the use of complex apparatus is as effective as the specific training of a particular muscle with the use of costly instrumentation. The question is related, of course, to the generality/specificity issue to be discussed in Chapter 7 and cannot be said to have been resolved at this point in time.

Voluntary Control of Tremor

Tremor in general, the finger tremor in particular, should be of considerable interest in the context of biofeedback because of its universality, its special characteristics, and the objectivity with which it can be measured, as well as its importance in certain well-known disorders such as Parkinson's disease. It has also been thought to represent a classic instance of servosystem control (although this has been disputed), involving the basal ganglia, supposed site of the control systems for balance. Thus far, however, with one or two notable exceptions little attention has been paid to tremor by workers in the field of biofeedback.

Modern techniques of recording finger tremor derive from the work of Cooper, Halliday, and Redfearn (1957), Chase (Chase & Cullen, 1962; Chase, Cullen, Sullivan, & Ommaya, 1965), and Van Buskirk and Fink (1962). All these investigators developed techniques for measuring finger tremor which involved a photoelectric device sensitive to oscillations of the finger in the vertical plane. The finger, held in free space, interrupts a beam of light and the rate of interruption represents the frequency of oscillation (i.e., tremor rate) of the finger.[2]

The characteristics of tremor measured with these devices are quite clear.

---

[2]Full details will be found in the articles cited.

Normal adults show a constant spectrum of tremor frequency in the range 5–15 Hz, with amplitude varying considerably from one person to another (Halliday & Redfearn, 1956). Marshall (1959)[3] and Van Buskirk and Fink (1962) have confirmed these results, and additionally have shown that the average level of tremor frequency is less in young children (up to 9 years of age) and elderly people.

As has been pointed out, little work has been reported on the voluntary control of finger tremor when feedback is provided. However, the neglected work of Chase (Chase & Cullen, 1962; Chase *et al.*, 1965) is extremely important. Chase required his subjects to attempt to superimpose their own finger tremor onto a reference line displayed on an oscilloscope and thus to reduce the amplitude of finger tremor as much as possible since the reference line, of course, showed no amplitude fluctuations. Chase examined the effect of providing various kinds of visual feedback on performance. Proportional, logarithmic, integral, and derivative forms of feedback were examined, as well as intermittency versus continuity of the display. The results obtained with proportional feedback were particularly interesting. By proportional, Chase referred to the degree of amplification of the "error" signal, that is, the extent to which the tremor fluctuated around the steady reference line. Chase found that the greater the amplification of the error signal (up to the limit he used of 40 times amplification), the more accurately the subject could match the target line. Unfortunately, Chase provided only demonstrational examples of his results and his pioneering studies have never been followed up, despite their obvious importance and their possible implications for the treatment of disorders involving uncontrolled tremor.

The theoretical interpretation of tremor has given rise to a considerable amount of controversy, which has been reviewed by Brumlik (1962). Halliday and Redfearn (1956) showed that finger tremor frequency was unaffected if the finger was loaded with 50- or 100-g weights, in marked contrast, of course, to the amplitude of tremor. They considered that tremor in adults may result from oscillation round a servo-loop from muscle spindle to muscle. Both Marshall (1959), and Van Buskirk and Fink (1962) rejected the servo-loop explanation of tremor; Marshall (1959) on the grounds that since the reflex arc constituting the servo-loop would be shorter in children, tremor should be faster (but the reverse is the case); Van Buskirk and Fink (1962) on the grounds that other evidence indicated that finger tremor is a ballistocardiographic effect, a position also taken by Brumlik (1962). The closed-loop model has, however, been reactivated recently by Zipp (1975) and by Stein and Oğuztöreli (1976). The latter distinguish between two types of oscillation, one arising from a muscle interacting with its load, the other from high gain in a reflex pathway.

---

[3]Marshall's results were actually obtained from tremor of the whole hand while the subject was grasping a valve.

Table 1. Symptoms of Temporomandibular Joint Dysfunction Syndrome

Gelb & Tarte (1975)	Gessel & Alderman (1971)
Head, ear, neck, facial pain	Pain in muscles of mastication
Tinnitus (subjective ear noise)	Fullness, buzzing or ringing in ear
Clicking and crepitation of joint	Clicking or crepitation of joint
Difficulty in swallowing	Difficulty in chewing
Subluxation of mandible	Subluxation
Vertigo without nystagmus	Limitation in mandibular movement
Burning sensations of side of tongue and roof of mouth	Deviation of mandible on opening
Fatigue	Bruxism
Diverse muscle spasm throughout the body	
Forgetfulness	

Whether finger tremor is ultimately shown to be under peripheral, central, or both peripheral and central control, remains to be determined. Nonetheless, the systematic investigation of the feedback control of finger tremor remains an important area of neglect within biofeedback research, given its potential importance, both theoretically and empirically, and in relation to the treatment of disorders like Parkinson's disease.

Disorders of Muscle Function

Temporomandibular Joint (TMJ) Dysfunction Syndrome

This syndrome is referred to by a number of different terms: myofascial pain-dysfunction syndrome, craniocervical-mandibular syndrome, dysfunctional temporomandibular joint arthritis. There is by no means complete agreement concerning the most important symptoms of the disorder. Table 1 shows the main symptoms as described by Gessel and Alderman (1971) on the one hand, and by Gelb and Tarte (1975) on the other, from which it will be clear that there are some symptoms in common, but a good deal of differential stress as well.

Personality characteristics have been implicated in the disorder, although whether as cause or effect is unclear. Gelb and Tarte (1975) claimed that of 205 patients referred to them with an initial diagnosis (in a separate headache unit) of migraine, no less than 200 were found to be suffering from the TMJ syndrome when carefully assessed by their criteria.[4]

[4]For a recent comprehensive review of theoretical interpretations of this syndrome, see Rugh and Solberg (1976).

The masseter muscle has been the principal focus of attention for biofeedback training in the TMJ syndrome. Specificity of training requires that it be demonstrated that resting levels of masseter activity be shown to be greater in TMJ dysfunction patients than in controls not suffering from the disorder. Most investigators have ignored this question, but a recent study by Dohrmann and Laskin (1978) provides a positive answer, although the number of control subjects is small. The normal subjects ($n = 7$) showed a mean resting level of activity of 4.0 μV; the group of TMJ dysfunction patients treated with biofeedback, a level of 6.31 μV; and a group of patients not treated, a level of 11.7 μV. The control/patient group differences were significant. It has been shown that the "silent period" in EMG activity recorded from various masticatory muscles (including the masseter) and jaw motion error are larger in TMJ dysfunction patients than in normals, and both are reduced by successful treatment (Altug, Childress, De Mund, McCall, & Ash, 1976; Bailey, McCall, & Ash, 1977).

The treatment of the TMJ dysfunction syndrome using techniques involving training in relaxation has a long history. Usually termed "myofunctional therapy," its development was associated particularly with the work of Alfred P. Rogers, which has recently been described and reviewed in some detail by Cottingham (1976). Rogers devised exercises for the pterygoid and masseter-temporal muscles as well as the tongue as aids to overcoming malocclusion difficulties which lead to muscle tension. The influence of Rogers may be seen in recent work by Boos (1965), who stressed the importance of the muscles in jaw activity and described isotonic and isometric exercises as a way of controlling muscle tension; and by Gessel and Alderman (1971), who used the Jacobson/Wolpe approach to train their patients first in general muscle relaxation and then in the relaxation of specific muscles, starting with the arms and moving eventually to the jaw (e.g., clenching teeth, opening jaw only), but without, in this study, making use of biofeedback. They reported good results with half their patients although none were incapacitated or had severe emotional difficulties. These patients cooperated well in the training and applied themselves diligently to their task. The patients considered to be failures, on the other hand, had a high level of social disability, greater than would be expected from their symptomatology. They tended to be depressed, to have multiple symptoms, and to discontinue treatment, even when some degree of success was being achieved. Similar favorable results using general relaxation training were obtained by Reading and Raw (1976) with four patients.

The biofeedback studies, sparse though they are, have generally obtained good results with this syndrome, using masseter muscle reduction training in uncontrolled single-case (Carlsson & Gale, 1976; Carlsson, Gale, & Ohman, 1975) or group (Carlsson & Gale, 1977) studies. Not much better controlled was a study by Gessel (1975) in which it was claimed that 15 of 23 patients benefited in 3–10 sessions from masseter muscle relaxation training with auditory (a tone) feedback. Patients not benefiting from biofeedback training within six sessions were transferred to an amitriptylene regimen. The patients who benefited from biofeedback training were described as having lower covert and overt depression ratings than the failures, the latter also having a higher degree of social disability as well as being older. No control group or untreated patient group was included in this study, and baseline levels and changes in masseter EMG activity during training were not reported.

The recent study by Dohrmann and Laskin (1978), however, was much more carefully conducted. A group of 24 patients with the TMJ dysfunction syndrome was allocated to biofeedback or control, no-treatment conditions; and a small group of 7 normal subjects was also studied. The experimental treatment consisted of 12 ½-h sessions with feedback from the masseter muscle being provided in auditory form. A shaping procedure was used and the patients also practiced at home, using a portable apparatus. Dohrmann and Laskin measured the differential effects of training/no training on no less than six dependent variables: EMG feedback levels during the 5-min baseline and at 10 and 30 min after training started; limitation of jaw opening due to pain; tenderness (determined by palpation of masticatory musculature bilaterally, and by subjective report); presence of joint sounds on opening and closing the jaw; ratings by the patient and the experimenter of degree of success attained; and evaluation of change by an unbiased, independent observer. As indicated earlier, the patient and control groups were successfully differentiated on level of masseter activity during the pretreatment baseline. The treated patients showed a significant reduction in EMG levels whereas the untreated patients did not (but no curve of learning was apparent). Of 13 patients who complained of pain, 11 reported after treatment that the pain had gone, compared with 4 of 8 untreated patients. Similar positive changes were found for the other dependent variables in the treated patients but not in the untreated patients. However, at follow-up after 6 months, both groups of patients had apparently recovered in that only one patient in each group reported still having difficulties. At an even later (7–12 months) follow-up, two of the treated patients required further treatment. Thus, Dohrmann's results must be treated cautiously as clearly spontaneous recovery occurred in both the patient groups and the possibility of an attention placebo effect during treatment for the biofeedback group cannot be ruled out.

Two other related studies may be mentioned here. Farrar (1976) has reported a single-case study of the biofeedback treatment of a patient suffering from orofacial dyskinesia, a neurologic disorder characterized by excessive uncoordinated movements of the face, jaw, tongue, and neck. The disorder usually occurs in patients over 50 years of age who complain that the base of the tongue is being elevated and flattened, that their speech is slurred, and that their tongue and jaws show a mild quiver. Excessive jaw movement develops and the muscles of the lip, throat, and neck become hyperactive and uncoordinated. The disorder can usually be treated successfully by prosthetic devices, but the tremors often remain. The patient seen by Farrar had been successfully treated prosthodontically but tremors persisted in the hyoid region and the platysma and lip muscles, which drugs, speech therapy, and exercises had failed to alleviate (it is interesting to note that the patient had developed a stutter). Farrar placed electrodes over the affected areas (the triangularis and quadratus labii inferioris muscles) and provided auditory feedback of the muscle activity with instructions to the patient to relax the muscles, using the feedback as a guide. After initial laboratory training, the patient was given a small portable unit and instructed to practice daily for 2 h. Three weeks later the patient returned, showing remarkable improvement in muscle control and a significantly improved social interaction capacity. No quantitative data of any kind were, however, provided in this study.

TMJ dysfunction may be produced by many factors, operating alone or interacting with one another. The problem of adapting to the fitting of complete dentures may affect the delicate balance of muscular adjustment. Kleinman and Lidsky (1976)[5] recorded the mandibular rest position cephalometrically with and without the dentures in place, both before and after biofeedback training in masseter muscle relaxation with auditory feedback (a tone varying in frequency). In five of six subjects, they found a reduction in masseter muscle activity following biofeedback training without any effect on the mandibular rest position.

These studies point out clearly the possibility of fruitful collaboration between dentists and psychologists in the area of TMJ dysfunction as well as other areas of difficulty associated with dentistry. It may be confidently expected that a good deal of collaborative research will develop in this area in the near future.

Tension Headache

As Bakal (1975) has pointed out in a recent survey of the literature on headache, there is a surprising lack of hard information about headache, despite the fact that headaches of various kinds afflict most people from time to time with varying degrees of severity. Tension headaches will be dealt with separately from migraine headaches largely for theoretical reasons, although it is undeniable that it is possible for the same person to experience both tension headaches and migraine headaches (the extent to which they may occur simultaneously is unknown). Tension (or muscle contraction) headache is characterized by "sensations of tightness and persistent band-like pain located bilaterally in the occipital and/or forehead regions" (Bakal, 1975, p. 370). Migraine headache, on the other hand, tends to be unilateral and associated with nausea, vomiting, and anorexia, as well as striking sensory, motor, and affective disturbances. Few well-controlled studies comparing patients suffering from tension headache with those suffering from migraine headache have been carried out. The most comprehensive study appears to be that of Friedman, von Storch, and Merritt (1954), who carefully examined 2000 patients over 7 years. Their results are shown in Table 2. In general, the comparative figures confirm the clinical impressions

---

[5]This account is based on only an abstract of the work.

Table 2. Characteristics of Migraine and Tension Headaches[a]

Characteristics	Percentage manifesting	
	Migraine	Tension headache
1. Family history	65	40
2. Age of onset		
< 20 years	55	30
> 20 years	45	70
3. Frequency		
Daily	3	50
< 1 per week	60	15
4. Duration		
Daily	0	20
1–3 days	35	10
5. Type - throbbing	80	30
6. Location		
unilateral	80	10
bilateral	20	90
7. Associated symptoms		
vomiting	50	10

SOURCE: Friedman, A. P., von Storch, T. J. C., & Merritt, H. H. Migraine and tension headaches: A clinical study of 2000 cases. *Neurology,* 1954, *4,* 773-788, Table 1. Reprinted by permission of the publisher.
[a]2000 cases.

mentioned above. The groups were found not to differ on: incidence, sex, precipitating causes, occurrence (time of day, season), mood change, or abruptness of onset or termination. However, in a recent study using small numbers of patients classified as migraine, tension headache, or combined tension headache/migraine, Bakal and Kaganov (1977) found that the migraine patients could be differentiated only in terms of more frequently reported nausea and vomiting.

Theories of tension headache tend to stress the role of muscle tension, especially in the frontal and occipital areas of the head, but involving also the neck muscles and even the trapezius. Onel, Friedman, and Grossman (1961) attempted to test the hypothesis that tension headaches are accompanied (caused ?) by local tissue ischemia resulting from muscle contraction, but could find no support for the hypothesis. During a severe tension headache, patients tended to show a faster rate of blood flow in the splenius capitis muscle (contrary to hypothesis) and no difference in rate of flow was found between normal subjects and patients when the latter were not experiencing a headache.

The application of biofeedback to tension headaches has usually been based on the specificity assumption (see Chapter 7), in this case that tension headaches are associated with specific muscle dysfunction (usually the frontalis muscle has been implicated). If, therefore, the patient can be trained with biofeedback to reduce the activity of the frontalis muscle, it is assumed that there will be a concomitant reduction in the frequency and severity of the tension headaches. For the assumption to be valid, it is necessary to show that a tension headache is indeed accompanied by a rise in frontalis muscle activity and (preferably) that tension headache patients show a higher resting level of frontalis muscle (in the absence of a tension headache) activity than controls. The evidence in favor of these assumptions is, however, equivocal. Davis and Malmo (1951) found a high correlation between frontalis muscle activity and headache occurrence report in one of two patients undergoing therapy. Sainsbury and Gibson (1954) recorded muscle activity in the resting state in 30 patients (anxiety cases) from three sites (frontalis, arm, neck). While a general heightened activity was found which was proportional to the level of anxiety, specific relationships were also found. Thus, if the patient complained of tension headache, an elevated level of frontalis muscle activity was found compared with arm activity (or frontalis activity if tension headache was not being experienced). Budzynski, Stoyva, Adler, and Mullaney (1973) stated that the patients in their biofeedback study showed frontalis muscle activity levels in the resting state before treatment which were twice as high as those found in normal subjects (no quantitative data are provided in support of this statement—the comparison is with "young normal subjects" in their laboratory). Acosta, Yamamoto, and Wilcox (1978) reported that a small group of tension headache patients had higher pretreatment frontalis muscle activity levels than did schizophrenics or neurotics. Also using very small numbers of patients, Vaughn, Pall, and Haynes (1977) found that baseline frontalis muscle activity levels were significantly higher in patients with a reported high frequency of tension headaches compared with patients who reported a low frequency. Under stress the low-frequency headache patients showed greater increase in frontalis activity than the high-frequency headache patients (indicating perhaps the effect of the law of initial values) and returned to baseline level faster. Support for the specific association of elevated frontalis muscle activity with tension headaches was also obtained in a study by van Boxtel and van der Ven (1978), who showed that tension headache patients had higher levels of frontalis activity than normal controls, both in the resting state and during mental effort, whereas no differences were found between the groups in either the resting state or in response to stress in respect of activity in the temporalis, trapezius, and left-forearm flexor muscles. On the other hand, Bakal and Kaganov (1977) reported that migraine patients had significantly higher levels of frontalis muscle activity than did tension headache patients, both in headache-free and actual headache states. The tension headache patients, in fact, did not differ from normal controls in level of frontalis muscle activity. Neither of the headache groups showed a significant increase in frontalis muscle activity during an actual headache.

The original studies of Budzynski, Stoyva, and Adler (1970), and Budzynski et al. (1973) demonstrated clearly the beneficial effects of biofeedback training for tension headache reduction. Subsequent studies have largely been directed toward determining whether the specific frontalis muscle training provided by them produces results superior to those obtained with other approaches, and to taking account of methodological problems arising from the studies of Budzynski and his colleagues. Alternative feedback training procedures have also been tried which bear directly on the specificity assumption.

The first study, by Budzynski et al. (1970), was a pilot study, since only five patients were trained and no controls whatever were employed. The results of this pilot study, however, encouraged Budzynski et al. (1973) to carry out an altogether more ambitious investigation which incorporated many of the procedures now regarded as standard. The daily headache activity and frontalis muscle activity of 18 tension headache patients (16 were female) aged 22–44 were recorded and the patients were then allocated to one of three groups. The first group was given auditory feedback of frontalis muscle activity in the form of clicks. The second group represented an ingenious and (up to that time) little-used form of control: patients in this group were given apparently true feedback which was actually false. What they heard was the feedback provided to a previously treated patient who had brought his frontalis muscle under control. Hence, instead of just random auditory feedback, the patients in this group heard a pattern of clicks which appeared to indicate that they were being successful. Such a control group represents a much more sophisticated test of the experimental training than does random feedback. The third group was a no-treatment control. Sixteen sessions of training were given to the two treated groups and they were followed up over 3 months.

Figure 6 shows the results of the frontalis muscle training, from which it can be seen that the true-feedback group showed a significant reduction in frontalis muscle activity as a function of biofeedback training whereas the pseudofeedback group did not. Concomitant significantly greater reductions in headache activity occurred in the biofeedback group. Furthermore, while the correlation between headache activity and frontalis activity levels (calculated across baseline and training weeks) was $+0.90$ for the biofeedback group, it was -0.05 for the pseudobiofeedback group. Further indications of the success of biofeedback training came from the dramatic drop in drug usage in the biofeedback group, and the improvement in respect of levels of depression, tension, anxiety, insomnia, and so on.

The success achieved by Budzynski and his colleagues was repeated on a smaller scale by Wickramasekera (1972, 1973), and it appeared that here was a therapy for a relatively specific disorder that really did work. However, methodological and theoretical issues remained. Budzynski had not really shown conclusively that there was a specific link between frontalis muscle activity and tension headaches. He had shown that frontalis muscle activity reduction was sufficient to produce a reduction in tension headaches, but he had not shown that it was necessary. To demonstrate necessity, he needed at least one additional

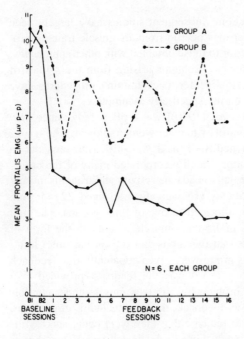

Figure 6. Mean frontalis EMG levels across sessions. Group A = true feedback; group B = pseudofeedback. (From Budzynski, T. H., Stoyva, J. M., Adler, C. S., & Mullaney, D. J. EMG biofeedback and tension headache: A controlled outcome study. *Psychosomatic Medicine,* 1973, *35,* 489, Figure 3. Reprinted by permission of the author and the publisher.)

control group which was trained to reduce activity in a muscle hypothesized to have no relationship with tension headaches, the prediction being that successful reduction of muscle activity would have no effect on the tension headaches. The other main question which needed to be answered related to the use of pseudofeedback control. While this clever device provided a useful control for the relevance of frontalis muscle activity (and in a sense also for reinforcement as opposed to informational feedback), it had no bearing on the question of whether general training in relaxation would be as effective in reducing tension headaches as specific training in reduction of frontalis muscle activity.

Four studies have examined this latter question with results which are reasonably clear-cut and consistent (although not entirely so, as was the case in studies of muscle control with normal subjects considered earlier in this chapter). Cox, Freundlich, and Mayer (1975) assigned 27 tension headache patients to one of three treatment groups:

I. Biofeedback training (auditory feedback)
II. Relaxation training (actually described as a verbal relaxation instruction group, but proper relaxation training was given)
III. Medication placebo group (given glucose tablet during weekly 1-h sessions)

All patients signed a treatment contract and kept daily records of headache activity. After two baseline sessions in which frontalis muscle activity was recorded, the differential treatment procedures were carried out for eight 1-h sessions followed by a 2-week posttreatment assessment and a further assessment 4 months later.

The results showed that the biofeedback and relaxation training groups both did significantly better than the control group, but did not differ from each other on such variables as reduction in headache activity, in frontalis muscle activity, and in psychosomatic complaints. These results were maintained at the 4-month follow-up assessment. The correlation between reduction in headache activity and reduction of frontalis muscle activity was found to be +0.42, considerably lower than the figure of +0.90 reported by Budzynski *et al.* (1973). A serious criticism of this study relates to the failure to report the quantitative changes in frontalis muscle activity—it is impossible to determine how successful the biofeedback training was. For example, it would have been interesting to know how

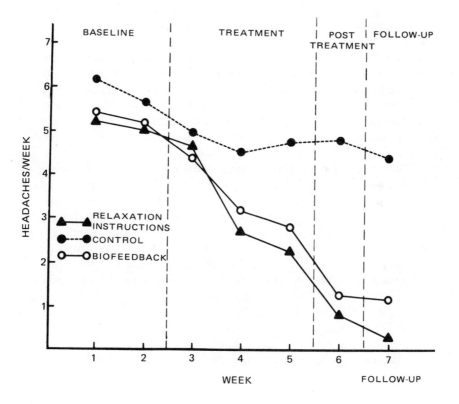

Figure 7. Mean headache rate (headaches/week) for the 2-week pretreatment phase, the week following treatment, and at follow-up as a function of intervention procedure. (From Haynes, S. N., Griffin, P., Mooney, D., & Parise, M. Electromyographic biofeedback and relaxation instructions in the treatment of muscle contraction headaches. *Behavior Therapy*, 1975, *6*, 676, Figure 1. Reprinted by permission of the author and the publisher.)

much reduction in frontalis muscle activity was produced by the specific feedback training as compared with the general relaxation training.

A very similar study was carried out by Haynes, Griffin, Mooney, and Parise (1975) except that a no-treatment control group was used instead of the medication placebo group used by Cox *et al.* (1975). The results were also similar in that biofeedback and relaxation training were both superior to no treatment, but did not differ in effectiveness. Figure 7 shows clearly the differential reduction in headache rate as a function of treatment, the course of change being quite similar to that reported by Budzynski *et al.* (1973, Figure 4). Haynes, Griffin, Mooney, and Parise (1975) also failed to report the changes in frontalis muscle activity as a function of treatment.

The third and fourth studies to be considered here reported somewhat different results. Chesney and Shelton (1976) conducted a study very similar to that of Cox *et al.* (1975) with the addition of a group given biofeedback *and* muscle relaxation training. They found that muscle relaxation training alone and a combination of muscle-relaxation training and biofeedback were equally effective and both were superior to biofeedback training alone, in respect of producing changes in headache frequency, duration, and severity. Once again, however, no quantitative details of changes in frontalis muscle activity were given, so it is impossible to say how successful the training was. On the other hand, Hutchings and Reinking (1976) claimed that their results indicated that the addition of relaxation training to biofeedback training did not improve the effectiveness of the biofeedback training which, given by itself, they found superior to relaxation training given alone.

These studies provide fairly compelling evidence that biofeedback training directed toward reduction in the activity of a specific muscle may be no more effective in alleviating the associated disorder than more general relaxation training which does not concentrate on specific muscle activity reduction. In the absence of precise information on the success of the specific muscle activity training, however, it would be premature to conclude that the specificity assumption has been seriously undermined by these studies.

Indirect support for the proposition that training in general relaxation will produce a beneficial result in tension headache sufferers was provided by Tasto and Hinkle (1973), who found a decline in tension headache frequency and duration 2½ months after muscle relaxation training and practice at home. However, the study was poorly designed, no objective data on muscle activity (frontalis or otherwise) being reported and no control being used, in addition to which their patients (only six) were students with only a short history of tension headaches.

In terms of the specificity hypothesis, it would be inappropriate to use peripheral temperature control training in the biofeedback treatment of tension headaches since there is no reason to link temperature at the forehead or the extremities with tension headache. Sargent, Green, and Walters (1972) did, however, treat a large group of patients (mainly migraine patients, but including some with tension headaches) in this way. But they provided no data specifically relating to the tension headache patients. In a subsequent similar study (Sargent, Green, & Walters, 1973), they reported that the peripheral temperature control training was much less successful in alleviating tension headaches as compared with migraine, a result which would be expected in terms of the specificity hypothesis. Both of these studies were poorly designed and heavily confounded. Raskin, Johnson, and Rondestvedt (1973) treated chronic anxiety patients with frontalis muscle training and found that the training was successful in alleviating tension headaches in the few patients in their study who suffered from anxiety *and* tension headaches (however, the frontalis muscle training, although successful in reducing frontalis muscle activity in the anxiety patients, had only minor beneficial effects on the anxiety, again in line with the specificity assumption). Medina, Diamond, and Franklin (1976) treated a group of patients half of whom had migraine only and half both migraine and tension headaches. All of the patients were first trained in frontalis muscle activity with auditory feedback and then in increasing peripheral finger temperature. They claimed that half of the patients showed a significant reduction in the number and severity of their headaches and medication and that the improvement was maintained at follow-up. Greater improvement was found in the migraine patients (64%) than in the migraine/tension headache patients (30%). Unfortunately, this study could lay claim to being one of the most confounded ever. In addition to training the patients sequentially in frontalis and finger temperature control (and not at least reporting the effects separately), autogenic phrases were used, verbal reinforcement provided, and what is described as "verbal therapy" given. It is thus impossible to interpret their results in any meaningful way.

McKenzie, Ehrisman, Montgomery, and Barnes (1974) trained eight tension headache patients to produce enhancement of alpha and beta brain-wave activity on the assumption that such enhancement would lead to increased muscle relaxation. An equal number of control patients were trained in general muscle relaxation. The experiment was quite carefully designed and carried out, and detailed graphs of the performance of individual patients provided in respect of EEG activity and splenius capitis and frontalis EMG activity. McKenzie *et al.* (1974) reported that there was an average reducton of 79.4% in the hours of headache activity reported by the 5th week of treatment, compared with pretreatment levels, and that this reduction was maintained in most patients at a 2-month follow-up. Frontalis muscle activity was reported to have declined in most of the patients. The control group showed similar changes but they took longer to appear. No statistical data were provided, however, to support these claims.

Bakal and Kaganov (1977) provided frontalis muscle activity reduction training with feedback to groups of tension headache and migraine patients (as mentioned earlier, migraine headache patients have been found to have higher levels of frontalis muscle activity than tension headache patients). It was found that the training was equally effective both in reducing levels of muscle activity and alleviating the headaches, thus again casting doubt on the specificity of the association between tension headaches and frontalis muscle activity.

Mention may be made here of a study by Gannon and Sternbach (1971), who trained five patients with incapacitating headaches resulting from head injuries to increase percentage of alpha, using music or tone as the feedback. The training was quite prolonged (a total of 70 sessions) with various procedural modifications introduced during the course of training. Some success in alpha enhancement was apparently achieved but the increased control had no observable effect on the headache. It seems likely that these headaches were organically determined.

The biofeedback treatment of tension headaches is commonly regarded as one of the cornerstones of the new approach, but this review of the work accomplished so far throws considerable doubt on the claim that frontalis muscle training for tension headaches is superior to general relaxation training. It may be that more careful examination and manipulation of the variables involved in frontalis training (such as type of feedback) will refine the technique to the point at which the investment in complex equipment (as compared with the simplicity of the relaxation training approach) will be justified. Clearly, however, that point has not yet been reached.

Tics and Torticollis (Torsion Dystonias)

There is no need here to review the present state of knowledge concerning the problems of differential diagnosis, etiology, and treatment of tics and torticollis as this task has been performed elsewhere (Yates, 1970a, b), while Eldridge (1970) has exhaustively reviewed all aspects of the torsion dystonias in general. What is surprising is the lack of interest shown in the possibility of using biofeedback training procedures in the therapy of tics, in spite of the fact that multiple tics have proved to be notoriously refractory to medical forms of treatment (Meares, 1971a, b). Indeed, even straightforward EMG recordings from the tic site are so rare that Moldofsky (1971) felt constrained to publish a figure illustrating the electrophysiological characteristics of a simple tic involving the right mid-deltoid muscle. At about the same time, Meares and Lader (1971) recorded activity in the sternomastoid (contralateral to the site of the head turned), the postcervical, and forearm extensor muscles in eight patients with spasmodic torticollis. The patients were trained in relaxation (not using biofeedback) and were then required to do mental arithmetic under the stress of exhortation to work faster. The stress operation was preceded by periods of relaxation, using the techniques in which they had been trained. Meares and Lader found no difference between the relaxation and stress periods in level of activity at any of the three recording sites. However, in the absence of a normal control group it was not possible to determine whether the resting levels of activity in the three muscle sites were significantly elevated or not.

Biofeedback training appears thus far to have been used only in the treatment of spasmodic torticollis, which may be regarded as a special subclass of tics in general. Torticollis involves both spasmodic activity in the sternocleidomastoid muscle (usually unilateral) together with a generally elevated background level of activity. As a result, the patient holds his head twisted to one side and somewhat elevated (in retrocollis, the side displacement is minimal and the backward elevation of the head maximal). The muscle contralateral to the direction of displacement may undergo marked hypertrophy (i.e., development) while the muscle on the ipsilateral side may show marked atrophy. The first application of biofeedback to spasmodic torticollis appears to be the study by Cleeland (1973). He placed surface electrodes near the anterior border and just above the clavicular attachment of both left and right sternocleidomastoid muscles and examined the effects of providing auditory feedback (a continuous pitch change or a binary tone whenever a spasm occurred) or shock, alone or in combination. He studied nine patients with spasmodic torticollis and one with retrocollis, aged between 15 and 64 years and with symptom durations ranging from 4 months to 5 years (four patients were male). The results for each individual patient were presented separately in the form of spasm frequency change as a function of treatment and overall improvement, crudely estimated by means of a rating scale. Although the individual and combined effects of feedback and shock could not adequately be separated out in the design used, quite dramatic reductions in spasm activity were obtained in half the patients, with all but one of the ten patients showing some improvement, and the improvement tended to be maintained at follow-up which varied from 17 to 40 months.

However, the most substantial biofeedback training studies in relation to spasmodic torticollis have come more recently from the clinic of Brudny and Korein. In their first report, Brudny, Grynbaum, and Korein (1974) provided results on nine patients (seven of whom were male) aged 20–58 years, with symptom duration of 9 months to 15 years. These patients were characterized by a lack of family history of torticollis, additional complications (e.g., some had dorsolumbar scoliosis and various dystonic signs), much drug therapy, and poor previous results from the various treatments they had undergone. The patients were trained using both visual (meter with scale and pointer) and auditory (variable click rate) feedback to *decrease* spasticity in the contralateral hypertrophied muscle and to increase tone in the ipsilateral atrophied muscle (usually the sternocleidomastoid or trapezius). Training sessions lasted between 30 and 60 min and continued 3–5 times a week for an average of 10 weeks. Table 3 shows the dramatic results obtained with respect to EMG activity in the hypertrophied and atrophied muscles as a result of biofeedback training (the units of activity shown in the table are approximately proportional to the integrated EMG

Table 3. Results of EMG Feedback Training in Spasmodic Torticollis[a]

Case no.	Head rotation	Hypertrophied muscle (resting condition)		Atrophied muscle (at rest) (max. contraction)	
		Before	After	Before	After
1	80° to R	> 120	6	10	> 120
2	60° to L	> 120	5	6	> 120
3	45° to L	> 120	6	12	> 120
4	30° to L	60	4	6	> 120
5	90° to L	> 120	6	10	> 120
6	30° to L	60	5	6	> 120
7	30° to R	90	4	8	> 120
8	30° to R	45	4	6	> 120
9	90° to L	> 120	6	10	90

[a]Adapted from Brudny, J., Grynbaum, B. B., & Korein, J. Spasmodic torticollis: Treatment by feedback display of the EMG. *Archives of Physical Medicine and Rehabilitation*, 1974, *55*, Table 2. Reprinted by permission of the author and the publisher.)

activity). All patients showed significant improvement in their ability to maintain normal head posture without pain or discomfort and without having to resort to various strategies, such as holding the head in the correct position with the hand.

Subsequently, Korein, Brudny, Grynbaum, Sachs-Frankel, Weisinger, and Levidow (1976) produced a more detailed report on a series of 55 patients with spasmodic torticollis, while Korein and Brudny (1976) were able to extend the series to 80 patients. Their work therefore represents one of the most extensive and important large-scale contributions to the use of biofeedback in abnormalities of function.[6] Korein and Brudny (1976) provide a very detailed account of their procedures which merit very careful study by anyone working in *any* remedial area involving biofeedback. In selecting patients for treatment, Korein and Brudny (1976) specify that the disorder must have been evident for at least 9 months; that previous therapeutic endeavors must have been unsuccessful; that the patient be adequately motivated; and that there be no evidence of an organic basis, receptive-communication disorder, severe psychiatric disturbance, carcinoma, or cardiac disease. The most recent sample on which they have reported consisted of 69 patients with torticollis and 11 patients with dystonic syndromes (i.e., involving movements of parts of the body other than the neck area), of whom 7 also manifested torticollis. The procedures used have generally followed those devised with the initial group of patients (Brudny, Grynbaum, and Korein 1974) with follow-up at 3- to 6-month intervals for as long as 4 years in some

[6]In both these recent reports, many informative photographs of patients taken before, during, and after treatment are presented.

cases. More sophisticated visual feedback displays have been developed and the training procedures refined.

It is impossible to convey briefly the richness of detail and clinical sophistication evident in these two reports, and the reader must refer to the original reports to obtain the full flavor of their work. Their results are reported cautiously and their claims with respect to positive results are modest. By the end of treatment significant improvement was found in 45 of 80 (56%) of the sample studied by Korein and Brudny (1976), while 24 patients were regarded as showing limited improvement but could not subsequently sustain control, and 11 patients were essentially unchanged. During the follow-up period, track was kept of 35 of the 45 "successes" and 9 of these showed a significant degree of relapse. Improvement was not related to sex, handedness, laterality, or type of torticollis, or to any etiological factors. Nor was improvement related to duration of illness, a factor which had appeared to be significant in the earlier study (Korein *et al.*, 1976) with the smaller sample. In general, therefore, no success has been achieved thus far in detecting factors which enable a prediction to be made of likely success or failure with biofeedback training in spasmodic torticollis.

Korein and Brudny (1976) provide a great deal of ancillary information which is important both theoretically and for future empirical therapeutic work. Following successful treatment, implanted EMG recordings usually showed that there was continuing abnormal activity in the *hyper*trophied muscle (i.e., the muscle under tension when the head is laterally twisted). Thus, the degree to which successfully treated patients had achieved correct head posture through obtaining voluntary control of the relevant musculature remains in doubt. Korein and Brudny (1976) also carried out a careful analysis of the patients who failed to improve and discovered some interesting facts. Many of these patients could not achieve voluntary control of the movement of the head, even with feedback. Even if control of the spasmodic EMG activity in the hypertrophied muscle could be achieved with feedback, the control was lost as soon as an attempt to turn the head was made,[7] apparently because of the inability of the patient to exercise reciprocal inhibition of the activity in the contralateral muscle. In these cases, attempts to increase activity in the contralateral muscle were no more successful. In other failures, control of movements was achieved with feedback but could not be sustained when feedback was withdrawn.

The major conclusion drawn by Korein and Brudny (1976) with respect to failure is very important:

> The difficulty was in learning to incorporate the SCM [sternocleidomastoid] activity into the patterned movement and not primarily related to inability of controlling the individual muscle itself. (p. 408)

---

[7]The reader will recall the work of Simard and Ladd (1969a) on the control of SMU activity while actively using the muscle concerned.

This suggests (in line with the general theoretical position taken in this book) that although the unsuccessful patients were able to utilize feedback information to gain some degree of control over their muscle activity (in the absence of skeletal movement), they failed to learn sufficient about the components of the servosystem controlling head and neck *movement,* so that while they were able to reset some components of the system to achieve individual muscle control, they had not learned sufficient to enable them to control the entire system.

Korein and Brudny (1976) in fact have adopted a general framework of servosystem control to explain the disorder and the treatment rationale. As they point out, "self-induced sensory feedback" occurred in 85% of their patients:

> The observance of this phenomenon suggested to us that these patients with torticollis were attempting to supply themselves with additional sensory feedback (tactile or kinaesthetic) in order to rectify the dysfunction of a servo system. (p. 417)

There is no need here to describe in detail the conceptions of Korein and Brudny (1976) in relation to servocontrol in general, as these are congruent with the account given in Chapter 7. They tentatively locate the faulty servosystem in the basal ganglion interactions with higher cortical centers.

The work of Korein, Brudny, and their colleagues on spasmodic torticollis is a landmark in the history of the application of biofeedback techniques. It can be expected that not only will this work be continued and extended, but that attention will also be turned to the application of biofeedback training to tics, for there are important differences between tics and torticollis which may shed light on the difficulties involved in the treatment of torticollis, as well as possibly having theoretical implications. One such difference which could be important is the fact that torticollis usually involves the maintenance of a set position for long periods of time, whereas a tic often involves a fairly sharp, repetitive movement separated from the next movement by an interval of time. The EMG activity patterns are therefore likely to be quite different in tics as compared with torticollis, and the servocontrol dysfunction may be less complex in tics and therefore more readily overridden. Here is a fertile field for future investigation.

Tardive dyskinesis is a condition involving constant, stereotyped, involuntary movements of the mouth, lips, and tongue, accompanied sometimes by choreiform movements of the limbs and trunk. The movements are absent during sleep and increase when the patient is anxious. Albanese and Gaarder (1977) have reported complete elimination of the abnormal movements in two patients given biofeedback training in relaxation of the right masseter muscle. There was a follow-up, of 3 months, of only one of the two patients.

Muscle Paralysis and Spasticity Resulting from Cerebral Trauma

One of the most promising areas of biofeedback training lies in the rehabilitation of physical function which has been impaired as a result of cerebral trauma, usually, but not necessarily always, a cerebrovascular accident (CVA);

and indeed as we saw in Chapter 1, historically the potential importance of biofeedback in this area was recognized in the work of Marinacci and Horande (1960) and Andrews (1964), long before the term biofeedback came into common use.

Broadly speaking, the effects of CVA which are of primary interest to the biofeedback worker fall into two categories. The patient may be left with a weakened muscular system on the side opposite to the CVA, resulting in apparent total or partial paralysis of the limb or limbs involved. In this case, the importance of biofeedback lies in its potential for detecting and displaying residual functioning in the muscle where, in terms of patient performance and conventional medical assessment, no function at all is present. In extreme cases, residual function may only be detectable by the use of implanted electrodes; in other instances, the use of surface electrodes may suffice. The effect of demonstrating to a patient with apparent total paralysis that residual function remains and can be "seen" to be able to be varied by voluntary effort can be quite dramatic. A CVA may, however, result in spasticity rather than paralysis, that is, the affected muscle overreacts in an uncontrollable (and often unpredictable) manner. The aim of biofeedback training will be, of course, quite different in each case. Where muscle paralysis is involved, it will be necessary to try to assist the patient to build up and capitalize on the residual function; in the case of spasticity, however, the aim will be to damp down spasticity when it occurs, or preferably to prevent it altogether or bring it under control as soon as it occurs (the latter may be impossible or very difficult, as in the similar case of a tic movement). Of course, paralysis accompanied by spasticity is not uncommon as a result of a CVA. Similar considerations apply to the other large class of paralyses, those resulting from injury to the spinal cord, producing paraplegia or quadriplegia. The possibilities of demonstrating some residual function and building on it are as great as in the case of disabilities resulting from a CVA.

There is one quite common feature of the results of a CVA, in particular, which produces a unique possibility in biofeedback training in the rehabilitation of physical function. This is the fact that a CVA may produce unilateral muscle paralysis or spasticity, leaving the functioning of the contralateral muscle either completely or only minimally impaired. Where this is so, it is possible to provide the patient with a target at which to aim; that is, simultaneous feedback may be provided (in a form which enables direct comparison by the patient) which shows the differential functioning of the unimpaired and impaired muscles, the patient's task being that of increasing the functioning of the impaired muscle (in the case of paralysis) until it matches the functioning of the unimpaired muscle. As we shall see, this training strategy has occasionally been used, but has not yet received the attention it deserves, possibly because of a lack of the sophisticated equipment needed (a computer-controlled system for generating the necessary displays is probably needed for really effective work along these lines).

In this section, traditional medical and more sophisticated methods of evaluating the presenting disability will first be considered. Then the use of feedback training will be reviewed, with the work being considered in relation to impaired lower limb control, impaired upper limb control, facial paralysis and spasticity, and other disabilities resulting from CVAs and spinal cord damage. Some account will also be given of the use of feedback incorporated into prosthetic devices, an area of growing importance in the rehabilitation of the physically handicapped.

The problem of describing adequately the neurological, physical, and social adjustment status of the physically handicapped person remains a matter of perennial interest. The clinical neurologist is a specialist whose authority and experience may be such as to override the results of objective measurement (no doubt, in many cases, rightly so). Often, however, these judgments are exactly that, with no necessary validity following from the judgments, as when Landau (1974) described "six varieties of spasticity" as if they were mutually exclusive. The neurologist's subjective judgment is, of course, supplemented by neurological tests. Attempts to objectify and quantify neurological test batteries are made from time to time. For example, Potvin and Tourtellotte (1975) recently presented a detailed description of the test battery used by them. It was made up of a total of 57 tests grouped into three categories: tests of vision, tests relating to the upper extremities, and tests relating to the lower extremities. As an example, the tests for sensation in the lower extremities included distal touch (finger), the length of filament for which three out of three strokes are felt; proximal touch, upper arm; finger pad vibration; elbow vibration; finger two-point discrimination; distal to proximal joint position; and thermal pain, dorsum of hand. Each of the tests is carefully described and quantification has been attempted.[8] Similarly, Taylor (1968) devised a test battery for evaluating dysfunction in left hemiplegia following stroke, based on the assumption that in left hemiplegia:

> the patient's ability to move and position his limbs may be thwarted by his inability to discern and sense his position in relation to other objects. (p. 512)

Consequently, her battery consisted of tests of the sensation of kinesthesis and proprioception, vision and tactile discrimination, right–left discrimination, body visualization, number skills, and fine motor planning for upper extremity performance and three-dimensional constructional praxis. In addition to this, the evaluation involves ratings of 53 variables related to daily living activities (such as self-dressing, use of wheelchair, etc.). Taylor (1968) provides quantitative data for this test battery on 210 nonhandicapped adults aged 40–75 (seven groups of 30 subjects each in 5-year age intervals) as a basis for evaluating the deficit in 35 patients (average age 62) with left hemiplegia resulting from a CVA. The

---

[8]The appropriate references will be found in the paper by Potvin and Tourlettotte (1975).

detailed results of this study will not be presented here, but many interesting and significant differences were found between the normal controls and the patients.

These kinds of studies represent an increase in sophistication over the clinical neurological examination but remain locked into the framework. A closer approach to a true behavioral analysis of deficit resulting from neurological insult is to be found in those studies which are more experimental in nature or which attempt a more integrated form of analysis. Thus, Chyatte and Birdsong (1971) used a motor task involving measurement of the separate components involved in performing the task. The motor task involved reach, move, grasp, position, and release components, and the relative deficit in carrying out each of these component parts of the task could be evaluated, using the patient as his own control by comparing impaired limb performance with unimpaired limb performance in left and right hemiplegics. No significant improvement as a result of practice was discernible in the hemiplegic limb, but clearly the method (virtually identical with that developed by K. U. Smith 20 years earlier) has possibilities for the examination of within-patient differential performance.

Very specific studies may yield important information relating, for example, to prognosis of recovery. Thus, Gottlieb, Tichauer, and Davis (1975) compared the performance of hemiplegic patients and normal controls, using the venerable patellar tendon reflex. They measured angular leg accelerations, velocity, displacement, and surface EMG from the femoral muscle and found that patients who subsequently recovered most function manifested EMG levels 2–15 times greater than patients who did not recover.

The studies just considered represent, of course, only a small sample of the more traditional ways (clinical and experimental) of investigating the effects of cerebral insult or spinal injury. They are not particularly relevant to the measurement of the effects of biofeedback training, except in terms of a global assessment of improvement. It was clearly implied in K.U. Smith and Henry's (1967) review of the cybernetic foundations for rehabilitation that biofeedback techniques themselves might be used to elucidate more precisely the nature of the defects and thus provide a more rational basis for biofeedback training. Very little has been accomplished along these lines because most of the effort so far (as in other areas) has been put into treatment. However, three studies may be mentioned as illustrative of the important findings which may be obtained by what might be termed biofeedback behavioral analysis.

The first of these studies is by Carmon (1970) who worked with patients who had incurred right or left anterior or posterior hemisphere lesions and a group of control subjects. The task was to maintain the needle of a visual meter within specified limits by depressing a spring with the finger (each hand being tested) toward a proximity detector which activated the meter needle according to the distance of the spring from it. The task was performed with the spring allowing either 150 g or 450 g maximum pressure to be exerted; while in a control condition, the spring was absent and the finger alone approached the proximity detector. Carmon wanted to examine the differential extent to which the brain-damaged subjects could utilize proprioceptive feedback to control the meter needle. The dependent variable was the time in seconds the needle was held within the specified range during a 30-sec trial. The results are shown in Figure 8. The controls showed no hand difference and their performance improved as pressure required to activate the proximity detector increased from 200 to 450 g. When no pressure was required, the brain-damaged groups were all significantly poorer than the controls but did not differ from each other. As the pressure (and hence proprioceptive feedback) increased, however, the left-hemisphere (both anterior and posterior) patients improved their performance and at 450 g pressure their performance approximated that of the normal controls. However, while the performance of the anterior right-hemisphere patients showed some improvement, that of the posterior right-hemisphere patients did not improve at all. These patients were apparently unable to make effective use of the increased proprioceptive feedback to control the meter needle and were out of range for more than half of the 30-sec trial period. These results were replicated very closely by Levin (1973a,b) and further extended by Levin and Benton (1976) using slightly different pressures to those of Carmon (1970). In the Levin and Benton study, the hand itself was not visible while the task was being performed, thus removing a confounding source of feedback. It is true, of

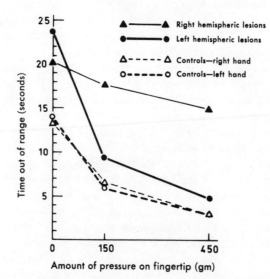

Figure 8. Means of time out of range in each pressure condition. (From Carmon, A. Impaired utilization of kinesthetic feedback in right hemisphere lesions. *Neurology,* 1970, *20,* 1033–1038, Figure 3. Reprinted by permission of the author and the publisher.)

course, that this task involves a further confounding of proprioceptive with visual feedback from the meter, and indeed approximates the situation studied by K. U. Smith where these two sources of feedback were shown to be capable of disturbing fine motor control when not congruent. Levin and Benton (1976) concluded that posterior right-sided focal lesions impair the control of spatial (positional) information which is not offset by increasing proprioceptive feedback, a conclusion in line with Carmon's explanation that the posterior right cerebral hemisphere mediates the utilization of proprioceptive cues to monitor the spatial location of body parts and to maintain their position. Clearly, however, results of this kind may also be of vital importance in determining the approach to retraining within a biofeedback context. Studies of this kind represent an essential groundwork for biofeedback training in specific disorders of function resulting from cerebral insult; thus far, not enough preliminary behavioral analysis of this kind has been carried out as a prelude to biofeedback training.

It has already been pointed out that a CVA (or spinal cord injury) is likely to have widespread effects on the functioning of the person afflicted. Nevertheless, it is not unreasonable, in the early phases of studying the applicability of a new approach, to concentrate on one or more functions which are commonly affected and in respect of which any improvement which might result from training can be quantified. Thus, it is not surprising that most of the work done so far on the effects of CVAs on *lower limb dysfunction* has related to the disability known as foot-drop. Foot-drop is produced by paralysis or weakness in the tibialis anterior muscle and is characterized by a gait in which the foot cannot be placed firmly on the ground in the usual heel-to-toe movement in walking, but rather drags. The abnormal gait results from the patient's inability to dorsiflex the ankle (i.e., to bend the foot upward from the horizontal toward the calf), a movement primarily initiated by the tibialis anterior muscle. The degree of disability varies, of course, and may be assessed in three ways: (1) the degree of strength in the tibialis anterior muscle; (2) the range of movement (ROM) in the ankle (the angular difference between maximum dorsiflexion and maximum plantar flexion—in the latter case, the foot is bent downward away from the calf); (3) the ability of the patient to walk without support. Inversion (the sole of the foot is twisted inward) or eversion (the sole of the foot is twisted outward) is also often present to add to the difficulties of the patient.

Basmajian, Kukulka, Narayan, and Takebe (1975) worked with 20 patients ranging in age from 30 to 63 years, all of whom had suffered CVAs resulting in residual foot dorsiflexion paresis. Half of the patients received the standard therapeutic physiotherapy training directed toward improving gait (such as practicing swing-through of the affected leg, progressing to walking with the support of parallel bars, and so on), while the other half received both the physiotherapy training and biofeedback training involving both auditory and visual feedback. The muscle trained was the tibialis anterior and the results of training were assessed in relation to the three aspects of gait control mentioned earlier—

strength of dorsiflexion, active ROM, and functional improvement in walking. The training was carried out three times a week for 5 weeks. The results were regarded as encouraging. The patients given physical therapy only showed an average increase of 5.7° in ROM and of 1.07 kg in strength of muscle activity; the corresponding figures for the patients given both physical and biofeedback training were 10.8° and 2.45 kg. Thus, biofeedback appeared to increase the effectiveness of physical therapy alone to a significant degree. Improvements in walking also occurred. In a subsequent report, Takebe, Kukulka, Narayan, and Basmajian (1976) reported the results of measuring peroneal nerve conduction velocity, skin temperature, and lower limb circumference in these patients on both the affected and unaffected sides. Prior to training, it was found that in the unaffected limb nerve conduction velocity was faster, temperature higher, and circumference larger, and Takebe et al. (1976) expected that these pretreatment differences would be reduced if training were successful. However, the expected changes were not found. They also examined the effect of training on the exaggerated patellar tendon reflex present in six patients and attributed to spasticity. Again, no difference was observed in spasticity after training. These results certainly make it difficult to interpret the results obtained by Basmajian et al. (1975) unequivocally, although Takebe et al. (1976) did not appear to believe that the former's results were rendered of doubtful significance. However, Fish, Mayer, and Herman (1976) have criticized the study by Basmajian et al. (1975) on several points. They point out that the groups were not equated for time elapsed since the CVA was experienced (the discrepancy is large—44.7 months for the group given physical therapy only as against only 22.5 months for the group given physical therapy and biofeedback), that they differed in average posttreatment time at which evaluation was made, and that proper statistical analysis of the quantitative data relating to changes in strength and ROM reveal that only strength showed a significant change. It needs to be remembered, of course, that the patients in the study by Basmajian et al. (1975) received a total of only about 12 h of training which is not a great deal by comparison with the amount of attention a CVA patient will normally receive. Thus, it must be concluded that this research produced encouraging but not decisive results in respect of the biofeedback component of the training. The results have, however, been replicated by Takebe and Basmajian (1976).

H. E. Johnson and Garton (1973) reported on the effects of biofeedback training in 11 patients (aged 27–73 years) who experienced foot dorsiflexion paralysis, resulting in all but two cases from a CVA (head injury was the trauma experienced in the other two cases). In all the patients studied, the foot dorsiflexion paralysis had lasted for more than 1 year. The initial training involved the use of electrodes implanted in the paralyzed tibialis anterior muscle. Motor unit action potentials (SMUs) were elicited in several ways: attempted mass flexion of the involved lower extremity, crossed facilitation, use of the stretch reflex, or use of the contralateral unimpaired muscle. Both auditory and visual feedback were provided and no more than three 30-min trials were given during this initial period of training. The patients were then placed on a self-training schedule, using a portable feedback unit and surface electrodes (although apparently they were able to use needle electrodes if the surface electrodes did not produce adequate feedback—it is not clear how the patients managed to use the needle electrodes). In the self-training period, auditory feedback was used rather than visual, which was found to be fatiguing and less helpful. The patients carried out at least two 30-min training sessions each day but overuse of the technique was discouraged. Unfortunately, in this study the number of weeks the patients spent in training was very variable, ranging from only 2 to as long as 16 weeks; and the assessment of change in motor function was very crude, being assessed on a simple scale ranging from zero, trace, poor, fair, good, up to normal gross foot dorsiflexion. Prior to training, six patients showed zero, one trace, two poor, and one fair dorsiflexion (the results of one patient were omitted); at final assessment, two patients showed good, seven fair, and one poor dorsiflexion, and all were considered improved. In some cases, successful training was hampered by the appearance of foot inversion during dorsiflexion, in which case retraining of the peroneus muscle was instituted. The criterion for ending training was the abandonment of the foot brace to assist ambulation (in the successful cases) or a failure of any return of function after 1 month. H. E. Johnson and Garton (1973) were sufficiently impressed by these clinical results to recommend the much wider use of biofeedback training in the rehabilitation of physical function, including retraining of shoulder, elbow, wrist and knee activity; the relaxation of spastic muscles; and the integration of separate muscle groups producing coordinated movements.

In these studies, the age range of the patients was very wide and several elderly patients were included. Flom, Quast, Boller, Berner, and Goldberg (1976) specifically investigated whether biofeedback training could be used successfully in elderly patients and reported detailed results on three patients aged 73–82. As might be expected, good motivation was found to be an important requirement. The training approach was similar to that used by Basmajian *et al.* (1975), but the training was more intensive and prolonged (five times a week for 1 h each time over a period of 12 weeks). Changes in muscle strength (as assessed by therapists, not as measured by level of EMG activity in the tibialis anterior muscle), ROM, gait (assessed from a motion-picture film of the patient walking), and neurological status were all assessed before and after training, with a 3-month follow-up. Considering the advanced age of the three patients who completed the training program and the multiple disabilities from which they suffered, the results obtained were regarded as quite promising. Two of the three patients were able to discard their leg braces and were able to walk without assistance or with the use of a cane.

Other studies have extended the basic observations and techniques described above. Amato, Hermsmeyer, and Kleinman (1973) attempted to retrain a 22-

year-old male with left hemiparesis (with spastic overlay) resulting from a traumatic right-sided head injury incurred 9 years earlier. The patient manifested a typical spastic hemiparesis gait with the left foot inverted and dorsiflexed in toe-off, and the hip circumducted, while knee flexion was minimal. At heel strike, the foot often contacted the floor on the lateral surface, thus barely allowing weight bearing on the sole of the foot. Before training began, with the hip and knee flexed to 90°, dorsiflexion of the left ankle was zero degrees with 10° inversion, while plantar flexion of 35° was present. Ankle motions were minimal because control of flexion via the tibialis anterior muscle was seriously interfered with by hypertonicity of the gastrocnemius-soleus muscles. The primary aim of training therefore became inhibiting gastrocnemius activity while the ankle was being dorsiflexed. In training, therefore, visual feedback was provided of the activity arising from the belly of the left medial gastrocnemius and the task of the patient was to attempt dorsiflexion of the left ankle while simultaneously inhibiting (that is, relaxing) the gastrocnemius muscle (surface electrodes were used). The training was carried out by the patient at home (after initial demonstrations) on a daily basis. After 2 months, the patient was able to dorsiflex the foot 15° (compared with zero dorsiflexion before training) with neutral supination and pronation maintained. His gait had improved and he was able to place his foot flat on the floor from heel strike into midstance. The main interest in this study lies in its demonstration of the importance of considering the interactions between the main muscle (tibialis anterior) involved in dorsiflexion and other muscles which normally act in a synergistic fashion but which, if affected by a CVA (or in this case a head injury) may need to be brought under control before training in control of the tibialis anterior muscle can be successfully instituted. In another single-case study, Nafpliotis (1976) successfully trained a 61-year-old male with right hemiplegia resulting from a CVA to increase dorsiflexion to the point at which the active ROM was equal to the passive (visual feedback was used in this case).

A significant innovation in biofeedback treatment has been described by Vodovnik and Rebersek (1973), who attempted to determine whether biofeedback training would be more effective if supplemented by electrical stimulation of the paralyzed muscle. The system used by Vodovnik and Rebersek (1973) is shown in Figure 9. The patient's leg is put in a brace which holds the ankle joint in a fixed position. Strain gauges are used to measure the amount of isometric torque generated. The patient watches the panel T_0 which displays the torque exerted. The lamp S_0 is illuminated when electrical stimulation is applied to the common peroneal nerve behind the fossa poplitea, resulting in involuntary foot dorsiflexion. When the lamp V_0 is illuminated, the patient is required to exert isometric torque voluntarily. In a third condition, both lamps are illuminated and the patient voluntarily exerts isometric torque while being "assisted" by the involuntary torque produced by electrical stimulation. Vodovnik and Rebersek (1973) consistently found that the combined effects of electrical stimulation and voluntary effort were greater than the effects of stimulation alone or the additive effects of stimulation alone and voluntary effort alone in producing increased torque. This was so even when the electrical stimulation was adjusted to a level where the resulting force was much smaller than the force obtained with volitional effort alone. Using this approach, Vodovnik and Rebersek (1973) reported significant improvements in voluntary control of dorsiflexion in four out of six patients with hemiplegia resulting frm CVAs. The main interest and importance of this study, however, lies in its demonstration of the fact that involuntarily produced torque may help in the acquisition of voluntary control.

Teng, McNeal, Kralj, and Waters (1976) attempted to confirm and extend the findings of Vodovnik and Rebersek (1973). The latter's work was based on the knowledge that automated stimulation of the peroneal nerve during the swing phase of walking has been shown to reduce foot-drop significantly in hemiplegic patients and that the effect may persist for some time. Teng *et al.* (1976) were concerned to try to separate out more clearly the effects of stimulation and visual feedback which had been confounded in the study of Vodovnik and Rebersek (1973). They had available for their work four patients who had used implanted stimulation for several years as an attempted correction for foot-drop. Torque was measured by a semiconductor strain gauge incorporated in a short leg brace. Training involved both visual and auditory feedback for torque magnitude. The patient was then required to walk for 20 min under several different conditions involving assistance by feedback or electrical stimulation or a combination of

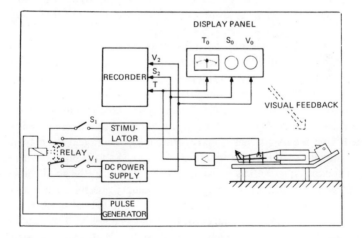

Figure 9. System for measuring foot torque under conditions of feedback, electrical stimulation, and combined feedback and electrical stimulation. (From Vodovnik, L., & Rebersek, S. Improvement in voluntary control of paretic muscles due to electrical stimulation. In W. S. Fields & L. A. Leavitt (Eds.), *Neural organization and its relevance to prosthetics.* New York: Intercontinental Medical Book Corporation, 1973, p. 102, Figure 1. Reprinted by permission from the author and Symposia Specialists, Inc. P. O. Box 610397, Miami, FL 33161.)

both, after which torque measurements were made while the patient attempted maximum dorsiflexion of the paretic foot while seated. The overall results were very variable and no clear conclusions could be drawn as to the comparative effects of electrical stimulation and feedback, alone or in combination. Thus, as indicated earlier, this new approach at present represents no more than a promising new development in the treatment of foot-drop.

All of the previous studies have dealt with foot-drop. Swann, van Wieringen, and Fokkema (1974) studied seven patients with either hemiplegia (the cause of which is not stated) or residual effects of poliomyelitis resulting in undesirable contractions of the peroneus longus muscle (in the back of the calf) when contracting the quadriceps muscle (in the thigh) during knee extension, which interfered with normal walking (the activity of the muscle was normal at rest). Using surface electrodes, EMG activity was recorded from the peroneus longus muscle and the patient was required to suppress the activity of the muscle as much as possible while stretching the leg (the patient sat on a chair with the lower part of the legs hanging freely). Using the patients as their own controls, a comparison was made between the effects of providing auditory feedback of peroneus longus muscle activity and conventional treatment by a physiotherapist, the dependent variable being pre–post training EMG activity and knee angle recordings while the patient stretched his leg. There were six training sessions with the treatment order varied within each session. The results indicated that the EMG training was superior to the physiotherapy, but the difference between the two methods must be interpreted cautiously as the study was not a well-controlled one and clear-cut results were obtained for only two of the seven patients.

To some extent at least, the difficulties encountered in the research and clinical treatment studies just reviewed arise from the complexity of the effects produced by CVAs, spinal cord injuries, and brain damage. It may well be that careful studies of the normal functioning of normal subjects in the activities impaired by cerebral insult will yield information which permits a more rational approach to therapeutic intervention. Little work in this direction has yet been reported. One such study has been reported by Kukulka and Basmajian (1975), who examined the ability of normal subjects to abduct the big toe with visual or auditory feedback, as well as in the absence of feedback (the abductor hallucis is a muscle which is difficult to bring under voluntary control). The subjects' task was to control both range of motion of the big toe and to control EMG activity, at first separately and later simultaneously but independently. The detailed results of this study need not be presented here except to indicate that successful control of both functions was achieved with adequate training. Kukulka and Basmajian (1975) stress the importance of studies such as this for elucidating the most effective procedures to be used in training patients with loss of function.

The studies of upper limb movement control are more diverse but less comprehensive than those dealing with lower limb movement control. The only study involving substantial numbers of patients is an early one by Andrews (1964) which can only be regarded as exploratory in nature. He reported on a group of 20 patients with hemiplegia who had no apparent residual function in the biceps and triceps muscles. Needle electrodes were first inserted into the contralateral normal muscle so that its activity could be observed by the patient with visual and auditory feedback provided. The electrodes were then inserted into the paretic muscle and the patient asked to contract it. If no action potentials appeared, the limb was moved passively and the patient asked to sustain the potentials which appeared. Only 5 min was spent with each patient if no success was obtained. Andrews (1964) reported that 17 of 20 patients developed many motor unit action potentials which could be utilized to produce voluntarily controlled muscle action. No quantitative data were provided by Andrews and the study can be regarded as of historical significance only.

The most important study of upper limb movement control is that by Simard and Ladd (1971), who implanted electrodes at three sites in the trapezius and frontalis muscles of ten quadriplegic patients who had suffered spinal cord lesions between C5 and C7. In the first stage of training, the patients were familiarized, using auditory and visual feedback, with the effects of activating each of the three segments of each muscle where the electrodes were implanted. Next, training in the separate activation and inhibition of SMUs in each segment of the muscle was undertaken. Then (using only visual feedback) simultaneous differential control of SMU activity in the three segments of the muscle was instituted. Finally, the patient was required to maintain SMU control in the trapezius muscle while the shoulder moved to convey a glass of water (actively or passively) from table level to mouth. Not all of the quadriplegic patients participated in all levels of the training, and at all stages of training except that involving control of a single segment the patients were, as might be expected, significantly poorer at achieving the control attained by normal subjects. Nevertheless, a significant degree of control was undoubtedly achieved by the quadriplegic patients with the assistance of feedback. Although there was no control for training without feedback, it seems most unlikely that the degree of success achieved would have been equalled in the absence of feedback.

An ingenious study by Sachs, Talley, and Boley (1976) investigated the possibility of training a 28-year-old female with right hemiparesis of upper and lower extremities and generalized spasticity following a car accident to hold a cup while drinking from it without spilling the contents. A plastic cup was fitted with mercury switches which allowed an operational definition of the degree of tilt and produced auditory feedback whenever a specified degree of tilt was exceeded (direct visual feedback was excluded). Auditory feedback and reinforcement in the form of tokens were provided alone and in combination for achieving a specified tilt criterion, a total of 25 training sessions being given. Feedback was found to be more important in producing and maintaining success, the role of reinforcement being to act as an incentive to attend to the information provided by the feedback. A considerable reduction in the amount of tilt in the cup was achieved in the training sessions, with some carrying over to the real-life situation.

In a study referred to earlier, Nafpliotis (1976) improved ankle dorsiflexion in a 61-year-old patient with right hemiplegia resulting from a CVA. This patient also showed difficulties in hand-grasp and finger-motion control which severely impaired his writing ability. Following training with visual feedback from the right forearm extensors, a dramatic improvement in handwriting took place while handgrasp was approximately 30–50% of normal performance.

An unusual study by MacPherson (1967) dealt with a female patient suffering from Huntington's chorea resulting in involuntary movements. Training in general relaxation was first given, followed by training in attending to sensory afferent input associated with beginning of an involuntary movement. Implanted electrodes were used to provide auditory feedback from the muscle under training and the patient attempted to relax the muscle whenever the feedback signal indicated that an involuntary movement was commencing. A major aim of the training was to help the patient initiate voluntary movement in one limb while inhibiting the involuntary movements that tended to accompany the voluntary movement. Although no quantitative data were provided by MacPherson (1967) and the difficulty of assessment was fully recognized, significant improvement (as assessed by husband's report) appeared to occur over a 1-year follow-up period.

The application of biofeedback training to physical rehabilitation of impaired function caused by physical injuries or other causes not involving brain damage or spinal cord lesions is only in its infancy. Two such studies may conveniently be included here, as both involve upper limb dysfunction. Kukulka, Brown, and Basmajian (1975) reported the results of biofeedback training with three patients who had suffered severe lacerations of various extrinsic flexor tendons of the hand. Surgical repair of the long flexor tendons may lead to dysfunction as a result of scar tissue's inhibiting tendon gliding. Surface electrodes were placed over the belly of the flexor digitorum superficialis and the patient was required to perform various exercises with the forearm both pronated and supinated, such as: isometric contractions in varying finger and wrist positions, mass flexions of the fingers with the wrist in a functional or random position, grasping built-up dowel rods of various sizes, making isolated proximal interphalangeal (PIP) motions, isolated flexion of the distal interphalangeal (DIP) joint, and indulging in active ranges of motion (ROM) of joints (e.g., ''make a fist''). Both auditory and visual feedback were provided. The training resulted in a significant increase in active ROM in all three patients. Simard and Ladd (1969b) attempted to train a group of thalidomide children (comparing their performance with that of normal children) in the control of SMU activity during movement of the ipsilateral upper limb, using implanted electrodes in the right rhomboid muscle. Not very much success was obtained but it should be borne in mind that the children were very young, being aged between 4 and 7 years.

feedback, are already familiar to the reader. The follow-up period has ranged from 3 months to 3 years. Attention will be concentrated here on their results with patients suffering from disabilities other than torticollis patients, who are also included in the results presented in these three papers.[9] The main findings may be summarized briefly as follows:

1. In 39 patients with hemiparesis of the upper extremity, 27 acquired prehension (60%), 4 had spasticity relieved, 4 showed no change in status, and 4 could not be properly evaluated because of insufficient therapy. No differences were found in the results as a function of whether the paresis was on the left or the right side.

2. In six patients with hemiparesis of the lower extremity, three achieved ankle dorsiflexion which had previously been absent.

3. In two quadriparetic patients (C5- or C6-level damage), prehension was achieved.

4. In two patients with facial spasm, voluntary control of the spasm over long periods was achieved.

5. In two patients with severe secondary quadriceps muscle atrophy (in each case, the patient needed a wheelchair to get about), increased strength of quadriceps muscle activity was achieved to the point at which the patient could walk.

6. In an unstated number of patients with peripheral nerve injury, return of muscle function was speeded up.

7. In two patients with brachial plexus avulsion, similar results were obtained. Overall, in light of their experience these authors are satisfied that biofeedback training is a useful technique in a wide variety of disabilities resulting from CVAs or spinal cord injury.

Basmajian, Regenos, and Baker (1977) have summarized the results of their work with foot-drop, shoulder subluxation, and reduced hand function. Of 25 patients who had been rendered ambulatory by the use of a short leg brace, 16 were able to discard the leg brace completely after an average of 16 training sessions (range: 3–25) but 9 showed little improvement for various reasons. Considerable further improvement with biofeedback training was obtained in nearly all of the 16 patients with foot-drop who prior to training had been able to ambulate without the use of a short leg brace. Improvement was obtained with biofeedback training in most of the 13 patients with shoulder subluxation and equally good results were obtained with an unspecified number of patients with impaired hand function. It may be pointed out here that Baker, Regenos, Wolf, and Basmajian (1977) have recently described in some detail their general clinical approach to the evaluation and training of neurologically handicapped patients.

---

[9]Their results with torticollis and dystonic patients have been more fully reported in the papers discussed in an earlier section of this chapter.

What conclusions can be drawn from this survey of the use of biofeedback training in the rehabilitation of physical function? A recent review by Inglis, Campbell, and Donald (1976) has clearly summarized the deficiencies in the work accomplished thus far:

> There were no control subjects and . . . little description has been given of the condition of the patients; for example, usually no details are given about sensory deficits due to the CNS lesions in the case of stroke patients, or about loss of function due to the disuse of muscles and joints. Little information has been provided about the feedback procedures, nor has consideration been given to the placebo effects likely to be produced by a novel kind of treatment and impressive electronic gear. (p. 318)

It should be noted that most of the above criticisms refer to the inadequacy of clinical description of the patients, rather than to formal requirements of experimental control. In addition, Inglis *et al.* (1976) stress the need for appropriate control groups to allow for spontaneous recovery of function, improved motivation, and other placebo effects. The comparative effects of skilled physiotherapy and the combined effects of physiotherapy and biofeedback also need much more study than has so far been given them. The reasons for failure need careful examination since failure may arise because of irreversible loss of function, use of inappropriate feedback, or poor planning. The transfer of results from the controlled laboratory situation to the real-life situation needs careful monitoring with appropriate follow-up of adequate duration. All these criticisms are well taken, but there is no doubt that studies of the rehabilitation of physical function pose real difficulties, given the extraordinary diversity of the disabilities that may result from a CVA or spinal cord lesion, not to mention the great variability that may manifest itself from day to day within the same patient. One aspect of this problem which has been sadly neglected thus far relates to the natural history of recovery. Van Buskirk (1954), for example, showed that a considerable amount of recovery of motor function in hemiplegics takes place with repeated testing of the affected limb (with the unaffected limb used as a control). The role of reinforcement in maintaining motivation and attention to the feedback display also needs to be examined more carefully (Peck, 1976). Goodkin (1966), for example, claimed that verbal reinforcement increased speed of responding in the affected hand paralyzed by a CVA in a 41-year-old female. Unfortunately he confounded reinforcement with informational feedback and withheld the latter whenever the patient performed more slowly. Nevertheless, the importance of adequate motivation in severely impaired patients can scarcely be overestimated.

Before completing this survey of the use of biofeedback in the rehabilitation of physical function, brief mention needs to be made of a new and potentially exciting area of collaborative effort involving the use of biofeedback in training severely disabled persons to use prosthetic devices. Clippinger (1973), for example, has stressed the need for the movements of a prosthetic device to provide feedback and has reviewed attempts to do this. He describes the use of a strain gauge incorporated into the stationary finger of a hook or control cable and has reported that the feedback eventually produces "sensations" or "images" of, for example, fist clenching:

> Physiological nervous system stimulation with appropriate interpretation of varying pressure and mental image can be obtained by the use of an implanted, induction-powered peripheral nerve stimulator. . . . (p. 172)

Similarly, Fernie, Kostuik, McLaurin, and Zimnicki (1976) have reported on the use of a buzzer to indicate when the knee is flexed or fully extended so that the patient is aware of when he may place his full weight on the prosthetic device. Although Fernie et al. (1976) use a binary on–off signal, they point out that proportional feedback would almost certainly be even more useful. In rather similar vein, Herman (1973) has described the use of a device called a Limb Load Monitor which is a transducer used to measure partial weight bearing in training patients to walk again. Clearly, feedback could be provided here also. Mann (1973) has described the Boston Arm, a device incorporating a feedback system which detects the amount of error between the signal transmitted to the prosthetic device from muscle and the actual resulting force exerted by the device. Scott, Bradley, and Timm (1973) have described the successful use of an implantable urinary sphincter which returns volitional control of urination to incontinent patients, while Trombly (1968) developed a Myoelectric Torque Motor Unit which could be used by C4 and C5 quadriplegic patients to perform skilled movements which were otherwise impossible. Childress (1973) has pointed out that devices of this kind should be fitted as early as possible in the case of congenital amputees (such as thalidomide children) so that in a very real sense the developing neural system could incorporate the prosthetic device and feedback resulting from it into its organization. Anani, Ikeda, and Körner (1977) have claimed that normal subjects with little training can discriminate different levels of direct nerve stimulation and hence such differences could be used as feedback stimuli for the control of prosthetic movements in amputees.

However, it should be noted that there are alternative approaches of more direct relevance to psychologists than, for example, the urinary prosthetic device described by Scott et al. (1973). Ince, Brucker, and Alba (1976) produced reflex urination in two patients with lower limb paralysis and no voluntary control of urination by strong shock to the abdomen. This was paired with mild electrical stimulation to the thigh as a conditioned stimulus. Subsequently, it was found that the patients were able to induce urination by applying the conditioned stimulus alone.

Such work is in its infancy and the difficulties involved in developing prosthetic devices with built-in feedback and interfacing them to the nervous system of the patient can hardly be exaggerated (Hogan, 1976). Indeed, a study by Warren and Lehmann (1975) has shown some of the difficulties involved in training normal subjects to achieve and maintain partial weight-bearing loads, intially with feedback, and later after the feedback is withdrawn. A force plate was used to determine the vertical load applied to the limb during the standing phase, after which the subject took four steps, using parallel bars (the situation was similar to that in which paralyzed patients attempt recovery of walking function). The results of several experiments were very disappointing. Thus, when subjects attempted to produce a force of between 29 and 34 kg while stepping on bathroom scales without visual feedback, they failed miserably. No greater success was obtained when a system called SCAP-III (involving the use of discs in an overshoe) was used, even though the device provides feedback in the form of an auditory alarm whenever the specified pressure is exceeded. As revealed in subsequent experiments, the major problem is that the subject has already committed himself to the force of the step by the time the alarm sounds and is then unable to avoid the overshoot, even though the alarm continues to sound. Further variations in the subtlety of the feedback system did not produce improvement. The difficulties experienced appear to arise from the fact that discrepant feedback information is being provided through two channels, the auditory and the sensory, producing a situation akin to delayed auditory feedback and consequent breakdown of the skill.

Cerebral Palsy

Cerebral palsy is the result of damage to the motor and speech areas of the brain and produces widespread difficulties in coordination of skilled motor movements and speech which may result in the child's being considered to be mentally retarded. In fact, the range of intelligence in cerebral-palsied children is probably not different than that found in an unselected sample of children—hence, the exceptional amount of effort which has been expended in trying to help the cerebral-palsied child overcome his often appalling difficulties.

The difficulties experienced by the cerebral-palsied child in coordinating his motor behavior have usually been regarded as a direct result of the damage to the motor areas of the cerebral cortex. The athetoidlike or spastic movements are explained as due to an absence of sensory feedback from the muscles involved. Harris (1971) has recently suggested that the basic defect in cerebral palsy may not be in the efferent motor system at all, but rather in the afferent system, that is, it may involve a faulty servomechanical feedback control system. He argues that the uncoordinated movements may result from inadequate peripheral stretch receptor function which produces false feedback information to the central comparator which determines when a movement has achieved its target. Let us suppose that a reaching movement is initiated toward an object with the ulimate intention of grasping the object. The progress of the reaching movement will be continuously (or at least intermittently) monitored and a halt command issued when the target is reached, to be succeeded by a grasp command. The latter command, however, can only be issued after the reaching movement has been successfully completed. Harris's model for the control of the reaching movement is shown in Figure 10. The comparator which monitors the movement is located by Harris in the cerebellum where the difference between the intended and actual positions of the limb is compared to drive an error signal. The signal for the intended position reaches the cerebellum via collateral branches of corticospinal tract fibers which excite the alpha motoneurones at the spinal cord level, whereas the signal for the actual position at any given moment arrives at the cerebellum via sensory projections from three sensory feedback sources (the visual system, the muscle stretch receptors, and the receptors which sense changes in joint angles). A difference or error signal is thus computed by the comparator, which issues instructions resulting in corrections in the form of increased or decreased output to the muscle systems involved. Thus, undershooting or overshooting the target can be corrected. When the error signal is equal to zero, the reaching movement is complete and the appropriate commands to grasp the object may be instituted. The control system for reaching involves reticular system control of the gamma efferents which in turn stimulate the stretch receptors. If this system is faulty, the gamma efferents may fail to perform their stimulatory function correctly, as a result of which the intrafusal fibers may remain slack and the

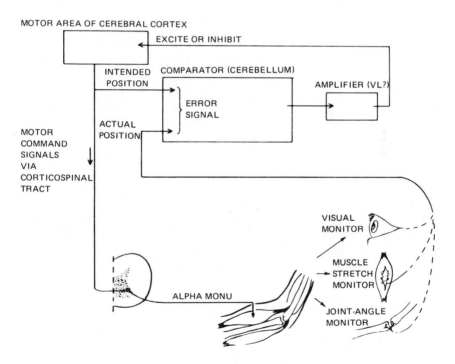

Figure 10. Control system for reaching movements. (From Harris, F. A. Inapproprioception: A possible sensory basis for athetoid movements. *Physical Therapy,* 1971, *51,* 763, Figure 1. Reprinted by permission of the author and the publisher.)

stretch receptors may not be adequately stimulated. The important point to note is that as a result of these failures the information fed back to the monitoring system may be incorrect. Thus, when the limb has actually reached the target, the feedback may be indicating that it is not yet there, as a result of which the error signal in the comparator will not be zero and the movement will be continued, resulting in overshooting the target. When the error signal does reach zero and it becomes apparent that the target has been overshot, a compensatory reversal will occur in an attempt to correct for the overshoot, but this in turn may lead to an overshoot in the opposite direction and an oscillatory movement about the target will result (it is assumed that feedback from the visual system is not adequate to override the effects of the faulty sensory feedback system). The primary defect in cerebral palsy may therefore be a faulty feedback control system rather than a faulty motor system. But such an interpretation of the basic defect in cerebral palsy has important implications for the approach to treatment. Instead of directly attempting to train the motor system, it may be more appropriate to intervene in the sensory feedback system (hence the term "inapproprioception" used by Harris).

No provision is made in Harris's feedback model (Figure 10) for the possibility of local, faster feedback loops to influence ongoing control of the response, and these may be particularly important in cerebral palsy. As Harrison (1976a) has pointed out, a local comparator mechanism may operate whereby feedback from the stretch receptors may directly modify the spinal-level alpha motoneurone activity, resulting in a modification of the motor command to the extrafusal fibers, "corrective action" (which may, in fact, be inappropriate if the feedback signal is faulty), resulting much more quickly than if the feedback signal had to reach the central comparator before "corrective action" could be taken. There is, in fact, direct experimental evidence that very rapid adjustments may be made to alterations of force impinging on a muscle system while it is in motion (Marsden, Merton, & Morton, 1972).

The contributions of Harris (1971) and Harrison (1976a) have not, however, been only at the theoretical level. Harris and his colleagues (Harris, Spelman, & Hymer, 1974; Harris, Spelman, Hymer, & Chase, 1973) have developed what they have called exoskeletal electronic sensory aids to provide feedback to the cerebral-palsied child which it is hoped will assist him in compensating for the faulty internal system which produces incorrect feedback. The most important devices developed by Harris and his colleagues are the Head Control Device, which provides auditory feedback of the position of the head as it varies in the vertical and horizontal planes, with no sound representing the normal upright position; and the Limb Position Monitor, which provides visual feedback of the angle of rotation about the axis of individual joints (e.g., elbow or wrist) while auditory feedback indicates the degree of undershoot or overshoot.

Harris *et al.* (1974) have described preliminary results obtained with the use of these devices with 18 athetoid cerebral-palsied children aged 7–18 years,

trained over periods varying between 2 and 12 months. All of the children trained
with the Head Control Device showed significantly improved head stability. The
results for one child over 2 months of training with the Head Control Device are
shown in Figure 11. The vertical changes indicate head position and the horizontal axis indicates time in seconds. The top tracing represents tilt from left to
right, and the bottom tracing tilt from front to rear. The large arrowheads indicate
the neutral position for each plane of tilt and the small arrowheads the beginning
and end of periods of stability. Similarly, all of the children using the Limb

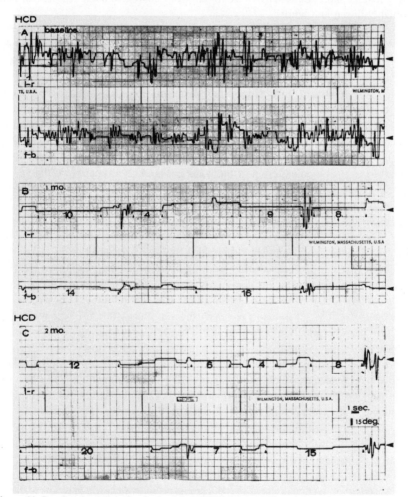

Figure 11. Results of training a cerebral-palsied child in head stability with the Head Control Device.
(From Harris, F. A., Spelman, F. A., & Hymer, J. W. Electronic sensory aids as treatment for
cerebral-palsied children: Inapproprioception: Part II. *Physical Therapy,* 1974, *54,* 359, Figure 4.
Reprinted by permission of the author and the publisher.)

Position Monitor improved their arm stability and range of motion. These results are demonstrations rather than definitive evidence of the validity of Harris's interpretation of the basic problem in cerebral palsy, but they indicate the exciting possibilities of these new techniques such as training in the simultaneous control of head position and arm movements. Harris *et al.* (1974) also reported that associated movements not directly trained appeared to show some improvement and there was some indication that the improvement could be sustained in the absence of the devices. Subsequent studies (Harris, 1978) have extended these results and comprehensive treatment programs have been devised for individual children and adults.

The use of a similar head control device with feedback has been described by Halpern, Kottke, Burrill, Fiterman, Popp, and Palmer (1970) who found that using such a device correct head posture could be maintained for 3–4 h without interfering with other activities and the posture could be maintained when the device was removed. Two points may be made about this study. First, other involuntary movements appeared to act as noise and interfere with control—a point also made by Harris, who stressed the need to restrain these other movements in the initial stages of training, and Halpern *et al.* (1970), who appeared to use their head halter in such a way as to produce aversive consequences in the form of increasing constriction of the head and neck as a function of the amount of movement away from the correct position, thus confounding informational feedback and reinforcement, whereas Harris, of course, provided informational feedback only.

Wooldridge and Russell (1976) have also described the use of a Head Position Trainer (HPT) similar to that used by Harris. In addition to an auditory feedback signal to indicate head position, an accumulated performance indicator (API) is used which provides essentially visual meter feedback enabling targets to be set. A clock device provides additional information while reinforcement in the form of a TV set is also provided (the set shuts itself off whenever head position is incorrect). Training is given in the real-life situation (e.g., while the subject is eating). Using this device and the various forms of feedback and reinforcement, Wooldridge and Russell (1976) reported very encouraging results with 12 cerebral-palsied children aged 3–10 years, and with a 7-year-old boy with a habitual head tilt to the left diagnosed as a congenital condition of os terminale with C_1–C_2 subluxation (Russell & Wooldridge, 1975).

Following preliminary investigations (Harrison & Connolly, 1971), Harrison (1976b,c) has reported the results of a series of important experimental investigations designed to determine the degree to which cerebral-palsied adults could exercise various kinds of muscle control compared with normal subjects in the absence of feedback, and the degree to which the provision of feedback produced an improvement in the control. In one experiment, for example (Harrison, 1976b, Experiment I), the maximum tension level which spastics and normal controls could achieve in the forearm flexor group of muscles was established. An arbitrary scale of 1–9 was determined covering the range of activity and the subject was required to try to produce each tension level. Visual feedback was not provided: the experimenter initially indicated verbally when each required tension level was reached, then the subject indicated on subsequent trials when he thought the specified level had been achieved. The results showed that the spastic patients were least accurate at low and high tension levels whereas the normal subjects were least accurate at intermediate tension levels (the spastics were, of course, less accurate than the normal controls at all tension levels). The spastics tended to overshoot at low, and undershoot at high, tension levels. A subsequent experiment (Harrison, 1976b, Experiment II.2) indicated that the spastic patients appeared to have an abnormally high threshold for the detection of muscular activity. Harrison (1976b,c) also measured the changes occurring in forearm extensor activity while the subject was engaged in forearm flexor activity and obtained results which suggested that spastics have great difficulty in differentiating flexor and extensor activity. Spastics also take much longer to return to resting level of muscle activity after tensing the muscle voluntarily (Harrison, 1976c, Experiment I) although substantial improvement in time to relax was obtained when visual feedback was provided (Experiment II). Similarly, the impairment in ability to maintain a voluntarily induced tension was significantly increased when feedback was made available (Experiment IV), while feedback also improved the ability of spastics simultaneously to control forearm and biceps muscle activity. These experiments by Harrison were not primarily intended as therapeutic; their importance lies in the empirical and theoretical foundations they provide on which attempts to improve difficulties in real-life tasks must ultimately be based.

So far, the great significance of the contributions made by Harris and by Harrison to both the theory and treatment of cerebral palsy (and their potential significance for other areas of rehabilitation) appears to have escaped the attention of workers in the biofeedback area, and it is hoped that this account will correct this state of affairs.

A study by Spearing and Poppen (1974) also indicated the promising possibilities of the use of feedback training in cerebral palsy. They attempted to relieve foot-drop in a young cerebral-palsied male. The shoe worn on the foot was modified so that a switch on the toe closed (producing an auditory tone) whenever the patient dragged his foot. He was instructed to try not to drag his foot, thus preventing the tone from occurring. Training was carried out over a 4-month period, using an A (no feedback) –B (feedback) –ABC (verbal feedback)– A design with a follow-up (no feedback) 3 months later. Foot-drop was reduced virtually to zero (without feedback) at the end of training but the improvement was not maintained at follow-up. In this instance, at least, however, there seems no reason why the feedback device should not have been available on a permanent basis, rather than dispensing with it at the end of the training period. The study also showed that the improvement could be maintained for a significant period of time as the feedback was gradually faded out.

Rugel, Mattingly, Eichinger, and May (1971) studied an 8-year-old boy with cerebral palsy who could walk or sit with difficulty, but who tended to take the weight off his legs whenever possible by supporting himself by his arms, thus being unable to carry out activities involving the use of his arms. In an attempt to train the child to support more of his body weight on his legs, he was stood on a scale with a walk support. Whenever the scale (which was not visible to the child) read 39–44 lb (the child's body weight was 44 lb), visual feedback in the form of a light was provided, and a toy car on a rail track was activated depending on how long the light remained on. After 4 weeks of training, full body weight was being supported by the legs for about 77% of trial time (the light alone was found to be sufficient to induce unsupported standing to a significant degree).

Sachs, Martin, and Fitch (1972)[10] illustrated the possibility of improving fine motor control in the cerebral-palsied child. Five metal tips were attached to the fingers of each hand of an 11-year-old child who was requested to touch each finger in turn to the thumb. A timer was activated by each touch provided the correct sequence of touches was followed, enabling individual finger latencies and total time for the entire sequence to be measured. A bank of four lights provided external feedback, the lights being activated only if the correct sequence of movements was produced. An A–B–C–A–C design was used, involving: baseline (no feedback), noncontingent visual feedback (the order of light activation was random with respect to the touch sequence), contingent visual feedback (the lights were sequentially activated if the touch sequence was performed correctly), baseline, and contingent visual feedback again. Two interesting controls were used: one hand of the cerebral-palsied child (the touch sequence required under baseline conditions only), and the performance level of the child's normal 8-year-old sister under both baseline and feedback conditions. A practice effect was found, but when this was allowed for, an improvement attributable to the visual feedback manipulation was still demonstrable. In other studies, Sachs and Mayhall (1971) obtained similar improvements in the control of spasms in a cerebral-palsied adult.

It is perhaps surprising that little evidence is available concerning the effects of specific or general relaxation training with feedback on spasticity. Presumably, expectations of success have been small, the spasticity being unlikely to be modifiable on a voluntary control basis. That this assumption may be false is indicated by three studies. Wolpert and Wooldridge (1975) investigated a 14-year-old girl with spastic quadriplegia and faulty head posture. The head was

---

[10]In a later paper, Martin and Sachs (1973) refer to the above study as if it were a different one. However, both papers appear to be a report on the same individual.

rotated to the right and tilted toward the left while sitting or standing. Excessive activity was found in the left sternomastoid muscle while little or no activity was present in the right. The patient was successfully trained to relax the left and tense the right sternomastoid muscles on command, using continuous proportional auditory and visual feedback while lying supine on the floor, sitting cross-legged on the floor, sitting in a chair, and standing. This control was maintained at a 4-month follow-up, but did not at any stage of training generalize to the normal life situation of the patient. Finley and his colleagues (Finley, Niman, Standley, & Ender, 1976; Finley, Niman, Standley, & Wansley, 1977) trained athetoid and spastic cerebral-palsied children in relaxation of frontalis muscle activity and measured the effects of the training on performance on speech and fine and gross motor skills. They were successful in training both athetoid and spastic children to reduce frontalis muscle activity levels and reported that a significant improvement was apparent in the motor performance of the children after training. Some degree of generalization of the frontalis muscle activity relaxation training to the forearm was also evident.

It may be concluded that biofeedback training procedures hold considerable promise for the treatment of the motor disabilities which afflict cerebral-palsied children and adults, and a considerably increased effort in this important area may be expected in the future.

Abnormal Tremor

Very little remedial work within the framework of biofeedback has thus far been carried out on disorders involving disturbances of the control of tremor in spite of the potential importance of feedback training in these disorders (even though they may usually have an organic basis). Recent studies which throw a good deal of light on the nature of abnormal tremor and its control, however, indicate that feedback training could indeed be helpful.

Most of these studies have concentrated on three aspects of abnormal functioning where tremor is disturbed, as in Parkinson's disease. There is the question of differences between patients and normal subjects while the affected limb is at rest, the problem of changing from rest to movement of the limb, and the question of differences in voluntary movement once the limb is in motion. Andreeva and Shafranova (1975) studied the EMG activity in the muscles controlling movement in a large sample of patients suffering from Parkinson's disease and showed that the main characteristics of the EMG activity in both the resting state and during movement were the same in patients and control subjects. However, significant differences did occur at the interface between the resting state and movement. The critical rate of muscle activity (i.e., the electrical potentials, not the movement of the limb itself) at which a change occurred from the steady state to movement was significantly higher in the patients, and in the advanced stage of the disease it was found that the critical change might never take place (patients with Parkinson's disease often show resistance to movement when a joint is flexed passively). If, however, the patient could exceed the critical rate of electrical activity, the change to movement would occur, and during the movement the EMG activity would be similar to that shown by normal subjects. Patients with Parkinson's disease also tended to show bursts of 5-Hz activity whereas this was never found in the normal subjects. Andreeva and Shafranova (1975) consider that the control mechanisms for posture have become predominant in this disorder, thus accounting for the failure of the patient to shift to sufficiently fast rates of EMG activity for movement to occur.

Clearly, if the analysis of Andreeva and Shafranova (1975) is correct, experimental studies of the performance of patients with Parkinson's disease in tracking tasks, with the extremities loaded or unloaded, become of great importance in further elucidation of the nature of the disorder. Such studies have a long history, of course, but more recently some very sophisticated and careful work has advanced knowledge in this area significantly. Flowers (1975) compared the performance of patients with Parkinson's disease, patients with essential tremor, patients with cerebellar disease, and normal controls, on a step-tracking task, using a joystick control and an oscilloscope display consisting of a small moving circle. The task involved moving the joystick so as to track the circle with a dot of light in such a way as to get the dot into the circle and then keep it there. The initial ballistic movement or excursion could be small (5 cm) or large (12.5 cm) and to the left or right. Flowers measured reaction time (RT) to move the joystick in response to the circle movement, initial movement time to reach the circle, corrective movement time, and total movement time. He found that the normal subjects had an initial RT of about 240 msec and a fast initial movement which got them to within about 20% (either side) of the target position. A series of corrections was then produced to get the spot inside the circle. The patients with essential tremor showed a longer RT; once started, however, their initial movement time was similar to that of the normal subjects, but subsequent corrective movements were not so accurate. The patients with Parkinson's disease also showed a longer RT but this was followed by a "slow creep" rather than a fast initial movement, and they were better at making subsequent corrections than the patients with essential tremor. Flowers (1975) concluded that patients with Parkinson's disease have lost the ability to generate initial fast ballistic movements compared with normal subjects. He points out that this suggests that Parkinson's disease cannot simply be explained as a loss of feedback control since the difficulty involves the initiation of movement rather than its control once the movement is underway. In subsequent studies, Flowers (1978a) has replicated these results with other wave forms and also showed that practice at the task does not lead to improvement in the performance of patients with Parkinson's disease (Flowers, 1976) and that these patients do not show the anticipatory behavior characteristic of normal performance in tracking (Flowers, 1978b).

While Flowers's results are in line with the findings of Andreeva and Shaf-ranova (1975) in that they both find the primary difficulty to lie at the interface between the resting state and the beginning of movement, the conclusion by Flowers (1975) that a feedback deficit is not the explanation of the difficulty would seem to be unwarranted. If the EMG activity in the muscle has to change from one level to a critically higher level before a change can occur from the resting state to movement, then malfunctioning of a feedback loop which pre-vents the critical rate of EMG activity from being reached is certainly a possibil-ity. There is no reason to suppose that feedback control systems operate only while movement is present; the maintenance of the resting state, the change from resting state to movement, and the movement itself all may involve different levels of feedback control.

Studies rather similar to those conducted by Flowers (1975, 1976) have been carried out by Tatton and Lee (1975) and by Hallett, Shahani, and Young (1975a,b, 1977) building on earlier work by, for example, Halliday and Redfearn (1958) and Van Buskirk and Fink (1962). Tatton and Lee (1975) utilized a task in which the subject grasped a handle coupled to a precision torque motor set to deliver step-loads of 300–500 g (the rise time to maximum torque being 3.2 msec). The load, which was imposed unexpectedly, caused passive flexion or extension displacement of the wrist. The subject was instructed to allow the passive wrist displacement and then respond by moving the handle as rapidly as possible in the direction opposite to the displacement. EMG activity was re-corded from the wrist flexor and extensor muscles. Detailed analysis of the results showed that the normal subjects in this study showed three short latency EMG responses at 29–32 msec (M1), 58–62 msec (M2), and 85–90 msec (M3) with higher amplitude, prolonged EMG activity being initiated at a latency of 110–116 msec—this latter activity represented initiation of the voluntary an-tagonistic movement by the subject. Patients with Parkinson's disease, however, showed a highly significant increase in M2 and M3 activity in both the passive and active phases of the task, compared with the normal subjects. According to Tatton and Lee, the M1 response involves spinal reflexes whereas the M2 and M3 responses are mediated by "long-loop" pathways involving the supraspinal centers. Tatton and Lee also confirmed the existence of the 5-Hz/sec rest tremor and its independence of peripheral input, concluding that it is generated by central oscillators. Thus, they conclude that feedback control is involved in the initiation of movement in Parkinson's disease (at least in those patients who manifest extreme rigidity). Harris (1971) also stressed the importance of the feedback loop in intention tremor.

Hallett, Shahani, and Young (1975a), however, working with normal sub-jects who were required to track a visual step function, considered that both central preprogramming mechanisms and gamma efferent–Ia feedback gain are involved in such tasks, with central programming being the important factor in fast flexion while segmental feedback is predominant in smooth reactions. Thus, control is exercised at different levels, depending on the particular task stage involved. Using a tracking task similar to that employed by Flowers (1975, 1976), they investigated the performance of 20 patients suffering from the effects of cerebellar degeneration, most of whom manifested ataxic tremor. They measured the levels of EMG activity in the biceps and triceps muscles when these muscles were in an antagonistic relationship. The patient's task was to match a step-function oscilloscope display by adjusting the angle of his elbow approximately 10°. The task was to be performed either quickly or carefully and slowly under each of five conditions: fast flexion (FF) without weights applied to the forearm; antagonist inhibition (AI), in which the triceps was made to contract tonically by a weight which would flex the elbow if unopposed; smooth flexion (SF) without weights; passive extension of the elbow during fast flexion effort (PE), in which two weights were attached so that their pull was neutralized but, just before biceps began, the weight pulling in the direction of the elbow flexion was released, causing passive elbow extension, thus reducing tension on the triceps (that is, biceps contraction did not lead to elbow flexion or triceps stretching); and, finally, smooth unload (SU), in which the weight was attached to the lever pulling in the direction of elbow extension, thus requiring tonic activity in the biceps to maintain an elbow flexion of 90°, and the weight was released unexpectedly. Hallett *et al.* (1975b) found a prolongation of the initial biceps reaction in FF as compared with normal reaction time. During AI, they found that there was a tendency in the patients for triceps activity not to cease before the biceps activity began (as happens in normal subjects), whereas in the SF condition no difference was found in the relationship between biceps and triceps activity when the patients' performance was compared with that of the normal subjects. The results suggested that the failure of control occurs at the suprasegmental level and involves central programming.

These rather complex studies indicate that the breakdown of the control of tremor involves several levels of servomechanical interaction which needs to be taken into account in devising biofeedback-based therapy. Thus far, little work has been reported in this important area, probably because of a lack of awareness of these fundamental studies. Chase *et al.* (1965) pointed out that in Parkinson's disease tremor tends to be present at rest but reduced or absent during voluntary movement, whereas the reverse tends to be the case with tremor associated with lesions of the cerebellar system. They investigated the performance of patients with Parkinson's disease or cerebellar deficits and of normals on a tracking task in which the task was to try to make a visual display of their tremor coincide with a reference bar on an oscilloscope display by reducing the amplitude of the tremor as much as possible. Increasing the gain of the display (that is, providing a larger vertical displacement for a specified magnitude of tremor) improved the tracking performance of both groups of patients as well as of the normal subjects, suggesting that all three groups used the same techniques to control tremor. However, when the matching task had to be performed against an upward-moving force of 25, 50, 75, or 100 g, intention tremor was also significantly reduced in the normals and patients with cerebellar deficits but not in the patients with Parkinson's disease. When a downward-directed force was used, tremor increased markedly in all groups as a function of the magnitude of the force. This study appears to be the only one so far on the effect of biofeedback on intention tremor. There is here a fertile field for future fundamental research and clinical treatment.

A study by Netsell and Cleeland (1973) is, however, relevant to the treatment of Parkinson's disease with biofeedback. The patient (a 64-year-old patient with a 15-year history of Parkinsonism) manifested a bilateral retraction of the upper lip following bilateral thalamic surgery for the disease. The bilateral retraction exposed the upper gum and precluded bilabial closure for sounds like /p/, /b/, and /m/. The lower lip closed against the upper teeth in compensation, leading to extreme eye squint and wrinkling of the forehead, and the patient also showed speech defects characteristic of Parkinson's disease. Surface electrodes were placed over the levator labii superioris (the muscle which elevates the upper lip) and over the orbicularis ori. Both speech and nonspeech behaviors were studied, with auditory feedback reflecting the level of EMG activity in the muscles. With respect to nonspeech activities, the patient was required to assume and maintain one of four distinct postures of the upper lip for 3–5 min at a time, ranging from a resting posture to complete retraction of the upper lip; and to produce continuous variation in the EMG feedback for 10-sec periods. The speech activities were selected so as not to involve the upper lip (phonate /a/ for 3–5 sec; repeat /a/, /ka/, /ta/, five times at a rate of two repetitions per second; read a passage devoid of lip consonants and vowels which would require lip rounding or spreading). These activities were also practiced at home. Complete restoration of the upper lip to the normal resting position was achieved and the retracted posture was never again assumed while control of the lip position during speech was also rapidly achieved. As a result of the successful lip-position training, the eye squint and forehead wrinkling also disappeared. This isolated study also indicates clearly the possibilities of biofeedback training in Parkinson's disease, although in this case the disabilities resulted from surgical intervention.

Excessive tremor, of course, does not always result from organic disease—it is a common concomitant of neurotic states of anxiety. Le Boeuf (1976) has shown that biofeedback may be helpful in such cases. He studied a 41-year-old socially introverted male with a history of obsessional checking behavior and depression who developed a marked tremor of the right hand and arm in stressful situations (when he believed he was the center of attention) and when required to write in front of people. The EMG activity of the forearm extensor muscle was recorded and auditory feedback provided. Following several baseline sessions in which the patient tried to relax the muscle without feedback, false feedback was provided and succeeded by true feedback, during both of which periods relaxation attempts were continued. This was in turn followed by a period of stress-management training during which the patient first reduced the EMG activity with true feedback and then imagined stressful situations. The latter led to an increase in EMG activity which was then reduced, using feedback. The results of this study are shown in Figure 12. The beneficial effects of the feedback training were maintained when feedback was no longer presented and produced positive benefits in the patient's real-life stress situations, the improvement being maintained at a 6-month follow-up.

This concludes our survey of muscle paralysis and spasticity resulting from innate or acquired cerebral insult. It is clear that the rehabilitation of physical function represents one of the most important areas for the application of biofeedback techniques. Thus far, however, the applications, though widespread, have been limited in scope and have not, of course, reflected the extremely diverse consequences of such afflictions and the complicated interactions between different systems which are involved. Proper control is very difficult for this very reason and it would be unfair to expect that the clinical studies would be able to be carried out under ideal experimental conditions. Thus, possible confounding of results by uncontrolled variables is highly likely. It will probably be necessary to rely on the overall impressiveness of the results obtained in diverse areas to conclude that biofeedback does have an important role to play in the rehabilitation of physical function. The results to date, however, do seem to be very promising.

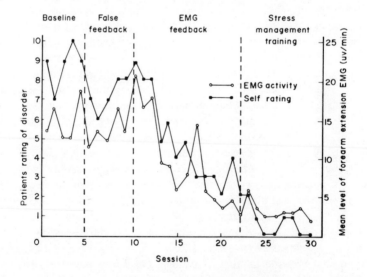

Figure 12. Results of biofeedback training on a severe tremor. (From Le Boeuf, A. The treatment of a severe tremor by electromyogram feedback. *Journal of Behavior Therapy and Experimental Psychiatry,* 1976, 7, 60, Figure 1. Reprinted by permission of the author and the publisher.)

Dysfunction of Muscle Activity in Speech and Breathing

In this section, we will deal with subvocalization in reading, esophageal dysfunction, nasality, and stuttering.

Subvocalization. Subvocalization (or silent speech) in reading has been of theoretical interest in the history of psychology since extreme behaviorists have tended to point to it as justification for their arguments that thinking is merely a form of talking to oneself quietly instead of out loud, and it has intermittently been of interest to education as it was long regarded as a hindrance to efficient reading. Only its relevance within the biofeedback context will be considered here. Jacobson (1973) has pointed out that he used biofeedback (a visual display of the muscle activity) in the context of subvocalization in reading at an early stage of his investigations, but the first systematic investigation of the phenomenon on a larger scale appears to have been that of McGuigan, Keller, and Stanton (1964).[11] They carried out three experiments on different age levels—children aged 6–11 years, elementary school children, and female college students—with EMG recordings from the chin muscle in the case of the first group and recordings from the lip muscle in the other two. They measured activity levels during a prereading baseline period, during silent reading of a lengthy passage of prose, and during a postreading baseline period. The difficulty level of the material was varied and the maximum amplitude of EMG activity at each difficulty level was measured. They found an increase in chin and lip activity during the silent reading period as compared with baseline activity in all three groups and concluded that subvocalization was associated with increased lip movements.

The first biofeedback study of subvocalization, however, appears to have been that by Hardycke, Petrinovich, and Ellsworth (1966), who recorded from surface electrodes placed over the thyroid cartilage of 17 college students who subvocalized while reading. They were able to distinguish clearly the levels of activity involved in the resting state, while reading silently, and while reading aloud (the greatest activity, of course, taking place during reading aloud). Auditory feedback was then provided and the task of the subject was to keep the auditory feedback (proportional to the amount of subvocalizing) as low as possible while reading silently. In all 17 subjects, a single training session of from 5 to 30 min was sufficient to eliminate the subvocalization completely. These impressive results were confirmed 1 month and 3 months later when the subjects were required to read for 30 min without feedback and subvocalization was found to be completely absent. Instructions alone, it was claimed, were not sufficient to eliminate subvocalization since the subject was usually unaware of his tendency until the feedback display drew his attention to it.

No quantitative data were provided to substantiate these claims and the study was criticized on this and and other grounds by Camacho (1967) and

---

[11]Some of the earliest references on subvocalization are provided by these authors.

McGuigan (1967). Camacho (1967) pointed out that no measures of comprehension were used by Hardycke *et al*. (1966) and hence there was no evidence that the subjects were actually still reading when they stopped vocalizing. McGuigan (1967), on the basis of some additional data he had collected, considered that continuous reading *per se* would lead to a reduction in EMG levels and hence the results obtained by Hardycke *et al*. (1966) could not be attributed to feedback training in the absence of proper controls. However, Hardycke, Petrinovich, and Ellsworth (1967) rejected these criticisms and reported further data in a subsequent study (Hardycke & Petrinovich, 1969). They conducted two further investigations, one with university students of high intelligence and reading ability, and another with high-school students. The results with the university students confirmed the original findings but less clear-cut results were obtained with the high-school students. Only those high-school students of high intelligence showed rapid favorable results with biofeedback training and the students of lower intelligence tended to relapse at follow-up. The elimination of subvocalization did not have any dramatic effect on reading speed.

In their earlier paper, McGuigan *et al*. (1964) had raised an important question which was subsequently echoed by Hardycke and Petrinovich (1969). It had long been assumed that subvocalization was undesirable because it interfered with reading speed and comprehension. However, there is evidence that subvocalization increases in normal readers (who do not usually subvocalize) when they are required to read increasingly difficult material, and that subvocalization will increase even in very efficient and highly intelligent subjects as the material becomes harder. Thus, it has been suggested that subvocalization may serve an important purpose, namely, to determine an optimal reading speed which maximizes comprehension. When the reading material is very easy no subvocalization at all will occur, but as it becomes more difficult subvocalization will increase to the point at which it slows reading rate so as to maximize comprehension. If this is so, then the elimination of subvocalization may actually have deleterious effects on comprehension. It is surprising that no definitive study on this important matter, with proper quantification of reading speed and comprehension, appears to have yet been carried out. Thus, the question of whether biofeedback training should be used to reduce or eliminate subvocalization remains unresolved.

Esophageal Dysfunction. Two studies of esophageal dysfunction are of interest because, although biofeedback was not used, its application might be of considerable assistance in overcoming the dysfunction. Jacobson (1925) trained three subjects successfully in relaxation of the esophagus to control excessive esophageal spasms which prevented ingested food from leaving the esophagus rapidly. Light, Silverman, and Garfinkel (1976) have described the development of a palatal prosthesis designed to improve proper tongue movement in patients who have undergone a laryngectomy operation. Esophageal speech production which must be learned following the operation involves making use of the

cricopharyngeus musculature as new substitute vocal cords or neoglottis to produce vibration of air from the esophageal reservoir. Failure to establish good
esophageal speech is often due to inability to learn to use the tongue correctly.
The patient must learn to contact the hard palate with the tongue sharply in order
to inject air back into the esophagus. Instead of using a prosthesis, it might well
be possible to provide feedback of the tongue activity together with a target
display representing correct performance. More generally, of course, implanted
electrodes in the esophagus could be used to generate a display of esophageal
activity in disorders involving dysfunction of this system.

    Nasality. An excessive degree of nasal speech is characteristic of some
retarded children, of children with special disabilities (such as cleft palate), and
of many deaf persons. The use of biofeedback to correct such problems is only in
its infancy, but the work that has been carried out so far is of quite extraordinary
interest and importance. Velopharangeal closure, involving contact of the soft
palate with the posterior pharangeal wall, is achieved by elevation of the soft
palate which prevents air from being expelled through the nose and hence prevents or reduces nasality. The elevation of the soft palate is accomplished by the
levator palatini muscle, which functions variably to achieve greater or lesser
elevation as required by the characteristics of the particular speech sounds being
uttered at a given moment (Bell-Berti, 1976; Moller, Path, Werth, & Christiansen, 1973). Velopharangeal closure is often defective in the conditions described
above, thus producing excessive expulsion of air through the nasal cavities, with
consequent nasalized speech. Several ingenious techniques have been developed
to measure the degree of nasality in speech. Fletcher (1972) has described the

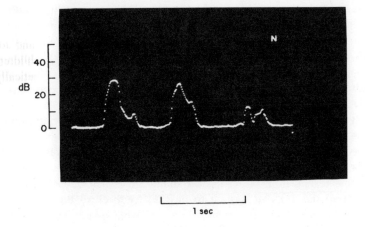

Figure 13. Display of nasal acceleromotor output for the three words, *cinder, sinner,* and *sitter.*
(From Stevens, K. N., Nickerson, R. S., Boothroyd, A., & Rollins, A. M. Assessment of nasalization in the speech of deaf children. *Journal of Speech and Hearing Research,* 1976, *19,* 404, Figure
8. Reprinted by permission of the author and the publisher.)

TONAR (the oral/nasal acoustic ratio) device which separates and utilizes sound levels from the oral and nasal channels to detect, quantify, and display the degree of nasalization in connected speech. The device produces a meter reading which indicates the momentary ratio and generates tonagrams if required. The material read using this device should be devoid of nasal consonants. Moller *et al.* (1973) have described the development of displacement transducers which monitor velar movement directly. A finger-spring sensor wire is attached to the free end of a cantilever beam strain-gauge transducer which is rigidly attached to an orthodontic band and cemented to a maxillary molar tooth. The sensor contact tip is positioned on the middle third of the soft palate at the midline and follows the movement of the soft palate. The movement of the soft palate can be displayed to provide the patient with visual or other feedback. Less sophisticated devices for measuring degree of nasality have been described by Roll (1973), who recorded the vibrations of the nasal cavity by means of a contact microphone placed on the nose, the vibrations being transduced into a white light when very small (low nasality) or a red light when large (high nasality); and by Stevens, Kalikow, and Willemain (1975) and Stevens, Nickerson, Boothroyd, and Rollins (1976), who used a miniature accelerometer in a way similar to that of Roll (1973) to generate an oscilloscope display of degree of nasality. An example of the display generated by three words, two nasal, one nonnasal, is shown in Figure 13.

Data are now available for degree of nasalization in abnormal and normal speakers which provide baselines from which efforts can be made to reduce the degree of nasality within normal limits. Daly (1974) compared the nasality of 50 educable retarded children (aged 7–19 with IQs from 56 to 80) and 78 nonretarded children while reading a 75-word passage containing all of the spoken sounds of English except the nasal consonants. The mean nasality ratio for the retarded children was 15% (range 0–70%) whereas for the nonretarded children it was only 9.4% (range 0–24%). Hypernasality was found to be present in 38% of the retarded children, but in only 4% of the nonretarded children. The hypernasality was not associated with significant oral structural defect, except in one case of cleft palate. Hypernasality is found even more frequently in severely retarded children (Daly, 1977). Stevens *et al.* (1976) have provided comparative data on degree of nasality in deaf children as compared with hearing children and hearing adults in a wide range of reading conditions. Figure 14 shows the results obtained in the utterance of ten different nondiphthongized vowels. Similar data have been provided for contextual material.

Some results from biofeedback training are available. Daly and Johnson (1974) used the TONAR system to provide feedback to three children with hypernasality (one with cleft palate) while they were speaking phonetically controlled phrases involving progressively harder articulation. Training was carried out over 3 weeks, involving a total of 30 sessions. A daily goal ratio of nasality was set. If the goal was surpassed, a panel light was activated and verbal praise was administered intermittently. Nasality was reduced on average by 21% with

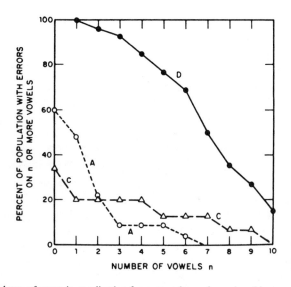

NUMBER OF VOWELS n

Figure 14. Incidence of errors in nasalization for nonnasal vowels produced in monosyllabic words by deaf children (D), hearing children (C), and hearing adults (A). (From Stevens, K. N., Nickerson, R. S., Boothroyd, A., & Rollins, A. M. Assessment of nasalization in the speech of deaf children. *Journal of Speech and Hearing Research,* 1976, *19,* 405, Figure 9. Reprinted by permission of the author and the publisher.)

the ratio for two of the children falling within the normal range by the end of treatment. Intelligibility errors decreased significantly, but errors of articulation remained fairly high.

Roll (1973) provided a binary information signal to provide feedback to two children with cleft palate while requiring them to produce continuous vowel sounds and compared the results with those obtained when feedback was not provided. A striking reduction in hypernasality occurred in one of the children but not in the other. Moller *et al.* (1973) have described the use of their feedback system (described above) in a study of a child with cleft palate resulting in moderate hypernasality. Objective measurements showed that the child had a velopharangeal gap of 2–3 mm. Visual feedback was provided representing the degree of nasality, and a criterion reference point for the child to aim at was also provided. Later in the treatment a digital meter which accumulated points indicating monetary reward was introduced (thus confounding informational feedback and reinforcement). Considerable success was achieved in training the child to close the velopharangeal gap while emitting the /u/ sound. Perhaps the most interesting finding, however, was the discovery that at the end of training, although velar elevation had increased by the very large amount of 8–9 mm (which should have resulted in the elimination of the velopharangeal gap), the gap remained as large as it had been before training commenced. The anomaly was convincingly explained by a demonstration (through radiography) that during the treatment the posterior pharangeal wall had progressively retropositioned itself, thus maintaining the original gap in spite of the increase in velar elevation. (It was believed that the retropositioning was due to atrophy of the adenoid tissue in the nasopharynx.) This study can only be regarded as a demonstration of the possibilities of feedback in the treatment of nasality, but it must rank as one of the most ingenious and careful examples of the possibilities of biofeedback in breaking new ground. The nasality of the child's speech was not improved, but the authors regarded their approach as a promising one, which indeed it is.

Stevens, Nickerson, Rollins, and Boothroyd (1974) trained nine deaf children aged 8–17 years in velar control with visual feedback. Various exercises were used (such as sustaining isolated vowels with nasalization readings below a specified criterion, and producing isolated nonnasal consonant–vowel syllables) and progress was judged by recordings of speech made under both naturalistic and experimental conditions (with and without feedback and using both familiar and unfamiliar material). All the subjects succeeded in suppressing nasalization to a significant degree with feedback under experimental conditions, and objective measures indicated that a considerable degree of generalization to natural speaking situations occurred, although ratings of speech improvement made by judges did not correlate too well with the objective indices.

Guralnick and Mott (1976) studied an 11-year-old boy with a wide range of developmental difficulties, including an inability to control respiratory movements. The provision of visual feedback (in the form of lights) in an effort to shape breathing rate and depth proved unsuccessful, but when the child was allowed to observe a continuous-strip chart showing the course of his breathing, he was able by manipulating his own breathing rate and depth and observing the result directly on the chart to bring his breathing under control to a considerable degree. This study can be regarded as a demonstration only.

Stuttering. No disorder has been investigated more thoroughly than stuttering; theories to account for it are legion. The present writer has reviewed the empirical data relating to stuttering and the theories about stuttering on several occasions (Yates, 1963, 1970a, 1975) and repetition of that material here is not necessary. It is assumed that although learning plays an important role in determining the final form stuttering takes in an individual, the uniqueness of the individual's stutter is superimposed on a basic, inborn deficit which involves feedback control systems which are faulty and hence provide the stutterer with conflicting information about the progress of his speech, leading to attempts to correct for what is perceived as faulty utterance, the "correction" being the stutter itself, manifested in the form of repetitions, prolongations, and blockages. This interpretation of stuttering remains controversial but can be supported by an impressive array of evidence, reviewed in the publications of the author, referred to above.

The feedback control theory of stuttering as a perceptual defect has problems, however, in accounting for the fact that the stutterer experiences most of his difficulty at the point of initiation of a word, that is, before any auditory feedback is experienced. Recent investigations have thrown considerable light on this aspect of stuttering (and, indeed, speech in general) but without suggesting that the servomechanical control theory of stuttering needs to be abandoned. Thus, the explanation of stuttering requires a two-stage approach to account for (a) the initial difficulty, experienced at the onset of a speech unit, and (b) the subsequent difficulties experienced as a result of faulty feedback during the utterance of the speech unit itself. In what follows we will be concerned entirely with the events which lead up to the initiation of a speech unit, but it should be remembered that this new approach is not considered to be in any way incompatible with the earlier servomechanical theories of stuttering.

The remarkable studies of Hixon and his colleagues (e.g., Hixon, 1972, 1973; Hixon, Goldman, & Mead, 1973; Hixon, Mead, & Goldman, 1976) have not only served to remind us of the extraordinarily complex sequence of events involved in the generation of a speech unit, but have also provided new levels of sophisticated devices for measuring and interpreting these events and their interrelationships. The dynamics and kinematics of the chest wall during speech production have been investigated in detail to demonstrate the functions of the thorax, rib cage, diaphragm, and abdomen. Volume–pressure body plethysmography has been used by Hixon (1972) to measure changes in lung volume, alveolar pressure, and so on during speech production, while sophisticated techniques have been developed to examine laryngeal mechanics, articulatory events, upper airway and transglottal flow, tongue movements, and so on. It is not feasible to describe Hixon's work here in the detail it deserves, but it provides an essential groundwork for an examination of what might possibly go wrong in the sequence of events leading up to a speech utterance. The detailed studies largely still remain to be done, but examples can be given. Fritzell and Kotby (1976) implanted electrodes in the thyroarytenoid and palatal levator muscles of normal subjects and examined the relative activity of the two muscles while 11 test sentences, each with a different initial sound, were being read. It was found that the thyroarytenoid muscle was always active (even when the subject was inactive and not speaking), whereas the palatal levator was usually completely silent during rest periods. Immediately preceding speech onset both muscles became active, but at different times and in different ways. The thyroarytenoid muscle showed a gradual onset of activity which preceded activation of the palatal levator by an average of 29 msec. Furthermore, once an utterance had commenced, the relationship of the activity of the two muscles varied in respect of the onset of individual words, depending on whether the word commenced with a vowel, whether nasalization was required, and so on. Thus, thyroarytenoid activity preceded palatal levator activity in the case of vowels, nasals, and voiced plosives, whereas the reverse was the case for unvoiced plosives and fricatives. The average latency from onset of thyroarytenoid activity to the onset of sound was about 300 msec for voiced sounds, but only about 100 msec for unvoiced sounds. During speech, thyroarytenoid activity tended to be continuous and showed little variation, whereas palatal levator activity followed the sounds more closely.

The importance of events occurring in the half second preceding an utterance has become apparent in recent years, but more important, the complexity of the events both prior to and during this critical period is only now being fully recognized. Platt and Basili (1973) made EMG recordings from the right masseter and anterior suprahyoid group of muscles in three adult male stutterers (not necessarily representative of all stutterers) during the period 1400–400 msec prior to the onset of utterance of 12 words with the initial /p/ sound and another 12 with the initial /b/ sound. They measured the tremor frequency (the number of amplitude-modulated peaks during a 1-sec period) and the tremor amplitude (the average voltage values for each EMG peak during the same period) during the preutterance period, as well as the frequency and amplitude of isometric tremor while the stutterer voluntarily opened and closed his jaw without teeth contact (to determine whether muscular frequencies matched the isometrically obtained frequencies). They found that tremor frequencies were similar across the two tasks (/p/, /b/) both between and within the three stutterers, and were similar to the isometrically obtained frequencies. With respect to tremor amplitude, suprahyoid activity was greater than masseter activity in all three stutterers on both tasks, and the same finding held for isometric activity. These results suggest that prestuttering jaw tremor may involve isometric muscular activity which prevents the normal execution of a speech unit. It seems reasonable to assume that in order for a speech unit to be executed efficiently, the correct relative tension of the speech musculature must be established prior to the utterance's being initiated. If this is not achieved (and particularly if a breakdown in the correct balance occurs immediately prior to the utterance), it would not be at all surprising if a failure of utterance occurred. The study by Platt and Basili (1973) suggests that precisely this failure of preutterance muscle coordination occurs. Perkins, Rudas, Johnson, and Bell (1976) have more recently provided more comprehensive evidence of the nature of the preutterance difficulty. Following Hixon (1972, 1973), they have examined indirectly the relationships among phonation, articulation, and respiration in speech, and attributed stuttering to a breakdown in the correct relationships of these three activities. Phonation refers to those laryngeal adjustments which coordinate the breath stream with the utterance of syllables in voiced and whispered speech (that is, where sound is actually produced). Articulation and respiration, on the other hand, involve subglottal processes. Thus, phonation differentiates laryngeal from sub- and supraglottal activities:

> Respiratory mistimings could disrupt phonatory and articulatory processes, and conversely oral articulatory or phonatory mistimings could impair the smooth management of subglottic, transglottic, and supraglottic pressures required for fluent speech. (Perkins et al., 1976, p. 510)

A reduction of the complexity of the motor coordinations required in speech can be achieved by requiring the stutterer to engage in three kinds of phonation changes: voiced speech, whispering, and lipped speech (that is, articulation without breath-stream management in which the observer lip-reads what the stutterer is "saying"). In the experiment of Perkins *et al.* (1976), 30 stutterers who stuttered while reading aloud or whispering (although the stuttering was markedly reduced during whispering) read syllabic excerpts under the three conditions listed above. In all of the stutterers, stuttering was reduced virtually to zero in lipped reading; that is, as the complexity of phonatory and respiratory coordination was reduced, so stuttering was reduced from an average of 24.6% of syllables disfluent for voiced speech, through an average of 10.3% of syllables disfluent for whispered speech, down to an average of only 0.8% of syllables disfluent for lipped speech. These results were shown not to be a function of a slower rate of speaking for whispered and lipped speech (indeed, the stutterers spoke faster in the lipped-speech condition) and lipped speech reduced stuttering more in the severe than in the mild cases.

The servomechanical control systems mediating these complex coordinations can only be speculated about at present. Ertl and Schafer (1967), using normal subjects, have provided evidence suggesting that time-locked EEG activity from the right motor area of the cortex occurs just prior to speech and motor activity. For both speech (uttering the word *tea*) and motor activity (clenching the left fist) a positive peak occurs 70–170 msec before the activity, while a negative peak occurs 10–70 msec before the activity. Wyke (1971), in an important integrative paper, has stressed the complexity of the neuromuscular mechanisms involved in speech production—especially the reflex actions involved in the control of the respiratory, laryngeal, pharyngeal, glottal, mandibular, and oral musculature—and has provided a detailed account of the control of the larynx muscle. Mechanoreceptor nerve endings have been demonstrated in the tissues of the larynx, and Wyke considers that afferent discharges from the mucous membrane, intrinsic muscles, and the capsules of the intercartilaginous joints play a vital role in the regulation of the activity of the intrinsic muscles of the larynx during respiration and phonation. Basing his views mainly on studies with cats, he considers the empirical evidence dealing with the laryngeal mucosal mechanoreceptors (which have a very low threshold for mechanical deformation by subglottic air pressure), the laryngeal myotatic mechanoreceptors (a reflex system which operates to oppose the stretch displacement of the intrinsic laryngeal muscles that would otherwise result from fluctuating increases in the intralaryngeal air pressures associated with vocalization), and the laryngeal articular mechanoreceptors (which are embedded in the capsules of each of the laryngeal joints, including the cricoarytenoid and cricothyroid joints). These three reflex systems are involved in the feedback regulation of the musculature, the precisely controlled activity of which is responsible for normal speech.

Wyke produces evidence to show that immediately prior to a sound utterance, there is a brief burst of vocalis muscle motor unit potentials associated with a sharp increase in its tension:

This observation reveals that, in order to utter an intended sound, the tone of the intrinsic laryngeal musculature has to be *preset* to the correct pattern some 0.05–0.55 sec before the expiratory air stream begins to deliver the audible sound . . .during normal speech, the tone of each of the laryngeal muscles is repeatedly adjusted to the required tension, just prior to the production of each audible sound . . . thus continuous *pre-phonatory tuning* of the laryngeal musculature is the principal voluntary contribution to speech regulation (along with coincident voluntary control of the respiratory musculature) that is made through the cortical projections to the laryngeal motor neurons located in the nucleus ambiguus in the medulla oblongata. (Wyke, 1971, p. 429; italics in original)

Thus, the speaker voluntarily presets the tension pattern of the laryngeal musculature (as well as the tension of the other muscles involved—diaphragm, intercostal, pharangeal, glottal, oral) into a state that is determined by an interaction between past experience and present situational circumstances with the expectation that an appropriate sound will result.

Wyke believes that stuttering may result from either of two breakdowns in the pattern of control: on the one hand, an abnormally slow or inaccurate voluntary presetting of the laryngeal and respiratory musculature may occur; on the other hand, inefficient or disorganized reflex maintenance of the preset pattern of muscle tone may occur because of abnormal action of one or more of the laryngeal, myotatic, or articulator reflex systems described above. Thus, two types of stuttering may be distinguished: voluntary or cortical stuttering, associated with presetting failure; and reflex stuttering, associated with the maintenance of the presetting. Stuttering, for Wyke, is a manifestation of phonatory ataxia, resulting from a temporal dysfunction in the operations of the voluntary and/or reflex mechanisms that continuously regulate the tone of the phonatory musculature during speech.

No doubt this increased interest in the integration of the complex physiological events leading up to a speech utterance, coupled with the ever-increasing sophistication of techniques of measurement, will lead to an increase of studies in this area. Already there is evidence that stutterers manifest an increased latency of onset of vocalization of nonstuttered words (Starkweather, Hirschman, & Tannenbaum, 1976) and a significantly increased jaw velocity during the release of a stuttering moment (Hutchinson & Watkin, 1976).

All of this work suggests that it may be possible to make use of biofeedback training techniques to help the stutterer overcome the difficulties he has in presetting the musculature involved in speech. If the initial stutter occurs because of a failure to achieve the correct balance of forces in the musculature involved in speech with a resultant breakdown in the utterance, then it might be possible for the stutterer to make use of biofeedback to establish the correct balance of forces just prior to the utterance, in which case the initial stutter should not occur. In Wyke's terms, we are referring to the presetting phase of speech. Of course, if, as Wyke suggests, the maintenance of speech, even if initiated adequately, may be impaired by a different kind of failure, then this approach may only be partially successful or successful only with some stutterers. Although most of the work to be reported here has in effect dealt with the presetting phase, it should be possible to utilize similar techniques with respect to the maintenance of the utterance, once initiated.

Guitar (1974) studied three adult stutterers who had difficulty with the initial sounds of at least 39 of a list of 78 sentences. For each stutterer, the most frequently stuttered phoneme in each of the vowel, labial consonant, and lingual consonant classes was selected and incorporated into lists of sentences to be spoken. Recordings were made from the orbicularis oris superior muscle, the anterior belly of the digastric muscle, the larynx (just above the thyroid cartilage, oriented horizontally), and the frontalis muscle (the latter being a control for general head relaxation). After baseline recordings (without feedback) had been made from these four sites while the lists were read, training in the relaxation of each muscle was carried out separately, using auditory feedback (a tone varying in pitch) and progressive shaping until muscle activity could not be reduced further. Then the stutterer was instructed to keep a specified muscle at the trained low level while a 7-sec warning light was on, at the end of which the sentence was again read, with feedback provided on alternate trials. Guitar found that successful training in reduction of muscle activity with feedback only reduced stuttering frequency when the stuttering was correlated with a high level of activity at the site trained. Thus, in one stutterer, facial grimacing around the lip area was correlated with stuttering and it was found that the percentage decrement in stuttering associated with successful training at each of the four sites was: chin, 1%, frontalis, 18%; larynx, 44%; and lip, 89%. Similar differential findings were reported for the other two stutterers. A fourth stutterer who showed a similar relationship (between stuttering and lip activity) was trained in a conversational situation. The mean frequency of stuttering was reduced from 17% to zero, an improvement which was maintained at a follow-up 9 months later.

Hanna, Wilfling, and McNeill (1975) reported some success with a male stutterer, using auditory feedback from electrodes placed 2 cm bilateral to the center line of the body and 1 cm above the thyroid prominence. During the training period, they included one session in which fake but plausible feedback (the record of another patient) was presented. Biofeedback training reduced stuttering frequency to less than 50% of baseline levels; false feedback was less effective and the patient complained that the apparatus must be malfunctioning. Speech was faster when feedback was available, ruling out slowing of speech as a factor in the reduction of stuttering.

The most substantial studies to date on the application of biofeedback techniques to stuttering have been carried out by Lanyon and his colleagues (Lanyon, 1977; Lanyon, Barrington, & Newman, 1976). Lanyon et al. (1976) trained eight severe stutterers in the control of masseter and suprahyoid activity with visual feedback. Two of the patients were given an oscilloscope display (in waveform) as feedback and practiced reducing muscle activity while counting. The remaining patients were systematically trained in control of masseter muscle activity with meter feedback while not speaking. They were then given speech training on 100 one-syllable words by being required first to look at each word while relaxing the muscle, and then to speak the word. This training was terminated only when a criterion of 95% muscle relaxation was reached. They then read 200 one-syllable words with the feedback present or absent. After this, the training was extended progressively to two-syllable words, to three-syllable phrases, and to four-syllable sentences (not all patients did all of these tasks, the procedures being developed gradually as a result of experience). All six stutterers who received multiple training showed a highly significant reduction in stuttering under biofeedback conditions and achieved control of masseter muscle activity to the criterion set. The reduction in stuttering was greater, as might be expected, when feedback was present as compared with when it was not; nevertheless, a significant transfer to reading without feedback was also achieved.

Subsequent studies have extended the training techniques used in the initial study. Lanyon (1977) studied a total of 19 stutterers in three experiments. The first exactly replicated the work of Lanyon *et al.* (1976). In the second, the patients were first trained in muscle relaxation while uttering one- and two-syllable words and two-syllable phrases. They then prepared a short statement on a neutral topic and spoke it one word at a time, with feedback, relaxing the masseter muscle between each word until a criterion of 5 or fewer stuttered words in a sequence of 40 was achieved. They were then taught to say words without feedback whenever they felt they had relaxed the masseter muscle sufficiently, with the therapist monitoring their EMG activity and stopping them from saying the word if he felt the muscle was insufficiently relaxed. At the end of each training segment, test data were collected. This method of training proved to be highly successful. In the final study, similar procedures were used with spontaneous speech. Again, considerable success was achieved, with stuttering reduced to an average of only 2.38 words per 100 words spoken when feedback was available. These studies by Lanyon and his colleagues are particularly valuable for the progressive training techniques used and lay the foundation for future work.

A rather different approach was used by Moore (1978), who recorded activity from the right masseter muscle and the chin in three stutterers while they read prose passages. Feedback in the form of noise was presented whenever muscle activity exceeded a specified criterion. Thus, the noise functioned as an aversive stimulus and the task could be described as one of obtaining negative reinforcement by reducing muscle activity so as to escape or avoid the aversive stimulus. A shaping technique was employed, involving progressive lowering of the criterion muscle activity level, while the tasks were similar to those used by Lanyon. All three subjects succeeded in reducing muscle activity levels and amount of stuttering, but the results were not particularly impressive, perhaps because of the aversive nature of the feedback signal.

Reference should be made to a study which was not strictly carried out within a biofeedback framework but which confirms the importance of the coordination of prespeech activities. Azrin and Nunn (1974) have developed a complex procedure for dealing with severe stutterers. First, the patient is required to review the inconveniences under which he labors because of his stuttering. This is followed by "awareness training" in which the patient stutters deliberately and then describes in great detail the nature of the stuttering episode, his awareness of associated body movements, and so on. Next, he is taught to anticipate a stuttering episode and to identify it by a pause in his speech. He is then trained to relax his posture and his breathing when tense, and to let his abdominal and throat muscles go limp. He is also trained in various activities which are regarded as being incompatible with stuttering: discontinuing speaking, mentally formulating words before speaking, speaking for a short duration and then pausing, taking a deep breath before speaking, starting speech immediately after inhaling (rather than holding his breath), and emphasizing the first few words of a statement. The use of symbolic rehearsal is encouraged, as is the use of "positive practice" (for example, gradually increasing the number of words spoken during one breathing episode). Practice in speaking on the telephone is introduced, family support enlisted, and finally practice in public places undertaken. While the number of techniques used makes it impossible to sort out the relative contribution of each, the most striking feature is the emphasis on the events immediately preceding utterance, thus placing this study within the framework adopted here. Azrin and Nunn (1974) applied this multimodal approach to 14 stutterers aged 4–67 years who had stuttered for 2–65 years and whose self-reported rate of stuttering varied from 2 instances per day up to 1000 per day (the average being 372 per day). It was reported that stuttering decreased by 94% on the first day of treatment and by 99% at a 3-month follow-up. Most of the patients reported that stuttering was no longer a social problem, and in telephone conversation with the experimenter were observed to be almost completely fluent.

It may be concluded that a new and promising orientation toward stuttering therapy has developed over the past 5 years, concentrating on the preliminaries to speech rather than the speech itself, and that biofeedback may have an important role to play in the future application of these techniques.

Henschen and Burton (1978) treated two patients with spastic dysphonia, a disorder which involves stuttering-like speech, a creaking, squeezed voice, strained hoarseness, normal laughter, periods of normal speech, intermittent whispering, jerkiness, and sometimes tic-like contractions in the mandible and upper arm. The disorder usually has its onset later on in life. Training in reduction of both frontalis and larynx muscle activity was successful, but the spastic dysphonia symptoms were unaffected. Holbrook, Rolnick, and Bailey (1974) devised a simple system to provide auditory feedback indicating loudness of speech and employed it in training subjects who had abused their vocal system to speak more quietly. Results were reported on 32 subjects who were candidates for surgery, Of these, 11 achieved complete resolution of identified vocal nodules, polyps, or contact ulcers without the need for surgery; a further 8 subjects had sufficient reduction of the lesions that surgery was not necessary.

The remainder were not helped and had surgery (3), dropped out of the training program (5), or used the procedure successfully for voice problems not associated with identifiable lesions.

Miscellaneous Dysfunctions

Some loose ends remain to be tied up, relating to dysfunctions which clearly involve abnormal muscle activity but do not fit easily into any of the categories so far discussed. The application of biofeedback techniques to the treatment of psychogenic cramps would appear to hold much promise, but as yet little work has been reported. Ballard, Doerr, and Varni (1972) provided both auditory biofeedback and aversive stimulation to a patient with blepharospasm (involuntary clonic and tonic spasms of the eyelids and accessory musculature). They considered that the biofeedback training was more successful than the avoidance conditioning, the spasms being absent 9 months later. Peck (1977) has reported a remarkable success with a 50-year-old female with a 7-year history of spasmodic, frequent blinking involving primarily the orbicularis oculi and frontalis muscle groups. Frontalis muscle activity and frequency of blinking were recorded by means of electrodes attached over the left frontalis and lower orbicularis muscles. Two baseline sessions without feedback were followed by two placebo sessions involving white noise with the suggestion to the patient that this would act as a distractor, reducing the intensity and frequency of the spasms. Then, 17 sessions were given with feedback of frontalis muscle activity. Mean frontalis muscle activity level was reduced from 25 μV p-p during baseline to 7 μV p-p by the seventh training session, after which it remained constant at this relatively normal level. The frequency of eyelid spasms was, however, reduced from no less than 1600 in the first 20-min baseline session to 15 normal blinks during the last three treatment sessions. The control achieved over the left eye generalized to the right eye. Increased control over the spasm outside the experimental situation was achieved. By the end of training it had been absent entirely for 1 week and a follow-up 4 months later revealed that the improvements had been maintained. Norton (1976) investigated a 34-year-old female with a 13-year history of difficulty in opening her eyes following the death of her brother, the problem manifesting itself particularly in social situations. Careful behavioral analysis revealed that her eyes were closed on 69% of the occasions on which observations were made; concomitant behavior included eyelash plucking and occasional eye rolling. Treatment included general relaxation training, negative practice (in which the eye closures were voluntarily practiced in exaggerated form), verbal punishment for eyelash plucking, and frontalis muscle relaxation training with auditory feedback (to reduce the facial muscle tension manifested when the patient tried to open her eyes). In the biofeedback training, a successive approximation technique was used, the feedback being provided initially with eyes closed, then with eyes partially open in a darkened room, and finally with eyes open in a fully lit room. The verbal punishment was successful in reducing the eyelash plucking to a significant degree but had no effect on eye closure or eye rolling. The relaxation training apparently reduced self-recorded eye closure (observations made by the patient at home) but had no effect on eye closure in the experimental situation. The feedback training (which was the last to be given), however, reduced all three abnormalities to zero and the improvement was maintained at a 6-month follow-up. However, this study was seriously confounded.

It will be recalled that Basmajian carried out some interesting studies of the ability of musicians to control the muscles involved in playing their instruments. Levee, Cohen, and Rickles (1976) treated a 52-year-old male musician who played the flute, clarinet, and saxophone and who was hospitalized with complaints of tightness of the jaw and constriction of the throat which were interfering seriously with his playing and hence his job opportunities. He was also handicapped by alcoholism and dexamyl dependence, both of which appeared to be the result of his shattered career. An earlier course of general relaxation training had not succeeded in resolving his problems. A visual feedback display of seven lights arranged in a vertical column was used, with each light representing a specified gain in muscle tension. There were four phases in the training program. In the first phase feedback was provided from the frontalis muscle and from the orbicularis oris muscle midway below and between the quadratus labii superior, infraorbital heads, and zygomaticus muscles on both the left and right sides in alternate sessions. Under instructions to turn off as many lights as possible (where each light turned off represented a drop of 10 μV, the patient succeeded in reducing his starting level of 70 μV to 10–20 μV in one session and maintained the new level over two succeeding sessions. In the second phase, the target area became the larynx to which the tension appeared to have shifted following the success in the first phase. Feedback was now provided of the activity of the infrahyoid muscle area alongside the trachea and larynx. With some difficulty, a significant reduction of muscle tension was achieved in this area. In phase three, feedback from the same area was displayed while the patient practiced instrument playing in a sound-reduced chamber between periods of attempted muscle relaxation. He was able to reduce muscle tension in the area of the larynx to 10–15 μV and maintain this level. Further reduction occurred when the instrument playing and relaxation training were shifted outside the sound-reduced chamber. The patient was followed up at 1-month intervals for 6 months by which time he had resumed his normal career and was still able to maintain low levels of muscle activity in the appropriate muscles. Levee *et al.* (1976) considered that the muscle dysfunction which affected his playing and hence job opportunities were probably directly responsible for his alcoholism and addiction (rather than the reverse), and these in turn produced family problems. The treatment plan was to deal with this sequence in reverse order so that the attack on the muscle dysfunction was last in sequence.

Writer's cramp would appear to be a natural target for biofeedback training, and indeed the common earlier methods of treatment involved a biofeedback component (for example, placing a stylus in progressively smaller holes, with feedback—often in the form of shock—whenever the stylus touched the side of the hole). Reavley (1975) retrained a male with writer's cramp in more precise control of his writing by providing feedback from the muscles involved in writing (upper arm, forearm, hand/wrist) which assisted the patient in relaxing the muscles before beginning to write. Additional aid involved the use of graded physical aids such as lines between which to write. The treatment was apparently successful and the improvement maintained at an 8-month follow-up, but quantitative comparisons (for example, pre–post comparison of handwriting) were not provided in this study. Bindman and Tibbetts (1977) attached surface electrodes to the skin over the tendons of the flexors to the index finger and thumb on the palmar surface of the hand. Auditory feedback was given to illustrate muscle activity and the six patients treated were then asked to write while keeping the auditory feedback as low as possible. A high initial level of auditory feedback for muscular spasm proved to be an aversive situation (producing increased anxiety) but encouraging results were obtained with four of the six patients when the initial auditory feedback level was lowered and the gains were maintained at follow-up in two of these patients. The results with feedback were considered somewhat better than those obtained with four patients treated with psychotherapy and reeducation or hypnosis. Two cases of writer's cramp were treated by Uchiyama, Lutterjohann, and Shah (1977) by a combination of biofeedback-assisted relaxation training of the muscles involved in writing, followed by imaginary or real systematic desensitization training. In both patients, muscle relaxation and writing improvement were obtained which were maintained at follow-up and both patients were in employment which necessitated writing. The contribution of feedback could not, of course, be disentangled in this study.

References

Acosta, F. X., Yamamoto, J., & Wilcox, S. A. Application of electromyographic biofeedback to the relaxation training of schizophrenic, neurotic, and tension headache patients. *Journal of Consulting and Clinical Psychology*, 1978, *46*, 383–384.

Albanese, H., & Gaarder, K. Biofeedback treatment of tardive dyskinesia: Two case reports. *American Journal of Psychiatry*, 1977, *134*, 1149–1150.

Alexander, A. B. An experimental test of assumptions relating to the use of electromyographic biofeedback as a general relaxation training technique. *Psychophysiology*, 1975, *12*, 656–662. (1975/76:20)

Alexander, A. B., French, C. A., & Goodman, N. J. A comparison of auditory and visual feedback assisted muscular relaxation training. *Psychophysiology*, 1975, *12*, 119–123.

Altug, S. S., Childress, C. T., De Mund, S. M., McCall, W. D., & Ash, M. M. An interactive computer peripheral to measure the electromyographic silent period. *IEEE Transactions on Biomedical Engineering*, 1976, *23*, 160–164.

Amato, A., Hermsmeyer, C. A., & Kleinman, K. M. Use of electromyographic feedback to increase inhibitory control of spastic muscles. *Physical Therapy*, 1973, *53*, 1063–1066.

Anani, A. B., Ikeda, K., & Körner, L. M. Human ability to discriminate various parameters in afferent electrical nerve stimulation with particular reference to prostheses sensory feedback. *Medical and Biological Engineering and Computing*, 1977, *15*, 363–373.

Andreeva, E. A., & Shafranova, E. I. Muscular activity control systems for Parkinson's disease. *Automation and Remote Control USSR*, 1975, *36*, 596–605.

Andrews, J. M. Neuromuscular reeducation of the hemiplegic with the aid of the electromyograph. *Archives of Physical Medicine and Rehabilitation*, 1964, *45*, 530–532.

Azrin, N. H., & Nunn, R. G. A rapid method of eliminating stuttering by a regulated breathing approach. *Behavior Research and Therapy*, 1974, *12*, 279–286.

Bailey, J. O., McCall, W. D., & Ash, M. M. Electromyographic silent periods and jaw motion parameters: Quantitative measures of temporomandibular joint dysfunction. *Journal of Dental Research*, 1977, *56*, 249–253.

Bair, J. H. Development of voluntary control. *Psychological Review*, 1901, *8*, 474–510.

Bakal, D. A. Headache: A biopsychological perspective. *Psychological Bulletin*, 1975, *82*, 369–382.

Bakal, D. A., & Kaganov, J. A. Muscle contraction and migraine headache: Psychophysiologic comparison. *Headache*, 1977, *17*, 208–214.

Baker, M., Regenos, E., Wolf, S. L., & Basmajian, J. V. Developing strategies for biofeedback: Applications for neurologically handicapped patients. *Physical Therapy*, 1977, *57*, 402–408.

Ballard, P., Doerr, H., & Varni, J. Arrest of a disabling eye disorder using biofeedback. *Psychophysiology*, 1972, *9*, 271. (Abstract)

Basmajian, J. V. Control and training of individual motor units. *Science*, 1963, *141*, 440–441. (R:45)

Basmajian, J. V. Methods in training the conscious control of motor units. *Archives of Physical Medicine and Rehabilitation*, 1967, *48*, 12–19.

Basmajian, J. V. Electromyography comes of age. *Science*, 1972, *176*, 603–609. (1972:21)

Basmajian, J. V., & Newton, W. J. Feedback training of parts of buccinator muscle in man. *Psychophysiology*, 1974, *11*, 92. (Abstract)

Basmajian, J. V., & Simard, T. G. Effects of distracting movements on the control of trained motor units. *American Journal of Physical Medicine*, 1967, *46*, 1427–1449.

Basmajian, J. V., & White, E. R. Neuromuscular control of trumpeters' lips. *Nature*, 1973, *241*, 70.

Basmajian, J. V., Baeza, M., & Fabrigar, C. Conscious control and training of individual spinal motor neurons in normal human subjects. *Journal of New Drugs*, 1965, *2*, 78–85.

Basmajian, J. V., Kukulka, C. G., Narayan, M. G., & Takebe, K. Biofeedback treatment of foot-drop after stroke compared with standard rehabilitation technique: Effects on voluntary control and strength. *Archives of Physical Medicine and Rehabilitation*, 1975, *56*, 231–236. (1975/76:56).

Basmajian, J. V., Regenos, E. M., & Baker, M. P. Rehabilitating stroke patients with biofeedback. *Geriatrics*, 1977, *32*, 85–88.

Bell-Berti, F. An electromyographic study of velopharyngeal function in speech. *Journal of Speech and Hearing Research*, 1976, *19*, 225–240.

Bindman, E., & Tibbetts, R. W. Writer's cramp—A rational approach to treatment? *British Journal of Psychiatry*, 1977, *131*, 143–148.

Booker, H. E., Rubow, R. T., & Coleman, P. J. Simplified feedback in neuromuscular retraining: An automated approach using electromyographic signals. *Archives of Physical Medicine and Rehabilitation*, 1969, *50*, 621–625.

Boos, R. H. Preliminary treatment of prosthetic patients. *Journal of Prosthetic Dentistry*, 1965, *15*, 1002–1009.

Bouisset, S., & Maton, B. Quantitative relationship between surface EMG and intramuscular electromyographic activity in voluntary movement. *American Journal of Physical Medicine*, 1972, *51*, 285–295.

Brucker, B. S., & Ince, L. P. Biofeedback as a treatment for postural hypotension in a spinal cord lesion patient. *Archives of Physical Medicine and Rehabilitation,* 1975, *56,* 532. (Abstract)

Brudny, J., Grynbaum, B. B., & Korein, J. Spasmodic torticollis: Treatment by feedback display of the EMG. *Archives of Physical Medicine and Rehabilitation,* 1974, *55,* 403–408.

Brudny, J., Korein, J., Levidow, L., Grynbaum, B., Lieberman, A., & Friedmann, L. W. Sensory feedback therapy as a modality of treatment in central nervous system disorders of voluntary movement. *Neurology,* 1974, *24,* 925–932. (1975/76:53)

Brudny, J., Korein, J., Grynbaum, B. B., Friedmann, L. W., Weinstein, S., Sachs-Frankel, G., & Belandres, P. V. EMG feedback therapy: Review of treatment of 114 patients. *Archives of Physical Medicine and Rehabilitation,* 1976, *57,* 55–61. (1976/77:3)

Brumlik, J. On the nature of normal tremor. *Neurology,* 1962, *12,* 159–179.

Budzynski, T. H., & Stoyva, J. M. An instrument for producing deep muscle relaxation by means of analog information feedback. *Journal of Applied Behavior Analysis,* 1969, *2,* 231–237.

Budzynski, T. H., & Stoyva, J. M. An electromyographic feedback technique for teaching voluntary relaxation of the masseter. *Journal of Dental Research,* 1973, *52,* 116–119.

Budzynski, T. H., Stoyva, J. M., & Adler, C. S. Feedback-induced muscle relaxation: Application to tension headache. *Journal of Behavior Therapy and Experimental Psychiatry,* 1970, *1,* 205–211. (1970:31)

Budzynski, T. H., Stoyva, J. M., Adler, C. S., & Mullaney, D. M. EMG biofeedback and tension headache: A controlled outcome study. *Psychosomatic Medicine,* 1973, *35,* 484–496. (1973:19)

Camacho, E. O. Feedback of speech muscle activity during silent reading: Two comments. *Science,* 1967, *157,* 581.

Carlsöö, S., & Edfeldt, A. W. Attempts at muscle control with visual and auditory impulses as auxiliary stimuli. *Scandinavian Journal of Psychology,* 1963, *4,* 231–235.

Carlsson, S. G., & Gale, E. N. Biofeedback treatment for muscle pain associated with the temporomandibular joint. *Journal of Behavior Therapy and Experimental Psychiatry,* 1976, *7,* 383–385.

Carlsson, S. G., & Gale, E. N. Biofeedback in the treatment of long-term temporomandibular joint pain. *Biofeedback and Self-Regulation,* 1977, *2,* 161–171.

Carlsson, S. G., Gale, E. N., & Ohman, A. Treatment of temporomandibular joint syndrome with biofeedback training. *Journal of the American Dental Association,* 1975, *91,* 602–605.

Carmon, A. Impaired utilization of kinesthetic feedback in right hemisphere lesions. *Neurology,* 1970, *20,* 1033–1038.

Chase, R. A., & Cullen, J. K. Experimental studies on motor control systems in man. Unpublished manuscript, 1962. (Available from author.)

Chase, R. A., Cullen, J. K., Sullivan, S. A., & Ommaya, A. K. Modification of intention tremor in man. *Nature,* 1965, *206,* 485–487.

Chesney, M. A., & Shelton, J. L. A comparison of muscle relaxation and electromyogram biofeedback treatments for muscle contraction headache. *Journal of Behavior Therapy and Experimental Psychiatry,* 1976, *7,* 221–225. (1976/77:13)

Childress, D. S. Neural organization and myoelectric control. In W. S. Fields & L. A. Leavitt (Eds.), *Neural organization and its relevance to prosthetics.* New York: Intercontinental Medical Book Corporation, 1973, pp. 117–130.

Chyatte, S. B., & Birdsong, J. H. Assessment of motor performance in brain injury: A bioengineering method. *American Journal of Physical Medicine,* 1971, *50,* 17–30.

Clamann, H. P. Activity of single motor units during isometric tension. *Neurology,* 1970, *20,* 254–260.

Cleeland, C. S. Behavior technics in the modification of spasmodic torticollis. *Neurology,* 1973, *23,* 1241–1247. (1973:23)

Clippinger, F. W. A system to provide sensation from an upper extremity amputation prosthesis. In

W. S. Fields & L. A. Leavitt (Eds.), *Neural organization and its relevance to prosthetics.* New York: Intercontinental Medical Book Corporation, 1973, pp. 165–176.

Cooper, J. D., Halliday, A. M., & Redfearn, J. W. Apparatus for the study of human tremor and stretch reflexes. *EEG and Clinical Neurophysiology,* 1957, *9,* 546–550.

Cottingham, L. L. Myofunctional therapy: Orthodontics—tongue thrusting—speech therapy. *American Journal of Orthodontics,* 1976, *69,* 679–687.

Coursey, R. D. Electromyograph feedback as a relaxation technique. *Journal of Consulting and Clinical Psychology,* 1975, *43,* 825–834. (1975/76:19)

Cox, D. J., Freundlich, A., & Meyer, R. G. Differential effectiveness of electromyograph feedback, verbal relaxation instructions and medication placebo with tension headaches. *Journal of Consulting and Clinical Psychology,* 1975, *43,* 892–898. (1975/76:15)

Daly, D. A. Quantitative measurement of nasality in EMR children. *Journal of Communication Disorders,* 1974, *7,* 287–293.

Daly, D. A. Bioelectronic measurement of nasality in trainable mentally retarded children. *Journal of Speech and Hearing Disorders,* 1977, *42,* 436–439.

Daly, D. A., & Johnson, H. P. Instrumental modification of hypernasal voice quality in retarded children: Case reports. *Journal of Speech and Hearing Disorders,* 1974, *39,* 500–507.

Daniel, B., & Guitar, B. EMG feedback and recovery of facial and speech gestures following neural anastomosis. *Journal of Speech and Hearing Disorders,* 1978, *43,* 9–20.

Davis, F. H., & Malmo, R. B. Electromyographic recording during interview. *American Journal of Psychiatry,* 1951, *107,* 908–916.

Dohrmann, R. J., & Laskin, D. M. An evaluation of electromyographic biofeedback in the treatment of myofascial pain-dysfunction syndrome. *Journal of the American Dental Association,* 1978, *96,* 656–662.

Eldridge, R. The torsion dystonias: Literature review and genetic and clinical studies. *Neurology,* 1970, *20,* 1–78.

Epstein, L. H., & Webster, J. S. Instructional, pacing, and feedback control of respiratory behavior. *Perceptual and Motor Skills,* 1975, *41,* 895–900.

Ertl, J., & Schafer, E. W. P. Cortical activity preceding speech. *Life Sciences,* 1967, *6,* 473–479.

Farrar, W. B. Using electromyographic biofeedback in treating orofacial dyskinesia. *Journal of Prosthetic Dentistry,* 1976, *35,* 384–387.

Fernie, G. R., Kostuik, J. P., McLaurin, C., & Zimnicki, B. Biofeedback applied to patients with above-knee amputations. *Canadian Journal of Surgery,* 1976, *19,* 331–332. (Abstract)

Finley, W. W., Niman, C., Standley, J., & Ender, P. Frontal EMG–biofeedback training of athetoid cerebral palsy patients: A report of six cases. *Biofeedback and Self-Regulation,* 1976, *1,* 169–182.

Finley, W. W., Niman, C. A., Standley, J., & Wansley, R. A. Electrophysiologic behavior modification of frontal EMG in cerebral-palsied children. *Biofeedback and Self-Regulation,* 1977, *2,* 59–79.

Fish, D., Mayer, N., & Herman, R. Biofeedback (letter to the editor). *Archives of Physical Medicine and Rehabilitation,* 1976, *57,* 152.

Fletcher, S. G. Contingencies for bioelectronic modification of nasality. *Journal of Speech and Hearing Disorders,* 1972, *37,* 329–346.

Flom, R. P., Quast, J. E., Boller, J. D., Berner, M., & Goldberg, J. Biofeedback training to overcome post stroke foot-drop. *Geriatrics,* 1976, *31,* 47–52.

Flowers, K. Ballistic and corrective movement on an aiming task: Intention tremor and Parkinsonian movement disorders compared. *Neurology,* 1975, *25,* 413–421.

Flowers, K. A. Visual "closed-loop" and "open-loop" characteristics of voluntary movement in patients with Parkinsonism and intention tremor. *Brain,* 1976, *99,* 269–310.

Flowers, K. Some frequency response characteristics of Parkinsonism on pursuit tracking. *Brain,* 1978, *101,* 19–34. (a)

Flowers, K. Lack of prediction in the motor behavior of Parkinsonism. *Brain*, 1978, *101*, 35–52. (b)

Frankstein, S. I., Sergeeva, L. N., Sergeeva, Z. N., & Ivanova, E. S. Muscular respiratory receptors in self-regulation of normal breathing in man. *Experientia*, 1975, *31*, 1431–1432.

Friedman, A. P., von Storch, T. J. C., & Merritt, H. H. Migraine and tension headaches: A clinical study of 2000 cases. *Neurology*, 1954, *4*, 773–788.

Fritzell, B., & Kotby, M. N. Observations on thyroarytenoid and palatal levator activation for speech. *Folia Phoniatrica*, 1976, *28*, 1–7.

Fukushima, K., Taniguchi, K., Kamishima, Y., & Kato, M. Peripheral factors contributing to the volitional control of firing rates of the human motor units. *Neuroscience Letters*, 1976, *3*, 33–36.

Gannon, L., & Sternbach, R. A. Alpha enhancement as a treatment for pain: A case study. *Journal of Behavior Therapy and Experimental Psychiatry*, 1971, *2*, 209–213. (1971:38)

Gelb, H., & Tarte, J. A two-year clinical dental evaluation of 200 cases of chronic headache: The craniocervical-mandibular syndrome. *Journal of the American Dental Association*, 1975, *91*, 1230–1236.

Gessel, A. H. Electromyographic biofeedback and tricyclic antidepressants in myofascial pain-dysfunction syndrome: Psychological predictors of outcome. *Journal of the American Dental Association*, 1975, *91*, 1048–1052.

Gessel, A. H., & Alderman, M. M. Management of myofascial pain dysfunction syndrome of the temporomandibular joint by tension control training. *Psychosomatics*, 1971, *12*, 302–309.

Goodkin, R. Case studies in behavioral research in rehabilitation. *Perceptual and Motor Skills*, 1966, *23*, 171–182.

Gottlieb, G. R., Tichauer, E. R., & Davis, S. W. A biochemical approach to the study of the hemiplegic patient. *Bulletin of the New York Academy of Medicine*, 1975, *51*, 1265–1280.

Gray, E. R. Conscious control of motor units in tonic muscle: Effect of motor unit training. *American Journal of Physical Medicine*, 1971, *50*, 34–40.

Green, E. E., Walters, E. D., Green, A. M., & Murphy, G. Feedback technique for deep relaxation. *Psychophysiology*, 1969, *6*, 371–377. (R:48)

Grynbaum, B. B., Brudny, J., Korein, J., & Belandres, P. V. Sensory feedback therapy for stroke patients. *Geriatrics*, 1976, *31*, 43–47.

Guitar, B. Reduction of stuttering frequency using electromyographic feedback of muscle action potentials (Occasional Paper No. 2). Human Communications Laboratory, University of New South Wales, Australia, 1974.

Guralnick, M. J., & Mott, D. E. W. Biofeedback training with a learning disabled child. *Perceptual and Motor Skills*, 1976, *42*, 27–30.

Hallett, M., Shahani, B. T., & Young, R. R. EMG analysis of stereotyped voluntary movements in man. *Journal of Neurology, Neurosurgery, and Psychiatry*, 1975, *38*, 1154–1162. (a)

Hallett, M., Shahani, B. T., & Young, R. R. EMG analysis of patients with cerebellar deficits. *Journal of Neurology, Neurosurgery, and Psychiatry*, 1975, *38*, 1163–1169. (b)

Hallett, M., Shahani, B. T., & Young, R. R. Analysis of stereotyped voluntary movements at the elbow in patients with Parkinson's disease. *Journal of Neurology, Neurosurgery and Psychiatry*, 1977, *40*, 1129–1135.

Halliday, A. M., & Redfearn, J. W. T. An analysis of the frequencies of finger tremor in healthy subjects. *Journal of Physiology*, 1956, *134*, 600–611.

Halliday, A. M., & Redfearn, J. W. T. Finger tremor in tabetic patients and its bearing on the mechanisms producing the rhythm of physiological tremor. *Journal of Neurology, Neurosurgery and Psychiatry*, 1958, *21*, 101–108.

Halpern, D., Kottke, F. J., Burrill, C., Fiterman, C., Popp, J., & Palmer, S. Training of control of head posture in children with cerebral palsy. *Developmental Medicine and Child Neurology*, 1970, *12*, 290–305.

Hanna, R., Wilfling, F., & McNeil, B. A biofeedback treatment for stuttering. *Journal of Speech and Hearing Disorders,* 1975, *40,* 270–273. (1975/76:59)

Hardycke, C. D., & Petrinovich, L. F. Treatment of subvocal speech during reading. *Journal of Reading,* 1969, *1,* 361–368, 419–422.

Hardycke, C. D., Petrinovich, L. F., & Ellsworth, D. W. Feedback of speech muscle activity during silent reading: Rapid extinction. *Science,* 1966, *154,* 1467–1468. (R:44)

Hardycke, D. C., Petrinovich, L. F., & Ellsworth, D. W. Feedback of speech muscle activity during silent reading: Two comments. *Science,* 1967, *157,* 581.

Harris, F. A. Inapproprioception: A possible sensory basis for athetoid movements. *Physical Therapy,* 1971, *51,* 761–770.

Harris, F. A. Muscle stretch receptor hypersensitization in spasticity: Inapproprioception. Part III. *American Journal of Physical Medicine,* 1978, *57,* 16–28.

Harris, F. A., Spelman, F. A., Hymer, J. W., & Chase, C. E. Application of electronic prostheses in rehabilitation and education of multiply handicapped children. *Proceedings of the 1973 Carnahan Conference on Electronic Prostheses.* Lexington: University of Kentucky, 1973.

Harris, F. A., Spelman, F. A., & Hymer, J. W. Electronic sensory aids as treatment for cerebral-palsied children: Inapproprioception. Part II. *Physical Therapy,* 1974, *54,* 354–365.

Harrison, A. Components of neuromuscular control. In K. S. Holt (Ed.), *Movement and child development* (Clinics in Developmental Medicine, No. 55). London: Heinemann, 1976, pp. 34–50. (a)

Harrison, A. Studies of neuromuscular control in normal and spastic individuals. In K. S. Holt (Ed.), *Movement and child development.* (Clinics in Developmental Medicine, No. 55). London: Heinemann, 1976, pp. 51–74. (b)

Harrison, A. Training spastic individuals to achieve better neuromuscular control using electromyographic feedback. In K. S. Holt (Ed.), *Movement and child development* (Clinics in Developmental Medicine, No. 55). London: Heinemann, 1976, pp. 75–101. (c)

Harrison, A., & Connolly, K. The conscious control of fine levels of neuromuscular firing in spastic and normal subjects. *Developmental Medicine and Child Neurology,* 1971, *13,* 762—771.

Harrison, V. F., & Mortensen, O. A. Identification and voluntary control of single motor unit activity in the tibialis anterior muscle. *Anatomical Record,* 1962, *144,* 109–116.

Haynes, S. N., Griffin, P., Mooney, D., & Parise, M. Electromyographic biofeedback and relaxation instructions in the treatment of muscle contraction headaches. *Behavior Therapy,* 1975, *6,* 672–678. (1975/76:16)

Haynes, S. N., Moseley, D., & McGowan, W. T. Relaxation training and biofeedback in the reduction of frontalis muscle tension. *Psychophysiology,* 1975, *12,* 547–552. (1975/76:17)

Hefferline, R. F. The role of proprioception in the control of behavior. *Transactions of the New York Academy of Science,* 1958, *20,* 739–764.

Henschen, T. L., & Burton, N. G. Treatment of spastic dysphonia by EMG biofeedback. *Biofeedback and Self-Regulation,* 1978, *3,* 91–96.

Herman, R. Augmented sensory feedback in the control of limb movement. In W. S. Fields & L. A. Leavitt (Eds.), *Neural organization and its relevance to prosthetics.* New York: Intercontinental Medical Book Corporation, 1973, pp. 197–215.

Hixon, T. J. Some new techniques for measuring the biomechanical events of speech production: One laboratory's experiences. *American Speech and Hearing Association Reports,* 1972, *7,* 68–103.

Hixon, T. J. Respiratory function in speech. In F. Minifie, T. Hixon, & F. Williams (Eds.), *Normal aspects of speech, hearing and language.* Englewood Cliffs, N.J.: Prentice-Hall, 1973, pp. 73–125.

Hixon, T. J., Goldman, M. D., & Mead, J. Kinematics of the chest wall during speech production: Volume displacements of the rib cage, abdomen and lung. *Journal of Speech and Hearing Research,* 1973, *16,* 78–115.

Hixon, T. J., Mead, J., & Goldman, M. D. Dynamics of the chest wall during speech production: Function of the thorax, rib cage, diaphragm, and abdomen. *Journal of Speech and Hearing Research,* 1976, *19,* 297–356.

Hogan. N. A review of the methods of processing EMG for use as a proportional control signal. *Biomedical Engineering,* 1976, *11,* 81–86.

Holbrook, A., Rolnick, M., & Bailey, C. Treatment of vocal abuse disorders using a vocal intensity controller. *Journal of Speech and Hearing Disorders,* 1974, *39,* 291–303.

Huffman, A. L. Biofeedback treatment of orofacial dysfunction: A preliminary study. *American Journal of Occupational Therapy,* 1978, *32,* 149–154.

Hutchings, D. F., & Reinking, R. H. Tension headaches: What form of therapy is most effective? *Biofeedback and Self-Regulation,* 1976, *1,* 183–190. (1976/77:12)

Hutchinson, J. M., & Watkin, K. L. Jaw mechanics during release of the stuttering moment: Some initial observations and interpretations. *Journal of Communication Disorders,* 1976, *9,* 269–279.

Ince, L. P., Brucker, B. S., & Alba, A. Behavioral techniques applied to the care of patients with spinal cord injuries. With an annotated reference list. *Behavioral Engineering,* 1976, *3,* 87–95. (1976/77:40)

Inglis, J., Campbell, D., & Donald, M. W. Electromyographic biofeedback and neuromuscular rehabilitation. *Canadian Journal of Behavioral Science,* 1976, *8,* 299–323. (1976/77: 2)

Jacobs, A., & Felton, G. S. Visual feedback ot myoelectric output to facilitate muscle relaxation in normal persons and patients with neck injuries. *Archives of Physical Medicine and Rehabilitation,* 1969, *50,* 34–39.

Jacobson, E. Voluntary relaxation of the esophagus. *American Journal of Physiology,* 1925, *72,* 387–394.

Jacobson, E. Electrophysiology of mental activities and introduction to the psychological process of thinking. In F. J. McGuigan & R. A. Schoonover (Eds.), *The psychophysiology of thinking.* New York: Academic, 1973, pp. 3–31.

Johnson, C. P. Analysis of five tests commonly used in determining the ability to control single motor units. *American Journal of Physical Medicine,* 1976, *55,* 113–121.

Johnson, H. E., & Garton, W. H. Muscle reeducation in hemiplegia by use of an electromyographic device. *Archives of Physical Medicine and Rehabilitation,* 1973, *54,* 320–325. (1974:23)

Kato, M., & Tanji, J. Volitionally controlled single motor units in human finger muscles. *Brain Research,* 1972, *40,* 345–357.

Kinsman, R. A., O'Banion, K., Robinson, S., & Staudenmayer, H. Continuous biofeedback and discrete posttrial verbal feedback in *frontalis* muscle relaxation training. *Psychophysiology,* 1975, *12,* 30–35. (1975/76:18)

Kleinman, A., & Lidsky, A. Biofeedback and rest position in denture subjects. *Journal of Dental Research,* 1976, *55,* B100. (Abstract)

Korein, J., & Brudny, J. Integrated EMG feedback in the management of spasmodic torticollis and focal dystonia: A prospective study of 80 patients. In M. D. Yahr (Ed.), *The basal ganglia.* New York: Raven, 1976, pp. 385–424.

Korein, J., Brudny, J., Grynbaum, B., Sachs-Frankel, G., Weisinger, M., & Levidow, L. Sensory feedback therapy of spasmodic torticollis and dystonia: Results in treatment of 55 patients. In R. Eldridge & S. Fahn (Eds.), *Advances in neurology* (Vol. 14). New York: Raven, 1976, pp. 375–402.

Kukulka, C. G., & Basmajian, J. V. Assessment of an audio-visual feedback device used in motor training. *American Journal of Physical Medicine,* 1975, *54,* 194–209. (1975/76:54)

Kukulka, C. G., Brown, D. M., & Basmajian, J. V. A preliminary report: Biofeedback training for early joint finger mobilization. *American Journal of Occupational Therapy,* 1975, *29,* 469–470. (1975/76:55)

Landau, W. M. Spasticity: The fable of a neurological demon and the emperor's new therapy.

Archives of Neurology, 1974, *31,* 217–219.

Lanyon, R. I. Effect of biofeedback-based relaxation on stuttering during reading and spontaneous speech. *Journal of Consulting and Clinical Psychology,* 1977, *45,* 860–866.

Lanyon, R. I., Barrington, C. C., & Newman, A. C. Modification of stuttering through EMG biofeedback: A preliminary study. *Behavior Therapy,* 1976, *7,* 96–103. (1976/77:46)

Le Boeuf, A. The treatment of a severe tremor by electromyogram feedback. *Journal of Behavior Therapy and Experimental Psychiatry,* 1976, *7,* 59–61.

Leibrecht, B. C., Lloyd, A. J., & Pounder, S. Auditory feedback and conditioning of the single motor unit. *Psychophysiology,* 1973, *10,* 1–7. (1973:11)

Levee, J. R., Cohen, M. J., & Rickles, W. H. Electromyographic biofeedback for relief of tension in the facial and throat muscles of a woodwind musician. *Biofeedback and Self-Regulation,* 1976, *1,* 113–120.

Levin, H. S. Evaluation of the tactile component in a proprioceptive feedback task. *Cortex,* 1973, *9,* 197–203. (a)

Levin, H. S. Motor impersistence and proprioceptive feedback in patients with unilateral cerebral disease. *Neurology,* 1973, *23,* 833–841. (b)

Levin, H. S., & Benton, A. L. Proprioceptive feedback performance in patients with focal brain lesions. *Journal of Neurology,* 1976, *212,* 117–121.

Light, J., Silverman, S. I., & Garfunkel, L. The use of an intraoral training aid in the speech rehabilitation of laryngectomy patients. *Journal of Prosthetic Dentistry,* 1976, *35,* 430–440.

Lloyd, A. J. Auditory EMG feedback during a maintained submaximum isometric contraction. *Research Quarterly,* 1972, *43,* 39–46.

Lloyd, A. J., & Leibrecht, B. C. Conditioning of a single motor unit. *Journal of Experimental Psychology,* 1971, *88,* 391–395.

Lloyd, A. J., & Shurley, J. T. The effects of sensory perceptual isolation on single motor unit conditioning. *Psychophysiology,* 1976, *13,* 340–344.

McGuigan, F. J. Feedback of speech muscle activity during silent reading: Two comments. *Science,* 1967, *157,* 579–580.

McGuigan, F. J., Keller, B., & Stanton, E. Covert language responses during silent reading. *Journal of Educational Psychology,* 1964, *55,* 339–343.

McKenzie, R. E., Ehrisman, W. J., Montgomery, P. S., & Barnes, R. H. The treatment of headache by means of electroencephalographic biofeedback. *Headache,* 1974, *13,* 164–172.

MacPherson, E. L. R. Control of voluntary movement. *Behavior Research and Therapy,* 1967, *5,* 143–145.

Mann, R. W. Prostheses control and feedback via noninvasive skin and invasive peripheral nerve techniques. In W. S. Fields & L. A. Leavitt (Eds.), *Neural organization and its relevance to prosthetics.* New York: Intercontinental Medical Book Corporation, 1973, pp. 177–195.

Marinacci, A. A., & Horande, M. Electromyogram in neuromuscular re-education. *Bulletin of the Los Angeles Neurological Society,* 1960, *25,* 57–71.

Marsden, C. D., Merton, P. A., & Morton, H. B. Servo action in human voluntary movement. *Nature,* 1972, *238,* 140–143.

Marshall, J. Physiological tremor in children. *Journal of Neurology, Neurosurgery and Psychiatry,* 1959, *22,* 33–35.

Martin, J., & Sachs, D. A. The effects of visual feedback on the fine motor behavior of a deaf cerebral palsied child. *Journal of Nervous and Mental Disease,* 1973, *157,* 59–62.

Maton, B. Motor unit differentiation and integrated surface EMG in voluntary isometric contraction. *European Journal of Applied Physiology,* 1976, *35,* 149–157.

Meares, R. Natural history of spasmodic torticollis and the effect of surgery. *Lancet,* 1971, *2,* 149–150. (a)

Meares, R. Features which distinguish groups of spasmodic torticollis. *Journal of Psychosomatic Research,* 1971, *15,* 1–11. (b)

Meares, R., & Lader, M. H. Electromyographic studies in patients with spasmodic torticollis. *Journal of Psychosomatic Research,* 1971, *15,* 13–18.

Medina, J. L., Diamond, S., & Franklin, M. A. Biofeedback therapy for migraine. *Headache,* 1976, *16,* 115–118.

Moldofsky, H. A psychophysiological study of multiple tics. *Archives of General Psychiatry,* 1971, *25,* 79–87.

Moller, K. T., Path, M., Werth, L. J., & Christiansen, R. L. The modification of velar movement. *Journal of Speech and Hearing Disorders,* 1973, *38,* 323–334.

Moore, W. H. Some effects of progressively lowering electromyographic levels with feedback procedures on the frequency of stuttered verbal behaviors. *Journal of Fluency Disorders,* 1978, *3,* 127–138.

Nafpliotis, H. Electromyographic feedback to improve ankle dorsiflexion, wrist extension, and hand grasp. *Physical Therapy,* 1976, *56,* 821–825.

Netsell, R., & Cleeland, C. S. Modification of lip hypertonia in dysarthria using EMG feedback. *Journal of Speech and Hearing Disorders,* 1973, *38,* 131–140.

Norton, G. R. Biofeedback treatment of long-standing eye closure reactions. *Journal of Behavior Therapy and Experimental Psychiatry,* 1976, *7,* 279–280.

Onel, Y., Friedman, A. P., & Grossman, J. Muscle blood flow studies in muscle contraction headaches. *Neurology,* 1961, *11,* 935–939.

Peck, D. F. Operant conditioning and physical rehabilitation. *European Journal of Behavioural Analysis and Modification,* 1976, *3,* 158–164.

Peck, D. F. The use of EMG feedback in the treatment of a severe case of blepharospasm. *Biofeedback and Self-Regulation,* 1977, *2,* 273–277.

Perkins, W., Rudas, J., Johnson, L., & Bell, J. Stuttering: Discoordination of phonation with articulation and respiration. *Journal of Speech and Hearing Research,* 1976, *19,* 509–522.

Platt, L. J., & Basili, A. Jaw tremor during stuttering block: An electromyographic study. *Journal of Communication Disorders,* 1973, *6,* 102–109.

Potvin, A. R., & Tourtellotte, W. W. The neurological examination: Advancements in quantification. *Archives of Physical Medicine and Rehabilitation,* 1975, *56,* 425–437.

Raskin, M., Johnson, G., & Rondestvedt, J. W. Chronic anxiety treated by feedback-induced muscle relaxation. *Archives of General Psychiatry,* 1973, *28,* 263–267. (1973:22)

Reading, A., & Raw, M. The treatment of mandibular dysfunction pain. *British Dental Journal,* 1976, *140,* 201–205.

Reavley, W. The use of biofeedback in the treatment of writer's cramp. *Journal of Behavior Therapy and Experimental Psychiatry,* 1975, *6,* 335–338.

Reinking, R. H., & Kohl, M. L. Effects of various forms of relaxation training on physiological and self-report measures of relaxation. *Journal of Consulting and Clinical Psychology,* 1975, *43,* 595–600. (1975/76:21)

Roll, D. L. Modification of nasal resonance in cleft-palate children by informative feedback. *Journal of Applied Behavior Analysis,* 1973, *6,* 397–403.

Rugel, R. P., Mattingly, J., Eichinger, M., & May, J. The use of operant conditioning with a physically disabled child. *American Journal of Occupational Therapy,* 1971, *25,* 247–249.

Rugh, J. D., & Solberg, W. K. Psychological implications in temporomandibular pain and dysfunction. *Oral Science Reviews,* 1976, *7,* 3–30.

Russell, G., & Wooldridge, C. P. Correction of an habitual head tilt using biofeedback techniques: A case study. *Physiotherapy Canada,* 1975, *27,* 181–187.

Sachs, D. A., & Mayhall, B. Behavioral control of spasms using aversive conditioning in a cerebral palsied adult. *Journal of Nervous and Mental Diseases,* 1971, *152,* 362–363.

Sachs, D. A., Martin, J. E., & Fitch, J. L. The effect of visual feedback on a digital exercise in a functionally deaf cerebral palsied child. *Journal of Behaviour Therapy and Experimental Psychiatry,* 1972, *3,* 217–222.

Sachs, D. A., Talley, E., & Boley, K. A comparison of feedback and reinforcement as modifiers of a functional motor response in a hemiparetic patient. *Journal of Behavior Therapy and Experimental Psychiatry,* 1976, *7,* 171–174. (1976/77:41)

Sainsbury, P., & Gibson, J. G. Symptoms of anxiety and tension and the accompanying physiological changes in the muscular system. *Journal of Neurology, Neurosurgery and Psychiatry,* 1954, *17,* 216–224.

Sargent, J. D., Green, E. E., & Walters, E. D. The use of autogenic feedback training in a pilot study of migraine and tension headache. *Headache,* 1972, *12,* 120–125.

Sargent, J. D., Green, E. E., & Walters, E. D. Preliminary report on the use of autogenic feedback training in the treatment of migraine and tension headaches. *Psychosomatic Medicine,* 1973, *35,* 129–135. (1973:21)

Scott, F. B., Bradley, W. E., & Timm, G. W. Electromechanical restoration of micturition. In W. S. Fields & L. A. Leavitt (Eds.), *Neural organization and its relevance to prosthetics.* New York: Intercontinental Medical Book Corporation, 1973, pp. 311–318.

Scully, H. E., & Basmajian, J. V. Motor-unit training and influence of manual skill. *Psychophysiology,* 1969, *5,* 625–632.

Simard, T. G. Fine neuromuscular control of the posterior deltoid muscle during resistance to finger extension. *American Journal of Physical Medicine,* 1977, *56,* 275–292.

Simard, T. G., & Basmajian, J. V. Methods in training the conscious control of motor units. *Archives of Physical Medicine,* 1966, *48,* 12–19.

Simard, T. G., & Ladd, H. W. Pre-orthotic training: An electromyographic study in normal adults. *American Journal of Physical Medicine,* 1969, *48,* 301–312. (a)

Simard, T. G., & Ladd, H. W. Conscious control of motor units with thalidomide children: An electromyographic study. *Developmental Medicine and Child Neurology,* 1969, *11,* 743–748. (b)

Simard, T. G., & Ladd, H. W. Differential control of muscle segments by quadriplegic patients: An electromyographic procedural investigation. *Archives of Physical Medicine and Rehabilitation,* 1971, *52,* 447–454.

Smith, H. M., Basmajian, J. V., & Vanderstoep, S. F. Inhibition of neighboring motoneurones in conscious control of single spinal motoneurones. *Science,* 1974, *183,* 975–976. (1974:25)

Smith, K. U., & Henry, J. P. Cybernetic foundations for rehabilitation. *American Journal of Physical Medicine,* 1967, *46,* 379–467.

Spearing, D. L., & Poppen, R. The use of feedback in the reduction of foot dragging in a cerebral palsied client. *Journal of Nervous and Mental Disease,* 1974, *159,* 148–151.

Starkweather, C. W., Hirschman, P., & Tannenbaum, R. S. Latency of vocalization onset: Stutterers versus nonstutterers. *Journal of Speech and Hearing Research,* 1976, *19,* 481–492.

Stein, R. B., & Oğuztöreli, M. N. Tremor and other oscillations in neuromuscular systems. *Biological Cybernetics,* 1976, *22,* 147–157.

Stevens, K. N., Nickerson, R. S., Rollins, A. M., & Boothroyd, A. Use of a visual display of nasalization to facilitate training of velar control for deaf speakers (Report No. 2899). Cambridge, Mass.: Bolt Beranek & Newman Inc., 1974.

Stevens, K. N., Kalikow, D. N., & Willemain, T. R. A miniature accelerometer for detecting glottal waveforms and nasalization. *Journal of Speech and Hearing Research,* 1975, *18,* 594–599.

Stevens, K. N., Nickerson, R. S., Boothroyd, A., & Rollins, A. M. Assessment of nasalization in the speech of deaf children. *Journal of Speech and Hearing Research,* 1976, *19,* 393–416.

Susset, J. G. The electrical drive of the urinary bladder and sphincter. In W. S. Fields & L. A. Leavitt (Eds.), *Neural organization and its relevance to prosthetics.* New York: Intercontinental Medical Book Corporation, 1973, pp. 319–342.

Sussman, H. M., MacNeilage, P. F., & Powers, R. K. Recruitment and discharge patterns of single motor units during speech production. *Journal of Speech and Hearing Research,* 1977, *20,* 613–630.

Swaan, D., van Wieringen, P. C. W., & Fokkema, S. D. Auditory electromyographic feedback therapy to inhibit undesired motor activity. *Archives of Physical Medicine and Rehabilitation,* 1974, *55,* 251–254. (1974:24)

Takebe, K., & Basmajian, J. V. Gait analysis in stroke patients to assess treatments of foot-drop. *Archives of Physical Medicine and Rehabilitation,* 1976, *57,* 305–310.

Takebe, K., Kukulka, C. G., Narayan, M. G., & Basmajian, J. V. Biofeedback treatment of foot drop after stroke compared with standard rehabilitation technique. Part 2. *Archives of Physical Medicine and Rehabilitation,* 1976, *57,* 9–11.

Tasto, D. L., & Hinkle, J. E. Muscle relaxation treatment for tension headaches. *Behavior Research and Therapy,* 1973, *11,* 347–349.

Tatton, W. G., & Lee, R. G. Evidence for abnormal long-loop reflexes in rigid Parkinsonian patients. *Brain Research,* 1975, *100,* 671–676.

Taylor, M. M. Analysis of dysfunction in left hemiplegia following stroke. *American Journal of Occupational Therapy,* 1968, *22,* 512–520.

Teng, E. L., McNeal, D. R., Kralj, A., & Waters, R. L. Electrical stimulation and feedback training: Effects on the voluntary control of paretic muscles. *Archives of Physical Medicine and Rehabilitation,* 1976, *57,* 228–233.

Thysell, R. V. Reaction time of single motor units. *Psychophysiology,* 1969, *6,* 174–185.

Trombly, C. A. Myoelectric control of orthotic devices for the severely paralyzed. *American Journal of Occupational Therapy,* 1968, *22,* 385–389.

Uchiyama, K., Lutterjohann, M., & Shah, M. D. Biofeedback-assisted desensitization treatment of writer's cramp. *Journal of Behaviour Therapy and Experimental Psychiatry,* 1977, *8,* 169–171.

van Boxtel, A., & van der Ven, J. R. Differential EMG activity in subjects with muscle contraction headaches related to mental effort. *Headache,* 1978, *17,* 233–237.

Van Buskirk, C. Return of motor function in hemiplegia. *Neurology,* 1954, *4,* 919–928.

Van Buskirk, C., & Fink, R. A. Physiologic tremor: An experimental study. *Neurology,* 1962, *12,* 361–370.

Vaughn, R., Pall, M. L., & Haynes, S. N. Frontalis EMG responses to stress in subjects with frequent muscle-contraction headaches. *Headache,* 1977, *16,* 313–317.

Vodovnik, L., & Rebersek, S. Improvement in voluntary control of paretic muscles due to electrical stimulation. In W. S. Fields & L. A. Leavitt (Eds.), *Neural organization and its relevance to prosthetics.* New York: Intercontinental Medical Book Corporation, 1973, pp. 101–116.

Wagman, I. H., Pierce, D. S., & Burger, R. E. Proprioceptive influence in volitional control of individual motor units. *Nature,* 1965, *207,* 957–958.

Warren, C. G., & Lehmann, J. F. Training procedures and biofeedback methods to achieve controlled partial weight bearing: An assessment. *Archives of Physical Medicine and Rehabilitation,* 1975, *56,* 449–455.

Wickramasekera, I. Effects of EMG feedback training on susceptibility to hypnosis: Preliminary observations. *Proceedings of the 79th Annual Convention of the American Psychological Association,* 1971, 783–784. (1971:30)

Wickramasekera, I. Electromyographic feedback training and tension headache: Preliminary observations. *American Journal of Clinical Hypnosis,* 1972, *15,* 83–85. (1973:20)

Wickramasekera, I. The application of verbal instructions and EMG feedback training to the management of tension headache—preliminary observations. *Headache,* 1973, *13,* 74–76.

Wolpert, R., & Wooldridge, C. P. The use of electromyography as biofeedback therapy in the management of cerebral palsy: A review and case study. *Physiotherapy Canada,* 1975, *27,* 5–9.

Woodworth, R. S. On the voluntary control of the force of movement. *Psychological Review,* 1901, *8,* 350–359.

Wooldridge, C. P., & Russell, G. Head position training with the cerebral palsied child: An application of biofeedback techniques. *Archives of Physical Medicine and Rehabilitation* 1976, *57,* 407–414. (1976/77:42)

Wyke, B. The neurology of stammering. *Journal of Psychosomatic Research*, 1971, *15*, 423–432.

Yates, A. J. Recent empirical and theoretical approaches to the experimental manipulation of speech in normal subjects and in stammerers. *Behavior Research and Therapy*, 1963, *1*, 95–119.

Yates, A. J. *Behavior therapy*. New York: Wiley, 1970. (a)

Yates, A. J. Tics. In C. G. Costello (Ed.), *Symptoms of psychopathology: A handbook*. New York: Wiley, 1970, pp. 320–335. (b)

Yates, A. J. *Theory and practice in behavior therapy*. New York: Wiley, 1975.

Yemm, R. The orderly recruitment of motor units of the masseter and temporal muscles during voluntary isometric contraction in man. *Journal of Physiology*, 1977, *265*, 163–174.

Zipp, P. Übertragungsverhalten des motorischen Systems der Hand bei elektrischer Anregung und seine Bedeutung für den Krafttremor. *European Journal of Applied Physiology*, 1975, *34*, 233–248.

CHAPTER 4

Voluntary Control of Autonomic Functions

Introduction

In discussing the historical antecedents of biofeedback in Chapter 1 it was evident that one of the developments which aroused most interest was the alleged demonstration of voluntary control over functions mediated via the autonomic nervous system (ANS) since it had long been considered that these functions could not be voluntarily controlled. The experiments of N. E. Miller and his colleagues with curarized rats appeared to overcome the difficulty raised by those who argued that the apparent direct (whatever "direct" might mean) operant conditioning of autonomically mediated functions was in fact indirectly achieved by voluntary control of other nonautonomically mediated functions which produced a parallel change in the autonomically mediated function. The subsequent failure to replicate these results with animals did not in any way diminish the enthusiastic search for evidence in humans of ability to exercise voluntary control over heart rate, blood pressure, GSR, temperature, and other functions dependent on autonomic activity. As a result, a very large and complex literature has accumulated, which will be reviewed in this chapter.

Voluntary Control of Autonomic Function

Voluntary Control of Heart Rate

In order to understand studies on the voluntary control of various functions of the cardiovascular system (and in particular to understand the application of biofeedback to abnormalities of cardiac function), some knowledge of the structure and functioning of the cardiovascular system is essential. The following account provides the bare minimum description of the system but should be sufficient to enable the reader to comprehend the technical details of the studies to be discussed. A much more detailed and authoritative account will, of course, be found in any standard textbook of physiology.

The heart is divided into right and left halves, each half comprising an upper chamber (the atrium) and a lower chamber (the ventricle). Blood flows from the atrium to the ventricle, but not vice versa, on each side (but the right and left halves do not communicate with each other). Oxygenated blood in the left ventricle commences its journey through the systemic circulatory system (that is, to all parts of the body except the lungs) when the left ventricle contracts and forces the blood in the ventricle into the aorta, the main artery providing exit from the heart. The aorta distributes the blood into the large arteries and thence into the smaller arterioles which themselves branch into the capillaries. At these points, the main exchanges of the contents of the blood occur, after which the blood is ready to begin its return journey to the heart. The equivalent of the arterioles on the return journey are the venules, which take the blood into the larger veins which in turn unite to form the inferior vena cava (receiving blood from the lower parts of the body) and the superior vena cava (receiving blood from the upper parts of the body). The final common path of the inferior and superior venae cavae leads the returning blood into the right atrium. The oxygenation of the blood occurs as a result of the returned blood's being pumped from the right ventricle through the pulmonary system before it returns to the left ventricle for a further journey around the body. Thus, in summary, the right half of the heart is responsible for circulating blood through the pulmonary system where it is oxygenated; the left half of the heart then pumps the oxygenated blood through the systemic system from whence it returns to the right half of the heart.

It is important to understand that the heart is essentially a large muscle system with the special characteristic that it is autorhythmic; that is, it beats spontaneously. The heart rate of an individual is determined primarily by a pacemaker which in the normal heart is the sinoatrial node (SA node), located near the top of the right atrium, embedded in its wall. When depolarization occurs, the SA node transmits excitatory potentials in all directions across both the left and right atria. Since the transmission is completed in less than 0.1 sec, all parts of both atria contract virtually simultaneously. It should be noted that no special conducting system is involved in the distribution of the excitation. However, part of the excitation wave makes contact with a small group of specialized cells at the base of the atrium known as the atrioventricular node (AV node), which provides the only link between the atria and the ventricles. The corresponding contraction of the AV node, when it is stimulated by excitation from the SA node, is delayed by about 0.1 sec, allowing time for the blood in the atria to empty into the ventricles before ventricular contraction occurs. As will be seen later, several cardiac abnormalities arise from a failure of the SA node to operate efficiently (in which case its pacemaking function may be taken over by the AV node) or by other potential pacemakers in the heart competing with the AV node for control of heart function. These malfunctions will be described at the appropriate points in this chapter.

Although the SA node has a spontaneous firing rate which determines the normal heart rate (number of beats per minute), it is richly supplied with inputs from both the sympathetic and parasympathetic divisions of the ANS and its rate of firing can be significantly influenced by changes in these inputs. Increased sympathetic stimulation of the SA node will increase its rate of discharge, whereas increased parasympathetic stimulation will slow the rate of discharge and may even stop the heart altogether. Similar effects can be obtained by the use of locally injected drugs which affect SA node activity (for example, acetylcholine slows the heart whereas norepinephrine increases it). If the parasympathetic nerves are severed, heart rate will increase, indicating that parasympathetic activity is normally predominant over sympathetic and acts to damp down the natural autonomous discharge rate of the SA node which may be as high as 100 contractions per minute. Heart rate may also be influenced by hormonal activity, temperature, and plasma electrolyte concentrations. Finally, mention should be made of the vagus nerve, a peripatetic wanderer through the body, which impinges also on the sinoatrial node as part of the parasympathetic influence on heart rate, and which almost certainly plays an important role in the inhibition of heart rate.

Nonpolarizing surface electrodes are usually used in studies of human heart rate and heart-rate variability, the two main dependent variables. The electrodes detect the action potentials of cardiac muscle, and with suitable amplification and recording devices the sequence of events occurring during the cardiac cycle can be reproduced by measuring the potential difference between any two sites on the surface of the body. Three standard configurations of electrodes are commonly used: in the lead I configuration, electrodes are attached to each of the upper arms; in the lead II configuration, they are attached to the right upper arm and lower left leg; and in the lead III configuration, to the left upper arm and lower left leg. However, these configurations are not critical, and in biofeedback work a quite remarkable variety of configurations has been employed in addition to the standard ones. Lang and his colleagues have preferred the anterolateral lower ribs (Gatchel, 1974; Lang, Troyer, Twentyman, & Gatchel, 1975; Lang & Twentyman, 1974, 1976); Headrick, Feather, and Wells (1971) used the extreme lateral margins of the chest, McCanne and Sandman (1976) the left lower rib cage and right collar bone, Wells (1973) the shin and medial portion of the collar bone (female subjects), Johnston (1976) the top and bottom of the sternum or chest bone, and McFarland and Coombs (1974) the wrists, to name but a few of the many possible variations. This variety of approaches arises from the fact that heart rate is usually measured as the interval between successive R waves, which are relatively easy to detect and are readily distinguishable from artifacts, provided the subject is supine and does not move about. The R wave is a segment of the electrocardiogram, of which a typical segment is shown in Figure 1. The segment comprises a P wave, the QRS complex, and a T wave. The low-amplitude P wave represents atrial depolarization, that is, the propagation of a wave of excitation from the SA node. The QRS complex, which occurs between 0.1 sec and 0.2 sec after the SA node fires, represents ventricular depolarization, that is, the ventricular contraction (which reaches its maximum, or systole, near the end of the R wave) which sends a volume of blood on its way through the aorta. The T wave indicates the occurrence of ventricular repolarization (atrial repolarization is not represented because it is occurring during ventricular de-polarization and hence is masked by the QRS complex). As can be seen from Figure 1, the R wave is readily detectable and hence the time interval between successive R waves may be used as an indicator of heart rate, while the variabil-ity in R wave intervals may be used as a measure of heart-rate variability. In abnormal conditions, of course, the characteristics of the P wave and its time relationships with the R wave may be important indications of the interaction between atrial and ventricular functioning (and of the effects of biofeedback training in such abnormal states).

In later sections of this chapter we will provide, as appropriate, further simplified details of the functioning of the cardiovascular system, but the above account will suffice for the discussion of studies of normal and abnormal heart functioning as such.

Let us now turn to the biofeedback studies of heart-rate control. As pointed out in Chapter 1, the apparent ability to induce, voluntarily, large increases or (more rarely) decreases in heart rate had been repeatedly reported since the original observations of Tarchanoff (1885). Most of the early studies of the control of heart rate, however, were carried out in attempts to determine whether

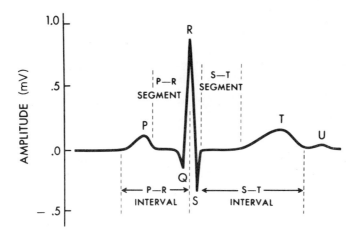

Figure 1. Characteristics of a normal electrocardiogram (see text for explanation).

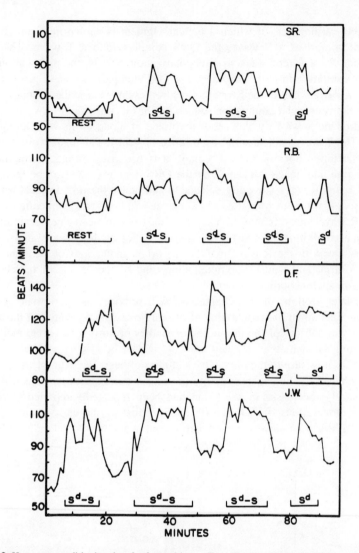

Figure 2. Heart rate conditioning data for four subjects. (From Frazier, T. W. Avoidance conditioning of heart rate in humans. *Psychophysiology,* 1966, *3,* 191, Figure 1. Reprinted by permission of the publisher.)

or not heart rate could be instrumentally conditioned and thus demolish the belief that only classical conditioning of heart rate was possible. Hence, the question of voluntary control was ignored; hence, too, not only was the subject usually not informed that heart rate was the response under investigation but it was considered undesirable that he should be aware of the fact since such knowledge, it was argued, might actually interfere with the establishment of external control of heart rate which it was the experimenter's ambition to achieve. These early studies (1962–1968) fall into three groups. In the first group are those studies which used a Sidman avoidance paradigm. Shearn (1962) made delay of shock contingent on acceleration of heart rate. His experimental subjects had to produce a sequence of five heartbeats at a higher rate than average baseline rate within a specified time interval in order to postpone shock. A yoked control group received the same number of shocks which were, however, unrelated to heart-rate performance (the control group was actually a classical conditioning group since some of the shocks would coincide with a heartbeat and thus produce an increase). Feedback in the form of an illuminated reset timer and an auditory representation of the heartbeat was also given. The group subjected to the avoidance schedule demonstrated a significant increase in the percentage of temporary heart-rate accelerations reaching criterion magnitude whereas the control group showed a decrease mainly produced by adaptations occurring after the initial shock-produced increase. Frazier (1966) likewise used a Sidman avoidance technique together with a visual feedback display which acted as a discriminative stimulus (S^d) during which shock was "available." Figure 2 shows the results for the four subjects used in the experiment (S^d– S refers to the period in which the display was on and shock was "available"). All four subjects showed an increase in heart rate during S^d– S periods, but when the visual stimulus was discontinued, heart rate fell rapidly to a stable baseline. This suggested that S^d was operating, after training, as a conditioned stimulus. When Frazier investigated this, he found that S^d alone, after training, could maintain an elevated heart rate for quite long periods of time, and furthermore, that it was possible to produce continuous oscillations in heart rate over prolonged periods of time by repeatedly presenting and withdrawing the S^d, as shown in Figure 3. A study carried out by Brener (1966) demonstrated that heart rate could also be slowed as well as increased to avoid shock. In none of these studies were the subjects informed that heart rate was the response under investigation. In Brener's study, for example, the subjects were:

> told that the purpose of the experiment was to determine their physiological reactions to a variety of peripheral stimuli. No hint was given that they were in any way able to control the experimental stimuli or that there was a special interest in their cardiac behaviour. (1966, p. 331)

A second group of three studies during this period also used uninformed subjects but combined the use of feedback[1] with positive reinforcement. Engel and Hansen (1966) provided feedback in the form of a light which came on whenever heart rate was slowed beyond a set criterion while reinforcement consisted of a cumulative clock which indicated that money had been earned each time a correct response was made. Six sessions of training were given, each consisting of adaptation and baseline periods involving neither feedback nor reinforcement, followed by a 25-min training period during which both feedback

---

[1]The feedback was, however, described as a "cue for correct response."

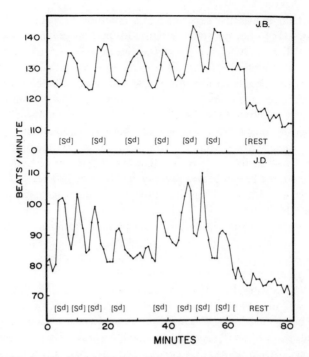

Figure 3. Results of employing the visual stimulus alone to induce continuous oscillations in heart rate for two subjects. (From Frazier, T. W. Avoidance conditioning of heart rate in humans. *Psychophysiology*, 1966, *3*, 195, Figure 5. Reprinted by permission of the publisher.)

and reinforcement were provided for heart-rate slowing. An important innovation in this study was the use of equipment enabling feedback or reinforcement to be given on a beat-by-beat basis. The results showed that some of the experimental subjects were able to slow their heart rate significantly while none of the control subjects was able to do so, as indexed by three measures of change (percentage time the light was kept on, decrease in heart rate, and number of beats at or below baseline average rate). It was this study particularly that gave rise to the short-term belief that knowledge of the response might interfere with the acquisition of control. In a parallel study, Engel and Chism (1967) provided evidence of heart rate speeding, using the same techniques. Levene, Engel, and Pearson (1968) extended these results by showing that following separate training in speeding and slowing heart rate it was possible alternately to speed and slow heart rate in successive trials, with the results shown in Table 1.

A third group, also of three studies, differed from the preceding two groups in that feedback only was provided while the subjects in the experimental groups were (except in one study) fully informed that they were to try to control their heart rate. In the earliest of these, Hnatiow and Lang (1965) provided half of their subjects with visual feedback which reflected heart-rate variability. The

Table 1. Mean Heart Rate in Rest and Alternating Slowing and Speeding Trials
(average over six sessions)[a]

Subject	Mean heart rate		
	Slow	Rest	Speed
1	76.5	79.6	79.9
2	80.1	79.2	84.3
3	71.8	70.7	78.3
4	84.3	87.7	97.3
5	74.8	78.1	79.5

[a]Adapted from Levene, H. I., Engel, B. T., & Pearson, J. A. Differential operant conditioning of heart rate. *Psychosomatic Medicine*, 1968, *30*, Table 1. Reprinted by permission of the author and the publisher.

display took the form of a pointer on a white field, the center of which was defined by a red stripe flanked by blue stripes. The width of each stripe was equal to a change of two beats per minute in heart rate, with the midline defining average heart rate at the start of each training trial. The task of the subject was to keep the pointer as vertical as possible. The control group was also provided with the same kind of display which, however, merely simulated heart-rate changes, and they were instructed to watch the display and track the pointer. These subjects were not informed about heart rate but were told instead that they were to try to keep their bodily processes at a steady level. The results indicated that the experimental subjects remained on target to a significantly greater extent during display trials than during trials in which there was no display, and that there was a corresponding reduction in variability of heart rate during display trials as compared with the control subjects. Brener and Hothersall (1966) provided auditory feedback to subjects attempting to increase and decrease their heart rate (with instructions to keep the tone high when increasing, and low when decreasing, heart rate). All of their subjects succeeded in lowering their heart rate with feedback, but none was successful in raising it, although the difference between lowering and raising was significant. The subjects of this study were not informed that heart rate was the target response. Finally, Lang, Sroufe, and Hastings (1967), in the first large-scale study of heart-rate control, allocated 60 male subjects to one of four experimental conditions. Group I was told that the display represented beat-to-beat changes in their own cardiac rates and that they were to maintain the pointer in the center of the meter so as to produce a steady heart rate, while group II was informed that the display was a tracking task and that they were to press a switch whenever the pointer was in the defined area (the display was the same as that used by Hnatiow & Lang, 1965). Subgroups of each group were in fact provided either with feedback of their own cardiac activity or the activity of a yoked control. The results of this study presented the first clear refutation of the suggestion made by Engel and Hansen (1966) that knowledge by the subject about the response under investigation might interfere with the establishment of control (and thus that subjects should be uninformed). For Lang *et al.* (1967) found that of the two subgroups provided with true feedback of their heart rate, the subgroup which was informed that the display represented heart rate showed a greater ability to reduce heart-rate variability than did the subgroup told that the display was a tracking task.

These early studies provided the framework for the explosion of activity which was about to occur in relation to the voluntary control of heart rate. However, most of them contained serious weaknesses which were quickly pointed out. Murray and Katkin (1968) made specific criticisms of the studies by Engel and Hansen (1966) and by Engel and Chism (1967), while Katkin and Murray (1968), and H. D. Kimmel (1967), in the course of more general reviews of the instrumental conditioning of autonomically mediated behavior, were severely critical of all of the above studies which were available to them. It is unnecessary to repeat these criticisms here since the methodological inadequacies of these studies derive from the problems already discussed in Chapter 2. From these reviews it is clear that up to this point in time the evidence for voluntary control of heart rate was inadequate, to say the least.

It is not intended here to provide a complete critical review of the very large number of studies carried out since 1968 which deal with the voluntary control of heart rate since this would occupy far too much space. It will be shown, however, that what might have seemed initially to be a relatively simple task (namely, to show that voluntary control of heart rate is possible) has turned out to be a question of bewildering complexity, the solution to which is even now not absolutely clear. The increasingly sophisticated methodology developed over the last 10 years in this area has been aimed primarily at clarifying the factors which produce changes in heart rate with the aim of demonstrating that if these factors are adequately controlled, a voluntary control component still remains. The research which has been carried out may be conveniently, if somewhat arbitrarily, grouped into a number of categories.

The first group of studies to be considered essentially deals with the question of the instructional control of heart rate in the absence of feedback and the extent to which this control may be partially accounted for by the drift phenomenon discussed in Chapter 2, and the extent to which achieved control can be maintained in a subsequent transfer situation. Even more recently, the extent to which heart-rate changes induced by various activities of a ''mental'' kind may confound voluntary control has also been examined. It should be noted carefully that some of these studies involve a repeated-measures design in which the same subjects proceed sequentially through various conditions, whereas others involve between-group designs in which the various conditions are applied to different groups matched on baseline performance.

The more important issue relates to the question of whether instructional control of heart rate is possible in the absence of any feedback at all. Brener,

Kleinman, and Goesling (1969) appear to have been the first to investigate this question. Subjects were instructed to increase or decrease their heart rate on alternate trials, 12 50-beat trials being given in each condition. A significant separation between heart-rate levels was obtained but the results were obscured by a consistent drift downward in heart rate across the 24 trials. Bergman and Johnson (1971) obtained more satisfactory results using a between-groups design. Separate groups of subjects were instructed to increase or decrease their heart rate whenever a tone was presented, while a control group was simply informed that their heart rate was being measured whenever the tone was on. A significant separation of the experimental groups from the control group in the appropriate direction up or down was obtained in the absence of informative feedback, providing the first clear evidence of voluntary control under instructional conditions alone. In a study concerned primarily with the relative effects of feedback and reinforcement, Blanchard, Young, Scott, and Haynes (1974) obtained significant increases in heart rate as a function of an instructional-only condition, while Blanchard, Young, Haynes, and Scott (1975) confirmed the results obtained by Bergman and Johnson (1971). Blanchard, Young, Haynes, and Scott (1975) instructed one group of subjects to raise their heart rate by "mental means" whereas a second group of subjects was told to "pay special attention" to their heart rate. Initial and final baseline levels were the same in both experimental and control groups, but the experimental group showed an increase of 6 bpm in the instructional control condition whereas the control group showed no such change.

As a result of these studies it was suggested that an instructional control group represented the appropriate "baseline" from which to assess the effects of informational feedback, and the next group of studies to be considered involves such comparisons. Finley (1971), using uninformed subjects (told to reduce the level of a "physiological" variable which would produce a change in the display), compared the effect of an instructed condition (in which no display of heart rate was available) with the effects of veridical and nonveridical displays of heart rate. The veridical display group showed significantly greater reduction in heart rate when the display was available as compared with when it was not, and greater reduction in the display condition as compared with the group given a nonveridical display. Thus, Finley did not appear to obtain voluntary control of heart rate in the absence of feedback, but of course his subjects were uninformed. The question of awareness in relation to voluntary control is discussed elsewhere in detail in this book, but awareness of the response to be controlled (as opposed to awareness of how control is exercised) may be very important in the absence of feedback. Johnston (1976) fully informed his subjects about the response in his study, and found that the control achieved in the absence of feedback was not enhanced by the addition of feedback information. Similar results were obtained by Levenson (1976) in two studies, one using a repeated-measures design, the other a between-groups design. In the first study, all subjects were required to increase and decrease heart rate in the absence of feedback (instructional control), with visual digital feedback provided on a 7-point scale and with both visual digital and respiratory feedback (where the respiratory feedback was to be used to maintain a steady respiratory rate). In the second study the same procedures were utilized, but different groups were used for the various conditions. In both studies, voluntary control of heart-rate increase and decrease was obtained, with the provision of visual or visual and respiratory feedback failing to improve the degree of voluntary control found in the absence of feedback.

However, other studies comparing the effects of instructional control with feedback control have claimed an effect of feedback over and above the effects of instructions without feedback. Davidson and Schwartz (1976), using a repeated-measures design, instructed their subjects first to increase and decrease heart rate without feedback, and then to perform the same task with auditory feedback. Instructions to raise and lower heart rate without feedback resulted in a rise of 4.53 bpm on average compared with baseline level, and a fall of 1.45 bpm on average compared with baseline level. When feedback was provided, the increase–decrease difference of 5.98 bpm was magnified to 11.39 bpm, indicating enhanced control with feedback. However, the increased difference with feedback was mainly the result of enhanced control of increased heart rate (the suggestion that it is easier to increase heart rate than it is to decrease it is a fairly common finding, probably attributable to the fact that resting level heart rate is close to the physiological lower level attainable in normal subjects). Similarly, Ray (1974) and Ray and Lamb (1974) found that the provision of visual feedback led to larger increases and decreases in heart rate than was the case with instructional control only; that is, feedback primarily affects the magnitude of the changes produced rather than the consistency of the change. Put another way, heart rate can be increased or decreased in the absence of feedback, but the provision of feedback will enable larger magnitude changes to be produced.

In many of the studies thus far considered, the amount of training given was comparatively restricted, even though it is clear that mastery of heart-rate control might prove to be a very difficult task. Stephens, Harris, Brady, and Shaffer (1975), however, conducted a much more prolonged study. Using a repeated-measures design, they trained their subjects over five sessions, each lasting 95 min. In each session, a 15-min baseline period was followed by four 4-min periods and four 8-min periods during which the subject attempted to raise and lower heart rate respectively. Each of the raise and lower periods was separated by a 4-min rest period, and a 4-min postexperimental period concluded the day's training. On the first day, voluntary control of heart rate without feedback was attempted, while on succeeding days various combinations of feedback and reinforcement were provided. The data of interest here relate to the comparison of day 1 (no feedback) with days 2 and 3 on which feedback was provided. On day 1 an average rise of 6.3 bpm (range: -9 to $+29$) and an average decrease of 1.7 bpm (range: -12 to $+3$) were obtained with instructional control only. On day 2, the average rise was 9.5 bpm (range: -10 to $+46$) and the average fall was 2.2 bpm (range: -14 to $+2$); while on day 3, the average rise was 12.3 bpm (range: -1 to $+37$) and the average fall was 3.1 bpm (range: -11 to $+4$). Substantial individual differences in ability to raise and lower heart rate were found in both the instructional and feedback conditions, although within-subject consistency was high from day to day. Thus, the provision of feedback does appear to aid the subject in increasing control over heart-rate increases and decreases. It should be pointed out, however, that the use of a repeated-measures design makes it impossible to determine whether the increases achieved with the addition of feedback might not have been equally readily achieved had the instructional control condition merely been continued. To control for this possibility, independent control groups are required (this difficulty will be seen to apply to some important studies still to be considered). The relatively large-magnitude changes obtained by Stephens *et al.* (1975) were also found in a repeated-measures study by Wells (1973), who also exposed his subjects to prolonged training under instructional and feedback control conditions and found large-magnitude changes for six of his nine subjects in respect of heart-rate increases (but not decreases).

The remaining studies relevant to the question of the instructional control of heart rate represent the most sophisticated investigations so far carried out. Foremost among these, perhaps, are those by Lang and his colleagues. The basic procedures used by Lang have already been described in detail and need only be summarized here. Following two 45-min habituation sessions (essentially baseline periods), four speeding and slowing training sessions were given. These consisted of a 3-min baseline period, a 1-min instructional control period, a 3-min feedback period, a 1-min instructional control period (to measure transfer effects), a 1-min baseline period (called a "time-out" period), and a final 3-min baseline period. The feedback, transfer, and time-out periods were presented five times in succession before the final baseline period. The data of interest here relate to the two instructional control periods compared with the feedback period. In the first study, by Lang and Twentyman (1974), no difference was found between the initial baseline level of heart rate and the levels achieved during the initial instructional control period. The results for the second instructional control period are complicated by the differential exposure of one group of subjects to a binary feedback condition and the other to analog feedback. Maintenance of the voluntary control of speeding and slowing of heart rate with feedback was maintained during the transfer period only for increasing heart rate in the group provided with analog feedback. Similar results were obtained by Gatchel (1974) in respect of transfer, although he did not report the results of the initial instructional control period. In a subsequent study, however, Lang and Twentyman (1976) did obtain a significant degree of voluntary control of heart rate by means of instructional control—but the control mainly applied to increasing heart rate and was manifested most strongly when an incentive in the form of expected monetary reward was available. Transfer trials with instructional control only likewise showed successful maintenance of the control achieved by feedback training for both increase and decrease conditions, and again the role of incentive was significant. More recently, Whitehead, Drescher, Heiman, and Blackwell (1977) have confirmed that control of heart-rate increases and decreases initially obtained without feedback may be extended significantly when feedback is introduced, and this control may be retained for several prolonged sessions when feedback is absent.

The two final studies represent the culmination of all of this work for they introduce the effects of various tasks on heart rate—effects which could be present during attempted control and thus confound the results attributed to voluntary control. The first of these studies, by Lang, Troyer, Twentyman, and Gatchel (1975), was primarily concerned with the voluntary control of heart rate by young and older normal subjects as compared with patients suffering from ischemic heart disease. However, in respect of the young normal subjects, it compared the effects of performing a perceptual-motor tracking task with the effects of instructional and feedback control. Performance of the tracking task (which did not involve muscular effort by the subject) produced only a transitory increase in heart rate, suggesting that the effects of paying attention to a visual display did not *per se* produce significant increases in heart rate. Instructional control led to significant increases in heart-rate speeding, but not slowing, while control acquired under feedback was maintained during the transfer trials. Bell and Schwartz (1975) introduced a "reactivity" condition, designed to investigate the influence on heart rate of various kinds of "mental activity." Following adaptation and baseline periods, the subjects, during a "reactivity" period, were required to recite the alphabet backward and carry out backward subtraction on the one hand, and on the other hand to listen to tones and watch lights. The purpose was to determine whether active mental activity would elicit increased heart rate while passive mental activity would decrease heart rate. Following the reactivity period, the subjects attempted to increase and decrease heart rate in an instructional condition without feedback, to do so with visual feedback, and finally again to exercise instructional control without feedback (transfer situation). Bell and Schwartz (1975) found that the reactivity "up" tasks (mental arithmetic) did indeed produce large average increases of 12 bpm in heart rate, while the reactivity "down" tasks (attending to tones and lights) produced small average decreases of about 1.5 bpm. When these tasks were followed by instructional control, significant increases in heart rate (but smaller than those produced by the reactivity tasks) were produced, but not decreases. In the feedback condition, significant increases and decreases were found with the decreases being greater than those found in the reactivity condition. These increases were maintained in the transfer period.

Thus, a decade of intensive research has demonstrated that instructional control of heart rate without feedback is possible and that control achieved with feedback is maintained in transfer, no-feedback trials. However, the results are complex and difficult to evaluate (especially as the most sophisticated studies have tended to use a repeated-measures design) and the relative contribution of feedback over and above instructional control remains unclear. Furthermore, the demonstration by Bell and Schwartz (1975) of the eliciting capability of "mental activities" represents a potential confounding variable in both instructional and feedback conditions if it is assumed that these conditions are not under the control of the experimenter. (Bell and Schwartz were primarily interested in the possibility that "mental activities" might serve as cognitive mediators for raising and lowering heart rate—this aspect of their work is dealt with elsewhere.) The relatively large changes in heart rate which have been shown to occur whenever "mental activities" occur suggests that the most careful attention to instructional control is necessary and also makes the case for relatively short baseline and training periods to attempt to overcome the possibility that "mental activity" may be engaged in progressively more often as the subject becomes bored with the task.

By comparison with studies in other areas, little attention has so far been paid to the production of heart-rate decreases by more general relaxation techniques as compared with feedback. DeGood and Adams (1976) were primarily concerned with the effects of the acquisition of heart-rate control on subsequent exposure to excessive stimulation. In the first part of their study, however, they compared the effects of biofeedback (a bank of lights representing a range of 10 bpm), progressive muscle-relaxation training, and instructions (no feedback but relaxing music tapes were played) in producing reductions in heart-rate. The relaxation training was not as effective as either feedback or instructional control, but it should be borne in mind that the relaxation training involved both relaxing and tensing and the latter may have offset the relaxing effects to some degree, even though the effects of the training were assessed during periods when muscle activity was minimized.

The question of whether heart-rate variability can be brought under voluntary control has also received some attention. The pioneering study of Hnatiow and Lang (1965) which has already been described in detail indicated that a reduction in variability could be achieved (although their subjects were not informed what function was being investigated, and this was confirmed in subsequent studies by Lang et al. (1967), also described earlier, which demonstrated that knowledge of the function under investigation improved the degree of control obtained, and Sroufe (1969, 1971). A particularly interesting study was carried out subsequently by Hnatiow (1971), who found voluntary control of variability[2] and reported that subjects successfully reducing variability showed significant changes in P–R wave relationships. There appeared a bimodal distribution of the P wave during the display trials which was absent during the nondisplay

[2]Probably for procedural reasons, however, the differences between his experimental and control groups were not significant.

trials (it will be recalled that the P wave represents atrial depolarization, while the R wave represents ventricular depolarization), suggesting that the interval between the P wave and the QRS complex varied systematically in length during the display trials, tending to be either very long or very short. Examples of the bimodality obtained in display trials are shown in Figure 4. While the significance of this finding is unclear, it points up the fact that thus far virtually no attention has been devoted to the detailed analysis of changes in the electrocardiogram during the acquisition and maintenance of control of heart rate and heart-rate variability.

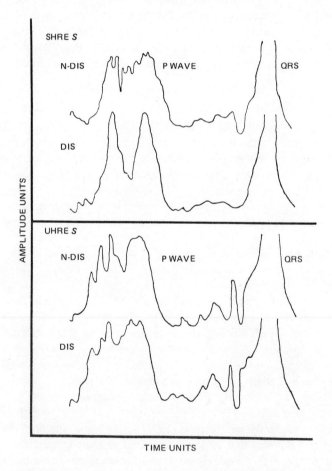

Figure 4. Averaged raw EKG wave forms time-locked to the R wave. (From Hnatiow, M. J. Learned control of heart rate and blood pressure. *Perceptual and Motor Skills*, 1971, *33*, 224, Figure 2. Reprinted by permission of the author and the publisher.)

The methodology of these studies was severely criticized by Harrison and Raskin (1976). They pointed out that subjects in the experimental and control groups had not been given equivalent tasks to perform; that the training periods were very short; that, even so, the initial control apparently achieved seemed to be breaking down toward the end of training; that the rest periods between training trials could produce abnormally high variances in heart rate as a result of the subjects' stretching and altering respiration; and that heart-rate levels did not remain constant over the training periods (the drift phenomenon). In their own study, they allocated 30 subjects (matched for resting levels of heart-rate variability) to one of three groups receiving contingent, noncontingent, or no feedback. Three 64-min training sessions were given on consecutive days, a 15-light display being used to provide feedback. The center light of the display corresponded to the subjects' mean heart rate (reset every minute on the basis of performance during the preceding 3 min) while the six lights immediately to the left indicated the number of beats the heart rate fell below the mean, and the six to the right correspondingly indicated the number of beats the heart rate rose above the mean. The two end lights indicated that the display range had been exceeded. The noncontingent subjects received the same feedback protocol as the matched contingent subjects. Both the contingent and noncontingent feedback groups showed a significant drop in variability of heart rate in the early stages of training compared with the control group (but did not differ from each other), followed by a gradual return to baseline. Thus, veridical feedback was not necessary to reduce variability, nor was the reduced variability maintained. Harrison and Raskin had suggested in reviewing the earlier studies that performance of a tracking-like task might itself result in reduced heart-rate variability, and their own results appear to support the conjecture. In this study, at least twice the amount of training was provided as compared with that given in previous studies, so their conclusion that voluntary control of heart-rate variability has not yet been convincingly demonstrated is one which is difficult to dispute. This conclusion also receives some support from an earlier study by McFarland and Coombs (1974), using a very different procedure. They first provided their subjects with auditory clicks through headphones with the click rate set at approximately the baseline heart rate of the individual subject, whose task was to try to synchronize his heart rate with the click rate in such a way that an individual heartbeat immediately followed the click. In a subsequent augmented feedback condition, the subjects both heard the clicks and received visual feedback via an oscilloscope display which informed them whether or not they had emitted a heartbeat within 200 msec of the click and thus succeeded in their task. The subjects were neither required nor requested to raise or lower their heart rate and the experiment could be regarded as training the subjects to reduce the variability of heart rate so as to match the click rate as closely as possible, with or without augmented visual feedback. It was found that the subjects were able to place significantly more heartbeats within 200 msec of the clicks in both the augmented and nonaugmented feedback conditions as compared with the matching that occurred during rest periods, but that there was no difference in success rate as between the augmented and nonaugmented conditions.

Thus, as with heart-rate control, the studies of heart-rate variability control have not yet convincingly demonstrated that augmented feedback is necessary to bring heart-rate variability under control. McFarland and Coombs (1974) attributed the success of their subjects to an ability to discriminate internal feedback processes without, as well as with, augmented external feedback, but as we shall see, it is doubtful whether this interpretation of their results can be sustained.

A good deal of attention has been given to the feedback display which the subject attempts to utilize to control his heart rate, with interesting results. Blanchard, Scott, Young, and Haynes (1974) examined the effects of providing proportional or binary visual feedback in a crossover design involving switching from proportional to binary feedback (or vice versa) after completion of the initial training. When proportional feedback was available, a pointer was deflected on a scale proportionally to increases (or decreases) in the subject's heart rate, the task being to move the pointer to a target line. When binary feedback was available, a red light came on whenever the criterion level was reached or exceeded.[3] The results indicated that when heart rate was to be raised, proportional feedback was more helpful than binary feedback, whereas when heart rate was to be lowered, neither proportional nor binary feedback was superior to performance in the absence of feedback. Gatchel (1974), using the same oscilloscope type of visual display as Lang and Twentyman (1974), assigned subjects to conditions involving feedback after every single heartbeat (that is, the R–R interval) or after every 5th or 10th heartbeat, and compared the performance of these groups in increasing and decreasing heart rate. The results of this study are shown in Figure 5 and indicate clearly that control is better when more frequent feedback is given, with the results being significant for speeding, but not for slowing, heart rate. A rather similar study, using various types of visual feedback, was carried out by Manuck, Levenson, Hinrichsen, and Gryll (1975), who allocated subjects to a binary feedback condition (in which a light signaled whenever the interbeat interval changed in the instructed direction), a "real-time" proportional feedback condition (in which information about the relative duration of successive interbeat intervals was provided by a bank of 16 lights), and a numerical proportional feedback condition (in which each successive interbeat interval was represented by a number from 2 to 8). Although significant increases and decreases in heart rate were obtained (as compared with a no-feedback baseline condition), no differences were found between the various feedback conditions. In this study, of course, there was confounding within the feedback conditions since both lights and numbers were used to provide proportional feedback. The study also had other defects of which the authors were well aware.

---

[3] A better form of binary feedback would have used the same display, with the pointer moving to the criterion line in a single sweep whenever the criterion rate was achieved.

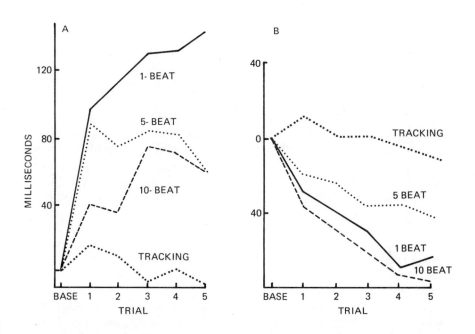

Figure 5. Changes in average median interpulse interval length over feedback trials for the tracking group and three feedback groups. **A.** Speeding Session 2. **B.** Slowing Sessions 1 and 2 combined. (From Gatchel, R. J. Frequency of feedback and learned heart rate control. *Journal of Experimental Psychology*, 1974, *103*, 278–279, Figures 2, 4. Copyright by the American Psychological Association. Reprinted by permission of the author and the publisher.)

The effect of different kinds of auditory feedback has also been investigated in relation to the control of heart rate: Brener *et al.* (1969), in the second part of a study previously mentioned, used binary feedback, a high and low tone corresponding to increased and decreased heart rate being presented whenever a set criterion (the high or low modal value of the basal interbeat interval distribution) was achieved. The feedback was presented either on all trials, half the trials, or none of the trials during training, and the relative efficacy of the differing levels of feedback was assessed on interspersed test trials. The degree of voluntary control achieved was found to be a direct function of the percentage of feedback trials during training, as assessed by the mean intermedian interbeat interval differences between increase and decrease heart rate test trials, with the differences being particularly striking by the end of the second session. Further statistical tests, however, showed that the 100% feedback condition was not significantly different from the 50% condition, while the latter was not significantly different from the 0% condition, although these differences would probably have become significant had training continued further. Young and Blanchard (1974) compared five kinds of auditory feedback: continuously available proportional auditory feedback; similar feedback which, however, became available only after a specified criterion was achieved; binary feedback in which a tone of constant pitch was available whenever the criterion was achieved; the subject's own heartbeat; and a control no-feedback condition. The proportional auditory feedback was a change in frequency of 5 Hz for every 1-bpm change in the heart rate, whereas the binary feedback was a 1000-Hz tone. All forms of feedback were equally helpful in raising heart rate (and superior to the no-feedback condition), but none of them was superior to the control condition in lowering heart rate.

The remaining studies of the effects of type of feedback on heart-rate control either compare across the auditory and visual or other modalities or represent special investigations. Blanchard and Young (1972) ran their subjects under visual or auditory proportional feedback in the first session; in a second session 1 week later, half the subjects in each group received the same type of feedback while the other half switched to the other feedback (i.e., visual to auditory, or vice versa). Visual and auditory feedback were found to be equally efficacious in raising heart rate and, not unexpectedly, a change to the alternative feedback a week later did not interfere with control. However, as in studies mentioned earlier, the feedback was helpful only in raising heart rate, not in lowering it. Lang and Twentyman (1974), in a study aiming to compare proportional and binary feedback, provided either visual feedback in their customary form (a line sweeping across the face of an oscilloscope toward a target line on each heartbeat) or binary feedback. However, the latter consisted of the word *good* appearing on the oscilloscope whenever the target line was exceeded (heart-rate slowing) or fallen short of (heart-rate speeding). These two conditions are not directly comparable,[4] even though in the proportional feedback condition the word *good* was additionally provided whenever the criterion set was achieved. Once again, however, analog feedback was found to be superior to binary for speeding, but not for slowing, heart rate. Stephens *et al.* (1975), using a repeated-measures design and no control groups, after assessing the ability of their subjects to raise and lower heart rate without feedback on the first day, provided both visual and auditory proportional feedback on the second day, while on the third day binary feedback was added to the proportional. However, as this study was primarily concerned with the relationship of other variables to heart-rate performance, it is impossible to tease out the relative effects of the proportional and binary feedback, within or across modalities. Finally, Headrick *et al.* (1971) compared the effects on increasing and decreasing heart rate of providing proportional auditory feedback which changed in the same or opposite direction as the heart-rate change. It might well be that a tone which rose in pitch as the subject decreased heart rate would prove confusing as compared with a tone which changed in the same direction. However, in this situation at least, the

[4]See Chapter 2 for a detailed analysis of the meaning of analog (proportional) and binary feedback, with particular reference to this study.

direction of the feedback made no difference to the degree of success attained in raising or lowering heart rate.

On the whole, these studies appear to show that proportional feedback is superior to binary feedback when the task involves raising heart rate but not when the task is to lower it. There does not appear to be any advantage to either mode (visual or auditory) of feedback.

A large number of studies has been carried out in attempts to determine what might be the variables which mediate heart-rate control (thereby, of course, abandoning the fiction of heart rate as a pure operant). The role of muscle tension has received much attention, as have autonomic awareness, mental activity, and affective states. Consideration of these matters will, however, be postponed until later (see Chapter 7).

Voluntary Control of Blood Pressure

Ventricular contraction ejects blood into the arteries during systole (the period during which the contraction persists). After initial rapid ejection, the pressure wave falls off as the contraction of the ventricle diminishes (diastole). The arteries expand during the systole to accommodate the fact that only about one-third of the blood ejected from the ventricle leaves the arteries during systole. The maximum pressure determining this expansion is termed the systolic blood pressure (SBP). As the ventricular contraction ends, the arterial walls recoil, driving the remaining blood along. The lowest pressure reached during this recoil is termed the diastolic blood pressure (DBP). The arterial pressure does not fall to zero because the next ventricular contraction pumps more blood into the arteries before such an event can occur. In measuring blood pressure, the results are usually reported as millimeters of mercury (mm Hg) with the SBP being given first (e.g., 125/70 means that SBP was recorded as 125 mm Hg and DBP as 70 mm Hg). Pulse pressure is represented as the difference between SBP and DBP, being, of course, 55 in the above example. Since the diastolic period usually lasts longer than the systolic period, and since arterial pressure is varying continuously during the cardiac cycle, mean arterial pressure (MAP) is not simply the average of SBP and DBP but may be represented reasonably accurately by the formula

$$MAP = DBP + \tfrac{1}{3} \text{ pulse pressure}$$

In the above example, therefore, MAP would be 87 mm Hg. Arterial pressure (whether measured as systolic, diastolic, or mean pressure) is determined by a wide range of factors, including heart rate, force of ventricular contraction, distensibility of the artery walls, and so on. For example, if ventricular contraction is strong, SBP will be elevated because a greater volume of blood will be pumped into the arteries during the systole, stretching the walls of the arteries more. On the other hand, a decrease in heart rate will produce a lower DBP because more blood can be evacuated from the arteries into the arterioles before the next ventricular contraction occurs. Disease of the arteries can affect their distensibility, producing changes in pressure due to their reduced flexibility.

In order to obtain a direct measure of arterial blood pressure, it is necessary to make intraarterial recordings by means of which the moment-to-moment fluctuations in SBP and DBP may be determined. However, this technique is not normally used even by physicians for either clinical or research purposes, and hence indirect measurements must be relied on. The standard clinical technique makes use of the sphygmomanometer. This involves inflating a hollow cuff (wrapped around the upper arm) with air to a pressure which is greater than SBP. As a result, the arteries under the cuff are collapsed and the passage of blood through them prevented. To determine SBP and DBP, a phenomenon known as the Korotkoff sound (detected through a stethoscope or microphone placed over the brachial artery below the cuff) is utilized. With the artery occluded, no sound is heard as no blood is flowing. As pressure is released in the cuff and falls just below SBP, the arterial blood pressure at the peak of systole is greater than the cuff pressure, causing the artery to expand and blood to flow. The high-velocity blood flow which results causes turbulence in the artery and a soft, intermittent tapping sound is heard which changes to a loud sound as pressure is lowered further. At DBP level, the K sound becomes muffled and disappears altogether as pressure in the cuff drops below DBP and there is no impediment to blood flow through the artery. Thus, SBP and DBP may be defined as the cuff pressures at which the K sound appears and disappears, respectively.

Intraarterial recordings have shown clearly that both SBP and DBP vary significantly (and independently, to some degree) over very short periods of time, of the order of 50 successive heartbeats, and this variability itself varies widely from individual to individual. Variations of the order of 10–34 mm Hg have been recorded in SBP and DBP over a period of only a few seconds. But this variability means that the occlusion method described above is not suitable to serious research purposes because that method, as normally applied, results in a single reading of SBP and DBP. Such a reading may not be representative of the MAP, nor indeed of SBP or DBP. Furthermore, as Tursky, Shapiro, and Schwartz (1972) have pointed out, the method introduces constant errors into the determination of SBP and DBP. Consequently, a good deal of effort has been expended in recent years in attempts to devise recording techniques which would enable continuous recording of blood pressure, preferably on a beat-to-beat basis, which would also overcome the major difficulty produced by repeated complete occlusion of the artery, namely, congestion in the return of the venous blood to the heart, resulting in a discomfort for the patient and the consequent requirement that blood pressure readings be taken only over very short periods of time.

Tursky *et al.* (1972) developed the automated constant-cuff-pressure system in a successful attempt to overcome these difficulties. The technique makes use of the presence or absence of the K sound, but obviates prolonged occlusion of the artery and hence enables continuous monitoring of blood pressure for longer periods of time than are usually possible without producing discomfort in the subject. The cuff is inflated above SBP but pressure is then immediately reduced until the first K sound is detected. The applied pressure is then adjusted so that K sounds occur on 50% of the heartbeats in a specified heart cycle (usually set at 50 heartbeats). Tursky *et al.* (1972) were able to show empirically that a 2-mm Hg increase in cuff pressure at the median systolic level reduced the average percentage of K sounds from 59 to 29, while a decrease of 2 mm Hg in cuff pressure increased the average percentage of K sounds to 76. A similar procedure may be followed in respect of DBP. In this case, the cuff is deflated until the K sound characteristic of DBP is detected and the pressure is held at this level for the duration of the heart cycle. The median DBP is defined as the pressure at which the criterion diastolic sound is heard on 50% of the heartbeats of the cycle; similarly, the median SBP is defined as the pressure at which the criterion systolic sound is heard on 50% of the heartbeats of the cycle. The same relationship between change in percentage of the criterion sound up or down and change in blood pressure was found for DBP as for SBP.

The validity of this technique as a measure of SBP and DBP was demonstrated by Tursky *et al.* (1972) by comparing results obtained using the method with results obtained using intraarterial recordings. Figure 6 shows the very close correspondence in results, even though different subjects were used with each technique. In a minor variation of this technique, Brener and Kleinman (1970) applied to the left index finger an occluding cuff which was slightly less in circumference than the finger itself, thus allowing venous return more readily. Various other modifications of the technique have been developed which need not be detailed here, as the most recent approach incorporates them into the latest system, developed by Elder, Longacre, Welsh, and McAfee (1977). In their system, the subject is fitted with a cuff on each arm. A tracking device detects the upper or lower K sounds, depending on whether SBP or DBP is being monitored, and initiates slow cuff inflation or deflation so as to track the lower or higher pressure threshold. Thus, either baseline pressure or changes occurring as a result of voluntary control may be recorded. An auditory feedback signal is generated to provide information to the subject. The alternating-cuff procedure was originally intended to obviate possible discomfort when measuring SBP, but as the authors point out, the use of a cuff on each arm enables SBP to be recorded from one arm while DBP is simultaneously recorded from the other. With the use of a computer and software programs, the procedures developed by Elder, Longacre, Welsh, and McAfee (1977) could readily be duplicated.

It will be clear that sophistication in the measurement of blood pressure has taken giant strides in recent years, but all of the techniques so far discussed have

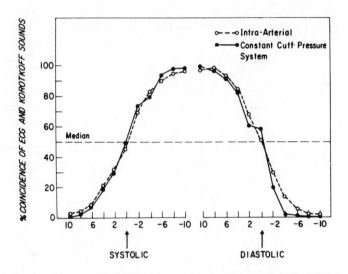

Figure 6. Percent change in R–K coincidence around systolic and diastolic levels for constant cuff-pressure system ($N = 6$) as cuff pressure is reduced in 2-mm Hg steps from above systolic to below diastolic pressure. This function is compared to data from intra-arterial records ($N = 5$) treated in a similar manner. (From Tursky, B., Shapiro, D., & Schwartz, G. E. Automated constant cuff-pressure system to measure average systolic and diastolic blood pressure in man. *IEEE Transactions on Biomedical Engineering*, 1971, *19*, 273, Figure 3. Reprinted by permission of the author and the publisher.)

been unable to avoid the need to reduce blood flow in the arteries with all its possible, and sometimes actual, disadvantages.[5] A new approach which obviates the need for a cuff altogether has recently been described by Jernsted and Newcomer (1974) and by Steptoe, Smulyan, and Gribbin (1976). The technique measures the transit time (TT) between the occurrence of an R wave and the arrival of the resulting pressure wave along the artery at a site where the pulse may be detected. Pulse wave velocity (PWV), of which TT is the inverse (i.e., the higher the velocity, the shorter the TT), is preferred over measurement of the TT between successive pulses detected at two points on the one artery because of the difficulty of monitoring the pulse-to-pulse interval. Some contamination may be caused by the failure of the technique to allow for the delay caused by intracardiac events, but this is not likely to be a serious matter when blood pressure is being monitored in the resting subject. Steptoe *et al.* (1976) compared TTs obtained in this manner with MAPs obtained by arterial cannulation in a group of subjects under a variety of conditions expected to produce variations in blood pressure (Valsalva's maneuver, mental arithmetic, isometric muscle contraction) and very high correlations (negative, of course) were found, of the order of -0.90 or greater when group comparisons were made between the various

[5]These disadvantages have been clearly detailed by Gribbin, Steptoe, and Sleight (1976).

conditions. Intraindividual correlations were even higher when values obtained were grouped over conditions. Heart rate, on the other hand, was not found to influence TT. The advantages of the pulse wave velocity technique are that it is relatively simple to use and is completely noninvasive. Instrumentation is not complex, although computer-controlled detection of the R wave and the pulse wave (enabling the TT to be calculated) is a great advantage.[6]

The feedback displays used in blood pressure studies have to a degree reflected the technical difficulties involved in detecting arterial pressure on a beat-to-beat basis since unless the detection problem is solved, the feedback display necessarily must be less than continuous. D. Shapiro, Tursky, Gershon, and Stern (1969) provided a 100-msec flash of red light and a simultaneous 100-msec tone of moderate intensity on a beat-to-beat basis each time pressure was raised or lowered in the approporiate direction, but confounded this informational feedback by presenting a reinforcer (a slide of a nude figure in the early studies plus additional reinforcing pictures in later studies) for 5 sec after a specified number of light flashes. Elder, Leftwich, and Wilkerson (1974) varied the stimulus feedback somewhat, although their description of their procedure is unclear:

> Stimulus feedback consisted on presenting the green indicator light whenever a minimum change of at least 5 mm Hg in S's blood pressure was observed and flashing the red light whenever S's pressure showed no change or S either failed to display an increase or a decrease, respectively. (p. 173)

Brener and Kleinman (1970) presented two types of feedback simultaneously: the reading on a manometer gauge, and a digital reading on an electromagnetic counter. Thus, the feedback displays have included binary (lights or tones on or off) and proportional (visual digital and scale readings) information. Blanchard, Young, Haynes, and Kallman (1974) photographed and displayed a graph on which the blood pressure was entered by hand by the experimenter every 1 min (proportional discontinuous). Steptoe and Johnston (1976a) adapted the display technique used by Lang and his colleagues for the display of heart rate with the addition of stars (representing reinforcement amount) which were progressively eliminated as reinforcement was earned.

The methodology of blood pressure biofeedback studies has followed that of heart-rate studies fairly closely. The procedures used by Fey and Lindholm (1975) will serve as an illustration. A 10-min adaptation period was followed by detection of the cuff pressure at which the first systolic K sound was detected. Several trials were than given to determine baseline SBP level, defined as the cuff pressure at which K sounds occurred coincident with 40–60% of a 50-heartbeat trial period. Each succeeding training session was made up of 25 trials, each trial consisting of 50 heartbeats duration. Prior to each trial, a short period (about 5 sec) must be allowed for cuff inflation and stabilization, and an intertrial

---

[6]Steptoe et al. (1976) report difficulties in real-time computer control, but it should be possible to overcome these.

interval of ½–1 min must be allowed for blood pressure to return to normal and to prevent venous congestion. Transfer trials may be used in which the subject is requested to continue to try to raise (or lower) his blood pressure (as opposed to resting and not trying) and a shaping procedure is commonly used in which the task is made progressively more difficult if the subject succeeds in raising or lowering blood pressure during the preceding training trial. Of course, some of the above requirements will be modified as a result of the more sophisticated instrumentation described earlier. The drift effect has been shown to be an important contaminating variable in blood pressure control and the use of pretrial rest scores (rather than initial baseline) as the point from which to measure degree of control exercised is becoming common. The use of appropriate control groups (rather than merely a repeated-measures within-group design) has been recognized as being important. The simultaneous measurement of DBP and SBP is relatively uncommon although it has been undertaken. As with heart rate, many of the early studies did not fully inform the subjects about the response being studied but rather simply informed them to keep the tone or the light from coming on or going off, although subjects have been fully informed in most of the recent studies.

In the early studies, as with heart rate, the subjects tended to be uninformed about the control to be achieved and there was a failure to exercise proper control over confounding variables, while the degree of which instructional control without feedback was possible was neglected. Later work has largely been directed toward correcting these deficiencies. It should be noted carefully that where subjects are fully informed, they are almost always instructed to control their "blood pressure"—only recently have studies appeared in which instructions to control systolic or diastolic blood pressure have been given specifically (e.g., Surwit, Hager, & Feldman, 1977). Presumably, this is because it is assumed that it would be extraordinarily difficult, if not impossible, to discriminate systolic from diastolic pressure. The dependent variable most often reported is SBP, although, as will be seen, there are important exceptions.

The earliest study on control of blood pressure demonstrated most of the major points which have made interpretation of results in this area difficult. D. Shapiro et al. (1969) used a between-groups design with uninformed subjects told only that the experiment was concerned with the ability of individuals to control certain physiological responses and that such control could often be achieved when information was provided about their own responses. It may seem unlikely that subjects having their blood pressure recorded would not be aware of the fact, but it should be remembered that heart rate and respiration rate were being recorded as well as blood pressure, and the subjects reported afterward that they were not aware which bodily function was related to the feedback and reinforcement. Feedback consisted of a 100-msec red light flash and tone provided on a beat-by-beat basis, while reinforcement consisted of a slide of a nude presented for 5 sec after every 20 flashes. Half of the subjects were provided with feedback and reinforcement for raising SBP and half for decreasing SBP. Only one session of training was given, consisting of 25 65-sec trials. Baseline and transfer trials were not given and no control group for possible drift effects was used. The results are shown in Figure 7. As is clear from the graph, the decrease group showed a significant drop in SBP whereas the increase group showed a small initial rise, followed by a return to starting level. These results are understandable if a downward drift in SBP is present, exaggerating the decrease effect and masking any increase effect. D. Shapiro, Tursky, and Schwartz (1970a) replicated and extended these results. A control group provided with random feedback and reinforcement was used in addition to the increase/decrease groups of the earlier experiment, and a wider range of reinforcement slides was employed. A second session was added in which all subjects were given feedback and reinforcement for decreasing SBP. In the first session, the results for the increase/decrease groups were replicated, but neither group was significantly differentiated from the control group. In the second session, the decrease group showed a further sharp drop in SBP while the control group continued the gradual drift downward manifested in the first session and the increase group also showed a decline. In neither of these studies was there any evidence of a relationship between changes in SBP and heart rate or respiration rate.

Encouraged by these results, D. Shapiro, Schwartz, and Tursky (1972) investigated the effect of feedback and reinforcement on DBP. Again, a single training session was used with a between-groups design. At the end of training, transfer of control was assessed in half of the subjects in each of the increase and decrease groups by instructing them to continue to maintain control in the absence of feedback and reinforcement, while the remainder were put on an extinction schedule, being instructed to rest quietly. This time the results were in the opposite direction to those obtained with SBP, since increases in DBP during the

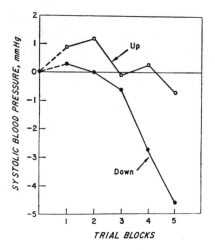

Figure 7. Average approximate systolic pressures in groups reinforced for increasing *(up)* and decreasing *(down)* blood pressure. (From Shapiro, D., Tursky, B., Gershon, E., & Stern, M. Effects of feedback and reinforcement on the control of human systolic blood pressure. *Science,* 1969, *163,* 589, Figure 2. Reprinted by permission of the author and the publisher.)

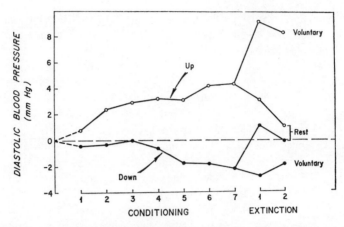

Figure 8. Average diastolic blood pressure in groups reinforced for increasing *(up)* and decreasing *(down)* diastolic blood pressure. (From Shapiro, D., Schwartz, G. E., & Tursky, B. Control of diastolic blood pressure in man by feedback and reinforcement. *Psychophysiology,* 1972, *9,* 301, Figure 1. Reprinted by permission of the author and the publisher.)

training period were more readily obtained than decreases, as is clear from Figure 8. A transfer effect is apparent as compared with the effect of rest during the posttraining period.

In all three of these studies, feedback and reinforcement were confounded and appropriate control groups not used (except in the third study). Brener and Kleinman (1970) remedied some of these defects in a study dealing only with decrease of SBP recorded from an occluding cuff on the left index finger. Two kinds of feedback were provided simultaneously: readings on a manometer gauge which provided continuous information of absolute SBP values, and digital read-out from an electromagnetic counter operating at a rate directly proportional to cuff pressure. A between-groups design was used with the experimental group fully informed (instructed to decrease blood pressure) and the control group not informed but instructed to pay close attention to the two displays. Two training sessions consisting of 20 trials each of 50 sec duration were given. In the first session the feedback group declined from a starting level of about 135 mm Hg[7] to about 115 mm Hg while the control group fluctuated markedly, but overall neither increased nor decreased. These differences were maintained during the second session but were obscured to some degree by an adaptation (drift) effect. No difference in heart rate was found between the two groups.

Blanchard, Young, Haynes, and Kallmann (1974) carried out two studies with the primary purpose of discovering whether instructional control in the absence of feedback was possible when the subjects were fully informed. In the

[7]These high values do not indicate that the normal subjects used were suffering from hypertension but are a function of recording from the finger rather than the arm.

first study, the subjects were instructed to increase SBP, initially without feedback and then with feedback provided in the form of a graph constructed on a minute-by-minute basis by the experimenter. Four sessions were run, each consisting of adaptation, baseline, trial, rest, and trial periods, with feedback provided during the trial periods only in the final two sessions. Using the baseline/trial (not the rest/trial) differences as the dependent variable, a significant superiority of feedback over instructional control was found. This experiment was a repeated-measures design but the second experiment used a between-groups design involving three groups. One group was given the discontinuous proportional feedback used in the first experiment; the second was provided with discontinuous binary verbal feedback (the subject was told only that his pattern of responding in the previous minute was "correct" or "incorrect," where "correct" indicated a decrease of SBP of at least 5 mm Hg); the third group was merely instructed to decrease blood pressure. The baseline/trials difference measure was again used as the dependent variable. While all three groups showed a significant reduction in SBP over the three training sessions given, the proportional feedback group was more successful in reducing blood pressure than the other two groups, which did not differ from each other.

Fey and Lindholm (1975) extended these results in a study involving four groups. Two of the groups were given visual feedback (a dim light on or off) on a beat-by-beat basis for increasing and decreasing SBP, respectively; a third group was provided with noncontingent (random) feedback following 50% of their heartbeats; while the fourth group (rather inaccurately termed a "no-feedback" condition) was given the same random pattern as the third group, but told to count the number of times the light came on. The first three groups were told that the experiment had to do with control of blood pressure but not instructed about the direction of change required, while the fourth group was told that the experiment was concerned with the relation of blood pressure to vigilance. To some degree the feedback was confounded with reinforcement since differential verbal praise was provided at the end of each trial, depending on performance. The results of this study are shown in Figure 9. Baseline/trial differences were also used as the dependent variable in this study. Once more, the decrease group was able to reduce SBP whereas the increase group (as well as the two control groups) showed a failure to achieve control. The difference between the decrease group and the other groups was significant across but not within sessions. The failure to inform the subjects fully may, of course, have diminished the magnitude of the differences which might otherwise have been obtained.

Surwit et al. (1977) randomly assigned subjects to four conditions. In the experimental condition, feedback (in the form of a light flash) was provided for each heartbeat which was accompanied (increase trials) or not accompanied (decrease trials) by a K sound. The first control group received the same number of feedback signals as the experimental group, but the signals were not informative, being produced by a random generator (although all were programmed to

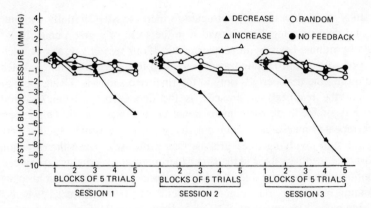

Figure 9. Systolic blood pressure for the four groups expressed as difference scores. (From Fey, S. G., & Lindholm, E. Systolic blood pressure and heart rate changes during three sessions involving biofeedback or no feedback. *Psychophysiology*, 1975, *12*, 515, Figure 1. Reprinted by permission of the author and the publisher.)

occur within ½ sec of a heartbeat). A second control group was treated similarly to the first except that the feedback signal occurred at longer intervals after the heartbeat, while a third control group was required to increase and decrease heart rate without feedback. All subjects were fully informed that the task was to increase/decrease systolic blood pressure. The results indicated that increases, but not decreases, in systolic blood pressure were obtained but no group differences were evident, suggesting that instructions alone were sufficient to produce increases and decreases in systolic blood pressure, even when inaccurate feedback was being presented. However, it should be noted that only a single training session of 20 trials (each trial being 50 heartbeats in length) was used. On the other hand, Elder, Welsh, Longacre, and McAfee (1977) reported that instructions alone did not lead to significant control of blood pressure increases and decreases, even when training was extended over ten sessions.

Studies of the control of arterial pressure changes using the pulse wave velocity technique have recently been reported by Steptoe and Johnston (1976b) and Steptoe (1977). The former involved a repeated-measures design in which the subjects were trained to increase and decrease blood pressure over four alternating sessions, each session consisting of adaptation and baseline periods followed by ten 4-min feedback or transfer trials. The feedback was similar to that used in Lang's studies of heart-rate control, an oscilloscope display involving a target line continuously visible with beat-by-beat information, and a summary display at the end of each trial as well as reinforcement in the form of stars, the progressive removal of which indicated that monetary reward had been earned. Analysis of the results was based both on baseline/trial and pretrial rest/trial difference scores. Steptoe and Johnston (1976b) found that decreases in arterial pressure could be obtained, but not increases, as was the case in many of the earlier studies. The increase trials showed a TT change of $+1.67$ msec (indicating an actual decrease in pressure) whereas the change in the decrease trials was $+7.26$ (that is, a much greater decrease than for the increase trials).[8] On the final feedback trials, the difference in TT was more than 11 msec (approximately equivalent to 11 mm Hg). It was also found that these differences were not apparent within trials—on the contrary, the increase trials showed significant changes in the expected direction, whereas the decrease trials showed no change. Thus, the decrease instructions produced changes from trial to trial but not within trials, whereas the increase instructions produced changes in the correct direction within a trial but this change was not maintained from one trial to the next. These results were based on baseline/trial difference analysis; when the pretrial rest/trial differences were analyzed, the opposite results were obtained. Transfer effects were obtained in the decrease condition, and a decline in control occurred from the first to the second session. The second study (Steptoe, 1977) took up the question of instructional as compared with feedback control and used a between-groups design. Subjects were allocated to groups instructed to increase or decrease arterial pressure with or without feedback. When change scores using baseline/trial differences were analyzed, feedback was superior to instructions alone for the increase groups, but not for the decrease, as shown in Figure 10. However, when pretrial scores were used as the reference level, feedback was superior to instructions for both decrease and increase conditions, indicative once again of properly allowing for the drift effect. Overall, the control achieved was greater for the decrease than for the increase conditions. When feedback was withdrawn, control deteriorated. However, these results were not confirmed by Steptoe and Johnston (1976a), who compared groups instructed to decrease blood pressure with and without visual feedback and found that both groups were equally successful. Johnston (1977) also found instructions without feedback to be as effective as instructions with feedback in the control of changes in digital pulse amplitude.

Only one investigator appears thus far to have measured and analyzed simultaneously both SBP and DBP in studies with normal subjects, although it is a matter of considerable interest whether changes in these two aspects of blood pressure vary together when blood pressure is being trained. Elder *et al.* (1974), using a between-groups design, trained four groups of subjects. Two groups were trained to raise or lower SBP; the other two were trained to raise or lower DBP. Three training sessions were given after a baseline session. The results for the two groups trained to increase or decrease SBP are shown in Figure 11, which shows both the SBP and DBP changes which resulted. Raw scores over the four sessions were analyzed in preference to difference scores. The usual results obtained for the increase and decrease conditions are shown in the top half of

[8]TT and pressure are related inversely.

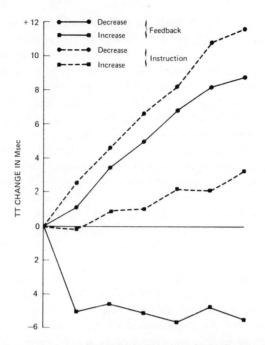

Figure 10. Transit time mean change from the initial baseline: feedback trials. (From Steptoe, A. Blood pressure control with pulse wave velocity feedback: Methods of analysis and training. In J. Beatty & H. Legewie (Eds.), *Biofeedback and Behavior*. New York: Plenum, 1977, p. 360, Figure 5. Reprinted by permission of the author and the publisher.)

Figure 11; the increase group showed an initial increase in session 2 but no change overall, whereas the decrease group showed a steady decline. Both groups showed a steady decline in DBP over the sessions (lower half of Figure 11). The groups trained to increase or decrease DBP showed a different pattern: increases were obtained in DBP in the group trained to increase DBP, but the group trained to decrease DBP showed no change. There were no corresponding changes in SBP in either group. The results for training in DBP control are in agreement with those obtained by D. Shapiro *et al.* (1972), and it is noteworthy that in neither of these studies were the subjects informed that blood pressure was the response to be controlled. It should also be noted that in the Elder *et al.* (1974) study, feedback was presented only every 2 min, contingent on change or no change and taking the form of presentation of a light.

Apart from the investigation of instructions alone without feedback, little has so far been reported relating to other conditions which might produce increases or decreases in blood pressure in the absence of feedback. Tasto and Huebner (1976), however, constituted four groups matched on the basis of baseline levels of DBP and SBP averaged over trials. One group was then given relaxation training while two others served as wait-controls. Following the training, one further relaxation training period was given to the first group; the second was subjected to stress; the third read for an equivalent period. The fourth group was given control reading sessions while the first group trained, then a further reading session. The blood pressure of all four groups was then measured. While stress led to a significant increase in blood pressure, the other three manipulations (including relaxation training) produced no change in blood pressure levels as compared with baseline.

As will be seen when the question of reducing hypertension is considered, these results should not be interpreted as indicating that relaxation training without feedback is incapable of producing decreases in blood pressure. Tasto and Huebner's (1976) study does, however, raise an important methodological point: it may be difficult to obtain significant decreases in blood pressure in nomotensive subjects because there may be a lower level below which blood pressure will not go, irrespective of how relaxed a person becomes. This suggests that the relatively small average decreases in blood pressure obtained in most of the studies discussed above may be somewhat misleading. There appears to be no study of blood pressure control in which a levels design has been used, that is, in which subjects have been grouped according to their baseline levels into high, medium, and low groups. It is quite possible that an interaction effect would be found if a levels design were used. Subjects with high initial levels might well

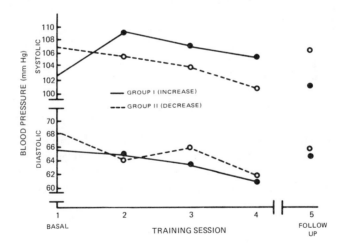

Figure 11. Mean systolic and diastolic blood pressures obtained from groups trained to increase or decrease systolic blood pressure. (From Elder, S. T., Leftwich, D. A., & Wilkerson, L. A. The role of systolic versus diastolic–contingent feedback in blood pressure conditioning. *Psychological Record,* 1974, *24,* 173, Figure 1. Reprinted by permission of the author and the publisher.)

show a greater ability to decrease blood pressure than subjects whose initial levels are low.

Blanchard, Haynes, Kallmann, and Harkey (1976) have reported an unusual control study. All of their subjects were required to lower blood pressure by "mental means." One group was given graphical feedback of changes in SBP, a second group was given frontalis EMG feedback, and a third group was given no feedback (instructional control). In the first training session, the SBP-feedback group produced a lower level of SBP than did the EMG-feedback group; however, the difference disappeared during the subsequent three training sessions, in the course of which both groups decreased their SBP further, while over all sessions the instructional control group showed no change. The comparison of the two feedback groups, however, was not really valid, since the SBP-feedback group received feedback information only every 1 min, while the EMG-feedback group received continuous auditory feedback.

Several conclusions may be drawn from the work so far reported on control of blood pressure. There is good agreement that decreases in SBP are more readily obtainable than increases, although the results are contaminated by a failure to take account of the drift effect and to block subjects by baseline levels. On the other hand, there is some, but not much, evidence that increases in DBP are more readily obtainable than decreases. Both of these conclusions make sense. The role of feedback by comparison with instructional control remains unclear, and a high proportion of the studies involve confounding of reinforcement with feedback. The importance of the baseline from which difference scores are taken remains unresolved although baseline/trial difference scores tend to produce a different result from pretrial/trial difference scores. Thus, it may be concluded that much more, and more carefully controlled, work still needs to be done before the extent to which voluntary control of blood pressure is possible, with or without the aid of feedback, is resolved.

Voluntary Control of Heart Rate and Blood Pressure

If the evidence reviewed above does indeed indicate that voluntary control of heart rate and blood pressure is possible, then three related questions arise. First, is it possible to raise and lower heart rate independently of changes in blood pressure, and vice versa? Second, is it possible to raise or lower blood pressure and heart rate simultaneously, that is, to produce an integrated response? Third, is it possible to raise heart rate while simultaneously lowering blood pressure, and vice versa? The first of these questions has been touched on throughout the previous discussion—here it is only necessary to refer to a study by D. Shapiro, Tursky, and Schwartz (1970b) which was specifically directed toward answering it. The results were positive, with heart-rate increases and decreases being obtained while SBP remained constant (the results for heart-rate increases are, however, subject to the usual qualifications). Two other studies are of considerably greater significance. Schwartz, Shapiro, and Tursky (1971) provided light and tone feedback to one group of subjects whenever they produced a simultaneous elevation of blood pressure and heart rate, while a second group was similarly treated for decreases in blood pressure and heart rate. The subjects were not specifically informed and the usual confounding with reinforcement occurred. Only a single training session was given, consisting of adaptation trials followed by 40 training trials, each 50 heartbeats in duration, with rest periods of 20–30 sec between each trial. While the superiority of decrease training was again evident, the results supported the hypothesis that integrated control of blood pressure and heart rate is possible. An average rise of 1 bpm in heart rate and 2 mm Hg in SBP was obtained in the up–up group, compared with an average fall of 6 bpm in heart rate and 5 mm Hg in SBP in the down–down group. These results were replicated in a study by Schwartz (1972) in which he additionally attempted to train a third group to raise heart rate while simultaneously lowering blood pressure and a fourth group to do the reverse. The results of this study are shown in Figure 12. The attempt to differentiate heart rate and blood pressure was not as successful as the attempt to integrate them, and appears to have retarded the successful control of both functions compared with their integration. Once again, integrated deceleration of SBP and HR was accomplished more successfully than integrated acceleration (Figure 12A). In view of the potential importance of these results, it is strange that no attempt to replicate them with the available improvements in methodology appears to have been made.

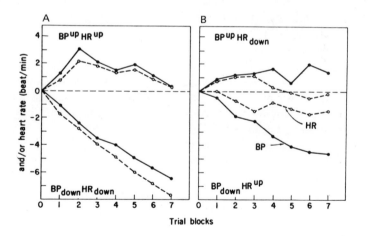

Figure 12. A. Average heart rate (HR) and systolic blood pressure (BP) in groups trained to raise and lower HR and BP simultaneously; **B.** In groups trained to raise HR and lower BP (or the reverse) simultaneously. (From Schwartz, G. E. Voluntary control of human cardiovascular integration and differentiation through feedback and reward. *Science,* 1972, *175,* 92, Figure 2. Reprinted by permission of the author and the publisher.)

One final point needs to be made with respect to the studies of the voluntary control of blood pressure and its integration with and differentiation from heart rate. Comparative studies of the helpfulness of different kinds of feedback are lacking in this area, and as has been pointed out, the relative importance of feedback and reinforcement has not really been investigated at all, the two variables usually being confounded. Methodological sophistication in this area has been at once considerable and weak. Until all aspects of methodology in this area are brought to the same high level as obtains with some, the results will continue to be unclear and puzzling.

Voluntary Control of Electrodermal Responding

Studies of the so-called galvanic skin reflex (GSR) stretch back to the beginnings of experimental psychology. Compared with the measurement and analysis of most other directly recordable behavior, quite extraordinary methodological and measurement problems have been experienced in this area, which has nevertheless maintained its popularity with research workers, in part at least because of the presumed relationship between electrodermal activity and emotional changes, enshrined, for example, in the misnamed "lie detector." It is a striking fact, however, that although electrodermal responding was one of the first areas in which attempts were made to show that instrumental conditioning of an autonomically mediated response was possible, resistance seems to have continued to the notion that voluntary control may be possible so that scarcely any studies exist as yet which could properly be called biofeedback experiments in the sense that subjects are specifically instructed to increase or decrease electrodermal responding, whether the study is carried out within a feedback or reinforcement framework.

In order to understand the work which has been carried out in this area, it is necessary to provide a brief account of basic concepts. The account given here will be kept to a bare minimum and the reader interested in carrying out research in this area will find it essential to consult the many detailed accounts available of methodology and procedures.[9]

The term "galvanic skin reflex" (GSR) and its equivalent, "psychogalvanic reflex" (PGR), have been replaced in recent years by the more general and more accurate term "electrodermal response" (EDR). Although still a matter of controversy, it may be accepted as a working hypothesis that electrodermal activity reflects changes occurring as a result of excitation of the eccrine sweat glands located in the subdermis (secretory portion) and dermis (excretory portion) of the various layers of the skin. Superimposed on a fluctuating resting level of activity, specific responses may occur as a result of external or internal stimulation. Psychological interest has mostly centered on sudden decreases in

[9]Of particular value are the short papers by Fowles (1974) and Grings (1974).

resistance to the passage of an electric current because these decreases are believed to be particularly associated with the occurrence of changes in emotional state.

These changes (as well as the steady state) have been measured in two main ways. Skin potential level (SPL) and response (SPR) may be measured as the voltage (expressed as milliamps) recorded between two electrodes placed at different points on a skin location (often the palm of the hand) where sudorific activity is normally present. If a very small constant current (varying, in the studies to be considered below, from about 20 μA to about 70 μA) is passed between the electrodes, the electrodermal activity is measured in terms of the resistance occurring in the steady rate or the change in resistance which occurs either spontaneously or to an internal or external stimulus. The measurement is usually expressed as the skin resistance level (SRL) and response (SRR) in ohms.[10] Skin potential is usually referred to as an endodermal phenomenon, whereas skin resistance (conductance, impedance) is referred to as an exodermal phenomenon. The great majority of studies of electrodermal reactivity utilize changes in resistance (SRL and SRR) as the dependent variable, although important investigations of potential (SPL and SPR) have been carried out.

The methodology of research into electrodermal phenomena within an operant framework may be illustrated by reference to one of the earliest studies to investigate the instrumental control of such responding. Fowler and Kimmel (1962) measured changes in skin resistance by passing a 40 μA dc current between electrodes placed on the palm and back of the subject's right hand. A criterion skin resistance response (SRR) was defined as one the magnitude of which was equal to or less than half of the average magnitude of the responses emitted by the same subject during a baseline period of measurement. The "reinforcement" for such responses was the presentation of a light stimulus of 1-sec duration, and the dependent variable was the number of criterion responses emitted by a group so reinforced as compared with a group given an equal number of reinforcements at times when a criterion SRR was not being emitted. Because a light stimulus, especially in the early stages of training, is capable of eliciting an SRR, a 5-sec "dead" period was defined immediately following the light stimulus during which any criterion SRRs were ignored. The subjects were uninformed, being told only to relax and refrain from abrupt movements and deep or uneven breathing, but to remain alert and attentive. Because measures of skin resistance are usually skewed, the frequency scores were transformed to generate a percentage score. The results are shown in Figure 13. In interpreting the figure, it should be remembered that a *decrease* in percentage of criterion scores indicates an *increase* in resistance, and vice versa. Thus, these results

---

[10]Skin conductance level (SCL) and response (SCR) are the reciprocal of SRL and SRR respectively expressed in microhms. In both cases, dc current is used; if ac current is used, the appropriate measures are of skin impedance level (SZL) and response (SZR) expressed in ohms.

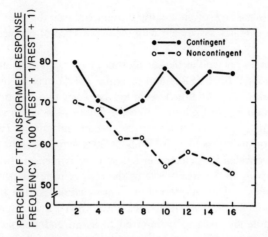

Figure 13. Percentage of transformed response frequencies during 16 min of reinforcement. (From Fowler, R. L., & Kimmel, H. D. Operant conditioning of the GSR. *Journal of Experimental Psychology,* 1962, *63,* 575, Figure 1. Copyright 1962 by the American Psychological Association. Reprinted by permission of the author and the publisher.)

indicated that there was no change in resistance in the reinforced group while the group reinforced at times when a criterion response was not being emitted showed a gradual increase in resistance, the difference between the two groups being significant in the later stages of training. While such a result has usually been interpreted as indicating that instrumental conditioning serves to retard the appearance of the adaptation effect (Gavalas, 1967), two points should be noted: first, the drift effect, of which these results are yet another example, could be masking a genuine increase in response frequency; and second, the "adaptation" effect apparent in Figure 13 for the control group might actually represent true instrumental control over and above the drift effect, since the light was in effect presented as a reinforcer for not increasing responding and hence on occasion would have been presented when a decreased response frequency was being manifested.

As pointed out earlier, only a few of the subsequent studies have involved instructing the subjects to increase or decrease response frequency (that is, the subjects have mostly been uninformed). It is not intended here to provide a comprehensive review of the literature on the instrumental control of the electrodermal response with uninformed subjects, but some knowledge of the main findings of subsequent research is essential to provide a framework for discussion of the biofeedback studies. A brief account will therefore be given of subsequent research and the principal results.

The initial results obtained by Fowler and Kimmel (1962) have been replicated on several occasions, not only for SRR (e.g., E. Kimmel & Kimmel, 1963;

H. D. Kimmel & Hill, 1960), but also for SPR (Crider, Shapiro, & Tursky, 1966; D. Shapiro, Crider, & Tursky, 1964; D. Shapiro & Watanabe, 1971).[11] The results obtained using skin potential are particularly interesting because they showed that SPR could be differentially manipulated without any corresponding differentiation occurring in SPL. Within this operant framework it has been shown that training under different schedules of reinforcement produces the results expected if the electrodermal response is truly being instrumentally controlled (e.g., Greene, 1966, and H.D. Kimmel & Gurucharri, 1975, using SRR; D. Shapiro & Crider, 1967, and D. Shapiro & Watanabe, 1971, using SPR). As in the early studies on control of heart rate, H. J. Johnson and Schwartz (1967) and Martin, Dean, and Shean (1968) have shown that SRR will be modified in order to avoid shock; it has also been shown that the elicited electrodermal response may be modified if it is differentially reinforced. Indeed, some of the earliest studies utilized an internally elicited response. For example, Crider *et al.* (1966) instructed their subjects to "recall and actively think about situations in your life in which you have felt especially emotional" (p. 21). In two control experiments, they showed that thinking emotional thoughts, on the one hand, or simply resting quietly on the other, were not sufficient to produce significant changes in the frequency of SPRs unless those responses were followed by reinforcement. Shnidman (1969, 1970) elicited the SPR by illuminating a small red triangle. The group that was reinforced for the response so elicited showed a similar pattern of responding to the experimental group used by Fowler and Kimmel (1962; that is, no change in rate), whereas the control group which was not reinforced for the elicited response showed the usual adaptation effect. In a subsequent study, Shnidman and Shapiro (1970) used two tones as eliciting stimuli, only one of which was followed by reinforcement, the other being followed by "punishment" (where the reinforcement consisted of a slide indicating the cumulative amount of money earned, and punishment a slide indicating a decrease in amount of money earned). A differential rate of SPR rate was obtained. Similar control over the SRR rate has been obtained (Edelman, 1970; H. D. Kimmel, Pendergrass, & Kimmel, 1967; Martin & Dean, 1971). These studies essentially involve learning to respond differentially to different stimuli, with instrumental reinforcement (Defran, Badia, & Lewis, 1969).

Finally, the role of muscle activity as a possible skeletal mediator or instrumental control of electrodermal activity has been investigated. In respect of SPR frequency, D. Shapiro *et al.* (1964) found that groups differentiated on SPR frequency after training did not show corresponding changes in heart or respiration rate. Birk, Crider, Shapiro, and Tursky (1966), in a dramatic single-case study, found that control could be achieved by a person totally paralyzed (except for breathing) by curare (although, of course, the possibility of some residual muscle function's influencing the control obtained could not be completely ruled

---

[11]D. Shapiro and Watanabe (1972) replicated the results in Japan in a cross-cultural study.

out). A number of studies of the possible mediation by muscle activity of the SRR have also agreed in concluding that such mediation could not account for the results obtained (e.g., Gavalas, 1967, 1968; Rice, 1966; Van Twyver & Kimmel, 1966), the only discordant note being sounded by Edelman (1970).

In the studies so far reviewed, the "reinforcers" used could, of course, be described as discontinuous binary information provided to the subject for performing correctly a task about which he was uninformed. The work to be considered now provided the subjects with more-or-less continuous feedback about electrodermal activity, and they were better informed about the nature of their task, although not always specifically that they were to control electrodermal activity. This work received its impetus from two studies by Stern and his colleagues. In the first, Stern and Kaplan (1967) provided half of their subjects with a visual meter display of changes in resistance, the needle moving to the left or right of a center point depending on whether resistance increased or decreased.

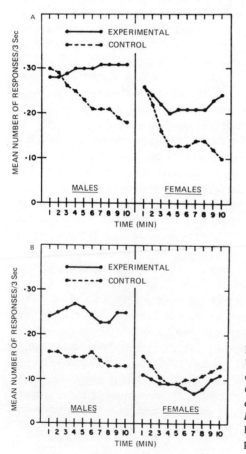

Figure 14. Mean number of GSRs per 3 sec: A. Under respond condition; B. Under relax condition. (From Stern, R. M., & Kaplan, B. E. Galvanic skin response: Voluntary control and externalization. *Journal of Psychosomatic Research,* 1967, *10,* 350–351, Figures 1, 2. Reprinted by permission of the author and the publisher.)

These subjects were told that thinking of emotional events would move the needle to the left, whereas relaxing (it is not clear whether the subjects were instructed merely to relax or to think of relaxing events) would make the needle go to the right. Control subjects were required to perform the same tasks but were not provided with feedback. The results are shown in Figure 14. It is clear that in the respond condition the provision of feedback produced differential performance, whereas this was not the case for the relax condition. The results are in fact identical with those obtained by Crider *et al.* (1966), who also instructed their subjects to think about emotional topics or relax. There was no control in this study for the effects of feedback alone on the control of electrodermal activity occurring spontaneously without instructions to engage in internal eliciting activities. In a second study, Stern and Lewis (1968) compared the ability of "method-trained" and "non-method-trained" actors and actresses to control electrodermal activity by thinking of emotional events or relaxing and concluded that method trained actors (who tend to express emotion by reliving earlier emotional experiences) were better able to differentiate increases and decreases in skin resistance than non-method-trained actors (who tend to communicate emotion by the use of standard facial expressions and other bodily movements). The studies by Stern and his colleagues also indicated that sex differences might be important in this area of research.

Klinge (1972) has carried these studies a step further. Her first experiment was virtually a successsful replication of the Stern and Kaplan (1967) investigation except that she found a main effect (that is, emotional thinking produced a decrease in resistance, rather than merely retarding the adaptation effect). In her second experiment, she provided subjects with either veridical feedback of resistance changes, nonveridical "positive" feedback (that is, feedback from the veridical group), negative feedback (that is, feedback from the emotional veridical condition in the veridical group when these subjects were relaxing, and vice versa), or noncontingent feedback. The results indicated that veridical feedback produced superior performance compared with positive nonveridical feedback, the latter, however, being more helpful than negative or noncontingent feedback. Although the differential instructions to relax or think about emotional events produced changes in heart and respiration rate, these changes were not correlated with the electrodermal changes, and she concluded that the latter were not mediated through muscular alterations.

Similar facilitating effects of veridical feedback in enhancing control of electrodermal responding in situations where responses are elicited by internal activities have been reported by Ikeda and Hirai (1976; using SPRs as the dependent variable) and by Wagner, Bourgeois, Levenson, and Denton (1974). Whether it is possible for the subject to detect changes in electrodermal responses directly, rather than produce them reliably by indirect means, however, is a question which has received little attention so far. An important study by Diekhoff (1976) has thrown light on this matter. The experiment was conducted within a signal-detection theory framework. Subjects were run over three 1-h sessions with resistance recorded from the left arm. During each session, a series of "trials" was run where a trial consisted of a point where a resistance change either was or was not occurring, according to specified criteria. At the given point a respond light was activated and the subject was required to indicate whether a resistance change had or had not occurred. Subjects were fully informed about the task and they were to attempt to attend to whatever (unspecified) physical sensations they could detect in order to discriminate a "yes" situation from a "no" situation (no mention was made of the fact that thinking about emotional events or relaxing could enhance or diminish electrodermal responding). Immediately after a decision had been communicated by the subject as to whether a response had occurred or not, one of four types of feedback was presented. One group received veridical information as to whether a response had occurred or not, and its relative magnitude (the feedback consisted of pilot lamps). A second group received "correctness" feedback (they were told only that a response had or had not occurred). A third group was provided with no feedback of any kind, and a fourth group with conflicting feedback (on all occasions when no response occurred, and on half the trials on which a response did occur, they were told that a response had occurred; on the remaining trials on which a response had occurred they were informed that it had not occurred). Receiver operating characteristic (ROC) curves and joint probability plots of each subject's true-positive and false-positive responses at each of three response bias levels were calculated for each subject enabling each subject's ability to detect and identify resistance changes to be assessed. From the ROC curves, two dependent measures were calculated: detection, defined as the absolute difference between the areas above and below each ROC curve (reflecting ability to differentiate between response and no-response trials); and identification, defined as the area below each ROC curve (reflecting ability correctly to label response trials as response trials and no-response trials as no-response trials). The results showed that only those subjects who did not receive any feedback at all showed significant improvement in detection of change in resistance over the training period, and even these subjects were able to detect the changes only when they were of large magnitude. None of the subjects showed any significant improvement in resistance identification as a function of training. Diekhoff (1976) concluded that not only did feedback not improve performance but it interfered with the discrimination of changes in internal state; however, external feedback may improve the labeling of internal states when they are correctly detected.

However, positive results have been obtained in other studies. Kotses, Rapaport, and Glaus (1978) presented a flashing white light for criterion increases or decreases in tonic skin resistance levels, and found that this produced significant changes in the required direction in uninformed subjects (told only to "keep the white light flashing") compared with the performance of subjects who received inaccurate feedback. However, in a second session reversal of the effects could not be obtained. Lacroix (1977) provided a considerable amount of training in the voluntary control of skin potential changes in fully informed subjects who were given accurate, inaccurate, or no feedback and found that the subjects given accurate feedback were able to raise and lower skin potential whereas the subjects given inaccurate or no feedback were not able to do so. Only a very small transfer effect to a no-feedback situation was shown, however, by the accurate-feedback training group.

Currently, therefore, the precise role of feedback in the voluntary control of electrodermal responding remains uncertain although it seems clear that such control can be achieved. In spite of the technical hazards of research in this area, its potential importance to the understanding of emotional disorders ensures that research will continue and become more sophisticated, perhaps within the framework of signal-detection theory as illustrated by the pioneering study of Diekhoff (1976).

Voluntary Control of Salivation

As C. C. Brown (1970) has pointed out:

The saliva exquisitely reflects the functioning of the organism. It mirrors the nutrition (through its chemical composition), the state of arousal of the organism (through modifications in flow rate and pattern), and portrays both individual and circadian patterns in both composition and flow. (p. 67)

As Brown's review clearly shows, however, formidable technical difficulties (as great as those applying to the study of the electrodermal response) stand in the way of competent research in this area, although the results of the few studies on instrumental or voluntary control of the salivary response are of great interest.

The principal salivary gland is the parotid, which secretes saliva from Stenson's duct located in the wall of the cheek below and in front of the external ear. Saliva can be collected from the duct by placing a capsule over the gland to trap and transmit the saliva in tubes. Modern techniques involve the use of a high-resolution, liquid-displacement sialometer, incorporating a photoelectric drop-counting system. From this point on, modular equipment or a computer may be used to provide feedback of various parameters of the secretion and to analyze the data. When the saliva is being spontaneously secreted, flow volume or flow rate are commonly used as dependent variables. In some studies, however, an external stimulus (usually acetic acid to the tongue) is applied to induce an initial flow which is then allowed to decline to a specified level before the operant rate is recorded. Discontinuities in flow rate occur and this may also yield a dependent variable. Most of the work to be considered has measured saliva secreted from the parotid gland as technical difficulties make accurate recordings from the two other major glands (submandibular, located beneath the root of the tongue; and sublingual, located under the tongue at the front of the mouth) difficult, and only the crude method of weighing a wad of cotton wool before and after it has been located under the tongue or at the side of the cheek are available. White (1977) has recently comprehensively reviewed various techniques used in measuring salivation and has shown experimentally that several techniques may be used reliably.

Only a few studies are available for consideration in relation to operant or voluntary control of salivation. Brown and Katz (1967) first measured baseline rates of salivation (number of drops of saliva secreted and number of peaks reaching a specified criterion), and number of swallows (known to affect secretion rate) over a period of 1 h on each of 3 days. The 18 male and female subjects were then divided into two groups. Subjects in one group were provided with a sign which lit up to indicate that a bonus had been earned whenever a spontaneous increase in salivary rate occurred (the criterion was three drops in 5 sec). Subjects in the other group received a bonus for not producing an increase (not for reducing salivary rate). The subject was informed that the study involved salivation and that a counter visible to him would keep track of the bonuses earned but that there was nothing he could do to affect the number of bonuses received. Two days of training were given. The results indicated that the subjects receiving bonuses for increasing salivation were able to achieve increases in the number of peaks compared with baseline, but not in the number of drops by comparison with baseline rates, whereas the control group showed no change. However, the experimental subjects also manifested a significant increase in the number of swallows and hence the results were confounded.

Delse and Feather (1968) attempted to overcome the movement (swallowing) problem by measuring EMG activity in the mouth region. They also used two groups, one provided with auditory feedback (a 1000-Hz tone at 60 db for 0.1 sec for each drop of saliva produced), the other without feedback, and subjects in both groups were required to both increase and decrease salivary rate. Each trial was preceded by a period of elicited salivation produced by acetic acid to the tongue, and a training trial did not commence until the secretion rate fell to less than 30 drops per min. No actual baseline levels of spontaneous rate were determined. The results of this study were somewhat inconclusive. The differences between increase and decrease training trials were significant in the feedback group but not in the no-feedback group, however, indicating that feedback was of assistance in achieving control of salivary rate. Frezza and Holland (1971) did record baseline rates. Their small group (only four subjects) was then provided with feedback for every drop secreted in the form of a counter (indicating money earned) on two sets of trials, following which they were alternately provided with feedback for salivating and not salivating. Swallowing was controlled by instructing the subjects only to swallow when instructed to do so. Three out of four subjects showed successful acquisition of the required increases and decreases.

Wells, Feather, and Headrick (1973) compared the effects of immediate and delayed feedback (an auditory tone for each drop of saliva in the case of immediate feedback, and a verbal report of the "score" obtained at the end of each trial in the case of delayed feedback). Subjects in both groups were required to increase and decrease salivation and an elicited salivation response preceded each training trial. In the first part of the experiment, the immediate and delayed groups were differentiated; in the second part, both groups received delayed feedback only. All subjects were fully informed. The results indicated that subjects provided with immediate feedback could produce significant decreases in salivary rate but could not produce corresponding increases, whereas subjects provided with delayed feedback could produce neither increases nor decreases. When the immediate feedback group was switched to delayed feedback, some transfer of control was found. There were no controls in this study for voluntary control without feedback.

White (1978) reported the results of five experiments in which he attempted to elucidate the role of imagery in the control of salivation. He was able to show that food imagery led to increased salivation whereas anxiety imagery was accompanied by a decrease in salivation, that persons with vivid imagery salivated more than persons with weak imagery when imagining food and less when imagining anxiety, and that vividness of imagery interacts with food preferences (for example, vivid images produce more salivation for preferred food than do weak images). White's final experiment suggested that imagery is a stronger determinant of salivation than instructions to increase or decrease imagery.

Although the number of studies on salivation in relation to feedback is small, and methodological criticisms can be lodged against all of them, the overall results suggest that voluntary control of salivation is possible with immediate feedback. The unidirectional effect obtained (significant decreases but not increases in salivation) is, as has been seen, not uncommon in the voluntary control of autonomically mediated responses.

Voluntary Control of Peripheral Temperature and Circulation

Peripheral finger temperature is a variable of particular, and perhaps critical, interest to biofeedback since changes in peripheral finger temperature can not only be measured objectively with near-perfect validity and reliability, but the changes which do occur are relatively slow as a function of time; hence, "noise" relative to signal is relatively low and it would seem to be a straightforward matter to determine whether or not peripheral finger temperature can be brought under voluntary control. Unfortunately, this has not turned out to be the case, mainly because most of the research carried out thus far has neglected the most elementary principles of research design.

The actual measurement of peripheral finger temperature is a relatively simple matter, provided elementary precautions are taken. Modern thermistors are available which are extremely sensitive to very small temperature changes; for biofeedback purposes, however, a unit of one-tenth of a degree change is quite sufficient while the sensitivity to change of the commercial thermistors available ensures that tracking is more than adequate. Amplification is a much simpler matter than is the case with other variables of interest in biofeedback while feedback displays may be of any required kind. It might, however, be reiterated that the most obvious kind of display (digital, providing a changing display of the actual temperature) is in this instance not necessarily the most helpful, since rapidly changing numbers are not at all easy to follow and compare with earlier values. With regard to metholodology, apart from specific matters which will be taken up when individual studies are discussed below, some general points need to be stressed. Not only is the drift effect of special importance when evaluating whether or not voluntary control has been achieved (particularly with respect to increases in temperature) but careful control of many other potentially confounding factors is of special importance. Subjects should always be adapted for a period of at least 30 min in a room temperature not less than 20° C (this may necessitate using a waiting room at this controlled temperature in addition to the experimental room, if the latter is to be set at a lower temperature) since Boudewyns (1976) has shown that different start temperatures will otherwise be obtained as a function of outside temperature. An adaptation period will also help to control for differential activity levels prior to arriving at the laboratory. There is good evidence that quite striking sex differences exist in baseline levels of peripheral temperature, with females tending to have colder extremities than males (Boudewyns, 1976; Livesey & Kirk, 1953; Sheridan, Boehm, Ward, & Justesen, 1976). Differences in mood state have been shown to produce quite remarkable and rapid changes in peripheral finger temperature (Mittelman & Wolff, 1939) and many other intra- and extrapersonal factors are known to have similar, although smaller, effects (Cabanac, Hildebrandt, Massonet, & Strempel, 1976; Flecker, 1951). Taub, Emurian, and Howell (1975) have stressed the importance of the "personal factor." They claimed that when the experimenter adopted an "impersonal" attitude toward the subject, only 2 of 22 subjects in their study succeeded in bringing peripheral finger temperature under voluntary control, whereas 20 of 21 subjects succeeded when a more informal, warm, and friendly approach was adopted. It is, of course, essential that the temperature of the experimental cubicle be controlled, as peripheral temperature will tend to drift toward the room temperature. As will be seen later, and as was described in detail in Chapter 2, "ceiling" and "bottoming" effects as a function of starting temperature can produce very misleading results unless both room temperature and starting levels (i.e., the level at which experimental manipulations begin) are very carefully controlled. Thus, the apparently simple matter of investigating the voluntary control of peripheral finger temperature is complicated by a large number of traps for the unwary; unfortunately, most of the investigations so far conducted have failed to avoid these traps.[12]

---

[12] Hardy (1961) has provided the most comprehensive review of all aspects of temperature regulation, while Hwang and Konz (1977) have recently reviewed the main theories of control.

Hadfield (1920) reported that a patient of his could produce large differential changes in hand temperature rapidly whenever it was suggested that he do so. Feedback of temperature was not, of course, provided. More recently, several studies have produced results which suggest that peripheral finger temperature changes may result from experimental procedures not involving the use of feedback. Boudewyns (1976) found that training in relaxation alone led to a significant increase in finger temperature, while subjecting the same subjects to a stressful situation produced a decrease in temperature. The results for successive periods of relaxation, stress, and relaxation are shown in Figure 15, which also shows the corresponding changes in level of arousal as subjectively assessed by the subjects. These results confirm the earlier findings of Mittelman and Wolff (1939), who found large decreases in temperature when difficult problems were attempted or the subjects discussed personal problems. Clearly, experimental results may be seriously confounded if normal subjects are tested when they are experiencing personal stress. Dugan and Sheridan (1976) found that instructing subjects to imagine their hands in very warm water or in ice-cold water (but with no feedback available) produced significant increases and decreases in peripheral finger temperature, respectively. All ten subjects using cooling imagery showed a significant change in one hand (an average of nearly 2°F over only 15 min)

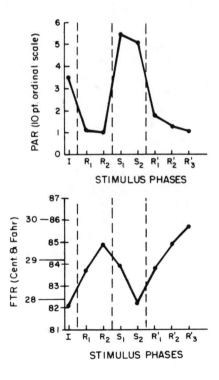

Figure 15. Mean finger temperature and arousal level ratings across the three stimulus phases of Experiment 2 (R, R_1 refer to relaxation phases; S to stress phase). (From Boudewyns. P. A. A comparison of the effects of stress vs. relaxation instruction on the finger temperature response. *Behavior Therapy.* 1976, 7, 61, Figure 3. Reprinted by permission of the author and the publisher.)

while six showed corresponding changes in the other hand as well. The results were less striking for warming imagery but the drift effect could have been operative in this study (the ambient room temperature was not stated).

In a study primarily concerned with the formation of blisters as a result of hypnotic suggestion, R. F. Q. Johnson and Barber (1976) incidentally found a rise in finger temperature of about half a degree following suggestions that the hand had been accidentally burned. In a study which acted as a trigger for much of the subsequent work, Maslach, Marshall, and Zimbardo (1972) induced a hypnotic state in a small group of subjects and then instructed them to make one hand hotter and the other colder, using imagery. Subsequently, they tried to equalize temperature in the two hands. A larger group of subjects attempted the same tasks in the normal state.[13] All three of the subjects who were hypnotized were able to produce differential bilateral changes in finger temperature of up to 4°C, with the decreases being larger than the increases, whereas the control subjects, using imagery alone, were unable to produce such differences. The results are not necessarily in conflict with those of Dugan and Sheridan (1976) since the production of differences between corresponding fingers of the two hands is clearly a much more difficult task than increasing or decreasing temperature alone.

Most of the studies which have used feedback suffer from serious confounding. Roberts and his colleagues have reported two studies which follow on from the work of Maslach et al. (1972). In the first, Roberts, Kewman, and MacDonald (1973) hypnotized six subjects who were all highly hypnotizable and then provided them with feedback (an auditory tone which, heard in stereo headphones, moved from left to right and also rose and fell in pitch) while they attempted to warm one hand and simultaneously cool the other. Subsequently, two of the subjects attempted differential control without feedback but while they were in the hypnotic state. The results for nine alternating trials over three training sessions with feedback indicated that four of the six subjects showed significant differences in the required direction over the course of training, while one was successful to begin with but not later, and the other could not produce differences at any stage of training. The maximum temperature differential produced was 5.6°C. No instructions regarding the use of imagery were provided, but the hypnotic state and provision of feedback were, of course confounded while the drift effect (ambient room temperature was only 22.5°C) could have obscured the degree of control achieved. The two subjects subsequently run without feedback were able to maintain control, although for an unstated reason ambient room temperature was changed to 28°C. A subsequent study by Roberts, Schuler, Bacon, Zimmerman, and Patterson (1975) used two groups of subjects, one scoring high, the other low, on both the Harvard Group Scale of Hypnotic

[13]It is not clear whether the two groups of subjects were equally susceptible to hypnotic induction or not.

Susceptibility and the Tellegen Absorption Scale (the latter is designed to measure the ability to concentrate). Auditory feedback was provided of the difference in temperature between corresponding fingertips of the two hands. Following a 10-min baseline, the subjects were required alternately to increase temperature in one finger while decreasing it in the other, and vice versa. The results are shown in Figure 16. Significant differential control of finger temperature was achieved, but as can be seen from Figure 16, no differences were found between the groups high and low in hypnotic susceptibility and absorption. In this study also, no instructions as to the use of imagery were given and it remained an uncontrolled variable, and no control group without feedback was used. The results, of course, do not support the original possibility that induction of a hypnotic state will facilitate voluntary control.

W. C. Lynch, Hama, Kohn, and Miller (1976) confounded feedback with reinforcement in their study of differential peripheral finger temperature control in children. They provided both visual meter feedback of temperature differential (with the needle changing toward the warmer hand) and a digital counter display which indicated how much money the child had earned. The children were aged 10–11½ years and the task was presented as a game called "moving the needle" (although it can be inferred that the children were informed that temperature change was the task). Three of the four children were able to warm one hand relative to the other. W. C. Lynch *et al.* (1976) pointed out that a difference

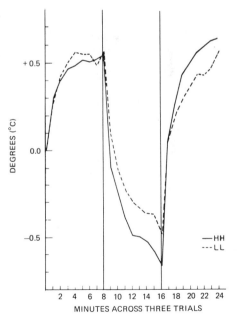

Figure 16. Average finger differential of seven high-absorption-hypnotic (HH) and seven low-absorption-hypnotic (LL) subjects for the last eight sessions. (From Roberts, A. H., Schuler, J., Bacon, J. G., Zimmerman, R. L., & Patterson, R. Individual differences and autonomic control: Absorption, hypnotic susceptibility, and the unilateral control of skin temperature. *Journal of Abnormal Psychology*, 1975, *84*, 275, Figure 1. Copyright 1975 by the American Psychological Association. Reprinted by permission of the author and the publisher.)

between the two hands could be produced by warming one hand and cooling the other, maintaining the temperature in one hand stable while cooling or warming the other, as appropriate, or warming/cooling both hands simultaneously, but at different rates. Analysis of the data suggested that success was mostly achieved by cooling both hands differentially and simultaneously. The authors do not speculate on the meaning of this finding, but given that the room temperature was only $25°C \pm 1°C$, the influence of the drift effect seems a likely candidate. The possibility that the results could be explained in terms of differential muscle activity affecting thoracic outflow to the two arms was ingeniously ruled out in a further study of two of the children who successfully produced temperature differentials between two fingers of the same hand, although significant differences were obtained for only one of the children.

The above studies set their subjects the very difficult task of acquiring differential finger temperature control without prior training on individual finger temperature increases and decreases as separate tasks. The remaining studies to be considered dealt with the simpler task. McDonagh and McGinnis (1973) successfully trained their subjects to produce quite large increases in finger temperature (of the order of $8°F$) if they started from an initial low level, whereas subjects starting from a high level did not produce such increases. This differential result was attributed to a ceiling effect but the use of an ambient room temperature of only $21°C$ may well have produced a drift effect in the high-starting-level subjects which would have masked any control achieved. In this study also, the differential effects of feedback (the type used was not stated) and training in the use of autogenic phrases were completely confounded.

Surwit, Shapiro, and Feld (1976) carried out two studies which, although confounding of feedback and reinforcement (as well as imagery) was involved, in many ways represent the most carefully conducted investigations to date, although the number of subjects was very small. They measured both peripheral temperature (from the middle finger on both hands) and blood flow (by means of a plethysmograph placed distally to the thermistor), as well as pulse amplitude, heart rate, and respiration. Half of the subjects were instructed to increase, and half to decrease, finger temperature, being told to think of their hands as being warm or cool. Two 45-min baseline sessions preceded the training sessions, each of which consisted of a stabilization period without feedback (lasting until temperature variability was equal to or less than one-fifth of a degree over 4 consecutive min, or 30 had passed), followed by 20 75-sec trials with feedback from the nondominant hand. Analog visual meter feedback was provided with full-scale deflection equaling one half of a degree change (changes of $0.01°C$ could be detected on the meter). At the end of each trial, a digital meter indicated the amount earned on that trial at 25c for each $0.1°C$ change from baseline. Across trials within each session there was evidence of success in decreasing temperature (an average of $2.0°C$) but not in increasing temperature. No changes occurred across the 5 training days, however, indicating that all of the control was achieved on the first day of training. Surwit *et al.* (1976) considered that the failure to obtain voluntary control of increases in peripheral finger temperature may have been due to a ceiling effect since the average starting temperature of their subjects was 33–34°C and hence little opportunity for increasing temperature was available. In an attempt to overcome this obstacle, they reduced the room temperature in a second study and succeeded thereby in reducing starting temperature to under 30°C during baseline recordings. In this second experiment eight new subjects were required only to increase temperature. However, the results showed that these subjects were not only not able to increase finger temperature, but that they showed a slight decrease over trials within sessions, while tending to show an increase in temperature over days. It would be tempting to attribute all of the results obtained by Surwit *et al.* (1976) to the drift phenomenon were it not for one awkward fact. Although the ambient temperature in the first experiment was only 22.5°C and in the second only 19.5°C, thus providing maximum opportunity for the drift phenomenon to manifest itself, no such drift occurred during the two initial baseline sessions without feedback (it is not clear, however, whether the authors analyzed the baseline records on a minute-by-minute basis or merely compared the two means). As pointed out earlier, this study was heavily confounded and the small number of subjects available may have led to nonrepresentative results.

A similarly confounded study was reported by Taub and Emurian (1976). They failed to separate out the effects of feedback, reinforcement, and imagery instructions in a study which was, furthermore, admittedly exploratory and carried out over several years. Their results, which in general supported the notion that voluntary control of peripheral finger temperature is possible, can hardly be regarded as more than demonstrational in nature in spite of the careful description of their procedures and recognition of the methodological hazards of research in this area of biofeedback. In a more recent study, Herzfeld and Taub (1977), using a small number of subjects, have produced evidence suggesting that a combination of suggestions (imposed externally, not self-induced) of warmth or cold by various means in combination with biofeedback is more successful than biofeedback alone in aiding voluntary control of finger temperature.

Several studies exist in which an attempt has been made to control possible confounding variables such as reinforcement and the use of imagery. Hunter, Russell, Russell, and Zimmerman (1976) unfortunately confounded feedback and reinforcement but attempted to control for imagery by instructions given to the children who were subjects of the experiment. They trained 30 "learning-disabled" children of low average intelligence and 30 carefully matched "normal" controls to produce increases in finger temperature in the presence of proportional feedback (a variable-intensity lamp) and reinforcement (a train which ran whenever an increase of 0.5°F was obtained). The children were adapted for at least 20 min to the experimental room temperature (70°F) and were given uniform instructions to "think your fingers warm." All of the subjects in both groups received veridical feedback on the first training day; on 4 subsequent days, half of the subjects in each group continued to receive veridical feedback whereas the other half received "inconsistent" feedback (that is, the light changed in intensity and the train ran for no change, a decrease in temperature, or an increase in temperature, irregularly). Over all subjects in both groups an average increase of 0.38°F was obtained, and consistent feedback produced a significantly greater rise in temperature than inconsistent feedback, both within and across days. Unexpectedly, the learning-disabled children showed significantly greater voluntary control of temperature than the "normal" children within days but not across days (in the authors' view, the learning-disabled children manifested equal learning, but better performance of what they had learned).

Steptoe, Mathews, and Johnston (1974) carried out a study which varied the usual pattern in that they investigated voluntary control of differential temperature in the earlobes, rather than the fingers. They chose the earlobes primarily because of the absence of active skeletal musculature and the specificity of the response which could be obtained. Both visual (meter) and auditory (frequency modulated tone) feedback were provided and the subject's task was to make one earlobe warmer than the other. Extended baseline measurements were not taken, only a 10-min stabilization period being recorded. The task proved to be a difficult one but only 25 min of training was given which, after an initial tendency to produce excursions in the wrong direction, resulted in an average temperature change (in the eight subjects used) of only 0.3°C in the right direction (no instructions concerning the use of imagery were given).

Keefe (1975) was well aware of the methodological deficiencies of the earlier studies, but unfortunately failed to heed his own warnings since he succeeded in confounding imagery instructions with feedback. His small number of subjects was divided into two groups with instructions to increase or decrease peripheral finger temperature relative to forehead temperature, with continuous auditory and visual feedback provided. The predicted differential increases and decreases in finger temperature relative to forehead temperatures, small in magnitude, were obtained, although the drift effect would have contaminated the data as the room temperature was kept at 21°C.

Finally, Sheridan et al. (1976) randomly allocated their subjects to one of four training conditions: an autogenic training group, a group given autogenic training and feedback, a feedback-only group, and a control group given neither feedback nor autogenic training. All groups were trained to increase peripheral finger temperature. All three experimental groups were more successful than the control group at acquiring control, but did not differ from one another.

Ohno, Tanaka, Takeya, and Ikemi (1977) trained independent groups of subjects to raise and lower peripheral finger temperature with veridical feedback, but the absolute magnitude of the changes after three ½-h sessions were very small, and although the increase and decrease groups differed significantly after training neither had succeeded in obtaining a significant change from its own baseline level. Two control groups (no feedback and false feedback) produced results which indicated that very little success had been achieved in this study. The subjects of this experiment were, however, uninformed about the nature of the task.

The methodological sophistication of many of these studies can only be categorized as deplorably defective insofar as the most elementary principles of research design have been cavalierly ignored. The relative significance of feedback and imagery instructions has, in particular, been very poorly handled. For the most part, complete confounding has occurred, but it is also not sufficient to try to control for the effects of imagery by simply not giving the subjects any instructions about imagery or by giving all subjects the same instructions. Both variables should obviously be treated as independent variables. In the case of imagery, for example, the correct method of investigating the effects of imagery would be to constitute groups which are (a) given no instructions about imagery; (b) given specific instructions about the kind of imagery to use; (c) given specific instructions not to use imagery. If significant differences between groups are obtained, the role of imagery is elucidated; if differences are not obtained, uncertainty would remain since it could be, of course, that groups given no instructions will use imagery and groups instructed not to use imagery might nevertheless use it. Similar considerations apply to the elucidation of the role of feedback on the one hand and reinforcement on the other. The result of the near-total failure to exercise even the most elementary design principles has been a situation in which the relative importance of feedback, imagery, and reinforcement remains virtually completely unknown. A second major criticism of the work carried out in this area relates to the extraordinary attraction for investigators of differential control studies. If it is true, as far as can be determined from the studies so far carried out, that voluntary control of increases and decreases in finger temperature is itself a difficult task, then it simply does not make sense to carry out experiments on the more difficult task of differential control. Before differential control is attempted comprehensive studies of increase/decrease control with adequate methodology (proper and extensive baselines; proper instructional control of imagery, feedback, and reinforcement; allowance for the drift effect) should be undertaken. Apart from providing reliable and valid indications as to whether voluntary control of peripheral finger temperature really is possible, the results of these experiments would identify those subjects (likely to be few in number) who can exercise a high degree of such control. It is *these* subjects who should then be used in studies of differential control. Studies in which all the subjects are required as their initial task to exercise differential control are likely to result in failure or minimally significant results simply because most of the subjects will have only limited capacity to control individual increases and decreases of peripheral temperature, let alone differential temperature. In short, this area of research appears to represent yet another example of workers in the area of biofeedback wanting to run before they have learned to walk.

Work on the voluntary control of peripheral finger temperature has been conducted on the assumption that changes in temperature at the periphery directly reflect (and indeed are produced by) changes in peripheral blood volume and/or blood flow resulting from vasodilation and vasoconstriction respectively. As Surwit (1973) has pointed out, however, changes in peripheral finger temperature can result either from a change in deep arterial and venous flow without corresponding changes in the peripheral tissues, or alternatively can result from change in blood volume in the peripheral tissues themselves. As will be seen later, these alternative possibilities are of considerable importance in relation to the treatment of Raynaud's disease (and possibly also in relation to the treatment of migraine) by means of peripheral finger temperature training. The question of whether voluntary control of peripheral finger temperature increases and decreases is accompanied by corresponding changes in vasodilation and vasoconstriction therefore becomes a matter of interest, as does the question of whether direct voluntary control of vasodilation and vasoconstriction is possible.

Measurement of vasodilation and vasoconstriction (as indicators of peripheral blood volume and/or flow) may be achieved by use of the technique called plethysmography. The different techniques for measuring local vasomotor status have been described by Brown, Giddon, and Dean (1965). *Rheoplethysmography* requires the fingertip to be sealed in a rigid, air-tight, water-filled capsule. The associated cuff is inflated to a pressure level which exceeds venous occlusion pressure but is less than systolic arterial pressure. This has the effect of altering blood outflow while leaving inflow unaffected. When fingertip volume increases, fluid is displaced from the capsule, activating a pneumatic-to-electrical sensing device. *Electrical impedance plethysmography* takes advantage of the fact that living tissue shows a characteristic impedance to the passage of a high-frequency alternating electric current, the measured impedance being a function of the tissues through which the current is passing and the volume of blood in the finger at any given time. Changes in the total observed impedance reflect changes in the ratio of blood volume to tissue. A third technique utilizes the fact that changes in blood volume are indexed by changes in circumference of the digit, but this method is not sufficiently reliable to be very satisfactory. The most favored technique currently in use involves *photoplethysmography,* which is based on the detection of changes in the opacity of a tissue segment exposed to a constant source of transillumination. Surwit *et al.* (1976) employed both circumference plethysmography (using a strain gauge to measure changes in digital diameter) and photoplethysmography, however, and found high positive correlations between the two measures.

The relationship between changes in peripheral skin temperature and blood volume/flow changes is critically dependent on a number of factors. As Fetcher, Hall, and Shaub (1949) pointed out, skin temperature depends on both the rate of

Table 2. Design of Experiment by Mitchell and White (1977)[a]

	Stage I	Stage II	Stage III	Stage IV
Group I ($n = 3$)	SR	SR	SR	SR
Group II ($n = 3$)	SR	SR + SM	SR + SM	SR + SM
Group III ($n = 3$)	SR	SR + SM	SR + SM + SA(I)	SR + SM + SA(I)
Group IV ($n = 3$)	SR	SR + SM	SR + SM + SA(I)	SR + SM + SA(I) + SA(II)

[a]SR = self-record; SM = self-monitor; SA(I) = skill acquisition, Stage I; SA(II) = skill acquisition, Stage II. (See text for explanation.)

realized that there is now good evidence that techniques are available which appear to achieve a high success rate without the use of biofeedback. Paulley and Haskell (1975) have reported 75% long-lasting success with relaxation training in a series of over 800 patients, although lack of detail makes it impossible to evaluate this claim. Similarly, Hay and Madders (1971) reported that 69 patients in a series of 98 were improved after relaxation training, although again the documentation of the claim was inadequate. However, the work and results of Mitchell offer a convincing demonstration of the efficacy of nonbiofeedback training techniques in the alleviation of migraine. In the first major study, Mitchell and Mitchell (1971) carried out two experiments. In the first, 17 patients with migraine were allocated to three treatment conditions: relaxation training only, combined systematic desensitization (SD) training, and a no-treatment control condition. A reduction of 76% in migraine frequency and 50% in duration of attack was obtained in the group treated with combined SD training, compared with only a 24% reduction in migraine frequency and no reduction in duration of attack in the group treated only with relaxation training (the improvement in these aspects being negligible in the untreated control group). A second experiment along similar lines produced similar results. Since this initial study, Mitchell has systematically developed procedures for training in behavioral self-management and self-control. The application for these training techniques is described in some detail in recent publications (Mitchell & White, 1976, 1977); they are similar to the cognitive training techniques described by Meichenbaum (1976).[25] In a study of 12 migraine patients, Mitchell and White (1977) used the interesting multiple-baseline design shown in Table 2. In stage I, all of the patients engaged only in recording details of their migrane headaches for a period of 12 weeks. Group I continued with this activity for the remainder of the training period, while the remaining three groups were then trained and required both to self-record and to monitor the circumstances preceding the onset of a migraine headache. At the end of this 12-week period, group II continued to perform these activities for the remainder of the study while groups III and IV proceeded to training in skill acquisition. The subsequent course of the

[25]Complete details of the techniques will be found in published manuals by Mitchell, Piatkowska, and White (1974), and Mitchell and White (1974).

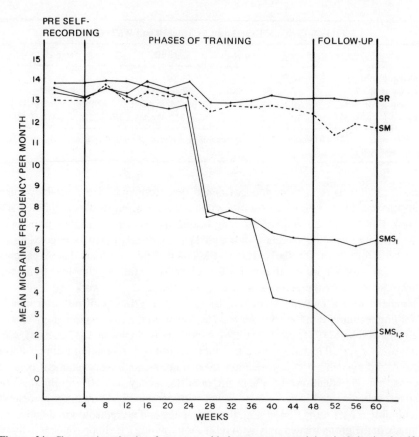

Figure 24. Changes in migraine frequency with increments to training in behavioral self-management: SR = self-recording only; SM = self-monitoring only; SMS_1 = self-recording, self-monitoring, and skill acquisition stage I; $SMS_{1,2}$ = self-recording, self-monitoring, and skill acquisition stages I and II. (From Mitchell, K. R., & White, R. G. Behavioral self-management: An application to the problem of migraine headaches. *Behavior Therapy*, 1977, *8*, 219, Figure 1. Reprinted by permission of the author and the publisher.)

study can readily be deduced from Table 2. The results are shown in Figure 24. It is clear that neither self-recording the occurrence of migraine attacks, nor recording them and identifying the precipitants, is sufficient to produce significant reductions in migraine frequency, whereas training in skill acquisition does have a very significant effect indeed. A reduction of 73% in mean monthly migraine frequency was obtained for the three patients who completed the entire training package, compared with no reduction at all in group I, 3.7% reduction in group II, and 44.9% reduction in group III. The skill acquisition training packages involved cue-controlled progressive muscle relaxation, mental and differential relaxation, and self-desensitization (stage I), and more advanced techniques for dealing with stress which are too complex to summarize here (stage II). The findings of Mitchell and White (1977) are entirely consonant with those of Reeves (1976) for tension headache patients, using the techniques developed by Meichenbaum (1976), although Mitchell and White (1977) did not examine changes in peripheral temperature and/or blood volume and flow, analogous to Reeves's measurement of frontalis muscle activity.[26] Mitchell and White (1977) stress the importance in the treatment of migraine of an approach which takes into account all of the factors involved in the production of a migraine pattern of response to stress, and deprecate the use of peripheral temperature and/or blood volume and flow training only. As already pointed out, it remains to be seen whether such training would increase the effectiveness of the Mitchell approach if introduced at a late stage of his training regimen.

Finally, it may be mentioned that there have been recent accounts of the use of multimodal methods of treatment of migraine, including the use of biofeedback techniques as part of the treatment package. Daniels (1977) treated a female patient with a long history of migraine, using deep muscle and cue-controlled relaxation training, hypnosis with hand warming, cognitive behavior therapy, and thought stopping. The use of all of these techniques was based on the assumption that the vasoconstrictive phase of the headaches experienced by the patient resulted from increased tension and anger produced by the behavior of other people. The treatment was reported as successful. Stambaugh and House (1977) treated a patient who had previously had frontalis and sternomastoid muscle reduction training with feedback, but without success. The use of relaxation training was likewise without effect, as was the use of heterohypnosis and autogenic training. However, the introduction of autohypnotic anesthesia training to relieve the headache pain was apparently successful and headache activity (which was of 23 years duration) was still significantly reduced at an 8-month follow-up.

In concluding this section it must be pointed out that the technical standard of the biofeedback work in relation to migraine has so far been deplorably poor in quality, so that none of the claims thus far made for its effectiveness can be considered to have been sustained. There are, however, hopeful signs that this situation is changing, reflected in the recent studies by Friar and Beatty (1976) and Price and Tursky (1976). It is also essential that the theoretical rationale for peripheral temperature and/or blood volume and flow training (whether in the direction of increasing vasoconstriction or vasodilation) be more rigorously examined in relation to the known two-stage process of vasoconstriction followed by vasodilation which is characteristic of migraine headaches.

[26]See Chapter 3 for an account of the study by Reeves (1976).

Raynaud's Disease

Raynaud's disease may be defined as:

> episodic attacks of decreased finger circulation characterized by white fingers, pares-
> thesia and a subsequent hyperemic phase with reddening of the skin and an increased
> cutaneous circulation. In advanced cases a continuous cyanotic phase is a predominant
> feature. (Thulesius, 1976, p. 5)

It will be noticed that Thulesius's definition makes no mention of the more unpleasant features (e.g., gangrene) with which most of the patients described by Raynaud in the mid-19th century were afflicted. Subsequent to Raynaud's discovery of the disease which bears his name, a distinction was drawn between Raynaud's disease (which might well be renamed essential Raynaud's disease, since its etiology remains mysterious) and Raynaud's phenomenon, in which the same symptoms are present but a specific cause is usually evident. The patients described by Raynaud in fact probably manifested the Raynaud phenomenon rather than Raynaud's disease, which nowadays is regarded as a relatively benign condition, with favorable prognosis, mainly affecting females and having its onset early in life (Thulesius, 1976). The classification adopted by Thulesius distinguishes two forms of primary Raynaud phenomena (Raynaud's disease and episodic acrocyanosis), and no fewer than ten forms of secondary Raynaud phenomena, each form with a specific etiology. The cases reported by Raynaud himself were probably the most common of the secondary form, resulting from peripheral obstructive arteriopathies, probably of arteriosclerotic origin.

Primary Raynaud's disease (as we shall term it from now on) remains a puzzle. There is evidence that these patients will show a steep decline in peripheral finger temperature if placed in a cool environment (lower than about 22°C). But such a decline is also characteristic of many females (and some males) placed in a similar environment, and furthermore the rate of decline tends to be identical in both patients and normal subjects, room temperature being reached in about 50 min. However, when peripheral finger temperature reaches room temperature, the normal subjects will report merely that their hands are "cool" and the appearance of the hands will be unchanged; the fingers of the patients, however, will be whitish/blue and appear almost frostbitten. Thus, the peripheral temperature change is clearly not the most critical factor, and it is therefore possible (as Surwit, 1973, pointed out) that peripheral finger temperature is not the most appropriate biofeedback method of treatment. Studies of peripheral blood flow and volume in patients with primary Raynaud's disease, in fact, support Surwit's observations, as blood flow to the peripheries may be essentially normal in the resting state and only be affected when an attack is actually occurring (Bollinger & Schlumpf, 1976; Edwards, Ottinger, & Ruberti, 1959; Mendlowitz & Naftchi, 1959; Zweifler, 1976). However, the position regarding both peripheral finger temperature and blood flow in primary Raynaud's disease compared with normal subjects remains controversial. Mittelman and Wolff (1939) reported that one patient:

had shown in control experiments, i.e. when adequately covered and relaxed, that she
was able to maintain the temperature of her fingers at 32°C to 33°C for three hours in
environmental temperatures of both 20° and 26°C. (p. 286)

However, her peripheral finger temperature dropped significantly in a room
temperature of 20.5°C when inadequately clothed or when discussing emotional
problems. Mittelman and Wolff (1939) also report that another patient, if relaxed, could raise her peripheral finger temperature from room level (20.5°C) to
32°C in only 30 min. By contrast, a patient studied by the present writer invariably dropped to room temperature, never showed any ability (without feedback)
to reverse the drop, and dropped to room temperature in a control experiment
when she was very heavily clothed with essentially only her hand exposed. It is
surprising that 100 years after Raynaud identified the disease, the most elementary information concerning finger temperature changes and blood flow (and
their relationship) are still almost totally lacking in respect of primary Raynaud's
disease. Mittelman and Wolff (1939) also reported some interesting results with a
patient who had been assessed prior to sympathectomy (a fairly common and
rather drastic intervention procedure in primary Raynaud's disease, in spite of its
favorable prognosis). Following sympathectomy, the drop in finger temperature
which commonly occurs when the patient is emotionally disturbed still manifested itself in the hand unaffected by the operation (a unilateral one) but became
much less in the hand which had had its sympathetic innervation abolished by the
operation. It is interesting to note that vasodilator drugs appear to be of little
value in the treatment of Raynaud's disease (Hansteen, 1976).

The biofeedback treatment of primary Raynaud's disease is in its infancy,
despite the prominence given to it in the biofeedback literature. Surwit (1973)
gathered together what information he could find in the literature, but all of it was
essentially anecdotal and uncontrolled. The study by A. M. Jacobsen, Hackett,
Surman, and Silverberg (1973) was not primarily biofeedback oriented and the
effects of peripheral finger temperature training were not reported in sufficient
detail for an evaluation to be made. Blanchard and Haynes (1975) reported in
some detail on the treatment of a single case in which successive attempts to
warm the fingers with and without feedback were compared (the feedback consisted of the difference between forehead and finger temperatures with instructions to make the hands warmer). Attempts to raise finger temperature without
feedback were unsuccessful, but at the end of treatment absolute hand temperature data indicated a rise from a baseline level of 79°F to a final level of 88°F,
which was maintained at a 7-month follow-up. Sunderman and Delk (1978) have
reported the successful results of 13 months of treatment of a 40-year-old female
with a 15-year history of migraine. She was provided with three kinds of feedback (flashing red and blue lights to indicate rises and falls in temperature, a
visual meter, and a rising and falling tone) to indicate progress. Starting temperature in a training session was always below 80°F (unless near the end of training, when it began to be higher) but rose ever more steeply during a session as

training progressed until it regularly reached over 90°F during the final 4 months of training. There was a marked improvement in the clinical condition of the patient. The authors stress the fluctuations which occur, and suggest that prolonged training may be necessary to achieve permanent success.

Recently, a substantial number of reports in abstract form have indicated a considerable degree of success in peripheral finger temperature training with cases of primary Raynaud's disease[27] with concomitant clinical improvement. One example (from another source) will suffice. Emery, Schaller, and Fowler (1976) studied 12 patients who were given 5 h in all of training, with visual feedback from one finger. All of the patients were able to raise digital temperature at least 4°C, some up to 10°C, and all of them reported clinical improvement as indexed by, for example, being able to swim or go about in cold temperatures without gloves (activities which prior to training would have resulted in severe vasoconstrictive attacks), while in one of the patients digital ulcers healed up. Thus, the outlook for biofeedback training with primary Raynaud's disease looks quite promising, although hard data are as yet lacking and the theoretical rationale for using peripheral temperature training (rather than control of blood flow and/or volume) remains as obscure as in the case of migraine. The lack of essential data is clearly indicated by the total lack of knowledge of whether peripheral finger temperature in the resting state is the same in patients with primary Raynaud's disease as it is in patients with migraine, and of whether both kinds of patients react similarly to being placed for a time in a cool or cold environment. It is quite possible that patients with primary Raynaud's disease start at a relatively high temperature (provided they have first been adapted to control for the effects of outside temperature) but drop sharply in a cool environment, whereas patients with migraine start off at a low temperature, whether they are placed in a warm or cool environment. It is a deplorable state of affairs that such basic information should be lacking.

Gastrointestinal Disorders

In spite of the impetus provided by the major review of Razran (1961) of the Russian work on interoceptive conditioning, little progress has subsequently been made in using biofeedback in the treatment of patients with internal dysfunctions which are not as readily measurable as blood pressure and heart rate, no doubt largely because of the technical difficulties involved in measurement. Nevertheless, what little work has been carried out so far is of very considerable interest. Two areas of research will be considered. The first deals with fecal incontinence. Elimination of feces is accomplished by relaxation of the internal and external anal sphincters. The events leading up to this final sequence are important. The entry of feces into the rectum produces a rise in pressure which

[27]See, for example, several abstracts in the journal *Biofeedback and Self-Regulation* (Vol. 1, No. 2, 1976).

leads in turn to relaxation of the internal sphincter. The normal reaction to this is contraction of the external sphincter which prevents expulsion of the contents of the rectum until adaptation occurs to the increased contents and the internal sphincter contracts, thus preventing evacuation of the rectum and allowing the external sphincter to relax without loss of the contents of the rectum. When the rectum is sufficiently full, voluntary defecation may be initiated by relaxation of the external sphincter following on relaxation of the internal sphincter. The internal sphincter is composed of smooth muscle and hence under autonomic control, and its innervation is normally involuntary, whereas the external sphincter is composed of striate muscle and is under voluntary control.[28] Fecal incontinence is usually caused by a failure of the external sphincter to contract when the internal sphincter relaxes consequent on the entry of a fecal mass into the rectum. However, it may also be due to a failure on the part of the patient to contract the internal sphincter muscle following initial relaxation, thus allowing a constant dribble of fecal material past the relaxed external sphincter with the patient receiving no feedback stimulation from the external sphincter to indicate that anything is amiss. As Goligher and Hughes (1951) have pointed out, this feedback failure may be the result of anal surgery which preserves the striated muscle of the external sphincter (thus enabling strong contraction) but accidentally destroys the feedback mechanism (the sensory nerves embedded in the rectum).

Engel and his colleagues have made use of the fact that the internal sphincter reacts to increased pressure in the rectum by making use of the inflated-balloon technique (Goligher & Hughes, 1951) to train patients with fecal incontinence to become more aware of both internal and external sphincter responding and of their mutual relationships. Engel, Nikoomanesh, and Schuster (1974) studied six patients with daily bowel incontinence (attributed to physical causes) of 3–8 years duration. They first determined that inflation of a balloon inserted into the rectum produced relaxation of the internal sphincter, but that the usual reflex external sphincter contraction was absent or much diminished. Visual feedback of the increased pressure produced by inflation of the balloon was provided to the patients, whose task was to associate the sensations produced by internal sphincter relaxation with a voluntarily produced external sphincter contraction. Engel *et al.* (1974) reported that "each patient was able to sense the rectal distention and each patient knew that this stimulus was the cue to initiate sphincteric control" (p. 647). The patients were trained to approximate normal external sphincter reaction to internal sphincter relaxation, and eventually to do so without the aid of externalized feedback. The results were evaluated objectively as indicated by the presence of external sphincter contraction, the time relationships between internal sphincter relaxation and external sphincter contraction, and changes in the relative amplitude of the responses, as well as by assessment of the clinical

---

[28]Hence, the material considered here could have been included in Chapter 3, rather than in this chapter, since the focus of some of the studies has been entirely on the external sphincter.

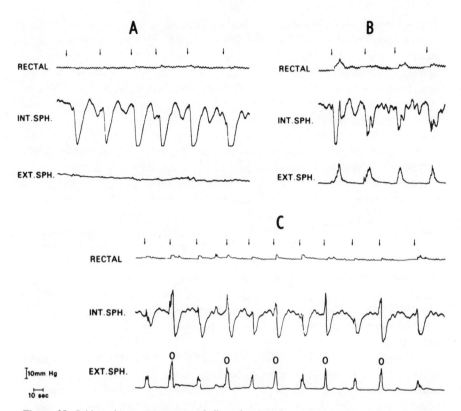

Figure 25. Sphincteric responses to rectal distension (→) in a representative patient. **A.** before training; **B.** during early training; **C.** after training, without feedback. (From Engel, B. T., Nikoomanesh, P., & Schuster, M. M. Operant conditioning of rectosphincteric responses in the treatment of rectal incontinence. *New England Journal of Medicine*, 1974, *290*, 648, Figure 1. Reprinted by permission of the author and the publisher.)

changes which took place. Typical results of training are shown in Figure 25, which shows the response in one patient to 25 ml distention before training (A), during early training (B), and after training, without feedback (C). Four of the six patients became completely continent after training, and the other two virtually free of incontinence over follow-up ranging from 6 months to 5 years. Engel *et al.* (1974) also studied a 6-year-old child who had neither internal nor external sphincter control, and reported successfully training her to control the internal as well as the external sphincter. The importance of this demonstration lies, of course, in the fact, as pointed out earlier, that the internal sphincter is under autonomic control. Subsequently, Cerulli, Nikoomanesh, and Schuster (1976) have provided a brief report of highly successful training of external sphincter control in a series of 40 patients with severe daily fecal incontinence for periods ranging from 1 to 38 years (and age ranges of 6–90 years!). Of the 40 patients,

28 reduced incontinence by more than 90% while the minimal volume of distention in the rectum required to produce an external sphincter contraction was reduced from an average of 35 ml to 20 ml in the successful cases. In follow-up ranging from 4 months to as long as 8 years, only two patients relapsed and they were successfully retrained. Although verbal reinforcement was used in these studies as well as biofeedback, it was not considered that the reinforcement served as other than an initial motivator.

The irritable bowel syndrome involves chronic abdominal pain (colonic spasm), accompanied by diarrhea or constipation, or alternating periods of each. Bueno-Miranda, Cerulli, and Schuster (1976), using the balloon technique, have shown that the spastic contractions are produced by rectosigmoid distention. Snape, Carlson, Matarazzo, and Cohen (1977) have suggested that the distention may be related to emotional stress, the administration of cholinergic drugs, gastrointestinal hormones, and other factors. Using implanted electrodes attached to the colonic mucosa 5–22 cm from the anus, they have shown that colonic contractions are associated to a higher degree with slow wave activity (3 Hz/min) in patients compared with normals (6 Hz/min). The administration of pentagastrin (a drug which increases colonic motor activity) led to a significant increase in 3-Hz contractile activity. Bueno-Miranda *et al.* (1976), in a brief report, successfully used biofeedback to raise the threshold (volume of distention) required to produce spastic contractions in a group of patients suffering from the irritable bowel syndrome. Two-thirds of the patients showed improvements which were maintained at a short follow-up 8 weeks later.

Furman (1973) used an electronic stethoscope to amplify bowel sounds assumed to represent colon and/or small intestine peristaltic activity, and trained five patients with functional diarrhea to increase or decrease peristaltic activity by increasing or decreasing the sounds produced by that activity. All five patients achieved some degree of control within five training sessions with corresponding clinical improvement, the latter occurring in each case at approximately the same time that control of the peristaltic activity was achieved. Since peristaltic activity is under autonomic control, this would appear to represent a case of voluntary control of an autonomic function. Young (1973) trained 14 children with encopresis to become more sensitive to their gastroileal and gastrocolonic reflexes (of which they appeared to be completely unaware). His technique involved providing the child with food or drink on awakening and then putting the child on the toilet 20–30 min later when gastroileal and gastrocolic reflexes should be maximized, the procedure being repeated during the day after each meal. No external feedback of the reflex activity was provided. All but two of the children were successfully treated in this way within a 12-month period.

As pointed out earlier, biofeedback training of the external sphincter represents an example of voluntary striate muscle control. Nevertheless, the study by Kohlenberg (1973) may be considered here. Gray (1971) has shown that it is possible to isolate and bring under voluntary control SMU activity in the external anal sphincter muscle, using inserted electrodes, and this approach may well be a useful technique for training in the development of control of incontinence. However, Kohlenberg (1973) made use of the balloon technique in his study of a patient with a history of continuous soiling believed to be due to inadequate external sphincter tone, resulting in continuous relaxation of the muscle. The balloon was placed so that contraction of the external sphincter on it forced up a column of water, the height of which could be read off on a scale, the reading serving as visual feedback for the patient. The baseline level of pressure in the resting state formed the criterion level, the patient's task being to force the column of water above that level by contracting the external sphincter muscle. The provision of visual feedback alone did not result in any improvement in sphincter control, so Kohlenberg introduced operant procedures. First, monetary reinforcement was provided whenever responding pressure exceeded the criterion (baseline level), using a fixed-interval (FI) schedule of 10 sec. Increased anal sphincter pressure was indeed obtained with this schedule, but the usual FI effects were also found, that is, a gradual increase in pressure during the 10-sec period, followed by a marked reduction immediately after the reinforcer (which was visible to the patient) was delivered. To overcome this problem, Kohlenberg introduced a new reinforcement schedule. Whenever pressure exceeded the criterion, two timers (T_1 and T_2) were activated. Initially, T_1 was set at 10 sec. If increased pressure was achieved during T_1, T_2 was activated at the end of the 10-sec period and ran for 4 sec, at the end of which reinforcement was delivered and T_2 recycled for a further 4 sec. If, however, pressure fell below criterion at any time during T_2, the cycle was broken and T_1 reactivated. The training accomplished with this technique was compared with interspersed extinction periods in which reinforcement was not delivered. With the use of this procedure, a striking increase in both the pressure and duration of external sphincter responses was obtained (it is not entirely clear whether during the operant training phase the visual feedback of pressure was still available to the patient, but it appears that it was probably not available). Independent measures of resting yield pressure indicated a pre–post treatment change from 35 mm Hg to 50 mm Hg. Some degree of clinical improvement was evident on follow-up, but this was admittedly primarily an experimental study.

It will be recalled that work with normal subjects has been carried out on the voluntary control of gastric acid secretion. Only one clinical application of this work has thus far been reported. Welgan (1974) studied ten patients with duodenal ulcers, whose pH levels were ≤ 3.5, the volume of stomach secretions being at least 10 cc every 30 min. Peptic ulcer is believed to result from excessive secretion of hydrochloric acid in the stomach, leading to ulceration and digestion of stomach tissues, as well as reducing the neutralizing capability of stomach mucus secretions. Acid secretions may be reduced if the pH of the stomach contents are increased; hence, if feedback training can lead to an increase in pH concentration, stomach acidity may decrease and the ulcer helped to heal. Welgan (1974) used the technique of stomach aspiration by continuous suction and displayed the acid changes in gastric secretions (as determined by a pH meter) in visual meter and auditory form, which indicated increases in pH. A shaping procedure was used. Following a baseline period of 15 min without feedback, three 15-min training periods with feedback were given, separated by two rest periods without feedback. The patients were fully informed about the procedures. No difference was found between the feedback and rest conditions in pH levels, acid concentrations per liter, or stomach secretion volumes. Welgan (1974) then allocated a new sample of ten patients to one of two conditions: one group was run under a baseline (30 min), rest (15 min), feedback (two 15-min periods) condition; the other was run under a baseline (30 min), treatment (15 min), rest (15 min), treatment (15 min) condition. It was found that increases in pH levels and decreases in acid concentrations and stomach secretion volumes were found only when feedback was introduced. Thus, the overall hypothesis was supported by the second study. As pointed out earlier (and, of course, recognized by Welgan), the significant time delay between stomach activity and the display of that activity, which is an inevitable consequence of using the aspiration technique, may well have set the patients a very difficult task and even produced the same kind of problems found in speech control under delayed auditory feedback. There is an urgent need for a replication of Welgan's study using electronic methods of recording which will abolish the delay in generating a display of pH and other changes. The results obtained by Welgan (1974) under these difficulties are, nevertheless, encouraging.

Schuster (1974, 1977) has reported some important work on the biofeedback treatment of a disorder known as esophageal reflux. The lower esophageal sphincter consists of smooth muscle which is under autonomic nervous system control. Reflux disorders are associated with impaired contraction of the sphincter resulting in lower pressures and a consequent inability to resist upward intragastric pressure. As a result, the contents of the stomach may be regurgitated involuntarily. The object of the biofeedback training is "to teach the patient to maintain a higher ratio of resting sphincter pressure to intragastric pressure" (Schuster, 1974, p. 138). The technique used and clearly described by Schuster (1974, 1977) is ingenious and contains its own inbuilt controls. Three perfused open-tipped catheters are carefully positioned so as to measure separately esophageal, sphincter, and intragastric pressures. Visual meter feedback is presented to the subject or patient from the middle tip (that is, the one in the sphincter) and the subject's task is to increase esophageal pressure without using the abdominal muscles or respiration as an aid. Schuster (1977) has shown that esophageal pressure is indeed significantly lower in patients with reflux disorders than in normal subjects. Both patients and normal subjects can produce very marked increases in pressure when provided with feedback, although even after training the patients will have lower pressures than the normals before training (pressure in normals averages 16 mm Hg before training, whereas in patients it averages from 5 mm Hg to 8 mm Hg, rising to 7.5–10.5 mm Hg after training). Anticipatory pressure increases, preventing reflux, may be acquired after training. Skeletal mediation is discounted by Schuster on the basis of simultaneous readings taken from the other two catheters and lack of change in breathing rate.

References

Abboud, F. M. Relaxation, autonomic control and hypertension. *New England Journal of Medicine*, 1976, *294*, 107–109.

Adler, C. S., & Adler, S. M. Biofeedback psychotherapy for the treatment of headaches: A 5-year follow-up. *Headache*, 1976, *16*, 189–191.

Andreychuk. T., & Skriver, C. Hypnosis and biofeedback in the treatment of migraine headache. *International Journal of Clinical and Experimental Hypnosis*, 1975, *23*, 172–183. (1975/76:12)

Bakal, D. A. Headache: A biopsychological perspective. *Psychological Bulletin*, 1975, *82*, 369–382.

Bell, I. R., & Schwartz, G. E. Voluntary control and reactivity of human heart rate. *Psychophysiology*, 1975, *12*, 339–348. (1975/76:34)

Benson, H., Shapiro, D., Tursky, B., & Schwartz, G. E. Decreased systolic blood pressure through operant conditioning techniques in patients with essential hypertension. *Science*, 1971, *173*, 740–742. (1971:37)

Benson, H., Rosner, B. A., Marzetta, B. R., & Klemchuk, H. P. Decreased blood pressure in borderline hypertensive subjects who practised meditation. *Journal of Chronic Disease*, 1974, *27*, 163–169. (a)

Benson, H., Rosner, B. A., Marzetta, B. R., & Klemchuk, H. M. Decreased blood pressure in pharmacologically treated hypertensive patients who regularly elicited the relaxation response. *Lancet*, 1974, *1*, 289–291. (b) (1974:50)

Bergman, J. S., & Johnson, H. J. The effects of instructional set and autonomic perception on cardiac control. *Psychophysiology*, 1971, *8*, 180–190. (1971:17)

Birk, L., Crider, A., Shapiro, D., & Tursky, B. Operant electrodermal conditioning under partial curarization. *Journal of Comparative and Physiological Psychology*, 1966, *62*, 165–166. (R:23)

Blanchard, E. B., & Haynes, M. R. Biofeedback treatment of a case of Raynaud's disease. *Journal of Behavior Therapy and Experimental Psychiatry*, 1975, *6*, 230–234.

Blanchard, E. B., & Young, L. D. The relative efficacy of visual and auditory feedback for self-control of heart-rate. *Journal of General Psychology*, 1972, *87*, 195–202.

Blanchard, E. B., & Young, L. D. Self-control of cardiac functioning: A promise as yet unfulfilled. *Psychological Bulletin*, 1973, *79*, 145–163. (1973:30)

Blanchard, E. B., Scott, R. W., Young, L. D., & Haynes, M. R. The effects of feedback signal information content on the long-term self-control of heart rate. *Journal of General Psychology*, 1974, *91*, 175–187.

Blanchard, E. B., Young, L. D., Haynes, M. R., & Kallman, M. D. A simple feedback system for self-control of blood pressure. *Perceptual and Motor Skills*, 1974, *39*, 891–898.

Blanchard, E. B., Young, L. D., Scott, R. W., & Haynes, M. R. Differential effects of feedback and reinforcement in voluntary acceleration of human heart rate. *Perceptual and Motor Skills*, 1974, *38*, 683–691.

Blanchard, E. B., Young, L. D., & Haynes, M. R. A simple feedback system for the treatment of elevated blood pressure. *Behavior Therapy*, 1975, *6*, 241–245. (1975/76:47)

Blanchard, E. B., Young, L. D., Haynes, M. R., & Scott, R. W. Long-term instructional control of heart rate without exteroceptive feedback. *Journal of General Psychology*, 1975, *92*, 291–292.

Blanchard, E. B., Haynes, M. R., Kallman, M. D., & Harkey, L. A comparison of direct blood pressure feedback and electromyographic feedback on the blood pressure of normotensives. *Biofeedback and Self-Regulation,* 1976, *1,* 445–451.

Bleecker, E. R., & Engel, B. T. Learned control of ventricular rate in patients with atrial fibrillation. *Psychosomatic Medicine,* 1973, *35,* 161–175. (a) (1973:24)

Bleecker, E. R., & Engel, B. T. Learned control of cardiac rate and cardiac conduction in the Wolff–Parkinson–White syndrome. *New England Journal of Medicine,* 1973, *288,* 560–562. (b) (1973:25)

Bollinger, A., & Schlumpf, M. Finger blood flow in healthy subjects of different age and sex and in patients with primary Raynaud's disease. *Acta Chirurgica Scandinavica,* 1976, Suppl. 465, 42–47.

Boudewyns, P. A. A comparison of the effects of stress vs. relaxation instruction on the finger temperature response. *Behavior Therapy,* 1976, *7,* 54–67.

Brady, J. P., Luborsky, L., & Kron, R. E. Blood pressure reduction in patients with essential hypertension through metronome-conditioned relaxation: A preliminary report. *Behavior Therapy,* 1974, *5,* 203–209. (1974:21)

Brener, J. Heart rate as an avoidance response. *Psychological Record,* 1966, *16,* 329–336.

Brener, J., & Hothersall, D. Heart rate control under conditions of augmented sensory feedback. *Psychophysiology,* 1966, *3,* 23–28. (R:4)

Brener, J., & Kleinman, R. A. Learned control of decreases in systolic blood pressure. *Nature,* 1970, *226,* 1063–1064. (1970:22)

Brener, J. P., Kleinman, R. A., & Goesling, W. J. The effects of different exposures to augmented sensory feedback on the control of heart rate. *Psychophysiology,* 1969, *5,* 510–516.

Brown, C. C. The parotid puzzle: A review of the literature on human salivation and its application to psychophysiology. *Psychophysiology,* 1970, *7,* 66–85.

Brown, C. C., & Katz, R. A. Operant salivary conditioning in man. *Psychophysiology,* 1967, *4,* 156–160. (R:27)

Brown, C. C., Giddon, D. B., & Dean, E. D. Techniques of plethysmography. *Psychophysiology,* 1965, *1,* 253–266.

Bueno-Miranda, F., Cerulli, M., & Schuster, M. M. Operant conditioning of colonic motility in irritable bowel syndrome (IBS). *Gastroenterology,* 1976, *70,* 867. (Abstract)

Bulpitt, C. J., Dollery, C. T., & Carne, S. A symptom questionnaire for hypertensive patients. *Journal of Chronic Disorders,* 1974, *27,* 309–323.

Cabanac, M., Hildebrandt, G., Massonet, B., & Strempel, H. A study of the nycthemeral cycle of behavioral temperature regulation in man. *Journal of Physiology,* 1976, *257,* 257–291.

Cardus, D., Fuentes, F., & Srinivasan, R. Cardiac evaluation of a physical rehabilitation program for patients with ischemic heart disease. *Archives of Physical Medicine and Rehabilitation,* 1975, *56,* 419–425.

Cerulli, M., Nikoomanesh, P., & Schuster, M. M. Progress in biofeedback treatment of fecal incontinence. *Gastroenterology,* 176, *70,* 869. (Abstract)

Christie, D. J., & Kotses, H. Bidirectional operant conditioning of the cephalic vasomotor response. *Journal of Psychosomatic Research,* 1973, *17,* 167–170.

Clark, R. E., & Forgione, A. G. Gingival and digital vasomotor response to thermal imagery in hypnosis. *Journal of Dental Research,* 1974, *53,* 792–796.

Conway, J. Labile hypertension: The problem. *Circulation Research,* 1970, *27,* Supl. I-43 to I-47.

Crider, A., Shapiro, D., & Tursky, B. Reinforcement of spontaneous electrodermal activity. *Journal of Comparative and Physiological Psychology,* 1966, *61,* 20–27. (R:22)

Dalessio, D. J. Headache. In C. G. Costello (Ed.), *Symptoms of psychopathology.* New York: Wiley, 1970, pp. 624–639

Daniels, L. K. The effects of automated hypnosis and hand warming on migraine: A pilot study. *American Journal of Clinical Hypnosis,* 1976, *19,* 91–94.

Daniels, L. K. Treatment of migraine headache by hypnosis and behavior therapy: A case study. *American Journal of Clinical Hypnosis*, 1977, *19*, 241–244.

Datey, K. K., Deshmukh, S. N., Dalvi, C. P., & Vinekar, S. L. "Shavasan": A yogic exercise in management of hypertension. *Angiology*, 1969, *20*, 325–333. (R:67)

Davidson, R. J., & Schwartz, G. E. Patterns of cerebral lateralization during cardiac biofeedback versus the self-regulation of emotion: Sex differences. *Psychophysiology*, 1976, *13*, 62–68.

Davis, J. D., & Levine, M. W. A model for the control of ingestion. *Psychological Review*, 1977, *84*, 379–412.

Defran, R. H., Badia, P., & Lewis, P. Stimulus control over operant galvanic skin responses. *Psychophysiology*, 1969, *6*, 101–106.

DeGood, D. E., & Adams, A. S. Control of cardiac response under aversive stimulation: Superiority of a heart-rate feedback condition. *Biofeedback and Self-Regulation*, 1976, *1*, 373–385.

Delse, F. C., & Feather, B. W. The effect of augmented sensory feedback on the control of salivation. *Psychophysiology*, 1968, *5*, 15–21.

Diekhoff, G. M. Effects of feedback in a forced-choice GSR detection task. *Psychophysiology*, 1976, *13*, 22–26.

Dugan, M., & Sheridan, C. Effects of instructed imagery on temperature of hands. *Perceptual and Motor Skills*, 1976, *42*, 14.

Edelman, R. I. Effects of differential afferent feedback on instrumental GSR conditioning. *Journal of Psychology*, 1970, *74*, 3–14.

Edmeads, J. Cerebral blood flow in migraine. *Headache*, 1977, *17*, 148–152.

Edwards, E. A., Ottinger, L., & Ruberti, U. Pulse registration as a means of evaluating peripheral vascular potency and vasomotor activity. *American Journal of Cardiology*, 1959, *4*, 572–579.

Elder, S. T., & Eustis, N. K. Instrumental blood pressure conditioning in out-patient hypertensives. *Behavior Research and Therapy*, 1975, *13*, 185–188. (1975/76:46)

Elder, S. T., Ruiz, Z. R., Deabler, H. L., & Dillenkoffer, R. L. Instrumental conditioning of diastolic blood pressure in essential hypertensive patients. *Journal of Applied Behavior Analysis*, 1973, *6*, 377–382. (1973:26)

Elder, S. T., Leftwich, D. A., & Wilkerson, L. A. The role of systolic- versus diastolic-contingent feedback in blood pressure conditioning. *Psychological Record*, 1974, *24*, 171–176.

Elder, S. T., Longacre, A., Welsh, D. M., & McAfee, R. D. Apparatus and procedure for training subjects to control their blood pressure. *Psychophysiology*, 1977, *14*, 68–72.

Elder, S. T., Welsh, D. M., Longacre, A., & McAfee, R. Acquisition, discriminative stimulus control, and retention of increases/decreases in blood pressure of normotensive human subjects. *Journal of Applied Behavior Analysis*, 1977, *10*, 381–390.

Emery, H., Schaller, J. G., & Fowler, R. S. Biofeedback in the management of primary and secondary Raynaud's phenomenon. *Arthritis and Rheumatism*, 1976, *19*, 795. (Abstract)

Engel, B. T. Operant conditioning of cardiac function: A status report. *Psychophysiology*, 1972, *9*, 161–177. (1972:13)

Engel, B. T., & Bleecker, E. R. Application of operant conditioning techniques to the control of the cardiac arrhythmias. In P. Obrist *et al.* (Eds.), *Contemporary trends in cardiovascular psychophysiology*. Chicago: Aldine–Atherton, 1974, pp. 456–476.

Engel, B. T., & Chism, R. A. Operant conditioning of heart rate speeding. *Psychophysiology*, 1967, *3*, 418–426.

Engel, B. T., & Hansen, S. P. Operant conditioning of heart rate slowing. *Psychophysiology*, 1966, *3*, 176–187. (R:3)

Engel, B. T., & Melmon, I. Operant conditioning of heart rate in patients with cardiac arrhythmias. *Conditional Reflex*, 1968, *3*, 130. (Abstract)

Engel, B. T., Nikoomanesh, P., & Schuster, M. M. Operant conditioning of rectosphincteric responses in the treatment of rectal incontinence. *New England Journal of Medicine*, 1974, *290*, 646–649. (1974:38)

Eustis, N. K., & Elder, S. T. Instrumental blood pressure conditioning in outpatient hypertensives. Paper presented at the 18th International Congress of Applied Psychology, Montreal, 1974.

Fahrion, S. L. Autogenic biofeedback treatment for migraine. *Mayo Clinic Proceedings,* 1977, *52,* 776–784.

Fetcher, E. S., Hall, J. F., & Shaub, H. G. The skin temperature of an extremity as a measure of its bloodflow. *Science,* 1949, *110,* 422–423.

Feuerstein, M., Adams, H. E., & Beiman, I. Cephalic vasomotor and electromyographic feedback in the treatment of combined muscle contraction and migraine headaches in a geriatric case. *Headache,* 1976, *16,* 232–237.

Fey, S. G., & Lindholm, E. Systolic blood pressure and heart rate changes during three sessions involving biofeedback or no feedback. *Psychophysiology,* 1975, *12,* 513–519. (1975/76:40)

Finley, W. W. The effect of feedback on the control of cardiac rate. *Journal of Psychology,* 1971, *77,* 43–54.

Flecker, R. Skin temperature as a psychophysical variable. *Australian Journal of Psychology,* 1951, *3,* 109–120.

Fleming, D. S., Finkelstein, S., Papra, J. G., & Twogood, G. R. Hypertension control. *Minnesota Medicine,* 1975, *58,* 895–898.

Floyer, M. A. Renal control of interstitial space compliance: A physiological mechanism which may play a part in the etiology of hypertension. *Clinical Nephrology,* 1975, *4,* 152–156.

Fowler, R. L., & Kimmel, H. D. Operant conditioning of the GSR. *Journal of Experimental Psychology,* 1962, *63,* 573–577.

Fowles, D. C. Mechanisms of electrodermal activity. In R. F. Thompson and M. M. Patterson (Eds.), *Bioelectric recording techniques* (Part C) *Receptor and Effector Processes.* New York: Academic, 1974, pp. 232–271.

Frazier, T. W. Avoidance conditioning of heart rate in humans. *Psychophysiology,* 1966, *3,* 188–202.

Frezza, D. A., & Holland, J. G. Operant conditioning of the human salivary response. *Psychophysiology,* 1971, *8,* 581–587. (1971:18)

Friar, L. R., & Beatty, J. Migraine: Management by trained control of vasoconstriction. *Journal of Consulting and Clinical Psychology,* 1976, *44,* 46–53. (1976/77:14)

Friedman, H., & Taub, H. A. The use of hypnosis and biofeedback procedures for essential hypertension. *International Journal of Clinical and Experimental Hypnosis,* 1977, *25,* 335–347.

Friedman, H., & Taub, H. A. A six-month follow-up of the use of hypnosis and biofeedback procedures in essential hypertension. *American Journal of Clinical Hypnosis,* 1978, *20,* 184–188.

Furman, S. Intestinal biofeedback in functional diarrhea: A preliminary report. *Journal of Behavior Therapy and Experimental Psychiatry,* 1973, *4,* 317–321. (1974:39)

Gatchel, R. J. Frequency of feedback and learned heart rate control. *Journal of Experimental Psychology,* 1974, *103,* 274–283. (1975/76:39)

Gavalas, R. J. Operant reinforcement of an autonomic response: Two studies. *Journal of the Experimental Analysis of Behavior,* 1967, *10,* 119–130.

Gavalas, R. J. Operant reinforcement of a skeletally mediated autonomic response: Uncoupling of the two responses. *Psychonomic Science,* 1968, *11,* 195–196.

Goldman, H., Kleinman, K. M., Snow, M. Y., Bidus, D. R., & Korol, B. Relationship between essential hypertension and cognitive functioning: Effects of biofeedback. *Psychophysiology,* 1975, *12,* 569–573. (1975/76:45)

Goligher, J. C., & Hughes, E. S. R. Sensibility of the rectum and colon: Its role in the mechanism of anal continence. *Lancet,* 1951, *1,* 543–548.

Gray, E. R. Conscious control of motor units in tonic muscle: The effect of motor unit training. *American Journal of Physical Medicine,* 1971, *50,* 34–40.

Greene, W. A. Operant conditioning of the GSR using partial reinforcement. *Psychological Reports*, 1966, *19*, 571–578.

Gribbin, B., Steptoe, A., & Sleight, P. Pulse wave velocity as a measure of blood pressure change. *Psychophysiology*, 1976, *13*, 86–90.

Griggs, R. C., & Stunkard, A. The interpretation of gastric motility: Sensitivity and bias in the perception of gastric motility. *Archives of General Psychiatry*, 1964, *11*, 82–89. (R:34)

Grings, W. W. Recording of electrodermal phenomena. In R. F. Thompson & M. M. Patterson (Eds.), *Bioelectric recording techniques* (Part C) *Receptor and Effector Processes*. New York: Academic, 1974, pp. 273–296.

Hadfield, A. The influence of suggestion on body temperature. *Lancet*, 1920, *2*, 68–69.

Hansteen, V. Medical treatment in Raynaud's disease. *Acta Chirurgica Scandinavica*, 1976, Suppl. 465, pp. 87–91.

Hardy, J. D. Physiology of temperature regulation. *Physiological Review*, 1961, *41*, 521–607.

Harrison, R. S., & Raskin, D. C. The role of feedback in control of heart rate variability. *Psychophysiology*, 1976, *13*, 135–139.

Hay, K. M., & Madders, J. Migraine treated by relaxation therapy. *Journal of the Royal College of General Practitioners*, 1971, *21*, 664–669.

Headrick, M. W., Feather, B. W., & Wells, D. T., Unidirectional and large magnitude heart rate changes with augmented sensory feedback. *Psychophysiology*, 1971, *8*, 132–142. (1971:16)

Henryk-Gutt, R., & Rees, W. L. Psychological aspects of migraine. *Journal of Psychosomatic Research*, 1973, *17*, 141–153.

Herzfeld, G. M., & Taub, E. Suggestion as an aid to self-regulation of hand temperature. *International Journal of Neuroscience*, 1977, *8*, 23–26.

Hnatiow, M. J. Learned control of heart rate and blood pressure. *Perceptual and Motor Skills*, 1971, *33*, 219–226.

Hnatiow, M. J. & Lang, P. J. Learned stabilization of cardiac rate. *Psychophysiology*, 1965, *1*, 330–336. (R:2)

Hubel, K. A. Voluntary control of gastrointestinal function: Operant conditioning and biofeedback. *Gastroenterology*, 1974, *66*, 1085–1090. (1974:37)

Hunter, S. H., Russell, H. L., Russell, E. D., & Zimmermann, R. L. Control of fingertip temperature increases via biofeedback in learning-disabled and normal children. *Perceptual and Motor Skills*, 1976, *43*, 743–755.

Hwang, C. L., & Konz, S. A. Engineering models of the human thermoregulatory system—a review. *IEEE Transactions on Biomedical Engineering*, 1977, *BME-24*, 309–325.

Ikeda, Y., & Hirai, H. Voluntary control of electrodermal activity in relation to imagery and internal perception scores. *Psychophysiology*, 1976, *13*, 330–333.

Jacobson, A. M., Hackett, R. P., Surman, O. S., & Silverberg, E. L. Raynaud's phenomenon: Treatment with hypnotic and operant technique. *Journal of the American Medical Association*, 1973, *225*, 739–740.

Jacobson, E. Variation of blood pressure with skeletal muscle tension and relaxation. *Annals of Internal Medicine*, 1939, *12*, 1194–1212.

Jernsted, G. C., & Newcomer, J. P. Blood pressure and pulse wave velocity measurement for operant conditioning of autonomic responding. *Behavior Research Methods and Instrumentation*, 1974, *6*, 393–399.

Johnson, H. J., & Schwartz, G. E. Suppression of GSR activity through operant reinforcement. *Journal of Experimental Psychology*, 1967, *75*, 307–312. (R:25)

Johnson, R. F. Q., & Barber, T. X. Hypnotic suggestions for blister formation: Subjective and physiological effects. *American Journal of Clinical Hypnosis*, 1976, *18*, 172–181. (1975/76:10)

Johnson, W. G., & Turin, A. Biofeedback treatment of migraine headache: A systematic case study. *Behavior Therapy*, 1975, *6*, 394–397.

Johnston, D. Criterion level and instructional effects in the voluntary control of heart rate. *Biological Psychology*, 1976, *4*, 1–17. (1976/77:22)

Johnston, D. Feedback and instructional effects in the voluntary control of digital pulse amplitude. *Biological Psychology*, 1977, *5*, 159–171.

Kahn, A., Morris, J. J., & Citron, P. Patient-initiated rapid atrial pacing to manage supra-ventricular tachycardia. *American Journal of Cardiology*, 1976, *38*, 200–204.

Katkin, E. S., & Murray, E. N. Instrumental conditioning of autonomically mediated behavior: Theoretical and methodological issues. *Psychological Bulletin*, 1968, *70*, 52–68. (R:50)

Keefe, F. J. Conditioning changes in differential skin temperature. *Perceptual and Motor Skills*, 1975, *40*, 283–288. (1975/76:31)

Kimmel, E., & Kimmel, H. D. A replication of operant conditioning of the GSR. *Journal of Experimental Psychology*, 1963, *65*, 212–213.

Kimmel, H. D. Instrumental conditioning of autonomically mediated behavior. *Psychological Bulletin*, 1967, *67*, 337–345. (R:49)

Kimmel, H. D., & Gurucharri, F. W. Operant GSR conditioning with cool air reinforcement. *Pavlovian Journal of Biological Science*, 1975, *10*, 239–245.

Kimmel, H. D., & Hill, F. A. Operant conditioning of the GSR. *Psychological Reports*, 1960, *7*, 555–562.

Kimmel, H. D., Pendergrass, V. E., & Kimmel, E. B. Modifying children's orienting reactions instrumentally. *Conditional Reflex*, 1967, *2*, 227–235.

Kleinman, K. M., Goldman, H., Snow, M. Y., & Korol, B. Relationship between essential hypertension and cognitive functioning. II. Effects of biofeedback training generalize to nonlaboratory environment. *Psychophysiology*, 1977, *14*, 192–197.

Klinge, V. Effects of exteroceptive feedback and instructions on control of spontaneous galvanic skin response. *Psychophysiology*, 1972, *9*, 305–317. (1972:23)

Kohlenberg, R. J. Operant conditioning of human anal sphincter pressure. *Journal of Applied Behavior Analysis*, 1973, *6*, 201–208.

Koppman, J. W., McDonald, R. D., & Kunzel, M. G. Voluntary regulation of temporal artery diameter in migraine patients. *Headache*, 1974, *14*, 133–138.

Kotses, H., Rapaport, I., & Glaus, K. D. Operant conditioning of skin resistance tonic levels. *Biofeedback and Self-Regulation*, 1978, *3*, 43–50.

Kristt, D. A., & Engel, B. T. Learned control of blood pressure in patients with high blood pressure. *Circulation*, 1975, *51*, 370–378. (1975/76:43)

Lacroix, J. M. Effects of biofeedback on the discrimination of electrodermal activity. *Biofeedback and Self-Regulation*, 1977, *2*, 393–406.

Lang, P. J., & Twentyman, C. T. Learning to control heart rate: Binary vs. analog feedback. *Psychophysiology*, 1974, *11*, 616–629. (1974:16)

Lang, P. J., & Twentyman, C. T. Learning to control heart rate: Effects of varying incentive and criterion of success on task performance. *Psychophysiology*, 1976, *13*, 378–385. (1976/77:20)

Lang, P. J., Sroufe, L. A., & Hastings, J. E. Effects of feedback and instructional set on the control of cardiac rate variability. *Journal of Experimental Psychology*, 1967, *75*, 425–431.

Lang, P. J., Troyer, W. G., Twentyman, C. T., & Gatchel, R. J. Differential effects of heart rate modification training on college students, older males, and patients with ischemic heart disease. *Psychosomatic Medicine*, 1975, *37*, 429–446. (1975/76:37)

Lantzsch, W., & Drunkenmöller, C. Kreislaufanalytische Untersuchungen bei Patienten mit essentieller Hypertonie während der ersten und zweiten Standardübung des autogenen Trainings. *Psychiatria Clinica*, 1975, *8*, 223–228.

Levene, H. I., Engel, B. T., & Pearson, J. A. Differential operant conditioning of heart rate. *Psychosomatic Medicine*, 1968, *30*, 837–845. (R:7)

Levenson, R. W. Feedback effects and respiratory involvement in voluntary control of heart rate. *Psychophysiology*, 1976, *13*, 108–114.

Livesey, P. J., & Kirk, R. L. Chronic extinction of conditioned vaso-motor responses in man. *Australian Journal of Psychology*, 1953, *5*, 133–145.

Lynch, J. J., Paskewitz, D. A., Gimbel, K. S., & Thomas, S. A. Psychological aspects of cardiac arrhythmia. *American Heart Journal*, 1977, *93*, 645–657.

Lynch, W. C., Hama, H., Kohn, S., & Miller, N. E. Instrumental control of peripheral vasomotor responses in children. *Psychophysiology*, 1976, *13*, 219–221. (1976/77:16)

McCanne, T. R., & Sandman, C. A. Proprioceptive awareness, information about response-reinforcement contingencies, and operant heart-rate control. *Physiological Psychology*, 1976, *4*, 369–375.

McDonagh, J. M., & McGinnis, M. Skin temperature increases as a function of base-line temperature, autogenic suggestion, and biofeedback. *Proceedings of the 81st Annual Convention of the American Psychological Association*, 1973, 547–548.

McFarland, R. A., & Coombs, R. Anxiety and feedback as factors in operant heart rate control. *Psychophysiology*, 1974, *11*, 53–57.

Manuck, S. B., Levenson, R. W., Hinrichsen, J. J., & Gryll, S. L. Role of feedback in voluntary control of heart rate. *Perceptual and Motor Skills*, 1975, *40*, 747–752. (1975/76:32)

Martin, R. B., & Dean, S. J. Instrumental modification of the GSR. *Psychophysiology*, 1971, *7*, 178–185.

Martin, R. B., Dean, S. J., & Shean, G. Selective attention and instrumental modification of the GSR. *Psychophysiology*, 1968, *4*, 460–467.

Maslach, C., Marshall, G., & Zimbardo, P. G. Hypnotic control of peripheral skin temperature: A case report. *Psychophysiology*, 1972, *9*, 600–605. (1972:32)

Medina, J. L., Diamond, S., & Franklin, M. A. Biofeedback therapy for migraine. *Headache*, 1976, *16*, 115–118.

Meichenbaum, D. Cognitive factors in biofeedback therapy. *Biofeedback and Self-Regulation*, 1976, *1*, 201–216. (1976/77:4)

Mendlowitz, M., & Naftchi, N. The digital circulation in Raynaud's disease. *American Journal of Cardiology*, 1959, *4*, 580–584.

Miller, N. E. Learning of glandular and visceral responses. In D. Singh & C. T. Morgan (Eds.), *Current status of physiological psychology*. Belmont: Wadsworth, 1972. (1972:8)

Mitch, P. S., McGrady, A., & Iannone, A. Autogenic feedback training in migraine: A treatment report. *Headache*, 1976, *15*, 267–270.

Mitchell, K. R., & Mitchell, D. M. Migraine: An exploratory treatment application of programmed behavior therapy techniques. *Journal of Psychosomatic Research*, 1971, *15*, 137–157.

Mitchell, K. R., & White, R. G. *The prevention and self-management of anxiety: II.* Sydney: Psychological Behavior Associates Press, 1974.

Mitchell, K. R., & White, R. G. Control of migraine headache by behavioral self-management: A controlled case study. *Headache*, 1976, *16*, 178–184.

Mitchell, K. R., & White, R. G. Behavioral self-management: An application to the problem of migraine headaches. *Behavior Therapy*, 1977, *8*, 213–221.

Mitchell, K. R., Piatkowska, O. E., & White, R. G. *The prevention and self-management of anxiety: I.* Sydney: Psychological Behavior Associates Press, 1974.

Mittelman, B., & Wolff, H. G. Affective states and skin temperature: Experimental study of subjects with "cold hands" and Raynaud's syndrome. *Psychosomatic Medicine*, 1939, *1*, 271–292.

Mullinix, J. M., Norton, B. J., Hack, S., & Fishman, M. A. Skin temperature biofeedback and migraine. *Headache*, 1978, *17*, 242–244.

Murray, E. N., & Katkin, E. S. Comment on two recent reports of operant heart rate conditioning. *Psychophysiology*, 1968, *5*, 192–195.

Norman, A. Response contingency and human gastric acidity. *Psychophysiology*, 1969, *5*, 673–682.

Ohno, Y., Tanaka, Y., Takeya, T., & Ikemi, Y. Modification of skin temperature by biofeedback procedures. *Journal of Behavior Therapy and Experimental Psychiatry*, 1977, *8*, 31–34.

Patel, C. H. Yoga and biofeedback in the management of hypertension. *Lancet,* 1973, *2,* 1053–1055. (1973:27)

Patel, C. Twelve-month follow-up of yoga and biofeedback in the management of hypertension. *Lancet,* 1975, *1,* 62–64. (a) (1975/76:8)

Patel, C. Yoga and biofeedback in the management of hypertension. *Journal of Psychosomatic Research,* 1975, *19,* 355–360. (b)

Patel, C. Yoga and biofeedback in the management of "stress" in hypertensive patients. *Clinical Science and Molecular Medicine,* 1975, *48,* 171–174. (c) (suppl.)

Patel, C. Reduction of serum cholesterol and blood pressure in hypertensive patients by behavior modification. *Journal of the Royal College of General Practitioners: British Journal of General Practice,* 1976, *26,* 211–215.

Patel, C. H. Biofeedback-aided relaxation and meditation in the management of hypertension. *Biofeedback and Self-Regulation,* 1977, *2,* 1–41.

Patel, C., & Carruthers, M. Coronary risk factor reduction through biofeedback-aided relaxation and meditation. *Journal of the Royal College of General Practitioners: British Journal of General Practice,* 1977, *27,* 401–405.

Patel, C., & Datey, K. K. Relaxation and biofeedback techniques in the management of hypertension. *Angiology,* 1976, *27,* 106–113.

Patel, C., & North, W. R. S. Randomized controlled trial of yoga and biofeedback in management of hypertension. *Lancet,* 1975, *2,* 93–95.

Paulley, J. W., & Haskell, D. A. L. The treatment of migraine without drugs. *Journal of Psychosomatic Research,* 1975, *19,* 367–374.

Philips, C. Headache and personality. *Journal of Psychosomatic Research,* 1976, *20,* 535–542.

Pickering, T., & Gorham, G. Learned heart-rate control by a patient with a ventricular parasystolic rhythm. *Lancet,* 1975, *1,* 252–253. (1976/77:27)

Pickering, T. G., & Miller, N. E. Learned voluntary control of heart rate and rhythm in two subjects with premature ventricular contractions. *British Heart Journal,* 1977, *39,* 152–159.

Pollack, A. A., Weber, M. A., Case, D. B., & Laragh, J. H. Limitations of transcendental meditation in the treatment of essential hypertension. *Lancet,* 1977, *1,* 71–73.

Price, K. P., & Tursky, B. Vascular reactivity of migraineurs and nonmigraineurs: A comparison of responses to self-control procedures. *Headache,* 1976, *16,* 210–217.

Rappaport, A. F., & Cammer, L. Breath meditation in the treatment of essential hypertension. *Behavior Therapy,* 1977, *8,* 269–270.

Ray, W. J. The relationship of locus of control, self-report measures, and feedback to the voluntary control of heart rate. *Psychophysiology,* 1974, *11,* 527–534. (1974:14)

Ray, W. J., & Lamb, S. B. Locus of control and the voluntary control of heart rate. *Psychosomatic Medicine,* 1974, *36,* 180–182.

Razran, G. The observable unconscious and the inferable conscious in current Soviet psychophysiology. *Psychological Review,* 1961, *68,* 81–147. (R:56)

Reading, C., & Mohr, P. D. Biofeedback control of migraine: A pilot study. *British Journal of Social and Clinical Psychology,* 1976, *15,* 429–433.

Redmond, D. P., Gaylor, M. S., McDonald, R. H., & Shapiro, A. P. Blood pressure and heart-rate response to verbal instruction and relaxation in hypertension. *Psychosomatic Medicine,* 1974, *36,* 285–297.

Reeves, J. L. EMG-biofeedback reduction of tension headache: A cognitive skills training approach. *Biofeedback and Self-Regulation,* 1976, *1,* 217–225.

Rice, D. G. Operant conditioning and associated electromyogram responses. *Journal of Experimental Psychology,* 1966, *71,* 908–912.

Richter-Heinrich, E., Knust, U., Müller, W., Schmidt, K-H., & Sprung, H. Psychophysiological investigations in essential hypertensives. *Journal of Psychosomatic Research,* 1975, *19,* 251–258.

Roberts, A. H., Kewman, D. G., & MacDonald, H. Voluntary control of skin temperature: Unilateral changes using hypnosis and feedback. *Journal of Abnormal Psychology*, 1973, *82*, 163–168. (1973:1)

Roberts, A. H., Schuler, J., Bacon, J. G., Zimmerman, R. L., & Patterson, R. Individual differences and autonomic control: Absorption, hypnotic susceptibility, and the unilateral control of skin temperature. *Journal of Abnormal Psychology*, 1975, *84*, 272–279. (1975/76:30)

Sargent, J. D., Green, E. E., & Walters, E. D. The use of autogenic feedback training in a pilot study of migraine and tension headache. *Headache*, 1972, *12*, 120–125.

Sargent, J. D., Green, E. E., & Walters, E. D. Preliminary report on the use of autogenic feedback training in the treatment of migraine and tension headaches. *Psychosomatic Medicine*, 1973, *35*, 129–135. (1973:21)

Sargent, J. D., Walters, E. D., & Green, E. E. Psychosomatic self-regulation of migraine headaches. *Seminars in Psychiatry*, 1973, *5*, 415–428.

Schuster, M. M. Operant conditioning in gastrointestinal dysfunctions. *Hospital Practice*, 1974, *9*, 135–143.

Schuster, M. M. Biofeedback treatment of gastrointestinal disorders. *Medical Clinics of North America*, 1977, *61*, 907–912.

Schwartz, G. E. Voluntary control of human cardiovascular integration and differentiation through feedback and reward. *Science*, 1972, *175*, 90–93. (1972:14)

Schwartz, G. E., & Shapiro, D. Biofeedback and essential hypertension: Current findings and theoretical concerns. *Seminars in Psychiatry*, 1973, *5*, 493–503. (1973:29)

Schwartz, G. E., Shapiro, D., & Tursky, B. Learned control of cardiovascular integration in man through operant conditioning. *Psychosomatic Medicine*, 1971, *33*, 57–62. (1971:15)

Scott, R. W., Blanchard, E. B., Edmunson, E. D., & Young, L. D. A shaping procedure for heart rate control of chronic tachycardia. *Perceptual and Motor Skills*, 1973, *37*, 327–338.

Scott, R. W., Peters, R. D., Gillespie, W. J., Blanchard, E. B., Edmunson, E. D., & Young, L. D. The use of shaping and reinforcement in the operant acceleration and deceleration of heart rate. *Behavior Research and Therapy*, 1973, *11*, 179–185.

Shapiro, A. P., Redmond, D. P., McDonald, R. H., & Gaylor, M. Relationships of perception, cognition, suggestion and operant conditioning in essential hypertension. *Progress in Brain Research*, 1975, *42*, 299–312.

Shapiro, D., & Crider, A. Operant electrodermal conditioning under multiple schedules of reinforcement. *Psychophysiology*, 1967, *4*, 168–175. (R:24)

Shapiro, D., & Watanabe, T. Timing characteristics of operant electrodermal modification: Fixed-interval effects. *Japanese Psychological Research*, 1971, *13*, 123–130. (1972:24)

Shapiro, D., & Watanabe, T. Reinforcement of spontaneous electrodermal activity: A cross-cultural study in Japan. *Psychophysiology*, 1972, *9*, 340–344.

Shapiro, D., Crider, A. B., & Tursky, B. Differentiation of an autonomic response through operant reinforcement. *Psychonomic Science*, 1964, *1*, 147–148. (R:21)

Shapiro, D., Tursky, B., Gershon, E., & Stern, M. Effects of feedback and reinforcement on the control of human systolic blood pressure. *Science*, 1969, *163*, 588–589. (R:16)

Shapiro, D., Tursky, B., & Schwartz, G. E. Control of blood pressure in man by operant conditioning. *Circulation Research*, 1970, *26*, Suppl. 1, 27, I-27 to I-32. (a) (1970:26)

Shapiro, D., Tursky, B., & Schwartz, G. E. Differentiation of heart rate and blood pressure in man by operant conditioning. *Psychosomatic Medicine*, 1970, *32*, 417–423. (b) (1970:27)

Shapiro, D., Schwartz, G. E., & Tursky, B. Control of diastolic blood pressure in man by feedback and reinforcement. *Psychophysiology*, 1972, *9*, 296–304. (1972:15)

Shearn, D. W. Operant conditioning of heart rate. *Science*, 1962, *137*, 530–531.

Sheridan, C. L., Boehm, M. B., Ward, L. B., & Justesen, D. R. *Autogenic biofeedback, autogenic phrases, and biofeedback compared.* Paper presented at Annual Meeting of Biofeedback Research Society, Colorado Springs, Colorado, 1976.

Shnidman, S. R. Avoidance conditioning of skin potential responses. *Psychophysiology,* 1969, *6,* 38–44.

Shnidman, S. R. Instrumental conditioning of orienting responses using positive reinforcement. *Journal of Experimental Psychology,* 1970, *83,* 491–494. (1970:33)

Shnidman, S. R., & Shapiro, D. Instrumental modification of elicited autonomic responses. *Psychophysiology,* 1970, *7,* 395–401.

Shoemaker, J. E., & Tasto, D. L. The effects of muscle relaxation on blood pressure of essential hypertensives. *Behavior Research and Therapy,* 1975, *13,* 29–43. (1975/76:42)

Simpson, D. D., & Nelson, A. E. Specificity of finger pulse volume feedback during relaxation. *Biofeedback and Self-Regulation,* 1976, *1,* 433–443.

Snape, W. J., Carlson, G. M., Matarazzo, S. A., & Cohen, S. Evidence that abnormal myoelectrical activity produces colonic motor dysfunction in the irritable bowl syndrome. *Gastroenterology,* 1977, *72,* 383–387.

Snyder, C., & Noble, M. Operant conditioning of vasoconstriction. *Journal of Experimental Psychology,* 1968, *77,* 263–268. (R:20)

Solbach, P., & Sargent, J. D. A follow-up evaluation of the Menninger pilot migraine study using thermal training. *Headache,* 1977, *17,* 198–202.

Sovak, M., Kunzel, M., Sternbach, R. A., & Dalessio, D. J. Effects of volitionally and/or thermally induced vasodilation in the upper extremities of the carotid hemodynamics of migraineurs. In J. I. Martin (Ed.), *Proceedings of the San Diego biomedical symposium* (Vol. 16). New York: Academic, 1977, pp. 221–224.

Sroufe, L. A. Learned stabilization of cardiac rate with respiration experimentally controlled. *Journal of Experimental Psychology,* 1969, *81,* 391–393.

Sroufe, L. A. Effects of depth and rate of breathing on heart rate and heart rate variability. *Psychophysiology,* 1971, *8,* 648–655.

Stambaugh, E. E., & House, A. E. Multimodality treatment of migraine headache: A case study utilizing biofeedback, relaxation, autogenic and hypnotic treatments. *American Journal of Clinical Hypnosis,* 1977, *19,* 235–240.

Stephens, J. H., Harris, A. H., Brady, J. V., & Shaffer, J. W. Psychological and physiological variables associated with large magnitude voluntary heart rate changes. *Psychophysiology,* 1975, *12,* 381–387. (1975/76:33)

Steptoe, A. Blood pressure control with pulse wave velocity feedback: Methods of analysis and training. In J. Beatty & H. Legewie (Eds.), *Biofeedback and behavior.* New York: Plenum, 1977.

Steptoe, A., & Johnston, D. The control of blood pressure with instructions and pulse wave velocity feedback. *European Journal of Behavioral Analysis and Modification,* 1976, *3,* 147–154. (a)

Steptoe, A., & Johnston, D. The control of blood pressure using pulse-wave velocity feedback. *Journal of Psychosomatic Research,* 1976, *20,* 417–424. (b)

Steptoe, A., Mathews, A., & Johnston, D. The learned control of differential temperature in the human earlobes: A preliminary study. *Biological Psychology,* 1974, *1,* 237–242. (1974:41)

Steptoe, A., Smulyan, H., & Gribbin, B. Pulse wave velocity and blood pressure change: Calibration and applications. *Psychophysiology,* 1976, *13,* 488–493.

Stern, R. M., & Kaplan, B. E. Galvanic skin response: Voluntary control and externalization. *Journal of Psychosomatic Research,* 1967, *10,* 349–353.

Stern, R. M., & Lewis, N. L. Ability of actors to control their GSRs and express emotions. *Psychophysiology,* 1968, *4,* 294–299. (R:26)

Stern, R. M., & Pavlovski, R. P. Operant conditioning of vasoconstriction: A verification. *Journal of Experimental Psychology,* 1974, *102,* 330–332.

Stone, R. A., & DeLeo, J. Psychotherapeutic control of hypertension. *New England Journal of Medicine,* 1976, *294,* 80–84. (1975/76:44)

Stunkard, A. J., & Fox, S. The relationship of gastric motility and hunger. *Psychosomatic Medicine,* 1971, *33,* 123–134.

Stunkard, A., & Koch, C. The interpretation of gastric motility: Apparent bias in the reports of hunger by obese persons. *Archives of General Psychiatry,* 1964, *11,* 74–82. (R:33)

Sundermann, R. H., & Delk, J. L. Treatment of Raynaud's disease with temperature biofeedback. *Southern Medical Journal,* 1978, *71,* 340–342.

Surwit, R. S. Biofeedback: A possible treatment for Raynaud's disease. *Seminars in Psychiatry,* 1973, *5,* 483–490.

Surwit, R. S., Shapiro, D., & Feldman, J. L. Digital temperature autoregulation and associated cardiovascular changes. *Psychophysiology,* 1976, *13,* 242–248. (1976/77:17)

Surwit, R. S., Hager, J. L., & Feldman, T. The role of feedback in voluntary control of blood pressure in instructed subjects. *Journal of Applied Behavior Analysis,* 1977, *10,* 625–631.

Surwit, R. S., Shapiro, D., & Good, M. I. Comparison of cardiovascular biofeedback, neuromuscular biofeedback, and meditation in the treatment of borderline essential hypertension. *Journal of Consulting and Clinical Psychology,* 1978, *46,* 252–263.

Tarchanoff, J. R. Uber die Willkurliche Acceleration der Herzschlage beim Menschen [Voluntary acceleration of the heartbeat in man]. *Pfluger's Archives,* 1885, *35,* 109–135. (1972:1)

Tasto, D. L., & Huebner, L. A. The effects of muscle relaxation and stress on the blood pressure levels of normotensives. *Behavior Research and Therapy,* 1976, *14,* 89–91.

Taub, E., & Emurian, C. S. Feedback-aided self-regulation of skin temperature with a single feedback locus. I. Acquisition and reversal training. *Biofeedback and Self-Regulation,* 1976, *1,* 147–168. (1976/77:18)

Taub, E., Emurian, C., & Howell, P. Further progress in training self regulation of skin temperature. *Journal of Altered States of Consciousness,* 1975, *2,* 201–202.

Taylor, C. B., Farquhar, J. W., Nelson, E., & Agras, S. Relaxation therapy and high blood pressure. *Archives of General Psychiatry,* 1977, *34,* 339–342.

Thulesius, O. Primary and secondary Raynaud phenomenon. *Acta Chirurgica Scandinavica,* 1976, Suppl. 465, 5–6.

Turin, A., & Johnson, W. G. Biofeedback therapy for migraine headaches. *Archives of General Psychiatry,* 1976, *33,* 517–519. (1976/77:15)

Tursky, B., Shapiro, D., & Schwartz, G. E. Automated constant cuff-pressure system to measure average systolic and diastolic blood pressure in man. *IEEE Transactions on Biomedical Engineering,* 1971, *19,* 271–276.

Van Twyver, H. B., & Kimmel, H. D. Operant conditioning of the GSR with concomitant measurement of two somatic variables. *Journal of Experimental Psychology,* 1966, *72,* 841–846.

Wagner, C., Bourgeois, A., Levenson, H., & Denton, J. Multidimensional locus of control and voluntary control of GSR. *Perceptual and Motor Skills,* 1974, *39,* 1142.

Walsh, P., Dale, A., & Anderson, D. E. Comparison of biofeedback pulse wave velocity and progressive relaxation in essential hypertensives. *Perceptual and Motor Skills,* 1977, *44,* 839–843.

Weiss, T., & Engel, B. T. Voluntary control of premature ventricular contractions in patients. *American Journal of Cardiology,* 1970, *26,* 666. (Abstract)

Weiss, T., & Engel, B. T. Operant conditioning of heart rate in patients with premature ventricular contractions. *Psychophysiology,* 1971, *8,* 263–264. (a)

Weiss, T., & Engel, B. T. Operant conditioning of heart rate patients with premature ventricular contractions. *Psychosomatic Medicine,* 1971, *33,* 301–321. (b) (1971:36)

Weiss, T., & Engel, B. T. Evaluation of an intra-cardiac limit of learned heart rate control. *Psychophysiology,* 1975, *12,* 310–312. (1975/76:38)

Welgan, P. R. Learned control of gastric acid secretion in ulcer patients. *Psychosomatic Medicine,* 1974, *36,* 411–419. (1974:39)

Wells, D. T. Large magnitude voluntary heart rate changes. *Psychophysiology,* 1973, *10,* 260–269. (1973:3)

Wells, D. T., Feather, B. W., & Headrick, M. W. The effects of immediate feedback upon voluntary control of salivary rate. *Psychophysiology,* 1973, *10,* 501–509. (1973:7)

White, K. D. Salivation: A review and experimental investigation of major techniques. *Psychophysiology,* 1977, *14,* 203–212.

White, K. D. Salivation: The significance of imagery in its voluntary control. *Psychophysiology,* 1978, *15,* 196–203.

Whitehead, W. E., Renault, P. F., & Goldiamond, I. Modification of human gastric acid secretion with operant-conditioning procedures. *Journal of Applied Behavior Analysis,* 1975, *8,* 147–156. (1975/76:58)

Whitehead, W. E., Drescher, V. M., Heiman, P., & Blackwell, B. Relation of heart rate control to heartbeat perception. *Biofeedback and Self-Regulation,* 1977, *2,* 371–392.

Wickramasekera, I. E. Temperature feedback for the control of migraine. *Journal of Behavior Therapy and Experimental Psychiatry,* 1973, *4,* 343–345. (1974:42)

Young, G. C. The treatment of childhood encopresis by conditioned gastro-ileal reflex training. *Behavior Research and Therapy,* 1973, *11,* 499–503.

Young, L. D., & Blanchard, E. B. Effects of auditory feedback of varying information content on the self/control of heart rate. *Journal of General Psychology,* 1974, *91,* 61–68. (1974:15)

Ziegler, D. K., Hassanein, R., & Hassanein, K. Headache syndromes suggested by factor analysis of symptom variables in a headache prone population. *Journal of Chronic Disease,* 1972, *25,* 353–363.

Zweifler, A. J. Detection of occlusive arterial disease in the hand in patients with Raynaud's phenomenon. *Acta Chirurgica Scandinavica,* 1976, Suppl. 465, 48–52.

CHAPTER 5

Voluntary Control of the Electrical Activity of the Brain

Introduction

The discovery that electrical activity could be recorded from the cortex of the brain by use of surface electrodes produced a whole new branch of medicine devoted to attempts to relate that activity to various psychiatric disorders associated with the effects of brain injuries, abnormal brain states, or simply disturbances of electrical activity *per se*. Alongside this research there also developed an interest in the relationship between various kinds of electrical discharge which were discovered and the different states of consciousness which had long fascinated psychologists and philosophers of the mind. More recently, the possibility that the relative balance of the various kinds of electrical activity might be altered voluntarily so as to induce altered states of consciousness has received much attention, resulting in a controversy that is still far from resolved.

In order to understand this controversy and the work to be reported in this chapter, it is essential to have some familiarity with the way in which the electrical activity of the brain is measured and of the principal kinds of electrical activity which can be detected. This account will inevitably be brief and selective, and the reader must be referred to the standard texts for more comprehensive accounts.

In recording electrical activity of the brain, a standard system (called the 10–20 system) is used to identify electrode placements. The standard system allows for the specific location of 21 electrodes (also enabling specification in clear terms of any additional special or unusual placements by reference to the standard locations). The positions are referenced to a grid consisting of one line drawn from the nasion (the depression lying between the top of the nose and the base of the forehead) to the inion (a bony projection which can be felt at the base of the skull at the rear of the head), and a second line drawn from the left to right preauricular points (which may be felt as depressions at the root of the zygoma just anterior to the tragus, or more simply, behind each ear). These lines are divided into proportional distances, with the distance from each outer point to the first electrode placement being 10% of the total distance, and the remaining intervals between electrodes being 20% of the total distance (hence the term "10–20 system"). Using this basic grid and the 10–20 system, 21 standard positions may be specified, enabling systematic sampling of electrical activity from the frontal, central, temporal, parietal, and occipital areas of the brain, on both the left and right sides. These positions, in schematic form, are shown in Figure 1. It will be seen that two electrodes are placed over the frontal pole area (F_{p1}, F_{p2}), five over the frontal area (F_7, F_3, F_z, F_4, F_8), four over the temporal

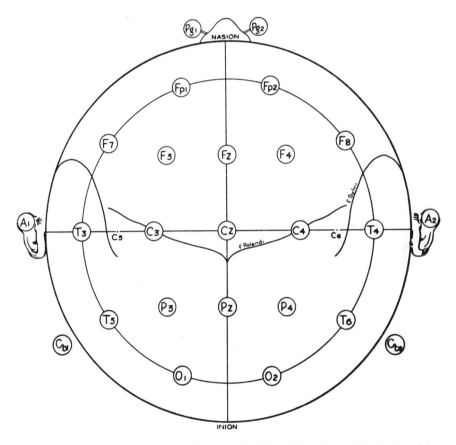

Figure 1. A single-plane projection of the head, showing all standard positions and the location of the rolandic and sylvian fissures. The outer circle was drawn at the level of the nasion and inion. The inner circle represents the temporal line of electrodes. This diagram provides a useful stamp for the indication of electrode placements in routine recording. (From Jasper, H. H. Report of the committee on methods of clinical examination in electroencephalography. *EEG and Clinical Neurophysiology*, 1958, *10*, 374, Figure 6. Reprinted by permission of the publisher.)

area (T_3, T_5, T_4, T_6), three over the central area (C_3, C_z, C_4), three over the parietal area (P_3, P_z, P_4), and two over the occipital area (O_1, O_2).[1] It will be noted that odd-numbered electrodes are placed over the left side of the cortex, even-numbered over the right side, while electrodes placed over the midline (F_z, C_z, P_z) are designated zero. The complete system is used, of course, for routine EEG examination; in psychological research electrode placements are usually restricted to one or two sites. Peper and Mulholland (1970), for example, recorded from O_2–P_4. The gaps in the numbering allow for specially placed electrodes to be designated by reference to standard position. Beatty (1971), for example, recorded from O_z, i.e., midway between O_1 and O_2.

Several different kinds of electrical activity have been identified and defined with a reasonable amount of agreement as to the characteristics of each kind, although no absolute standards have been set. The basic definition is made in terms of the frequency of the electrical activity, with four main types being identified in this way:

Delta   =   0.5–6.0 Hz
Theta   =   3.5–7.0 Hz
Alpha   =   8.0–12.0 Hz
Beta   =   13.0 Hz and above

At least 90% of all the work to be considered in this chapter has been concerned with alpha activity with some attention being paid to beta and theta activity, but none at all to delta, largely because the latter is associated with states of sleep. Identification of a particular pattern of activity and its discrimination (by the experimenter) from other patterns is by no means as easy as it may appear and a significant degree of difference of opinion as to the criteria for the presence of, say, alpha becomes evident on careful examination of reported work. Thus, Nowlis and Kamiya (1970) defined alpha as the occurrence of 8- to 13-Hz activity but only if the amplitude exceeded 20 μV, whereas Peper and Mulholland (1970) also defined alpha as the occurrence of 8- to 13-Hz activity but required it to exceed 25% of the maximum level of alpha recorded in a resting, baseline condition. Mulholland (1962), on the other hand, used a very strict criterion of 10 Hz $\pm$ 1 Hz to define alpha but required an amplitude of only 5–7 μV. Brown (1970) defined alpha as the occurrence of 7–15 Hz. There are many other problems involved in the definition of alpha for experimental purposes. These will be mentioned later, but it should be noted here that the lack of agreed criteria for specifying the presence or absence of alpha makes it very difficult to compare studies in which contradictory results are obtained. It should also be noted that quite sophisticated equipment (whether computerized or not) is required to discriminate alpha activity from other electrical activity; for example, sharp filtering is required to detect 8 Hz while eliminating 7 Hz.

---

[1]The remaining positions designated in Figure 1 need not concern us here.

Research into the voluntary control of the electrical activity of the brain has followed a fairly clear-cut pattern. Initially, it appeared that voluntary control had been demonstrated. The enthusiasm thus generated (for reasons which will become clear) was sharply tempered by the appearance of some severe criticisms of this initial work and appeared to demonstrate that the alleged control was probably artifactual. Subsequent work was largely concerned with attempts to refute these criticisms and show that voluntary control could indeed be obtained. Quite recently, however, a second wave of criticism has again shaken the foundations of the claims that voluntary control is possible and current research is endeavoring to overcome these latest criticisms.

Voluntary Control of Alpha: Early Studies

Three main approaches may be distinguished within the early studies of the voluntary control of alpha activity, of which the earliest was not in fact primarily concerned with voluntary control as such, but rather with the relationship between attention and alpha. The work of Mulholland, which is only now receiving adequate recognition, represents a very important example of the demonstration of feedback control of cortical activity by establishing a genuine feedback loop of which the subject is not necessarily aware. Mulholland (1962)[2] devised a very simple but ingenious method for demonstrating how changes in the electrical activity of the brain could be used to program the environment. The subject was informed that he would be presented with a sequence of 15 light flashes. In one condition, he was requested merely to observe passively as the lights appeared and disappeared; in a second condition, he was to count the lights silently as they appeared and to judge whether the 15th flash was brighter than the 14th; while in a third condition, he was asked to be prepared for a sudden, loud sound that might occur simultaneously with the 15th flash (it never did occur, in fact). Thus, as far as the subject was concerned, the experimenter was presenting him with a series of light flashes together with instructions as to how he was to behave in this situation. In actual fact, however, the situation was quite different. Mulholland's study was based on the known fact that alpha tends to increase as attention is relaxed and to diminish as orientation or alertness increases. Thus, at the beginning of a trial, with the first light not yet having appeared, alpha would gradually increase as the subject relaxed. When alpha attained a specified level (5–7 μV) the first light was automatically displayed. The appearance of the light produced an orientation or attentional response which had the effect of suppressing alpha below the specified level and this event turned off the light. The second light came on when alpha again increased above threshold and went off when alpha

---

[2]Mulholland (1968) has provided a detailed survey of the historical antecedents of his work together with a broad perspective of research within this framework.

decreased below threshold, and so on until all 15 lights had been displayed. Thus, the appearance and disappearance of the lights, their duration, and the interval between their successive appearances was entirely determined by increases and decreases in alpha amplitude although the subjects had no knowledge whatever that it was self-produced changes in alpha amplitude which were responsible for the sequence of lights. The results of this experiment are shown in Figure 2. With simple observing of the lights, time in alpha initially decreased, while time in no-alpha increased significantly, but the difference was rapidly abolished. When active counting of the flashes was required, however, there was a dramatic and sustained drop in time in alpha, coupled with an equally dramatic and sustained increase in time in no-alpha. These results confirmed earlier findings by Mulholland and Runnals (1962) and were extended in a subsequent study by Mulholland and Runnals (1963). In the first experiment, subjects were required to observe the sequence of 30 flashes; count to the 15th flash, then observe another 15 flashes; count to the 30th flash; or count to the 15th flash and judge

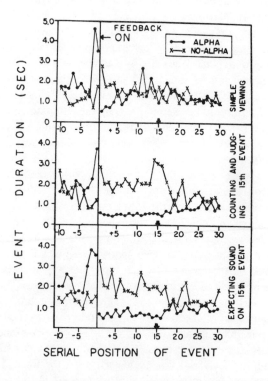

Figure 2. Mean event durations for alpha and no-alpha before and during feedback stimulation during internal gradients of attention. (From Mullholland, T. The electroencephalogram as an experimental tool in the study of internal attention gradients. *Transactions of the New York Academy of Sciences,* 1962, *24,* 668, Figure 3. Reprinted by permission of the author and the publisher.)

the comparative brightness of the 14th and 15th flashes. In the second experiment, subjects were required to observe only, or count and then judge to the 7th, 13th, or 23rd flash in a sequence of 30 flashes. In both experiments the existence of a gradient of attention was demonstrated, indexed by the relationship of alpha and no-alpha activity. For our purposes, however, the main point of interest is the interaction between an environmental event and changes in the alpha amplitude, in spite of the subject's lack of awareness of what was going on and his probable belief that the light flashes were being presented by the experimenter.

Mulholland's findings were independently confirmed in the USSR by Bundzen (1966), who found that at the beginning of a trial, light-on duration ranged from 0.5 sec to 1.2 sec, considerably shorter than light-off duration. As autoregulation proceeded, however, the light-on duration became longer and the interval between flashes became shorter so that after 30–50 sec of stimulation the light-on and light-off durations were equalized. A return to the initial state occurred after 60–110 sec of stimulation and was followed by another trend toward equalization, a cyclic pattern thus being established. Mulholland and Evans (1966) extended these findings to show that enhancement and suppression of alpha could be used to control the position of a meter needle on a dial so as to maintain it within defined limits.

Ingenious though Mulholland's technique is, it is no different, of course, from the presentation of feedback for the production of a specified amount of alpha or no alpha, which was the approach adopted by Kamiya, whose work has received much more attention than that of Mulholland, even though the latter's work has temporal priority and is much the more sophisticated and interesting. Kamiya apparently began his work about the same time as Mulholland, but did not formally publish his work until later; indeed, his first account (Kamiya, 1968) was a popular article.[3] Kamiya claimed to have demonstrated both enhancement and suppression of alpha with auditory feedback (the feedback was apparently not proportional to the amount of alpha, the tone being on when alpha was present and off when it was absent). Kamiya (1968) also claimed to have trained subjects to increase or decrease alpha frequency. Kamiya (1969) reviewed his work over 10 years, paying particular attention to the suppression of alpha by imagery and drawing attention to the possible importance of the "drift" effect as a confounding variable. When he trained subjects to alternately enhance and suppress alpha with feedback and interspersed the training trials with rest periods, he obtained the results shown in Figure 3. Clearly a baseline drift effect is present in this study with a tendency for alpha to increase spontaneously as a function of time in the experimental situation.

Nowlis and Kamiya (1970) provided the first full account of the experimental procedures used by Kamiya. The subjects were informed that the exper-

[3]The two other main accounts given by Kamiya of his work (Kamiya, 1969, 1974) are also general papers constituting a review of his work.

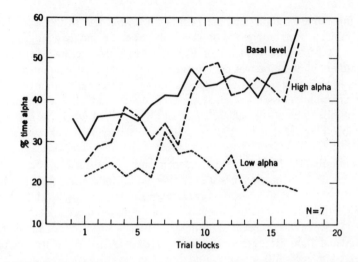

Figure 3. Enhancement and suppression of alpha compared with baseline changes. (From Kamiya, J. Operant control of the EEG alpha rhythm and some of its reported effects on consciousness. In C. Tart (Ed.), *Altered states of consciousness.* New York: Wiley, 1969, p. 513, Figure 2. Reprinted by permission of the author and the publisher.)

iment was concerned with the control of "brain waves," but not that alpha control was involved. Auditory feedback (not proportional to amount of alpha) was provided for 8- to 13-Hz activity of at least 20 μV amplitude. After a 2-min period to adjust to the tone's coming on and going off, a 2-min baseline was run with eyes closed and the tone presented whenever alpha, as defined, was present. This was followed by a period of up to 15 min during which the subject tried in a relaxed way to discover how to make the tone come on and go off. Finally, a 2-min trial period was given during which the subject tried to keep the tone on, followed by a 2-min period during which he tried to keep the tone off. One group of subjects performed throughout with eyes closed; a second group, which manifested a high baseline level of alpha (with eyes closed) was given a second baseline period with eyes open and also kept their eyes open during the feedback training trials. The subjects who kept their eyes closed throughout showed an average of 35 sec tone-on during the baseline, which increased to 53 sec in the last "on" trial and decreased to 26 sec in the last "off" trial, whereas the subjects who kept their eyes open during the feedback training trials showed an average of 57 sec tone-on during the baseline (eyes closed), which increased to 77 sec during the last "on" trial and decreased to 16 sec during the last "off" trial. All of the subjects manifested more alpha in the final "on" trial as compared with the final "off" trial, and nearly all showed significantly increased and decreased alpha in the appropriate "on" or "off" trials compared with baseline. High levels of baseline alpha appeared to be positively correlated with success in controlling alpha. No sex differences were found, nor was there any correlation between alpha control and heart rate, blood pressure, respiration rate, or GSR.

The third of the early approaches to the control of the electrical activity of the brain was that of B. B. Brown, who was particularly interested in determining whether "feeling states" could be induced by her subjects which would modify alpha amplitude and hence control a stimulus. This aspect of her research will be dealt with in Chapter 7; here we are concerned with whether alterations in alpha are correlated with changes in the stimulus situation. Her approach was virtually identical to that of Mulholland, except for the instructions given to the subject. In her first study, Brown (1970) used a visual stimulus (a blue lamp) which was on whenever alpha (defined as 7–15 Hz) exceeded 15 μV. The subject was instructed to identify a "feeling state" which would keep the light on, with the intensity of the light varying as a function of the strength of the "feeling state" (in fact, of course, it varied as a function of the alpha amplitude). No mention was made of alpha to the subject. Following a 10- to 15-min adaptation period, 5-min baselines with eyes open and closed were recorded, followed by five 10-min periods with feedback, alternating with 3-min rest periods without feedback with eyes open throughout the training period. Of 47 subjects used, 23 completed one training session, 14 completed two, and 10 completed four. The results showed that a significant increase in alpha activity took place within each 10-min feedback period, whereas no such change occurred within any rest period, and that the difference between changes with and without feedback within periods of training and rest were significant. However, there was no evidence that these increases in alpha abundance *within* periods were maintained *across* periods. Furthermore, the levels of alpha activity achieved with feedback (with eyes open) did not exceed (and mostly did not even approach) the levels of alpha activity manifested in the baseline condition with eyes closed, although they did tend to exceed the levels manifested in the baseline condition with eyes open.[4]

The perceptive reader unfamiliar with this area of research will have noticed the gradual introduction of new variables into the studies described, such as "eyes open" and "eyes closed," and findings suggesting that the amount of alpha produced with feedback never exceeded the amount manifested in the resting state with eyes closed. The mounting suspicion that something might be very seriously wrong with the methodology of these early studies was confirmed by the work of Peper and Mulholland (1970). Using a rather peculiar sample of subjects (hospital employees, children, and college students), they carried out two experiments. In the first, auditory feedback was given for alpha whenever it reached 25% of the maximum resting amplitude (again, the feedback was not proportional to alpha amplitude but simply on or off). Baseline trials of 2-min duration with eyes open and closed (without feedback) were given, followed by

---

[4]The second study by Brown (1971) was concerned solely with subjective correlates of EEG activity and will be dealt with in Chapter 7.

Table 1. Mean Percent Time Alpha before, during, and after Feedback Training[a]

Stimulation	2-min trial	% Time alpha	
No feedback	1st	40.7	Eyes open
	2nd	56.5	Eyes closed
			Autoregulation training to keep tone
Feedback	3rd	57.5	On
(eyes closed)	4th	51.6	Off
	5th	55.0	On
	6th	43.3	Off
	7th	54.5	On
	8th	42.0	Off
	9th	57.5	On
	10th	41.7	Off
	11th	54.5	On
	12th	38.3	Off
			Autoregulation test
No feedback	13th	51.0	On
(eyes closed)	14th	40.8	Off

[a]SOURCE: Peper, E., & Mulholland, T. Methodological and theoretical problems in the voluntary control of electroencephalographic occipital alpha by the subject. *Kybernetik*, 1970, 7, Table 1. Reprinted by permission of the author and the publisher.

10 training trials, also of 2-min duration, in which the subject was required alternately to keep the tone on (alpha above criterion) and off (alpha below criterion), all of these trials being administered with eyes closed. Finally, two trials without feedback were given in the first of which the subject was asked to keep the tone on, and in the second to keep it off (in both cases, with eyes closed). The results are shown in Table 1 and are quite clear-cut. When instructed to keep the tone on with feedback available, the percentage time in alpha was about the same as the baseline level of alpha without feedback with eyes closed and no evidence of learning was demonstrated over trials. On the other hand, when instructed to keep the tone off with feedback available, the percentage time in alpha decreased (from 51.6% on average to 38.3% on average) to the level of alpha manifested in baseline without feedback and with eyes open. After training was completed, the two test trials showed that these subjects were able to maintain alpha on (51%) or off (40.8%) to about the same degree as during the training period. In a second experiment, 8 of the 21 subjects who had just been trained were given further training for five more sessions, just as described above. However, no further differentiation between alpha on and alpha off was obtained. Peper and Mulholland (1970) concluded, not unnaturally, that subjects could be trained to decrease alpha with feedback, but could not be trained to

$$\begin{aligned}
\text{Delta} &= 0.5\text{–}6.0 \text{ Hz} \\
\text{Theta} &= 3.5\text{–}7.0 \text{ Hz} \\
\text{Alpha} &= 8.0\text{–}12.0 \text{ Hz} \\
\text{Beta} &= 13.0 \text{ Hz and above}
\end{aligned}$$

increase alpha to levels exceeding those obtained at rest with eyes closed. It should be noted in passing that the problem of drift is clearly a possible confounding variable in this study since on/off times with feedback were compared with preexperimental baselines, rather than with a running baseline.

The First Critiques

The growing suspicion that something was not quite right with the earlier studies culminated in a flurry of critical analyses. These were directed both at the methodological inadequacies of the reported studies and their philosophical underpinnings. With respect to the latter, it was charged that much of the work was not directed to a scientific understanding of alpha control so much as to using alpha enhancement as a pathway toward higher (mystical) states of consciousness (Grossberg, 1972). This aspect will be dealt with elsewhere. Of more immediate concern are the methodological criticisms and the alternative explanations advanced to account for increases and decreases in alpha in contrast to the subjective state explanations provided by workers such as B. B. Brown (1970, 1971) and Kamiya (1968, 1969). The most comprehensive review was provided by Lynch and Paskewitz (1971), who particularly concentrated on the role of attentional factors in increasing and decreasing alpha. They pointed out that alpha abundance could be affected by direct visual stimulation, differential attention to visual stimulation, and oculomotor activity. Although alpha is normally blocked by visual stimulation, paradoxical stimulus-induced alpha has been observed, while alpha may be reduced by too much *or* too little arousal in the subject. The role of cognitive and expectancy factors, the effect of various kinds of feedback stimuli, and many other factors were stressed. The failure adequately to control such parameters as the ambient illumination of the room, whether baselines and experimental periods were run with eyes open or eyes closed, and in particular the neglect of the proper establishment of baseline levels all came under heavy criticism.[5] Lynch and Paskewitz (1971) are particularly critical of attempts to interpret alpha enhancement and suppression in reinforcement terms, but this aspect of their critique will be dealt with elsewhere (see Chapter 7). Relying heavily on the indication that enhanced alpha with feedback never exceeds baseline alpha levels with eyes closed, they contended:

> *Alpha activity occurs in the feedback situation when an individual ceases to pay attention to any of a number of stimuli which normally block this activity.* These stimuli may be cognitive, somatic, emotional, or anything, in fact, which will lead to alpha blocking. The alpha densities which can occur in the feedback situation may approach those seen in that same individual under optimal baseline conditions, but will not significantly exceed them. While the feedback process may yield trial-to-trial increases which resemble learning curves, these curves are the result of inhibition, as the S gradually removes from his attention most, or all of the influences which block

---

[5]However, like Kamiya (1968), Lynch and Paskewitz seem to assume that a baseline must involve unchanging levels of performance. As demonstrated in Chapter 2, this assumption is of course false.

the production of alpha activity. The resulting density is limited only by the S's own
natural ability to generate this activity. (p. 213, italics in original)

Peper (1971b) argued along much the same lines, but in conjunction with
Mulholland and Evans (1966) he proposed a more specific hypothesis to account
for alpha enhancement and suppression in the feedback situation. He argued that
corrective commands to the oculomotor system, causing movement in the extrinsic eye muscles and lens adjustment, are responsible for the suppression of
occipital alpha; that somatic commands to many muscle groups block or suppress
central alpha; and that, hence, the absence of such commands may be a precondition for an altered state of consciousness that produces alpha enhancement
with feedback:

the underlying mechanism involved in alpha training experiments is the cessation of
the functions that block alpha. Specifically, this alpha "blocking" at the alpha–beta
transition is due to activity in those areas of the brain that are involved in generating
efferent motor commands to muscles. (Peper, 1971b, p. 226)

Peper provides examples illustrating alpha blocking occurring immediately before muscle (in this case, arm) activity occurs (that is, it is the efferent motor
command which produces the blocking, not feedback from the muscle activity
itself).

Thus, the position had been reached that interpretation of the studies so far
carried out was unclear because of severe methodological inadequacies on the one
hand, while on the other hand alternative explanations to those customarily given
of the results obtained were available (the oculomotor hypothesis as compared
with the generation of altered states of consciousness). Research over the next
few years was to be directed toward an examination of the oculomotor
hypothesis, improvements in methodological control, and more sophisticated
investigation of the factors in the voluntary control of alpha enhancement and
suppression.

Alpha Research Comes of Age

The oculomotor hypothesis as an explanation of alpha enhancement and
suppression had been investigated very quickly in an ingenious study by Dewan
(1967). He instructed three subjects to control alpha amplitude in two ways. To
obtain maximum alpha amplitude, the subject was to turn his eyes to the extreme
upward position consistent with comfort while avoiding fixation or convergence
and accommodation. Minimal or blocked alpha was to be obtained by opening
the eyes and fixating a nearby object, or by keeping the eyes closed and fixating
an imaginary point located almost immediately in front of the eyelids. Information about the presence or absence of alpha was provided by means of a pulse
from a Schmitt trigger or verbal information given by the experimenter. The
ingenious part of this study, however, lay in the fact that by generating sequences

of high and low alpha of specified duration, the subject would in effect transmit Morse code sequences which would be interpreted by a computer as letters of the alphabet and displayed on a readout. Dewan found that, with some difficulty and many errors, his subjects were able to transmit letters. Dewan considered that these results could not be accounted for in terms of "attention" since attention to the feedback stimuli (and the letter display) was required throughout the experiment. The study is, of course, confounded, since it was not demonstrated whether the alpha on/off pattern could have been generated with the feedback alone and in the absence of the oculomotor maneuver.

A new type of procedure to examine the oculomotor hypothesis was introduced by Peper (1970). Arguing that oculomotor activity is involved in tracking a target, he reasoned that tracking should be facilitated if the target is visible when and only when alpha is reduced, whereas tracking should be more difficult if the target is visible when and only when alpha is present (because the presence of alpha indicates reduced attention, whereas its absence indicates increased attention). He reported the results of four experiments designed to test this hypothesis. In the first, the subjects tracked a target which was visible when alpha was either enhanced or suppressed. All of the subjects behaved in an identical fashion. When the target was visible only when alpha was enhanced, they oscillated between alpha and no-alpha; however, when the target was visible only when alpha was suppressed, no-alpha predominated for long periods of time, with the consequence that continuous tracking was predominant. In the second experiment, a light with slow rise and decay times was on whenever the subject produced alpha and the subject was instructed to "pay attention to" or "not to pay attention to" the light whenever it came on. Under the first set of instructions alpha and no-alpha states alternated, whereas under the second set of instructions the alpha/no-alpha ratio became unstable. The third experiment was similar to the second except that pictures were used, while the fourth was similar to the experiment carried out by Peper and Mulholland (1970), discussed previously. Peper (1970) interpreted these results as due to the presence or absence of oculomotor commands. However, although electrooculograms were recorded (from electrodes attached to the outer canthi of the eyes), the interpretation of the results was based on inferences from the assumed relationships among attention requirements (resulting from the tracking task), alpha enhancement and suppression, and the known relationship between tracking and oculomotor activity, rather than by correlating oculomotor activity as directly measured and changes in alpha.

The results obtained by Peper (1970) were confirmed by Mulholland and Peper (1971), who also carried the investigation of the oculomotor hypothesis a stage further. They required their subjects either to focus on a target or to let it blur while tracking or not tracking the target, which was stationary, moving predictably, moving unpredictably, or increasing or decreasing in its speed of movement. The results showed that alpha amplitude was greater when the subject blurred the target while tracking it as compared with keeping it in focus. Since oculomotor activity is crucial to focusing and blurring, the results provided support for the hypothesis, although once again the interpretation was based on indirect rather than direct evidence.

If alpha enhancement produced by elevating the eyes is related to the resultant divergence of the eyes and relaxation of accommodation, then it should follow that far vision (involving divergence and relaxed accommodation) should enhance alpha by comparison with near vision. If this were so, then elevation of the eyes would be a sufficient but not a necessary condition for alpha enhancement. Eason and Sadler (1977) have shown that this is the case. Increased convergence led to a drop in alpha while the reverse was the case when the eyes diverged. It was also shown that direct feedback from the electrooculogram was as effective as feedback of alpha itself.

The relationship between oculomotor activity and alpha amplitude as put forward by Mulholland and Peper has not been without its controversial aspects. Chapman, Shelburne, and Bragdon (1970) provided evidence that alpha amplitude is related to visual input rather than eye movement, to which Mulholland and Peper (1971) replied that Chapman et al. had produced less than optimal eye movement in their subjects. The two interpretations have recently been put to the test by Goodman (1976), who used eye movement as the independent variable. He instructed his subjects to move their open eyes (while in total darkness) toward tones coming from five different loudspeakers located in different positions around a perimeter in front of the subject. An appropriate control condition was also used, consisting of the amount of alpha manifested with eyes open in total darkness and the tones presented, but with no movement required. The results are shown in Figure 4 and clearly support the oculomotor hypothesis. All of the eye-movement conditions produced a significant reduction in alpha as compared with the equivalent no-eye-movement conditions, and this was so even though visual input in all conditions was essentially zero. Thus, it may be concluded that to demonstrate voluntary control of alpha as a function of some change of internal state, it is necessary to control for the effects of oculomotor movements.

It will be recalled that the methodological adequacy of the early studies of alpha enhancement and suppression had been called into question by Grossberg (1972) and by Lynch and Paskewitz (1971). In particular, the question of the adequacy of control of the conditions under which alpha had been measured was raised with reference especially to levels of alpha recorded under baseline conditions with eyes open and closed under varying conditions of room illumination. The studies to be considered now attempted to throw light on these matters and to establish the boundaries for alpha from which true enhancement and suppression could be measured. Paskewitz and Orne (1973) defined alpha as 8- to 12-Hz activity recorded from the occipital region (specifically, the O_2 position) and provided auditory feedback (not proportional) for alpha levels exceeding 15 μV.

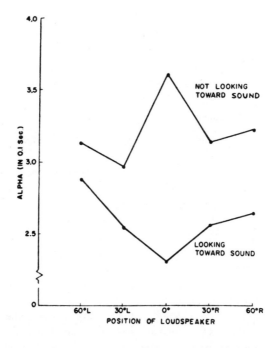

Figure 4. Mean alpha duration (in 0.1-sec units) during the 1-sec interval following tone presentation from each loudspeaker, with and without eye movements. (From Goodman, D. M. The effect of oculomotor activity on alpha blocking in the absence of visual stimuli. *Psychophysiology*, 1976, *13*, 464, Figure 1. Reprinted by permission of the author and the publisher.)

Six training sessions were given, each consisting of two 3-min baseline periods (eyes closed, then open); a 5-min orientation period with feedback present and the subject encouraged to experiment in turning the tone on and off; and ten 2-min feedback training trials, interspersed with 1-min rest periods. The subjects were instructed to keep the tone on (that is, enhance alpha) as much as possible and were in total darkness with eyes open during the training trials. In addition to the auditory feedback, a digital display of the cumulative total of alpha activity was presented at the beginning of each rest period. The results showed that an initial steep drop in alpha activity occurred when the subject was switched from eyes closed to eyes open in the baseline period, followed by a significant recovery of alpha toward the eyes-closed level during the orientation period, but no further change occurred during the feedback training trials and no difference was found during this period between feedback and rest trials. The experiment was repeated with a new group of subjects, the only difference being that the training was carried out in dim, ambient light rather than total darkness. The same baseline drop was found, but less recovery occurred during the orientation period and a significant difference between feedback and rest periods was found, with the latter resulting in less alpha activity. Alpha activity also tended to increase across the feedback trials. Paskewitz and Orne (1973) conclude from these results that previous findings are artifactual, being produced by an artificial lowering of alpha before feedback training is introduced, leading to apparent but spurious voluntary control. They comment that:

> subjects can acquire volitional control over alpha activity only under conditions which normally lead to decreased densities. . . . . we have not seen alpha densities beyond an individual's initially demonstrated normal physiological range. (Paskewitz & Orne, 1973, p. 363)

In a further three experiments, Lynch, Paskewitz, and Orne (1974) confirmed and extended these results. In the first experiment, following the usual eyes-open/eyes-closed baseline trials in total darkness, one group was trained to enhance alpha with visual feedback (a green light which came on whenever alpha exceeded the criterion set, and a red light whenever it did not) while a second group was provided with similar feedback from the experimental group subject who showed the median value of alpha density for that group. The results showed that the resting[6] level of alpha (that is, the levels obtained in rest trials interspersed between the training trials) was significantly higher in both the experimental and control groups than the alpha levels obtained when either contingent or noncontingent visual feedback was available. Both the contingent and noncontingent feedback groups showed a gradual increase in alpha during the training trials, but never achieved the resting levels of alpha and there was no difference in final levels of alpha achieved by the two groups at the end of training. A high correlation ($+0.74$) was found between baseline (eyes-open) level of alpha and the level achieved during training. In the second experiment (using 13 of the 16 subjects from the first) differential training was attempted with six training trials in which the subject attempted to enhance alpha and six in which he attempted to suppress alpha by keeping either the red light (indicating alpha suppression) or the green light (indicating alpha enhancement) on. The results are shown in Figure 5. Bidirectional control was achieved, but once again alpha enhancement did not reach resting level. Of course, one of the major problems inherent in all of the studies discussed so far relates to the use of visual feedback which (except in some of the early studies by Mulholland) requires that eyes be kept open during the training trials and involves repeated visual orientation. In their third experiment, Lynch *et al.* (1974) used auditory feedback instead of visual, and the results from five of the original subjects showed that under these conditions of training the subjects achieved but did not exceed the resting levels manifested without feedback. Furthermore, these resting levels were the same as those which had been manifested in the first two experiments when visual feedback was used. However, no curve of learning was found; that

---

[6]It is not clear whether eyes were open or closed during the rest trials; clearly, they had to be open during the experimental trials.

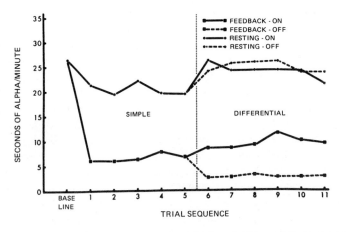

Figure 5. Alpha densities for the 13 subjects during simple and differential feedback trials. (From Lynch, J. J., Paskewitz, D. A., & Orne, M. T. Some factors in the feedback control of human alpha rhythm. *Psychosomatic Medicine,* 1974, *36,* 405, Figure 3. Reprinted by permission of the author and the publisher.)

is, the resting and feedback levels of alpha were essentially the same from beginning to end of the training trials. Thus, once again it was concluded that the increased amounts of alpha which had been attributed in earlier studies to voluntary control resulted in fact from the disinhibition of stimuli which normally block alpha activity.

Several subsequent studies have examined closely the effects of eyes open and closed in varying levels of ambient illumination on alpha activity in relation to changes which take place with feedback. Bridgwater, Sherry, and Marczynski (1975) recorded from the right occipital lobe between the vortex and the O_2 electrode placement (10–20 system) and defined alpha as 9–10.5 Hz occurring with an amplitude between 10 μV and 23 μV. In a single experimental session, they ran eight 10-min trials, each separated by 2-min rest periods, in which they varied the ambient illumination. First, three trials without feedback were given (eyes closed, then open in darkness, followed by eyes open in light of 3-footcandle intensity). Then four trials with auditory feedback (not proportional) for alpha responses within the amplitude range specified were run with eyes open in darkness, and in illumination of 1, 3, and 15 footcandles (the order of the conditions being varied randomly across subjects). A final no-feedback trial was then given with eyes open in illumination of 3 footcandles. Throughout the experiment the subjects wore light-diffusing goggles to prevent patterned vision. The dependent variable in this study was the number of single alpha waves which met the specified criterion. Large individual differences in alpha activity were found together with a significant effect of ambient illumination, the amount of alpha activity being greater during the feedback trials in darkness as compared with the trials run in ambient illumination of 3 or 15 footcandles. However, feedback itself did not produce any increase of alpha activity over that manifested during the baseline or posttraining no-feedback trial. Although these results in general were consonant with those obtained by Paskewitz and his colleagues, one discrepancy was found in that Bridgwater *et al.* found no difference in alpha activity between any of the baseline conditions; specifically, they did not find the drop in alpha activity reported by Paskewitz when the switch from eyes closed to eyes open was made (this could, of course, have been due to the wearing of light-diffusing goggles, which would tend to eliminate the distinction between eyes closed and open). However, Mulholland, McLaughlin, and Benson (1976), using psychiatric patients as well as normal subjects and recording from O_1-P_3 and O_2-P_4 (occipital/parietal regions) reported that alpha durations did tend to be longest in the eyes-closed resting position, decreased with eyes open (in both cases the subjects were in darkness), and decreased further in their usual feedback-loop condition, using visual stimulation. Leib, Tryon, and Stroebel (1976), also using psychiatric patients as subjects, studied the differential effects of eyes open/closed in relation to attempts to enhance and suppress alpha with feedback. Contrary to all of the studies so far discussed, the subjects of this experiment were fully informed about the purpose of the training trials. Baseline recordings of alpha were taken with eyes open and eyes closed, followed by 20 30-min training sessions, each of which involved 2-min periods of enhancement and suppression of alpha with auditory feedback in dim ambient light with eyes open, interspersed with rest trials. The presence of alpha within the range of 0.5 Hz above a subject's dominant baseline frequency turned the auditory feedback signal off, whereas the presence of alpha within the range of 0.5 Hz below the dominant baseline frequency turned the tone on. The results of this study are shown in Figure 6. It is evident from the figure that the level of alpha could be enhanced with feedback (tone off) to the level of alpha manifested in the eyes-closed baseline condition, whereas the level of alpha could be suppressed with feedback (tone on) to the level of alpha manifested in the eyes-open baseline condition. Furthermore, the amount of alpha generated in the eyes-closed and tone-on conditions was greater than that generated in the eyes-open and tone-off

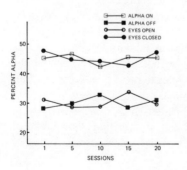

Figure 6. The percentage of alpha observed over 20 sessions as a function of instructions to turn alpha on, turn alpha off, keep eyes open, and keep eyes closed. (From Leib, W., Tryon, W. W., & Stroebel, C. S. Alpha biofeedback: Fact or artifact? *Psychophysiology,* 1976, *13,* 543, Figure 1. Reprinted by permission of the author and the publisher.)

conditions. No evidence of any learning occurring in the feedback conditions was obtained. Once more, the conclusion was reached that none of the subjects succeeded in enhancing or suppressing alpha levels above or below those manifested in the eyes-closed and -open baseline conditions, respectively. As also previously found, there was a gradual increase in alpha production within each session, but not across sessions.

Orenstein and McWilliams (1976) were critical of certain aspects of the study by Paskewitz and Orne (1973), discussed earlier, and repeated that study with additional controls. Monopolar occipital to right mastoid EEG signals (8–13 Hz above a threshold of 15 μV) were recorded, but the amplitude threshold levels for feedback were determined during an eyes-open baseline period, being set at 10 μV if less than 20% alpha was produced during this period, at 15 μV if 20–80% alpha was produced, and at 20 μV if more than 80% alpha was produced. Following 3-min baseline recordings with eyes closed and then open, two groups were given a 5-min orientation period during which proportional auditory feedback was available and the subjects were instructed to experiment to try to increase the pitch of the tone with eyes open. Then ten 2-min trials with eyes open and auditory feedback were given, interspersed with 1-min rest periods. Additionally, the subjects were shown the percentage time spent in alpha at the end of each trial. One group of subjects was run in darkness with eyes open for six sessions, followed by a seventh session in dim light, also with eyes open, while a second group followed the reverse procedure (six sessions in dim light, followed by a single session in darkness). The first group showed a significant drop in alpha activity during the eyes-closed baseline, followed by some recovery during the eyes-open baseline, a further recovery (to the level manifested in the eyes-closed baseline) during the orientation period, this level being maintained but not exceeded during the feedback trials, with drops in alpha during the rest periods. In the seventh session (in dim light) a drop was shown in the eyes-closed baseline with no recovery. The second group also showed a significant drop in the eyes-closed baseline, but manifested no recovery at any subsequent stage and no difference between feedback and resting levels of alpha. In the seventh session (in darkness) the results were similar to those of the first group. These authors considered that their results in general supported the position taken by Paskewitz and Orne (1973) with respect to results obtained when subjects are run in darkness but not when subjects are run in dim illumination.

More recently, Cram, Kohlenberg, and Singer (1977) have examined the effects of three levels of illumination (bright, ambient, and dark) and two levels of eyelid position (eyes open or closed) on enhancement and suppression of alpha. In a single session of training, they claimed to find significant suppression and enhancement of alpha in all six conditions, but that the combination of eyes open and ambient illumination facilitated alpha control best.

The results of all of these studies demonstrate the complexity of the problem of determining whether voluntary control of alpha can genuinely be obtained and the importance of controlling factors such as eyes open/closed and ambient illumination There does seem, however, to be general agreement that feedback training does not lead to the enhancement or suppression of alpha to levels beyond those which are manifested in conditions which optimize the levels of alpha (up or down) without feedback. Thus, considerable doubt remains as to whether genuine voluntary control of alpha has been demonstrated.

While these special investigations, as they might be called, were being carried out, there was a great upsurge of studies designed to investigate the parameters of alpha enhancement and suppression within the framework of voluntary control. These studies fall fairly clearly into a number of categories. One group concerned itself with investigating the relevance of true feedback to the establishment of voluntary control. Travis, Kondo, and Knott (1974a) provided visual nonproportional feedback for "criterion alpha" (recorded from the O_z position) defined as 0.07–0.13 sec of 8- to 13-Hz activity which was 50% or more of the amplitude of maximum eyes-closed alpha, determined individually for each subject during the initial baseline period. The subjects (who were fully informed) were divided into an experimental group (receiving feedback for enhancing alpha), a yoked control group (receiving feedback from a matched experimental group subject), and a control group which received no feedback. Twelve 10-min training sessions were given over 2 days, including one session without feedback on each day for the two experimental groups. On the second day, both experimental groups were given veridical feedback. The results are shown in Figure 7. On the first day, the true-feedback group produced significantly more alpha than the yoked-feedback group which, however, produced significantly more alpha than the no-feedback group, but the true- and yoked-feedback groups did not differ in the no-feedback session. On the second day, the two experimental groups (both now receiving verdical feedback) did not differ but produced significantly more alpha again than the control group, the levels being maintained during the no-feedback session. In a second experiment these results were replicated in all essential details, while in a third the level of alpha reached during training was maintained when feedback was withdrawn for a longer period of time. Lynch, Paskewitz, and Orne (1974), however, in the study described earlier, found no difference between true- and yoked-feedback groups, but these groups were run in total darkness. On the whole, the results obtained by Lynch et al. (1974) have been supported, rather than those obtained by Travis et al. (1974a). Thus, Brolund and Schallow (1976), using partially informed subjects (told their brain waves were being studied) with nonproportional auditory feedback for alpha (minimum duration of 0.07–0.13 sec with amplitude exceeding 15 μV) found no difference in alpha production between groups given true feedback, yoked feedback, or an auditory stimulus not presented as feedback. Rouse, Peterson, and Shapiro (1975) compared groups given nonproportional auditory feedback for enhancement of alpha in the ranges 8–13 Hz or 9–11 Hz with yoked control groups and found no differences attributable to the feedback conditions. Rather an "entrainment" phenomenon was found; that is, subjects tended toward a narrowing of the alpha frequency band toward a stable frequency of 10 Hz.

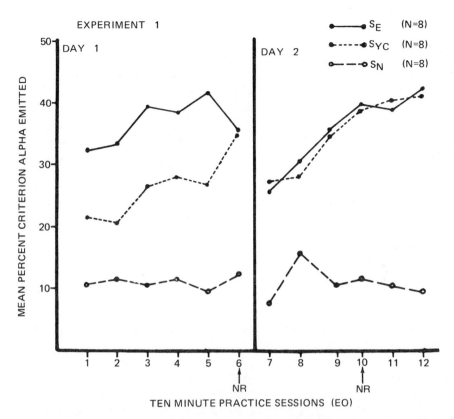

Figure 7. Mean performance of all groups averaged for all practice sessions. Abbreviations: S_E = contingent reinforcement; S_{YC} = yoked controls; S_N = no-reinforcement controls; NR = nonreinforced session. (From Travis, T. A., Kondo, C. Y., & Knott, J. R. Alpha conditioning: A controlled study. *Journal of Nervous and Mental Disease*, 1974, *158*, 166, Figure 1. Reprinted by permission of the author and the publisher.)

Several studies have used somewhat different approaches to the problem of the role of feedback in the voluntary control of alpha. Grynol and Jamieson (1975) presented one group with true auditory feedback whenever alpha was present, whereas a second group was presented alternately with correct and incorrect feedback. All subjects were fully informed. The duration of time in alpha increased in the true-feedback group from 6.35 sec to 13.49 sec per minute over three 30-min training sessions, but in the other group duration of time in alpha decreased from 12.70 sec to 9.75 sec.[7] Prewett and Adams (1976) compared the performance of four groups, all fully informed, with nonproportional auditory feedback, two of the groups being required to enhance alpha and two to decrease alpha. One of the enhance groups was given (true) feedback whenever alpha was in fact enhanced, whereas the other group was given (false) feedback

[7]It is not stated why there should have been such a large difference between the two groups in the first session.

whenever alpha was in fact decreased. Similar true and false feedback was given in respect of the groups required to decrease alpha. They found that alpha enhancement occurred independently of whether the feedback was true or false, but that alpha suppression was dependent on the provision of true feedback. Kuhlman and Klieger (1975), also using nonproportional auditory feedback, provided feedback whenever alpha (8–12 Hz) was above criterion level (20 μV) for one group, the subjects being instructed to keep the tone on. A second group was provided with feedback whenever alpha fell below the criterion, and was instructed to keep the tone off. A control group received no feedback. The group given feedback when alpha was above criterion showed an increase in alpha across trials, but did not exceed baseline (eyes-closed) levels. The group given feedback when alpha was below criterion did exceed the baseline levels but did not show an increase across trials. Hord and Barber (1971) conducted two sessions of alpha training with auditory feedback. In the first, the presence of the tone indicated that alpha was present and the subjects were instructed to produce or suppress alpha, using the presence or absence of the tone as a guide. In the second session, the task was the same except that now the presence of alpha was indicated by the absence of the tone and vice versa. They found that alpha enhancement could be produced irrespective of whether the presence of the tone indicated the presence or absence of alpha. On the other hand, alpha suppression was able to be produced only when the presence of the tone signaled that alpha was absent.

In all of the studies so far discussed, feedback, whether auditory or visual, has been nonproportional. In a complex study which involved both relevant and irrelevant feedback, Travis, Kondo, and Knott (1974b) also investigated the role of binary and proportional feedback. Alpha was recorded from the O_z position. Two days of training were given, each consisting of ten 5-min training periods, preceded by two no-feedback periods. Two groups of subjects received relevant proportional auditory feedback (a tone varying in pitch from 300Hz to 500 Hz as a function of 0–100% alpha present) while two other groups received relevant binary feedback (a 400-Hz tone which was on whenever criterion alpha—defined as 0.07–0.13 sec of 8- to 13-Hz activity with an amplitude 50% or more of the amplitude of maximum eyes-closed alpha—was present) during the training trials. All of these subjects received both eyes-open and eyes-closed training trials, with the order of training reversed for half the subjects in each group. When training involved eyes open, the rest periods involved eyes closed, and vice versa. Three other groups were also run: one receiving random proportional feedback, with eyes closed; another, random binary feedback, also with eyes closed; and a group which received no feedback but sat quietly with eyes closed for periods equivalent to those of the experimental groups. Both criterion and integrated alpha scores were examined for changes related to the various experimental and control conditions. Overall, the groups receiving relevant feedback produced significantly more alpha than the groups receiving random or no feedback. However, relevant binary feedback was not superior to random binary or

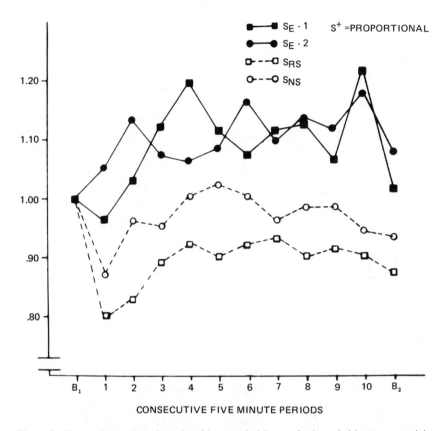

Figure 8. Changes in number of epochs of integrated alpha per 5-min period in groups receiving relevant (S_E–1 and S_E–2), random (S_{RS}) and no (S_{NS}) proportional feedback. Group S_E–1 received eyes-closed training first; S_E–2 received eyes-open training first. (From Travis, T. A., Kondo, C. Y., & Knott, J. R. Parameters of eyes-closed alpha enhancement. *Psychophysiology*, 1974, *11*, 678, Figure 2. Reprinted by permission of the author and the publisher.)

no feedback. Figure 8 shows the relative effects of relevant proportional feedback (for the two groups given the different sequences of eyes-open, eyes-closed training), random proportional feedback, and no feedback, using integrated alpha as the dependent variable. Both groups receiving relevant proportional feedback were superior to the random- and no-feedback groups. No differences were, however, found between these four groups in changes in criterion alpha, highlighting for the first time the importance of using all of the information available regarding changes in alpha rather than an arbitrary threshold (such as alpha greater than 20 μV) as has been customary in most experiments. There was some suggestion in the results that binary feedback might be more effective in establishing eyes-open alpha training, whereas proportional feedback might be more effective in establishing eyes-closed alpha training.

Not a great deal of work has been carried out as yet to determine whether alpha can be enhanced or suppressed voluntarily in the absence of feedback. No doubt this is mainly due to the fact that in most experiments the subjects have not been fully informed, that is, they have not been told that their task is to increase or decrease alpha, but only that their "brain waves" were being studied. No doubt also the reason for not informing subjects is that most experimenters find it difficult to conceive what it could mean to tell subjects to "control alpha" (as opposed, say, to telling them to "control heart rate" or "blood pressure"). This, of course, once more raises the specter of "awareness" in relation to voluntary control, a matter which is dealt with elsewhere. Hord and Barber (1971), in the study discussed earlier, did, however, instruct their subjects to try to increase and decrease alpha in the absence of feedback, and found that significant increases in alpha could be produced under this condition. More generally, the important role of instructions and the expectations induced by them have been demonstrated in several studies. Valle and Levine (1975) allocated their subjects to alpha enhancement and suppression groups and they were provided with nonproportional auditory feedback with tone on indicating alpha enhancement and tone off indicating alpha suppression. Half of the subjects whose task was to enhance alpha were told that tone on indicated the presence of alpha (Enhancement–Expectation Enhancement group), while the other half were told that tone off indicated the presence of alpha (Enhancement–Expectation Suppression). Similarly, half the subjects whose task was to suppress alpha were told that tone on signaled the presence of alpha (Suppression–Expectation Suppression), while the other half were informed that tone off indicated the presence of alpha (Suppression–Expectation Enhancement). Although the group differences in percentage alpha change during training relative to eyes-closed baseline alpha levels were small, an expectation effect was demonstrated, with greater voluntary control being found for the groups expecting to enhance alpha:

> *Regardless* of the direction of alpha change dictated by Task instructions, S's who thought they were enhancing alpha (Expectation Enhancement) exhibited significantly greater ability to control alpha than did S's who thought they were suppressing alpha (Expectation Suppression). Thus, S's in the Task Enhancement–Expectation Enhancement condition ($\bar{X} = 13.91$) *increased* alpha more than S's in the Task Enhancement–Expectation Suppression condition ($\bar{X} = 11.59$), while S's in the Task Suppression–Expectation Enhancement condition ($\bar{X} = 12.74$) *decreased* alpha more than S's in the Task Suppression–Expectation Suppression condition ($\bar{X} = 12.31$). (Valle & Levine, 1975, p. 308, italics in original)

In a subsequent study, however, DeGood, Elkin, Lessin, and Valle (1977) found no difference in ability to enhance and suppress alpha levels in groups with natural positive or neutral expectations regarding the potential of alpha training to enhance relaxation.

Prewett and Adams (1976), in the study discussed in more detail earlier, also found that instructions played an important role in the voluntary enhancement and suppression of alpha. In addition to the four fully informed groups required to increase or decrease alpha while being given feedback for increases or decreases *within* the increase/decrease conditions, two other groups were given ambiguous information on conditions in which increases and decreases in alpha were attempted. The ambiguous instructions actually consisted of a failure to tell the subjects that alpha was being monitored or that the tone they would hear was related to the amount of alpha being produced. They were told only that they were to try to determine what the tone meant. Dummy electrodes were attached to the arms and legs of all groups, and in the case of the two ambiguous groups were intended to ensure that it was not obvious that the tones were related to activity from the electrodes attached to the scalp. When all six groups were compared, alpha activity was greatest in the groups given ambiguous instructions, whether the feedback was given for enhancement or suppression of alpha in these two groups. Furthermore, in these groups alpha activity exceeded resting baseline levels. Rouse *et al.* (1975), in the study already described, paid particular attention to inducing positive expectations in both their feedback and yoked control subjects and considered that their results indicated that the effects of induced expectations were more important in enhancing alpha than whether feedback was available or not, or whether feedback was given for wide-band or narrow-band activity. These conclusions have recently been supported in a study by Williams (1977). He gave two groups of subjects false feedback (auditory feedback from a subject in another experiment). One group was told that the tone would sound whenever "a certain brain wave" was present and were instructed to "keep the tone on"; the other group was told that the sound was feedback from a previous subject, but that the experimenter merely wished to determine what effect it would have on this subject's brain-wave pattern. The subjects in both groups were given 5 min of adaptation during which the tone sounded intermittently, a 2-min baseline without feedback, and four 10-min feedback trials with 2-min rests between each trial. A low level of ambient illumination was used with eyes open and alpha recorded from the O_2-P_4 positions. The percentage alpha activity increased in the group given false feedback but told to keep the tone on from 23.1% during baseline to 36.9% during the fourth "training" trial, whereas it decreased from 25.5% to 17.2% over the same period in the other group. Thus, Williams was able to replicate the earlier alpha-enhancement results solely by the use of appropriate instructions, even in the presence of false feedback.

The role of "reinforcement" may be briefly touched on here (see Chapter 7 for a more detailed account). Kondo, Travis, and Knott (1975) allocated female subjects to four groups given differential monetary rewards ($0, $2.50, $5.00, and $10.00) for exceeding first-trial performance by 20% on all of the last five training trials, using auditory feedback and found no differential effect of reward. On the other hand, Brolund and Schallow (1976), in a study discussed earlier, compared the effects of auditory feedback alone, auditory feedback plus backup reinforcement (class credit or monetary reward if final-session activity increased one and one-half times the baseline activity), yoked feedback, and random feedback, and found that backup reinforcement coupled with feedback produced the best performance (it should be noted, however, that no reinforcement-only group was used, nor a yoked control group receiving feedback and reinforcement from another subject).

Several studies not fitting into any of the above categories may also be mentioned. It will be recalled that the Sidman avoidance technique was used in several studies of heart-rate control (see Chapter 4). The only study using this methodology in the area of alpha control appears to be that by Orne and Paskewitz (1974), who were interested in demonstrating whether increased anxiety would lead to a decrease in alpha and the corollary that training in alpha enhancement would produce increased control over anxiety. They set up a situation in which the presence of one tone indicated the presence of alpha, the presence of a second tone indicated the absence of alpha, and the presence of a third tone indicated the possibility of shock, but the tone only occurred in conjunction with the tone which indicated the absence of alpha—that is, the more alpha the subject produced, the less likely was the shock-threatening tone likely to occur. Although subjects reported experiencing anxiety whenever an anticipatory shock tone occurred, no effect of the tone on alpha density was found. Albert, Simmons, and Walker (1974) examined the effects of massed and spaced practice (involving intersession intervals of 90 sec and 24 h, respectively) on alpha-enhancement training with nonproportional auditory feedback for alpha of 8–12 Hz and amplitude exceeding 29 μV, and found that spaced practice led to higher alpha percentages on all trials except the first of the five given. Regestein, Pegram, Cook, and Bradley (1973) seem to be alone in examining the effects of prolonged feedback periods (they were mainly interested in the degree to which enhanced alpha could offset the usual effects of prolonged sleep deprivation). A group of subjects was given a 30-min baseline followed by 30 min of practice with auditory feedback available, being instructed to enhance alpha by keeping the tone on. They then attempted to maintain alpha at the level achieved during the training period for a further 4 h. Some of the subjects were paid for producing alpha, some were not. Those subjects who produced the most alpha during this 4-h period were then put through two further 12-h periods in which they were first paid for maintaining high alpha levels and then paid for maintaining low alpha levels. In the initial part of the study the amount of alpha dropped during the baseline period, increased significantly during the practice period, and was maintained at this level during the remaining 4 h. In the second part, very high levels of activity (relative to baseline) were maintained when the subjects were paid for high levels, but dropped to very low levels when the subjects were paid for low levels (these levels were not percentages of baseline activity, but actual levels and hence were truly above and below baseline levels). The results for the two 12-h sessions are shown in Figure 9. Regestein *et al.* (1973) point out that it did not seem to matter during these prolonged periods whether the subjects were paid or not, or whether they received feedback or not.

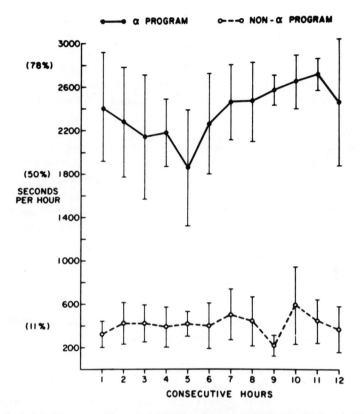

Figure 9. A plot of the mean and standard deviation of alpha maintenance in a 12-h performance for subjects ($N = 6$) under two experimental conditions: reinforced for maintaining alpha, and reinforced for maintaining nonalpha. The same subjects were used in both conditions and were selected on their ability to maintain high levels of alpha. (From Regestein, Q. R., Pegram, G. V., Cook, B., & Bradley, D. Alpha rhythm percentage maintained during 4- and 12-hour feedback periods. *Psychosomatic Medicine*, 1973, *35*, 220, Figure 3. Reprinted by permission of the author and the publisher.)

The difficulties involved in demonstrating whether voluntary control of alpha is or is not possible have not deterred workers in this area from attempting to show that even more complex forms of voluntary control are possible. In particular, efforts have been made to determine whether or not differential control can be established. Such a demonstration would be particularly important since it would be less easy to explain away as artifactual. The work to be considered falls into two categories: differential control of different EEG activities, and differential control of the same EEG activity emanating from different areas of the brain.

It is surprising that so little work has so far been reported relating to the differential control simultaneously of more than one kind of electrical activity.

Beatty (1971) recorded occipital EEG from the O_z position and provided non-proportional auditory feedback for either alpha (8–12 Hz) or beta (14+ Hz) with separate visual stimuli indicating which brain-wave activity was associated with the presence of the auditory feedback (the subjects were not informed about alpha and beta). Backup reinforcement (class credit) was available for doubling alpha and beta activity appropriately as compared with baseline levels. For reasons not explained, 27 of the 36 subjects were given ten feedback trials of 200 sec duration (in half the feedback was for alpha, in half for beta) while the remaining 9 subjects were run as yoked controls. Differentiation of the two states with feedback was successfully achieved, whereas it did not occur in the yoked control group. These results were replicated and extended by Beatty (1972), again training for alpha and beta differentiation. In this study, five groups were used. The first group (information only) was not provided with feedback but was told that alpha and beta were being measured, and instructions were given about the internal states believed to be associated with the production of alpha and beta, respectively. The second group (feedback only) was told that two EEG response patterns had been chosen for study and that a tone would increase in loudness whenever a computer detected the presence of the required activity (identified in each trial, of course, only as ''activity one'' or ''activity two''). No mention was made of alpha or beta, or of associated internal states. The third group (information plus feedback) was given the same information as the first group and additionally the feedback provided to the second group. The fourth group (control) was given neither information nor feedback, while the fifth group (information plus false feedback) was given the same information as the first group but was given beta feedback when trying to increase alpha, and vice versa. The training procedures were the same as those used by Beatty (1971). The results are shown in Figure 10. The subjects in the first three groups (information only, feedback only, information plus feedback) were equally well able to achieve differentiation of alpha and beta activity and did significantly better than the other two groups (no information/no feedback, and information/false feedback). Inspection of the graphs suggests, however, that the differentiation was achieved primarily by the enhancement and suppression of alpha rather than by the active differential control of both states. The results also support the conclusions reached in some of the experiments reviewed earlier that feedback is not essential for the achievement of control:

> The similarity in both the development and the final magnitude of differential responsiveness in the groups which learned, either with or without feedback, emphasizes the difficulty in ascribing learned changes to the effects of feedback when subjects are also informed about the nature of the task. Further, these data suggest that, while proper feedback may be used by naive subjects to produce significant changes in the EEG spectra, it is not the only method by which such changes may be quickly and easily produced. Feedback about alpha or beta frequency activity does not provide unique access to these possible physiological substrates of conscious states. (Beatty, 1972, p. 154)

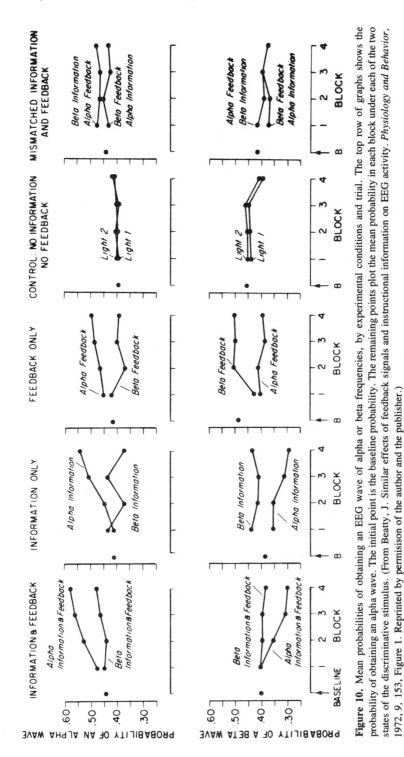

Figure 10. Mean probabilities of obtaining an EEG wave of alpha or beta frequencies, by experimental conditions and trial. The top row of graphs shows the probability of obtaining an alpha wave. The initial point is the baseline probability. The remaining points plot the mean probability in each block under each of the two states of the discriminative stimulus. (From Beatty, J. Similar effects of feedback signals and instructional information on EEG activity. *Physiology and Behavior,* 1972, 9, 153, Figure 1. Reprinted by permisison of the author and the publisher.)

Beatty and Kornfeld (1973) also obtained successful alpha and beta differentiation.

   Peper (1971a) appears to have been the first to investigate the voluntary
control of alpha asymmetry, that is, the production of differential amounts of
alpha in each hemisphere. Alpha was recorded from sites O_2-P_4 and O_1-P_3 and
subjects (informed only that different brain-wave patterns were under investigation) provided with auditory feedback whenever asymmetry was present. Their
task was alternately to keep the tone on (produce asymmetry) or off (produce
symmetry). Asymmetry was defined in terms of alpha being "present" in one
hemisphere and "absent" in the other, using the criteria established earlier in
Mulholland's studies. Following 2-min baseline trials without feedback with
eyes open, then closed, and an 8-min practice period with eyes closed and
auditory feedback, 12 training trials of 2 min each were given with the subject
alternately keeping the tone on and off. A 2-min transfer trial without feedback
and final baseline trials with eyes open and closed completed the experiment.
The striking results obtained are shown in Figure 11. Peper seems somewhat
suspicious of his own results, however, considering that genuine asymmetry
control may not have occurred. Rather, if genuine asymmetry is present initially

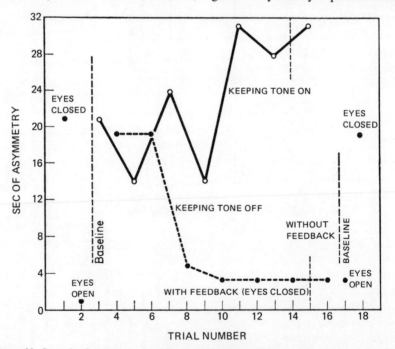

Figure 11. Seconds of asymmetry between the left and right EEG recording for each condition.
(From Peper, E. Comment on feedback training of parietal-occipital alpha asymmetry in normal
human subjects. *Kybernetik,* 1971, *9,* 157, Figure 2. Reprinted by permission of the author and the
publisher.)

(which is very likely) the subject may merely have been trained to increase the total number of alpha events, which would in itself have increased the asymmetry. He makes the valuable suggestion that the experiment be repeated using separate tones to index the presence of symmetry and asymmetry. An attempt to do just this by Peper (1972) produced equivocal results, with only one subject of the eight tested demonstrating clear control.

Using the Mulholland technique described earlier (in which alpha above criterion produces a visual stimulus and alpha below criterion then turns it off), Eberlin and Mulholland (1976) investigated the effects of linking the appearance and disappearance of various visual stimuli with alpha abundance and suppression in one hemisphere while no such relationship was present for alpha occurring in the other hemisphere. After 30 events (where an event is defined as the occurrence of an alpha/no-alpha sequence) had been obtained in the dark with eyes closed and eyes open, a further 10 events were collected with eyes open in the dark (no feedback) followed by 30 presentations of eight slides (four consisting of the words *child, bitch, broom,* and *raped,* and four consisting of perceptual illusions such as the Necker cube) were given, the appearance, duration, and disappearance of the slides depending on alpha abundance and suppression occurring on the specified hemisphere side (left or right), following which a further 30 events were collected with eyes closed and eyes open in the dark. Alpha levels were also allowed to return to resting levels after each set of slide presentations. Independent pretraining calibration of each hemisphere prior to training was carried out to allow for natural differences in resting levels of alpha in each hemisphere. In line with earlier results obtained by Mulholland, increased control of alpha responding was obtained in the hemisphere forming part of the feedback loop as compared to the hemisphere not forming part of the feedback loop. In a single-case study, O'Malley and Conners (1972) successfully trained a 14-year-old boy to increase alpha in the left hemisphere while simultaneously increasing beta or theta responding in the right hemisphere. Davidson, Schwartz, Pugash, and Bromfield (1976) recorded alpha from sites P_3 and P_4, and using auditory feedback attempted to train males and females to differentiate right- from left-hemisphere alpha. The subjects were required to suppress alpha in both hemispheres and to suppress it in one hemisphere while enhancing it in the other. Successful differentiation between hemispheres was obtained, with females proving to be more skillful at the task than males, whereas no sex difference was found in the integration (keep alpha off on both sides) task. Similar results were obtained by Schwartz, Davidson, and Pugash (1976). Nowlis and Wortz (1973) trained subjects to differentiate alpha within a single hemisphere. Following initial training in alpha control with proportional auditory feedback at occipital, parietal, and frontal sites, training in increasing alpha in the frontal site while simultaneously decreasing it in the parietal site was followed by training in the reverse task. Some of the subjects also attempted to institute differential control without the aid of feedback. Although the results of this experiment were not particularly clear-cut, some evidence of differential control was obtained which was maintained in the absence of feedback. Once again, however, there seemed to be a strong tendency for control to be exercised in one direction only, irrespective of the differential instructions given; that is, alpha would be greatest in the parietal region whether the subject was trying to generate more parietal *or* more frontal alpha, and vice versa. For example, subject JR, when instructed to generate frontal alpha, showed 20.70% frontal alpha and 31.91% parietal alpha; when instructed to generate parietal alpha, he showed 12.95% frontal alpha and 34.44% parietal alpha. Subject PC generated 31.60% frontal and 13.90% parietal alpha when instructed to generate frontal alpha; but when instructed to generate parietal alpha he showed the same amount of frontal alpha (32.58%) while showing increased parietal alpha (21.92%). Ray, Frediani, and Harman (1977) successfully trained their subjects to control the output of electrical activity of each hemisphere separately. The feedback in this case was a visual display of the ratio of one hemisphere to the other, based on average EEG power derived from analysis of frequencies between 0.5 and 30 Hz.

On the whole these results on the differential control of alpha between or within hemispheres are quite encouraging. These studies have the advantage that they help to reduce the effects of the large individual differences in level and variability of resting alpha since the subject is used as his own control.

It will be evident that a great deal of attention has been paid to the alpha rhythm in studies of the voluntary control of the electrical activity of the brain. It is quite surprising how little attention has been directed toward other rhythms, although, as we have seen, Beatty and his colleagues have investigated the differential training of alpha and beta rhythms. However, the theta rhythm is beginning to attract a significant degree of attention.[8] Beatty, Greenberg, Deibler, and O'Hanlon (1974) carried out a study on the control of theta which is of special significance, since they tried to show that the establishment of theta control would have important consequences for another activity. They noted that there is evidence that a decrement in vigilance behavior is usually accompanied by an increase in theta activity, from which it follows that subjects trained to increase theta activity should show impairment on a vigilance task; on the other hand, subjects trained to decrease theta activity should manifest an improvement in vigilant behavior. They set up a complex and realistic radar system involving the detection of visual targets from a background of visual noise displayed on an oscilloscope, the dependent variable being the number of sweeps made across the screen in any trial by the combined noise and target before the target was detected. The subjects were first trained in target detection until stable performance was achieved. This was followed by a 2-h vigilance task with five targets occurring in each 15-min period at irregular times. Half of the subjects were then given two 60-min training sessions in the suppression of theta activity, while the

[8]For a comprehensive review of all aspects of theta research, see Schacter (1977).

other half were similarly trained to enhance theta activity, using nonproportional auditory feedback whenever theta met or exceeded the criterion set. The radar-monitoring task was then repeated under both regulated and unregulated conditions, where the unregulated condition was the same as the initial monitoring setup and the regulated condition involved the subject in controlling theta activity while simultaneously performing the vigilance task. Theta enhancement and suppression were successfully achieved and the effects of this training on vigilance performance are shown in Figure 12. The subjects trained to augment theta showed a significant decrement in vigilance performance in the regulated condition as compared to their performance in the unregulated condition, whereas the subjects trained to suppress theta performed better in the regulated condition than they did in the unregulated condition. In terms of actual improvement on the vigilance task the effects of suppression of theta activity were quite striking. In the third half hour of the vigilance task (and therefore uncontaminated by the

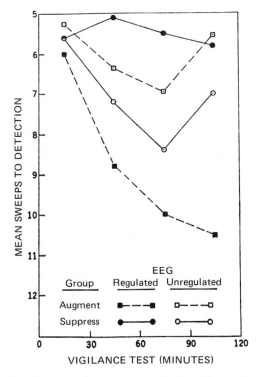

Figure 12. Mean number of sweeps to detect targets as a function of time in the vigilance test for the theta-augment group and the theta-suppress group with regulated and unregulated EEG (ordinate scale inverted). (From Beatty, J., Greenberg, A., Deibler, W. P., & O'Hanlon, J. F. Operant control of occipital theta rhythm affects performance in a radar monitoring task. *Science*, 1974, *183*, 872, Figure 2. Reprinted by permission of the author and the publisher.)

usual end-spurt improvement in vigilance which commonly occurs toward the end of a vigilance task, the duration of which is known to the subject), theta suppression improved detection by an average of 18 sec faster detection of targets, while the theta-enhance subjects showed a very significant degree of deterioration in vigilance performance.

Sittenfeld, Budzynski, and Stoyva (1976) pointed out that training in theta control is difficult and attempted to capitalize on the finding that a reduction in frontalis muscle activity is often accompanied by an increase in theta activity. On the basis of baseline levels of frontalis activity, they allocated subjects to four experimental conditions. One group of subjects with high levels of baseline frontalis activity was given eight sessions of feedback training in theta enhancement (one-phase training). A second group, also with high levels of baseline frontalis activity, was given four sessions of muscle activity relaxation training (one session involving reduction of forearm muscle activity, and three involving reduction of frontalis muscle activity) followed by four sessions of feedback training in theta enhancement while continuing to receive feedback relating to forearm and frontalis muscle activity (two-phase training). Two other groups, manifesting low baseline levels of frontalis muscle activity, were similarly trained. Proportional auditory feedback in the form of clicks was provided for theta activity, while visual feedback was provided for forearm and frontalis muscle activity. The feedback training sessions were preceded and followed by no-feedback baseline sessions. The results are shown in Figure 13.[9] The high frontal EMG two-phase group showed a significant pre–post baseline increase in theta level ($5.5 \mu V$ to $10.2 \mu V$) as did the low frontal EMG single-phase group ($6.9 \mu V$ to $11.8 \mu V$). The other two groups did not show these increases, indicating an interaction between EMG frontalis baseline levels and one- and two-phase training; that is, if EMG frontalis baseline level is high, that level should be reduced first if theta training is to be successful. On the other hand, if EMG frontalis baseline level is low, theta training will be successful even if unaccompanied by a reduction in EMG level through prior training, whereas combined training in this instance seems to interfere with the theta training. Sittenfeld *et al.* (1976) draw the important conclusion (assuming their results are replicable) that "biofeedback techniques must be adapted to the physiological characteristics of the subjects" (p. 40). There is, however, a significant degree of confounding in this study, for in the two-phase groups the effects of pretraining on muscle activity is not separated out from the effect of the continuation of that training while the theta training is in progress. Hence, the facilitation of theta control could have been due to the effects of the continuation of the training rather than to the effects of the pretraining.

Lutzenberger, Birbaumer, and Wildgruber (1975) were critical of this ear-

---

[9]The original figure is incorrectly labeled—the *solid* lines indicate EMG activity, and the *dashed* lines indicate theta activity. The error has been corrected in the figure as reproduced here.

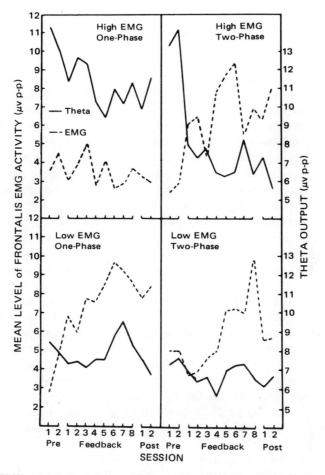

Figure 13. EMG and theta levels in four different training groups (see text for explanation). Left: Theta feedback only (8 sessions). Right: EMG feedback (4 sessions) and Theta feedback (4 sessions). (From Sittenfeld, P., Budzynski, T., & Stoyva, J. Differential shaping of EEG theta rhythms. *Biofeedback and Self-Regulation,* 1976, *1,* 38, Figure 1. Reprinted by permission of the author and the publisher.)

lier work on theta control[10] on methodological grounds. They gave ten fully informed subjects ten training sessions with feedback and instructions to increase theta by keeping a tone on for as long as possible, theta being defined as 3- to 7.8-Hz activity from site C_Z–P_4 of at least 10 μV amplitude. For half the subjects, the feedback was contingent on theta production in the first five ses-

[10]Sittenfeld's results (published in 1976) were available to them, having been published in thesis form in 1973.

sions, then noncontingent; for the remaining subjects, the reverse procedure was employed. No differences were found between contingent and noncontingent feedback, nor was there any evidence of an increase in theta activity over baseline levels. Unfortunately, however, although the subjects were not told how to try to increase theta, they were told that the experiment was to investigate whether theta is an indicator of deep relaxation. Hence, a set to relax both in the contingent and noncontingent conditions may have overridden any effect of feedback. Furthermore, the use of a very soft pink noise as the feedback may have induced relaxation *per se*.

In a subsequent study, the interaction between frontalis muscle relaxation training and theta-enhancement training was also not replicated by Lutzenberger, Birbaumer, and Steinmetz (1976). Using a Lang-type visual display which provided simultaneous feedback for heart rate and frontalis muscle activity, they first trained their subjects to reduce both heart rate and frontalis muscle activity before proceeding to theta-enhancement training, using nonproportional soft pink noise feedback to indicate the presence of theta. Eight 40-min sessions in theta-enhancement training were given with each session consisting of 5 min of relaxation followed by three periods of 7 min of training, 2 min of attempted theta enhancement without feedback, and 2 min of relaxation. In half the sessions the feedback was contingent on the presence of theta and in half it was noncontingent. A small but significant increase in theta was found across, but not within, sessions when feedback was contingent as compared with when it was noncontingent, but no influence of pretraining in heart rate and frontalis muscle activity training was found. There were, however, some very important procedural differences between this study and that of Sittenfeld *et al.* (1976). In this study the subjects were not informed about theta activity and how to increase it, no differentiation was made between subjects with high and low baseline levels of frontalis muscle activity, and feedback for frontalis muscle activity was not provided during the theta training. Hence, the results of the two studies may not be as discrepant as they appear at first sight.

Biofeedback training in voluntary control of 40-Hz activity has received increasing attention in recent years. Sheer (1975) has argued that beta, alpha, and theta enhancement are all associated with impairment or inhibition of performance. Facilitation of performance, on the other hand, tends to be associated with desynchronization of the EEG, involving very low amplitudes and mixed fast frequencies (defining an arousal state). Sheer suggests that as learning progresses the initial desynchronization is replaced by specific, localized "subassemblies." However, special analysis is required to separate out these subassemblies from the overall diffuse patterns. Sheer further maintains that a narrow frequency band centered at 40 Hz reflects the state of "focused arousal" produced by learning. Sheer (1975) has described the technical problems of measuring 40-Hz activity reliably (it is particularly easily confused with muscle activity) and has described in detail a system by which a slide projector will be turned on whenever a specified level of 40-Hz activity occurs (but not if this activity is accompanied by a burst of 70-Hz muscle activity recorded within 20 msec either side of the 40-Hz burst from electrodes placed over the neck and temporal muscles). Recordings of 40-Hz activity are usually made from $O_1 - P_3$.

Bird, Newton, Sheer, and Ford (1978a) trained normal subjects to increase or decrease 40-Hz activity using the techniques described above. These results were replicated by Bird, Newton, Sheer, and Ford (1978b), who additionally demonstrated transfer of the ability to a no-feedback situation, alternation of increase/decrease control, and differential hemisphere control. The control was exercised independently of changes in heart rate, EMG activity with the same frequency characteristic, and beta, theta, and alpha responding.

The studies on theta training indicate the increasing sophistication in the design of experiments in this area which has occurred in recent years. This has been paralleled in the area of alpha research as well, partly as a result of a second wave of critical analysis of the problems of research design in studies of alpha control.

The Second Wave of Criticism

In spite of the concentrated research that was carried out following the first wave of criticism, serious doubts remained concerning what if anything had been demonstrated concerning the voluntary control of the electrical activity of the brain. The distinguished French neurophysiologist Gastaut delivered a withering attack on what he called the "cult of alpha" and the "alpha culture," describing Kamiya as the high priest of the cult and the institute where he did his work as its Mecca. In his address to the Eighth International Congress of Electroencephalography and Clinical Neurophysiology, few of those whose work has been discussed in this chapter escaped his scorn (Gastaut, 1974) and he was to return to the attack in English 1 year later in respect of the attempts to reduce epileptic seizures by brain-wave training, to be discussed below (Gastaut, 1975). Critics were not wanting in the United States either, and the criticisms which still seemed relevant in spite of all the work that had been done were brought together in a substantial review by Plotkin (1976a). He considered first the strategies and factors implicated in alpha control: the role of attention, the role of the oculomotor system (including the significance of convergence and accommodation), the role of arousal (making an important distinction between oculomotor and behavioral arousal in relation to the frequency and amplitude characteristics of the alpha response), the role of somatic processes such as heart rate, blood pressure, and respiration rate (the influence of which on alpha he rejects), and the role of cognitive and emotional factors. As a result of this survey, he highlights the roles of the oculomotor system and cognitive factors and their possible interaction. He also points out the degree to which feedback has been confounded with instructions to the subject about strategies of control in most of the studies on alpha control. Finally, Plotkin carefully considers the methodology of alpha research in relation to the measurement of alpha, stressing the need to measure alpha amplitude continuously (rather than using a threshold above which alpha is arbitrarily said to be present and below which it is equally arbitrarily said to be absent), the need to use proportional rather than discontinuous feedback, the need to control for the effects of fatigue and sleepiness, and particularly the need to measure alpha enhancement and suppression by reference to the immediately preceding baseline level (that is, to use the pretrial baseline rather than the running baseline technique—this is in effect a recognition of the problem of the drift effect, although Plotkin does not refer to it directly as such). It will be seen that there are no new points in Plotkin's review of the problem associated with alpha control research, but he succeeded in bringing them all together to a degree which had not previously been achieved.

Plotkin (1976a) then proceeded to carry out a complex experiment in which he attempted systematically to vary the factors he believed most clearly implicated in alpha control, while eliminating the less important but possibly confounding variables by controlling them out. He incorporated five variables into his study: two between (auditory feedback versus no auditory feedback, and instructions type—cognitive versus oculomotor versus no instructions), and three within (total darkness versus low ambient light; trial type—generate alpha, suppress alpha, and rest; and trial blocks). It should be noted that a condition involving neither feedback nor instructions was not included in the experimental design. Alpha was recorded from the right occipital and right frontal lobes (O_2–F_4) and the feedback was an intensity-modulated tone proportional to alpha amplitude. The subjects were not specifically informed about alpha but were instructed in the feedback conditions to increase or decrease the tone appropriately (an attempt was made to control subjects' activity during the rest periods by instructing them not to try to imagine increasing or decreasing tones). At all times during the training sessions the subjects kept their eyes open. Cognitive instructions involved telling the subjects to relax (etc.) in the increase-alpha condition, and to concentrate (etc.) in the decrease-alpha condition. Appropriate instructions were given for the oculomotor-strategy condition. As no mention of alpha was ever made (and the subjects were naive), the signal for generating alpha was "receptive state" and that for suppressing alpha was "action state." Only a single session of training was given, involving 5 min of relaxation, general instructions about biofeedback, two 3-min baseline trials (eyes open, then eyes closed), provision of instructions appropriate to the subject's training condition, and 18 3-min trials in six blocks of 3 trials each.

The main results of the experiment are shown in Table 2 and indicate that alpha was better controlled with lights on than with lights off, that feedback was a significant factor in successful control of alpha and its effect was enhanced with lights on, and that alpha was successfully enhanced, but not suppressed, as a

Table 2. Means for Trial Number Effects from Percent Success Score ANOVA 1[a]

Test	Trial number					
	1	2	3	4	5	6
Trial number	10.6	14.7	13.2	15.0	15.6	19.6
Trial no. × Fdbk						
Feedback	14.3	19.8	19.9	23.0	24.0	27.3
No feedback	6.9	9.6	6.5	7.1	7.3	11.8
Trial no. × Lights						
On	12.7	23.8	20.8	23.7	24.8	31.6
Off	8.6	5.6	5.6	6.7	6.4	7.6
Trial no. × Task						
Generate alpha	4.0	13.8	12.9	17.2	17.6	22.6
Suppress alpha	17.3	15.6	13.4	12.9	13.6	16.6

SOURCE: Adapted from Plotkin, W. B. On the self-regulation of the occipital alpha rhythm, control strategies, states of consciousness, and the role of physiological feedback. *Journal of Experimental Psychology: General*, 1976, *105*, Table 1. Copyright 1976 by the American Psychological Association. Reprinted by permission of the author and the publisher.
[a]ANOVA 1 = Analysis in which feedback/no-instruction group was omitted.

function of trials. However, feedback-augmented enhancement of alpha was always mediated by learned control of the oculomotor strategy rather than the cognitive strategy, as revealed by further analyses, the strategy involving learning ''not to look.'' Whenever the cognitive strategy was successful, it was so by virtue of mediating changes in the oculomotor processes. Plotkin concluded that the proposition that alpha control is intimately connected with oculomotor processes rather than cognitive mediational processes is supported by the results of his experiment.

Not surprisingly, Plotkin's critical review and his experimental study drew fire from those who had most strongly argued that alpha control was mediated through cognitive activities. Hardt and Kamiya (1976a) complained that Plotkin had recorded frontal rather than occipital alpha, had not made actual measurements of oculomotor activity (pointing out that alpha activity is present in eyeless subjects), and that he had trained his subjects for an insufficient period of time (72 min), whereas at least 2 h of preliminary training is required to deal with the effects of habituation and attention. They also complained about Plotkin's use of continuous feedback instead of discontinuous digital end-of-trial feedback, claiming that the latter provided a clearer indication of progress and increased motivation;[11] they considered that the eyes-open training used by Plotkin guaranteed alpha disruption, even in the dark; and they objected to the short trial durations as well as the alternation of training trials and rest periods. The instruction not to indulge in imaginal activities which might increase or decrease an

[11]See Chapter 2 for a discussion of types of feedback.

imaginary tone they regarded as "uninterpretable" by the subject. In short, they were not at all impressed with Plotkin's results or his interpretation of them. Plotkin (1976b) was unmoved, pointing out that Brown (1970) had obtained significant results with 70 min of training, while Kamiya (1969) himself had claimed to enhance alpha in less than 10 min of training. He also pointed out that Nowlis and Kamiya (1970) found no difference in alpha enhancement between subjects trained with eyes closed and those trained with eyes open, both groups in a moderately darkened room. In his reply, Plotkin stressed particularly the importance of suggestion and expectation in alpha experiments and the similarity of the situation created in many alpha studies to the situation created in sensory-deprivation experiments. More recently, Plotkin (1978) has conducted a further study in an effort to remove the flaws alleged to vitiate the results of his earlier work. A long period of training was given (9 h) and an integrated amplitude measure used, both of which should maximally facilitate alpha enhancement. The independent variables were electrode placement, uninterrupted versus interrupted training trials, high versus low sensory deprivation, and the effect of instructions. Once more, Plotkin reported a failure to find enhancement of alpha above levels reached during eyes-closed baseline periods. On the other hand, Pressner and Savitsky (1977) matched four groups on baseline alpha levels and then provided each group with a combination of contingent or noncontingent feedback and positive or negative expectation of a resultant mood experience if alpha were enhanced and found that contingent feedback did produce more alpha enhancement than did noncontingent feedback.

The evidence relating to the voluntary control of alpha which has been reviewed in this chapter is an excellent example of the interaction between empirical results, theory, and methodology by which science advances—except that in this case the advance appears to have come to a dead halt. It is clear that the major pathway to a resolution of the question of whether voluntary control of alpha is possible lies in the development of an adequate methodology. Before considering what might be involved in such a development, reference should be made to several recent papers which have touched on various methodological aspects of alpha research. Hardt and Kamiya (1976b), to some extent contradicting some aspects of their critique of Plotkin's work, have pointed out that those studies which have reported weak alpha enhancement have used percentage time in alpha as the dependent variable, together with discontinuous feedback, whereas those studies which have reported a strong alpha-enhancement effect have tended to use an integrated-amplitude alpha moving index as the dependent variable, together with continuous proportional feedback. The former method establishes a threshold above which alpha is deemed to be present and below which it is deemed to be absent, thus assigning equal significance to all values above the threshold and treating amplitudes below threshold as noise. They consider that this approach discards much useful information and recommend that all alpha should be incorporated into the measurement of the dependent variable. This is, of course, precisely what Plotkin (1976a) did in his experiment. Hardt and Kamiya (1976b) gave roughly 5½ h of training in alpha enhancement and suppression to 16 male subjects, providing both continuous auditory feedback and discontinuous feedback (a digital score after every 2 min). Alpha was recorded from O_1–O_3 sites and training was given with eyes closed in the dark (except that eyes were open briefly when the digital score was provided). In line with their criticism of the short training periods used by Plotkin, they gave 32 min of continuous enhancement training and 16 min of continuous suppression training, separated by 10–15 min of rest and an 8-min baseline. They found that the two measures of alpha they calculated (integrated, using all of the alpha present; and threshold, using alpha above and below threshold in the enhance and suppress conditions, respectively) were relatively independent of each other, and they recommend strongly the use of integrated amplitude in preference to the use of a threshold measurement.

Peper (1974) has also considered some of the methodological problems involved in alpha research, mainly relating to the definition of what constitutes alpha responding when feedback is provided and control achieved. He particularly raises the problems of the confounding of alpha with pathological spikes containing 8- to 13-Hz components, the threshold problem, the question of what constitutes "no-alpha" (usually defined as an absence of alpha but this may involve the presence of either beta or theta waves), and the site or sites from which recordings are taken, given that alpha activity may be present in almost any region of the cortex. He makes suggestions for overcoming these difficulties such as recording from multiple site locations and grouping subjects who have similar toposcopic EEG patterns, training subjects on multiple alpha parameters (amplitude, frequency, differential location) with no-alpha clearly defined, recording continuous frequency spectra, using single-subject research designs, and standardizing procedures across laboratories. It will be remembered (see Chapter 2) that Peper (1976) has also severely criticized the use of short alternating periods of enhance, rest, suppress alpha (in this he is in agreement with Hardt & Kamiya, 1976a, and in disagreement with Plotkin, 1976b).

Finally, Mulholland and Benson (1976) and Mulholland *et al.* (1976) have suggested new and sophisticated approaches to the quantification of alpha and no-alpha responding, with the aim of more clearly differentiating alpha from noise. The approach is based on the work of Goodman (1973) and involves the calculation of best-fit lines for alpha and no-alpha under various conditions of stimulation. The interested reader must be referred to the original papers for a detailed account of the methods used.

The inevitable conclusion to be drawn from all of the work reviewed in this chapter must be that research into the voluntary control of alpha is beset with methodological problems which have not yet been resolved. Indeed, it would perhaps not be going too far to suggest that research in this area might well start again from scratch, provided certain standards could be set up to ensure comparability of results across different laboratories and the collection of basic data from which the effects of attempted voluntary control could be assessed. Here, we can only attempt to draw together some of the main points, bearing in mind that it would of course be quite unreasonable to suppose that the question of the voluntary control of alpha will be solved by one gigantic experiment incorporating all of the variables in question.

The instructions and information given to the subject are clearly of prime importance. In most studies, even as recently as the one by Plotkin (1976a), subjects have not been informed that it is alpha activity that is being brought under control, yet in other experiments the subjects have been fully informed. The question of informing subjects is, as has been seen in previous chapters and as will be taken up generally in a later chapter, a perennial one in biofeedback research. The obvious answer to the problem is to treat the question of information as an independent variable and discover empirically the differential effect, if any, of informing or not informing subjects. Yet with few exceptions this has not been done, for reasons which appear to be related to the theoretical preconceptions of the research workers. The problem is, however, an empirical one which needs urgent resolution.

There are many unresolved (or at least not satisfactorily resolved) questions relating to the specific methodology of experimentation in relation to which straightforward studies to obtain reliable and valid empirical data are urgently needed. Such matters as the interaction between eyes open and closed and the levels of ambient illumination in baseline, no-feedback conditions remain unresolved and are linked with the need to investigate the drift effect which is obviously of crucial significance in alpha research. What does happen to alpha with eyes closed/open in various levels of illumination over prolonged periods of time in baseline without feedback? The answer to this simple but fundamental question remains unknown. Reliable information on this matter would help to resolve the questions of whether a running or a pretrial baseline should be used from which to assess the effects of alpha training, and of whether it is or is not possible to increase alpha beyond the baseline levels manifested with eyes closed in darkness when training is initiated after the dramatic drop in alpha which occurs when an eyes-closed baseline is succeeded by an eyes-open baseline and the subsequent recovery of alpha which takes place without feedback. The question of the effects on acquisition of control of alternating short training periods in enhancing and suppressing alpha with rest periods as compared with running relatively long enhancement and suppression trials needs much more investigation than it has so far been given, in spite of the claim by Plotkin (1976a) that alternating short training periods are quite satisfactory. Finally, insufficient attention has so far been paid to the ability of subjects to enhance and suppress alpha without feedback and simply under informed instructions to do so. Even less attention has been paid (compared with, for example, heart-rate control) to the maintenance of alpha control obtained with feedback after the feedback has been withdrawn (transfer effects). Many other methodological points could be made (such as the clearer definition of alpha and its discrimination from beta and theta, and the use of integrated amplitude as opposed to above- and below-threshold states), but enough has been said to make it clear that alpha research is, methodologically speaking, in a state of considerable disarray. Rarely can so much effort have been expended for so little result. This is not to imply that such a result was inevitable. The basic difficulty seems to be that the same kind of careful standardization which was given to defining uniformly the location of sites from which recordings could be taken in the 10–20 system has not yet been applied to the methodology of research into alpha in respect of the important basic variables (eyes open/closed, room illumination, and so on) which must be either controlled or treated as independent variables in alpha research.

The Treatment of Epilepsy

The attribution of epilepsy to disturbances of electrical activity in the brain represents one of the great advances of this century, removing epilepsy from the realm of the mystical which had led in the past to an association between epilepsy and mystical states of consciousness. Nevertheless, the clear demonstration of an organic basis for epilepsy does not in any way involve a denial that psychological factors may be implicated in both the production and inhibition of seizures. The clearest evidence for the operation of conditioning and learned elements in epilepsy has been found in that variety known as temporal lobe epilepsy[12] where it has been shown that a seizure may be invoked in some patients by quite specific "psychological" stimuli (as opposed to the induction of seizures by repetitive stimuli such as flickering lights).

Several examples of the role of psychological factors in the production and inhibition of seizures may be given. Robertson (1954) has described in detail seven cases in which seizures could be produced voluntarily by interrupting the sun's rays by moving the fingers across the eyes or by blinking rapidly to induce effects which can, of course, lead to an involuntary seizure in such patients if experienced naturally. According to Robertson the condition involves "the provocation of cerebral dysrhythmia by action of voluntary muscles" (1954, p. 248) without loss of consciousness. There is no doubt that these attacks were not simply self-induced alterations of overt behavior patterns since Robertson was able to show that they were accompanied by severe disturbances in the electrical activity of the brain. It proved possible to bring the seizures under control in some of these patients by training them to inhibit the finger movement or eye

[12]Temporal lobe epilepsy is associated with electrical disturbances in the temporal lobe, usually unilateral and involving short-term nonresponsiveness to the environment without a grand mal seizure or total loss of consciousness. Treatment often involves excision of the involved temporal lobe.

blinking when outside in sunlight. Efron (1956, 1957) described several cases in which it was possible to intervene during the aura phase of a seizure and abort the full seizure. Thus, in one case, where the aura consisted of sensations traveling up the leg or arm, application of a ligature aborted the seizure. More important, Efron also reported a case study in which the presentation of an unpleasant olfactory stimulus arrested a seizure in its early stages in a female epileptic. Efron then paired a neutral stimulus (a bracelet) with the unpleasant aroma every 15 min throughout the day for 8 days, establishing the connection in different places and in the presence of different people to obtain as much generalization as possible. The patient then reported that she could inhibit a seizure by staring at the bracelet as soon as the preseizure aura was experienced. Later on, inhibition could be induced merely by thinking of the bracelet. Further evidence of the inhibitory effect of the conditioned stimulus was obtained by showing that following the training the induction of a seizure by the administration of metrazol became less likely. This particular patient was reported by Efron to have been completely free of seizures for a long period of time and to have been able to resume a singing career. Tassinari (1968) reported that abnormal EEG patterns could be suppressed by passive or voluntary flexion or extension of the right foot, or by stroking or rubbing the sole of the right foot. This was not a therapeutic study so no attempt was made to determine whether the voluntary control could be used in that way by the patient on a permanent basis. De Weerdt and van Rijn (1975) described a case of specific reading epilepsy in a 19-year-old female who found that she had to stop reading after 15 min because of the occurrence of visual disturbances followed by muscular spasms, and on one occasion when she nevertheless continued to read, a generalized convulsion. The treatment consisted of instructing the patient to hit her thigh with her hand whenever the letter e occurred in what she was reading (later, other, less common vowels were specified). Treatment was prolonged over 38 weeks but eventually the abnormal spike and wave activity associated with the disturbance when reading disappeared, although the beneficial effects were present only if the patient restricted her reading to short periods of time. This approach was based on earlier studies of specific forms of epileptic responding by Forster, Paulsen, and Baughman (1969).[13]

The notion that seizure activity in the brain and/or actual epileptic attacks might be brought under more direct voluntary control, however, resulted from work by Sterman and his colleagues on the effects of increased amounts of sensorimotor rhythm (SMR) activity in the region of the brain adjacent to the central sulcus in the cat. Sterman noted that whenever cats are in a state of relaxation (involving a marked reduction in movement) there was a significant increase in 12- to 14-Hz activity recorded from the sensorimotor region, and was able to train cats, using operant conditioning, to assume stereotyped, motionless

[13]For a review of Forster's work on reflex epilepsy, see Adams (1976).

postures to produce SMR activity when this activity was rewarded.[14] Sterman (1973) wondered whether the frequency and severity of abnormal electrical activity in the brains of epileptics, and perhaps consequently the frequency and severity of epileptic attacks, might be reduced if the patients could be trained to increase the amount of SMR activity with feedback, provided, of course, some degree of such activity was already present in the appropriate area as a basis on which to build.

Sterman and Friar (1972) conducted the first trial of SMR training with a 23-year-old female with a 6-year history of convulsions consisting of a nocturnal, generalized major motor seizure, preceded by a nonspecific aura and with a frequency of about two per month. SMR activity was recorded from anterior leads placed between F_3-C_3 and posterior leads placed between C_3-P_3, while alpha was also recorded from leads placed at P_z-O_1. SMR activity was defined as 11–13 Hz of "large amplitude" emanating from the areas specified while alpha was defined as 9–11 Hz at P_z-O_1 of unspecified amplitude. Feedback (referred to as reward by Sterman and Friar) consisted of two rows of ten small lamps, together with auditory feedback presented simultaneously. As each successive criterion SMR response was detected, the lights in the top row lit up sequentially, accompanied each time by a single chime. When the 11th response was made, the first light in the second row lit up, accompanied by a double chime, while the first row of lights went out. The ten lights in the first row were then used again, followed by the second light in the second row, and so on. Thus, 200–300 feedback (reward) stimuli were given in training periods lasting ½–1 h, preceded and followed by 5-min no-feedback baseline periods. One to two sessions a week were given in this way for 4 months. The patient kept her eyes open during training and was instructed to "clear the mind and think of past experiences or of nothing at all in an effort to achieve the desired mental state" (Sterman & Friar, 1972, p. 90). The results with respect to progressive changes in SMR and alpha rhythms for sessions 2, 4, and 12 are shown in Figure 14. Initially, the level of both SMR and alpha activity was low but by session 12 SMR activity had increased significantly, whereas alpha activity, after initially increasing, had returned virtually to its original level. The introduction of a monetary reward late in training resulted in the highest levels of SMR activity achieved by the patient. The effect of the training on seizure rate is more difficult to determine. In the 12 months prior to the start of training the patient experienced 21 seizures, while during the 4-month training period she experienced 3.[15] It is impossible to know whether this represents a significant improvement in seizure rate or not.

Encouraged by these results, Sterman, MacDonald, and Stone (1974) investigated the effects of SMR training on four epileptic patients[16] and four

[14]For a detailed description of the animal studies, see Sterman (1973).

[15]Data calculated from Table 1 in Sterman and Friar (1972).

[16]The patients studied in this report are the same as those in an earlier report by Sterman (1973).

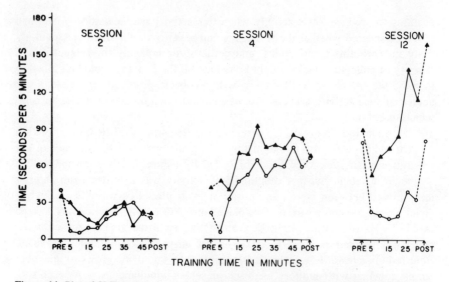

Figure 14. Plot of SMR (solid triangles) and alpha rhythm (open circles) production during SMR training and pre–post baseline recordings at three points in the training sequence. Output is expressed in terms of the total occurrence of these rhythms, at criterion amplitude and duration, in pre- and posttraining 5-min samples and in sequential 5-min epochs during training. Transitions between training and pre–post measures are indicated by broken line. (From Sterman, M. B., & Friar, L. Suppression of seizures in an epileptic following sensorimotor EEG feedback training. *Electroencephalography and Clinical Neurophysiology,* 1972, *33,* 92, Figure 2. Reprinted by permission of the author and the publisher.)

normal controls. Electrode placements and general procedures were similar to those in the earlier study, but much more sophisticated instrumentation was used to detect criterion SMR (13-Hz activity at minimum voltage and lasting at least 0.75 sec). The normal subjects were trained for 2–3 months while the epileptics were trained for much longer periods (6–18 months). In addition to the auditory and visual feedback for SMR activity, slide scenes were used as reinforcement. The results of this study threw up a number of new and important findings. The normal subjects were able to increase the rate of SMR activation, but the epileptics (who initially showed very low levels of SMR activity) were not. However, it is known that epilepsy is accompanied very often by rather specific epileptiform brain-wave activity consisting of 6- to 8- or 5- to 9-Hz trains with abnormal spike and wave discharge, and this activity was significantly reduced by the SMR training so that the EEG developed a more normal appearance. The use of power spectral analysis revealed clearly the presence of abnormal slow frequencies and their subsequent reduction during SMR training, as shown in Figure 15. A significant improvement in the clinical seizure records was evident in all four epileptics, although not sustained in one when feedback was withdrawn.

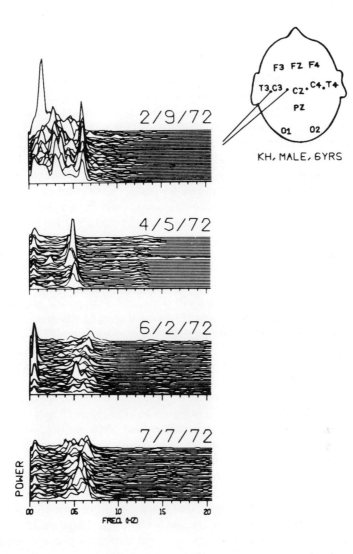

Figure 15. Sequential power spectral arrays computed from laboratory EEG recordings obtained during the first 10 min of SMR training (scale factor = 0). This subject was recorded from the left central cortex only during the first 6 months of training. Note marked occurrence of abnormal slow frequency associated with epileptiform discharge at the earliest stage of training. This activity was progressively reduced and essentially absent by the 4th month. A sustained frequency peak can also be noted at 5–7 Hz. Spectral traces represent sequential 17-sec epochs of EEG activity (From Sterman, M. B., MacDonald, L. R., & Stone, R. K. Biofeedback training of the sensorimotor electroencephalogram rhythm in man: Effects on epilepsy. *Epilepsia*, 1974, *15*, 408, Figure 5. Reprinted by permission of the author and the publisher).

Sterman (1977) has provided a preliminary report on SMR training results with 40 epileptics. Sterman has used an A–B–A design where A involves feedback if 6- to 9-Hz activity is present and 12- to 15-Hz activity is absent, while B involves the reverse. Training lasts for 1 year with the A and B conditions replacing one another at 3-month intervals without the patient's knowledge. The results obtained by Sterman look to be very encouraging although detailed quantitative analysis, as well as adequate follow-up, remains to be accomplished.

Finley, Smith, and Etherton (1975) used SMR training with a 13-year-old male patient who at the time training commenced was experiencing an average of 75 seizures for every 10 h of wakefulness. Each attack lasted about 30 sec and involved loss of consciousness and falling to the floor, although the attacks seemed to be exacerbation of petit mal (or perhaps even psychomotor) seizures experienced since the age of 4. Recordings were made from a single site (intermediate between F_3–C_3, as in Sterman's studies) with 12 ± 1 Hz and 5.5 ± 1.5 Hz being detected, using appropriate filtering. In the initial study, 1-h feedback training trials were given three times a week for a total of 80 trials. In trials 1–34, both visual (a blue light) and auditory (a 1500-Hz tone) feedback were provided whenever 5 μV or more of 12-Hz activity was detected. Additionally, every 5 sec of 12-Hz activity earned one point, and if the patient accumulated a certain number of points before a specified time elapsed he was given a monetary reward. False feedback (from previous trials) was given on trials 29–31. During trials 35–80, the occurrence of epileptiform activity (5.5 Hz) activated a red light, and while this light was on feedback for SMR activity was withheld. During this period the patient was instructed to try to turn off the red light whenever it occurred, as points could not be earned while the red light was on. The results of this study are shown in Figure 16. The top and bottom portions of the graph show the percentage epileptiform and SMR activity, respectively, while the center portion shows the seizure rate per hour, recorded at the same time each day by the parents, who were regarded as reliable observers. During trials 1–34, when feedback was provided only for SMR activity, significant negative correlations were found between home seizure rate and percentage SMR activity ($r = -0.42$) and percentage SMR activity and percentage epileptiform activity ($r = -0.53$). These correlations were negative and significant when calculated for trials 1–80, but tended to be nonsignificant during trials 35–80 when both feedback signals were in operation. A significant overall reduction in 5.5-Hz activity and a significant overall increase in 12-Hz activity was found over the whole training period, but when epileptiform activity was partialed out, the increase in SMR activity over trials remained highly significant ($r = +0.56$). The rate of clinical seizures (measured in the home situation) declined over the training period by a factor of ten. The introduction of false feedback produced an immediate increase in seizure rate at home, although neither the patient nor his parents were aware of the fact that false feedback had been introduced.

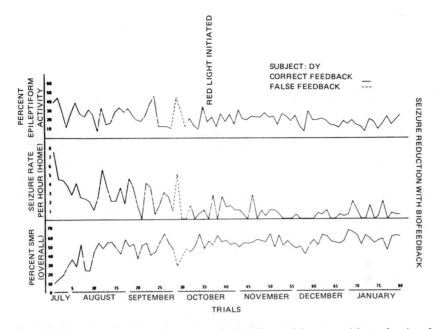

Figure 16. Seizure rate per hour and percentage of epileptiform activity across trials as a function of the percentage of SMR (overall). Seizure rate per hour was determined by the parents who observed their son's seizure rate between 7 and 8 P.M. each evening. The percentage of SMR (overall) was determined by averaging the percentage of SMR on pre- and postfeedback baselines and during the actual feedback period for each training trial. False feedback (noncontingent reinforcement) was instituted on trials 29, 30, and 31, as indicated by the dashed lines. The vertical dotted line (trial 35) depicts initiation of red light to inform the subject of the occurrence of epileptiform activity. (From Finley, W. W., Smith, H. A., & Etherton, M. D. Reduction of seizures and normalization of the EEG in a severe epileptic following sensorimotor biofeedback training: Preliminary study. *Biological Psychology,* 1975, *2,* 197, Figure 5. Reprinted by permission of the author and the publisher.)

The training of this patient was continued for a further 5 months, with results which have been reported in detail by Finley (1976). The seizure rate continued to decline during this period to the point at which clinical seizures were occurring less than once every 3–4 h compared with the pretreatment average of 7–8 per hour. During this same period, SMR activity equal to or greater than 5 μV occurred in the training situation for 70% of the time. To determine what would be the effect of discontinuing veridical feedback, false feedback only was provided for a 7-week period, after which veridical feedback was reintroduced for a further period.[17] The introduction of a sham period of feedback produced a significant decrease in the percentage of SMR activity and a significant increase

---

[17]The introduction of a prolonged period of false feedback without the knowledge of either the patient or his parents is fully explained by Finley, and seems to have been ethically justified.

in the percentage of epileptiform discharge, but no change in the clinical rate of seizures. However, the seizures which did occur became more severe as evidenced by increased incontinence during a seizure. When true feedback was reintroduced there was a rapid return to the improved status achieved with SMR training, and the gains made were maintained during a 6-month follow-up period following final termination of treatment.

Seifert and Lubar (1975) studied six epileptics refractory to treatment and two normal controls, and Lubar and Bahler (1976) have provided additional information on these patients and subjects, together with data on two more epileptics. The patients (four males, four females) had had seizures for 4–18 years and training lasted for 6–8½ months with three 40-min training sessions each week during this period. Each session consisted of a 5-min baseline recorded without feedback from either the left or right rolandic cortical area, followed by a 15-min period with feedback from the site of the baseline recording and a subsequent 15-min period with feedback from the contralateral site, and ending with a 5-min baseline, no-feedback recording from the original site. Feedback for SMR activity meeting a specified criterion (six wave forms of 12- to 14-Hz activity within ½ sec) consisted of a progressively lit bank of lights (plus auditory feedback if the patient desired it); while the occurrence of 4- to 7-Hz activity produced a green light indicating the presence of epileptiform spike activity, slow waves, or movement, the SMR feedback not being available as long as the green light remained on. The results for the eight epileptic patients are presented in great detail by Lubar and Bahler (1976), who conclude that most of them demonstrated SMR acquisition and a corresponding reduction of clinical seizure rate during training. Spectral analysis also indicated that there was a tendency toward normalization of the EEG. However, the improvement claimed in respect of seizures is largely based on qualitative judgments rather than quantitative changes, and the evidence for increased SMR activity is somewhat tenuous.[18] One conclusion that was tentatively drawn was that SMR training might be most suitable for cases of psychomotor epilepsy. Lubar (1977) has extended his sample size to 12 patients treated for periods of up to 2½ years. He has concluded that all but one of the patients have shown moderate to marked degrees of improvement during training.

These studies are noteworthy for several features: the highly sophisticated instrumentation used, the relatively great length of the training, the simultaneous attempt to increase SMR activity and decrease epileptiform activity, and the attempt to relate changes in cortical activity to changes in clinical seizure rate and severity. They represent a degree of dedication and persistence rarely seen in studies of the voluntary control of the electrical activity of the brain. Nevertheless, even though the conclusions drawn are stated very cautiously and with

[18] See the detailed graphical results for seizure data (Figure 3) and SMR acquisition (Figure 4) in Lubar and Bahler (1976).

appropriate reservations relating to possible placebo effects and the failure to control adequately for possible confounding factors, both the methodology and the tentative conclusions drawn as to the benefits of SMR training for epilepsy have come under severe scrutiny and criticism. One of the main criticisms relates to the failure to demonstrate whether training to increase (or, presumably, decrease) other brain rhythms might not result in a decrease in epileptiform activity and seizure rate and severity. As we have seen, attempts were made to reduce 5- to 7-Hz activity while increasing 12- to 14-Hz activity, but these studies were confounded in that the attempts were made simultaneously. Kaplan (1975a) carried out two experiments with five patients aged 20–30 years. In the first experiment, two of the patients were presented with individually preferred feedback (tone, music, colored lights, television, tape-recorded or slide-projected material) and were told that the feedback would be available whenever appropriate EEG activity (12–14 Hz) was present. The electrodes were sited 1 cm posterior to C_4. Three sessions of training per week were given, consisting of 2 min of baseline recording with eyes closed, then open, followed by 30 min with feedback and baseline repeat. Power spectral analysis was used to evaluate general EEG changes. Training appears to have continued for 3–4 months, but no significant changes took place in 12- to 15-Hz activity nor in the clinical EEGs. One patient did show a reduction in seizure activity, but this was attributed to a change in medication. In the second experiment, feedback was provided for 6- to 12-Hz activity to determine whether increases in this activity would be accompanied by a reduction in seizure activity. One patient showed an improvement in seizure activity (following a change in medication), but this was not correlated with any change in 6- to 12-Hz activity. The second patient showed no changes in either clinical EEG or power spectra, but did show a reduction in seizure activity. The third patient did, however, show a reduction in seizures and an increase in 6- to 12-Hz activity. In none of these patients could any changes in 6- to 12-Hz activity be attributed to the feedback training. Kaplan (1975a) concluded that the earlier studies had not been carried out under sufficiently controlled conditions to attribute clinical improvement unequivocally to the results of the SMR training or the inhibition of 5- to 7-Hz activity. In a comment on Kaplan's equivocal findings, Gastaut (1975) took the opportunity both to renew his earlier attack on alpha training and to extend it to the SMR studies in relation to epilepsy, an area in which he is, of course, an expert. Kaplan (1975b), however, in a comment on Gastaut's comment, was cautiously optimistic (or pessimistic, perhaps) about the eventual outcome of SMR research.

It has been recognized by all workers in this area that extreme caution is indeed necessary in interpreting the results obtained,[19] and Kaplan's (1975a)

---

[19]See, for example, the sophisticated discussion of technical and methodological issues in Finley (1977), Kuhlman and Allison (1977), Lubar (1977), and Lubar and Shouse (1977).

point that it is possible that general training of electrical activity of the brain in the sense of reducing its overall level of activity is what is involved in SMR training is well taken. A rather similar interpretation has been put forward by Wyler (1977; Wyler, Lockard, Ward, & Finch, 1976). Indeed, Rouse *et al.* (1975), in a study already referred to, had reported being able to train a patient with grand mal epilepsy to entrain a bimodal pattern of EEG responding with peaks at 6.5 Hz and 13 Hz towards one centered around 10 Hz, recorded from site C_2. Johnson and Meyer (1974) utilized what they termed a phased biofeedback approach in treating an 18-year-old female with a 10-year history of grand mal seizures. Two weeks of general relaxation training was first given, followed by forearm and frontalis EMG relaxation training (the kind of feedback used was not stated). A total of 36 sessions of EEG feedback training was then given, starting with alpha and proceeding to "alpha–theta," and finally to theta alone. Prior to the commencement of training a total of 67 seizures had been experienced over 2 years (a rate of nearly 3 per month), whereas during the 12 months of training only 18 seizures occurred (a rate of 1½ per month). This improvement was maintained during a follow-up of unspecified length. The patient seemed to be able, following training, to abort a seizure during its prodromal phase, but was unable to suppress it once it was fully under way. However, the absence of a detailed specification of the procedures and results makes it impossible to evaluate this study properly. The importance of general relaxation training has also been highlighted in several recent studies. Cabral and Scott (1976) treated three young female epileptics with a long and severe history with a combination of biofeedback, relaxation, and systematic desensitization. Some improvement was reported in all three patients after 6 months of treatment and at a 15-month follow-up. Ince (1976) treated a 12-year-old male with petit and grand mal seizures by systematic desensitization, deep relaxation, and a cue word associated with the relaxation and to be used whenever an aura occurred. Both petit and grand mal seizures reduced gradually to zero by the end of treatment and were still completely absent at a 9-month follow-up. Wells, Turner, Bellack, and Hersen (1978) obtained similar results with a 22-year-old girl.

Somewhat ironically, this brings us to the final study to be considered in this chapter. The important study by Zlutnik, Mayville, and Moffat (1975) represents, in fact, a return to the procedures rather casually reported before the institution of SMR training, but placed now within an operant framework involving much more careful observation and control of the patients' behavior. They systematically utilized two intervention techniques with five epileptic patients experiencing seizures reliably at least once a day and with a firm diagnosis of epilepsy. The first technique involved the contingent interruption of preseizure behavior (e.g., headaches, tinnitus, polydipsia, and localized spasms). The contingent interruption consisted of the experimenter's shouting "No!" loudly and sharply, and grasping the patient by the shoulder with both hands and shaking him once vigorously whenever a prodromal behavior was produced. This

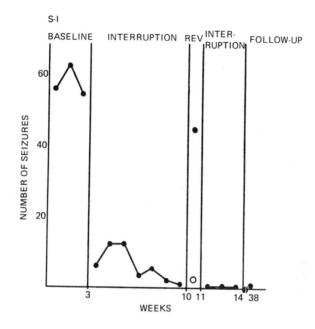

Figure 17. The number of minor motor seizures per week for Subject 1. The reversal is prorated for a 5 day week. During reversal, ● = A.M. and ○ = P.M. Follow-up data represent the absolute number of seizures for the next six months. (From Zlutnick, S., Mayville, W. J., & Moffat, S. Modification of seizure disorders: The interruption of behavioral chains. *Journal of Applied Behavior Analysis, 1975, 8,* 4, Figure 1. Reprinted by permission of the publisher. Copyright 1975 by the Society for the Experimental Analysis of Behavior, Inc.)

technique was applied to four of the five patients. The second technique was applied to the fifth patient and involved the reinforcement of incompatible behaviors. The preseizure behavior chosen was that of arm raising. Whenever this occurred, the experimenter placed the patient's hands down to her side (or on her lap if she was sitting) waiting for about 5 sec, and then providing a combination of primary and social reinforcement contingent on "arms down." Some degree of improvement was achieved in four of the five patients. The striking results obtained with one patient are shown in Figure 17. It will be seen that a baseline–intervention–reversal to baseline–interruption design was used. During the initial baseline period, seizure frequency was about 12 per day. The introduction of the interruption procedure led quickly to a drop in seizure frequency to about 1 or 2 per day and to zero by the 7th week of treatment. Withdrawal of the interruption procedure reinstated the baseline seizure pattern which dropped quickly to zero again when the interruption pattern was resumed. Only one seizure was reported to have occurred during a 6-month follow-up period.

It remains to be seen whether SMR training, training in the inhibition of epileptiform activity, training in the control of other forms of EEG activity, or other approaches such as general relaxation training or the operant control of preseizure activity will fulfill the possibilities suggested by the studies reviewed here. Perhaps the most encouraging aspect of all of this work lies in the reactivation of procedures which, if ultimately successful, will enable the treatment of at least some forms of epilepsy to be conducted within a framework which either does not require the use of drugs or at least enables the dependence on drugs to be significantly reduced.[20]

References

Adams, K. M. Behavioral treatment of reflex or sensory-evoked seizures. *Journal of Behavior Therapy and Experimental Psychiatry,* 1976, *7,* 123–127.

Albert, I. B., Simmons, J., & Walker, J. Massed and spaced practice in alpha enhancement. *Perceptual and Motor Skills,* 1974, *39,* 1039–1042.

Beatty, J. T. Effects of initial alpha wave abundance and operant training procedures on occipital alpha and beta activity. *Psychonomic Science,* 1971, *23,* 197–199. (1971:9)

Beatty, J. Similar effects of feedback signals and instructional information on EEG activity. *Physiology and Behavior,* 1972, *9,* 151–154. (1972:19)

Beatty, J., & Kornfeld, C. Relative independence of conditioned EEG changes from cardiac and respiratory activity. *Physiology and Behavior,* 1973, *9,* 733–736. (1973:15)

Beatty, J., Greenberg, A., Deibler, W. P., & O'Hanlon, J. F. Operant control of occipital theta rhythm affects performance in a radar monitoring task. *Science,* 1974, *183,* 871–873. (1974:33)

Bird, B. L., Newton, F. A., Sheer, D. E., & Ford, M. Biofeedback training of 40-Hz EEG in humans. *Biofeedback and Self-Regulation,* 1978, *3,* 1–11. (a)

Bird, B. L., Newton, F. A., Sheer, D. E., & Ford, M. Behavioral and electroencephalographic correlates of 40-Hz EEG biofeedback training in humans. *Biofeedback and Self-Regulation,* 1978, *3,* 13–28. (b)

Bridgwater, G., Sherry, C. J., & Marczynski, T. J. Alpha activity: The influence of unpatterned light input and auditory feedback. *Life Sciences,* 1975, *16,* 729–739. (1975/76:29)

Brolund, J. W., & Schallow, J. R. The effects of reward on occipital alpha facilitation by biofeedback. *Psychophysiology,* 1976, *13,* 236–241. (1976/77:32)

Brown, B. B. Recognition of aspects of consciousness through association with EEG alpha activity represented by a light signal. *Psychophysiology,* 1970, *6,* 442–452. (1970:15)

Brown, B. B. Awareness of EEG-subjective activity relationships detected within a closed feedback system. *Psychophysiology,* 1971, *7,* 451–464. (1971:8)

Bundzen, P. V. Autoregulation of functional state of the brain: An investigation using photostimulation with feedback. *Federation Proceedings Translation Supplement,* 1966, *25,* T551–T554.

Cabral, R. J., & Scott, D. F. Effects of two desensitization techniques, biofeedback and relaxation, on intractable epilepsy: Follow-up study. *Journal of Neurology, Neurosurgery and Psychiatry,* 1976, *39,* 504–507.

Chapman, R. M., Shelburne, S. A., & Bragdon, H. R. EEG alpha activity influenced by visual input and not by eye position. *EEG and Clinical Neurophysiology,* 1970, *28,* 183–189.

Cram, J. R., Kohlenberg, R. J., & Singer, M. Operant control of alpha EEG and the effects of illumination and eye closure. *Psychosomatic Medicine,* 1977, *39,* 11–18.

[20]Mostovsky and Balaschak (1977) have reviewed all aspects of the psychological control of epilepsy.

Davidson, R. J., Schwartz, G. E., Pugash, E., & Bromfield, E. Sex differences in patterns of EEG asymmetry. *Biological Psychology*, 1976, *4*, 119–138.

DeGood, D. E., Elkin, B., Lessin, S., & Valle, R. S. Expectancy influence on self-reported experience during alpha feedback training: Subject and situational factors. *Biofeedback and Self-Regulation*, 1977, *2*, 183–194.

Dewan, E. M. Occipital alpha rhythm, eye position, and lens accommodation. *Nature*, 1967, *214*, 975–977. (R:38)

de Weerdt, C. J., & van Rijn, A. J. Conditioning therapy in reading epilepsy. *EEG and Clinical Neurophysiology*, 1975, *39*, 417–420.

Eason, R. G., & Sadler, R. Relationship between voluntary control of alpha activity level through auditory feedback and degree of eye convergence. *Bulletin of the Psychonomic Society*, 1977, *9*, 21–24.

Eberlin, P., & Mulholland, T. Bilateral differences in parietal-occipital EEG induced by contingent visual feedback. *Psychophysiology*, 1976, *13*, 212–218. (1976/77:34)

Efron, R. The effect of olfactory stimuli in arresting uncinate fits. *Brain*, 1956, *79*, 267–281.

Efron, R. Conditioned inhibition of uncinate fits. *Brain*, 1957, *80*, 251–262.

Finley, W. W. Effects of sham feedback following successful SMR training in an epileptic: Follow-up study. *Biofeedback and Self-Regulation*, 1976, *1*, 227–235.

Finley, W. W. Operant conditioning of the EEG in two patients with epilepsy: Methodologic and clinical considerations. *Pavlovian Journal of Biological Science*, 1977, *12*, 93–111.

Finley, W. W., Smith, H. A., & Etherton, M. D. Reduction of seizures and normalization of the EEG in a severe epileptic following sensorimotor biofeedback training: Preliminary study. *Biological Psychology*, 1975, *2*, 189–203. (1975/76:48)

Forster, F. M., Paulsen, W. A., & Baughman, F. A. Clinical therapeutic conditioning in reading epilepsy. *Neurology*, 1969, *19*, 717–723.

Gastaut, H. Du rhythme de Berger au culte alpha et à la culture alpha. Revue E.E.G. *Neurophysiologie*, 1974, *4*, 5–20.

Gastaut, H. Comments on "Biofeedback in epileptics: Equivocal relationship of reinforced EEG frequency to seizure reduction" by Bonnie J. Kaplan, in *Epilepsia*, 1975. *16*, 477–485. *Epilepsia*, 1975, *16*, 487–488. (1975/76:50)

Goodman, D. ALFIE: Collection of EEG alpha under feedback control using time series analysis. *Psychophysiology*, 1973, *10*, 437–440.

Goodman, D. M. The effect of oculomotor activity on alpha-blocking in the absence of visual stimuli. *Psychophysiology*, 1976, *13*, 462–465.

Grossberg, J. M. Brain wave feedback experiments and the concept of mental mechanism. *Journal of Behavior Therapy and Experimental Psychiatry*, 1972, *3*, 245–251.

Grynol, E., & Jamieson, J. Alpha feedback and relaxation: A cautionary note. *Perceptual and Motor Skills*, 1975, *40*, 58. (1975/76:26)

Hardt, J. V., & Kamiya, J. Some comments on Plotkin's self-regulation of electro-encephalographic alpha. *Journal of Experimental Psychology: General*, 1976, *105*, 100–108. (a) (1976/77:29)

Hardt, J. V., & Kamiya, J. Conflicting results in EEG alpha feedback studies: Why amplitude integration should replace percent time. *Biofeedback and Self-Regulation*, 1976, *1*, 63–75. (b)

Hord, D., & Barber, J. Alpha control: Effectiveness of two kinds of feedback. *Psychonomic Science*, 1971, *25*, 151–154.

Ince, L. P. The use of relaxation training and a conditioned stimulus in the elimination of epileptic seizures in a child: A case study. *Journal of Behavior Therapy and Experimental Psychiatry*, 1976, *7*, 39–42.

Jasper, H. H. Report of the committee on methods of clinical examination in electroencephalography. *EEG and Clinical Neurophysiology*, 1958, *10*, 370–375.

Johnson, R. K., & Meyer, R. G. Phased biofeedback approach for epileptic seizure control. *Journal of Behavior Therapy and Experimental Psychiatry*, 1974, *5*, 185–187. (1974:27)

Kamiya, J. Conscious control of brain waves. *Psychology Today*, 1968, *1*, 57–60.

Kamiya, J. Operant control of the EEG alpha rhythm and some of its reported effects on consciousness. In C. Tart (Ed.), *Altered states of consciousness*. New York: Wiley, 1969, pp. 507–517. (R:36)

Kamiya, J. Autoregulation of the EEG alpha rhythm: A program for the study of consciousness. In M. H. Chase (Ed.), *Operant control of brain activity* (Perspectives in the Brain Sciences, Vol. 2). Los Angeles: Brain Information Service/Brain Research Institute, UCLA, 1974. (1975/76:22)

Kaplan, B. J. Biofeedback in epileptics: Equivocal relationship of reinforced EEG frequency to seizure reduction. *Epilepsia*, 1975, *16*, 477–485. (a) (1975/76:49)

Kaplan, B. J. Reply to Professor Gastaut's comments on "Biofeedback in epileptics." *Epilepsia*, 1975, *16*, 488–489. (b) (1975/76:51)

Kondo, C. Y., Travis, T. A., & Knott, J. R. The effect of changes in motivation on alpha enhancement. *Psychophysiology*, 1975, *12*, 388–389.

Kuhlman, W. N., & Allison, T. EEG feedback training in the treatment of epilepsy: Some questions and some answers. *Pavlovian Journal of Biological Science*, 1977, *12*, 112–122.

Kuhlman, W. N., & Klieger, D. M. Alpha enhancement: Effectiveness of two feedback contingencies relative to a resting baseline. *Psychophysiology*, 1975, *12*, 456–460.

Leib, W., Tryon, W. W., & Stroebel, C. S. Alpha biofeedback: Fact or artifact? *Psychophysiology*, 1976, *13*, 541–545.

Lubar, J. F. Electroencephalographic biofeedback methodology and the management of epilepsy. *Pavlovian Journal of Biological Science*, 1977, *12*, 147–185.

Lubar, J. F., & Bahler, W. W. Behavioral management of epileptic seizures following EEG biofeedback training of the sensorimotor rhythm. *Biofeedback and Self-Regulation*, 1976, *1*, 77–104. (1976/77:32)

Lubar, J. F., & Shouse, M. N. Use of biofeedback in treatment of seizure disorders and hyperactivity. In B. B. Lahey & A. E. Kazdin (Eds.), *Advances in clinical child psychology* (Vol. 1). New York: Plenum, 1977, pp. 203–266.

Lutzenberger, W., Birbaumer, N., & Wildgruber, C. An experiment on the feedback of the theta activity of the human EEG. *European Journal of Behavioral Analysis and Modification*, 1975, *2*, 119–126.

Lutzenberger, W., Birbaumer, N., & Steinmetz, P. Simultaneous biofeedback of heart rate and frontal EMG as a pretraining for the control of theta activity. *Biofeedback and Self-Regulation*, 1976, *1*, 395–410.

Lynch, J. J., & Paskewitz, D. A. On the mechanisms of the feedback control of human brain wave activity. *Journal of Nervous and Mental Disease*, 1971, *153*, 205–217. (1971:12)

Lynch, J. J., Paskewitz, D. A., & Orne, M. T. Some factors in the feedback control of human alpha rhythm. *Psychosomatic Medicine*, 1974, *36*, 399–410. (1974:29)

Mostovsky, D. I., & Balaschak, B. A. Psychobiological control of seizures. *Psychological Bulletin*, 1977, *84*, 723–750.

Mulholland, T. The electro-encephalogram as an experimental tool in the study of internal attention gradients. *Transactions of the New York Academy of Sciences*, 1962, *24*, 664–669.

Mulholland, T. Feedback electroencephalography. *Activitas Nervosa Superior* (Prague), 1968, *10*, 410–438. (R:39)

Mulholland, T., & Benson, F. Detection of EEG abnormalities with feedback stimulation. *Biofeedback and Self-Regulation*, 1976, *1*, 47–61.

Mulholland, T., & Evans, C. R. Oculomotor function and the alpha activation cycle. *Nature*, 1966, *211*, 1278–1279.

Mulholland, T. B., & Peper, E. Occipital alpha and accommodative vergence, pursuit tracking, and fast eye movements. *Psychophysiology*, 1971, *8*, 556–575. (1971:10)

Mulholland, T., & Runnals, S. Evaluation of attention and alertness with a stimulus–brain feedback loop. *EEG and Clinical Neurophysiology*, 1962, *14*, 847–852.

Mulholland, T., & Runnals, S. The effect of voluntarily directed attention on successive cortical activation responses. *Journal of Psychology*, 1963, *55*, 427–436.

Mulholland, T., McLaughlin, T., & Benson, F. Feedback control and quantification of the response of EEG alpha to visual stimulation. *Biofeedback and Self-Control*, 1976, *1*, 411–422.

Nowlis, D. P., & Kamiya, J. The control of electroencephalographic alpha rhythms through auditory feedback and the associated mental activity. *Psychophysiology*, 1970, *6*, 476–484. (1970:14)

Nowlis, D. P., & Wortz, E. C. Control of the ratio of midline parietal to midline frontal EEG alpha rhythms through auditory feedback. *Perceptual and Motor Skills*, 1973, *37*, 815–824.

O'Malley, J. E., & Conners, C. K. The effect of unilateral alpha training on visual evoked response in a dyslexic adolescent. *Psychophysiology*, 1972, *9*, 467–470.

Orenstein, H. B., & McWilliams, B. Variations in electroencephalographic alpha activity under conditions of differential lighting and auditory feedback. *Biofeedback and Self-Regulation*, 1976, *1*, 423–432.

Orne, M. T., & Paskewitz, D. A. Aversive situational effects on alpha feedback training. *Science*, 1974, *186*, 458–460. (1974:28)

Paskewitz, D. A., & Orne, M. T. Visual effects on alpha feedback training. *Science*, 1973, *181*, 360–363. (1973:13)

Peper, E. Feedback regulation of the alpha electroencephalogram activity through control of internal and external parameters. *Kybernetik*, 1970, *7*, 107–112. (1970:17)

Peper E. Comment on feedback training of parietal-occipital alpha asymmetry in normal human subjects. *Kybernetik*, 1971, *9*, 156–158. (a) (1971:11)

Peper, E. Reduction of efferent motor commands during alpha feedback as a facilitator of EEG alpha and a precondition for changes in consciousness. *Kybernetik*, 1971, *9*, 226–231. (b)

Peper, E. Localized EEG alpha feedback training: A possible technique for mapping subjective, conscious, and behavioral experiences. *Kybernetik*, 1972, *11*, 166–169. (1972:20)

Peper, E. Problems in heart rate and alpha electroencephalographic feedback—is the control over the feedback stimulus meaningful? *Kybernetik*, 1974, *14*, 217–221. (1974:32)

Peper, E. Problems in biofeedback training: An experiential analogy—urination. *Perspectives in Biology and Medicine*, 1976, *1*, 404–412.

Peper, E., & Mulholland, T. Methodological and theoretical problems in the voluntary control of electroencephalographic occipital alpha by the subject. *Kybernetik*, 1970, *7*, 10–13. (1970:16)

Plotkin, W. B. On the self-regulation of the occipital alpha rhythm, control strategies, states of consciousness, and the role of physiological feedback. *Journal of Experimental Psychology: General*, 1976, *105*, 66–99. (a)

Plotkin, W. B. Appraising the ephemeral "alpha phenomenon": A reply to Hardt and Kamiya. *Journal of Experimental Psychology: General*, 1976, *105*, 109–121. (b) (1976/77:30)

Plotkin, W. B. Long-term eyes-closed alpha-enhancement training: Effects on alpha amplitudes and on experiential state. *Psychophysiology*, 1978, *15*, 40–52.

Pressner, J. A., & Savitsky, J. C. Effect of contingent and noncontingent feedback and subject expectancies on electroencephalogram biofeedback training. *Journal of Consulting and Clinical Psychology*, 1977, *45*, 713–714.

Prewett, M. J., & Adams, H. E. Alpha activity suppression and enhancement as a function of feedback and instructions. *Psychophysiology*, 1976, *13*, 307–310.

Ray, W. J., Frediani, A. W., & Harman, D. Self-regulation of hemispheric asymmetry. *Biofeedback and Self-Regulation*, 1977, *2*, 195–199.

Regestein, Q. R., Pegram, G. V., Cook, B., & Bradley, D. Alpha rhythm percentage maintained during 4- and 12-hour feedback periods. *Psychosomatic Medicine*, 1973, *35*, 215–222. (1973:14)

Robertson, E. G., Photogenic epilepsy: Self-precipitated attacks. *Brain*, 1954, *77*, 232–251.

Rouse, L., Peterson, J., & Shapiro, G. EEG alpha entrainment reaction within the biofeedback setting and some possible effects on epilepsy. *Physiological Psychology*, 1975, *3*, 113–122.

Schacter, D. L. EEG theta waves and psychological phenomena: A review and analysis. *Biological Psychology*, 1977, *5*, 47–82.

Schwartz, G. E., Davidson, R. J.. & Pugash, E. Voluntary control of patterns of EEG parietal asymmetry: Cognitive concomitants. *Psychophysiology*, 1976, *13*, 498–504. (1976/77:33)

Seifert, A. R., & Lubar, J. F. Reduction of epileptic seizures through EEG biofeedback training. *Biological Psychology*, 1975, *3*, 157–184.

Sheer, D. E. Biofeedback training of 40-Hz EEG and behavior. In N. Burch & H. L. Altschuler (Eds.), *Behavior and brain electrical activity*. New York: Plenum, 1975, pp. 325–362. (1976/77:37)

Sittenfeld, P., Budzynski, T., & Stoyva, J. Differential shaping of EEG theta rhythms. *Biofeedback and Self-Regulation*, 1976, *1*, 31–46. (1976/77:35)

Sterman, M. B. Neurophysiologic and clinical studies of sensorimotor EEG biofeedback training: Some effects on epilepsy. *Seminars in Psychiatry*, 1973, *5*, 507–525. (1973:32)

Sterman, M. B. Sensorimotor EEG operant conditioning: Experimental and clinical effects. *Pavlovian Journal of Biological Science*, 1977, *12*, 63–92.

Sterman, M. B., & Friar, L. Suppression of seizures in an epileptic following sensorimotor EEG feedback training. *EEG and Clinical Neurophysiology*, 1972, *33*, 89–95.

Sterman, M. B., MacDonald, L. R., & Stone, R. K. Biofeedback training of the sensorimotor EEG rhythm in man: Effects on epilepsy. *Epilepsia*, 1974, *15*, 395–416. (1974:26)

Tassinari, C. A. Suppression of focal spikes by somato-sensory stimuli. *EEG and Clinical Neurophysiology*, 1968, *25*, 574–578.

Travis, T. A., Kondo, C. Y., & Knott, J. R. Alpha conditioning: A controlled study. *Journal of Nervous and Mental Disease*, 1974, *158*, 163–173. (a) (1974:31)

Travis, T. A., Kondo, C. Y., & Knott, J. R. Parameters of eyes-closed alpha enhancement. *Psychophysiology*, 1974, *11*, 674–681. (b)

Valle, R. S., & Levine, J. M. Expectation effects in alpha wave control. *Psychophysiology*, 1975, *12*, 306–309. (1975/76:24)

Wells, K. C., Turner, S. M., Bellack, A. S., & Hersen, M. Effects of cue-controlled relaxation on psychomotor seizures: An experimental analysis. *Behavior Research and Therapy*, 1978, *16*, 51–53.

Williams, P. EEG alpha feedback—a comparison of two control groups. *Psychosomatic Medicine*, 1977, *39*, 44–47.

Wyler, A. R. Operant conditioning of epileptic neurons in monkeys and its theoretical application to EEG operant conditioning in humans. *Pavlovian Journal of Biological Science*, 1977, *12*, 130–146.

Wyler, A. R., Lockard, J. S., Ward, A. A., & Finch, C. A. Conditioned EEG desynchronization and seizure occurrence in patients. *EEG and Clinical Neurophysiology*, 1976, *41*, 501–512. (1976/77:39)

Zlutnick, S., Mayville, W. J., & Moffat, S. Modification of seizure disorders: The interruption of behavioral chains. *Journal of Applied Behavior Analysis*, 1975, *8*, 1–12.

CHAPTER 6

Other Applications of Biofeedback

Introduction

In the three previous chapters, it has been tacitly accepted that it is legitimate to assume that some behaviors are related to the operation of the central nervous system, others to the operation of the autonomic nervous system, and yet others to specific electrical patterns of activity in the brain. This assumption is quite certainly incorrect (as will be seen in the next chapter), but it is not an unreasonable working assumption for the purpose of developing biofeedback training techniques in relation to some of the disabilities which have been considered. There are, however, a fairly large number of disorders to which biofeedback training has been applied which quite clearly cannot be subsumed at present, even on a pragmatic basis, under any of these three categories. In this chapter, the work done so far in relation to these disorders or problem behaviors will be considered. Since no adequate framework within which to place these disorders is currently available, they will be dealt with in alphabetical order. Many of the disorders to be dealt with are in fact of extreme complexity. However, no attempt will be made to provide a complete overview of the etiology and treatment of these disorders. Instead, each will be placed, as far as possible, within a framework which shows why biofeedback training is relevant to the particular disorder. It should be understood, of course, that it is not being suggested that biofeedback training is the only, or even the most relevant, approach to treatment of the particular disorder. In many instances, it will be clear that biofeedback may have only an ancillary or minor role to play in treatment. Nevertheless, that role may be an important one, both in practical terms and, in some cases, in suggesting new approaches to treatment.

Applications

Alcoholism

The relevance of biofeedback training to alcoholism derives from the refutation in recent years of one of the cornerstones of the treatment approach to alcoholism in modern times, namely, the loss-of-control or one-drink hypothesis. This hypothesis asserts that the alcoholic is unable to resist drinking in the presence of others who are drinking, that the alcoholic will always drink if alcohol is available, and most important, that if the alcoholic takes one drink he will be unable to control his subsequent behavior—that is, he will then take a second drink, followed by a third drink, and so on as long as alcohol is available. The interpretation of this alleged inability of the alcoholic to control his drinking behavior once he has taken one drink has varied, but the most commonly accepted view is that the ingestion of one drink produces physiological changes which create the need to ingest more alcohol (either to maintain the physiological state induced by the first drink, or to change that physiological state further). Whatever the explanation of the alleged fatal effects of indulging in just one drink following a period of abstinence from alcohol, two clear-cut conclusions follow if the loss-of-control hypothesis is true: first, that the aim of treatment must be total abstinence, and second, that it is impossible to train alcoholics to be social drinkers, that is, to drink in moderation without losing control. The great strength of the belief in the one-drink hypothesis is attested by the extraordinary reaction produced by the observation of Davies (1962) that some alcoholics do, in fact, become social drinkers without any treatment (or perhaps in spite of treatment) and do not as a consequence relapse into alcoholism. The reaction was immediate, indignant, and intense. It was denied that Davies's patients could have been "true" alcoholics since, if they were, they must inevitably have relapsed; and this position was maintained even when Davies (1963) subsequently showed that the patients met all of the criteria which were regarded as defining a true alcoholic.

Subsequent research has, however, strongly supported Davies's view that the one-drink hypothesis is not universally true in respect of alcoholics. Thus, Bailey and Stewart (1967) studied 13 patients (out of a group of 91 problem drinkers) who appeared to have changed to a normal drinking pattern. Of these, 6 were judged to be alcoholics who were currently able to drink within normal limits without having received psychotherapy. Cutter, Schwaab, and Nathan (1970) could find no evidence that alcoholics themselves fear an initial drink because they will then lose control and experience an irresistible craving for a second drink. The most direct evidence on this matter comes from a recent study by Orford, Oppenheimer, and Edwards (1976). They treated 65 couples (in all cases, the husband was the alcoholic) in a program aimed at total abstinence and followed up the patients over a 2-year period from commencement of treatment. A high relapse rate was found so that a satisfactory outcome was evident for only 26 of the patients. Of these patients 11 were abstinent, but 10 were drinking in a controlled manner, and it was evident that "when individualised data are examined, it emerges that a number of individual men are drinking in a virtually 'totally controlled' fashion in the second year" (Orford *et al.*, 1976, p. 415). These authors considered that their results "fairly unequivocally" ran contrary to the view that controlled drinking is a rare phenomenon and of no practical clinical significance.

There is also now a considerable amount of evidence from experimental studies of the behavior of alcoholics in simulated barroom situations which casts serious doubt on the one-drink hypothesis. This evidence need not be reviewed in detail here[1] but a brief summary may be helpful. It has been shown that alcoholics given unlimited access to alcohol will not necessarily drink at all; and that if they do drink, they may stop after a while even though alcohol is still freely available and their fellow alcoholics are continuing to drink (Gottheil, Alterman, Skoloda, & Murphy, 1973); that alcoholics will drink more if they believe a drink contains alcohol even though the drink may be nonalcoholic, demonstrating the importance of expectancy factors in the drinking behavior of alcoholics (Marlatt, Demming, & Reed, 1973); and that the behavior of alcoholics in respect of drinking patterns in a simulated barroom situation may not at all correspond to the stereotypes of how alcoholics behave in such situations (Schaeffer, Sobell, & Mills, 1971; Sobell, Schaeffer, & Mills, 1972). The reason this experimental evidence contradicts many of the accepted beliefs of experts in the field (that is, those who treat alcoholics in a clinical situation) is quite simple: most of the evidence on which these beliefs are based derives from contaminated sources—the alcoholic himself (who is usually seen first in an intoxicated state), his parents and friends, or the police. Only recently has the behavior of the alcoholic in the real-life situation begun to be investigated, rather than placing reliance on reports from biased witnesses. The development in recent years of careful behavior-analytic techniques has (or should have) resulted in a complete reappraisal of the behavior patterns of alcoholics in situations in which alcohol is readily available.[2]

While all of this evidence has had little impact on the traditional treatment settings to which alcoholics are usually referred, the conclusion has been drawn elsewhere that it might be possible to train at least a proportion of alcoholics to become controlled or social drinkers as an alternative to the total abstinence aim of most alcohol treatment programs. Comprehensive treatment programs aimed

[1]See Yates (1975, pp. 47–57) for a review of this evidence; Miller and Caddy (1977) have critically evaluated the use of abstinence as a sole criterion for treatment success or failure.
[2]Lloyd and Salzberg (1975) have provided a comprehensive review of all aspects of training in controlled social drinking.

at training alcoholics in controlled drinking are now being reported as having considerable success (e.g., Sobell & Sobell, 1973a,b). Within this new approach to treatment, the possible role that biofeedback training might play needs to be considered.

Most of the biofeedback research with alcoholics has been concerned with determining whether they are able to discriminate their own blood alcohol levels (BAL), or if they cannot do so initially, whether they can be trained to make such discriminations. Once discrimination has been achieved successfully, other training techniques may then be instituted in the hope that eventually the alcoholic will come to control his own drinking behavior so that, using his new discriminative ability, he will stop drinking at a point prior to intoxication and hence become a controlled or social drinker.

Until recently, little evidence was available in relation to the question of whether nonalcoholic social drinkers could discriminate their blood alcohol levels, particularly in the absence of obvious external cues as to how much alcohol they had consumed. Three recent studies have thrown considerable light on this matter. Bois and Vogel-Sprott (1974) provided nine nonalcoholic males with six training sessions in BAL discrimination. In the first three sessions both internal and external cues to BAL were available. They received a cocktail containing 0.9 ml of an alcohol solution (40% alcohol by volume) per pound of body weight (equivalent to 0.36 ml of absolute alcohol per pound). The alcohol was mixed with an equal volume of a carbonated beverage and a drop of peppermint oil, making it difficult to detect the presence of alcohol in the drink. In the first 10 min of a session the subject consumed one-quarter of the drink, and 10 min later reported his symptoms, estimated his BAL, and provided a breath sample for objective determination of his BAL. This procedure was repeated at 20-min intervals until the entire drink had been consumed, except that the fifth reading was taken 10 min after the fourth while the BAL level was still at its peak. A final five readings were then taken in a similar manner while the BAL was falling. Thus, errors in subjective estimates of BAL were assessed while BAL was rising, while it was at a peak, and while it was falling. In the first and third sessions, no feedback was given except after the fifth reading to provide a reference point for the subsequent fall in BAL, whereas during the second (training) session, feedback in the form of a breathalyzer readout was provided after each estimate. In the last three sessions, an attempt was made to eliminate external cues such as size of drink, its particular taste, the type of alcohol, and the rate of intake. The subject was required to nominate one particular low BAL in the range of 0.04–0.06% and to decide when, based on his own internal sensations, he had reached that point. Drinking was terminated at this point and the procedures used in the earlier sessions were instituted to determine whether the subject could learn to discriminate the subsequent rise, peaking, and fall in BAL within this much narrower range of BALs. The results of the experiment are shown in Figure 1. During the first three sessions the subjects learned to estimate

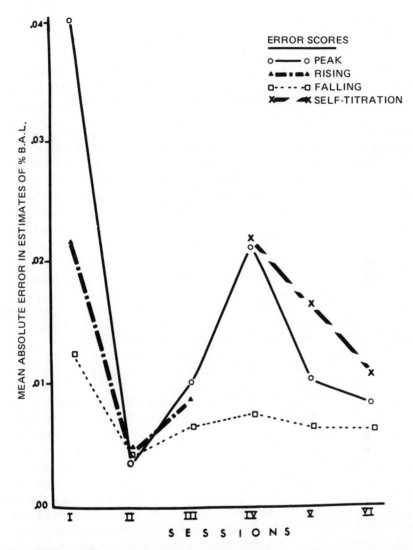

Figure 1. Group mean absolute error in blood alcohol level estimates over drinking sessions. (From Bois, C., Vogel-Sprott, M. Discrimination of low blood alcohol levels and self-titration skills in social drinkers. *Quarterly Journal of Studies on Alcohol*, 1974, *35*, 91, Figure 2. Reprinted by permission of the author and the publisher.)

rising and peak BALs when provided with feedback, as indicated by the smaller absolute error in session II as compared with session I, and retained this learned discrimination to a significant degree when feedback was withdrawn in session III. During the last three sessions, the subjects successfully learned to use internal cues only to estimate rising and peak BAL accurately. Much less success was achieved in estimating falling BALs, however, but the authors considered that this finding might have been a result of the methodology they used rather than the result of a genuine inability to learn to discriminate falling BALs. Ogurzsoff and Vogel-Sprott (1976) extended these results to show that subjects trained in BAL discrimination with feedback could successfully select a target BAL and self-titrate a drink so that the target BAL was closely approximated. They additionally demonstrated that the skill was equally well acquired by heavy and light, frequent and infrequent drinkers. However, Maisto and Adesso (1977), using an approach similar to that employed by Marlatt *et al.* (1973), concluded that their normal subjects did not learn to discriminate their BALs on the basis of internal cues because subjects consuming a nonalcoholic beverage (believing it to be alcoholic) showed BAL estimates which were similar to those made by subjects who were consuming alcohol.

The first study which suggested that BAL discrimination training might be an important adjunct in the treatment of alcoholism was that by Lovibond and Caddy (1971). They allocated 44 alcoholics (35 of whom were males), aged between 22 and 56 years who had been alcoholics on average for 10 years, to either a treatment or a control group. Actually, the BAL discrimination training formed a relatively small part of their treatment program, occupying only one training session lasting 1½–2 h. During this session, they were required to consume alcohol with subjective estimates of BAL being made every 15–20 min, with a visual meter then indicating the correct BAL. Sufficient alcohol was consumed to raise the BAL to 0.08%, after which it was allowed to return to normal, with subjective estimates continuing to be made. It was found that the alcoholics could estimate their BAL, given feedback training, very accurately to within ±0.01%. Following the BAL training, Lovibond and Caddy attempted to incorporate the new skill into an aversive training program involving quite a severe electric shock to the chin in an unpredictable manner. The subject was required to consume alcohol while continuing to estimate his BAL and being given feedback. He was allowed to drink with impunity as long as the BAL was less than 0.065%. Beyond this point, however (and the subject was required to continue drinking), intermittent intense to very intense shocks to the chin occurred on 80% of drinking occasions with shock duration varying from 1 sec to 6 sec and intensity from 4 mA to 7 mA. The point in the drinking sequence at which the shock occurred was also varied to induce maximum uncertainty. Sometimes the shock occurred when the subject picked up the glass, at other times when he was swallowing the drink, or at any point in between. The first three training sessions lasted 1½–2 h, were spaced 5–7 days apart, and involved a total of 8–10 shocks. Later sessions were spaced further apart and involved fewer shocks. Altogether, each subject underwent between 6 and 12 training sessions involving 30–70 shocks in all. An attempt was made to involve the family of the aloholic by having a family member attend the training sessions, if possible. The control subjects were treated similarly, except that the shocks were noncontingent with respect to alcohol consumption. The subjects were followed up for periods varying between 16 and 60 weeks. Of the 31 subjects allocated to the experimental group, 28 completed the full course of treatment. Of these, 21 were classified as "complete successes" (that is, were drinking moderately), three were rated as "considerably improved" (exceeding 0.07% once or twice a week), and four were regarded as only "slightly improved" (drinking only slightly less than before treatment). The control alcoholics showed an initial drop in alcohol consumption but relapsed almost immediately. The experimental subjects also showed a greater general improvement in adjustment as compared with the controls. Conditioned aversion to alcohol was, however, produced in only 20% of the experimental subjects. More commonly, these subjects reported a loss of the desire to continue drinking after three or four glasses of alcohol had been consumed; that is, a loss of motivation to consume alcohol rather than a conditioned fear of alcohol was the outcome of the treatment.

Caddy and Lovibond (1976) followed up this pioneering study with a more comprehensive one. A total of 60 alcoholics (49 of whom were males), aged between 21 and 69 years of age, were allocated to three treatment groups. The first group received aversion, BAL discrimination, and self-regulation training; the second group, BAL discrimination and self-regulation; and the third group, BAL discrimination and aversion training. In the self-regulation training:

> the patient was encouraged to see himself as a person with a behavioral disorder rather than a disease over which he could exert no control. From the beginning he was confronted with evidence of the nature of his drinking and its consequences, and encouraged to have a family member or other confederate monitor the behavior. The whole program was designed to convey that the patient can learn to exert decisive self-control. Any attempt by the patient to deny his ultimate responsibility or his ability to learn to control his drinking behavior was vigorously rejected and strongly criticized. (Caddy & Lovibond, 1976, p. 224)

All of the patients were also provided with general educational material concerning the effects of alcohol and general support. A total of 20 h of training was given. Two indices of drinking behavior were used: the total weekly consumption of alcohol, and the number of times each week the BAL exceeded 0.07%. The results indicated that 65% of the patients given aversion, self-regulation, and BAL discrimination training could be classified as "completely successful" at the end of treatment compared with 45% of the patients given self-regulation and BAL discrimination training, and only 20% of the patients given aversion and BAL discrimination training but not self-regulation training. At a 12-month follow-up, these percentages had dropped to 38, 29, and 10, respectively. Thus, the combination of aversion and self-regulation training was more successful than the other combinations, both at the end of treatment and at a 12-month follow-up. No evidence of conditioned aversion was obtained. However, the role played by BAL discrimination training remained unclear since all three groups were given this training, and it is not certain whether the combination of aversion and self-regulation training would have been as successful had BAL discrimination training not been included.

With one exception, subsequent work has tended to confirm the usefulness of BAL discrimination training as an adjunct to the treatment of alcoholism. Silverstein, Nathan, and Taylor (1974) carried out a complex series of procedures with four male chronic alcoholics involving BAL discrimination training. In the first phase (estimation training) a target was set to achieve 75% of all BAL estimates falling within 20 mg per 100 ml of the true BAL. Drinking was programmed to cause BAL to rise slowly to 150 mg per 100 ml on the first day, remain at that level overnight, and then fall to zero on the following day. Baseline levels of subjective accuracy were first assessed with no feedback or reinforcement provided. Then the subjects were alerted to the emotional and physical correlates of BALs while true BAL was provided as feedback and verbal reinforcement given for success. The BAL feedback was then given on a 50% random schedule, and finally a new form of reinforcement was added (points convertible to money or alcohol). Baseline trials were then reintroduced. The

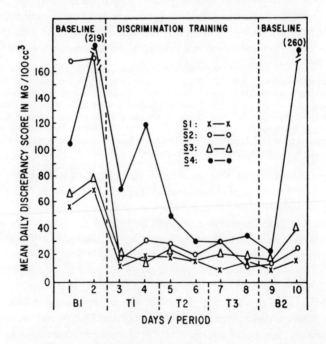

Figure 2. Accuracy of BAL estimation during phase I discrimination training. (From Silverstein, S.J., Nathan, P.E., Taylor, H.A. Blood alcohol level estimation and controlled drinking by chronic alcoholics. *Behavior Therapy,* 1974, *5,* 8, Figure 1. Reprinted by permission of the author and the publisher.)

results for this phase of training are shown in Figure 2. Without feedback, BAL estimation was inaccurate, the average discrepancy being 112 mg/100 cc. However, the introduction of feedback and verbal reinforcement led to an improvement in three of the patients, the discrepancy falling to 14 mg/100 cc. No further improvement occurred when the second form of reinforcement was introduced, and three of the patients maintained their newly acquired skill when feedback and reinforcement were withdrawn. The second phase of the experiment (control training) adopted as target the maintenance of BAL at 80 mg/100 cc. In an initial baseline period (BC1) the patients drank for 6 h to attain the target BAL and were then required to maintain this level for a further 10 h. During this period no feedback was available, and drinks were given on request unless an upper limit of 150 mg/100 ml was achieved. This baseline period lasted for 3 days and was succeeded by a 2-day reinforcement sampling (RS) period in which each patient experienced all of the contingencies associated with two routines: "drink call," in which the patient was required to pay a fine for a drink just consumed if his BAL then proved to be higher than the target level; and "BAL check," where no drink had been dispensed but the patient proved to be either above or below the target BAL level when checked. Feedback was provided during the RS period after each check. In the next segment of the control phase, three behavioral control procedures were instituted (C1, C2, C3): the responsibility for control was placed entirely on the patient, the range of positively reinforced BAL estimates was narrowed, and both feedback and reinforcement were gradually faded out. Two further segments followed: BC2, which was identical with BC1, and a period during which the patient was asked to maintain himself at an individually chosen level (G). The results for the three patients who completed this phase are shown in Figure 3. The control over BAL levels which had been achieved in phase 1 was lost during the initial baseline period of the control training but was subsequently reinstated during the C1–C3 segments, only to deteriorate again during BC2 and G. Two of the three patients were then followed up by mail for 40 days and reinterviewed after 80 days, while information on the third was obtained more indirectly. Some evidence of a modification of drinking behaviors was obtained in respect of each of the patients.

The remaining studies may be dealt with more briefly. Strickler, Bigelow, Lawrence, and Liebson (1976) combined positive reinforcement (rather than aversive) training with BAL discrimination training in a simulated barroom setting with three chronic alcoholics who were required to enter into a contractual arrangement involving a monetary deposit. The 7-week training program involved a 2-h group meeting twice weekly, during which abstinence was required for the first 2 weeks while information was given and relaxation training instituted. Then supervised drinking practice was given for 2 weeks, followed by BAL discrimination training for 2 weeks. Finally, a prolonged party was given at which alcohol was freely available. The patients all learned BAL discrimination successfully, and at a 6-month follow-up two of the patients were engaging in

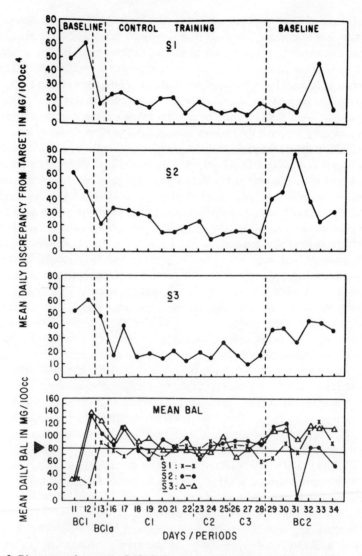

Figure 3. Discrepancy from target BAL during control training. (From Silverstein, S.J., Nathan, P.E., & Taylor, H.A. Blood alcohol level estimation and controlled drinking by chronic alcoholics. *Behavior Therapy,* 1974, *5*, 11, Figure 3. Reprinted by permission of the author and the publisher.)

stable forms of drinking within reasonable limits while the third remained highly variable.

The technique used by Lovibond and Caddy (1971) involved not only BAL training and punishment (shock) for drinking beyond a specified BAL level, but also avoidance training since shock could be avoided if the BAL level remained below the criterion level specified. A modification of this approach was used by

De Ricco and Garlington (1977), whose patients could avoid shock by sipping their drinks, ordering mixed rather than straight drinks, and showing a longer drink latency. Striking reductions in alcohol intake were shown by eight outpatient alcoholics who undertook this treatment and the results were maintained at an 18-month follow-up, although only one patient became and remained abstinent.

Paredes, Jones, and Gregory (1977) have reported the results of an interesting detailed study of a single alcoholic in relation to his ability to estimate his BAL under various conditions. The patient was first required to consume sufficient alcohol estimated to achieve a peak BAL of 0.06% while subjective estimates of level and feedback were made. An actual level of 0.095% was, however, reached and the subjective estimates were inaccurate. The dose was then increased to produce a level of 0.16% with feedback being given. Under these conditions, the patient's accuracy improved considerably and was maintained during the succeeding 6 h as BAL declined. On subsequent occasions, various procedures were tried involving subjective estimates of BAL in rising and falling conditions of actual BAL, and a considerable degree of success was obtained. A typical result at an advanced stage of training is shown in Figure 4. In this session, the patient was able to drink to achieve a BAL of 0.05%, maintain this level for 1 h,

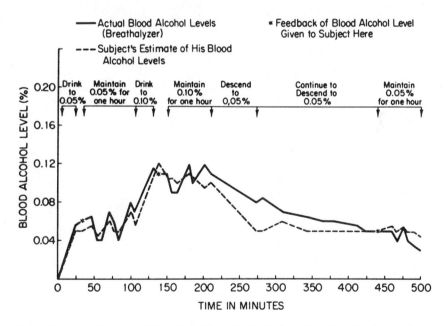

Figure 4. Actual and estimated blood alcohol levels for the ninth session. (From Paredes, A., Jones, B.M., & Gregory, D. Blood alcohol discrimination training with alcoholics. In F.A. Seixas (Ed.), *Currents in alcoholism,* Vol. 2. New York: Grune & Stratton, 1977, p. 137, Figure 2b. Reprinted by permission of the author and the publisher.)

increase his BAL to 0.10% and maintain this level for 1 h, with satisfactory accuracy. As found in other studies, he then had some difficulty in estimating falling BALs, but once 0.05% had been reached he could maintain that level successfully.

There have been several comparative studies of various therapeutic approaches which have involved BAL training. Vogler, Compton, and Weissbach (1975) compared the effectiveness of two package deals in the treatment of carefully selected groups of alcoholics. Although it is impossible to separate out the relative contribution of the BAL training given to one of the groups (but not the other), Vogler et al. (1975) concluded that this training was one of the most important components determining the success of treatment. Miller (1978) randomly assigned 29 self-referred and 17 court-referred alcoholics to one of three treatment conditions: aversive counterconditioning (involving shock for picking up a drink), behavioral self-control training (involving discussion of the antecedents of drinking and strategies for coping with drinking), and a controlled drinking composite treatment (involving BAL training, discriminated aversive counterconditioning, and self-control drinking). It was found that all three approaches were equally successful, both at the end of training and at a 1-year follow-up. Indeed, other work by Miller (1977) suggests that a self-help manual used alone or in a group setting with minimal therapist help may be as effective as the more expensive, unpleasant, and time-consuming effort involved in BAL and discriminated aversive counterconditioning.

Only one report has so far thrown doubt on the usefulness of BAL discrimination training as an adjunct to treatment. Ewing and Rouse (1976) applied Lovibond's discriminated aversive training procedures to 35 alcoholics and followed them up for 27–55 months beyond the time of completion of treatment. A very high dropout rate was found, only 14 patients attending at least six sessions of treatment (but many of these came from 12 to 24 times). Treatment sessions were held weekly and lasted at least 4 h. The patients who persisted did learn to discriminate BALs successfully and were able to control their drinking behavior as long as they were in treatment. But this control was not maintained after treatment ended and those patients who were "successes" at follow-up were completely abstinent rather than drinking in a controlled fashion. This was in spite of the fact that these patients were convinced at the end of treatment that they had reestablished control over their drinking (and had indeed apparently established control at that time). These expectations were not, however, fulfilled.

There seems no doubt, therefore, that it is possible to train a significant proportion of chronic alcholics to discriminate their blood alcohol levels and to utilize this skill in controlling their drinking behavior. The extent to which this training is subsequently instrumental (in conjunction with the usual training programs for alcoholism) in enabling the alcoholic to remain abstinent or become a controlled drinker, however, remains uncertain. Certainly, it seems that BAL discrimination training by itself will have no significant effect in the control of drinking behavior in the absence of positive effects produced by therapeutic procedures such as aversive training or more traditional therapy. Obviously, more research is needed to establish clearly the role of BAL discrimination training in the therapy of alcoholism.

Several other biofeedback-oriented approaches to the treatment of alcoholism have been reported, all of which appear to be based on the assumption that alcoholics drink to reduce anxiety, a proposition which, while long accepted as dogma, is of doubtful validity. There is now considerable objective evidence that alcoholics experience an *increase* in anxiety and depression *after* they have started a drinking episode (Mendelsohn & Mello, 1966; Nathan & O'Brien, 1971; Nathan, Titler, Lowenstein, Solomon, & Rossi, 1970). On the other hand, Steffen, Nathan, and Taylor (1974) provided free access to beverage alcohol (whisky) for 12 days to four male chronic alcoholics and took measures of BAL, frontalis muscle activity, and subjective anxiety every second hour while the patients were awake. They found that increased BALs tended to be accompanied by reduced frontalis muscle activity (which they took to be an objective measure of anxiety level), whereas subjective estimates of anxiety by the patients increased as BAL increased. The conclusion of Steffen *et al.* (1974), that the reduction in frontalis muscle tension as BAL increases supports the anxiety-reduction theory of alcoholism, depends, of course, on the validity of frontalis muscle activity as a measure of anxiety.[3] Steffen (1975) has subsequently reported the results of a complex study with four chronic alcoholics subjected to a ten-phase model II 2 × 2 replicated Latin square ANOVA for repeated-measures design comparing frontalis muscle training with placebo involving a reversal procedure with two patients in each condition in an inpatient setting. In phase I (orientation, 3 days) the patients were trained to reduce frontalis muscle activity with proportional auditory and nonproportional visual feedback. In phase II (baseline drinking, 12 days) liquor was made freely available via a dispenser as long as BAL did not exceed 250 mg/%. During this phase, BALs and frontalis muscle activity were regularly recorded. Detoxification (phase III, 2 days) followed, during which alcohol access was progressively reduced till BAL fell to zero. Phase IV (training period A, 6 days) followed, involving 14 sessions of training in general, forearm, and frontalis relaxation training with and without feedback. Free-drinking, training, and detoxification procedures were repeated until a total of 41 days had elapsed. The results indicated that the EMG training led to lowered levels of EMG activity and to lowered BALs, but not to a decrease in the number of drinks ordered during the free-drinking periods. The patients reported a decrease in subjective disturbance after the EMG training. Steffen explains these results as possibly due to a changed drinking pattern of behavior but provides no direct evidence on the point. It should be noted that Steffen did not test a crucial aspect of his theory, namely, that if frontalis muscle activity is a

[3]The specificity/generality issue will be discussed in detail in Chapter 7.

valid measure of anxiety in alcoholics, the resting level of frontalis activity just prior to indulgence in alcohol (and preferably after a period of enforced abstinence) should be higher than in nonalcoholic subjects. It should also be possible to demonstrate a gradient of increased frontalis muscle activity following abstinence if the hypothesis is true.

Training alcoholics to increase alpha activity is also based on the assumption that anxiety plays a major role in alcoholism and that the alcoholic drinks to reduce anxiety. Jacobson, Wilson, and La Rocca (1977) allocated 30 inpatient alcoholics, 30 abstinent alcoholics, and 30 nonalcoholic controls in groups of ten to each of three alpha training conditions: veridical auditory feedback, nonveridical auditory feedback, and no-feedback control. Alpha was recorded from the occipital area bilaterally and the feedback was a tone indicating the presence of alpha (the subjects were partially informed, but not told directly about alpha). Five training sessions were given, involving increasing and suppressing alpha for 2-min periods. The results could not be related to the alcoholism variable since successful alpha training was not achieved in any of the three conditions. Jones and Holmes (1976) found no difference between alcoholics and nonalcoholics in voluntary control of alpha with either true or false feedback, although this study has been criticized on methodological grounds (Glaros, 1977; Holmes, 1977). Twemlow and Bowen (1977) provided intensive training in alpha and theta enhancement to a large group of alcoholics and attempted to identify predictors of the degree of self-actualization achieved as a result of the training. They suggest that alpha- and theta-enhancement training might indicate the degree of self-actualization, but any feedback training effects were so hopelessly confounded with effects attributable to other therapeutic techniques (individual and group counseling, role playing, and art therapy) that no conclusions can possibly be drawn from this study. More encouraging results were obtained by Passini, Watson, Dehnel, Herder, and Watkins (1977), who allocated 50 alcoholics to experimental and control groups. The patients in the experimental group were given two sessions of finger temperature training followed by ten 1-h sessions of alpha-enhancement training with auditory feedback. These patients were fully informed and instructed in techniques believed to lead to increased alpha. The control patients did not receive any training but the groups were compared before and after the training of the training group on alpha production time percentage with eyes open and eyes closed. While both groups showed the same amount of alpha production in both eyes-open and eyes-closed conditions before training was begun, the controls showed no change after training of the experimental group was completed, whereas the latter group significantly increased alpha production in both eyes-open and eyes-closed conditions. This study did not investigate whether the training had any effect on patterns of alcoholic consumption, but it was found that the alpha training group did show a significant reduction in state and trait anxiety (although not on another anxiety inventory) as compared with the controls. Only minimal differences, however, were found on a number of measures of positive affective states.

Finally, it may be mentioned that Benson (1974) has reported an admittedly uncontrolled study of no less than 1862 alcoholics in which the practice of transcendental meditation supposedly led to a marked reduction in alcohol intake, while Green, Green, and Walters (1974) have reported cases where training in finger temperature increase was associated with decreased alcohol intake and improved personality functioning. In both cases the implication is that the training reduced anxiety and thus the need for alcohol as an anxiety-reducing agent. However, neither of these reports can be regarded seriously as no evidence whatever is presented to validate the assertions.

Thus, the role of biofeedback training in alcoholism remains obscure. Training in BAL discrimination certainly seems to be feasible with alcoholics and there seems no reason why alcoholics should not be trained to increase alpha (assuming this phenomenon to be genuine), relax various muscles, or learn to meditate. Whether the acquisition of these skills will significantly improve the effectiveness of traditional or behavioral approaches to the treatment of alcoholism remains to be seen.

Attempts to use biofeedback in the treatment of drug addiction are so recent that none are mentioned in the comprehensive review of behavioral approaches by Callner (1975), while a recent plea by Volpe (1977) for the use of feedback-facilitated relaxation training as a preventive method in relation to adolescent drug abuse (on the assumption that such use is primarily anxiety reducing) was not backed up by any empirical evidence other than non-drug-oriented biofeedback studies. Nevertheless, some studies have been carried out which have attracted little attention. The most ambitious are those by Lamontagne and his colleagues. Lamontagne, Hand, Annable, and Gagnon (1975) compared the effects of alpha-enhancement training with frontalis muscle reduction training on marihuana usage in students classified as light, medium, and heavy users. A yoked control group (which listened to a randomly varying tone) was also used. While all groups showed improvement in sleep patterns and a reduction in anxiety over the training and 3-month follow-up period, these changes were not reliably associated with any of the treatments and there was evidence of reduced drug usage only in the light users. Not much more impressive results were obtained in a subsequent large-scale study by Lamontagne, Beauséjour, Annable, and Tétreault (1977) in which three control groups (yoked feedback, no feedback, no treatment) were used in addition to the alpha-enhancement and frontalis muscle reduction groups. A significant reduction in drug usage occurred in the frontalis training group compared with the no-treatment group, but the group differences were not very striking.

Goldberg, Greenwood, and Taintor (1977) have discussed the use of alpha training with drug addicts while Goldberg, Greenwood, and Taintor (1976) trained four males on methadone maintenance to increase alpha on the assumption that drugs are used to produce an altered state of consciousness and that the induction of an alpha state may serve as a substitute for the drug-induced state. Control of alpha enhancement was apparently achieved and a posttraining interview revealed that the patients wanted to use the alpha state as a substitute, while reduced drug usage was confirmed by urine testing. However, no details are given of the alpha training or the results achieved in this study in quantitative terms. In another poorly controlled and reported study, Kuna, Salkin, and Weinberger (1976) reported that relaxation training produced increased tolerance of the side effects of methadone treatment (which may lead to symptoms similar to those experienced during withdrawal) together with high anxiety.

To date, the biofeedback work carried out in the area of drug addiction has largely been exploratory and poorly controlled so that virtually nothing can be said as yet about its potential value.

Anxiety

The different approaches to the use of biofeedback in the treatment of anxiety reflect assumptions relating to the generality/specificity issue, that is, whether it matters little which form of relaxation training (heart-rate reduction, frontalis muscle activity reduction, and so on) is used (generality assumption) or whether a specific function should be sought which is directly implicated in the anxiety displayed by a particular patient (specificity assumption). The importance of these assumptions is dealt with in Chapter 7, but mention may be made here of two studies which suggest that even in cases of apparent general anxiety, quite specific physiological correlates may be present and that biofeedback training might therefore be specific rather than general in nature. Thus, Cox and McGuinness (1977) trained nonclinical but highly anxious subjects to increase and decrease heart rate with visual feedback and compared their performance with that of low anxious subjects. The highly anxious subjects were able to increase their heart rate by 12 bpm on average but were not able to decrease heart rate, while the reverse was the case for the low anxious subjects. Sappington (1977), in fact, has suggested that anxious subjects should be trained to increase heart rate in the initial stages of therapy as this procedure leads to greater subsequent relaxation. Hama, Kawamura, Mine, and Matsuyama (1977) found that highly anxious subjects were able to reduce peripheral finger temperature to a greater degree than low anxious subjects, but the groups did not differ in the ability to increase finger temperature.

The first study of the use of biofeedback training for general anxiety was carried out by Raskin, Johnson, and Rondestvedt (1973) and was based on the generality assumption, namely, that successful training in reduction of frontalis muscle activity would have a generalized effect of reducing anxiety. The ten patients treated suffered from very severe generalized long-standing anxiety which had proved refractory to various forms of treatment (including 2 years of individual psychotherapy and medication). They were given 40 h of training in frontalis muscle activity reduction with proportional auditory feedback over a period of 8 weeks. Deep relaxation was considered to have been achieved when frontalis activity averaged less than 25 μV peak-to-peak (equivalent to about 8 μV rms) for at least 25 min of a 1-h trial. When this stage was reached, trials without feedback were interspersed every 2–3 days. In addition to frontalis muscle activity, subjective ratings of degree of calmness at the beginning and end of each session were made, the therapist rated the degree of anxiety, insomnia and tension headache ratings were made, a 65-item mood checklist was administered, and the patients kept sleep records and records of the occurrence of tension headaches. All ten patients were able to produce very significant reductions in frontalis muscle activity, the average baseline level of 14.1 μV peak-to-peak being reduced by from one-half to seven-eighths during the course of training. However, six of the ten patients showed no improvement in overall anxiety level while those who did could use the acquired relaxation skill to reduce anxiety when alone (although they could not prevent its onset). Only three of the patients reported some success in reducing their anxiety in social situations. Of six patients who suffered from insomnia, five reported an improvement in going to sleep but the training did not improve the tendency to wake up after going to sleep. An important finding was that deep relaxation was sometimes accompanied by profound subjective anxiety, and indeed, overall the frontalis muscle levels did not correlate significantly with the patients' subjective ratings of anxiety. Thus, the results of this pioneering experiment were not particularly encouraging, but it should be remembered that the patients were affected with exceptionally severe, long-standing, and socially crippling anxiety.

Townsend, House, and Addario (1975) also used frontalis muscle reduction training and compared its effects with those of short-term structured group therapy dealing specifically with anxiety and making use of TAT cards and discussion. The patients allocated to frontalis muscle training were provided with both visual and auditory feedback, 3 h of training being given over a period of 3 weeks; they also practiced general deep muscle relaxation during the feedback training period. Resting frontalis muscle activity levels were recorded for both groups before and at various times during treatment. Anxiety and mood were measured by the State–Trait Anxiety Inventory (STAI) and the Profile of Mood States (POMS) Inventory, which were also repeated several times. Of the 30 patients with anxiety neurosis who commenced treatment, only 18 completed the training course. The group given frontalis muscle training showed a significant drop in activity during treatment where the group therapy patients did not (although the difference had disappeared by the end of treatment, due to an increase in frontalis activity in the feedback group). No differences between the groups were found at any stage of the treatment in the POMS or STAI, but the frontalis muscle training group were reported as showing greater clinical improvement, although the assessment of clinical state was inadequate and only two patients were followed up. Not unexpectedly, perhaps, this study attracted some criticism, both with respect to the conclusions drawn and its alleged methodological inadequacies (such as the confounding of general relaxation training with specific frontalis muscle training; Frankel, 1975; Weiss, 1975), to which Townsend (1975) replied that his study was not primarily intended to be a comparative one of general versus specific relaxation training but rather a comparison of behavioral versus traditional therapy. Nevertheless, it must be admitted that the design of this study was inadequate and the results again not particularly encouraging.

While Townsend *et al.* (1975) had used a combination of general relaxation and specific frontalis relaxation training, Canter, Kondo, and Knott (1975) compared the relative efficacy of these two procedures. They treated 28 patients aged 19–48 years (13 of whom were females) diagnosed as anxiety neurosis with a high degree of anxiety and complaints of muscular tension and insomnia. Half of the patients suffered from chronic anxiety while the remainder reported acute panic episodes. All were taken off medication when treatment began. The patients were allocated to one of two treatments (with equal numbers of panic attack patients in each group): frontalis biofeedback treatment with proportional auditory feedback, and progressive relaxation training (not involving alternate tensing and relaxing of muscles), proceeding from one muscle group to another and including the frontalis, but without feedback. Between 10 and 25 training sessions were given over several weeks. In addition to measuring frontalis muscle activity at the beginning and end of each training session, patient and therapist ratings of anxiety were recorded. The groups were reasonably comparable in levels of frontalis muscle activity at the beginning of training. Both training techniques led to a significant reduction in frontalis muscle activity by the end of training but the decline was much greater in the feedback group than in the relaxation without feedback group (there were no important differences between the chronic anxiety and panic attack patients within either treatment technique). The reduction in frontalis muscle activity was accompanied by a reduction in anxiety as rated both subjectively and objectively. No follow-up data were reported.

Lavallée, Lamontagne, Pinard, Annable, and Tétreault (1977) treated 40 outpatients manifesting free-floating anxiety of at least 6 months duration (patients with phobias, obsessions, or depression, and those taking major tranquilizers were excluded). Four treatment groups were formed, involving combinations of feedback/no-feedback training and drug (diazepam)/placebo. The feedback groups were given frontalis muscle activity reduction training with auditory feedback while the no-feedback groups were asked (but not trained) to relax. The drug groups were given 5 mg of diazepam or placebo three times daily. A shaping procedure was used in the feedback training. Various anxiety measures (the Hamilton Anxiety Scale, the IPAT Anxiety Scale, and the de Bonis Trait–State Anxiety Scale) were taken before and after treatment and at follow-up sessions 1, 3, and 6 months after termination of treatment. The main results are shown in Figure 5. At the end of training, frontalis muscle training alone and diazepam administration alone were equally effective in reducing frontalis mus-

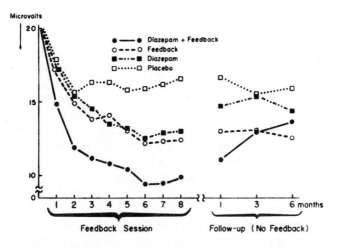

Figure 5. Mean EMG levels during treatment and follow-up. (From Lavallée, Y.-J., Lamontagne, Y., Pinard, G., Annable, L., & Tétreault, L. Effects of EMG feedback, diazepam and their combination on chronic anxiety. *Journal of Psychosomatic Research*, 1977, *21*, 68, Figure 1. Reprinted by permission of the author and the publisher.)

cle activity and even more effective when used in combination. However, although these differences were still present at the 1-month follow-up, they had disappeared at the time of the 3-month follow-up. The results for the anxiety rating scales were, however, different. The three treatment groups showed reduced anxiety at the end of treatment and at the 1-month follow-up, but anxiety had returned in full at the 6-month follow-up. Furthermore, while the no-treatment group showed no change in rated anxiety at the end of treatment, it had lower anxiety scores at the 6-month follow-up. Only low correlations were found between frontalis muscle and anxiety changes, and the suspicion cannot be avoided that the changes in the treatment groups may have been due to factors other than the feedback training and drug administration.

Kappes and Michaud (1978) compared the effects of contingent and non-contingent frontalis muscle reduction training on anxiety by varying the order in which the training was given. For one group, contingent feedback training was completed and followed by noncontingent training; for the other group, the reverse procedure was followed. The results indicated that contingent training led to a reduction in anxiety and that prior contingent training might interfere with the contingent training when it was introduced.

De Vries, Burke, Hopper, and Sloan (1977) investigated the potential of biofeedback training for reducing the high resting levels of forearm muscle tension manifested by ten nonpatient volunteers who exhibited one or more signs of a high level of anxiety (difficulty getting to sleep, general nervous tension, persistent feelings of tension or strain, irritability, unremitting worry, restlessness, inability to concentrate, or feelings of panic in everyday life situations). All of the subjects were tested on 12 occasions (four per day) over 3 days. On the first day, all subjects were provided with auditory (clicks) feedback for forearm muscle tension; on the second day, half continued to have auditory feedback while half tried to reduce tension without feedback; on the third day, the reverse procedure was employed. While feedback enabled significantly more reduction to be accomplished than no feedback, these differences were swamped by a time-of-day effect with forearm tension levels being very significantly lower late in the day as compared with early-morning levels. No attempt was made to relate the forearm muscle tension level changes to the adjustment difficulties of the subjects. It is interesting to note that in an earlier study De Vries and Adams (1972) had demonstrated that 15 min of walking-type exercise at rates which maintained heart rates of 100 or 120 bpm led to a significant reduction in resting levels of forearm muscle activity in middle-aged and elderly subjects complaining of anxiety symptoms. Matheson, Edelson, Hiatrides, Newkirk, Twinem, and Thurston (1976) had shown with normal subjects that electromechanical vibration to the feet led to a significant reduction in frontalis muscle activity, as compared with vibration applied to the back or a control condition involving no vibration. In a subsequent (although reported earlier) unpublished study (Matheson & Twinem, 1975) they investigated the effects of frontalis muscle activity auditory feedback, progressive relaxation training, and low-frequency vibration to the legs (alone and in various combinations) on the frontalis muscle activity of 40 nonpatient subjects who felt tense and anxious. The results suggested that a combination of the three treatments was more effective than any one alone. Beiman, Israel, and Johnson (1978) compared the effects of three kinds of relaxation training (live, taped, and self-administered) with frontalis muscle relaxation training in a large-scale study involving a substantial amount of training, including a final self-control assessment session, in which the subject was asked to relax as much as possible using the skills he had acquired during training. The subjects were not strictly anxiety cases but had reported tension as a serious problem. The biofeedback training was not found to be markedly superior to the other relaxation techniques and in some respects was inferior (for example, self-relaxation training reduced heart rate more than did frontalis muscle relaxation training).

Two other studies (both dealing with heart-rate control) relevant to the use of biofeedback training to relieve anxiety may be mentioned at this point. Blankstein.(1975) trained high, medium, and low trait-anxious groups to increase and decrease heart rate with visual meter feedback. He found that the high-anxious group was not very successful in lowering heart rate with feedback. McFarland and Coombs (1974), in the study described in detail in Chapter 4, also found that high-anxiety subjects had more difficulty in acquiring heart-rate control with feedback than low-anxiety subjects. Thus, although attempts have not yet been made to train generally anxious clinical patients in heart-rate reduction with feedback, the results of these two studies suggest that it might prove to be a difficult undertaking.

Clearly, the procedures so far described are intended to reduce overall tension level (that is, promote relaxation) in generally anxious persons by training them to reduce the level of activity in specific muscle groups. Since alpha enhancement is alleged to increase relaxation and feelings of well-being, it would not be surprising to find alpha-enhancement training used for the same purpose (as was the case with alcoholism). However, so far only tangential evidence is available as to the relationship between alpha levels and general anxiety. Orne and Paskewitz (1974) attempted to test the hypothesis that an increase in anxiety would be reflected by a drop in alpha activity and the corollary that the enhancement of alpha would increase control over anxiety. Using a Sidman avoidance paradigm (and normal subjects) they provided one tone for the presence of alpha, a second for the presence of no-alpha, while a third tone indicated the possibility of shock but the tone occurred only in the presence of no-alpha. Hence, the more alpha that was produced, the less likely the third tone (and the threat of shock) was to occur. The experiment was indecisive, however, because the anticipation of shock did not decrease anxiety even though the subjects reported anxiety during the shock jeopardy trials; hence, there was no base from which to assess the effects of alpha-enhancement acquisition. Grynol and Jamieson (1975) did succeed in differentiating between groups of normal females given correct as opposed to alternately correct and incorrect auditory feedback for alpha enhancement (the group given correct feedback producing more alpha) but both groups showed an equal decrease in anxiety (as measured by questionnaire) at the end of training. Nor did Valle and DeGood (1977) succeed in relating alpha control to anxiety level in another study with normal subjects. The State–Trait Anxiety Inventory (STAI) was given to 40 males who were allocated to enhance- and suppress-alpha training groups, using proportional auditory feedback. Subjects with low initial trait and state anxiety scores proved to be significantly better than high scorers in suppressing but not in enhancing alpha, but final state anxiety scores were unrelated to degree of alpha control and significant decreases in state anxiety which did occur over the training period were also unrelated to either enhancement or suppression of alpha, or to the degree of control achieved. Alpha training with biofeedback does not as yet, however, appear to have been used with clinically anxious patients.

Thus, no convincing evidence has yet been produced that biofeedback training has any special advantages in the amelioration of general anxiety as compared with more general relaxation training procedures or techniques such as transcendental meditation (e.g., Girodo, 1974).

Rather more success has attended the few attempts so far to use biofeedback training to overcome specific situational anxieties. Nearly all of these studies have involved training in heart-rate control. Blanchard and Abel (1976) were concerned with the therapy of a 30-year-old married female who had been raped at the age of 14 and subsequently experienced "spells" (feelings of nausea and vomiting, choking sensations, tachycardia, and numbness of the extremities) which were triggered by thoughts of other people evaluating her as a loose person. The patient was trained with binary visual feedback to control heart rate while various tape-recordings were played to her which contained neutral or rape-related sexual material. Control of heart rate was first established while listening to neutral material. One of the rape-related tapes (containing a detailed account of her own rape) did not produce tachycardia, but the second (containing a description of presumed disturbing events, such as men telephoning and propositioning her) produced a massive increase in heart rate (up to 150 bpm) prior to the feedback training. However, following feedback training with the neutral tape the patient was able to control her heart rate in the presence of the second tape and this effect was subsequently transferred to listening to this tape in the absence of feedback of heart rate, and eventually to a third tape containing similar material. Subsequent follow-up tests indicated continued heart-rate control in the presence of the second and third tapes (without feedback) and highly significant clinical changes were found to have occurred, the patient being able to return to her hometown (where the rape had occurred) and talk to acquaintances she had previously avoided because their presence precipitated the "spells."

The most important and comprehensive work so far reported in relation to the use of biofeedback training to overcome situational anxiety is undoubtedly that by Gatchel. In his first study (Gatchel & Proctor, 1976), normal subjects scoring high on two indices of situational anxiety ("speaking before a group," and Paul's Personal Report of Confidence as a Speaker, PRCS) were first required to prepare and deliver a short speech during which they were rated by two observers for overt signs of anxiety at ½-min intervals and completed a self-report measure of anxiety. They were then assigned to either training in the reduction of heart rate with visual feedback (using the Lang-type oscilloscope tracking display) or to a control condition involving tracking but without veridical heart-rate feedback. Following this training, half of the subjects in each group were led to believe that the training they had been given would assist them in preparing and giving two short speeches without experiencing anxiety while the remainder were given neutral instructions as to the benefits of the training. The speeches were then prepared and given while the anxiety ratings (subjective and objective) were repeated. Feedback for heart-rate reduction led to a significant reduction in heart rate as compared with the tracking task, and these differences were maintained in transfer, no-feedback trials. The main results of interest, however, are shown in Figure 6. The groups given feedback training in heart-rate reduction, regardless of the subsequent induced expectancy (high or neutral), showed significantly less rise in heart rate during both preparation and delivery of their speeches compared with the groups given tracking training. Furthermore, following training the feedback groups showed significantly greater reductions in both subjective and objective ratings of anxiety compared with the tracking

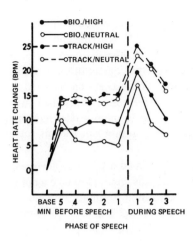

Figure 6. Mean heart-rate changes during speech preparation and presentation for the four experimental groups: Posttest Speeches 2 and 3 combined. (From Gatchel, R.J., & Proctor, J.D. Effectiveness of voluntary heart rate control in reducing speech anxiety. *Journal of Consulting and Clinical Psychology*, 1976, *44*, 386, Figure 3. Copyright by the American Psychological Association. Reprinted by permission of the author and the publisher.)

groups. A follow-up questionnaire revealed that the feedback-trained groups attributed their improvement in the speech situation to the feedback training they had received.

Some qualification of these results is necessary, however, in the light of subsequent results obtained by Gatchel, Hatch, Watson, Smith, and Gaas (1977), who compared the effects on speech anxiety of four training techniques: heart-rate deceleration training, general muscle relaxation training, a combination of these two methods, and a control condition involving false heart-rate feedback. The three experimental groups all slowed heart rate equally compared with the false-feedback group. The combined training group showed a significant reduction in heart rate and skin conductance during posttraining speech preparation and delivery compared with the other three groups. However, all four groups decreased significantly and to the same extent in both self- and observer-rated indices of anxiety. Thus, while the feedback training appeared to produce significant reductions in the physiological concomitants of anxiety, a powerful placebo effect (produced equally as well by the provision of false feedback) was present which was at least as important as the specific training given.

A very interesting related finding reported by Gatchel and Proctor (1976) was that similar changes occurred in relation to GSR measures with the feedback-trained groups showing a significant reduction in GSR during the preparation and delivery of the posttraining speeches, even though GSR itself had not been given any training. Only one study has been reported so far which involved GSR training in relation to alleviation of a specific anxiety. Corson, Bouchard, Scherer, Amit, Hisey, Cleghorn, and Golden (1973) treated a 20-year-old male with an intense fear of social situations accompanied by profuse perspiration. Training in progressive relaxation had been successful in inducing relaxation but had no effect on his social situation. The patient was presented with stories dealing with social situations which produced excessive perspiration. When his perspiration-induced GSR exceeded a specified level, a buzzer sounded, the tape stopped, and the subject attempted to turn off the buzzer by relaxing and reducing his GSR level. A significant decline in the amount of time the buzzer was on occurred over four sessions of training, even though the content of the recorded stories was gradually made more anxiety-inducing. This success encouraged the authors to pursue this line of training for 10 weeks, at the end of which the patient was engaging in increased social activity. A follow-up 15 months later indicated that the patient no longer had an excessive perspiration problem and his social phobia had disappeared.

Finally, Wickramasekera (1972) successfully treated a 42-year-old female with severe anxiety about taking examinations, who was required to take a public service examination within 3 weeks. Desensitization training was given, supplemented by EMG feedback training with auditory feedback. The examination was successfully taken but, of course, the study is confounded with respect to the effects of general as compared with specific relaxation training.

It is surprising that more work has not so far been reported with respect to the use of biofeedback training for general or specific anxiety. This is, perhaps, fortunate, for this is a critical area in relation to the generality/specificity assumption. In each case, the use of biofeedback will almost certainly be facilitated if the correct assumptions are followed, leading to an appropriate training schedule for the individual patient, whether afflicted with general or situational anxiety. This matter will be taken up in more detail in the next chapter.

Asthma

In spite of massive research efforts, asthma remains a puzzling and mysterious disorder and the subject of much controversy. About the only agreement that has been reached relates to the objective characteristics of asthma with respect to breathing patterns. An asthmatic episode is characterized by changed sensitivity of bronchial mucosa and musculature producing increased airways resistance, together with edema of the bronchial mucosa, blockage of the airways by secretions, and spasm of the bronchial muscles. The relative contributions of the autonomic and central nervous systems to these changes is a matter of dispute so that the degree to which classical and instrumental conditioning may be implicated in the genesis and maintenance of asthma is also uncertain. The role of psychological factors in asthma, however, seems well established and studies by Dekker and Groen (1956), Dekker, Pelser, and Groen (1957), Luparello, Lyons, Bleecker, and McFadden (1968), and Tal and Miklich (1976), among others, have strongly implicated conditioning as a factor in asthma.[4] Turnbull (1962)

---

[4]For a comprehensive short review of the role of psychological factors in asthma, see Purcell and Weiss (1970); for a brief account of conditioning factors and behavioral approaches to treatment, see Yates (1970, pp. 181–184), or more recently, Knapp and Wells (1978).

has advanced a theory of asthma as a conditioned avoidance response, while Miklich (1977) has defined asthma as:

> a state of chronic autonomic nervous system imbalance caused by normal homeostatic reductions in endogenous vagus nerve efferent activity in response to protracted "continuous and intense" bronchial obstruction which is usually, but not necessarily, allergic in origin. (p. 235)

And he cites a great deal of evidence in support of this viewpoint.

In order to understand the approach to treatment adopted in many biofeedback studies of asthma, some understanding of the basic measurements made of respiratory function in asthma is necessary. While total lung capacity and residual volume measures are commonly assessed routinely, certain special measures are used to assess the effects of treatment. Peak expiratory flow rate (PEFR) measures (in liters/sec) the maximum flow rate during the first 0.1 sec of a forced expiration (occasionally, the maximum midexpiratory flow rate— MMEF—has also been measured). A variant of this measure is the forced expiratory volume (FEV_1, measured in ml/sec). The other main measurement used is the total respiratory resistance (TRR or R_T) in which a forced oscillation technique is used involving the introduction of a small amplitude 3-Hz pressure variation continuously into the airways while the subject is breathing. The respiratory resistance to the passage of air during the breathing cycle may be assessed with the use of this technique, the resistance being expressed as cm H_2O of pressure/1 liter per sec of flow (the normal range being below 2.5 cm H_2O).[5]

Attempts to identify an "asthmatic personality" have met with little success and the multidimensionality of the symptomatology of asthma has been clearly shown in recent studies by Kinsman and his colleagues (Kinsman, Luparello, O'Banion & Spector, 1973; Kinsman, Spector, Shucard, & Luparello, 1974). They established a checklist of 77 subjective symptoms by detailed interviews of 29 adult asthmatics and then administered the checklist to 100 inpatient asthmatics between the ages of 14 and 67 years. Cluster analysis of the resulting data enabled identification of five main symptom clusters: two affective states (panic–fear and irritability), two somatic states (hyperventilation/hypocapnia and bronchoconstriction), and reduced energy level (fatigue). The most common symptom found was bronchoconstriction (reported by 91% of the patients), followed by fatigue (78%), panic–fear (42%), and irritability (34%), while hyperventilation and hypocapnia were relatively infrequently reported (9%). Bronchoconstriction did not correlate with the mood states but was related to fatigue, whereas the panic–fear symptom was associated with hyperventilation/hypocapnia and irritability. More detailed analysis of the clusters enabled the identification of 15 patterns represented by various combinations of the five clusters. For example, high fatigue was found to occur in patterns which included

[5]Levenson (1974) has described an automated system for the measurement of TRR by the forced oscillation technique.

high airway obstruction and high hyperventilation/hypocapnia scores. More significant, some possible patterns were not found; for example, low panic–fear states were never found in conjunction with high irritability states, and vice versa. Patients with high mood symptom scores tended to have higher steroid regimens on discharge, indicating more severe asthmatic states. The information obtained from these kinds of studies has important implications for therapeutic approaches since failure to take cognizance of such differences may well account for conflicting results in different therapy programs.

Studies in the use of biofeedback in the treatment of asthma fall into two clear-cut groups. In the first group, the assumption has been that asthmatics are characterized by high levels of anxiety and that training in relaxation will help to reduce the frequency of asthmatic attacks or to reduce the severity of an attack after it has started. In the second group, the assumption has been that it should be possible to help the patient control the events which are associated with impairment in the control of breathing so that, again, an attack is less likely to occur or can be better controlled when it does occur. The argument appears to be on the one hand that anxiety is the precipitant of an asthma attack, whereas on the other hand it appears to be that anxiety is probably the result of an attack.

Turning to the relaxation training studies first, Alexander, Miklich, and Hershkoff (1972) showed that training in relaxation produced a greater increase in PEFR in asthmatic children than did just sitting quietly. Subsequently, using a within-subjects design (each patient being given an equal number of sessions sitting quietly on the one hand, and practicing relaxation on the other), Alexander (1972) was able to replicate this result with a group of 25 asthmatic children aged 10– 15 years. Relaxation training produced an increase of 23.53 liters/min after relaxation training, compared with an increase of only 1.52 liters/min after sitting quietly for an equivalent period of time. No correlation was found between the change in PEFR in the two conditions; that is, resting PEFR was not predictive of the response to relaxation training. Nor was any correlation found between change in PEFR and an anxiety measure. Hence, although the patients with identifiable precipitating emotional factors benefited more from the relaxation training than did the patients without such a history, this result did not seem to be due to the effect of relaxation training on a conditioned anxiety response.

Neither of these studies involved the use of biofeedback. The first study to do so appears to have been that by Davis, Saunders, Creer, and Chai (1973). They allocated 24 asthmatic children, aged 6– 15 years (12 receiving steroid therapy, regarded as severe cases; 12 as nonsevere) to three treatment conditions: general relaxation training assisted by specific frontalis muscle relaxation training, general relaxation training alone, and instructed relaxation training while reading. Continuous proportional auditory feedback was used. Five days of training was preceded and followed by 8 days of baseline recording, PEFR being measured three times a day on each of the 21 days. The principal results obtained are shown in Figure 7. Neither of the training techniques was successful in the

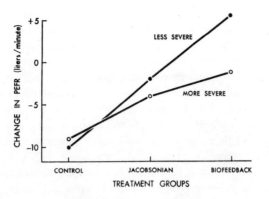

Figure 7. A comparison of treatment effects between groups identified as less severe and more severe. (From Davis, M.H., Saunders, D.R., Creer, T.L., & Chai, H. Relaxation training facilitated by biofeedback apparatus as a supplemental treatment in bronchial asthma. *Journal of Psychosomatic Research*, 1973, *17*, 123, Figure 1. Reprinted by permission of the publisher.)

case of the severe asthmatics, but in the case of the nonsevere asthmatics general relaxation combined with specific frontalis muscle reduction training produced a greater increase in PEFR than did general relaxation training alone or no training. Both the nonsevere training groups showed lower levels of frontalis muscle activity over the 5 days of training as compared with the control groups, although there was no evidence of a progressive reduction over the 5 days, indicating that the lower levels were achieved by reductions within each training session. The gains made during training were not, however, maintained during the second baseline session. Thus, these results, while encouraging, did not suggest that permanent improvement could be achieved with a comparatively short period of training in relaxation.

Kotses, Glaus, Crawford, Edwards, and Scherr (1976) carried out a similar study except that they provided training only in frontalis muscle activity reduction, not general relaxation as well. They allocated 36 asthmatic children to three groups matched for age, sex, race, and previous EMG experience, and equated roughly for severity of asthma and amount of drug therapy. One group was trained to reduce frontalis muscle activity with veridical proportional feedback, a second group with nonveridical feedback from a yoked patient in the first group, while the third group served as an untreated control. A total of nine training sessions over 3 weeks was given, including test periods for the maintenance of control in the absence of feedback. The group receiving veridical frontalis muscle activity feedback showed a significant reduction in that activity and a concomitant significant increase in PEFR, whereas the nonveridical frontalis muscle activity feedback group did not differ from the control group on either measure. The results were not a function of large changes in a small number of the children; rather, all of the children in the veridical feedback group showed improvement on both variables. In this study, the measures of PEFR were not recorded at the same time as the measures of frontalis muscle activity; hence, the possibility existed that the increases in PEFR may have been unrelated to the training in frontalis muscle activity reduction. This defect was remedied in a study by Kotses, Glaus, Bricel, Edwards, and Crawford (1978) which also examined the effects of brachioradialus muscle activity reduction training to determine whether frontalis muscle activity reduction training was both a necessary as well as a sufficient condition to produce increases in PEFR. Contingent frontalis feedback training produced an increase in PEFR of 11.1 liters/min whereas noncontingent frontalis and contingent and noncontingent brachioradialis training produced no change. Much less encouraging results, however, were obtained by Miklich, Renne, Creer, Alexander, Chai, Davis, Hoffman, and Danker-Brown (1977) using systematic desensitization training (sometimes in combination with frontalis muscle reduction training). They considered their results to be of no clinical significance. Thus, the results of biofeedback training of frontalis muscle activity in asthmatic children suggests that it may be a very promising approach to treatment. However, the long-term clinical effects remain as yet obscure and much more research is clearly needed before it is known whether significant clinical benefits can be obtained and sustained by the use of this technique.

Several attempts have been made to train asthmatic patients to establish control over the events which accompany (and perhaps directly cause) the breathing difficulties experienced in an asthmatic attack. Khan, Staerk, and Bonk (1973) first subjected 20 asthmatic children aged 8–15 years to a suggestion test (inhalation of neutral saline vapors on 3 days with the suggestion that they were inhaling a potent allergen) and on the basis of the results obtained, divided the children into ten reactors (those who developed bronchospasms, audible wheezing, and a 20% or greater reduction in FEV_1) and ten nonreactors. Half of the patients in each group then underwent biofeedback training while the other half were kept as controls. The training involved two phases. In the first, the training group patients were given five sessions in which they tried to increase FEV_1 (that is, produce bronchodilation) with nonproportional visual feedback (a light which came on whenever FEV_1 reached a criterion level). Verbal praise for success was also given. In the second phase (ten sessions), bronchospasm was induced by suggestion (recall of a previous attack, inhalation of saline vapors, listening to an audiotape of asthmatic wheezing, voluntary hyperventilation, exercise, or medication) after which the child attempted to use feedback to reduce the bronchospasm. Retraining with feedback was given at intervals up to 6 months later and a final follow-up was conducted after 1 year. This was a genuine clinical study in that the effects of the training were assessed in relation to changes in the number of emergency room visits, number of hospitalizations, amount of medication, and number of asthmatic attacks. The results of this study are shown in Table 1.

Table 1. Measures of Treatment Effectiveness

		Number of visits		Amount of medication		Number of attacks	
		Pre	Post	Pre	Post	Pre	Post
I. Experimental	$\overline{X}$	16.0	2.0	10.4	4.4	33.6	13.8
Reactors	Range	2–35	0–4	5–14	1–7	23–56	0–25
II. Experimental	$\overline{X}$	1.6	0.6	11.2	3.4	49.0	24.8
Nonreactors	Range	1–3	0–2	7–14	1–7	11–162	0–109
III. Control	$\overline{X}$	15.6	9.4	8.6	8.8	64.6	77.8
Reactors	Range	1–56	0–26	1–15	6–15	24–182	5–158
IV. Control	$\overline{X}$	4.8	3.4	8.0	6.4	30.8	39.8
Nonreactors	Range	1–14	0–12	3–13	1–14	12–71	3–79

Adapted from Khan, A.U., Staerk, M., & Bonk, C. Role of counterconditioning in the treatment of asthma. *Journal of Asthma Research,* 1973, *11,* 57–62, Table 1. Reprinted by permission of the publisher.

The pre–post differences between the treated and untreated groups as a whole in emergency room visits, amount of medication, and number of attacks were all significant but no differences were found between the treated reactors and the treated nonreactors. The effect of the training on PEFR was not reported. However, in a later larger scale study, Khan (1977) found much smaller differences between the experimental and control groups in relation to clinical changes occurring after a 1-year follow-up.

The study by Khan *et al.* (1973) was criticized by Danker, Miklich, Pratt, and Creer (1975) on the grounds that FEV_1 is a measure which is dependent on effort, the degree of effort exerted by the children not having been controlled.[6] They carried out two studies. In the first, six male asthmatic children aged 9–12 years were required to produce ten successive expirations in each trial. After three to six baseline trials without feedback, experimental trials were given in which visual feedback (a light) was provided for producing a "good" PEFR as compared with baseline levels, a shaping procedure being employed. No evidence of increased PEFR as a result of the feedback training was found. In the second study, a similar procedure with a new group of patients was employed, except that training lasted longer. While all of the patients showed a tendency to produce increased PEFR with feedback as compared with baseline levels, the change was significant for only three of the five patients. This study cannot be regarded as a significant gloss on the Khan *et al.* (1973) experiment. Apart from

[6]They also criticized it on the grounds that it was unclear whether classical or instrumental conditioning, or both, were involved. This criticism is irrelevant since feedback training was used and the results stand, whatever the theoretical framework.

the gratuitous interpretation of the study as an instrumental conditioning study when in fact it was a straightforward feedback study, the amount of training given does not compare with that provided in the earlier experiment. Its only value lies in demonstrating that the results obtained by Khan *et al.* (1973) might not have been related to changes in PEFR, data which, as pointed out earlier, were not provided by Khan *et al.* (1973).

Feldman (1976) attempted to control for possible confounding effects of the effort involved in the measurement of TRR by delivering simulated breathing sounds with a cycle time made up of 1.50 sec for inspiration and 1.75 sec for expiration. Four children with severe asthma attempted to match this breathing pattern, presented to them through headphones while they attempted to increase airflow by lowering the continuous auditory tone which reflected changes in TRR. Measurements were made of total lung capacity, residual value, FEV_1, MMEF, and PEFR during pre- and posttraining baseline sessions. The comparative effect of the administration of isoproterenol (a drug which induces bronchodilation) on these variables was also measured. The pretraining baseline measures indicated that all four patients manifested abnormal pulmonary function which showed significant improvement after the biofeedback training as indexed by changes in MMEF and TRR, but not in PEFR. Similar changes were produced by the administration of isoproterenol. In neither case, however, were normal levels of airways resistance achieved. Feldman considered that the improvement in TRR function could not be attributed to changes in the tone of the voluntary muscles of respiration or to the operation of other possible confounding variables, and concluded that relaxation of airways smooth muscle tone could well have been the mediating function (that is, that voluntary control of an autonomically mediated function had been achieved).

Positive results with feedback training were also obtained by Vachon and Rich (1976), using a large sample of mild asthmatics aged 18–30 years. The method of forced oscillation was used with visual feedback indicating when a preset target had been reached on each trial. In the first experiment, it was shown that TRR was reduced when feedback was available during either the inhalation phase only or during both the inhalation and expiration phases, but TRR was not reduced when nonveridical feedback was given. The second experiment attempted to control for the possible confounding effects of changes in thoracic gas volume (TGV), which is known to be inversely proportional to TRR. In this experiment, visual feedback was presented only if TGV was at baseline level at the time TRR had been reduced to the point at which feedback was due to be given. The results for groups of asthmatics given either veridical or nonveridical feedback (but in each case only when TGV was at baseline level) are shown in Figure 8. TRR was significantly reduced in the group given veridical feedback but not in the group given nonveridical feedback. As in the study by Feldman (1976), the reduction in TRR with feedback was equivalent to the reduction obtained after one inhalation of isoproterenol.

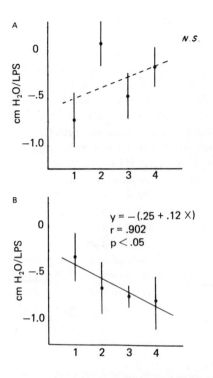

Figure 8. Change in resistance within trials. **A.** With noncontingent reinforcement. **B.** With contingent reinforcement. The ordinate presents the change in resistance at each trial. The group receiving the contingent reinforcement showed a clear tendency toward a greater reduction of their Rt (total respiratory resistance) over the four trials. (From Vachon, L., & Rich, E.S. Visceral learning in asthma. *Psychosomatic Medicine,* 1976, *38,* 122–130, Figure 4. Reprinted by permission of the publisher.)

A rather different biofeedback training approach has been suggested by Block, Lagerson, Zohman, and Kelly (1969), who argue that there may be merit in training patients with pulmonary insufficiency to change from thoracic to diaphragmatic breathing, thus achieving a more efficient mode of ventilation. They developed a simple feedback device (involving visual and/or auditory signals) to indicate to the patient when he is breathing incorrectly. Training in the mechanics of diaphragmatic breathing in conjunction with the use of the device to provide information whenever diaphragmatic breathing is not being used was found to be very effective when used with asthmatic children, although no quantitative data were presented. Mention may be made here of a recent study by Tiep, Mittman, and Tripp (1977) on the biofeedback treatment of emphysema. The major problem in breathing for the patient with emphysema occurs in the expiratory phase, resulting from collapsing airways due to the destruction of tissue elasticity. Using a transducer which measured suprasternal pressure changes (which have been shown to be linearly related to measurements made by a balloon in the esophagus), Tiep *et al.* (1977) were able to produce a 24% mean reduction in maximum voltage change during expiratory efforts, the patients using a feedback display which was both visual and auditory. Clinical observations suggested that changes in breathing patterns had occurred, involving a slowing of respiration (especially at the beginning of expiration) and a smoother, less forceful respiratory effort. The "expiratory catch" in breathing, characteristic of emphysema, also disappeared.

Wilson, Honsberger, Chiu, and Novey (1975) investigated the effects of transcendental meditation (TM) in two groups of adult asthmatics, using a crossover design (TM followed by placebo condition or the reverse procedure). Significant beneficial changes in FEV_1, PEFR, and TRR were found in the group given TM first, although the effects were lost during the subsequent control period. No beneficial effects were found during the initial placebo period for the second group, but the subsequent introduction of TM led to a significant improvement in TRR only. In both groups, however, an index of symptom severity showed a significant reduction throughout the study, indicating that an overall suggestion or expectation effect was mainly responsible for the results obtained. As pointed out earlier, suggestion and expectation effects are of considerable importance in asthma and have been clearly demonstrated in studies specifically designed to examine them. Nevertheless, the studies reviewed above lead to the conclusion that it may be possible to train asthmatic children (and possibly adults) to obtain at least some degree of voluntary control over the bronchoconstriction which is implicated in asthmatic attacks and thus either prevent or reduce the severity of the attack. This appears to be one of the more promising areas of the application of biofeedback training.

Blindness

Recent developments in two areas relating to difficulties experienced as a result of blindness are of particular interest for biofeedback research workers. The first relates to the problem of locomotion and the avoidance of obstacles by the blind, the second to the fact that facial expression in persons blind from birth may inadequately reflect the emotional state underlying the facial expression and thus lead to interpersonal communication difficulties. The problem of providing substitute feedback systems to enable blind persons to locomote successfully (or, of course, to read) has generated a vast literature which cannot be reviewed here. Reference to some recent work, however, may alert biofeedback workers to the possibilities inherent in the use of biofeedback techniques with the blind, currently a neglected area. Fish (1976)[7] has described the ingenious techniques which are being developed to enable the blind to substitute auditory feedback for the visual feedback which is not available to them and thus locomote successfully in a field containing obstacles. A simple example will suffice. A simple visual shape (e.g., a square) is scanned by a flying spot scanner system which detects and follows the sharp edge of the lines constituting the square. The tracking device essentially reduces to a moving point of light, the successive positions of

[7]See also Fish (1975) and Fish and Fish (1976). Fish's (1975, 1976) two papers contain a valuable selection of references which will enable the interested reader to pursue these developments further.

which are transduced into audio signals representing the momentary horizontal and vertical coordinates of the dot. The frequency of the feedback tone is used to represent the vertical position of the dot, while the amplitude of the tone is used to represent the horizontal position of the dot. The subject listens to the tone presented through stereophonic headphones and hears the dot moving from left to right or vice versa while simultaneously detecting the vertical position of the dot by discriminating the frequency. With relatively little practice, the subject is able to identify complex shapes (gaps in the shapes can, of course, be represented by the duration of interruption of the tone). The importance of the system lies mainly, however, in the fact that the subject can be trained to use a portable television scanner attached to his body to identify real objects (their shape and size) and thus move about confidently in the real world. Fish (1976) has shown that 10-year-old subjects can learn to identify patterns as complex as a star with 11 points in 4 h of training with auditory feedback and can become mobile in an unfamiliar environment with as little as 20 min of training with the TV camera attached to the body. Bach-y-Rita (1973) has developed a Tactile Vision Substitution System (TVSS) by means of which a TV camera transmits impulses in patterned form to an array of over 400 sensors which provide a differential pattern of tactile stimulation to the skin as a function of the particular pattern being transmitted. The TV camera may be mounted on a pair of spectacles, thus making the subject mobile as in the case of Fish's device. Using this technique, Bach-y-Rita (1973) has progressively trained blind subjects to discriminate lines, then circles and squares, followed by the identification of common objects. It has been found that eventually the subject "externalizes" the skin patterns and reacts to them as if they were real objects. Transfer of the learned discriminations to other skin areas is readily achieved and subjects can learn to compensate for the effects of camera tilt resulting from head movements.

The second development of interest relates to the role of facial expression in the expression of the emotions in blind persons. Several attempts have been made in recent years to explore these relationships using more sophisticated techniques than were available in earlier studies. Lehr, Blanton, Biggs, and Sewell (1974), for example, using inserted electrodes recorded bilaterally from the superior and inferior groups of circumoral facial muscles, and measured the changes in muscle activity which occurred when the normal subjects were required to perform a series of movements (smile, frown, pucker the lips, suck on a straw with resistance, raise the left or right upper lip, raise the nose, chew, or swallow). With recordings being made simultaneously from a large number of muscles, it was possible to determine which muscles were involved in particular movements, the order in which the muscles involved in a particular movement were innervated, and how they were integrated. Schwartz, Fair, Salt, Mandel, and Klerman (1976a,b) have examined in detail the facial muscle patterning in depressed and nondepressed patients while they are imagining happy, sad, and angry thoughts and feelings; thinking about a typical day; assuming happy, sad, and angry facial expressions; or indulging in maximal muscle contractions involving various areas of the face (horizontal and vertical wrinkling of the forehead, clenching the teeth, smiling, frowning, pouting, and opening the mouth). Schwartz *et al.* (1976a) found similar patterns of facial expression in both depressed and nondepressed patients when asked to imagine themselves as sad or angry (an increase in corrugator activity, but no change in depressor anguli oris activity), whereas when imagining themselves as happy the nondepressed patients showed a decrease in corrugator activity coupled with an increase in depressor anguli oris activity, but the depressed patients showed attenuated level of activity in these two muscle groups with a failure to produce the decrease in corrugator activity shown by the nondepressed patients. When asked to imagine a typical day's activities, the depressed patients produced a sadness pattern of activity. Schwartz *et al.* (1976b) examined the differential effects of thinking about emotional states without actually experiencing them with actually reliving the states, but the differences between normal and depressed subjects were not very striking.

The possibility of producing positive changes in these patterns of activity in depressed patients has not yet been investigated, but a little-known study by N.C. Webb (1974)[8] has shown that blind people tend to have facial expressions which are often inappropriate to their emotional state, and that they can be trained with biofeedback to acquire the facial expressiveness appropriate to different emotional states.[9] Webb began her study by requiring normal subjects to simulate the facial expressions they associated with happiness, anger, and surprise. The muscle groups consistently related to the three facial expressions were identified from film recordings. Happiness was found to be associated primarily with activity of the zygomaticus muscle (drawing backward and upward of the corners of the mouth), anger with activity of the corrugator muscle (originating at the arch of the eyebrow and extending to the bridge of the nose), and surprise with activity of the frontalis muscle. Having established the normal primary muscle activity correlates of these three facial expressions, Webb then placed surface electrodes bilaterally on the face of five blind[10] subjects as follows: right and left frontalis, origin and insertion of the corrugator, and origin and insertion of the zygomaticus. After baseline measures of muscle activity had been taken without feedback while the subjects adopted the three facial expressions (happiness, anger, surprise), training with auditory feedback for producing the correct (i.e., normal) muscle pattern for each facial expression was carried out until the specified criteria were met or 3 h of training had elapsed. Two of the subjects required only ½ h of training, one required 2 h, and two required 3 h. Following the feedback

---

[8] A brief account of the original study has been provided by C. Webb (1977). The present account is based on the original study.

[9] N.C. Webb (1974, pp. 231–239) also provides a comprehensive review of the literature on facial expression in the blind.

[10] The blind subjects were aged 18–45 years; two had been blind from birth and three from the age of 10 or 11 years.

training, tests were run to determine whether the correct expressions could be produced without feedback. Film recordings were made at all stages of the training and judges known to be expert at interpreting the film records judged the records in terms of identification of the emotion expressed and appropriateness of the facial expression displayed. The results showed that the correlation between expressions intended by the subjects and judged by the experts was much stronger after training than before training, and that a wider and more appropriate range of muscles were used in each expression after training than before. Prior to training, for example, the blind subjects tended not to use the frontalis muscle when expressing surprise, but it proved very easy to train them to do so. Webb (1974, p. 252) points out that her results suggest that there should be little difficulty in training blind persons with feedback to gain fine control over a much wider range of facial muscle activities than the three with which she concerned herself.

It may be concluded that the problems associated with blindness constitute a fertile field for the application of biofeedback training techniques.

Bruxism

The relationship between the temporomandibular joint dysfunction syndrome and bruxism (or teeth grinding, usually during sleep) remains somewhat obscure (particularly as to the direction of cause and effect) although there seems little doubt that both are quite commonly found together (Glaros & Rao, 1977b; Zarb & Speck, 1977). There is no doubt at all that teeth grinding produces excessive tooth wear and damage to the supporting bone so that elimination of the practice at an early stage would be beneficial. The recording of teeth grinding presents problems because apparatus is needed and the recording will usually need to be made while the patient is sleeping. Several techniques have been described (e.g., Dowdell, Clarke, & Kardachi, 1976; Gentz, 1972; Heller & Strang, 1973; Solberg & Rugh, 1972) which record the activity of the masseter muscle or the sounds produced by the teeth grinding. Using a portable apparatus, Dowdell *et al.* (1976) claim to have achieved outstanding results in the treatment of facial pain resulting from teeth grinding, but the quantitative results have not yet been published. Using a similar system, Solberg and Rugh (1972) reported that 2–7 days of training were sufficient to effect a significant reduction in tooth grinding in 10 out of 15 patients treated, but again quantitative details of the study were not reported. Butler, Abbott, and Bush (1976)[11] claimed that 1 week's training with either an occlusal guard or biofeedback (unspecified) was sufficient to reduce masseter muscle activity significantly in 20 patients afflicted with teeth grinding. Once more, however, no data were presented to substantiate the claim. Heller and Strang (1973) treated a 24-year-old student with bruxism.

[11]Published in abstract form only.

They positioned a microphone near the patient's ear and recorded the characteristic grinding sound on a time-sampling basis for a baseline period of 18 days. The patient manifested an audible grinding rate of 1.75 times per minute. An arrangement was then set up so that a 3-sec aversive sound blast was delivered whenever the grinding rate reached three per 5-sec interval. Seven training sessions with feedback for grinding were given, followed by 6 reversal sessions and another 21 feedback sessions. During feedback sessions teeth grinding was reduced by over 60%, with an increase (but not to the original baseline level) occurring during the reversal sessions. Indeed, the intensity of the teeth grinding eventually became so low that the resultant sound could not be detected by the microphone so that feedback was no longer able to be presented. No information was provided as to the subsequent course of the disorder. Since bruxism is surprisingly common (estimates as high as a 5% incidence in college students and 15% in school children have been reported), and since the practice can produce serious dental damage as well as masseter muscle tension, further investigation of these relatively simple techniques seems warranted. However, it may be noted that Ayer and Levin (1973) claim to have eliminated teeth grinding in 11 of 14 females by the simple use of massed practice, involving repeated clenching of the teeth together as hard as possible for a short period, followed by jaw relaxation for an equal period of time.[12]

Deafness

The speech defects manifested by profoundly deaf persons and the difficulties experienced in training children deaf from birth to generate adequate speech is a classic example of the importance of self-generated feedback in the control of skilled behavior. Nickerson (1975) has recently provided a comprehensive review of the deficits in timing and rhythm, pitch and intonation, velar control, articulation, and voice quality commonly found in the speech of deaf persons. As was pointed out in Chapter 1, the development of external aids to provide visual feedback of the characteristics of the speech defects of deaf people and the effects of altering those characteristics can be traced back to the pioneering work of the great inventor Alexander Graham Bell, who invented the Bell reduced visible-symbol method for teaching speech to the deaf. Subsequently, many attempts have been made to develop devices which will display specific characteristics of speech in efforts to obtain more precise control of vowel and consonant sounds, pitch, fricatives, rhythm, and intonation (Borrild, 1968; Levitt, 1973; Martony, 1968; Pickett, 1968; Risberg, 1968; Searson, 1965). As Borrild (1968) has pointed out, it is possible to teach deaf children the correct production of individual sounds without the use of such aids, but it remains very difficult for the

---

[12]Excellent critical reviews of theories of bruxism and its treatment have recently been published by Glaros and Rao (1977a,b).

child to integrate this accomplishment into normal flowing speech with the result that intonation and rhythm remain faulty. Until recently, the feedback displays used were not very successful in overcoming this problem because, like the normal teaching procedures, they were unable to reflect the natural flow of speech, displaying only, as it were, a frozen crosssection at a particular instant in the speech flow. The introduction of real-time computer-controlled displays of speech characteristics in more than one dimension simultaneously represents a major advance in this area of treatment. The system developed by Nickerson and his colleagues (Boothroyd, Archambault, Adams, & Storm, 1975; Nickerson, Kalikow, & Stevens, 1976; Nickerson & Stevens, 1972) has been described in Chapter 2. Here, it is only necessary to recall that the computer system involves the use of appropriate sensors (accelerometers attached to the throat and/or nose, and a head-mounted voice microphone), preprocessing devices (pitch extractor, spectrum analyzer, nasal output detector, and multiplexing to analog-to-digital converters), the computer itself (using a ring buffer to store a running record of the immediately preceding 2 sec of speech), and display devices of special kinds (the "ball game," the vertical spectrum, the cartoon face) in addition to the time plot, which displays any chosen aspect of speech (loudness, pitch, vowels, voicing, and so on) as a function of time. The computer also enables various display-mode options to be exercised. In other words, this flexibility enables much more realistic information to be presented to the deaf person as well as, for example, permitting the deaf person to match his own output to that of a model, correct form of speech. There is no suggestion here, of course, that the use of computer-generated displays makes it easier to teach correct speech to the deaf—indeed, the very sophistication itself only serves to emphasize the extreme complexity of the problem. As a result, detailed results of studies using the system are not yet available,[13] although preliminary findings have been described (Boothroyd et al., 1975). One study has, however, been reported in some detail. Boothroyd, Nickerson, and Stevens (1974) attempted to train eight profoundly deaf children aged 8–17 years to improve the temporal patterns of their speech. As Boothroyd et al. (1974) point out, defects in speech production attributable to distortions in timing are common in deaf persons:

> The speech is generally slow, the relative durations of speech sounds are inappropriate; stressed and unstressed syllables are temporally undifferentiated; voicing begins and ends at the wrong time, causing voiced/voiceless errors, or the introduction of extra syllables; and pauses are introduced at inappropriate places, leading to confusion about the locations of phrase and sentence boundaries. (pp. 1–2)

Boothroyd et al. first compared the speech characteristics of the deaf children while reading simple familiar sentences with those of normal subjects reading the same sentences. They measured the duration of syllables and of the gap between syllables and found that the deaf children took significantly longer to

---

[13]The use of the system to control inappropriate nasalization in deaf persons has been described in Chapter 3.

enunciate unstressed and secondary (but not primary) syllables and also manifested significantly longer between- and within-phrase gaps. So striking were
these differences that on average the deaf children took twice as long as the
normal subjects to read the sentences as a whole. Over a period of 7 weeks, the
deaf children were then given about 8 h of training in imitating nonsense
rhythmic patterns (e.g., /pa/) which were then incorporated into real words
(e.g., papa), followed by practice in producing sounds which matched a model
provided by a normal speaker. Figure 9 shows the main results obtained. A
significant improvement occurred in relation to unstressed syllables and the
within-phrase gap, but not in primary or secondary syllables or the between-
phrase gap. A significant carryover of the effects of training was found for
unrehearsed speech. However, when independent judges rated the intelligibility
of pretraining and posttraining speech of the deaf children, either no improvement was detectable or the natural speech of the children had actually become
worse. Thus, the point made by Borrild (1968) that training to improve specific
characteristics of speech may not result in improvement in general speech
characteristics remains a major stumbling block.

Procedures similar to those of Nickerson and his colleagues have been
developed by Fourcin with the use of the laryngograph which generates displays

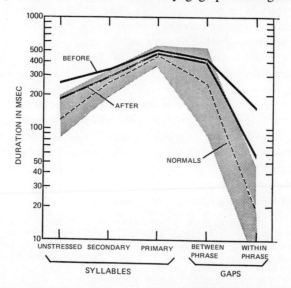

Figure 9. Mean values for duration of five durational categories are shown for the eight deaf students and
may be compared with the distribution found for normally hearing subjects. The two sets of data for the
deaf students were taken before training and after 450 min of training which included rehearsal of the test
material. (From Boothroyd, A., Nickerson, R.S., & Stevens, K.N. Temporal patterns in the speech of
the deaf—An experiment in remedial training. (SARP #15) Northampton, Mass: Research Department,
Clarke School for the Deaf, 1974, Figure 7. Reprinted by permission of the author and Clarke School for
the Deaf.)

of voice, pitch, and timing by detecting movements in the vocal folds (Fourcin, 1974; Fourcin & Abberton, 1971, 1976; A. Parker, 1974) but quantitative results are lacking. Holbrook and Crawford (1970) have described FLORIDA (Frequency Lowering or Raising Intensity Determining Apparatus), a device which employs operant conditioning techniques to shape pitch levels. When a white light is on, speech is being correctly produced; incorrect production is indicated by a red light. Partial reinforcement techniques are used to increase resistance to extinction. Good results were obtained when used with four deaf adult males with abnormally high pitch levels due to poor voice control of fundamental vocal frequency and intensity. Pitch fell to within the normal range and the improvement was maintained at a 3-month follow-up, with each subject able to speak correctly for long periods in the absence of the red and white lights. (Successful use of a similar device with two mildly retarded normal hearing adults has been described by Brody, Nelson, & Brody, 1975.)

Attempts have also been made to use tactile feedback displays with deaf people, analogous to those used to assist blind people. Bach-y-Rita (1973), for example, has reported the development of an electrotactile sound detector which converts sounds to a pattern of impulses delivered to the forehead, a device which may be useful in emergencies such as the need to detect a car horn where the car has not been noticed by the deaf person and the horn blast itself, of course, is not heard directly. Stratton (1974) presented a tactile display of the fundamental frequency of words and phrases to the fingers by means of solenoid-driven pins. As the pitch of the voice varies, the subject experiences the fundamental frequency contour as a tracing out of a localized mild vibration moving along the skin surface. Stratton's technique involved the experimenter in voicing words and phrases which the subject monitored and then attempted to match while receiving tactile feedback, first from the experimenter and then from his own speech. Twelve severely or profoundly deaf persons aged 12–16 years were given about 3 h of training in this manner. Independent judges rated the speech of the deaf persons before and after training in terms of its similarity to the normal speech model, and also, in the absence of the model, judged the "esthetic" quality of the speech of the deaf persons before and after training. The model was, indeed, found to influence the judgments made in that the same samples of speech from the deaf persons were judged more favorably when the model was available than when it was not. Nevertheless, the results obtained by Stratton were very encouraging. Figure 10 shows the changes in fundamental frequency contours for the phrase "A NEW day" in three deaf persons, and indicates the improvement which occurred in matching the contours of a normal speaker following training.

Thus, as in the case of blindness, it may be concluded that technological advances have opened up new vistas for the training of deaf persons in the production of normal speech patterns. The problem of generalizing from the specific improvements produced with feedback training to the characteristics of

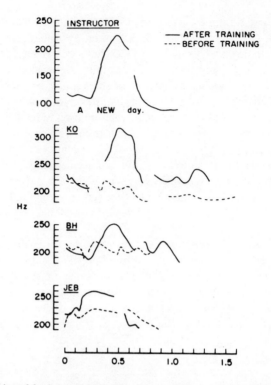

Figure 10. Matching of fundamental frequency contours of the speech of a normal person by deaf persons before and after training ("A NEW day"). (From Stratton, W.D. Intonation feedback for the deaf through a tactile display. *Volta Review*, 1974, *76*, 33, Figure 4. Reprinted by permission of the author and the Alexander Graham Bell Association, 3417 Volta Place N.W., Washington, D.C. 20007.)

speech in real situations remains unsolved, but this work is only in its infancy and significant advances may be anticipated in the future.

Dental Hygiene

The use of biofeedback to train persons in dental hygiene has been suggested and used by Godin (1973, 1974, 1976). The procedure involves the use of the dentiscope (Godin, 1973) which consists of a reflector with a focal length of 20 cm and a light designed so that it does not shine directly in the patient's eyes. Used in combination with a mouth mirror of the kind used by dentists for tooth inspection, the patient can examine his own teeth, learn self-scaling, improve his toothbrushing technique (especially by learning correct bristle pressure), and acquire the skill of flossing (using the special "string" to clean between the teeth; Godin, 1974).[14] Godin (1976) has provided evidence of

[14]Dramatic pictures of the improvement in teeth appearance obtainable by regular self-administration with feedback of these techniques will be found in Godin (1973, 1974).

the differential effectiveness of self-administered dental hygiene with feedback as compared with the same hygiene following instruction but without subsequent feedback in self-management. He assessed plaque and gingivitis levels in 12 patients aged 20–55 years requiring oral hygiene treatment. They were then paired according to age, sex, plaque, and gingivitis levels. One group was provided with a dentiscope, a large plane mouth mirror, a scaler, and 3 h of instruction in using the dentiscope, self-scaling, toothbrushing, and flossing. No professional scaling was carried out before they began self-treatment. The other group had their teeth professionally scaled, were then given instruction in oral hygiene over 3 h, and provided with a small mirror. Photographs of the teeth were taken 2 weeks after completion of the instructional phase and again 5 months later. No differences between the two groups were found in the plaque and gingival status of the teeth at the 2-week inspection (indicating that the self-treatment group had achieved the results obtained by professional scaling in the control group), but at the 5-month examination very significant differences were found in plaque control, the self-treated group achieving plaque indices two and one-half to three times those of the control group, the results being particularly striking for the first and second molars. Both groups, however, showed an equal improvement in the indices of gingival status. These results indicate that gingival status may be significantly improved provided minimal feedback is provided, whereas more precise feedback may be required to achieve a significant improvement in plaque control. The differential feedback in this study was essentially the more detailed visual feedback of the results of self-scaling as opposed to less detailed visual feedback of the results of brushing. There was, thus, confounding of scaling with brushing, but of course it is not meaningful to scale one's teeth unless detailed visual feedback is available via a suitable viewing mirror, so the results may be regarded as genuinely significant.

Diabetes

Diabetes is, of course, a very complex disorder known to be associated with arteriolar disease in long-term cases (although whether as cause or effect is unknown), and it has been demonstrated that autoregulation of cerebral blood flow breaks down sooner than it does in normal subjects, leading to a deficiency in the supply of oxygen (Bentsen, Larsen, & Lassen, 1975). It might be thought that biofeedback training has little to offer in the treatment of diabetes, but the fact that psychological factors (notably emotional lability) can affect the course and control of diabetes led Fowler, Budzynski, and VandenBergh (1976) to examine the effects of relaxation training on the control of diabetes in a single-case study. Their patient was a 20-year-old female who had suffered from diabetes for some 10 years and in whom physical or emotional stress produced severe keto-acedosis. The patient had become accustomed to taking insulin doses of 100 units per day with massive swings in blood sugar levels. Keto-acedosis often led to hypoglycemic reactions with resultant frequent hospitalization. Six weeks were spent in baseline recording of the daily insulin dose self-administered by the patient, who also kept a diary recording her diet, exercise, medication, infections, accidents, and emotional state. A daily assessment of her diabetic state and emotional state was also kept by the patient, while testing of urine content and blood sugar level was made at 2- to 4-week intervals. Following the baseline period, the patient was trained in both general relaxation and specific relaxation of the frontalis muscle activity, with both visual and auditory feedback, over a period of 6–7 weeks, twice a day, using a portable biofeedback unit.[15] At the conclusion of training the patient continued to practice the general relaxation technique until a follow-up could be carried out at the same time of year at which the original assessment had been made. The results showed that the average daily intake of insulin declined from 85 units during the initial baseline period to 59 units by the end of training and to 52 units at the 1-year follow-up assessment (carried out over a 2-month period). The variability of the daily intake had also declined. Self-ratings in the diabetic scale (which measured the degree of hypoglycemia by checking various symptoms) correlated $+0.77$ with insulin dose and showed a change from hyper- to hypoglycemia during the training phase (in fact, the patient showed a tendency to swing from one extreme to the other during the training phase, experiencing some extreme insulin reactions). A scale of emotional reactivity which was used showed an improvement in emotional stability, although the change did not correlate with insulin dose changes. These findings were corroborated in part by the fact that during the year over which the study was carried out the patient was not hospitalized. Three comments may be made in relation to this interesting study. In the first place, no data were provided to show that the patient manifested a significantly high level of frontalis muscle activity prior to the biofeedback training. Second, no evidence was given that frontalis muscle activity was in fact reduced as a result of the training given. Third, the effects of general relaxation training were confounded with the effects of specific frontalis muscle relaxation training. In spite of these defects, the results suggest that larger scale studies of the effects of relaxation training (general and/or specific) would be justified to determine whether the techniques are helpful in the control of diabetes. Guthrie, Moeller, and Guthrie (1976) have carried out a study of EMG training (the muscle site was not specified) on seven diabetics, but no results were presented in the abstract.

Eczema

Manuso (1977) treated a 60-year-old female with a 6-year history of chronic dermatitis of the hands (indexed by dryness, discoloration, scaling of skin, and multiple lesions) for which no organic basis could be found and after multiple treatments had proved ineffective. After baseline measures of finger temperatures were taken over a 4-week baseline, the patient was taught to relax (and

---

[15]It is unclear whether all of the training was carried out under direct supervision or not.

instructed to imagine vasodilation occurring in her hands), following which auditory feedback was provided of temperature change during each of 13 weekly sessions. Baseline finger temperature was low (about 73°F) but rose steadily to about 89°F during feedback training, and at a 6-month follow-up was about 89°F. During the treatment period the dermatitis cleared up, and the patient was medically free of it at the time of the follow-up. Naturally, a placebo effect producing both the temperature increase and the elimination of the eczema cannot be ruled out.

Hyperactivity

It appears that biofeedback training may be highly relevant to the treatment of hyperactivity. Braud, Lupin, and Braud (1975) studied a 6½-year-old boy with extreme hyperactivity. Auditory feedback from the frontalis muscle was provided, with the tone on whenever the muscle activity exceeded a specified level. The child's task was to keep the tone off. Activity levels while feedback was available were compared with pre–post feedback baseline levels. A considerable amount of training was given resulting in a dramatic reduction in frontalis muscle tension. The drop was maintained 7 months later and was accompanied by significant improvement in classroom and home behavior, as well as in objectively assessed test scores.

Encouraged by these findings, Braud (1978) launched a more ambitious study. A group of hyperactive children, aged 6–13 years, who scored 24 or more on a rating scale for hyperkinesis, was compared with a similarly aged group of normal children. Frontalis muscle activity and skin temperature from the forehead and right index finger were recorded while behavioral rating scales were completed and observation of behavior in the home situation made by the parents of the children. Various tests reflecting differences between hyperactive and normal children (the Bender Gestalt, the Visual Sequential Memory Test of the ITPA, and the Digit Span and Coding subtests of the WISC) were also administered. The children were allocated to one of three groups: relaxation training using Jacobson's technique, biofeedback relaxation training of frontalis muscle activity, and a no-treatment control. Twelve training sessions spread over 6 weeks were given to the experimental groups. In the hyperactive children biofeedback training produced a massive reduction of 87% in frontalis muscle activity, compared with 59% in the group trained in relaxation and only 5.5% in the control group. Little or no change occurred in the normal subjects; the biofeedback training reduced the level of frontalis muscle activity in the hyperactive group below that of the normal controls. An increase in hand temperature relative to head temperature occurred in the hyperactive children although no training was given, indicating, according to Braud, increased autonomic relaxation. Parental ratings indicated a significant drop in hyperactivity after both relaxation training and biofeedback training, the results generalizing to the home situation where, however, there was no difference in amount of reduction between the relaxation and the biofeedback techniques. Some improvement in performance on the objective tests was also found in the groups trained in biofeedback or relaxation. These results are distinctly encouraging and it may be anticipated that more work will be carried out on the application of biofeedback training to hyperactivity in the future.

Based on the assumption that breathing is a higher order behavior, increased control over which would lead to increased control of hyperactivity, Simpson and Nelson (1974) trained three young hyperactive boys to match their breathing to an ocsilloscope target display while three other boys were used as controls, being given feedback of the breathing pattern of one of the experimental children. Feedback assistance was gradually faded out to see whether control could be exercised in a more realistic social situation. Breathing control was achieved by both groups and parallel changes occurred on a number of tests requiring attention (in the direction of improved performance). Although Simpson and Nelson claimed that the biofeedback-trained boys did better than the controls, their data do not support this conclusion; rather, it appears that both groups improved to the same extent, suggesting an experimenter attention placebo effect. Furthermore, the control achieved in the laboratory setting did not transfer to the naturalistic situation.

The measurement of hyperactivity poses technical problems, of course. Schulman, Stevens, Suran, Kupst, and Naughton (1978) have described the use of a biomotometer which records the amount of activity being displayed and which can be set to deliver an auditory feedback signal whenever a preset criterion is exceeded. A major advantage of the device is its portability since it can be worn on the waist, with an earpiece. Results have been reported with one hyperactive and one hypoactive child for demonstrational purposes. Appropriate increases and decreases in amount of activity were obtained, but the effects did not persist when the device was disconnected, and feedback was confounded with reinforcement. Nonetheless, the device has interesting possibilities.

Insomnia

The relatively sparse literature on the behavioral treatment of insomnia has recently been critically reviewed by Ribordy and Denney (1977).[16] They are severely critical of the methodological inadequacies of studies which have used hypnotic drugs, systematic desensitization, applied relaxation, attribution-based therapy, and classical conditioning. Thus far, very little work has been carried out specifically within a biofeedback framework. The most important study to date is that by Freedman and Papsdorf (1976), although it dealt with relatively

[16]Their review, however, is inexplicably incomplete, no mention being made, for example, of the important studies by Gershman and Clouser (1974) or Good (1975). See also the earlier review by Montgomery, Perkin, and Wise (1975).

mild cases of insomnia (self-defined as inability to fall asleep within 1 h at least four nights a week for at least 6 months) in 18 normal subjects aged 17–39 years. The subjects were allocated to one of three treatment conditions: training in frontalis muscle activity reduction with auditory feedback, progressive relaxation training, or a combination of exercises and relaxation training. For each group the procedure involved sleeping two nights in the laboratory before and after the training sessions while recordings were made from two EEG channels (occipital and central), one (intraorbital) EOG channel, and the chin. Training consisted of six ½-h sessions over a 2-week period and involved recording the activity of the frontalis, masseter, and forearm muscles, as well as heart rate, while training was in progress. The biofeedback and progressive relaxation training groups showed a significant reduction in sleep onset time in the laboratory compared with the exercise–relaxation group which showed no change. No other sleep-related measures (e.g., time spent in the different stages of sleep as indexed by EEG performance, rapid eye movement behavior) were found which differentiated the treatment groups before or after training. The feedback and relaxation groups also showed significant reductions in heart rate and on all three muscle groups (frontalis, masseter, forearm), whereas the exercise-relaxation group did not. However, when regression toward the mean was allowed for, the changes in muscle tension did not correlate with sleep onset time (that is, muscle tension reduction was a function of starting levels of tension). At a follow-up 2 months later, subjective estimates of sleep onset time did not differentiate the groups. The finding that sleep onset latency is not related to levels of frontalis muscle activity has been reported in other studies (e.g., Good, 1975). In a very similar study, Haynes, Sides, and Lockwood (1977) found frontalis muscle activity reduction training similar in its effect on insomnia to general relaxation training, as indexed by time to fall asleep and number of times awake at night, both techniques producing better results than those obtained with a group simply given instructions to relax but no training in how to do it.

Nicassio and Bootzin (1974) assigned 30 subjects who had difficulty falling asleep to four treatment conditions: autogenic training, progressive relaxation training, self-relaxation control, and no-treatment control. Following a 4-week treatment period, the time to fall asleep was found to be significantly reduced in the groups given autogenic and progressive relaxation training as compared with the other two groups (although the authors relied on self-report of sleep onset latency). No differences were found in relation to other sleep characteristics (number of hours slept, number of nightly awakenings, how the subject felt on awakening, and the rated quality of the sleep). Gershman and Clouser (1974) found relaxation training and systematic desensitization to be equally effective in reducing sleep onset time as compared with no treatment.[17] One other incidental result should be mentioned. In their study of the treatment of chronic anxiety

---

[17]For other nonbiofeedback studies involving relaxation training, see Ribordy and Denney (1977).

with frontalis muscle reduction training, described earlier in this chapter, Raskin, Johnson, and Rondestvedt (1973) reported that five of the six patients who suffered from insomnia showed improved ability to go to sleep without, however, any beneficial effect on the tendency to wake up after being asleep for some time. Woolfolk, Carr-Kaffashan, McNulty, and Lehrer (1976) found meditation and relaxation training to be equally effective in reducing the latency of sleep onset compared with changes in a waiting-list control group, and these differences were maintained at a 6-month follow-up.

In general, it must be concluded that at this point in time biofeedback training has not been very successful in the treatment of insomnia. This may be, of course, in part because the training techniques used may not have been the relevant ones, relying as they have done on the generality principle rather than seeking the specific abnormal pattern of behavior related to insomnia. One such specific pattern of behavior, of course, may be the changes in the electrical activity of the brain which occur during the various stages of presleep and sleep itself.

Learning-Disabled Children

The deliberate application of biofeedback training techniques to the remedial treatment of learning-disabled children has not yet really gotten underway, although the potential of such techniques is probably very great. J.L. Parker, Rosenfeld, and Todd (1973), for example, have described a simple light box on which is placed a tracing of the design (for example, a letter) to be reproduced. The sheet on which the subject is to copy the design is placed over the tracing so that illumination of the box provides both a model (the tracing) of the design and immediate feedback of errors made. By progressively dimming the light, the feedback can gradually be faded out. This device can be used in almost unlimited ways, but one simple example would be the correction of confusion errors (e.g., b and d) in dyslexic children. More recently, J.L. Parker (1975) has developed a photoelectric pen constructed by fitting a small phototransistor into the tip of the plastic casing of an ordinary felt pen. When the subject uses the pen to trace a stimulus (such as a black line on a white background), auditory feedback can be provided to indicate errors (or, alternately, correct performance, with errors indicated by the sound's going off). Parker has reported its successful use in training a severely retarded, autistic child to write his own name and copy shapes. Gracenin and Cook (1977), on the other hand, compared two groups of learning-disabled children on reading ability before and after one group had been trained to increase and maintain alpha with visual and auditory feedback. Although the trained group apparently did succeed in increasing and maintaining alpha while reading, no differential improvement in reading skill between the two groups was found after training was completed. Carter and Synolds (1974) reported that training in relaxation significantly improved the handwriting of a group of boys with minimal brain injury; the improvement transferred to non-laboratory writing situations and was maintained at a 4-month follow-up (the writing samples were rated blind by two independent judges).

A study by Pohl (1977) is of considerable interest, although only indirectly relevant to biofeedback. He attempted to test the theory that stereotyped rocking behavior, often found in autistic and severely retarded children, is under internal, neurological control and is produced involuntarily. Three severely retarded children were individually studied when placed in a cubicle while an attempt was made to produce synchronization of the rocking with a flashing light via reinforcement so that if such control could be established, the flash rate could be slowed down to see whether the rocking behavior slowed down in tandem. The results were variable: one child's rocking behavior became perfectly synchronized with the flashing light at all rates, the behavior of a second child did not change at all, and a third child demonstrated a peculiar and special form of behavior. Of course, if this kind of behavior is produced by defects in or injury to the central nervous system, the prospects of using biofeedback training to alleviate the problem are fairly remote. That this is so is indicated by a study by Schroeder, Peterson, Solomon, and Artley (1977). They tried to discover whether the effects of restraint for self-injurious behavior in two severely retarded children could be increased by the provision of feedback of trapezius muscle activity and verbal reinforcement (the aim being, of course, to abandon the use of restraint if successful relaxation training itself reduced the incidence of self-injurious behavior). The major finding of this study was that little self-injurious behavior occurred when the subject was deeply relaxed but it proved difficult to establish a consistent relationship between level of trapezius muscle activity and likelihood of an instance of self-injurious behavior. In spite of the relatively disappointing results obtained so far with the application of biofeedback training to the intellectually handicapped, it seems that this may well prove to be a growth area over the next few years.

Obsessive-Compulsive Behavior

Little work has been reported in this area as yet. Boulougouris, Rabavilas, and Stefanis (1977) have produced evidence suggesting that heart rate is significantly elevated in obsessives when they imagine their obsessive fantasies or have them described by the therapist as compared with when they engage in neutral fantasies. Delk (1977) treated a young female with moderate to severe depression associated with an obsessive concern for the welfare of animals by using frontalis muscle activity relaxation training to reduce anxiety associated with visualizing items in a hierarchy relating to the ill-treatment of animals. The depressive thoughts were apparently reduced by the treatment and were absent at a 6-month follow-up. Mills and Solyom (1974) argued that obsessive thoughts might be interrupted or even reduced by the enhancement of alpha, and reported some confirmation of this in a study of five obsessive patients without, however, any carryover into the real-life situation.

Pain

It is a curious fact that the literature on biofeedback contains almost no empirical studies relating to chronic pain even though the promotional literature on biofeedback invariably refers to its usefulness in this area, often with special reference to low back pain. Pain, of course, is an ill-defined concept which is used in relation to many disorders with which we have already dealt (such as migraine and tension headaches)[18] but is more commonly, and perhaps more appropriately, thought of in reference to conditions involving intractable pain such as cancer and neuralgia. Given the lack of empirical studies dealing with the application of biofeedback techniques to the alleviation of pain, there is no point in providing a detailed account of the conflicting theories of the origin and maintenance of pain in relation to the very large individual differences which undoubtedly exist in the way in which pain is perceived and reacted to.[19] The recent study by Melzack and Perry (1975), however, represents an important first step in the direction of developing biofeedback techniques for the treatment of disorders involving pain. They point out the important role that expectations and suggestion play in the subjective reaction to pain. The control of pain (in the sense of reducing its subjectively reported intensity) may to some degree at least be increased if the subject can be trained to engage in activities which direct attention away from the pain, and this may be achieved in many different ways, including distraction of attention from a painful body site, the use of strong suggestion (provided the subject is sufficiently suggestible), training in relaxation to reduce the high state of arousal which pain often induces, and the induction of a belief that the pain can be brought under self-control. Melzack and Perry (1975) considered that successful training in alpha enhancement, carried out in an atmosphere of strong positive expectation of beneficial effects, might be of considerable assistance in producing a reduction in the level of self-reported pain. They collected a diverse group of 24 patients, all of whom were experiencing chronic pain which had proved refractory to numerous forms of medical treatment: back pain (10 patients), peripheral nerve injury (4), cancer pain (3), arthritis (2), phantom limb and stump pain (2), posttraumatic pain (2), and head pain (1). These patients were assigned at random to one of three training conditions: alpha-enhancement training combined with hypnotic training, alpha training alone, or hypnotic training alone. In all three groups, however, strong expectations were induced in the patients that the treatment would be successful. The "hypnotic" training essentially consisted of training in relaxation techniques

---

[18]For a comprehensive review of the large number of syndromes associated with muscle pain, see Simons (1975, 1976).

[19]The interested reader may be referred to a recent review by Weisenburg (1977).

as well as general coping behaviors in stressful situations.[20] The alpha-enhance-ment training involved the use of pleasant music which was present when alpha was "on." Baseline, training, and practice (no feedback) sessions were given, the total duration covering several hours of training over a number of sessions. The quality and intensity of pain were assessed by means of the McGill Pain Questionnaire[21] given before, during, and after training. All three groups were found to increase percentage alpha enhancement to the same extent, but only the group given both alpha training and hypnotic training showed a significant de-crease in pain as assessed by the questionnaire, an effect which persisted for several hours after the end of a training session. About half of the patients were found to be still using the techniques they had been taught with some success 4–6 months later. Melzack and Perry (1975) concluded that alpha-enhancement training alone was not sufficient to reduce the intensity of subjective pain unless it was combined with "hypnotic" training which emphasized "ego-strengthen-ing" and "progressive relaxation" techniques as well as the addition of distrac-tion and the reduction of anxiety consequent to the anticipation of pain relief. This study, of course, can be regarded only as a demonstration of the possibilities of biofeedback and related techniques since it did not begin to identify the relative contribution of the many variables which were incorporated into the experiment in a confounded way. Gannon and Sternbach (1971) successfully trained a patient with incapacitating headaches (apparently the result of several head injuries sustained over a short period of time) to increase percentage alpha with feedback. There was some evidence that the patient, following training, was occasionally able to prevent the onset of pain (in situations where it was likely to occur) by inducing a high alpha state, although he was not able to abolish the pain once it had begun.

Several recent studies have appeared which indicate the upsurge of interest in low back pain. Of course, a perennial problem relates to distinguishing psychological pain experience from pain which results directly from organic injury, although the two are not uncommonly found together. Ransford, Cairns, and Mooney (1976) have suggested using drawings of pain locations accom-panied by verbal descriptions of the pain characteristics as an aid in determining whether the pain has a clear organic basis or not. Cairns and Pasino (1977) have compared two methods of treating low back pain resulting in lack of mobility and hospitalization. Baseline rates of walking and bike riding were first assessed. Then one group of patients was verbally reinforced for these activities while a second group was initially given informational feedback only about the amount of walking and bike riding they had done, followed by various combinations of reinforcement and informational feedback. A control group was given neither informational feedback nor reinforcement. It was found that verbal reinforcement

[20]It is not made absolutely clear whether formal hypnotic induction procedures were carried out, but it may be assumed that they were.
[21]See Table 2 in Melzack and Perry (1975).

increased the amount of exercising and that informational feedback did not add to this effect, which was not sustained when reinforcement was withdrawn. This was a small-scale study (involving only nine patients), but Cairns, Thomas, Mooney, and Pace (1976) had earlier reported the results of a two-phase treatment program (initially drugs and recreational therapy, followed by the reinforcement program if the pain persisted) carried out on 175 patients. All of these patients were severely disabled by their pain. Of the 90 whose responses to a follow-up questionnaire over an average follow-up of 10 months were analyzed, it was found that 70% reported a reduction in pain level and/or increased activity.

Hendler, Derogatis, Avella, and Long (1977) trained a group of patients with low back and leg pain, or neck, shoulder, and arm pain, in frontalis muscle activity reduction with auditory and visual feedback. Negative expectations were induced as far as possible regarding outcome. About half of the patients reported a reduction in pain following the training but apparently frontalis muscle activity reduction was not in fact achieved. It is probable that negative expectations were not induced successfully and that the reduction in pain was a placebo effect. The importance of expectations (and cognitive factors in general) have, of course, been particularly stressed in pain research and are under investigation (e.g., Scott & Barber, 1977a,b). An equally interesting approach recently utilized by Pelletier and Peper (1977) involves the observation of skilled meditators inflicting "painful" stimuli (such as piercing the cheeks with a bicycle spoke) without apparently experiencing pain while simultaneous measurements are made of the electrical activity of the brain, muscle activity, heart rate, and so on. So far, the results have not been very clear-cut.

Phobias

As will be seen in Chapter 7, phobic conditions (both monosymptomatic and polysymptomatic) potentially represent a crucial testing ground for the relative validity of the generality and specificity assumptions which underly most approaches to biofeedback training (although this fact does not appear to have been generally appreciated, given the almost total neglect of the application of biofeedback techniques to the treatment of phobias). Here, therefore, only a brief account will be given of the sparse literature on the biofeedback treatment of the phobias. Nunes and Marks (1976) treated ten females with animal phobias by systematic desensitization involving graded exposure to the real objects of fear, with the experimenter modeling appropriate nonfearful responses. Each treatment session was divided into four 30-min periods, in two of which the patient was provided with visual feedback of her heart rate, a target line, and instructions to try to reduce the visual display magnitude to the target line while the phobic object was gradually brought closer.[22] In the other two periods, the target line was visible but feedback was not provided. The patients rated the strength of

[22]Four patients were additionally given auditory feedback.

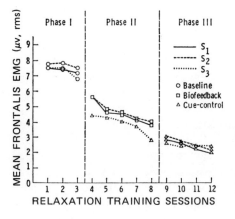

Figure 11. Mean level of frontalis EMG, in μV rms, for 20-min blocks. Phase I, baseline for all Ss; phase II, biofeedback-assisted relaxation for S_1 and S_2 (cue-controlled relaxation for S_3; phase III, cue-controlled relaxation for all Ss. (From Reeves, J. L., & Mealiea, W.L. Biofeedback-assisted, cue-controlled relaxation for the treatment of flight phobias. *Journal of Behavior Therapy and Experimental Psychiatry*, 1975, *6*, 107, Figure 1. Reprinted by permission of the author and the publisher.)

their tendency to avoid the phobic object before and after treatment on a 9-point scale, and within each session rated their degree of subjective anxiety every 10 min on a scale of 0–100. Heart rate was found to drop during feedback trials and increase when feedback was absent, while subjective anxiety declined steadily over feedback and no-feedback trials throughout the training. As the authors admit, this was a heavily confounded study and no data were provided as to whether the patients were better able to tolerate the animals they feared in real life after the training. Also heavily confounded was a study by Reeves and Mealiea (1975). They successfully treated three persons with extreme fear of flying, using biofeedback-assisted cue-controlled relaxation training combined with systematic desensitization. After three sessions in which frontalis muscle activity baselines were recorded, auditory feedback was provided for five sessions while two of the subjects attempted to reduce frontalis muscle activity. During this period, hierarchy construction was carried out. Then what the authors term "cue-controlled relaxation training" was carried out for three sessions (the third subject had been given this training also in the previous sessions). This training involved the subjects' covertly verbalizing the word *relax* and immediately thereafter relaxing the frontalis muscle as quickly as possible while exhaling. Deep inhalation followed and the procedure was repeated 20 times. In the final two training sessions, cue-controlled relaxation training was continued, the only difference being that the feedback tone was gradually faded out. The effects of the training on frontalis muscle levels of activity are shown in Figure 11. All three subjects showed a significant reduction in frontalis muscle activity. Systematic desensitization was carried out apparently after this training was completed.[23] However, instead of an anxiety scene being terminated whenever the subject experienced anxiety, he was instructed to use the cue ("relax") to reduce the experienced anxiety. This training was succeeded by graded real-life

---

[23]The text is not entirely clear on this point.

training (going to the airport initially, and finally, actually flying). In all three subjects, successful flights were made and at a 1-year follow-up all three were still able to fly.

In a study that was not intended to assess therapeutic effects, Shephard and Watts (1974) found that patients with monosymptomatic phobias were more successful in reducing heart rate with feedback than were patients with polysymptomatic phobias, although the decreases (significant for both groups) were small. Gatchell (1977) treated a patient with claustrophobia associated with elevated heart rate. Successful training in heart-rate reduction was achieved in a small enclosed subject cubicle and the patient reported a reduction in the anxiety produced by the enclosed space. The improvement was maintained at a 6-month follow-up. There was, of course, no control for the effects of "flooding" in this case—that is, the heart-rate reduction might have resulted from the continued exposure to the anxiety situation rather than the training in heart-rate control. Wickramasekera (1974) trained a 55-year-old male with an extreme fear of heart attacks (for which no organic basis could be found; he had experienced shortness of breath and palpitations which he interpreted as indicative of heart malfunction) to raise and lower his heart rate with visual (digital) feedback (no training in relaxation was given). Following initial success in raising and lowering heart rate, the patient was trained to monitor and tolerate increases in heart rate which occurred while he was under stresses such as imagining stressful situations or listening to the therapist talking about aspects of his fears. The patient was in this manner able to observe that increases in heart rate were not followed by fainting (which was his greatest fear). At a follow-up 12 months later, the patient reported that he was engaging in his normal range of activities and no longer experienced his former anxieties.

As pointed out earlier, all of these studies are confounded and it is impossible to extract the contribution of the biofeedback training to the beneficial results. Thus far, properly controlled studies of the role of biofeedback training in the alleviation of phobias have not been carried out. For reasons which will become apparent in the next chapter, such studies are urgently needed.

Psychopathic Behavior

One of the major characteristics of the psychopath is said to be lack of self-control. The possibility that biofeedback might be used to help train psychopaths in self-control is intriguing but has attracted little attention as yet. Steinberg and Schwartz (1976) measured the skin resistance level in the resting state of 10 primary psychopaths and 12 normal controls and then determined the extent to which they could increase and decrease skin resistance, with and without feedback. No difference in resting level between the two groups was found. However, the normal subjects were better able to increase the spontaneous number of responses when instructed to try to do so without the aid of feedback (although neither group was able to reduce responding under these circumstances). When feedback was introduced, the results in both groups were similar to those discussed in Chapter 4 and a pronounced drift effect was apparent. In subsequent transfer, no-feedback trials, both groups showed successful control in both directions. Further research is obviously warranted.

Sensory Loss

Apart from the work on sensory substitution systems for the blind and the deaf, reviewed earlier, virtually no studies of the provision of sensory substitution systems in other cases of sensory loss have been reported and the category is included here mainly to draw attention to its importance as an area of investigation. Bach-y-Rita (1973) has described a sensory substitution system intended for use with leprosy patients who have lost hand sensations as a result of their disease. A specially constructed glove has strain gauges built into each finger to record touch and pressure while thermistors also built in record temperature. The data generated by the sensors may be conveyed to other areas of the hand which remain sensitive to touch, pressure, and temperature by the use of electrodes taped to the hand. In this way, injuries (for example, burns) to the insensitive fingers may be avoided. No data were reported by Bach-y-Rita but the technique is obviously applicable to other areas of sensory loss, including congenital insensitivity to pain.

Sexual Problems

In no other area of human behavior has such a dramatic change taken place in the last 10 years in the approach to therapy by professionals as that of sexual behavior. The reference here is not so much to the striking increase in community tolerance of various forms of sexual behavior which 10 years ago were still widely regarded as abnormal and in need of treatment as to the concomitant (and sometimes slower) changes in the conceptualization of the problems involved in these forms of sexual behavior by therapeutically oriented professional workers. Thus, whereas 10 years ago (Yates, 1970) it was possible for the present writer to include a significant section in his book on the behavioral treatment of homosexuality, the inclusion of such a chapter in a book written now would be inconceivable. In brief, in relation to homosexuality, for example, the position now taken would have to be one in which difficulties relating to homosexual behavior are treated in exactly the same manner as difficulties relating to heterosexual behavior (or more broadly still, the emphasis might well be on the modification of societal attitudes toward homosexuality in much the same way the behavior therapist might be interested in modifying societal attitudes toward prostitution, rather than regarding prostitution as a disorder of behavior requiring change in the direction of "normal" behavior). In other words, the battle fought by homosexuals for the recognition of homosexual behavior as a variant of the vast range of sexual behaviors already accepted as normal appears to have been well and truly won. This is not, of course, to deny that some individuals may require individual therapy in relation to their sexual behavior, even in respect of developing heterosexual skills which might complement or replace their homosexual skills (the corollary of this, of course, is the heterosexual who might request assistance in developing homosexual skills—a possibility which has sparked off a lively debate among behavior therapists). These developments have yet to be fully assimilated in the biofeedback and behavior modification literature, and in this section, therefore, only a brief account will be given of the work so far carried out which seems relevant to the potential use of biofeedback in assisting individuals with sexual problems of whatever nature to cope with them.

Although sexual competence clearly involves more than the ability to obtain a sustainable erection followed by eventual ejaculation in males, and vaginal engorgement followed by an orgasm in females, the obvious most direct role that biofeedback training could play in the area of sexual competence would be in relation to the increased mastery of these skills. Thus, the development of appropriate measuring devices to assess such behaviors is essential. In the area of male sexual behavior, this specific problem has been satisfactorily solved by the development of various methods of penile plethysmography. The literature has been adequately reviewed quite recently by Rosen (1976), who distinguishes four main measurement techniques: the use of electromechanical strain gauges or mercury-in-rubber resistance gauges (both of which measure changes in penile circumference); the use of volumetric plethysmographs which, of course, measure changes in penile volume; and, less commonly, the use of temperature probes to assess changes in penile skin temperature during erection. While male sexual arousal may be readily indexed by changes in penile volume, circumference, and temperature, the measurement of analogous physiological changes in females has proved considerably more difficult. Zuckerman (1971) reviewed comprehensively all aspects of the measurement of physiological indices of sexual arousal in both males and females and concluded that precise physiological correlates of sexual arousal in the female had not been consistently achieved nor distinguished from changes occurring as a function of general, not necessarily specifically sexual, arousal. A significant advance, however, appears to have occurred with the development by Sintchak and Geer (1975) of a light reflectance plethysmograph consisting of an acrylic probe containing an incandescent light source which can be inserted into the vagina, the intent being to measure the blood flow and volume changes in vaginal tissues during sexual arousal. Geer, Morokoff, and Greenwood (1974) attempted to validate the technique by measuring vaginal tissue pulse pressure (reflecting the distensibility of the vascular bed in response to changes in blood pressure) and blood volume (reflecting the congestion caused by the pooling of blood in the vaginal tissues) in a group of normal females as they viewed an erotic and a nonerotic film. Significant and parallel changes in both pulse pressure and blood volume occurred in all of the subjects as they viewed the erotic film whereas no such changes occurred as they viewed tne nonerotic film. Although these changes did not correlate with subjective estimates of arousal or estimates of how sexually arousing the erotic film was, the technique appeared to have a reasonable degree of validity. This study, however, lacked important controls (particularly an estimate of the effects of arousing but nonerotic material) and a study by Hoon, Wincze, and Hoon (1976) attempted to remedy this deficiency. Using vaginal plethysmography and measuring six other physiological variables as well (skin conductance, systolic and diastolic blood pressure, heart rate, forehead temperature, and finger pulse amplitude) they presented neutral, sexually arousing, and generally arousing films to six normal females (the generally arousing or dysphoric film consisted of very unpleasant war atrocities). They were able to confirm that differential vasodilation of vaginal blood vessels did occur during the erotic film while blood pressure and forehead temperature also showed significant changes indicative of heightened sexual arousal. Thus, vaginal plethysmography appears to provide the equivalent measure to penile plethysmography in males as an indicator of degree of sexual arousal in females. Recent studies have provided strong supporting evidence for this conclusion. Sexual arousal in women is accompanied by temperature changes in the labia minora (Henson, Rubin, Henson, & Williams, 1977) and these changes correlate significantly with those recorded using vaginal plethysmography (Henson & Rubin, 1978; Henson, Rubin, & Henson, 1978). The relevance of other autonomic indices of sexual arousal (such as blood pressure) has also been confirmed (Wenger, Averill, & Smith, 1968), although it seems generally agreed that skin conductance is not a reliable indicator of degree of sexual arousal.

Whether penile tumescence can be brought under voluntary control has been the subject of several investigations. Laws and Rubin (1969) found that four male subjects (who all obtained full erections to an erotic film in a baseline condition) were all able to inhibit the erection (reducing it by at least 50%) in the presence of the film when instructed to do so, and were able to repeat the pattern of behavior required (alternately allowing and inhibiting an erection) on repeated occasions. They were also able to induce voluntary partial erection in the absence of the erotic film, although its characteristics differed somewhat from the erection obtained when the film was shown (manifested by longer latencies, lower peak levels, and greater variability). In a subsequent study, Henson and Rubin (1971) controlled for the possibility that the inhibition of the erection in the presence of the erotic film occurred because the subject directed his attention away from the film when requested to inhibit. This was accompanied by intermittently superimposing a brief light flash on the film and requiring the subject to detect its occurrence and respond by depressing a button. A further control of attention was achieved by requiring the subject, on some trials, to describe the film while inhibiting erection. The light signals were detected on 87% of the occasions on which they occurred and descriptions of the film were accurate so that adequate control of attention was, in fact, achieved. The results are shown in Figure 12. All of the subjects obtained full erection when instructed not to inhibit, whereas successful inhibition was obtained when required to respond to the light or give a verbal description of the film while inhibiting. While all of the subjects reported that they tried to inhibit erection by engaging in intellectual activity, the fact that inhibition was successfully achieved while describing the film indicates that self-generation of competing nonsexual cognitive activity is not essential to the successful inhibition of erection. Rubin and Henson (1975) have since shown that the degree of erection induced by viewing an erotic film may be enhanced by the use of fantasy or reduced by the use of relaxation techniques.

Rosen (1973) also showed that voluntary control of tumescence could be obtained with feedback. After measuring the baseline level of penile diameter recorded during a 3-min period spent listening to quiet music, he allocated 40 normal male subjects to four matched groups. One group was instructed to suppress erection (induced by listening to erotic stories told by a female) by keeping off a red light which came on whenever tumescence exceeded the baseline level by more than 0.5 mm (contingent feedback). A second group was given noncontingent feedback (actually the feedback given to a yoked subject from the first group). A third group was simply instructed to suppress tumescence while listening to the stories, while the fourth group simply listened to the stories, being given neither instructions nor feedback. Rosen (1973) found that successful inhibition of tumescence in the presence of erotic material was achieved only by the group given relevant (contingent) feedback. Thus, he did not find successful inhibition in those subjects who were merely instructed to suppress tumescence, his results in this respect conflicting with those obtained by Rubin and his colleagues. Rosen, Shapiro, and Schwartz (1975) investigated whether voluntary control of tumescence could be obtained in the absence of erotic material if appropriate feedback of penile diameter changes was provided. Subjects in the experimental and control groups were instructed to produce maximal erection. For the experimental group, a shaping procedure was used, involving visual feedback in the form of an orange light which changed in intensity in proportion to changes in penile diameter. The control group received noncontingent visual feedback. A reward was earned by the experimental group subjects if the criterion set for each trial was earned. The results are shown in Figure 13 and indicate quite clearly that over two sessions of training the combination of feedback and reward led to greater voluntary control over tumescence as compared with the absence of feedback and reward (these two variables were, of course, confounded in this study). However, the control group did show some degree of voluntary control.

It appears, therefore, to have been demonstrated reasonably clearly that voluntary control of tumescence is possible in males, whether erotic material is present or not. Similar demonstrations have now appeared indicating that voluntary control of the vaginal vasomotor response is possible. Hoon, Wincze, and

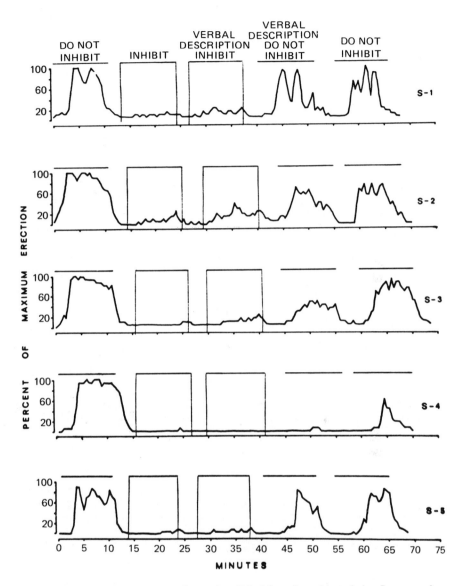

Figure 12. Percent of maximum penile erection elicited from five subjects during five successive presentations of an erotic film. The horizontal lines above each graph indicate those periods of time that the film was projected. Subjects were instructed to inhibit during presentations enclosed by dotted lines, and not to inhibit during all other presentations. Subjects were required to give a continuous account of the behavioral content of the film during those presentations labeled verbal description, and were required to make a detection response to the appearance of signal lights on the projection screen during all other presentations. (From Henson, D.E., & Rubin, H.B. Voluntary control of eroticism. *Journal of Applied Behavior Analysis*, 1971, *4*, 42, Figure 1. Copyright 1971 by the Society for the Experimental Analysis of Behavior, Inc. Reprinted by permission of the author and the publisher.)

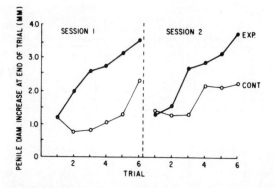

Figure 13. Mean penile diameter increase over six trials in the two experimental sessions. The 12 subjects receiving feedback and reward are indicated by the solid circles, and the controls by the open circles. (From Rosen, R.C., Shapiro, D., & Schwartz, G.E. Voluntary control of penile tumescence. *Psychosomatic Medicine,* 1975, *37,* 479–483, Figure 1. Reprinted by permission of the publisher.)

Hoon (1977) measured changes in vaginal blood volume (as well as taking other physiological measures) in two normal female volunteers under various conditions. First, substantial baseline readings were taken. Then feedback (not identified as vaginal blood volume) was presented (with no instructions to control the response) followed by instructions to the subjects to develop erotic fantasies (no feedback was presented during this condition). Finally, each subject was asked to develop erotic fantasies while feedback of vaginal blood volume was given and the subject was now fully informed that the task was to change the display which consisted of a vertical line on a TV monitor which moved to the right or left according to whether blood volume was increasing or decreasing. In both subjects the combination of fantasy, feedback, and instructions produced significant changes in vaginal blood volume in the required direction whereas feedback alone did not. In one subject, fantasy alone produced blood volume changes. No significant changes occurred in the other autonomic functions (systolic and diastolic blood pressure, finger pulse blood amplitude, heart rate, and skin conductance), indicating a high degree of specificity of control. Positive results were also obtained by Zingheim and Sandman (1978). They obtained measures of vaginal pulse amplitude and blood volume and found that control of the former, but not the latter, was obtained over five sessions of training with ten normal females. They also reported specificity of control. In neither of these studies was a learning curve apparent. The subjects of the experiment by Zingheim and Sandman (1978) were not instructed to use erotic fantasies but, of course, they may have done so.

It is not intended to review here those earlier "therapeutic" studies which have attempted to change the behavior of homosexuals in the direction of heterosexual behavior, even though some of them used biofeedback techniques.[24] Such studies were carried out, as has already been indicated, at a time when attitudes toward homosexuality were quite different to what they are at present. Furthermore, in at least some instances the therapy was presented as virtually a compulsory alternative to punishment in the form of legal punishment, the unfortunate person having already been convicted of the "crime" of homosexual behavior. Thus, the ethical status of many of these studies must be called seriously into question. Two recent studies, both carried out within an explicitly biofeedback framework, are, however, of considerable interest. Csillag (1976) attempted to modify erectile impotence in six males, one of whom engaged in both heterosexual and homosexual behavior. The patients were trained to fantasize a sexually arousing situation while relaxing without feedback, and to do the same while provided with visual (meter) and auditory feedback which indicated changes in penile diameter. They were also shown erotic pictures while relaxing without feedback, and instructed to try to achieve an erection while viewing the erotic slides and being given feedback. Six normal controls were also subjected to these procedures. The normal subjects showed initial penile responsiveness in the various situations but habituated rather rapidly. The patients, on the other hand, showed little initial penile reaction but improved steadily in their ability to initiate and maintain an erection as training proceeded. Three of the patients eventually were able to indulge in satisfactory sexual intercourse although one remained unable to ejaculate; one improved considerably but impotence was still easily induced by stressful situations; while the bisexual patient reported improvement in his homosexual performance but had not experienced heterosexual activity at the time of follow-up. One patient appeared to show no improvement at all. A rather similar attempt to overcome impotence in a 51-year-old male was reported by Herman and Prewett (1974). This patient was primarily homosexually oriented but was unable to maintain an erection even during masturbation. Slides of males and females, selected as attractive by the patient, were presented for 2-min periods while he imagined himself in a sexually arousing situation. Feedback was provided by a bank of ten lights with one light being added to those lit up each time penile diameter increased by 1 mm (which was subsequently determined to represent 4% of a full erection). A large number of training sessions was given (33 in all) involving a sequence of baseline, contingent feedback, noncontingent feedback, and more contingent feedback trials. Contingent feedback increased penile responsiveness to both the male and female slides while noncontingent feedback decreased penile responsiveness. The therapy was not successful in alleviating the patient's real-life difficulties, however, and he was readmitted to the hospital 7 months later following excessive drinking and sexual failure, at which point his penile responding in the presence of erotic stimuli was again very low.

As Herman and Prewett (1974) point out, biofeedback will probably have

---

[24]For a recent review, see Adams and Sturgis (1977).

only a limited and ancillary role to play in the treatment of sexual dysfunction as the sexually inadequate person almost always shows severe deficiencies in social skills in general.[25] Nevertheless, the work carried out so far with both normal and abnormal subjects suggests that the role is potentially an important one. There seems little doubt that a whole range of therapeutic studies using biofeedback will be carried out over the next few years.

So far, little work has been reported relating to the use of biofeedback training in the area of sexual offences. Keltner (1977) attempted to train a pedophiliac to inhibit penile tumescence in the presence of sexually arousing slides depicting pedophiliac activity. Penile arousal was reduced to zero in the presence of slides of both boys and girls and this result was maintained at a 4-month follow-up. Keltner reported a general improvement in the offender but no evidence relating to sexual offence rate is provided. Rather similar results were obtained with a second offender whose treatment was prematurely ended when he was chemically castrated.

References

Adams, H. E., & Sturgis, E. T. Status of behavioral reorientation techniques in the modification of homosexuality: A review. *Psychological Bulletin*, 1977, *84*, 1171–1188.

Alexander, A. B. Systematic relaxation and flow rates in asthmatic children: Relationship to emotional precipitants and anxiety. *Journal of Psychosomatic Research*, 1972, *16*, 405–410.

Alexander, A. B., Miklich, D. R., & Hershkoff, H. The immediate effects of systematic relaxation training on peak expiratory flow rates in asthmatic children. *Psychosomatic Medicine*, 1972, *34*, 388–394.

Ayer, W. A., & Levin, M. P. Elimination of tooth grinding habits by massed practice therapy. *Journal of Periodontology*, 1973, *44*, 569–571.

Bach-y-Rita, P. Sensory substitution: Neural mechanisms underlying prosthetic applications. In W. S. Fields & L. A. Leavitt (Eds.), *Neural organization and its relevance to prosthetics*. New York: Intercontinental Medical Book Corporation, 1973, pp. 149–164.

Bailey, M. B., & Stewart, J. Normal drinking by persons reporting previous problem drinking. *Quarterly Journal of Studies on Alcohol*, 1967, *28*, 305–315.

Beiman, I., Israel, E., & Johnson, S. A. During training and posttraining effects of live and taped extended progressive relaxation, self-relaxation, and electromyogram biofeedback. *Journal of Consulting and Clinical Psychology*, 1978, *46*, 314–321.

Benson, H. Decreased alcohol intake associated with the practice of meditation: A retrospective investigation. *Annals New York Academy of Sciences*, 1974, *233*, 174–177.

Bentsen, N., Larsen, B., & Lassen, N. A. Chronically impaired autoregulation of cerebral blood flow in long-term diabetics. *Stroke*, 1975, *6*, 497–502.

Blanchard, E. B., & Abel, G. G. An experimental case study of the biofeedback treatment of a rape-induced psychophysiological cardiovascular disorder. *Behavior Therapy*, 1976, *7*, 113–119.

Blankstein, K. R. Heart rate control, general anxiety, and subjective tenseness. *Behavior Therapy*, 1975, *6*, 699–700.

[25]For recent reviews of behavioral approaches to the treatment of sexual dysfunctions, see Reynolds (1977; males) and Sotile and Kilmann (1977; females).

Block, J. D., Lagerson, J., Zohman, L. R., & Kelly, G. A feedback device for teaching diaphragmatic breathing. *American Review of Respiratory Disease*, 1969, *100*, 577–578.

Bois, C., & Vogel-Sprott, M. Discrimination of low blood alcohol levels and self-titration skills in social drinkers. *Quarterly Journal of Studies on Alcohol*, 1974, *35*, 86–97.

Boothroyd, A., Nickerson, R. S., & Stevens, K. N. Temporal patterns in the speech of the deaf—an experiment in remedial training (SARP #15). Northampton, Mass.: Research Department, Clarke School for the Deaf, 1974.

Boothroyd, A., Archambault, P., Adams, R. E., & Storm, R. D. Use of a computer-based system of speech training aids for deaf persons. *Volta Review*, 1975, *77*, 178–193.

Borrild, K. Experience with the design and use of technical aids for the training of the deaf and hard of hearing children. *American Annals of the Deaf*, 1968, *113*, 168–177.

Boulougouris, J. C., Rabavilas, A. D., & Stefanis, C. Psychophysiological responses in obsessive-compulsive patients. *Behavior Research and Therapy*, 1977, *15*, 221–230.

Braud, L. W. The effects of frontal EMG biofeedback and progressive relaxation upon hyperactivity and its behavioral concomitants. *Biofeedback and Self-Regulation*, 1978, *3*, 69–89.

Braud, L. W., Lupin, M. N., & Braud, W. G. The use of electromyographic biofeedback in the control of hyperactivity. *Journal of Learning Disabilities*, 1975, *8*, 420–425.

Brody, D. M., Nelson, B. A., & Brody, J. F. The use of visual feedback in establishing normal vocal intensity in two mildly retarded adults. *Journal of Speech and Hearing Disorders*, 1975, *40*, 502–507.

Butler, J. H., Abbott, D. M., & Bush, F. M. Biofeedback as a method of controlling bruxism. *Journal of Dental Research*, 1976, *55*, B310. (Abstract)

Caddy, G. R., & Lovibond, S. H. Self-regulation and discriminated aversive conditioning in the modification of alcoholics' drinking behavior. *Behavior Therapy*, 1976, *7*, 223–230.

Cairns, D., & Pasino, J. A. Comparison of verbal reinforcement and feedback in the operant treatment of disability due to chronic low back pain. *Behavior Therapy*, 1977, *8*, 621–630.

Cairns, D., Thomas, L., Mooney, V., & Pace, J. B. A comprehensive treatment approach to chronic low back pain. *Pain*, 1976, *2*, 301–308.

Callner, D. A. Behavioral treatment approaches to drug abuse: A critical review of the research. *Psychological Bulletin*, 1975, *82*, 143–164.

Canter, A., Kondo, C. Y., & Knott, J. R. A comparison of EMG feedback and progressive muscle relaxation training in anxiety neurosis. *British Journal of Psychiatry*, 1975, *127*, 470–477. (1976/77:44)

Carter, J. L., & Synolds, D. Effects of relaxation training upon handwriting quality. *Journal of Learning Disabilities*, 1974, *7*, 236–238.

Corson, J. A., Bouchard, C., Scherer, M. W., Amit, Z., Hisey, L. G., Cleghorn, R. A., & Golden, M. Instrumental control of autonomic responses with the use of a cognitive strategy. *Canadian Psychiatric Association Journal*, 1973, *18*, 21–24.

Cox, R. J., & McGuinness, D. The effect of chronic anxiety level upon self control of heart rate. *Biological Psychology*, 1977, *5*, 7–14.

Csillag, E. R. Modification of penile erectile response. *Journal of Behavior Therapy and Experimental Psychiatry*, 1976, *7*, 27–29. (1976/77:47)

Cutter, H. S. G., Schwaab, E. L., & Nathan, P. E. Effects of alcohol on its utility for alcoholics and nonalcoholics. *Quarterly Journal of Studies on Alcohol*, 1970, *31*, 369–378.

Danker, P. S., Miklich, D. R., Pratt, C., & Creer, T. L. An unsuccessful attempt to instrumentally condition peak expiratory flow rates in asthmatic children. *Journal of Psychosomatic Research*, 1975, *19*, 209–213.

Davies, D. L. Normal drinking in recovered alcoholic addicts. *Quarterly Journal of Studies on Alcohol*, 1962, *23*, 94–104.

Davies, D. L. Normal drinking in recovered alcoholic addicts (comments by various correspondents). *Quarterly Journal of Studies on Alcohol*, 1963, *24*, 109–121, 321–332.

Davis, M. H., Saunders, D. R., Creer, T. L., & Chai, H. Relaxation training facilitated by biofeedback apparatus as a supplemental treatment in bronchial asthma. *Journal of Psychosomatic Research*, 1973, *17*, 121–128. (1974:52)

Dekker, E., & Groen, J. Reproducible psychogenic attacks of asthma: A laboratory study. *Journal of Psychosomatic Research*, 1956, *1*, 58–67.

Dekker, E., Pelser, H. E., & Groen, J. Conditioning as a cause of asthmatic attacks. *Journal of Psychosomatic Research*, 1957, *2*, 97–108.

Delk, J. L. Use of EMG biofeedback in behavioral treatment of an obsessive–phobic–depressive syndrome. *Diseases of the Nervous System*, 1977, *38*, 938–939.

De Ricco, D. A., & Garlington, W. K. An operant treatment procedure for alcoholics. *Behavior Research and Therapy*, 1977, *15*, 497–499.

De Vries, H. A., & Adams, G. M. Electromyographic comparison of single doses of exercise and meprobamate as to effects on muscular relaxation. *American Journal of Physical Medicine*, 1972, *51*, 130–141.

De Vries, H. A., Burke, R. K., Hopper, R. T., & Sloan, J. H. Efficacy of EMG biofeedback in relaxation training. *American Journal of Physical Medicine*, 1977, *56*, 75–81.

Dowdell, L. R., Clarke, N. G., & Kardachi, B. J. Biofeedback: Control of masticatory muscle spasm. *Medical and Biological Engineering*, 1976, *14*, 295–298.

Ewing, J. A., & Rouse, B. A. Failure of an experimental treatment program to inculcate controlled drinking in alcoholics. *British Journal of Addiction*, 1976, *71*, 123–134.

Feldman, G. M. The effect of biofeedback training on respiratory resistance of asthmatic children. *Psychosomatic Medicine*, 1976, *38*, 27–34. (1976/77:48)

Fish, R. M. Visual substitution systems: Control and information processing considerations. *New Outlook*, 1975, *69*, 300–304.

Fish, R. M. An audio display for the blind. *IEEE Transactions on Biomedical Engineering*, 1976, *BME-23*, 144–154.

Fish, R. M., & Fish, R. C. An electronically generated audio display for the blind. *New Outlook*, 1976, *70*, 295–298.

Fourcin, A. J. Laryngographic examination of vocal fold vibration. In B. Wyke (Ed.), *Ventilatory and phonatory control systems*. London: Oxford University Press, 1974, Chapter 19, pp. 315–326.

Fourcin, A. J., & Abberton, E. First applications of a new laryngograph. *Medical and Biological Illustration*, 1971, *21*, 172–182.

Fourcin, A. J., & Abberton, E. The laryngograph and the voiscope in speech therapy. In E. Loebell (Ed.), *XVIth international congress of logopedics and phoniatrics*. Basel: S. Karger, 1976, pp. 116–122.

Fowler, J. E., Budzynski, T. H., & VandenBergh, R. L. Effects of an EMG biofeedback relaxation program on the control of diabetes: A case study. *Biofeedback and Self-Regulation*, 1976, *1*, 105–112.

Frankel, B. L. Biofeedback and anxiety. *American Journal of Psychiatry*, 1975, *132*, 1223.

Freedman, R., & Papsdorf, J. D. Biofeedback and progressive relaxation treatment of sleep-onset insomnia: A controlled, all-night investigation. *Biofeedback and Self-Regulation*, 1976, *1*, 253–271.

Gannon, L., & Sternbach, R. A. Alpha enhancement as a treatment for pain: A case study. *Journal of Behavior Therapy and Experimental Psychiatry*, 1971, *2*, 209–213. (1971:38)

Gatchel, R. J. Therapeutic effectiveness of voluntary heart rate control in reducing anxiety. *Journal of Consulting and Clinical Psychology*, 1977, *45*, 689–691.

Gatchel, R. J., & Proctor, J. D. Effectiveness of voluntary heart rate control in reducing speech anxiety. *Journal of Consulting and Clinical Psychology*, 1976, *44*, 381–389. (1976/77:45)

Gatchel, R. J., Hatch, J. P., Watson, P. J., Smith, D., & Gaas, E. Comparative effectiveness of voluntary heart rate control and muscular relaxation as active coping skills for reducing speech anxiety. *Journal of Consulting and Clinical Psychology*, 1977, *45*, 1093–1100.

Geer, J., Morokoff, P., & Greenwood, P. Sexual arousal in women: The development of a measurement device for vaginal blood volume. *Archives of Sexual Behavior*, 1974, *3*, 559–564.

Gentz, R. Apparatus for recording of bruxism during sleep. *Swedish Dental Journal*, 1972, *65*, 327–342.

Gershman, L., & Clouser, R. A. Treating insomnia with relaxation and desensitization in a group setting by an automated approach. *Journal of Behavior Therapy and Experimental Psychiatry*, 1974, *5*, 31–35. (1974:51)

Girodo, M. Yoga meditation and flooding in the treatment of anxiety neurosis. *Journal of Behavior Therapy and Experimental Psychiatry*, 1974, *5*, 157–160.

Glaros, A. G. Comment on "Alcoholism, alpha production and biofeedback." *Journal of Consulting and Clinical Psychology*, 1977, *45*, 698–699.

Glaros, A. G., & Rao, S. M. Bruxism: A critical review. *Psychological Bulletin*, 1977, *84*, 767–781. (a)

Glaros, A. G., & Rao, S. M. Effects of bruxism: A review of the literature. *Journal of Prosthetic Dentistry*, 1977, *38*, 149–157. (b)

Godin, M. C. Patient behavior and calculus removal. *The Probe*, 1973, *14*, 392–394.

Godin, M. C. The dentiscope system of plaque control. *The Probe*, 1974, *15*, (Jan., Feb., Mar., Apr.).

Godin, M. C. The effect of visual feedback and self-scaling on plaque control behavior. *Journal of Periodontology*, 1976, *47*, 34–37.

Goldberg, R. J., Greenwood, J. C., & Taintor, Z. Alpha conditioning as an adjunct treatment for drug dependence. I. *International Journal of the Addictions*, 1977, *11*, 1085–1089.

Goldberg, R. J., Greenwood, J. C., & Taintor, Z. Alpha conditioning as an adjunct treatment for drug dependence. II. *International Journal of the Addictions*, 1977, *12*, 195–204.

Good, R. Frontalis muscle tension and sleep latency. *Psychophysiology*, 1975, *12*, 465–467.

Gottheil, E., Alterman, A. I., Skoloda, T. E., & Murphy, B. F. Alcoholics' patterns of controlled drinking. *American Journal of Psychiatry*, 1973, *130*, 418–422.

Gracenin, C. T., & Cook, J. E. Alpha biofeedback and LD children. *Academic Therapy*, 1977, *12*, 275–279.

Green, E. E., Green, A. M., & Walters, E. D. Biofeedback training for anxiety tension reduction. *Annals New York Academy of Sciences*, 1974, *233*, 157–161.

Grynol, E., & Jamieson, J. Alpha feedback and relaxation: A cautionary note. *Perceptual and Motor Skills*, 1975, *40*, 58. (1975/76:26)

Guthrie, D. W., Moeller, T., & Guthrie, R. A. Biofeedback and its application to the stabilization and control of diabetes mellitus. *Diabetes*, 1976, *25*, 350. (Abstract)

Hama, H., Kawamura, Y., Mine, H., & Matsuyama, Y. Anxiety as a factor of autonomic arousal in instrumental control of skin temperature. *Psychologia*, 1977, *20*, 55–63.

Haynes, S. N., Sides, H., & Lockwood, G. Relaxation instructions and frontalis electromyographic feedback intervention with sleep-onset insomnia. *Behavior Therapy*, 1977, *8*, 644–652.

Heller, R. F., & Strang, H. R. Controlling bruxism through automated aversive conditioning. *Behavior Research and Therapy*, 1973, *11*, 327–329.

Hendler, N., Derogatis, L., Avella, J., & Long, D. EMG biofeedback in patients with chronic pain. *Diseases of the Nervous System*, 1977, *38*, 505–509.

Henson, D. E., & Rubin, H. B. Voluntary control of eroticism. *Journal of Applied Behavior Analysis*, 1971, *4*, 37–44. (1971:39)

Henson, D. E., & Rubin, H. B. A comparison of two objective measures of sexual arousal of women. *Behavior Research and Therapy*, 1978, *16*, 143–151.

Henson, D. E., Rubin, H. B., Henson, C., & Williams, J. R. Temperature change of the labia minora as an objective measure of female eroticism. *Journal of Behavior Therapy and Experimental Psychiatry*, 1977, *8*, 401–410.

Henson, D. E., Rubin, H. B., & Henson, C. Consistency of labial temperature change measure of human female eroticism. *Behavior Research and Therapy*, 1978, *16*, 125–130.

Herman, S. H., & Prewett, M. An experimental analysis of feedback to increase sexual arousal in a case of homo- and heterosexual impotence: A preliminary report. *Journal of Behavior Therapy and Experimental Psychiatry*, 1974, *5*, 271–274.

Holbrook, A., & Crawford, G. H. Modification of vocal frequency and intensity in the speech of the deaf. *Volta Review*, 1970, *72*, 492–497.

Holmes, D. S. Reply to "A comment on alcoholism, alpha production, and biofeedback." *Journal of Consulting and Clinical Psychology*, 1977, *45*, 700–701.

Hoon, P. W., Wincze, J. P., & Hoon, E. F. Physiological assessment of sexual arousal in women. *Psychophysiology*, 1976, *13*, 196–204.

Hoon, P. W., Wincze, J. P., & Hoon, E. F. The effects of biofeedback and cognitive mediation upon vaginal blood volume. *Behavior Therapy*, 1977, *8*, 694–702.

Jacobson, G. R., Wilson, A., & La Rocca, L. Perceptual field dependence and biofeedback training (EEG alpha) among male alcoholics. In F. A. Seixas (Ed.), *Currents in alcoholism* (Vol. 2). New York: Grune & Stratton, 1977, pp. 197–206.

Jones, F. W., & Holmes, D. S. Alcoholism, alpha production, and biofeedback. *Journal of Consulting and Clinical Psychology*, 1976, *44*, 224–228. (1976/77:50)

Kappes, B., & Michaud, J. Contingent vs. noncontingent EMG feedback and hand temperature in relation to anxiety and locus of control. *Biofeedback and Self-Regulation*, 1978, *3*, 51–60.

Keltner, A. A. The control of penile tumescence with biofeedback in two cases of pedophilia. *Corrective and Social Psychiatry and Journal of Applied Behavior Therapy*, 1977, *23*, 117–121.

Khan, A. U. Effectiveness of biofeedback and counter-conditioning in the treatment of bronchial asthma. *Journal of Psychosomatic Research*, 1977, *21*, 97–104.

Khan, A. U., Staerk, M., & Bonk, C. Role of counterconditioning in the treatment of asthma. *Journal of Asthma Research*, 1973, *11*, 57–62.

Kinsman, R. A., Luparello, T., O'Banion, K., & Spector, S. Multidimensional analysis of the subjective symptomatology of asthma. *Psychosomatic Medicine*, 1973, *35*, 250–267.

Kinsman, R. A., Spector, S. L., Shucard, D. W., & Luparello, T. J. Observations on patterns of subjective symptomatology of acute asthma. *Psychosomatic Medicine*, 1974, *36*, 129–143.

Knapp, T. J., & Wells, L. A. Behavior therapy for asthma: A review. *Behavior Research and Therapy*, 1978, *16*, 103–115.

Kotses, H., Glaus, K. D., Crawford, P. L., Edwards, J. E., & Scherr, M.S. Operant reduction of frontalis EMG activity in the treatment of asthma in children. *Journal of Psychosomatic Research*, 1976, *20*, 453–459.

Kotses, H., Glaus, K. D., Bricel, S. K., Edwards, J. E., & Crawford, P. L. Operant muscular relaxation and peak expiratory flow rate in asthmatic children. *Journal of Psychosomatic Research*, 1978, *22*, 17–23.

Kuna, D. J., Salkin, W., & Weinberger, K. Biofeedback, relaxation training, and methadone clients: An inquiry. *Contemporary Drug Problems*, 1976. *5*, 565–572.

Lamontagne, Y., Hand, I., Annable, L., & Gagnon, M.-A. Physiological and psychological effects of alpha and EMG feedback training with college drug users: A pilot study. *Canadian Psychiatric Association Journal*, 1975, *20*, 337–349.

Lamontagne, Y., Beauséjour, R., Annable, L., & Tétreault, L. Alpha and EMG feedback training in the prevention of drug abuse. *Canadian Psychiatric Association Journal*, 1977, *22*, 301–310.

Lavallée, Y.-J., Lamontagne, Y., Pinard, G., Annable, L., & Tétreault, L. Effects of EMG feedback, diazepam and their combination on chronic anxiety. *Journal of Psychosomatic Research*, 1977, *21*, 65–71.

Laws, D. R., & Rubin, H. B. Instructional control of an autonomic sexual response. *Journal of Applied Behavior Analysis*, 1969, *2*, 93–99.

Lehr, R. P., Blanton, P. L., Biggs, N. L., & Sewell, D. A. Electromyographic analysis of the circumoral muscles of facial expression. *Journal of Dental Research*, 1974, *53*, 661–669.

Levenson, R. W. Automated system for direct measurement and feedback of total respiratory resistance by the forced oscillation technique. *Psychophysiology*, 1974, *11*, 86–90.

Levitt, H. Speech processing aids for the deaf. *IEEE Transactions on Audio and Electroacoustics*, 1973, *AU-21*, 269–273.

Lloyd, R. W., & Salzberg, H. C. Controlled social drinking: An alternative to abstinence as a treatment goal for some alcohol abusers. *Psychological Bulletin*, 1975, *82*, 815–842.

Lovibond, S. H., & Caddy, G. Discriminated aversive control in the moderation of alcoholics' drinking behavior. *Behavior Therapy*, 1971, *1*, 437–444. (1971:40)

Luparello, T., Lyons, H.A., Bleecker, E. R., & McFadden, E. R. Influences of suggestion on airway reactivity in asthmatic subjects. *Psychosomatic Medicine*, 1968, *30*, 819–825. (1973:18)

McFarland, R. A., & Coombs, R. Anxiety and feedback as factors in operant heart rate control. *Psychophysiology*, 1974, *11*, 53–57.

Maisto, S. A., & Adesso, V. J. Effect of instructions and feedback on blood alcohol level discrimination training in nonalcoholic drinkers. *Journal of Consulting and Clinical Psychology*, 1977, *45*, 625–636.

Manuso, J. J. The use of biofeedback-assisted hand warming training in the treatment of chronic eczematous dermatitis of the hands: A case study. *Journal of Behavior Therapy and Experimental Psychiatry*, 1977, *8*, 445–446.

Marlatt, A., Demming, B., & Reid, J. B. Loss of control drinking in alcoholics: An experimental analogue. *Journal of Abnormal Psychology*, 1973, *81*, 233–241.

Martony, J. On the correction of the voice pitch level for severely hard of hearing subjects. *American Annals of the Deaf*, 1968, *113*, 195–202.

Matheson, D. W., & Twinem, K. The effect of EMG biofeedback, progressive relaxation training, and vibrotactile stimulation on relaxation in high arousal individuals. Paper presented at Western Psychological Association Convention, Sacramento, California, 1975.

Matheson, D. W., Edelson, R., Hiatrides, D., Newkirk, J., Twinem, K., & Thurston, S. Relaxation measured by EMG as a function of vibrotactile stimulation. *Biofeedback and Self-Regulation*, 1976, *1*, 285–292.

Melzack, R., & Perry, C. Self-regulation of pain: The use of alpha-feedback and hypnotic training for the control of chronic pain. *Experimental Neurology*, 1975, *46*, 452–469. (1975/76:13)

Mendelson, J. H., & Mello, N. K. Experimental analysis of drinking behavior of chronic alcoholics. *Annals of the New York Academy of Science*, 1966, *133*, 828–845.

Miklich, D. R. Chronic homeostatic vagal efferent activity turndown: A theory of asthma. *Medical Hypotheses*, 1977, *3*, 226–237.

Miklich, D. R., Renne, C. M., Creer, T. L., Alexander, A. B., Chai, H., Davis, M. H., Hoffman, A., & Danker-Brown, P. The clinical utility of behavior therapy as an adjunctive treatment for asthma. *Journal of Allergy and Clinical Immunology*, 1977, *60*, 285–294.

Miller, W. R. Behavioral self-control training in the treatment of problem drinkers. In R. B. Stuart (Ed.), *Behavioral self-management: Strategies and outcomes*. New York: Brunner/Mazel, 1977, pp. 154–175.

Miller, W. R. Behavioral treatment of problem drinkers: A comparative outcome study of three controlled drinking therapies. *Journal of Consulting and Clinical Psychology*, 1978, *46*, 74–86.

Miller, W. R., & Caddy, G. R. Abstinence and controlled drinking in the treatment of problem drinkers. *Journal of Studies on Alcohol*, 1977, *38*, 986–1003.

Mills, G. K., & Solyom, L. Biofeedback of EEG alpha in the treatment of obsessive ruminations: An exploration. *Journal of Behavior Therapy and Experimental Psychiatry*, 1974, *5*, 37–41.

Montgomery, I., Perkin, G., & Wise, D. A review of behavioral treatments for insomnia. *Journal of Behavior Therapy and Experimental Psychiatry*, 1975, *6*, 93–100. (1976/77:7)

Nathan, P.E., & O'Brien, J. S. An experimental analysis of the behavior of alcoholics and nonalcoholics during prolonged experimental drinking: A necessary precursor of behavior therapy? *Behavior Therapy*, 1971, *2*, 455–476.

Nathan, P. E., Titler, N. A., Lowenstein, L. M., Solomon, P., & Rossi, A. Behavioral analysis of chronic alcoholism. *Archives of General Psychiatry,* 1970, *22*, 419–430.

Nicassio, P., & Bootzin, R. A comparison of progressive relaxation and autogenic training as treatments for insomnia. *Journal of Abnormal Psychology,* 1974, *83*, 253–260. (1974:48)

Nickerson, R. S. Characteristics of the speech of deaf persons. *Volta Review,* 1975, *77*, 342–362.

Nickerson, R. S., & Stevens, K. N. Teaching speech to the deaf: Can a computer help? *Proceedings of the Association for Computer Machinery,* 1972, 240–252.

Nickerson, R. S., Kalikow, D. N., & Stevens, K. N. Computer-aided speech training for the deaf. *Journal of Speech and Hearing Disorders,* 1976, *41*, 120–132.

Nunes, J. S., & Marks, I. M. Feedback of true heartrate during exposure *in vivo. Archives of General Psychiatry,* 1976, *33*, 1346–1352.

Ogurzsoff, S., & Vogel-Sprott, M. Low blood alcohol discrimination and self-titration skills of social drinkers with widely varied drinking habits. *Canadian Journal of Behavioral Science,* 1976, *8*, 232–242.

Orford, J., Oppenheimer, E., & Edwards, G. Abstinence or control: The outcome for excessive drinkers two years after consultation. *Behavior Research and Therapy,* 1976, *14*, 409–418.

Orne, M. T., & Paskewitz, D. A. Aversive situational effects on alpha feedback training. *Science,* 1974, *186*, 458–460. (1974:28)

Paredes, A., Jones, B. M., & Gregory, D. Blood alcohol discrimination training with alcoholics. In F. A. Seixas (Ed.), *Currents in alcoholism* (Vol. 2). New York: Grune & Stratton, 1977, pp. 125–148.

Parker, A. The laryngograph. *Hearing,* 1974, *29*, 256–261.

Parker, J. L. A photo-electric pen for producing action feedback to aid development in handicapped children of fine visual-motor skills: Tracing and writing. *The Slow Learning Child,* 1975, *22*, 13–22.

Parker, J. L., Rosenfeld, S., & Todd, G. Simple device for enhancing feedback in the acquisition of visual motor skills of slow learning children. *The Slow Learning Child,* 1973, *20*, 164–169.

Passini, F. T., Watson, C. G., Dehnel, L., Herder, J., & Watkins, B. Alpha wave biofeedback training therapy in alcoholics. *Journal of Clinical Psychology,* 1977, *33*, 292–299.

Pelletier, K. R., & Peper, E. Developing a biofeedback model: Alpha EEG feedback as a means for pain control. *International Journal of Clinical and Experimental Hypnosis,* 1977, *25*, 361–371.

Pickett, J. M. Recent research on speech-analyzing aids for the deaf. *IEEE Transactions on Audio and Electroacoustics,* 1968, *AU-16*, 227–234.

Pohl, P. Voluntary control of stereotyped behavior by mentally retarded children: Preliminary experimental findings. *Developmental Medicine and Child Neurology,* 1977, *19*, 811–817.

Purcell, K., & Weiss, J. H. Asthma. In C. G. Costello (Ed.), *Symptoms of psychopathology.* New York: Wiley, 1970, pp. 597–623.

Ransford, A. O., Cairns, D., & Mooney, V. The pain drawing as an aid to the psychologic evaluation of patients with low back pain. *Spine,* 1976, *1*, 127–134.

Raskin, M., Johnson, G., & Rondestvedt, J. W. Chronic anxiety treated by feedback-induced muscle relaxation. *Archives of General Psychiatry,* 1973, *28*, 263–267. (1973:22)

Reeves, J. L., & Mealiea, W. L. Biofeedback-assisted, cue-controlled relaxation for the treatment of flight phobias. *Journal of Behavior Therapy and Experimental Psychiatry,* 1975, *6*, 105–109.

Reynolds, B. S. Psychological treatment models and outcome results for erectile dysfunction: A critical review. *Psychological Bulletin,* 1977, *84*, 1218–1238.

Ribordy, S. C., & Denney, D. R. The behavioral treatment of insomnia: An alternative to drug therapy. *Behavior Research and Therapy,* 1977, *15*, 39–50.

Risberg, A. Visual aids for speech correction. *American Annals of the Deaf,* 1968, *113*, 178–194.

Rosen, R. C. Suppression of penile tumescence by instrumental conditioning. *Psychosomatic Medicine,* 1973, *35*, 509–514. (1973:28)

Rosen, R. C. Genital blood flow measurement: Feedback applications in sexual therapy. *Journal of Sex and Marital Therapy,* 1976, *2*, 184–196.

Rosen, R. C., Shapiro, D., & Schwartz, G. E. Voluntary control of penile tumescence. *Psychosomatic Medicine*, 1975, *37*, 479–483. (1975/76:57)

Rubin, H. B., & Henson, D. E. Voluntary enhancement of penile erection. *Bulletin of the Psychonomic Society*, 1975, *6*, 158–160.

Sappington, A. A. Direct manipulation of physiological arousal in induced anxiety therapy—biofeedback approach. *Journal of Clinical Psychology*, 1977, *33*, 1070–1075.

Schaeffer, H. H., Sobell, M. B., & Mills, K. C. Baseline drinking behavior in alcoholics and social drinkers: Kinds of drinks and sip magnitude. *Behavior Research and Therapy*, 1971, *9*, 23–27.

Schroeder, S. R., Peterson, C. R., Solomon, L. J., & Artley, J. J. EMG feedback and the contingent restraint of self-injurious behavior among the severely retarded: Two case illustrations. *Behavior Therapy*, 1977, *8*, 738–741.

Schulman, J. L., Stevens, T. M., Suran, B. G., Kupst, M. J., & Naughton, M. J. Modification of activity level through biofeedback and operant conditioning. *Journal of Applied Behavior Analysis*, 1978, *11*, 145–152.

Schwartz, G. E., Fair, P. L., Salt, P., Mandel, M. R., & Klerman, G. L. Facial muscle patterning to affective imagery in depressed and nondepressed subjects. *Science*, 1976, *192*, 489–491. (a)

Schwartz, G. E., Fair, P. L., Salt, P., Mandel, M. R., & Klerman, G. L. Facial expression and imagery in depression: An electromyographic study. *Psychosomatic Medicine*, 1976, *38*, 337–347. (b)

Scott, D. S., & Barber, T. X. Cognitive control of pain: Four serendipitous results. *Perceptual and Motor Skills*, 1977, *44*, 569–570. (a)

Scott, D. S., & Barber, T. X. Cognitive control of pain: Effects of multiple cognitive strategies. *Psychological Record*, 1977, *2*, 373–383. (b)

Searson, M. A speech-training program using the Kamplex visible speech apparatus. *Teacher of the Deaf*, 1965, *63*, 85–90.

Shepherd, G. W., & Watts, F. N. Heart rate control in psychiatric patients. *Behavior Therapy*, 1974, *5*, 153–154.

Silverstein, S. J., Nathan, P. E., & Taylor, H. A. Blood alcohol level estimation and controlled drinking by chronic alcoholics. *Behavior Therapy*, 1974, *5*, 1–15.

Simons, D. G. Muscle pain syndromes. I. *American Journal of Physical Medicine*, 1975, *54*, 289–311.

Simons, D. G. Muscle pain syndromes. II. *American Journal of Physical Medicine*, 1976, *55*, 15–42.

Simpson, D. D., & Nelson, A. E. Attention training through breathing control to modify hyperactivity. *Journal of Learning Disabilities*, 1974, *7*, 274–283.

Sintchak, G., & Geer, J. A vaginal plethysmographic system. *Psychophysiology*, 1975, *12*, 113–115.

Sobell, M. B., & Sobell, L. C. Individualized behavior therapy for alcoholics. *Behavior Therapy*, 1973, *4*, 49–72. (a)

Sobell, M. B., & Sobell, L. C. Alcoholics treated by individualized behavior therapy: One year treatment outcome. *Behavior Research and Therapy*, 1973, *11*, 599–618. (b)

Sobell, M. B., Schaeffer, H. H., & Mills, K. C. Differences in baseline drinking behavior between alcoholics and normal drinkers. *Behavior Research and Therapy*, 1972, *10*, 257–267.

Solberg, W. K., & Rugh, J. D. The use of biofeedback devices in the treatment of bruxism. *Journal of the Southern California Dental Association*, 1972, *40*, 852–853.

Sotile, W. M., & Kilmann, P. R. Treatments of psychogenic female sexual dysfunctions. *Psychological Bulletin*, 1977, *84*, 619–633.

Steffen, J. J. Electromyographically induced relaxation in the treatment of chronic alcohol abuse. *Journal of Consulting and Clinical Psychology*, 1975, *43*, 275.

Steffen, J. J., Nathan, P. E., & Taylor, H. A. Tension-reducing effects of alcohol: Further evidence and some methodological considerations. *Journal of Abnormal Psychology*, 1974, *83*, 542–547.

Steinberg, E. P., & Schwartz, G. E. Biofeedback and electrodermal self-regulation in psychopathy. *Journal of Abnormal Psychology*, 1976, *85*, 408–415.

Stratton, W. D. Information feedback for the deaf through a tactile display. *Volta Review*, 1974, *76*, 26–35.

Strickler, D., Bigelow, G., Lawrence, C., & Liebson, I. Moderate drinking as an alternative to alcohol abuse: A non-aversive procedure. *Behavior Research and Therapy*, 1976, *14*, 279–288.

Tal, A., & Miklich, D. R. Emotionally induced decreases in pulmonary flow rates in asthmatic children. *Psychosomatic Medicine*, 1976, *38*, 190–200.

Tiep, B., Mittman, C., & Tripp, M. A new biofeedback technique for controlling intrathoracic pressure in patients with pulmonary emphysema. In J. I. Martin (Ed.), *Proceedings of the San Diego biomedical symposium* (Vol. 16). New York: Academic, 1977, pp. 215–220.

Townsend, R. E. Dr. Townsend replies. *American Journal of Psychiatry*, 1975, *132*, 1224.

Townsend, R. E., House, J. F., & Addario, D. A comparison of biofeedback-mediated relaxation and group therapy in the treatment of chronic anxiety. *American Journal of Psychiatry*, 1975, *132*, 598–601. (1976/77:43)

Turnbull, J. W. Asthma conceived as a learned response. *Journal of Psychosomatic Research*, 1962, *6*, 59–70.

Twemlow, S. W., & Bowen, W. T. Sociocultural predictors of self-actualization in EEG-biofeedback-treated alcoholics. *Psychological Reports*, 1977, *40*, 591–598.

Vachon, L., & Rich, E. S. Visceral learning in asthma. *Psychosomatic Medicine*, 1976, *38*, 122–130. (1976/77:49)

Valle, R. S., & DeGood, D. E. Effects of state-trait anxiety on the ability to enhance and suppress EEG alpha. *Psychophysiology*, 1977, *14*, 1–7.

Vogler, R. E. Compton, J. V., & Weissbach, T.A. Integrated behavior change techniques for alcoholics. *Journal of Consulting and Clinical Psychology*, 1975, *43*, 233–243.

Volpe, R. Feedback facilitated relaxation training as primary prevention of drug abuse in early adolescence. *Journal of Drug Education*, 1977, *7*, 179–194.

Webb, N. C. The use of myoelectric feedback in teaching facial expression to the blind. *American Foundation for the Blind Research Bulletin*, 1974, *27*, 231–262.

Webb, C. The use of myoelectric feedback in teaching facial expression to the blind. *Biofeedback and Self-Regulation*, 1977, *2*, 147–160.

Weisenburg, M. Pain and pain control. *Psychological Bulletin*, 1977, *84*, 1008–1044.

Weiss, T. Weaning in biofeedback training. *American Journal of Psychiatry*, 1975, *132*, 1220.

Wenger, M.A., Averill, J. R., & Smith, D. D. B. Autonomic activity during sexual arousal. *Psycophysiology*, 1968, *4*, 468–478.

Wickramasekera, I. Instructions and EMG feedback in systematic desensitization: A case report. *Behavior Therapy*, 1972, *3*, 460–465.

Wickramasekera, I. Heart rate feedback and the management of cardiac neurosis. *Journal of Abnormal Psychology*, 1974, *83*, 578–580. (1974:18)

Wilson, A. F., Honsberger, R., Chiu, J. T., & Novey, H. S. Transcendental meditation and asthma. *Respiration*, 1975, *32*, 74–80. (1975/76:7)

Woolfolk, R. L., Carr-Kaffashan, L., McNulty, T. F., & Lehrer, P. M. Meditation training as a treatment for insomnia. *Behavior Therapy*, 1976, *7*, 359–365. (1976/77:8)

Yates, A. J. *Behavior therapy*. New York: Wiley, 1970.

Yates, A. J. *Theory and practice in behavior therapy*. New York: Wiley, 1975.

Zarb, G. A., & Speck, J. E. The treatment of temporomandibular joint dysfunction: A retrospective study. *Journal of Prosthetic Dentistry*, 1977, *38*, 420–432.

Zingheim, P. K., & Sandman, C. A. Discriminative control of the vaginal vasomotor response. *Biofeedback and Self-Regulation*, 1978, *3*, 29–41.

Zuckerman, M. Physiological measures of sexual arousal in the human. *Psychological Bulletin*, 1971, *75*, 297–329.

CHAPTER 7

Theoretical Aspects of Biofeedback

Introduction

When the biofeedback research worker or clinician conducts an experiment or carries out treatment using biofeedback displays, it is commonly observed by the experimenter or clinician that he is unable to provide the subject or patient with precise instructions as to how control may be achieved over the function that is being studied. Following the completion of the experiment or treatment, and assuming some success in obtaining control over the function, it is equally commonly observed by the subjects or patients that they are unable to describe what they did to achieve control. The inability on the part of the experimenter or clinician to instruct the subject or patient how to achieve control, and the inability of the subject or patient to tell the experimenter or clinician how control was achieved appear to have caused a great deal of concern. It is the primary intent of this chapter to show that the concern is misplaced and based on a fundamental misunderstanding of the nature of biofeedback and the purpose of biofeedback training. As a consequence, a good deal of inappropriate research has been carried out in a vain and unnecessary search for certain presumed ''mediators'' of biofeedback control. It is not, of course, being asserted that mediation does not occur in biofeedback; what is being asserted is that the mediation which occurs is quite other than that which it is commonly assumed to be and that it is not in the least surprising or a matter for concern that subjects and patients are unable to ''explain'' their success when they achieve it. Indeed, in terms of the theoretical position to be developed here, it would be neither expected nor desirable that increased control following biofeedback training will be accompanied by an ''understanding'' of how the increased control was achieved.

It will be argued that biofeedback training involves essentially teaching the subject or patient the ''language'' of his bodily systems, but the ''language'' is a nonverbal ''language'' of a special kind. In order to arrive at this point, however, consideration in some detail must first be given to a number of "issues" which have arisen in the biofeedback literature. The elucidation of these issues will establish a framework within which the true purpose of biofeedback training may be expounded. Each of these issues implicates major research areas of psychology and it would obviously be impracticable to review the entire literature pertinent to each of them. Hence, the issues will be discussed using a range of examples to illustrate the critical points to be made.

The Specificity/Generality Issue and Somatic Integration

The biofeedback treatment of tension headaches has been based on the assumption that there is evidence that tension headaches are correlated with a level of frontalis muscle activity which is significantly higher in the resting state and in the absence of a current headache than the level found in subjects who do not suffer from tension headaches (Vaughn, Pall, & Haynes, 1977). As we have seen, the biofeedback treatment of tension headaches has usually involved training the patient to reduce the level of frontalis muscle activity by providing feedback of that level and instructing the patient to effect a reduction in the level of frontalis muscle activity, with the biofeedback display providing information about his success in achieving his goal. If the patient succeeds in reducing the level of frontalis muscle activity, it has been found that a corresponding decrease in the frequency and intensity of the tension headaches is very likely to occur. Although not always made specifically clear (and perhaps not always recognized), frontalis muscle relaxation training in the treatment of tension headaches is based on the *specificity assumption* which may be stated as follows:

> If a clinical disorder is correlated with a specific dysfunction in an effector system, then if the dysfunction in the effector system can be brought under voluntary control and altered to normal levels, there will be a corresponding improvement in the clinical disorder.

Thus, in the case of the clinical disorder tension headaches the corresponding dysfunction is an abnormally high level of frontalis muscle activity. Reduction of frontalis muscle activity to normal levels will be accompanied by a reduction in tension headache activity, if the assumption is correct.

It is frequently asserted that alcoholism is associated with high levels of general anxiety and that excessive drinking is an attempt to reduce that anxiety. If by some means the high level of anxiety could be reduced, it is argued that there will be a corresponding decline in the tendency to drink heavily. General relaxation training is thus often used with alcoholics in an effort to reduce the anxiety. However, as we have seen, highly specific biofeedback training has been provided also, both for alcoholism and, indeed, for cases of general anxiety itself. This highly specific training is in fact based on the *generality assumption*, which may be stated as follows:

> If a clinical disorder (whether highly specific or more general in nature) exists, successful training in the reduction of levels of activity in any effector system will be accompanied by a corresponding improvement in the clinical disorder.

Thus, in the case of alcoholism it has been assumed that either general relaxation training or specific training in frontalis muscle activity, or even training in other specific systems (such as alpha enhancement), will be beneficial because any of these techniques will effect a general reduction in the anxiety level supposedly underlying the clinical disorder. Successful frontalis muscle training, for example, is assumed to generalize to other muscle systems while alpha-enhancement training is assumed to effect a general reduction in level of arousal and thus indirectly produce widespread reductions in tension levels.

The specificity/generality issue is not, of course, in any way a new issue. It has a long and contentious history in psychology. The relative validity of these two assumptions (which are important because to a significant degree they clearly dictate how the biofeedback clinician is likely to proceed in devising his treatment programs) will now be considered in more detail, drawing on various kinds of empirical evidence.

The first evidence to be considered relates to studies carried out using biofeedback itself. The specificity assumption leads to a number of predictions which are not too difficult to test:

1. Training in control of a dysfunction which covaries with the presenting disorder will reduce the severity of the disorder itself; and will be more successful than general relaxation training. Thus, frontalis muscle activity reduction will reduce tension headaches while extracranial blood volume and flow training will alleviate migraine headaches.

2. Training in control of a function which does not covary with the presenting disorder will not reduce the severity of the disorder. Thus, frontalis muscle activity reduction will not alleviate migraine headaches and training in extracranial blood volume and flow will not reduce tension headaches.

3. Where a nonspecific disorder exists (such as generalized anxiety), training in control of a specific function will not alleviate the nonspecific disorder unless the specific function has a specific role to play in the production and maintenance of the nonspecific disorder. Thus, training in frontalis muscle activity reduction or peripheral finger temperature control will not alleviate general anxiety unless these functions are an integrated part of the anxiety. In terms of the specificity assumption, an important implication of this prediction is that it is necessary to seek out the specific correlates of a generalized disorder, recognizing that these correlates may be unique to the individual patient (this point will be taken up in more detail later).

In a similar way, the generality assumption leads to a number of clear predictions:

1. Training in the voluntary control of a specific function will, if control of the function involves relaxation, lead to a generalization of that control to other

similar functions with a generally beneficial effect on any presenting disorder. Thus, training in frontalis muscle relaxation will generalize to other muscle groups and produce an increase in overall relaxation, thus benefiting the patient suffering from a generalized failure in relaxation (as in general anxiety).

2. Training in generalized relaxation will produce a beneficial effect on disorders such as anxiety.

3. Training in generalized relaxation will produce a beneficial effect on specific disorders even if generalized tension is absent. Thus, training in general relaxation will reduce tension headaches even if specific training in frontalis muscle activity reduction is not included as part of the general relaxation training.

These predictions have been formulated in relation to the treatment situation in which abnormalities of function have to be dealt with. However, analogous predictions can be made with respect to training in the voluntary control of various functions in normal subjects. Thus, the specificity assumption would predict that specific training in frontalis muscle activity reduction would not generalize to other muscles (such as forearm muscle activity) unless those muscles were closely related to, and usually covaried with, frontalis muscle activity (such as the muscles of the face and neck), and would predict that general relaxation training would effect much less reduction in frontalis muscle activity than would specific frontalis muscle activity reduction training. The generality assumption, on the other hand, would predict a spread of effect beyond any specific muscle training, while generalized muscle activity relaxation training would of course produce a significant overall beneficial effect.

As pointed out earlier, it is not intended to conduct an exhaustive review of the literature relevant to these predictions. Rather, it will be shown that evidence can be produced in favor of each assumption. There is, for example, quite cogent evidence that in normal subjects training in the control of a particular kind of activity does not usually generalize to different systems. Suter (1977), for example, showed that alpha training did not affect skin resistance, and vice versa. Alexander (1975) found that frontalis muscle reduction training did not generalize to forearm and leg muscle activity. Shedivy and Kleinman (1977) have recently reported the results of a study particularly relevant to this matter. They trained normal subjects to increase and decrease frontalis muscle activity with continuous proportional auditory feedback while simultaneously recording either sternomastoid or semispinalis/splenius activity (feedback of the activity of these muscle complexes was not, of course, provided). The results obtained are shown in Figure 1. The expected increases and decreases in frontalis muscle activity were obtained as compared with baseline levels, but no changes from baseline levels were evident for the other two muscle groups[1] except that semispinalis/splenius activity tended to *increase* during relaxation of the frontalis muscle.

[1]Thus refuting Basmajian's (1976) contention that frontalis muscle activity measurement with surface electrodes is inevitably contaminated with activity in a wide range of adjacent muscles.

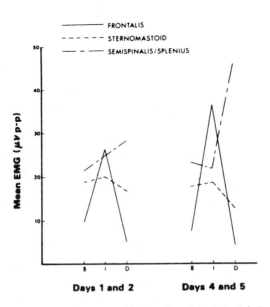

Figure 1. Mean frontalis ($N = 8$), sternomastoid ($N = 8$). and semispinalis/splenius ($N = 4$) EMG levels (in μV p-p) recorded during baseline, increase frontalis, and decrease frontalis periods during early (days 1 and 2) and late (days 4 and 5) feedback training. (From Shedivy, D. I., & Kleinman, K. M. Lack of correlation between frontalis EMG with other neck muscles and verbal ratings of tension or relaxation. *Psychophysiology*, 1977, *14*, 184, Figure 1. Reprinted by permission of the author and the publisher.)

Training in relaxation within one system does not necessarily benefit subsequent training in a different system. Alexander, White, and Wallace (1977), for example, showed that training in frontalis muscle activity reduction did not generalize to subsequent forearm muscle activity reduction training, and vice versa. Sittenfeld, Budzynski, and Stoyva (1976) found that prior training in frontalis muscle relaxation did not subsequently facilitate training in theta production even though enhancement of theta supposedly is an indicator of relaxation. Furthermore, there is now good evidence that it is possible to train subjects to produce enhanced alpha in one hemisphere of the cortex while simultaneously maintaining alpha at baseline levels in the other hemisphere; that is, generalization of enhancement does not inevitably take place (Mulholland & Eberlin, 1977). And, of course, the studies reviewed in Chapter 4 on the differentiation of heart rate from blood pressure point in the same direction. There is also cogent evidence from laboratory studies which tends to support the specificity hypothesis. Thus, Grings and Schandler (1977) trained normal subjects to produce a fear response (indexed by a specific electrodermal reaction) and then trained them to use an equally specific forearm relaxation response to reduce the magnitude of the fear response in the presence of the fear-inducing stimulus. In rather similar fashion, V. A. Harris, Katkin, Lick, and Habberfield (1976) have shown that training normal subjects to breathe at about half the normal rate with feedback enables the subjects to control their autonomic response to the anticipation of shock more successfully than attention and baseline control groups. Such highly specific control of functions merely reflects, of course, the evidence reviewed in Chapter 3 relating to the specific control of SMUs and the ability of the subjects in these experiments to suppress surrounding activity.

Another line of evidence supporting the validity of the specificity assumption comes from comparative studies of the effects of specific and general relaxation training on relaxation of a specific muscle complex. This evidence need not be reviewed in detail here, but the results of many studies indicate that specific relaxation training of a specific muscle group is either superior to (e.g., Coursey, 1975) or equally as beneficial as (e.g., S. N. Haynes, Moseley, & McGowan, 1975) general relaxation training.

Studies of biofeedback training to alleviate abnormalities of function may also be cited in support of the specificity assumption, such as frontalis muscle training for tension headache and extracranial blood volume and flow training for migraine headaches. In a few cases the specificity assumption has been shown to be relevant in studies where superficially it might appear not to be. Thus, the use of frontalis muscle training with cerebral-palsied children by Finley, Niman, Standley, and Ender (1976) and by Finley, Niman, Standley, and Wansley (1977) might appear to be a violation of the specificity assumption. However, they were able to show that elevated frontalis muscle activity is a characteristic of cerebral palsy and hence training in reduction of that activity does not, in fact, violate the assumption (although it will be realized that a much wider range of specific training might be necessary to effect overall improvement in a disorder such as this). A very interesting demonstration of the use of the specificity assumption is to be found in the work of Guitar (1974) on the biofeedback treatment of stuttering. He recorded muscle activity from a number of sites (lip, chin, larynx, frontalis) and found that successful muscle activity training at these sites only affected stuttering frequency when the stuttering was correlated with an abnormal amount of activity at the site trained.

In a number of studies it has been found that training in control of an irrelevant function does not lead to amelioration of the disorder under treatment, whereas if the irrelevant function happens in fact to be relevant to an accompanying disorder, a serendipitous therapeutic effect on that disorder will be obtained. The classic example is the study by Raskin, Johnson, and Rondestvedt (1973), who found that successful frontalis muscle relaxation training with biofeedback resulted in disappointing therapeutic effects on severe generalized anxiety. However, some of the patients also suffered from tension headaches and these were relieved by the frontalis muscle relaxation training. Similarly, Reading and Mohr (1976) reported success with peripheral finger temperature training for migraine but no effect of this training on concomitant tension headaches. Philips (1977) concluded from her study of biofeedback training of patients with tension headaches or mixed tension-migraine headaches that it was desirable to provide feedback of activity in the muscle group (usually frontalis or temporalis) which manifested most tension in the resting state, and that the subsequent training was successful with pure tension headache patients and unsuccessful with the mixed cases. Wickramasekera (1973) reported that frontalis muscle training had no beneficial effect on two patients with migraine headaches whereas the subsequent use of peripheral finger temperature training did lead to improvement.

It would seem, therefore, that there is a good deal of evidence in favor of the specificity assumption. Yet substantial evidence can be marshaled in support of the generality assumption, apart from the fact that training in general relaxation has been abundantly demonstrated to have beneficial effects, both with normal subjects and in relation to abnormalities of behavior. Even in studies where the specificity assumption would be most expected to hold up it has sometimes failed, as in the study by Blanchard, Haynes, Kallman, and Harkey (1976) in which it was found that training in the reduction of frontalis muscle activity was equally as efficacious as training in the reduction of systolic blood pressure in producing decreases in systolic blood pressure in normotensive males and females. Similarly, Bakal and Kaganov (1977) have provided evidence indicating that frontalis muscle activity levels are higher in migraine than in tension headache patients, both in the resting state and while a headache is being experienced. There is also now compelling evidence that training in the voluntary control of a specific function (not necessarily directly related to the presenting disorder) may have beneficial effects on that disorder. Since these studies have been discussed in detail in earlier chapters, only a selection of them need be mentioned here to make the point. Thus, frontalis muscle relaxation training has been shown to have generally beneficial effects in disorders as diverse as urinary retention (Pearne, Zigelbaum, & Peyser, 1977), diabetes (Fowler, Budzynski & VandenBergh, 1976), asthma (Davis, Saunders, Creer, & Chai, 1973; Kotses, Glaus, Crawford, Edwards, & Sherr, 1976), dysphagia (S. N. Haynes, 1976), alcoholism (Steffen, 1975), hyperactivity (Braud, Lupin, & Braud, 1975), and anxiety (Lavallée, Lamontagne, Pinard, Annable, & Tétreault, 1977; Townsend, House, & Addario, 1975). Training in alpha enhancement has been successfully used in the treatment of pain (Gannon & Sternbach, 1971), tension headaches (McKenzie, Ehrisman, Montgomery, & Barnes, 1974), and alcoholism (Passini, Watson, Dehnel, Herder, & Watkins, 1977). Finger temperature training has been applied with success in the treatment of vomiting (Schneider, 1976). Many of these studies were confounded since they tended to combine relaxation training of a specific kind with general relaxation training, and most of them are based on the belief that a high level of anxiety underlies and even determines the presenting disorder so that the specific training is directed toward inducing general relaxation as a state which will inhibit the general anxiety. There is also correlative evidence which supports the generality assumption. For example,

Brady, Luborsky, and Kron (1974) found that metronome-conditioned relaxation training reduced diastolic blood pressure in four patients with essential hypertension, while Mathews and Gelder (1969) showed that when anxious and/or phobic patients were given general relaxation training there was a decrease in level of frontalis muscle activity without any specific relaxation exercises being directed toward that muscle. Canter, Kondo, and Knott (1975) also found that general relaxation training led to a significant reduction in frontalis muscle activity in anxious patients, although the reduction was not as great as that obtained with specific frontalis muscle relaxation training. Similar results with "normal" subjects scoring high on the Manifest Anxiety Scale were reported by Edelman (1971).

Before considering the implications of these apparently conflicting results, it is necessary to look briefly at some quite different and earlier sources of evidence which are highly relevant to the specificity/generality issue. The issue has been repeatedly raised in the area of psychosomatic medicine. Although the belief in specificity of function goes back a long way in psychiatry, several sources of evidence appeared to converge some 25 years ago to suggest that specific physiological responses were associated with specific disorders. However, the "specificity" hypothesis has been put forward in a number of somewhat different guises which need to be distinguished. Figure 2 shows four well-known variants. The first (Figure 2A) was advanced by Lacy, Bateman, and VanLehn (1953), who subjected normal subjects to a variety of stressful situations while measuring a range of autonomic functions. On the basis of their results, they argued that:

> for a given set of autonomic functions, individuals tend to respond with a pattern of autonomic activation in which maximum activation occurs in the same physiological function, whatever the stress. (p. 21)

Figure 2B illustrates a similar hypothesis which was put forward by Malmo, Shagass, and Davis (1950) in relation to psychiatric disorders:

> In psychiatric patients presenting a somatic complaint, the particular physiolgic mechanism of that complaint is specifically susceptible to activation by stressful experience.

Using standard and stressful interviews, Malmo et al. (1950) attempted to answer the following question:

> Are tensional responses in an area of symptom reference (e.g., the head in a case of headache) more closely related to changes in the degree of stress, than tensional responses in other bodily areas? (p. 363)

In three patients (one with tension headaches, one with stiffness and cramps in the right arm and writer's cramp, and one with a head tic) they showed that in each case levels of activity in the "relevant" muscle groups were significantly higher in stressful activities than the level of activity in "irrelevant" muscle groups. This form of the specificity hypothesis differs from that of Lacey et al. in

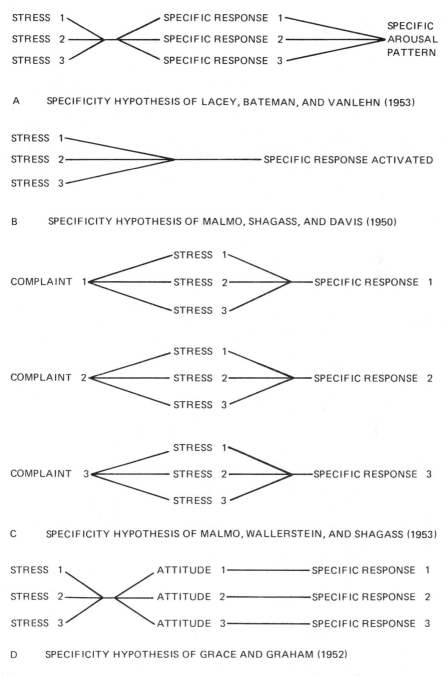

A   SPECIFICITY HYPOTHESIS OF LACEY, BATEMAN, AND VANLEHN (1953)

B   SPECIFICITY HYPOTHESIS OF MALMO, SHAGASS, AND DAVIS (1950)

C   SPECIFICITY HYPOTHESIS OF MALMO, WALLERSTEIN, AND SHAGASS (1953)

D   SPECIFICITY HYPOTHESIS OF GRACE AND GRAHAM (1952)

Figure 2. Four variations of the response specificity hypothesis in psychosomatic medicine.

that a particular relevant muscle (or autonomic function) will show a rise in activity in response to the induction of *any* stressful situation. Other research by Malmo and his colleagues tended to support the hypothesis. Malmo and Shagass (1949b) found that when subjected to a standard thermal stress stimulus, patients with complaints referred to the head and neck showed greater disturbance in neck muscle potentials than did patients free of such complaints. Similarly, patients with cardiovascular complaints tended to respond with raised autonomic activity when subjected to a thermal stress stimulus while anxiety neurotics tended to respond with heightened systolic blood pressure to three different kinds of stress (Malmo & Shagass, 1952). However, Malmo also provided evidence tending to support the Lacey *et al.* hypothesis (Figure 2A). Thus, Malmo and Shagass (1949a) found a general rise in respiration, neck muscle activity, heart rate, and finger movement in anxiety patients subjected to stress, and this finding was replicated by Malmo, Shagass, Belanger, and Smith (1951) with respect to finger movements and by Malmo, Shagass, and Davis (1951) with respect to neck and arm muscle activity. On the basis of all of this work, Malmo, Wallerstein, and Shagass (1953) attempted to test two alternative hypotheses: the "specific reaction" hypothesis (that, for example, in patients complaining of neck muscle pain, neck muscle activity will increase no matter what stress is applied; Figure 2C), and the "conflict" hypothesis (that muscle tension reflects a central conflict state so that neck muscle activity will increase if stress is applied to the head region, whereas arm muscle activity will increase if stress is applied to the arm area). The "specific reaction" hypothesis of Malmo is actually more general than the "conflict" hypothesis, the latter being more closely related to the specificity assumption as defined earlier in this section than is the former. Malmo *et al.* (1953) applied pain stimuli to the forehead and arm (at separate times) of patients with complaints referred to head and neck on the one hand, or not referred to these areas on the other hand (a normal control group was also run). Recordings were made from the forehead, neck, and right and left forearm extensors and flexors, while finger movements and heart rate were also recorded. The results showed that the headache-prone patients showed elevated forearm muscle activity whenever stress was applied to the forearm and elevated neck muscle activity whenever stress was applied to the head. This differential specificity of responding did not, however, occur in patients whose complaints were not referred to specific organ function, nor did it occur in the control subjects. Elevation of these functions did not occur in the headache-prone patients in nonstressful conditions, although their resting levels of activity were higher than those of the normal controls, as were the levels of the non-headache-prone patients. Specificity of response was also found in a study of depressive female patients by Goldstein, Grinker, Heath, Oken, & Shipman (1964). Furthermore, there is evidence from this study and others of response stereotypy, that is, the tendency to respond in a similar way, and on an individual basis, from one occasion to the next. Walker and Sandman (1977) showed that gastric activity in duodenal ulcer and rheumatoid arthritis patients could be differentiated in a stressful situation (viewing autopsy slides).

These studies were aiming to determine whether individual response specificity could be demonstrated, but a good deal of attention has also been paid to the question whether patients who present with the same or similar complaints (that is, referred to the same part of the body) tend to respond in the same way to stress. The work of Graham and his colleagues is relevant to this question. The argument is that particular psychosomatic disorders are associated with specific feelings or attitudes in the face of stress and that these attitudes are manifested both by verbalizations during stress and by a tendency to respond with specific changes in bodily function (Figure 2D). Thus, Grace and Graham (1952) interviewed 128 patients suffering from a variety of psychosomatic complaints and inquired of the patient "what he felt was happening to him, and what he wanted to do about it" at the time the symptom occurred. The particular complaints manifested by groups of patients and the most commonly expressed attitudes are shown in Table 1. Subsequent studies attempted to show that the "specificity of attitude" hypothesis and its relation to specific bodily dysfunction was valid. Graham, Stern, and Winokur (1958) induced under hypnosis two attitudes in normal subjects — "feeling unfairly treated and unable to do anything about it" (the "hives" attitude), and "feeling unfairly treated and wanting to respond aggressively" (the "Raynaud's disease" attitude) — and predicted that the "hives" attitude would lead to an increase in peripheral and/or forehead temperature whereas the reverse would happen when the "Raynaud's disease" attitude was induced (with resting level temperature while "relaxed" serving as the baseline from which to measure change). Unfortunately, the "drift effect" com-

Table 1. Attitudes Associated with Psychosomatic Complaints

Complaint	Attitude
Urticaria	Mistreatment and feeling of helplessness
Eczema	Interference from others; feelings of frustration
Raynaud's disease	Hostility
Rhinitis	Feeling that situation would go away
Asthma	As for rhinitis, but feeling more intense
Diarrhea	Wanting to be done with a situation
Constipation	Determination to persist with a job
Nausea/vomiting	Preoccupation with mistakes
Duodenal ulcer	Preoccupation with revenge
Migraine	Striving followed by relaxation
Hypertension	Need to be prepared for threat
Low back pain	Whole body action needed

SOURCE: Grace, W. J., & Graham, D. T. Relationship of specific attitudes and emotions to certain bodily diseases. *Psychosomatic Medicine*, 1952, *14*, 243–251. Reprinted by permission of the publisher.

plicated the interpretation of the results, but bearing this in mind the results provided some evidence in favor of the hypothesis. J. A. Stern, Winokur, Graham, and Graham (1961) repeated this experiment (again with normal subjects), adding a group in whom an attitude hypothesized to be characteristic of hypertension (anticipation of a stressful event) was induced, the prediction being that the attitude would produce a rise in diastolic blood pressure. Once again a reasonable degree of support for the hypothesis was found. Finally, Graham, Kabler, and Graham (1962) obtained results supporting the hypothesis when they compared the effects of the "hives" attitude with the "hypertension" attitude. On the basis of these experiments, it was concluded that:

> the specificity-of-attitude hypothesis . . .is compatible with a demonstration of either individual-specific or situation-specific patterns but suggests that the major effects of both of these factors may be accounted for by specific attitudes. (Graham, *et al.,* 1962, p. 166)

These four variants of the specificity hypothesis in fact represent more moderate statements of the extreme forms of the specificity/generality issue as defined at the beginning of this section. Additionally, it may be noted in passing that in a fairly large percentage of studies in which biofeedback has been used to bring a particular function under voluntary control, correlations have been reported between changes in the function being studied with biofeedback and changes occurring simultaneously in other functions not specifically the object of biofeedback training. Thus, when heart rate has been the object of study, changes in respiration rate, blood pressure, electrodermal responding, and so on have often been measured to determine the degree of specificity obtained in the function under study. It is unnecessary to coordinate and review the large amount of material potentially available since it is undoubtedly the case that a very confused picture would be the disheartening result. In any event, it seems clear that correlational data are not likely to be very helpful in elucidating the specificity issue. Of much more relevance, of course, are those studies in which a deliberate attempt is made to show whether or not a particular function can be brought under voluntary control while closely related functions remain unchanged, or those studies of the integration of closely related functions. It will be clear from the literature reviewed in previous chapters (for example, the work of Schwartz on the simultaneous raising and lowering of heart rate and blood pressure, or the simultaneous raising of heart rate while lowering blood pressure, or vice versa) that specificity of control is certainly possible to a limited degree. Once again, however, the basic question asserts itself: What is the true meaning of the results which have been obtained empirically in relation to the specificity/generality issue? A final answer to this question must be postponed until after a brief consideration of the integration or patterning of physiological processes, to which we must now briefly turn.

The classic work of Sherrington (1906) on the integrative action of the nervous system provided the empirical evidence which finally demolished the simplistic reflex arc explanation of behavior. In a sense, the extreme form of the specificity assumption is a modern equivalent of the reflex arc concept, but as Engel (1974) rather sarcastically pointed out, "If one taught an anxious patient to slow his heart, the end result would be an anxious patient whose heart beats slower" (p. 303).

It is, of course, obvious that the human organism functions in an integrated fashion and that it would not survive for more than a few minutes if that integration were to break down. This matter will be dealt with in detail later in this chapter. For the moment, only the practical implications of the integrative activity of the human organism in relation to the specificity assumption will be considered. The significance of the patterning of physiological processes in relation to the tendency of biofeedback studies to concentrate on narrowly defined response systems has been considered in some detail by Schwartz (1975, 1976), by Engel (1972), and by Obrist (1976). As Schwartz (1975) points out, the brain appears to have a remarkable capacity for producing both integrated ongoing activity while at the same time producing precisely controlled specificity of action when this is required. However, such apparent specificity of action is misleading in the sense that the precisely controlled action is performed against a background of controlled integrated activity. The precise activity is in no sense isolated from the general background activity, but is integrated with it, even though to the observer it appears as a "figure" against a "ground." It is precisely this failure of the integration of the specific activity with the accompanying background integration which produces a failure of practical functioning. As Schwartz (1975) has pointed out in relation to his own studies of heart rate and blood pressure, voluntary control of heart rate proceeds more rapidly when feedback is given for similar changes of direction in both heart rate and blood pressure than when feedback is provided only for appropriate changes in heart rate. Thus, heart rate can be successfully decoupled from blood pressure (and indeed, as Schwartz has shown, heart rate may be increased and blood pressure decreased simultaneously) but voluntary control will be more readily established if the natural patterning and integration of response systems are taken into account. Schwartz refers to the importance of biological constraints in voluntary control training and provides an important example from studies of the simultaneous control of heart rate and the electrical activity of the brain. After separate control was established in raising and lowering heart rate on the one hand, and enhancing and suppressing alpha on the other hand, the subjects were required simultaneously to raise or lower heart rate while enhancing or suppressing alpha. It was found that an alpha/heart-rate unidirectional constraint existed in that alpha control had a greater effect on heart rate than heart-rate control did on alpha (even though all possible combinations could be brought under voluntary control).[2] Thus, Schwartz has been led to the adoption of a gestalt point of view which

[2]Similar partial constraints with respect to frontalis muscle activity and alpha abundance have been demonstrated by DeGood and Chisholm (1977).

stresses the notion of an "emergent property" underlying the patterning or integration of somatic activity and control:

> Patterns of physiological processes can be both generated and processed by the brain, producing unique cross-system interactions and perceptual gestalts that make up a significant component of human behavior and subjective experience. The concept of pattern refers not simply to viewing, in isolation, combinations of physiological responses, but rather goes beyond the individual responses making up the pattern to recognize the novel, interactive or emergent property that patterns can acquire. Simply stated, the whole can be qualitatively different from the sum of its parts, and yet be dependent upon the organization of its parts for its unique properties. (1975, p. 323)

The point of view advanced by Schwartz may, however, be expressed in a somewhat different way in relation to the resolution of the problem of the specificity and generality assumptions which underly biofeedback research and therapy. To achieve this, it is necessary to refer to a quite different area of research which at first sight might appear to have no relevance whatever to biofeedback. The psychological effects of brain damage are a matter of great importance in clinical psychology, reflected in the continuing endeavor to construct tests of brain damage. Such tests are usually constructed by constituting a group of brain-damaged patients and attempting to show that they can be discriminated on one or more tests from a group of non-brain-damaged subjects (or better, patients with physical disorders not affecting brain functioning). With proper cross-validation of results, a test of brain damage will eventually result. The basic flaw in this procedure lies in the assumption that brain damage can be treated as a unitary concept. As Yates (1966) pointed out, however, it is necessary to adopt a hierarchical approach to this problem. That is, brain damage (of whatever kind) may be postulated to have general, group, specific, and "error" (random) effects in every patient who suffers a brain insult but the relative significance of each of these effects will differ from patient to patient. Thus, gradual deterioration of the blood supply to the brain (as in arteriosclerosis) will produce very general impairment of function but highly specific effects may not be readily apparent. A penetrating wound, on the other hand, may produce highly specific effects, depending on the exact site of the damage inflicted (such as blindness if the occipital cortex is destroyed) while at the same time producing only a small generalized impairment of functioning (which may not even be detectable). Hence, it does not make sense to ask whether the patient is "brain damaged" or not, or to attempt to construct *the* test of brain damage. Rather, the appropriate question is to what extent this patient demonstrates general, group, and specific effects of the brain damage suffered. The analogy, of course, is with the hierarchical structure of intelligence and personality (general, group, specific, and error factors).

The relevance of this framework for the specificity and generality assumptions in biofeedback should be obvious. A stark distinction between specificity and generality is both unhelpful and unnecessary, while a stress on the patterning of behavior to exclusion of specificity is also unhelpful. It is both possible and likely that extreme specificity may exist while at the same time it is both possible and likely that extreme generality may also exist. The problem is for each individual patient to discover the relative significance of the range of possibilities from specificity to generality. Thus, frontalis muscle training may be all that is needed in the treatment of tension headaches while blood flow and volume training may be all that is needed in the treatment of migraine headaches. In the case of generalized anxiety, however, a search for a single covariant physiological activity may be futile since anxiety may involve a wide range of dysfunctioning physiological systems.

The latter point, however, does not necessarily imply that generalized relaxation training in the case of anxiety will be more relevant or successful than specific training, provided in the latter case that a careful search is made to determine the specific physiological systems which are involved in anxiety. It should be stressed, of course, that this search will be for a pattern of dysfunction which is unique to the particular patient. If this unique pattern can be discovered, then specific training with biofeedback may be expected to be more effective than generalized relaxation training, the latter being the equivalent of the search for a single test of brain damage applicable to all brain-damaged patients.

The development of biofeedback instrumentation and methodology, in fact, provides a unique tool for the search for the physiological concomitants of behavioral abnormalities. This is clear in relation to certain abnormalities such as tension headaches but may be illustrated even more clearly with respect to disorders to which biofeedback has not yet been systematically applied. Phobias may be chosen as an example. The strength of a phobia is commonly assessed in three ways: a verbal report from the patient of the strength of his fear (either by questionnaire or in the presence of the feared object), a behavioral avoidance test (in which the patient attempts to approach the feared object), or physiological changes occurring in the presence of the feared object.[3] It is a striking fact that the correlations between these three measures tend to be low; indeed, following treatment (such as systematic desensitization) the patient might report a significant lessening of subjectively expressed fear and might approach close to or handle the feared object while simultaneously manifesting an unchanged level of physiological responsiveness. Within the framework developed here, it is suggested that the initial task of the biofeedback clinician must be to determine the specific physiological response systems which are correlated with the avoidance responding, that even for specific phobias the physiological pattern will be unique for each patient, and that biofeedback training will therefore need to be uniquely tailored for each patient. It is further being argued that the failure to obtain correlation between subjective, behavioral, and physiological measures of phobic fear in studies to date is the result of approaching the problem in the same way as the search for *the* test of brain damage. However, it is recognized that

[3]Such measures may, of course, be obtained while the patient is imagining the feared object rather than being in its presence.

even in the case of highly specific phobias, a search for a *single* physiological correlate (analogous to frontalis muscle activity in tension headaches) is likely to be futile. Even more futile, of course, would be a search for a single physiological correlate of generalized anxiety. Thus, Engel's dismissal of heart-rate training in anxiety and Schwartz's emphasis on the patterning of physiological responding are seen to be correct but at the same time the need to determine specific physiological responses need not be denied. Rather, the need is to determine in each individual case the relative contribution of general, group, and specific factors in the individual patient. In this connection appropriate research has hardly begun, but it is worth drawing attention to a recent study by McCutcheon and Adams (1975) which appears to support the position taken here. They used implosive therapy (which involves confronting the subject with the feared object directly) with a group of subjects who were unable to tolerate a film showing surgical procedures. They found that a reduction in anxiety to the film only occurred when implosive arousal of anxiety was relevant to the content of the film. Physiological arousal which was produced by a different kind of film had no effect on the anxiety which the surgical film produced; hence:

> It would appear that physiological arousal, observed in the Irrelevant Imagery Group, is not sufficient for change in the behavioral test to occur. Rather, there has to be physiological arousal in IT [implosive therapy] to anxiety-provoking cues which are relevant to the conditioned fear, and IT has to be continued until physiological habituation to these cues has taken place. (McCutcheon & Adams, 1975, p. 99)

The implications of this study for specific fears are clear: it is necessary to determine the precise link between specific physiological responding and the cues producing this responding if treatment is to be directed to voluntary control of the fear. But the argument can be extended to more general anxiety as well. Detailed behavioral and physiological analysis will lead to a more effective treatment program than will generalized relaxation training based on the assumption that a universal treatment procedure will be universally beneficial. It is not, of course, being argued here that general relaxation training is not beneficial, or indeed that specific relaxation training will not have favorable effects. What is being argued is that careful analysis of physiological responding in relation to anxiety-arousing situations will enable a treatment program to be devised that will be more effective than either a general, standard treatment or a highly specific treatment. It should be pointed out, of course, that the "anxiety-arousing situations" may refer to internal as well as external events. May (1977b) has demonstrated clearly that self-regulated phobic thoughts produce physiological changes that are similar to the changes produced by external phobic stimuli, and has stressed the importance of identifying specific phobic or obsessive thoughts and the possibility of eliminating them by biofeedback training directed toward control of identified physiological concomitants.

It may be concluded that the specificity/generality distinction is an inadequate basis from which to derive approaches to treatment. An integrated but hierarchical framework represents an alternative, viable approach. Such an approach may also appear to provide an answer to the question of what happens when biofeedback control is established, that is, when the subject or patient reestablishes a level of integration that has been lost by reintegrating the malfunctioning physiological response (or pattern of responses) into the general pattern of integrated responding. Hence, biofeedback training does indeed appear to teach the subject or patient the "language" of his somatic systems and their integration. That is not, however, the position that will finally be adopted here. Before proceeding to develop that position, however, several other important theoretical issues in biofeedback must be considered to complete the overall picture which provides the framework for the resolution of the problem of how control is exercised or reestablished after it has been lost.

The Role of Reinforcement in Biofeedback

The increase in voluntary control over a particular somatic function as the result of biofeedback training has been interpreted as, or even simply assumed to be, yet another example of the ubiquity of reinforcement as an explanatory principle in the explanation of behavior. Put in its simplest terms, the reinforcement explanation of biofeedback asserts that when a change in the display indicates to the subject that he has produced a response in the required direction, that change acts as a reinforcer which increases the probability that the response which produced it will be repeated by the subject and hence that learning will occur. By using appropriate shaping procedures the reinforced response may gradually be altered (made stronger or weaker as desired) until maximum learning has occurred. Of course, technically it is not necessary for the subject to be aware of the response which is being shaped, and indeed in many studies (for example, the earlier studies of Schwartz and his colleagues on heart rate and blood pressure) quite elaborate precautions were taken to prevent the subject from knowing which response was being trained. Although the intrusion of operant psychologists into the biofeedback area may seem somewhat surprising (since it was supposed by most research workers in the area that it was the informational aspects of biofeedback that were crucial), it is really no surprise at all since, just as psychoanalysts believe that all forms of human behavior are explainable in terms of psychodynamic factors, so the operant psychologists believe that all forms of human behavior are explainable in terms of reinforcement. In this, the psychoanalysts and the operant psychologists share a common rigidity and inflexibility of approach to the explanation of human behavior.

However, the meaningful question which requires serious discussion is whether reinforcement plays any role at all in biofeedback, and if it does, just what that role is. The answer to the question is not simple and indeed has not yet been fully determined, since the appropriately designed studies to work out the relative contributions of informational feedback and reinforcement have simply not yet been carried out, largely because *a priori* assumptions have made it seem unnecessary to carry out these experiments.

In order to understand why this is so, it is necessary to engage in a little history. As every psychologist knows, for the first half of this century a fairly clear distinction was made between classical and instrumental conditioning. In classical conditioning, the pairing of a neutral stimulus with an unconditioned stimulus (US) which produced an unconditioned response (UR) would eventually lead to the neutral stimulus's (such as a sound or light) becoming a conditioned stimulus (CS) for the unconditioned response (such as salivation) which was now termed a conditioned response (CR). The US was a primary reinforcer and the CS a secondary reinforcer. The operations defining the generation of a CR could be quite unequivocally specified and the precise conditions under which a CS could be generated, maintained, extinguished, and so on were investigated in great detail. In particular it was shown that the CR to the CS would extinguish quite rapidly unless periodical reestablishment of the pairing of the CS and US was instituted.

In the parallel field of instrumental or operant conditioning, a similar explanatory model for the acquisition of reliable responding to originally indifferent stimuli obtained with the important exception that the response to be conditioned was not an elicited response, or respondent (as in classical conditioning), but was an operant which had to appear spontaneously before reinforcement could begin to operate. The standard experiment to demonstrate operant conditioning involved, of course, the use of the Skinner box in which, for example, the rat would receive primary reinforcement for pressing a bar (a response it would originally perform occasionally but intermittently as part of its exploratory activity before training was instituted). Subsequently, following training the bar would be pressed to obtain a secondary reinforcer which had been paired with the primary reinforcer. Again, the operations defining operant or instrumental conditioning were quite clearly and unequivocally specified.

This very simple account of the basic features of classical and instrumental conditioning has been given because it enables two important points relevant to the role of reinforcement in biofeedback to be made. In the first place, a clear distinction was made in both classical and instrumental conditioning between primary and secondary reinforcers. A primary reinforcer (food, water, or sex in a situation where the animal had been deprived of food, water, or sex) was clearly distinguished from a secondary reinforcer (e.g., a light or sound), defined as a neutral stimulus which acquired reinforcing properties as a consequence of repeated presentations simultaneously with, or in a strictly specified temporal relationship with, the primary reinforcer. In the second place, the reinforcing properties of the secondary reinforcer would only be maintained, once training had occurred, if the primary reinforcer was occasionally paired with the secondary reinforcer. If this did not happen, then extinction of the CR would take place, although, in animals at least, it was shown that resistance to extinction could be greatly increased if partial reinforcement procedures were used during the acquisition training.

In general, therefore, control of behavior by secondary reinforcing stimuli could be demonstrated unequivocally by showing that a stimulus which originally had no effect on behavior could control behavior if it was repeatedly paired with another stimulus which did control that behavior, the latter stimulus being one that was related to primary drives such as hunger, thirst, and sex. The methodology of instrumental conditioning thus provided a strong definition of reinforcement and, specifically, of a secondary reinforcing stimulus.

However, it was eventually recognized that this model of reinforcement was simply inadequate to provide a basis for the explanation of the acquisition and maintenance of behavior in human subjects. The very tight experimental control which was necessary to demonstrate secondary reinforcement in the laboratory and the very fragile nature of the control then exercised by secondary reinforcement made it clear that secondary reinforcement as a controlling agent was simply inadequate as a basis from which to account for the maintenance of human behavior, or for changes in that behavior. The dilemma thus posed was resolved in an exceedingly simple, but equally unsatisfactory, manner. The distinction between primary and secondary reinforcement was simply abandoned and a reinforcer was defined as any stimulus consequent upon a response which increased the probability that the response would be repeated. Simultaneously, the "operant conditioners" or "reinforcement theorists" turned themselves into applied behavior analysts whose task became that of discovering empirically the stimuli (reinforcers) which controlled behavior, following which stimuli producing undesirable behaviors were eliminated and replaced by other stimuli associated with desirable alternative forms of behavior. Pragmatically, this changed approach (which may be termed the weak definition of reinforcement) has had some very beneficial consequences in the area of behavior modification. In other respects, however, its effect has been disastrous for it makes it impossible to develop a genuine theory of human behavior. The reason for this becomes evident if a comparison is made with a parallel weakness in the psychoanalytic approach. Let us suppose that a hypothesis derived from psychoanalytic theory predicts that a group of subjects will manifest anxiety in a specified situation. If the subjects do indeed manifest anxiety in the situation, the hypothesis is clearly supported. But if the subjects do not manifest anxiety in the situation, the psychoanalyst will be tempted to invoke the construct of reaction formation and argue that although anxiety was not manifested overtly, it was in fact induced but was repressed as a result of reaction formation. There is, of course, nothing inherently objectionable about the concept of reaction formation. What is objectionable is the *ad hoc* invocation of the concept to "save the hypothesis" so that there is no empirical result which could be obtained which would enable the hypothesis to be disproved. Clearly, the invocation of reaction formation to explain the unexpected results is valid only if its operation can be demonstrated independently of the operation which measures anxiety. Similarly, the weak form of the reinforcement principle leads to the situation where a stimulus is defined as reinforcing if its presence produces an increased probability of responding and as nonreinforcing if it does not. Theoretically, this is a very unsatisfactory position because it reduces psychology to the status of an empirical endeavor with no theoretical basis whatsoever. While this position is apparently quite acceptable to applied behavior analysts, it is not acceptable to many psychologists who regard psychology as more than just an empirical endeavor.

In the area of biofeedback, the pragmatic or weak definition of reinforcement has produced some curious consequences which will now be examined as a prelude to determining the role which reinforcement plays in biofeedback training.

Within the framework of the strong definition of reinforcement, a clear distinction was made, as we have seen, between primary and secondary reinforcers. Common examples of the latter would be lights or sounds which are originally neutral stimuli and become secondary reinforcers by being paired with primary reinforcers. But in the biofeedback situation, and within the framework of the weak definition of reinforcement, lights, sound, and other "neutral" stimuli have been described as reinforcers without ever having been paired with primary reinforcers.[4] A few examples chosen at random will illustrate the point. Elder and Eustis (1975) trained hypertensive patients to lower their diastolic blood pressure and presented a green light when reductions in diastolic blood pressure occurred and a red light when no change or an increase in diastolic blood pressure occurred. The study was described as one involving "instrumental blood pressure conditioning." Alpha enhancement produced an auditory tone in an experiment described as "operant conditioning" by Goesling, May, Lavond, Barnes, and Carreira (1974). Greene and Nielson (1966), in an experiment described as "operant GSR conditioning," presented "reinforcement" in the form of a digital counter display, while E. Kimmel and Kimmel (1963) used a dim light as the "reinforcer" for unelicited electrodermal responses. In some studies light has even been described as a secondary reinforcer within the strong definition of reinforcement in that it indicated monetary reward, even though it had never been directly paired with monetary reward (e.g., Rosenfeld, Rudell, & Fox, 1969, in their study of the "operant control" of the auditory evoked response).[5] In other studies, one visual stimulus has arbitrarily been

---

[4]It is not denied, of course, that strong lights and loud noises may act as primary aversive stimuli and hence their removal or cessation as a reinforcing situation.

[5]For other examples of light or sound described as a secondary reinforcer, see the studies by Beatty (1971), Engel and Hansen (1966), and Stephens, Harris, Brady, and Shaffer (1975), to cite but a few.

defined as a feedback stimulus with another visual stimulus equally arbitrarily defined as a reinforcing stimulus. Thus, Weiss and Engel (1971), in a study on the "operant conditioning" of heart-rate patients with premature ventricular contractions, used two lights (red and green) as "cue" lights indicating whether heart rate was to be increased or decreased, a visual meter display (described as "feedback") which indicated heart-rate increases and decreases, and a yellow light (described as a "reinforcer") which came on whenever a correct response was being made. Hamano and Okita (1972) have described the results of several Japanese studies in which, for example, light was used as a "reinforcer" in a study of heart rate and slides in a study of the electrodermal response. Bergman and Johnson (1972), in a study on the voluntary control of heart rate, used an auditory signal which was described as an informational or feedback stimulus, and a blue light which was activated whenever a specified criterion of responding was reached and which was described as a "reinforcer."

The confusion inherent in the use of reinforcement in its weak sense is compounded when it is realized that in many studies exactly the same stimuli have been used for display purposes without any reference whatsoever to reinforcement. Randomly chosen examples may include the studies by Brener, Kleinman, and Goesling (1969) in which "auditory feedback" was used in relation to heart-rate control; and by Brown (1970, 1971) in which "visual feedback" was used in relation to the control of alpha. And, of course, studies such as those by Lang and his colleagues have used complex visual displays described as feedback while simultaneously presenting other displays which are described as indicators of eventual (primary?) monetary reinforcement and thus could be regarded (although not necessarily specifically described) as secondary reinforcers (or, in effect, tokens) (e.g., Lang & Twentyman, 1974).

One of the major objections to the use of the weak definition of a reinforcer lies in the fact that a serious confounding thereby almost always exists in studies carried out within this framework between the *informational* and the *reinforcement* properties of the displays provided. That reinforcing stimuli may also have an informational component has not, of course, been denied by the applied behavior analysts, but it is almost always impossible to discriminate the informational from the reinforcement aspects of the displays as long as the weak definition of a reinforcer is employed. Such confounding was clearly present (and subsequently admitted to be present) in nearly all of the pioneering studies by Schwartz and Shapiro and their colleagues which have been discussed in detail in Chapter 4. The problem has, of course, been recognized and explicitly mentioned from time to time. Thus, Black (1972, pp. 107–112) discussed the relative significance of informational feedback and reinforcement in the voluntary control of neural events, while Brener (1975) has argued:

> Within the traditional framework of scientific explanation, the concept of events being the effects of their future consequences is totally alien. (p. 149)

Similar critical discussions of the use of reinforcement to explain the effects of biofeedback training may be found in many different sources.[6]

Whether or not a weak or a strong definition of reinforcement is adopted, two points need to be made. First, if reinforcement in its weak usage plays an important role in biofeedback training, then it should be possible to demonstrate even more readily the role of reinforcement in its strong usage. Second, if both reinforcement and informational feedback play important roles in biofeedback training, then it should not be too difficult a task to determine the relative role of these two factors by the use of appropriate experimental designs. Before considering the relatively sparse literature directly relating to these two points, let us consider the kind of experiment which might be conducted within the framework of a strong definition of reinforcement to determine whether increased voluntary control is a function of reinforcement or not. Within this framework, clearly there is a need to demonstrate that if a CS is paired with a US during a number of training trials, the control exercised by the US will be transferred to the CS and will continue to be exercised, at least for a time, by the CS after the US is withdrawn (it is assumed that the informational aspects of the CS and US remain constant, although in practice this might not be the case—however, other techniques, which are discussed below, would be needed to handle this aspect). The necessary experiment within the biofeedback situation is relatively easy to specify. In the case of training in voluntary control of frontalis muscle activity, for example, changes in muscle activity in the required direction would be followed by primary reinforcement such as food or water (the subject having been deprived of food or water for a period sufficient to induce a significant degree of deprivation), and the presentation of the primary reinforcer would be accompanied by the presentation of a neutral stimulus such as a dim light or a soft tone. The predictions would be quite clear: the availability of a primary reinforcer (the subject being in a state of deprivation) would induce learning of the required response (elevation or reduction of frontalis muscle activity) and the required response would then continue to be manifested after the primary reinforcer (food, water) is withdrawn, provided the originally neutral stimulus, which has now acquired secondary reinforcing properties, remains available (the subject continuing in a state of deprivation). Eventually, of course, if the primary reinforcer is never represented, extinction of the acquired control would be expected. It should, of course, also be possible to obtain all of the other characteristics of learning under these learning conditions, such as generalization, discrimination, spontaneous recovery, and so on. Furthermore, it should be possible to demonstrate the differential effects of the various kinds of schedules of reinforcement which can be introduced, and the expected curves of learning, extinction, spontaneous recovery, and so on should be manifested.

---

[6]See, for example, discussions in Brown (1977), Gaarder (1971), Lang (1974, 1975), Lynch and Paskewitz (1971), Peper and Mulholland (1970), Schwartz (1974), and Shapiro (1977).

Now it is a striking fact that no such demonstration has ever been obtained in biofeedback; indeed, no such research program has ever been undertaken, using positive primary and secondary reinforcers (that is, in an appetitive learning situation). Furthermore, it has been found again and again that the control achieved with feedback almost never shows the characteristics which would be expected if the control were a function of reinforcement variables (such as typical acquisition and extinction curves of learning). Nevertheless, it would be premature to conclude that reinforcement plays no role in the acquisition and maintenance of control in biofeedback. There is, in fact, one area of research where reinforcement (in its strong usage) has been unequivocally shown to play a very significant role. This is the area of escape-and-avoidance learning, using shock or other aversive consequences where the reinforcement is escape from or avoidance of the aversive stimulation. Some of these studies have been described in earlier chapters so that only a brief reminder of this work is needed here. Most of the studies deal with the control of heart rate or electrodermal responding. Brener (1966), for example, showed that subjects would learn to increase or decrease heart rate in order to avoid shock, compared with control subjects who received noncontingent shock. Similar results for heart rate were obtained by Cohen (1973) using an aversive tone, and by Shearn (1962) using shock. These studies do not represent a very satisfactory demonstration of the role of secondary reinforcement, however, because confounding by informational feedback was present and secondary reinforcers were not in fact established. A more important study in this respect is that by Frazier (1966), who used a discriminative avoidance-conditioning technique. The discriminative stimulus (S^d) was a light panel. During S^d epochs, shock was given after each minute in which heart rate decreased below the level of the previous minute. If the rate was maintained or increased, shock was withheld. Subsequently, the effect of the light panel alone as a secondary reinforcer was determined, shock not being presented. The results showed that the S^d (originally a neutral stimulus) acquired secondary reinforcing properties which were maintained for a considerable time after the primary reinforcer was completely withdrawn. Studies of the electrodermal response in a Sidman avoidance-type learning situation have also produced evidence of acquired avoidance responding in the presence of a secondary reinforcer and have been described in detail in previous chapters (e.g., Edelman, 1970; H. J. Johnson & Schwartz, 1967; H. D. Kimmel & Gurucharri, 1975; Martin & Dean, 1971; Martin, Dean, & Shearn, 1968).

There are several comparative studies which throw indirect light on the relative role of informational feedback and reinforcement in biofeedback control. Brolund and Schallow (1976) compared the effects on alpha enhancement of auditory feedback alone with the combined effect of auditory feedback and a backup reinforcer (class credit or a monetary reward if enhancement in the final training session was at least one and one-half times the original baseline level). The combined feedback/reinforcement group did significantly better than the feedback-only group, which did not differ from two control groups in alpha enhancement. However, a group receiving only reinforcement was not included in the design of the experiment. Reinking and Kohl (1975) compared five methods of relaxation training on frontalis muscle activity: general relaxation training alone, frontalis muscle activity reduction training alone, frontalis combined with general relaxation training, frontalis training combined with monetary reinforcement when a specified criterion was met, and simple instructions to relax generally. The three groups given frontalis muscle relaxation training were all more successful in reducing frontalis muscle activity levels but did not differ from each other, suggesting that the addition of general relaxation training or monetary reinforcement did not add to the effects of frontalis muscle training alone. Stephens *et al.* (1975), using a repeated-measures design, trained subjects to raise and lower heart rate: first without feedback or reinforcement, then with visual and auditory feedback (proportional initially, with binary added later), and finally with a combination of proportional and binary visual and auditory feedback, accompanied by a monetary reward when a specified criterion was met. The addition of monetary reward in the final stages did not appear to lead to any increase in the control which had been established with feedback, but of course the study is confounded and in any event ceiling effects may have been operating by the time monetary reward was introduced. McCanne and Sandman (1975) compared the effects of visual feedback[7] and monetary reinforcement on voluntary control of heart-rate increases and decreases. Some of the subjects were trained with visual feedback first, followed by training with monetary reinforcement; for others, the procedure was reversed. Control of heart-rate decreases was not demonstrated but for heart-rate increase training, increases were obtained when monetary reinforcement was given first and the effect persisted when a switch to visual feedback was made. However, when visual feedback was given first, increases in heart rate were not obtained, but did occur when the switch was made to monetary reinforcement (this latter change was not, however, attributed by the authors to the effects of reinforcement).

There are two studies in which the differential effect of monetary reinforcement has been examined. Kondo, Travis, and Knott (1975) randomly assigned female subjects to four conditions involving different monetary rewards ($0, $2.50, $5.00, or $10.00) for producing alpha enhancement which at the end of training exceeded initial training performance by at least 20%. The same kind of auditory feedback was provided for all groups. Alpha enhancement occurred in all four groups but a differential effect of amount of reward offered was not found. Similar results were found by Regestein, Pegram, Cook, and Bradley (1973) in a study of prolonged (12 h) maintenance of acquired alpha enhance-

---

[7]It should be noted that the study is described by the authors as one involving a comparison of two different reinforcers (a small green light and money), not as a comparison of feedback and reinforcement.

ment in subjects who had shown very high levels of alpha enhancement on initial 4-h training period. Payment or nonpayment of monetary rewards had no effect on the maintenance of high alpha levels. Malec, Sipprelle, and Behring (1978) provided continuous visual meter and auditory feedback in frontalis muscle activity reduction training while providing contingent, noncontingent, or no verbal "reinforcement." While this study was not primarily concerned with reinforcement, no differential effects were in fact found as a function of the amount of verbal "reinforcement" provided.

None of these studies represents an adequate test of the relative contribution of informational feedback and reinforcement to the voluntary control of behavior (or, if insisting on a total reinforcement framework, to the relative contribution of the informational and rewarding aspects of weak and strong reinforcers). The appropriate way to investigate this question, of course, requires the independent manipulation of informational feedback and reinforcement so that their separate effects and any possible interactions between the effects may be adequately determined. Thus, it would not be difficult to design an experiment in which the amount of informational feedback is systematically varied within a trial while at the same time the magnitude of a primary reward given at the end of each trial is also systematically varied. For reasons which are quite unclear, such an experiment appears not yet to have been carried out.

There is some even more indirect evidence from biofeedback studies which suggests that reinforcement may be an important variable in the establishment of control. Thus, Kohlenberg (1973), in a study described in detail in Chapter 4, found that feedback alone was not sufficient to produce anal sphincter pressure control in a child who soiled, but that the introduction of a schedule of reinforcement program involving monetary reward did lead to significantly improved control. The importance of rewards has often been demonstrated in the retraining of persons handicapped as a result of brain injury or cerebral vascular accidents (e.g., Goodkin, 1966; Meyerson, Kerr, & Michael, 1967). On the other hand, Sachs, Talley, and Boley (1976), who trained a female with hemiparesis to hold a cup without spilling liquid from it (see Chapter 3), and Silverstein, Nathan, and Taylor (1974), who trained alcoholics in blood alcohol level discrimination (see Chapter 6), concluded that informational feedback was more important than reinforcement in the acquisition of voluntary control.

What conclusion may then be drawn from all of this data about the role of reinforcement in biofeedback training? A good deal of consensus has in fact now been reached, and it may be illustrated by reference to the conclusion reached by Sachs *et al.* (1976) in the study just mentioned:

> The present data strongly suggest that behavioral improvement was the result of external feedback and not external reinforcement.... reinforcement provided the patient with sufficient incentive to utilize information to alter her behavior but, by itself, reinforcement was unable to produce consistent behavioral improvement. (p. 173)

Thus, the role of reinforcement in biofeedback is that of increasing motivational or incentive levels, rather than that of directly effecting learning or unlearning of responses. One effect of such an increase in motivation or incentive would be, of course, a heightened degree of attention to the informational content of the feedback display (although the implications of the Yerkes–Dodson law —which specifies that there is an optimal drive level which varies as a function of task difficulty—need to be borne in mind since too high a level of motivation may interfere with the acquisition of learning, just as may too low a level of motivation). Two comments should be made about this interpretation of the role of reinforcement in biofeedback training. The significance of the incentive role of reinforcement has been recognized for quite a long time in the area of biofeedback, in spite of the failure to carry out studies explicitly designed to test the proposition. Gaarder (1971) concluded that reinforcement helps to motivate the subject in the presence of informational feedback, while Schwartz and his colleagues (e.g., Schwartz, 1974; Shapiro & Schwartz, 1972; Shapiro & Watanabe, 1971), quite early in their studies which confounded informational feedback and reinforcement, recognized that the role of reinforcement was mainly if not wholly motivational. Second, the applied behavior analysts would not disagree that reinforcement has a motivational or incentive component. Thus, it would no doubt seem to them that the question of whether reinforcement is informational or motivational is a meaningless question and wonder what all the fuss is about. The question is not, however, a meaningless one. The applied behavior analysts tend to take the position that reinforcement affects responses which are already in the behavioral repertoire of the subject and that biofeedback training merely alters the relative probability of the emission of competing responses in a particular stimulus situation.[8] It will, however, be argued later in this chapter that biofeedback training is not in fact that kind of training at all, and hence that maintaining a distinction between informational feedback and reinforcement of responding is of vital importance. Finally, it should be noted that other criticisms of the reinforcement position (e.g., Gatchel, 1974; Lang, 1974, 1975; Lynch & Paskewitz, 1971; Peper & Mulholland, 1970) have been made for reasons other than those put forward here. (Lang, for example, has leaned toward a motor learning interpretation of biofeedback.) The question of the role of reinforcement in biofeedback will need to be taken up again briefly when the servomechanical model of biofeedback control is eventually considered.

The Role of Somatic Mediation in Biofeedback

As we have seen, the instrumental conditioning paradigm as it is applied to autonomic functions requires that an unelicited response (such as a change in

---

[8] The standard example is that in training a rat to turn right in a maze to receive reinforcement, the rat is not being trained in *how* to turn right (a response it already has in its repertoire) but rather is being trained to turn right in preference to turning left.

heart rate) be emitted and followed by "reinforcement" with the consequence that there will be an increase in the probability that the changed response will again be emitted the next time the (unspecified, and presumably unspecifiable) "stimulus complex" associated with the original response is present. The autonomic response is regarded as being directly conditioned in exactly the same way as a skeletal response to which the instrumental paradigm has always been regarded as being appropriately applied. Thus, the question of "mediation" of the acquired autonomic change in responding is regarded by the applied behavior analysts as a meaningless question, indeed as a relic of the "ghost in the machine" controversy. In relation to biofeedback, this point of view has perhaps been most forcefully expressed by H. D. Kimmel (1974):

> I believe that it is because of this unrecognized free will attributed to skeletal behavior that involuntary, autonomic behavior must be restricted to modifiability only by classical conditioning, that is, mechanically. Exclusion of autonomic responses from the elite domain of the instrumentally conditionable has the function of protecting the unrecognized dualism. Perhaps the influence of Skinner's (1971) *Beyond Freedom and Dignity* will ultimately sweep the ghost of this reverse dualism from autonomic behavior's closet. Surely, if we succeed in purging what Skinner calls "autonomous man" as an explanatory concept in dealing with skeletal behavior, we may also succeed in banishing him, in the guise of an unobservable central mediator, in dealing with the more mechanical autonomic responses. (p. 331).

The curare studies of Miller and his colleagues (see Chapter 1), of course, represent attempts to exorcise the "ghost in the machine." Unfortunately, the mediators refuse to fold up their tents and steal quietly away. Indeed, if the amount of empirical research in recent years is any criterion, the search for the mediators of biofeedback is flourishing as never before, even among the applied behavior analysts, and, even though it is true, as Kimmel and others have pointed out, it is still impossible to demonstrate conclusively that mediation is either a necessary or a sufficient condition for the voluntary control of automatic activity.

In direct constrast to Kimmel's plea for the exorcism of the "ghost," R. S. Lazarus (1975) has recently insisted on the necessity of finding and taking into account the mediators of autonomic behavior. Lazarus makes an important distinction between two kinds of coping or regulatory behavior in dealing with stress: direct action which involves attempts to deal with whatever problem generates stress in the first place, and palliative action which responds to the stress by reducing the emotional state arising from the stress without attempting to deal with the problem generating the stress. He provides as examples of the two reaction modes the student facing an important, stressful examination who responds by appropriate study on the one hand (direct action response), or by engaging in the use of tranquilizers or muscle relaxation (palliative response) on the other hand:

> The palliative form of control that aims at reducing somatic turmoil rather than at resolving its psychodynamic origins is the arena into which biofeedback research and

its use in therapy fall. It would argue that those who want to rule out cognitive or other mediators in biofeedback research miss the central point in the self-regulation of emotion. Not only does such an effort greatly narrow the scope of such self-regulation, but it misses the complexity of the problem and the diverse patterns by which it typically operates in all our lives. We need to have more knowledge of the myriad forms of self-regulation that are available and serviceable to given kinds of people and in given types of situations in managing their emotional lives.... as my opening statements suggest, a major virtue of the biofeedback movement lies in the opportunity it provides to test some of our ideas about the coping processes used by people and about those that are capable of influencing the emotional response. (Lazarus, 1975, p. 559)

Apart from the reinforcement approach (which could be regarded as a mediational interpretation) there are two main candidates for the role of mediation in biofeedback: the somatic and the cognitive. A very large literature now exists in relation to both these candidates and an attempt will be made here to place this literature in perspective. Before doing so, however, a major difficulty (which will no doubt confirm Kimmel in his view that the entire endeavor to establish mediating variables is futile) should be pointed out, one which has been largely, but not entirely, ignored. The difficulty applies particularly to the cognitive mediational position, but applies also, although less obviously, to the somatic mediational position. It becomes apparent most obviously in relation to the search for correlates of alpha enhancement. Does successful alpha enhancement produce changes in cognitive state or do changes in cognitive state produce changes in alpha enhancement? The studies by Kamiya and his colleagues were based on the assumption that alpha enhancement produced altered states of consciousness, whereas the studies by Brown (1970, 1971) were equally firmly based on the assumption that altered states of consciousness or affective state produced changes in alpha. Or do the alpha changes *and* the state of consciousness changes occur simultaneously, both being mediated by some common third variable? For Kimmel, of course, the mere posing of the questions is simply an indicator of the persistence of the mind/body dualism which has plagued psychology for centuries and which the applied behavior analysts have worked so hard to eradicate. Nevertheless, the question needs to be raised, given the nature of the empirical studies which are about to be reviewed. If the question is a meaningful one, then clearly the answer will not be forthcoming from correlational studies and hence the innumerable reports of correlations between biofeedback variables, gathered incidentally as part of the study in question, will not be considered here. Only experimental studies which have attempted to treat one variable as a dependent variable while manipulating the other as an independent variable will be examined.

Turning now to the somatic mediation hypothesis, most of the work to be considered relates to the possible role of inconspicuous muscle activity in producing the increases and decreases in heart rate which have been produced in biofeedback studies. It is, of course, obvious that massive increases in heart rate can readily be produced by vigorous exercise, but the activity of climbing a short flight of stairs or even of small movements can produce a detectable increase in heart rate. The possibility that the voluntary control of heart-rate increases is mediated via relatively small muscle activities cannot easily be ruled out. Lind, Taylor, Humphreys, Kennelly, and Donald (1964) and Lind and McNicol (1967), for example, showed that muscle contraction produced heart rate increases. Lind et al. (1964) measured the cardiovascular responses of four normal subjects before, during, and after sustained hand-grip contractions which were sustained at 10%, 20%, and 50% of maximum possible voluntary contraction. Cardiac output, systemic arterial pressure, and heart rate all showed graded responses proportional to the tension exerted. Similar effects of squeezing a dynamometer with one-sixth the maximum possible voluntary pressure were found by Peters and Gantt (1953), heart rate increasing by 8 bpm for the lesser exertion as compared with an increase of 27 bpm for maximal exertion. Belmaker, Proctor, and Feather (1972) required one group of normal subjects to "tense the chest muscles, as if a heavy pile of sand were on the chest and it were difficult to breathe," while a second group was instructed to "tense the diaphragm and abdominal muscles, as if expecting a blow." A shaping procedure was employed which rewarded heart-rate increases[9] while punishing respiratory changes, detectable EMG activity, and gross movement. It is important to note that the tensing activities required did not result in surface muscle activity that was detectable by surface electrodes. Each of the 11 subjects achieved heart-rate increases of 10 bpm or greater during at least one of the four trials given, but no correlation was found between EMG activity levels (recorded from the heart-rate electrodes) or respiratory patterns. The results of this study were regarded as evidence for the influence of low-level muscle activity deep within the body structure on heart rate.

One way of investigating the role of muscle tension in the voluntary control of heart rate would be to train subjects with feedback to produce and hold varying levels of increases and decreases in a muscle complex, increases and decreases in which are known to affect heart rate, and then to see whether or not heart-rate increases and decreases with and without feedback can be produced while the various levels of muscle tension are held without feedback. Successful voluntary control of heart rate in these conditions would be strong evidence that variations in muscle activity (at least in the muscle system involved) are not necessary to establish voluntary control of heart rate (of course, mediation could have occurred through uncontrolled muscle activity but the onus would then clearly be thrown on proponents of the mediation hypothesis to demonstrate which muscles are involved or progressively eliminate other muscle complexes as the mediators). This critical experiment does not appear to have been carried out, but a study by Magnussen (1976) contains elements of it. She assigned 30 female

---

[9]In fact, no feedback was provided in this study for heart-rate increases, and the subjects were given no information about heart rate.

subjects to one of three groups run over three sessions in varying combinations of visual meter feedback for raising heart rate, accompanied or not by the production of specified degrees of muscle tension obtained by squeezing a hand dynamometer at 20% of maximum possible tension. In the three sessions, one group was given feedback while tensing for the first two sessions, then given feedback only; a second group was given feedback only for all three sessions; and a third group was required to tense but was not given feedback for the first two sessions, followed by a session in which feedback only was given. The main result was that the first group, given feedback *and* required to tense in the first two training sessions, showed an increase in heart rate (compared with the other two groups) which was not maintained in the third session, when feedback only was available. Thus, muscle tension played a role in determining the heart-rate increases obtained but feedback was also shown to be significant, since the performance of this group in raising heart rate in the first two sessions was superior to the third group (not given feedback, but required to tense muscles) which showed a smaller rise in heart rate, equivalent to the levels achieved by the second group, given feedback only.

These studies indicate that small amounts of muscle tension do significantly influence heart rate but may not account for the whole of the increases obtained when feedback is provided. Evidence that muscle relaxation may correspondingly produce a reduction in heart rate (in the absence of feedback training) has been provided by E. Jacobson (1940), who also showed that decreases in blood pressure may result from muscle relaxation training (E. Jacobson, 1939), findings which have provided a basis for the use of general muscle relaxation training in cases of anxiety and tachycardia, as well as hypertension (see Chapters 4 and 6).

Respiration rate and depth is another muscle activity which, it has been suggested, may mediate heart-rate changes in biofeedback training. Correlational findings (which have been reported in a large number of biofeedback studies) have largely failed to show any consistent relationship between changes between heart rate and breathing rate and depth. However, experimental studies which treat breathing as an independent variable suggest that it is important to distinguish between rate and depth of breathing, whereas the correlations have almost always reflected rates of breathing and neglected depth. As with other muscle activities, there is some evidence that heart rate can be brought under voluntary control with respiration rate held constant. Brener and Hothersall (1967) measured resting respiration rate and instructed the subjects to breathe at the rate (in time with a light flashing at the resting breathing rate) while attempting to increase and decrease heart rate with auditory feedback (the subjects were uninformed, merely being told to control the tones). Control established before paced respiration was introduced was maintained when respiration rate was itself controlled. Sroufe (1969) controlled respiration rate by instructing his subjects to breathe in synchrony with a respiration simulator set for 14, 16, or 18 cycles per minute. With respiration rate thus controlled, the subjects who received visual feedback of their own heart rate were able to reduce heart rate variability better than subjects receiving nonveridical heart-rate feedback. The most rigidly controlled study, however, has been that by Vandercar, Feldstein, and Solomon (1977). They respirated their subjects at a constant rate and tidal volume, using a Bennett MA1 respirator, so that breathing rate and depth were definitely not under subject control. The ability to raise and lower heart rate with continuous visual and auditory feedback in this condition was compared with results obtained before and after this training in conditions where the subjects were instructed to control respiration rate and depth. Control of heart rate (indexed by differences between raise/lower periods) was achieved when respiration rate and depth were under instructional control. However, respiration rate was found to increase in the heart-rate increase condition suggesting possible mediation of heart rate by respiration, and this possibility was strongly supported by the finding that heart-rate control was not achieved when respiration rate was artificially controlled.

Epstein and Webster (1975) were primarily interested in determining the extent to which respiratory behavior itself could be controlled under conditions involving no instructions about breathing rate, instructions only in rate and depth of breathing, instructions in rate and depth of breathing combined with a pacing stimulus, and the addition of verbal discrete feedback to instructions and a pacing stimulus. While increased control of breathing behavior was successfully obtained, the resultant changes in respiration had no discernable effect on heart rate. However, it has been shown by Harrison and Raskin (1976) and by Sroufe (1971) that a rapid increase in rate of breathing may reduce heart-rate variability while respiration depth may affect both heart-rate level and variability (Sroufe, 1971), although the heart-rate changes produced in this way have been shown by Wells (1973) not to exceed those which can be produced by feedback. As with other kinds of muscle activity, therefore, while respiration rate and depth may be used to control heart rate and heart-rate variability, it seems possible that heart-rate control can be exercised when breathing rate and depth are reasonably well controlled.

Turning now to the voluntary control of the electrical activity of the brain, the oculomotor theory provides perhaps the clearest example of all of a somatic mediation hypothesis since it postulates that alpha control is mediated via the effects of eye movements. Since this theory was discussed in detail in Chapter 5 the reader need only be reminded that recent work reported by Eason and Sadler (1977) has shown fairly decisively that elevation of the eyes is not the critical factor in producing enhanced alpha; rather, the degree of convergence and divergence of the eyes plays the vital role, with increased convergence leading to decreased alpha and vice versa. Once again, this does not imply that convergence or divergence is necessary for increased or decreased alpha but only that such movements of the eyes are sufficient to produce alpha changes equal to those obtained with feedback. Sadler and Eason (1977) have also shown that physiological activity tends to increase as alpha abundance decreases, a finding which fits well with the evidence that physiological activity tends to be reduced in meditative states as alpha increases. Sadler and Eason (1977) also found that evoked potentials to visual stimuli tended to become more precise when alpha activity was lowered, indicating increased arousal. Spilker, Kamiya, Callaway, and Yeager (1969), on the other hand, showed that evoked responses to visual stimuli increased in amplitude (although not necessarily in precision) when alpha abundance was high. However, no change was found in auditory evoked responses. Schwartz (1975) has reported the results of studies which tend to indicate that voluntary control of heart rate may affect alpha levels whereas the reverse does not occur.

It remains unclear whether other forms of electrical activity may be mediated by muscle activity. Sittenfeld *et al.* (1976; see Chapter 5 for a detailed account of this study) claimed that training in frontalis muscle activity reduction facilitated subsequent training in the voluntary control of increases in theta activity, but their results were not replicated by Lutzenberger, Birbaumer, and Steinmetz (1976).

It will be apparent that all of the examples of somatic mediation discussed so far involve a relatively high degree of specificity of mediational control, as in the effect of variations in the rate and depth of breathing on the rate and variability of the heartbeat. And indeed, the great majority of biofeedback studies on both the control of normal and abnormal functions appear to be based on the assumption that specificity of control is a desirable achievement. If, however, it is accepted that the functioning of the organism in an integrated fashion is based on hierarchical systems of increasing complexity, then specificity of control may be, in some circumstances, actually harmful to efficient functioning. One possibility is that where an apparent specific dysfunction exists, the response in question has become "uncoupled" from the integrated system or subsystem and is behaving in a maverick way (that such "uncoupling" can be experimentally produced has been shown clearly in studies by Gavalas, 1968, and Gavalas-Medici, 1972, in relation to respiration and electrodermal responding). Brener (1975) has argued that specificity of control is important only when integrated activity is the norm. Thus, a demonstration that finger temperature can be modified without affecting movement of the big toe is trivial, whereas a demonstration that one toe can be moved independently of the other toes effectively "uncouples" a normally integrated activity. The point to be noted, however, is that biofeedback training in specific control of an "uncoupled" big toe may be irrelevant or even harmful if what is really required is a restoration of the lost integrated activity of toe movements. Adaptively, in most circumstances it may be highly inappropriate to have the ability to wiggle one's toes independently if this interferes with the "normal" ability to move them synchronously. Thus, the aim of biofeedback training cannot be divorced from a consideration of the integrative features of organismic activity, a consideration which may well explain some of the disappointing results which have been obtained with specific biofeedback training.

This question will be taken up again later, but reference needs to be made here to one aspect of the integrative activity of the nervous system in relation to specificity of control. It has been suggested by Brener (1975) and by Obrist, Webb, Sutterer, and Howard (1970), among others, that while it may be true that somatic events may mediate cardiovascular events, a higher level of central nervous system mediation may actually mediate both sets of events which are "coupled" together at this higher level. If this is so, then it becomes important to take account of, and perhaps bring under control, these higher level activities, rather than attempting to control the more specific relationships which are manifested at lower levels. One such integrative system which has been proposed will serve to illustrate the point, namely, the alleged ergotropic and trophotropic systems of autonomic-somatic integration, originally proposed by Hess (1925) and subsequently developed in detail by Gellhorn (1967). Activation of the ergotropic system occurs in situations of danger or apprehension, whereas activation of the trophotropic system occurs in situations where danger or anxiety are minimal. An ergotropic/trophotropic balance would be present in "normal" situations, with shifts in the balance occurring as a consequence of differential stimulation of the hypothalamus, depending particularly on the amount of proprioceptive feedback stimulation reaching the hypothalamus. The major effects of stimulation of the two systems on autonomic, somatic, and behavioral responding are shown in Table 2, while the effects of a change in the balance of the two systems are shown in Table 3. Clearly, biofeedback studies have not yet achieved the degree of sophistication needed to cope with such complicated integrative systems yet it may be essential to develop techniques which are able to handle the integrated nature of physiological events if real progress is to be made. In this connection, it may be noted that whereas the human organism routinely integrates its activities in an astonishingly complex manner quite automatically, there are no more than a handful of biofeedback studies which have attempted to train subjects in the control of more than a single response at any one time—and the situation seems to be that such attempted voluntary control would be exceedingly difficult to achieve. The question of why complex integrated activity should be the norm in human behavior yet voluntary control of complex behaviors with biofeedback training should present insuperable problems is one which has received little or no attention so far, in spite of its crucial relevance to present training procedures. This point will also be taken up again later in this chapter. As has already been pointed out, there has been some recognition of the problem (e.g., by Schwartz) and a few studies relating to somatic constraints have been carried out (e.g., Manuck, 1976; Obrist, Galosy, Lawler, Gaebelein, Howard, & Shanks, 1975). Obrist et al. (1975), for example, studied the effects of instructional control of somatic activity (chin muscle activity, general activity, eye movements, eyeblinks, respiration rate and amplitude),

Table 2. The Effects of Stimulation of the Ergotropic and Trophotropic Systems[a]

Autonomic effects	Somatic effects	Behavioral effects
A. Stimulation of the Ergotropic System		
Augmented sympathetic discharges 　1. Increased cardiac rate, blood pressure, sweat secretion 　2. Pupillary dilation and contraction of nictitating membrane 　3. Inhibition of GI motor and secretory function	Desynchrony of EEG, increased skeletal muscle tone, elevation of certain hormones: adrenaline, noradrenaline, adrenocortical steroids, thyroxin	Arousal, heightened activity, and emotional responsiveness
B. Stimulation of the Trophotropic System		
Augmented parasympathetic discharges 　1. Reduction in cardiac rate, blood pressure, sweat secretion 　2. Pupillary constriction and relaxation of nictitating membrane 　3. Increased GI motor and secretory function	Synchrony of EEG, loss of skeletal muscle tone, blocking of shivering response, increased secretion of insulin	Inactivity, drowsiness, and sleep

[a]SOURCE: Gellhorn, E., & Kiely, W. F. Mystical states of consciousness: Neurophysiological and clinical aspects. *Journal of Nervous and Mental Disease,* 1972, *154,* Table 1. Reprinted by permission of the author and the publisher.)

informational and noninformational feedback, and contingent or random aversive consequences, on the control of increases and decreases in heart rate in uninformed subjects. The instructions were varied so as to involve no control, minimum control, or maximal control over the somatic activities specified while heart-rate control was being established. The main results are shown in Figure 3. Instructional control of somatic activity had a highly significant effect on the control of heart-rate increases, but not on heart-rate decreases. While this study clearly indicates the interaction of various somatic activities, it does not, of course, directly address the question of integrative control but remains confined within the framework of examining what happens to one activity when other covarying activities are controlled to varying degress.

Two other lines of investigation are relevant to the question of the role of somatic mediation in biofeedback. One of the historically important antecedents

---

Table 3. Reciprocity between Ergotropic and Trophotropic Systems[a]

1. Shift in ergotropic–trophotropic balance through trophotropic stimulation

Excitation of trophotropic system	Effects on ergotropic system
a. Reflexly through baroreceptors by raising sinoaortic pressure b. Directly through low-frequency stimulation of medulla oblongata, supraoptic area, caudate nucleus, or basal forebrain area	a. Autonomic: inhibition of sympathetic discharges to pupil, nictitating membrane, heart, sweat glands b. Somatic: synchrony in EEG, lessened skeletal muscle tone c. Behavioral: inhibition of sham rage

2. Shift in ergotropic–trophotropic balance through ergotropic stimulation

Excitation of ergotropic system	Effects on trophotropic system
a. Reflexly through baroreceptors by lowering sinoaortic pressure b. Directly by stimulation of posterior hypothalamus or mesencephalic reticular formation	a. Autonomic: reduction in tonic state of oculomotor (3rd) nerve; diminution in parasympathetic responsivity b. Somatic: lessening of recruitment responses in EEG

3. Shift in ergotropic–trophotropic balance through CNS lesions

Reduction in ergotropic tone by lesions placed in:	Effects on trophotropic system
a. Posterior hypothalamus b. Mesencephalic reticular formation c. Transection brainstem at intracollicular level	Increase in parasympathetic reactions: reduction in blood pressure, cardiac rate, and skeletal muscle tone; cortical synchrony in EEG; somnolence

Reduction of trophotropic tone by lesions in:	Effects on ergotropic system
a. Septal and anterior hypothalamic areas b. Medial thalamic nuclei c. By midpontine transection	Increase blood pressure and cardiac rate; heightened arousal and activity; desynchrony in cortical EEG

---

[a]SOURCE: Gellhorn, E. & Kiely, W. F. Mystical states of consciousness: Neurophysiological and clinical aspects. *Journal of Nervous and Mental Disease*, 1972, *154*, Table 2. Reprinted by permission of the author and the publisher.)

---

of biofeedback was the attempt to show that instrumental conditioning of autonomic functioning could be obtained in rats whose skeletal functioning was totally paralyzed (see Chapter 1). There are a few studies with human subjects of a similar nature. The work of Lapides, Sweet, and Lewis (1957) in which voluntary control of the initiation of urination was achieved by subjects who were totally paralyzed has already been described (see Chapter 1), and it will be

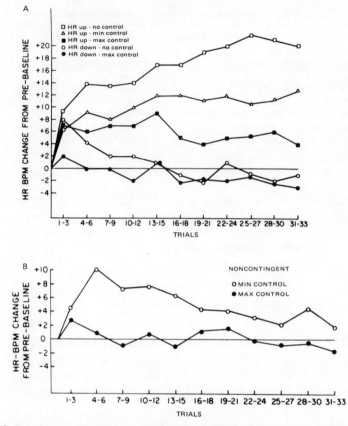

Figure 3. Base-S_D level HR differences averaged over blocks of three trials: **A.** contingent reinforcement groups; **B.** noncontingent groups (From Obrist, P. A., Galosy, R. A., Lawler, J. E., Gaebelein, C. J., Howard, J. L., & Shanks, E. M. Operant conditioning of heart rate: Somatic correlates. *Psychophysiology,* 1975, *12,* 448, Figure 1. Reprinted by permission of the author and the publisher.)

recalled that Birk, Crider, Shapiro, and Tursky (1966) obtained electrodermal control in a single subject under partial curarization (see Chapter 4). Two other studies may be mentioned here. Brucker, Dworkin, Eisenberg, Miller and Pickering (1975) attempted to train eight severely paralyzed patients (four as a result of poliomyelitis and four affected with muscular dystrophy) to increase and decrease diastolic blood pressure with the aid of auditory feedback. Most of the patients showed small but significant changes in blood pressure in the required direction. Attempted contraction of paralyzed muscles led to a rise in blood pressure and heart rate (an effect attributed by the authors to be mediated by "central commands" rather than residual muscle activity in the affected limb), while in a group of 16 patients with paralysis, attempted maximal hand grip produced a mean rise of 8.7 mm Hg in diastolic blood pressure and a mean rise of 9.1 bpm in heart rate after 1 min. Comparable rises were not found in normal subjects attempting the same task. In a later report,[10] Pickering (1976) found that one-quarter of a group of tetraplegic patients with complete cervical cord transections were able to produce increases in systolic blood pressure of between 7 and 24 mm Hg. This apparent voluntary control could be blocked by atropine (suggesting that a vagal mechanism was involved) and the patients could not produce equivalent blood pressure changes by using respiratory maneuvers or attempting muscle contractions. While these studies offer some support for the view that somatic mediation of autonomic functions may not be necessary for control to be achieved, their results can hardly be regarded as impressive evidence, given the known variability over short periods of time of both blood pressure and heart rate, and in the absence of data relating to such variability in these patients.

The second line of evidence relates to studies which have attempted to show whether the ability to discriminate levels of and changes in autonomic or somatic activity is related to the ability to bring these activities under increased voluntary control, with or without feedback. The first group of studies concerns the use of the Mandler Autonomic Perception Questionnaire (APQ), constructed by Mandler, Mandler, and Uviller (1958). The defined "autonomic feedback" as:

> the relationship between autonomic response and subjects' reported perception of such response-induced stimulation. (p. 367)

The full APQ consists of three parts dealing with subjective reports of feelings when anxious or pleased (part I); perception of bodily activity—heart rate, perspiration, temperature change, respiration, gastrointestinal upset, muscle tension, and blood pressure—when anxious (part II); and responses to 70 items from the Minnesota Multiphasic Personality Inventory, 50 dealing with aspects of anxiety and 20 dealing with reports of internal body stimulation (part III). The APQ was validated by comparing subjects scoring at the extreme ends of the test on performance on extremely difficult cognitive tasks (constituting a high-stress situation) and simultaneously recording measures of autonomic activity (heart rate, electrodermal responding, respiration rate, temperature of face and cheek, and blood volume). They found that the measures of autonomic activity tended to correlate positively and that high APQ scorers (supposedly able to perceive autonomic changes successfully) showed significantly greater autonomic activity and tended to overestimate autonomic response levels as compared with low APQ scorers. It has been assumed that differences in APQ scores reflect differences in the ability to detect autonomic activity and changes in that activity, and hence that high scorers will be more successful in bringing autonomic functions under voluntary control in the biofeedback training situation, whether or not external augmented feedback is presented. However, with one minor exception

[10]Reported in abstract form only.

the results of studies using either the whole questionnaire or part of it (e.g., the items relating to the perception of heart activity) have not confirmed this expectation. Bergman and Johnson (1971) demonstrated instructional control of heart-rate increases and decreases without feedback and reported that greater control was achieved by those subjects who obtained intermediate APQ scores as compared with those obtaining high or low scores, but the effect was a very weak one. Blanchard, Young, and McLeod (1972), using only the items relating to the perception of heart activity, found that, contrary to expectation, subjects who reported low awareness of heart activity were better able to produce increases and decreases of heart rate with feedback than subjects who reported high awareness of heart activity. McFarland (1975), also using the heart items of the APQ only, could find no relationship between APQ scores and control of heart-rate increases and decreases with feedback. Similar negative findings were reported by McCanne and Sandman (1976), and Leib, Tryon, and Stroebel (1976), using inpatients (not further defined), found no relationship between APQ scores and ability to enhance or suppress alpha, while Greene and Nielson (1966) reported that subjects with low APQ scores manifested better control of electrodermal responding than did subjects with high APQ scores. Thus, the evidence is strong that individual differences in APQ scores are either unrelated to individual differences in the ability to control autonomic functions or that high APQ scores lead to results opposite to those expected if sensitivity to autonomic changes facilitates autonomic control. Negative results were also obtained by Ikeda and Hirai (1976) in a study of the relationship between control of the skin potential response and a measure of the "intensity of autonomic self-perceptions in daily life."

The APQ relates to individual differences in the ability to discriminate within and between internal bodily states. A good deal of effort has been expended to determine whether individual differences in tendencies to be "inwardly" or "outwardly" oriented are related to the ability to gain voluntary control over internal bodily states. Studies of the field dependence/independence construct have been sparse and the results not encouraging. Leib et al. (1976), in the study just mentioned, used the Rod-and-Frame and Embedded Figures tests to form groups high and low in degree of field dependence but could find no difference between the groups so formed on alpha enhancement and suppression with feedback. G. R. Jacobson, Wilson, and La Rocca (1977) trained alcoholics to enhance and suppress alpha with feedback and reported that better control was achieved by those patients who were field independent (and therefore presumably "inwardly" oriented). Once again, however, the positive finding was a very weak one.

However, more encouraging results have been reported in studies utilizing the locus-of-control[11] construct developed by Rotter (1966). The Rotter I–E Scale was designed to measure individual differences in the extent to which the

[11]The inclusion of the locus-of-control variable as a possible somatic mediator is, of course, fairly arbitrary. It could just as easily have been included in the next section on cognitive mediation.

subject believes that he controls his own behavior as compared with a belief that his behavior is controlled by forces not under his control, or by chance. Ray and Lamb (1974) trained their subjects to increase and decrease heart rate with and without feedback and found that internally oriented subjects did better at increasing heart rate than externally oriented subjects, whereas the reverse was the case for decreasing heart rate. These results were replicated by Ray (1974), who additionally found that externally oriented subjects reported that they tried to decrease heart rate by paying increased attention to the environment (that is, directing their attention away from internal activities). Scores on a self-report affect scale showed no correlation with heart-rate control. The studies by Ray were criticized by Blankstein and Egner (1977) on the grounds that the training period he used was too short. When they gave a somewhat longer period of heart-rate increase and decrease training they found that internally oriented subjects were more successful at both tasks. However, Gatchel (1975), who gave far more extended heart-rate control training than either Ray or Blankstein and Egner, reported that whereas he found the same results as Ray in the first training session, no differences in heart-rate control as a function of locus-of-control scores were evident in any of the subsequent three training sessions. Positive results have also been found in relation to alpha-enhancement and suppression training. Goesling *et al.* (1974) found that internally oriented subjects were able to enhance alpha with auditory feedback more successfully than externally oriented subjects, and the differences increased as training progressed. R. K. Johnson and Meyer (1974), using a modified version of the Rotter Scale, confirmed this finding and showed additionally that internally oriented subjects who failed to demonstrate alpha enhancement showed a shift by the end of training toward being externally oriented, whereas internally oriented subjects who did achieve control showed no such shift. Negative results were, however, found by Brolund and Schallow (1976) in relation to alpha-enhancement and locus-of-control scores. Negative results were also found by Freedman and Papsdorf (1976) in a study described more fully in Chapter 6. They trained insomniacs in frontalis or general relaxation and were unable to find a relationship between success in achieving relaxation and locus-of-control scores. Similarly, Vogt (1975) reported no relationship between locus-of-control scores and either ability to tense and relax muscles or estimated degree of success in the tasks, while only a very tenuous relationship was found between locus-of-control scores and frontalis muscle reduction ability by Carlson (1977). Wagner, Bourgeois, Levenson, and Denton (1974) pointed out that the I–E scale appears to be multidimensional and to measure at least three separate components (I: expectancy that self-control is possible; P: expectancy that one is controlled by powerful others; C: expectancy that control is random). They predicted that only scores on the I component would correlate with voluntary control of electrodermal responding with feedback. When subjects who proved to be particularly good and poor at control of electrodermal responding were compared on each of the three components, only the I component discriminated, a high degree of electrodermal control being associated with high I component scores (that is, a belief in the ability to control one's own behavior). G. S. Stern and Berrenberg (1977) reported that successful reduction of frontalis muscle activity with feedback resulted in a significant increase in internality scores on the Rotter scale (that is, expression of a greater belief in personal control).

An important study which is also relevant to both the somatic and the cognitive mediation aspects of biofeedback control is that carried out by Davidson, Schwartz, and Rothman (1976) using the Telegen Absorption Scale (TAS), which is intended to measure the ability to focus attention. Their study was based on the hypothesis that mode-specific attentional behaviors (e.g., attend to or count flashes on the one hand, or attend to or count taps on the other hand, the former representing a visual and the latter a kinesthetic task) will be reflected by differential evoked potentials occurring in the occipital (when the stimuli are flashes) and the sensorimotor (when the stimuli are taps) regions of the cortex. These differences, they argued, will be related to individual differences in scores on the TAS. Two groups of subjects were formed respectively scoring high and low on the TAS. In the first phase of the study each subject was given two trials during which a large number of simple visual (a small flashing light) and kinesthetic (taps to right forearm) stimuli were presented, with the subject merely instructed to attend to the stimuli. Two trials were then given in which the visual and kinesthetic stimuli had to be counted. In the second phase of the study the subjects were required to tap sequentially, starting with the little finger and proceeding to the thumb via the other fingers, and to clench and release the right hand at a rate of about one operation per second. The percentage alpha present at the occipital and sensorimotor regions of the cortex in the different conditions was measured and related to the TAS scores. No differences in alpha activity in the two cortical regions were found between the high and low TAS groups in baseline conditions. In the simple attending tasks, task-specific differences were found in alpha activity at the two cortical regions but again the high and low TAS groups were not discriminated. However, in the counting condition, significant differences were found between the high and low TAS groups in cortical activity as a function of the task. These results are shown in Figure 4. Subjects with low TAS scores showed equal amounts of alpha in both cortical regions, whether counting visual or kinesthetic stimuli; but subjects with high TAS scores showed low alpha while counting visual stimuli but high alpha while counting kinesthetic stimuli. The shift in alpha activity with respect to visual and kinesthetic stimuli occurred in the occipital cortex, indicating that high and low levels of attention were related to alpha activity in that area; that is, attention in subjects with high TAS scores involves the ability to inhibit activity in the modality-irrelevant area rather than in the modality-relevant area.

In all of the studies considered so far, the measurement of the perception of autonomic or somatic activity has been indirect and it is surprising to find that

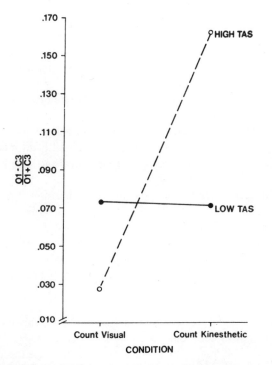

Figure 4. Mean EEG alpha ratio score for count-visual versus count-kinesthetic conditions separately for high- and low-absorption subjects (TAS = Tellegen Absorption Scale). (From Davidson, R. J., Schwartz, G. E., & Rothman, L. P. Attentional style and the self-regulation of mode-specific attention: An electroencephalographic study. *Journal of Abnormal Psychology,* 1976, *85,* 615, Figure 3. Copyright 1976 by the American Psychological Association. Reprinted by permission of the author and the publisher.)

few studies have so far been carried out which measure more directly the degree to which the subject can identify and monitor such activity. However, studies of this kind are becoming more frequent and an upsurge of research in this area can be anticipated. Taking heart rate as a convenient example, several basic areas of research may be identified. The first relates to the detection of the heartbeat itself and raises the following questions:

1. Are there individual differences in the ability to detect the occurrence of the heartbeat accurately?

2. If there are, is the accuracy with which the heartbeat can be detected related positively to the ability to control heart rate?

3. Can the ability to detect the heartbeat be significantly improved with biofeedback training?

4. If significant improvement in the ability to detect the heartbeat is achieved, will this lead to a significant improvement in the ability to control heart rate?

The ability to detect the heartbeat could be described as the ability to discriminate between a heartbeat event and the absence of a heartbeat event. The second area rather more obviously deals with the ability to discriminate a change in heart rate and raises questions similar to those associated with the detection of the heartbeat itself:

1. Are there individual differences in the ability to discriminate a change in heart rate accurately?

2. If there are, is the accuracy with which a change in heart rate can be discriminated related positively to the ability to control heart rate?

3. Can the ability to discriminate a change in heart rate be significantly improved with biofeedback training?

4. If significant improvement in the ability to discriminate a change in heart rate is achieved, will this lead to a significant improvement in the ability to control heart rate?

These first two areas are really concerned with the question of whether the ability to detect the heartbeat and/or discriminate changes in heart rate are necessary and/or sufficient conditions for the control of heart rate. Thus:

1. Can control of heart rate be achieved in the absence of the ability to detect the heartbeat?

2. Can control of heart rate be achieved in the absence of the ability to discriminate changes in heart rate?

3. Will successful training in heart-rate control increase the ability to detect the heartbeat?

4. Will successful training in heart-rate control increase the ability to discriminate changes in heart rate?

Finally, it should be pointed out that these questions must be kept separate from the rather similar questions which can be asked about awareness of the heartbeat and changes in heart rate. There are semantic difficulties here, of course, but it is probable that distinctions which can be made between detection, perception, discrimination, and awareness of heart activity are not just semantic quibbling but represent important differences in approach to these problems. As will be seen, many biofeedback workers assume that training in control of a function leads not merely to an increased ability to discriminate changes in that function, but to an increased awareness of those changes, and that it is the increased awareness that is the critical factor (whatever ''awareness'' may mean over and above discrimination in this context).

It will be evident that a very fertile field of investigation is opened up by these considerations since precisely the same questions can, of course, be asked of every function that has been investigated thus far. Most of the work to be discussed relates, as it happens, to heart rate.

The ability to detect the heartbeat and the effect of specific training in heartbeat detection have been examined in two studies. Brener and Jones (1974) required their subjects to indicate whether each of a series of stimulus trains (consisting of vibratory pulses applied to the left wrist) was or was not associated with the occurrence of a heartbeat. On half of the trials, the vibratory stimuli were triggered by the R wave; on the other half, the stimuli were triggered by a clock pulse generator set to produce a frequency equal to the subject's heart rate. Tests of whether the subjects could determine whether a vibratory stimulus train was associated with a heartbeat or not were conducted before and after training in detection with or without auditory feedback for correct responses. Prior to training detection of heartbeat was at chance levels, but veridical feedback training resulted in a significant posttraining improvement in the detection of heartbeats in the absence of feedback as compared with training in which no feedback was provided. Subjective reports obtained from the feedback subjects indicated that some had made use of the characteristics of the vibratory stimuli while others had apparently succeeded in relating the vibratory stimuli to sensations occurring simultaneously (and presumably "naturally") in the arm, face, or respiratory muscles. Hamano (1977) repeated this study in modified form (the vibratory train in the control group matching the subject's prerecorded heartbeats rather than being triggered by the pulse generator) and obtained essentially the same results. Karate experts were no better at detecting heartbeats than nonexperts before training, but acquired the ability to detect the heartbeat accurately much faster during training.

In neither of these studies was the effect of heartbeat detection training on heart-rate control examined. McFarland (1975) provided his subjects with visual feedback of their heartbeats in a resting situation and then required them, without feedback, to press a button every time they judged a heartbeat had occurred. Following this, they were required to increase and decrease heart rate with visual feedback. Ability to identify heartbeats without feedback was found to be related to the ability to increase heart rate, but the reverse was not the case. In another study by McFarland and Campbell (1975), however, perception of heart-rate activity was not related to the ability to alter heart rate so as to match a click rate set at resting heart-rate level. In neither of these studies did McFarland measure the ability to detect the heartbeat before training in heartbeat detection was given, so only indirect evidence of the success of the detection training was available and the results suggested that only small increases in detection ability were achieved.

Whitehead, Drescher, Heiman, and Blackwell (1977) developed an interesting method of determining the accuracy of heartbeat detection. They provided the subject with a light flash which was synchronous (actually occurring 128 msec after the R wave) or nonsynchronous (occurring 384 msec after the R wave) with a heartbeat. The subject's task was to indicate whether a succession of such flashes had occurred synchronously or not with the succession of heartbeats. Following a considerable amount of detection training, heart-rate control without feedback was assessed, followed by extensive training in heart-rate control with feedback and measurement of transfer of control to a no-feedback condition.

Successful heart-rate control and its retention when feedback was withdrawn was obtained, but no relationship between the ability to detect heartbeat and heart-rate control was found. (Unfortunately, no information is provided in this study on the degree to which the training in heartbeat detection was successful with immediate and delayed feedback.) In two subsequent experiments, similar negative results were found.

Several studies have examined the ability of subjects to discriminate changes in various functions, including heart rate, blood pressure, and frontalis muscle activity, and the effects of training in discrimination on that ability. Epstein and Stein (1974) requested their subjects to press a button whenever they thought their heart rate was above or below an average level. These assessments were made prior to, during, and following training in the detection of heart-rate levels above and below the average rate with feedback. The results are shown in Figure 5. Prior to training discrimination was at chance levels, but feedback training led to successful discrimination of heart-rate increases and decreases which, after feedback was withdrawn, was maintained above baseline but below the level achieved during training. These results were replicated and extended by Epstein, Cinciripini, McCoy, and Marshall (1977). In each session, the subject was required to "observe" his heart rate for 20 min (adaptation period) and was then subjected to a baseline or a training period. In a baseline period, a red light was presented four times each minute on a 6- to 15-sec schedule. Each time the light flashed, the subject pressed one button if he judged his heart rate was higher than during the preceding adaptation period and another if he judged his heart rate to be lower. In a training period, either feedback in the form of a light was provided for correct responses (trial-and-error learning) or the light came on

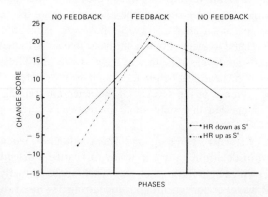

Figure 5. Stimulus control of the button-press response during no-feedback, feedback, and no-feedback phases when the positive stimulus (S$^+$) was heart-rate level above the preceding 10-min mean and S$^+$ was heart-rate level below the preceding 10-min mean. (From Epstein, L. H., & Stein, D. B. Feedback-influenced heart rate discrimination. *Journal of Abnormal Psychology*, 1974, *83*, 586, Figure 1. Copyright 1974 by the American Psychological Association. Reprinted by permission of the publisher.)

whenever the heart rate was equal to or greater than the adaptation rate and the subject responded to the light by pressing the increase button. The green light was gradually faded out so that the subject (presumably) had to rely more and more on internal cues as in the trial-and-error learning condition. A multiple-baseline design was used, with subjects being given different numbers of baseline trials before the trial-and-error or fading training was introduced. The results confirmed the findings of Epstein and Stein (1974), the fading training proving to be more effective in increasing discrimination ability than the trial-and-error training.

Whether systolic blood pressure can be correctly estimated has been the subject of an important recent study by Luborsky, Brady, McClintock, Kron, Bortnichak, and Levitz (1976). A five-stage program was carried out involving a group of normotensive subjects, including some who had relatively high systolic blood pressure (range: 115–136) and a group of moderately hypertensive patients (range: 143–156). Because of the relatively large degree of natural variation in systolic blood pressure both within and between sessions (see Chapter 4), subjective estimates of blood pressure were made on a scale which showed the true range of the subject's blood pressure as determined from baseline measurements. During each session within a stage, true blood pressure (both diastolic and systolic) was measured twice with a 2-min interval between each measurement, and these measurements were compared with the values estimated by the subject. The first stage consisted of eight baseline sessions, the subjects being provided with range information at the end of each session. In the second stage (ten sessions) the subjects estimated their systolic pressure but were given no feedback. For the third stage, two groups of subjects were formed, matched in pairs on level and range of systolic blood pressure. Subjects in one group made two estimates and were given the mean of their true blood pressure immediately after the second estimate; subjects in the other group were given the mean of their yoked subject after making their own estimates. Stage 4 (10 sessions) involved making estimates without feedback, while in stage 5 (15 sessions) the yoked subjects only were tested, being given veridical feedback after making their estimates. Three types of error scores were calculated: raw error (the differences between the subject's estimate and the true value), an error score corrected for differences in individual range of blood pressure, and an error score corrected for individual differences in scaling strategies.

The principal results obtained are shown in Figure 6. The natural variation between two adjacent true scores in the baseline condition was found to be ±6.00 mm Hg. This compares with a mean raw error score in stage 2 (estimates made, but feedback not given) of ±12.4 mm Hg. In stage 3, the group given veridical feedback reduced the error to ±7.4 mm Hg while the group given yoked non-veridical feedback reduced the error to ±8.5 mm Hg (the only difference between the groups being that the veridical feedback group improved its judgments at a faster rate). These gains were maintained during stage 4 (estimates made, but

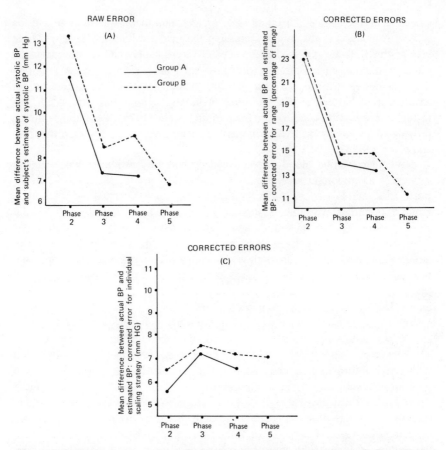

Figure 6. A. Raw error across phases; **B.** Range-corrected error across phases; **C.** The individual scaling strategy corrected error. (From Luborsky, L., Brady, J. P., McClintock, M., Kron, R. E., Bortnichak, E., & Levitz, L. Estimating one's own systolic blood pressure: Effects of feedback training. *Psychosomatic Medicine,* 1976, *38,* 432, Figure 2. Reprinted by permission of the author and the publisher.)

feedback not given), while in stage 5 the yoked group (now provided with veridical feedback) showed further improvement in assessment accuracy. It was concluded that the subjects were actually acquiring knowledge of range information concerning systolic blood pressure rather than specific values of systolic blood pressure. This is an important point, since it suggests that the kind of feedback information is of great importance in feedback training. The term "kind of feedback information" does not here refer to whether the information is proportional or binary, continuous or discontinuous, visual or auditory, and so on; rather, it refers to the relevance of the feedback (in whatever form it might be provided) to the natural characteristics of the response, changes in which the subject is attempting to discriminate. This explains why the yoked group improved as much as the veridical feedback group in stage 3; the yoked group was being given range information about the veridical feedback group rather than specific information about blood pressure change in that group, and that information was in fact quite relevant to the discrimination of changes in their own systolic blood pressure (there is, however, a confounding here with the effects of mere practice in estimating blood pressure levels, since an appropriate control group which simply continued to estimate blood pressure levels in the absence of any feedback was not used). It appeared that estimates were being based mainly on feedback information provided after the preceding estimation rather than on cues arising from the current blood pressure variation at the time the estimate was made. However, there was also evidence that the current level was being used to some extent. No correlation was found between degree of estimation accuracy attained and clinical levels of systolic blood pressure. In confirmation of findings discussed earlier in this section, no relationship was found between success in estimating blood pressure range and performance on the Rod-and-Frame test or the Embedded Figures test.

Staudenmayer and Kinsman (1976) trained groups of normal subjects to reduce frontalis muscle activity with or without auditory feedback.[12] At the end of each trial the subject was required to judge whether or not frontalis activity on the trial just concluded was greater or less than activity on the preceding trial. They found that where the difference in muscle activity between adjacent trials was small, the provision of feedback did not lead to more accurate judgments of comparative levels than was found with no feedback provided, but that feedback led to a significant improvement in correct judgment as the activity level between adjacent trials increased, as compared with the group not given feedback whose judgments remained at chance levels. But, of course, the improved judgments were most likely the result of directly interpreting the changes in the feedback display rather than acquiring an increased ability to discriminate between levels of activity in the frontalis muscle itself. However, they did also find that the group not given feedback was unable to discriminate large changes in muscle activity, which suggests, of course, that discrimination of different levels of muscle activity is normally very poor and does not improve with practice in making such judgments in the absence of feedback. As with the studies on heart rate and blood pressure, the crucial test with respect to discrimination of muscle activity levels necessitates the withdrawal of feedback after successful discrimination of levels has been achieved to determine whether discrimination accuracy will be maintained when only feedback stimulation for the frontalis muscle itself is available.

Although Epstein and Blanchard (1977) have stressed the role of discrimination in increasing voluntary control over a function, it is surprising that almost no work specifically directed to investigating this matter has so far been reported.

---

[12]They also provided verbal feedback or not at the end of each trial, but this variable had no effect on acquisition of control.

Ray (1974) allocated subjects to "awareness" and "nonawareness" training conditions. In the former condition, subjects were given visual feedback of 200 heartbeats and instructed to watch the display and correlate changes with changes in internal sensations; in the latter condition, the subjects were not shown the display, but instructed to remain calm for 200 beats. No difference between the groups in the ability to control heart rate was subsequently found. However, the ability to detect heart-rate changes was not measured before and after the awareness/nonawareness training so it is impossible to know whether the groups differed in the ability to detect changes in heart rate at any stage. Apart from this study, evidence is entirely lacking as to the effects of discrimination training on voluntary control.

Nor is the situation much better in relation to the question of the effects of successful training in control on subsequent discrimination ability compared with the level of ability present before control training. Lacroix (1977) found that subjects who successfully gained control of increases and decreases in skin potential activity with feedback showed increased ability to discriminate the presence and absence of negative skin potential responses. However, subjects who were given accurate feedback but misinformed that the feedback indicated the opposite, and who did not gain voluntary control, also showed increased discrimination ability (both groups being superior in posttraining discrimination ability to a no-feedback control group). Sime and DeGood (1977) essentially used the technique of Staudenmayer and Kinsman (1976) with the addition of training in frontalis muscle control and a postcontrol training test in discrimination. They found that judgments of changes in frontalis muscle tension before control training were at chance levels if the actual differences were low, but if the difference was high correct judgments rose to 70%. Following control training, the subjects given biofeedback showed a significant improvement in the discrimination of tension changes at all three levels of actual difference in magnitude (low, medium, high). These subjects improved more in discrimination ability than did subjects given progressive muscle relaxation training (mostly directed at the frontalis) without feedback. On the other hand, Epstein and Abel (1977) concluded that frontalis muscle reduction training with tension headache patients did not lead to an increase in the ability of the patients to discriminate small changes in muscle activity sufficiently well to be useful in controlling muscle activity in the absence of feedback.

Within the framework described, the results of the investigations so far carried out must be regarded as equivocal and disappointing, a conclusion recently arrived at by Carroll (1977). It should be noted that the ability to detect internal changes produced by the application of external stimuli is, of course, very substantial. For example, Molinari, Greenspan, and Kenshalo (1977) have shown using magnitude estimation techniques that human subjects can detect quite small changes in temperature resulting from the application of external stimulation, and that the ability to detect the changes is unrelated to the rate at which the changes take place (within the range 0.5–2.0°C per sec. However, what is in question here is the ability to detect the occurrence of and changes in internally arising stimuli which are not induced by external stimulation but are self-generated. Gannon (1977) has recently discussed one important aspect of this problem, namely, the relative lack of cortical representation of visceral afferent feedback, and indeed the lack of any evidence of afferent feedback channels in respect of some autonomically controlled functions such as the sweat glands (Good, 1975). Brener (1975) has discussed in detail the implications of the relative abundance of feedback channels from functions under central nervous system control and the relative scarcity of such channels from functions under autonomic nervous system control and has argued that external feedback is more crucial in achieving control of autonomically mediated functions since it enables a response image to be constructed which then serves the same function as the internal feedback derived from skeletal responses.[13] However, it will be recalled that Diekhoff (1976) concluded from his study of the detection of electrodermal responding that an internal imperfect schema for detecting internal events exists which may actually be upset by the provision of accurate external feedback although the feedback may assist in labeling these events accurately. We are here, of course, trespassing into the area of "awareness" and its relation to detection. The question of whether or not detection, perception, awareness, and discrimination do in fact form the basis of successful voluntary control will be taken up again later.

The Role of Cognitive Mediation in Biofeedback

In searching for possible mediators of the control achieved in biofeedback training, the role of cognitive behavior has received a good deal of attention. In spite of determined rearguard actions, it has appeared increasingly foolish to most behaviorists to ignore the significance of cognitive activity, provided it is recognized that cognitive activity is always an inference which at some point must be indexed by overt behavior.[14] Of course, what is subsumed under the term "cognitive activity" takes a wide variety of forms and there is no doubt that the notion of cognitive activity is a very slippery one. Nevertheless, significant advances have been made in recent years in solving the problem of indexing the occurrence of cognitive activities, advances which are particularly relvevant to the interpretation of biofeedback control. Several "dimensions" of cognitive activity will be considered here to see what light may be thrown on the relevance of such activity to biofeedback control.

---

[13]The only attempt so far to test Brener's neural response image theory (Wright, Carroll, & Newman, 1977) did not obtain results which supported the theory.

[14]The old saying: "Sometimes I sits and thinks, and sometimes I just sits." How can these two states be differentiated unless an observable behavior (such as a verbal response) occurs?

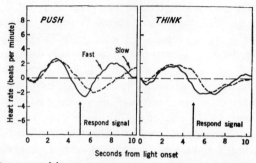

Figure 7. Computer-averaged heart-rate responses as a function of response mode ("push" or "think") and speed ("fast" or "slow"). Plots are in the form of difference scores relative to the basic measure. The wave form was moved back in time 0.75 sec to correct for cardiotachometer lag (warning stimulus at $\tau = 0$ sec, offset at $t = 5$ sec. (From Schwartz, G. E., & Higgins, J. D. Cardiac activity preparatory to overt and covert behavior. *Science*, 1971, *173*, 1144, Figure 1. Reprinted by permission of the author and the publisher.)

There is now an impressive amount of evidence that cognitive activity may be indexed by somatic changes. Schwartz and Higgins (1971) presented their subjects with a 5-sec warning light, at the end of which they were to respond either slowly or quickly with a covert ("think 'stop'") or overt ("press a key") response. Changes in heart rate over a 17-sec period, beginning 3 sec before the onset of the warning light, were examined. The results are shown in Figure 7 for the 5 sec of the warning light and the succeeding 5 sec. For both covert and overt responding, heart rate acceleration was produced by the onset of the warning light but deceleration occurred as the time to respond approached, heart rate reaching its lowest point just after the warning signal terminated, followed by another acceleration. The requirement to respond quickly produced more rapid deceleration and subsequent acceleration than did the requirement to respond in a leisurely fashion. Klinger, Gregoire, and Barta (1973) had shown that cognitive tasks such as simple addition produced increases in heart rate, whereas tasks such as imagining a liked person led to decreases in heart rate.[15] Bell and Schwartz (1975) extended this finding. After measuring baseline heart rate, they instructed their subjects to engage in two types of cognitive activity: "effortful" (reciting the alphabet backward and backward subtraction) and "relaxing" (listening to tones and watching lights). The "effortful" cognitive activity led to large increases in heart rate, averaging 12 bpm, whereas the "relaxing" cognitive activity led to small decreases in heart rate, averaging 1.5 bpm. Subsequent instructions to increase and decrease heart rate without feedback produced increases which were significant but smaller than those produced by cognitive activity but (in this study at least) did not lead to significant decreases in heart rate.

[15]It should be noted, however, that search and choice tasks did not produce heart-rate increases, indicating that the relationships are not simple.

It has also been shown that self-generated thoughts are correlated with specific changes in somatic activity. The methodology of this research requires that the subject be "paced" with an external signal, producing "thoughts" at a precisely defined point in time, as a result of which the occurrence of the "thought" can be correlated with physiological changes. Schwartz (1971) presented a series of tones through headphones at a rate of one tone of 0.1-sec duration every 1.25 sec. The subject was required to count silently in sequence in synchrony with the tones for one, two, or three sets of four tones and then produce one of two sets of four "thoughts" in synchrony with the tones, pressing a microswitch to indicate the end of the sequence and informing the experimenter of the thought set which had been produced. Two thought sets were used: neutral (the letters *A, B, C, D*), and affective (the words, *sex, rape, death,* and "a rude word for intercourse"). A significant difference was found in the effect of the two thought sets on heart rate, the affective thought sequence leading to an increase in heart rate and the neutral sequence to a decrease. May and Johnson (1973) assigned female subjects to one of two experimental conditions. One group was required on cue to think about arousing words, neutral words, or numbers, while the other group was required on cue to think about inhibitory (restful) words, neutral words, or numbers. The results are shown in Figure 8. While the groups did not differ in heart rate with respect to neutral words, and

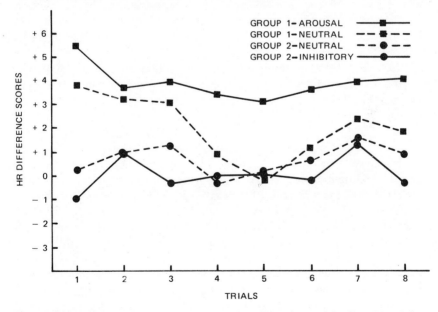

Figure 8. Mean heart-rate difference scores for the subconditions across trials. (From May, J. R., & Johnson, H. J. Physiological activity to internally elicited arousal and inhibitory thoughts. *Journal of Abnormal Psychology,* 1973, *82,* 242, Figure 2. Copyright 1973 by the American Psychological Association. Reprinted by permission of the author and the publisher.)

thinking inhibitory (relaxing) words produced the same heart rate scores as neutral words, a significant elevation of heart rate was produced by thinking about affective words, the effect being constant across all words of each category and consistent both within and across trials.

The importance of these findings has been highlighted by recent studies of the physiological effects of thoughts in abnormal conditions. Boulougouris, Rabavilas, and Stefanis (1977) studied changes in heart rate when obsessive-compulsives engaged in fantasy activity related or unrelated to their obsessive behavior and compared the effects with those obtained when the therapist described a neutral scene, a scene involving their obsession, or conducted *in vivo* "flooding" therapy. They found that when the patient engaged in fantasies related to his obsessive behavior, heart rate was significantly increased as compared with the effect of engaging in a neutral fantasy. It should be noted, however, that no control was exercised in this study for the effects on heart rate of cognitive arousal activity *per se,* a control which was found to be important in studies of sexual arousal (see Chapter 6).

May (1977a) conducted a rather similar study with snake-phobic subjects who were required on cue to think (subvocalize) or image affective (involving their phobia) or neutral sentences. The phobic subjects showed elevated heart rate while thinking and imagining the affective sentences compared with non-phobic subjects thinking and imagining the same sentences. In a subsequent study (May, 1977b), it was shown that these changes were as great as changes produced when the stimulation was externally imposed rather than internally generated.

Thus, the evidence is strong that internally generated thoughts of an affective kind on the one hand, and cognitive activities (such as solving arithmetic problems) on the other hand, produce an elevation of heart rate and can act as mediators of heart rate. The evidence with respect to other somatic variables is less clear. Diekhoff, Garland, Dansereau, and Walker (1978) recorded forearm EMG, skin conductance, and finger pulse volume from the left or right side while the subjects were performing two left-hemisphere (verb memorization and lyric recitation) and right-hemisphere (facial memorization and humming) controlled tasks. They found that forearm EMG was lower on the side contralateral to the hemisphere involved in task processing (thus, right-sided EMG levels were reduced when the verbal tasks were being performed while the opposite result obtained when nonverbal tasks were being performed). Shapiro, Crider, and Tursky (1964) instructed their subjects to think actively about emotional experiences while skin potential responses were monitored. The subjects were informed that a tone would occur whenever the apparatus "detected" the occurrence of a criterion response whereas, of course, the tone in fact occurred whenever a criterion skin potential response occurred. A control group was used which was given the same instructions but the tone was presented only when a skin potential response at criterion level was not occurring. They found that the experimental group maintained a stable response pattern while the control group showed a reduction in skin potential responding. Of course, this study did not directly investigate the effect of thinking on skin potential response, but it appears to have suggested the possibility of such investigations to later research workers. R. M. Stern and Kaplan (1967) instructed their experimental group to think of emotional events and provided visual feedback of electrodermal response activity, while a control group was similarly instructed but not given feedback. A crucial innovation, however, was that the experimental subjects were required to "control" the meter needle by making it go in one direction by thinking arousing thoughts and making it go in the other direction by thinking relaxing thoughts. As in the study by Shapiro et al. (1964), the experimental subjects in the "arousal" condition maintained the baseline level of electrodermal responding (but did not increase it), whereas the control group showed the drift effect. In the "relax" condition, however, both groups maintained their baseline levels of electrodermal responding. Klinge (1972) found that spontaneous fluctuations in electrodermal responding were greater when her subjects engaged in generating "stimulating" thoughts as compared with engaging in "relaxing" thoughts; the provision of veridical or false feedback, or no feedback at all, for electrodermal responding made no difference. However, more recent studies of electrodermal responding in obsessional and phobic patients have failed to find any clear effect of thinking on electrodermal responding (Boulougouris et al., 1977; May, 1977a, b; May & Johnson, 1973).

The role of cognitive activity in alpha enhancement and suppression has received surprisingly little attention.[16] Following an initial study (Martindale & Armstrong, 1974) which suggested that creativity might be related particularly to the suppression of alpha (but only three short enhancement and one suppression trials were given), Martindale and Hines (1975) carried out a more comprehensive investigation. Male subjects were divided into four groups according to whether they scored high or low on two tests of creativity (the alternate-uses test and the remote-associates test). They participated in two sessions, in the first of which baseline levels of alpha were recorded and alpha was then monitored while the subjects completed the two creativity tests again, together with the IPAT culture fair test. In the second session, baseline levels of alpha were again recorded, after which the subjects practiced making a feedback tone go on and off and then were given ten trials of alternately keeping the tone on and off. Baseline levels of alpha were found not to differentiate high- and low-creativity subjects (as measured by either of the tests), but during creative tasks performance subjects scoring high on creativity as measured by the alternate-uses test showed much higher levels of alpha as compared with low scorers. No such difference was found for creativity differences as measured by the remote-associates test. The ability to control alpha with feedback was unrelated to

[16]The studies by Mulholland and his colleagues, reviewed in Chapter 5, are, of course, relevant.

creativity as measured by either task. Ancoli and Green (1977) selected subjects on the basis of high and low self-rated scores on tendency to be introspective[17] and related these tendencies to alpha enhancement and suppression with auditory feedback. The high-introspection group showed significantly higher levels of alpha during baseline and maintained this level during alpha-enhancement trials when feedback was provided. This group also showed a larger difference between alpha-enhancement and suppression trials. Subjective state reports suggested that the high-introspection subjects used passive relaxation and concentration to keep alpha on, whereas the low-introspection subjects used active concentration to keep alpha on. Both groups used active concentration to keep alpha off, with the high-introspection group additionally using visual focusing to keep alpha off.

There are several studies which provide indirect evidence for the role of cognitive factors in biofeedback training. The effects of induced expectations have been shown to play a significant part in determining what happens in biofeedback training (that is, the precise instructions provided to the subject are of great importance). Thus, Valle and Levine (1975), Pressner and Savitsky (1977), and Walsh (1974) have examined, and verified, the effects of induced expectations and/or instructional control in relation to alpha enhancement and suppression.[18] Attempts have also been made to incorporate "cognitive training" into biofeedback remedial work. Meichenbaum (1976) had provided a detailed rationale for such procedures with his cognitive theory of self-control, involving training the subject to gain an increased awareness of his problem, to develop thoughts and behaviors which are incompatible with the thoughts and behaviors which Meichenbaum believes underly the disturbed functioning, and to engage in a continuous "internal" dialogue about the changes which may occur in the biofeedback training situation. Reeves (1976) has shown that it is possible to produce changes in the frequency and severity of tension headaches by cognitive training based on Meichenbaum's theory without any corresponding changes occurring in frontalis muscle activity until feedback of the frontalis muscle activity is introduced (see Chapter 3 for a detailed account of this study). Training in the development of similar cognitive strategies has been described by Barber (1974) within a hypnotic retraining situation. Kleinman, Goldman, Snow, and Korol (1977) found some evidence that hypertension leads to impaired cognitive functioning while Goldman, Kleinman, Snow, Bidus, and Korol (1975) claimed that successful training in reduction in blood pressure with feedback was accompanied by an improvement in cognitive functioning, although the evidence for this was not strong. Henson and Rubin (1971) found that their subjects reported engaging in cognitive activities when they were required to inhibit erection in the presence of an erotic film.

---

[17]It is impossible to determine whether the "introspective" tendency was a measure of "cognitive" activity or essentially a measure of somatic locus of control.

[18]Plotkin, Mazer, and Loewy (1976), however, found no expectation effect.

An important aspect of cognition which has received some (although inadequate) attention in the biofeedback literature is imagery. As Richardson (1969) has pointed out in his review of the topic, several categories of imagery may be distinguished. The kind of imagery which has been used in biofeedback studies falls under one of two categories: memory imagery (e.g., self-induction of warm or cold conditions, as in temperature control studies), and imagination imagery which is a term covering a wide variety of cognitive behaviors (hypnagogic, perceptual isolation, hallucinogenic drug, photic stimulation, pulse current, sleep deprivation, and meditation). Imagination imagery is distinguished from memory imagery mainly by its lack of personal experiential reference, by its being more vivid than memory imagery, and by its tendency to occur in unusual states of consciousness. The importance of imagination imagery lies in its potential link with the subjective states alleged to be associated with some kinds of biofeedback training (such as alpha enhancement) and the possibility that these states may act, via imagination imagery, as links with the somatic changes which biofeedback produces. These subjective states will be considered shortly.

Actually, not a great deal of work has been reported regarding the use of imagery in biofeedback training and the results thus far have generally been unclear. Dugan and Sheridan (1976) recorded baseline finger temperature in normal subjects for 15 min and found that in 13 of 16 subjects both hands became warmer (however, the ambient room temperature was not stated and, as was seen in Chapter 2, some rise in temperature, even in a cool room, in the first 10 min or so is not uncommon). Half the subjects were then asked to imagine their hands in very warm water; the other half were asked to imagine their hands in ice-cold water. All of the subjects asked to image a cooling situation showed a significant change downward in one hand and more than half changed downward on both. However, the mean change of about $-2.°F$ was well within the expected drift effect (if the ambient room temperature was 20–21°C). The subjects required to image warmth showed a small mean increase in hand temperature of $+.06°F$ (which would have been an underestimate if ambient room temperature was low). No feedback was provided in this study so some evidence, although weak, was provided that imagery may influence temperature. Blizard, Cowings, and Miller (1975) taught their subjects to image heaviness and warmth or coolness and lightness in their hands. Significant increases in heart rate and respiration rate accompanied the induction of coolness and lightness but the reverse was not the case for the induction of heaviness and warmth, and no differences in the electrical activity of the brain or finger temperature resulted from the differential induction of the two states. Clark and Forgione (1974) hypnotized normal subjects and tried to induce images that their hands or gingiva were getting hot or cold. Blood volume pulse and total blood volume were measured by means of photoplethysmographs attached to the finger pads of the distal phalanges of the second digits of both hands and to the gingiva above the maxillary lateral incisors. The results were somewhat disconcerting:

The digital vasomotor response of both hands to induction and to suggestion of either
hot or cold was one of initial vasoconstriction followed by progressive vasodilation . . :
variation of vascular response of the gingive was not significant. . . . (Clark & Forgione, 1974, p. 794)

A somewhat different approach was followed by Ikeda and Hirai (1976),
who trained their subjects in voluntary control of electrodermal activity with
visual feedback and claimed that voluntary control was facilitated in those subjects obtaining high scores on a richness of imagery questionnaire. However, the
reported correlations between richness of imagery and voluntary control achieved
were not, in fact, significant so that the role of imagery was at best a very weak
one. E. Jacobson (1973) claimed that muscle activity can be induced by imagining muscle activity and, of course, systematic desensitization as a technique is
based in part on the assumption that visual images of feared objects will result in
significant physiological changes.

A more sophisticated analysis of the possible role of imagery in biofeedback
training was introduced by Davidson and Schwartz (1976), who instructed their
subjects to self-induce covert affective and nonaffective states, using verbal and
visual strategies. The affective states involved images of angry or relaxing scenes
while the nonaffective states involved thinking about a typical day or performing
a verbal task. A mean difference of 3.31 bpm was found between the affective
and nonaffective states, but this difference was smaller than that found between
heart rate in the resting state and the level achieved when the subjects were
merely instructed to increase their heart rate, no feedback being provided. No
effect of relaxation imagery on heart rate as compared with resting baseline level
was found. However, Davidson and Schwartz (1976) also recorded alpha levels
bilaterally from the left and right parietal areas of the brain and found that
affective imagery was associated with right-hemisphere alpha activity whereas
nonaffective imagery had no differential alpha activity associated with it. No
cortical differential relationships were found with verbal as opposed to visual
types of imagery in spite of the fact that the left hemisphere is alleged to be
associated with verbal processing and the right hemisphere with nonverbal processing. An important sex difference was demonstrated: all females showed
greater relative right-hemisphere activity when anger imagery was invoked
(compared with baseline levels) but less than half of the males showed this effect.
Davidson and Schwartz (1977) recorded alpha activity from the O_1 (left occipital)
and C_3 (left sensorimotor) areas while subjects were presented with flashing
lights or taps to the forearm, and then asked the subjects to imagine the visual and
kinesthetic stimuli separately or occurring together. They found that activity at
C_3 was greatest when the subject was imagining the taps, least when he was
imagining the lights, and intermediate when both taps and lights were being
imagined together. Schwartz, Fair, Salt, Mandel, and Klerman (1976) were
responsible for another new and promising line of investigation where muscle
activity was recorded from four regions of the face (frontalis, currugator, masse-

ter, and depressor anguli oris) using depressed and nondepressed female subjects who were required to engage in various kinds of covert imagery (happy, sad, angry thoughts and feelings, and thinking about a "typical" day) as well as assuming voluntary facial expressions which represented being happy, sad, or angry. The various kinds of imagery were found to be correlated with different patterns of facial muscle activity in both the depressed and nondepressed subjects, some of the patterns being common to both groups and some unique to each group.

On the whole, the results of studies utilizing imagery in relation to biofeedback have failed so far to demonstrate clearly that it has an important role to play. It is worth pointing out that Schwartz (1975) has maintained that the role of cognitive states (including imagery) is to enable the subject to identify somatic states of which there may be a low level of awareness and hence that cognitive behavior serves as a mediator of somatic states which in turn then mediate overt behavior:

> The ability of affective imagery to produce discrete muscular patterns supports the view that specific self-induced cognitive states can generate discrete bodily patterns, and that these heretofore unnoticed somatic patterns may serve as a major physiological mechanism allowing imagery to elicit the subjective feelings associated with different emotions. In other words, a self-regulated internal feedback loop may be created, when the particular "thought" triggers a specific *pattern* of peripheral physiological activity which is then itself reprocessed by the brain, contributing to the unique "feeling" state associated with the image. (Schwartz, 1975, p. 320)

This quotation clearly shows the extraordinary complexity of the relationships between cognitive activities, somatic activities, and subjective states. Nowhere is this more clearly illustrated than in relation to the question of the subjective state correlates of biofeedback training, in particular in the area of alpha and theta enhancement. Much of the initial impetus in biofeedback research resulted from the early apparent demonstrations that alpha enhancement was associated with states of pleasantness and relaxation. Indeed, as we have seen (in Chapter 5), there was more than a suspicion that the principal interest in training in alpha enhancement lay in the possibility that it would serve as a convenient means of entry into "higher states of consciousness," in other words, into mystical states of higher degrees of awareness, communication with the "spiritual" nature of the cosmos, or whatever. Questions such as whether it was alpha enhancement which produced the higher state of consciousness or the achievement of the higher state of consciousness which produced the enhancement of alpha were conveniently ignored or regarded as no problem since the two were merely mirror images of each other. In spite of the duality of body/mind which was implied (not to mention their interaction), it was implicitly assumed that it was the production of the physiological changes in the brain which induced higher states of consciousness rather than the reverse, although no experiments were designed which might show the temporal relationships which were required to hold for the causal direction to be established. On the whole, subsequent research has not substantiated the alleged relationship, let alone the causal direction. In fairness, some subsequent positive results should, however, be mentioned. In a little-noticed study, Honorton, Davidson, and Bindler (1971) examined the ability of subjects (previously trained to enhance and suppress alpha) to demonstrate extrasensory perception in a card-guessing task while enhancing and suppressing alpha. They assessed their subjective state on a 5-point scale *during* the alpha training. Contrary to what might have been expected due to the effect of these complex activities on alpha enhancement, it was found that percentage alpha was significantly higher in enhancement than in suppression trials, even when the ESP task was being performed simultaneously, and enhanced alpha was subjectively assessed as being accompanied by an increased focus on internal state as opposed to external events. Success at the ESP task was not found to be related to enhancement, and suppression of alpha states was greater in those subjects who did succeed in experiencing internal states.[19] Hebert and Lehmann (1977), who showed that some highly practiced meditators manifest bursts of theta activity while meditating, interrupted the subjects at the time theta bursts were present and found that the subjects described their state as comfortable, peaceful, pleasant, "drifting," and "sliding," but that they were awake, with intact self-awareness and reality orientation. However, the early positive reports of similar states occuring in naive subjects have not been confirmed. Travis, Kondo, and Knott (1975) examined the subjective reports of 140 subjects who had participated in four experiments on alpha enhancement and found results which they described as equivocal and diverse. Not more than half of the subjects described alpha enhancement as being correlated with a pleasant or a relaxing state, and a substantial proportion described alpha enhancement as involving an unpleasant nonrelaxed state. Plotkin and his colleagues have also reported equivocal or negative results. Plotkin (1976), for example, found that enhanced levels of alpha were not usually accompanied by reports of the "alpha experience," as he termed it. This conclusion was confirmed by three subsequent studies. Plotkin and Cohen (1976) trained their normal subjects to practice the opposite poles of one of five subjective dimensions: degree of oculomotor processing ("not-looking" versus "looking"), degree of sensory awareness (nonsensory awareness of thoughts and feelings versus sensory awareness of the external world), degree of body awareness ("disembodied" or relaxed versus heightened body awareness), degree of deliberateness of thought (undirected, free-flowing, or absent thought versus intense concentration and problem solving), and degree of pleasantness of emotional state (pleasant and peaceful versus unpleasant and emotional). Having practiced one of these states, the subject was then required to use the skill to increase or decrease a tone which indicated the presence or absence of alpha (the subjects were not informed of the connection). Only oculomotor processing and sensory awareness were found to be related to

---

[19]The paper by Honorton *et al.* (1971) contains a good review of the literature on the relationship between ESP and alpha.

alpha enhancement. (Subjects trained in these strategies reported that they were able to use them appropriately to increase and decrease the tone.) Subjects trained in the other techniques in fact tended to discover the effective ones spontaneously during the course of the experiment. Plotkin et al. (1976) and Plotkin (1978) also found no relationship between alpha enhancement and subjective reports of the alpha experience. Brolund and Schallow (1976) reported that there was no relationship between success in achieving alpha enhancement and subjective reports of how the control was achieved, while Passini et al. (1977) found that alcoholics given alpha-enhancement training did not report experiencing positive states as a result of enhancing alpha.

Bird, Newton, Sheer, and Ford (1978a, b), on the other hand, claimed that subjects they trained to control 40-Hz activity showed appropriate awareness of subjective concomitants of that control and that clear-cut and differentiable patterns were obtained for theta, alpha, beta, and 40-Hz control by the use of Q sorts (details will be found in Bird et al., 1978b, Table II). Similar positive results were obtained by Schwartz, Davidson, and Pugash (1976) and by Davidson, Schwartz, Pugash, and Bromfield (1976). They trained subjects to decrease alpha in both the left and right parietal areas of the cortex, and to maintain alpha in the right hemisphere while decreasing it simultaneously in the left, or vice versa (that is, they trained the subjects to integrate and differentiate alpha, in much the same way Schwartz had earlier trained subjects to integrate and differentiate heart rate and blood pressure). After each period of training, the subjects completed a questionnaire designed to assess the cognitive strategies used (verbal, numerical, visual, musical, emotional, thinking about nothing). Significant regulation of all three patterns was found. The use of verbal cognitions was associated with decreasing left-sided alpha while maintaining right-sided alpha. The reverse accomplishment was associated with visual cognitions. However, integration was not found to be accompanied by a combination of verbal and visual cognitions but rather by an increase in "thinking nothing" coupled with intense concentration on one or a small number of images. Thus, integration is not simply the sum of the component parts.

Investigators in areas other than those related to alpha enhancement have occasionally tried to relate changes in somatic activity with changes in subjectively reported emotional states (e.g., Engel & Chism, 1967, and Engel & Hanson, 1966, in relation to heart rate) but the results have generally been negative and it is unnecessary to consider them in detail. Typical of such reports are those by Alexander (1975) and Coursey (1975) who found no correlation between frontalis muscle relaxation training and subjective reports of relaxation, following successful training. Lader and Mathews (1971) have discussed in some detail the difficulties of demonstrating a correlation between objective and subjective measures of tension, and the matter has been discussed elsewhere (see Chapter 6, "Anxiety") in relation to clinical states of anxiety and tension.

A similar lack of success has attended the small number of efforts to associate biofeedback training success or failure with personality measures.

Alexander, French, and Goodman (1975) were unable to relate scores on the State–Trait Anxiety Inventory (STAI) to success in frontalis muscle reduction training, and a similar lack of success attended Good's (1975) effort to relate various questionnaire measures of anxiety to frontalis muscle activity just prior to going to sleep. On the other hand, Valle and DeGood (1977) found that subjects with low pretraining STAI scores succeeded in suppressing alpha more readily than subjects with high STAI scores, but after training in alpha enhancement and suppression posttraining STAI scores did not correlate with success in either direction. Travis, Kondo, and Knott (1974) found that subjects with high neuroticism scores on Eysenck's EPI questionnaire enhanced alpha more successfully than subjects with low neuroticism scores. LeBoeuf (1977) found no relationship between introversion/extraversion and ability to reduce frontalis muscle activity levels in anxious introverts and extraverts. Pardine and Napoli (1977), however, found an interaction between personality characteristics and feedback in relation to heart-rate control, with neither variable predicting success in heart-rate reduction training. Success was associated with high exhibition and succorance and low deference and aggression scores on the Edwards Personal Preference Schedule, provided feedback was available.

All of the work reviewed in this section on cognitive and emotional subjective states in relation to biofeedback training seems to be predicated on the assumption that the aim of biofeedback is somehow to increase "awareness" of bodily functioning, in some sense (undefined) of "awareness." Whether this assumption is either a necessary or desirable one to make in the context of biofeedback training will be discussed later.

The Motor Skills Theory of Biofeedback

The operant–reinforcement interpretation of the acquisition of control in biofeedback training which was critically reviewed in an earlier section of this chapter has also been attacked by Lang (1974, 1975), who has suggested and attempted to demonstrate that:

> the training of human subjects to modify their own cardiac rate may be conceptualized as a skills learning task (Lang, 1975). Thus, variables which modulate skilled somato-motor performance would be presumed to influence similarly the acquisition of an ability to intentionally speed or slow heart rate. (Lang & Twentyman, 1976, p. 378)

In developing this interpretation, Lang has relied rather heavily on an unfortunate distinction between continuous proportional biofeedback and discontinuous proportional or binary feedback. Thus, he points out quite correctly that continuous proportional feedback may lead to superior control during the training trials with feedback, as compared with the presentation of information in discrete form only at the end of each trial. However, the former procedure may make the subject very dependent on the external feedback to the neglect of internal feedback sources, whereas the latter procedure may force the subject to pay more attention to the internal sources. Hence, when feedback is withdrawn and transfer trials instituted, there may be a greater loss of control in the subjects trained with continuous proportional feedback as compared with the group trained with discrete end-of-trial-only feedback. But the attempt to restrict the operant interpretation in this way is quite unfair since no such clear distinction can be made, as was indicated in Chapter 2. Feedback may be proportional or nonproportional; it may also be discrete or continuous, and any combination of these two dimensions may be involved in a particular training situation. More importantly, one of the most striking features of the data obtained in biofeedback training situations is the consistent failure to demonstrate the kind of learning curves within or between trials which would be expected if the motor skills hypothesis is valid. To a degree, the hypothesis can be saved by arguing that the ''skill'' is already present in the subject (in the sense in which it is clearly *not* present in most motor-skill learning tasks such as pursuit rotor learning where, in unskilled subjects initial time on target will be close to zero but final time on target will be up to 90%), and indeed Lang has indicated that this is the position he takes. But this brings Lang's interpretation closer to being a servocontrol system model (to be discussed shortly), a model which is not identical to the motor skills model.

The motor skills analogy has recently been examined by Johnston (1977a,b). He points out that motor skill learning manifests four main characteristics: dependence on knowledge of results, existence of a learning curve, which is a function of the amount of feedback provided during training, and increased precision of control with practice. Johnston found that examination of the empirical results of his own studies on heart rate and finger blood flow did not support the hypothesis that voluntary control of these functions manifested the characteristics required to support the motor skills hypothesis. Hence, it seems likely that the pursuit of Lang's analogy will not prove profitable. However, the motor skills theory may continue a precarious existence as a result of two recent studies. M. R. Haynes, Blanchard, and Young (1977) have provided some tenuous evidence for the superiority of spacing as opposed to massing of practice and for the existence of a learning curve in cardiac control. A more significant contribution has come from Schwartz, Young, and Vogler (1976). They used the Fleishman motor skills model in which complex skills are regarded as made up of several distinct underlying abilities which tend not to be correlated with one another. Thus, the separate parameters of a motor skill may include strength, endurance, steadiness, precision of control, and reaction time. The equivalent parameters of cardiac activity (conceived of as a motor skill) may be described as maximum and minimum heart rates that can be achieved (equivalent to strength), ability to hold the maximum or minimum rate (endurance), the minimum variability attainable (steadiness), cardiac control precision (motor control precision), and cardiac reaction time (motor reaction time). It was predicted that if the motor skills model is applicable to heart-rate control, then training in the ability to meet strength/endurance criteria (the usual biofeedback training situation) would not facilitate training in the ability to meet a reaction time criterion, and vice versa. In the strength/endurance (SE) task, the subject was required to increase or decrease heart rate as much as possible and maintain the maximum change achieved for 1 min; in the reaction time (RT) task, the subject had to reach 50% of the change from resting level achieved on the immediately preceding SE trial (in the same direction) as rapidly as possible and then maintain this level for 3 min. In brief, the SE task required the subject to make as large a change as possible in his own time and maintain it for a short period, whereas the RT task required the subject to make a much smaller change as quickly as possible, but maintain it longer (it is not clear why the RT task involved such a long mainte-nance time). It was found that independence between the two tasks did appear to exist: training in strength and endurance did not facilitate training in speed of reaction, and vice versa, thus offering some support for the motor skills model.

The Servomechanical Model of Biofeedback Control

The single most striking feature about the human organism is what Cannon long ago called the "wisdom of the body," that is, the fact that at any instant thousands of activities are simultaneously occurring which involve incredibly complex and delicate adjustments which are finely tuned relative to each other. These interactions and adjustments may be regarded as being controlled by extremely refined servosystems. The second most striking feature relates to the fact that for the most part these systems operate below the threshold of awareness and may only (and mostly not even then) arise above that threshold when one or more of the control systems malfunctions. Thus, it is evident that heart rate, blood pressure, breathing, and so on, are functions which are normally under automatic control, as are the adjustments involved in skilled forms of behavior such as walking, grasping objects, and so on. The dramatic effects of a failure in one of the automatic control systems are nowhere more apparent than in the disorder of locomotion control which may be manifest in tabes dorsalis (resulting from syphilis in which proprioceptive feedback from the muscle actions involved in walking is lost due to destruction of the motoneurones which mediate that feedback). The patient becomes dependent on the sight of his limbs to determine their relative position in space, as a result of which he is liable to lose his balance and fall if deprived of vision, whereas the normal person can locomote quite successfully if blindfolded (provided, of course, the terrain is reasonably even). In this section, the role of servocontrol systems in skilled behavior will be examined, following which its relevance to what happens in training with biofeedback will be considered.

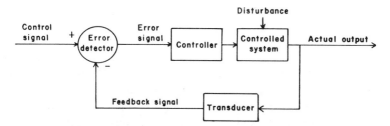

Figure 9. General characteristics of a feedback control system.

The general characteristics of a feedback control system are shown in Figure 9. Let us consider as the controlled system an aircraft and its required output as its prescribed flying speed. The controller generates various inputs (engine power, etc.) which, other things being equal, will maintain the required flying speed. However, the actual flying speed may differ from time to time from the required flying speed because of the operation of factors which vary from time to time, some of these factors being external to the aircraft (e.g., force of the headwind into which the plane might be flying) and some internal (e.g., loss of power in one engine). The actual speed resulting from the interaction of these factors will be measured by a device (the transducer in Figure 9) which generates a feedback signal and transmits it to the error detector, which in turn compares the feedback signal with the control signal, the latter being the expected feedback signal if the aircraft is meeting the specified flying speed requirement. The error signal thus generated may indicate that no adjustment is needed (if the error signal is zero or below some specified value) or an adjustment may be needed which is made by the controller so as to bring the actual flying speed closer to the prescribed flying speed. The feedback loop may be continuously operative but adjustments may be made only if the error signal exceeds specified values.

It is now generally accepted by physiologists that feedback control systems play a vital role in the maintenance of vital body systems within specified limits and that abnormalities result from a breakdown in such systems, involving malfunctioning of one or more of the component parts of the system. In the case of many physiological systems the components involved in the feedback control system relating to a particular function are known (e.g., in diabetes mellitus). In the case of other systems, the servocontrol mechanisms are more speculative, simply because of the extreme complexities involved. Thus, Fender (1964), Stark (1968), and Young and Stark (1963) have attempted to specify the servocontrol systems involved in eye movements, while Stark (1968) has provided models for the pupil, lens, and hand. The way in which body temperature is controlled has attracted a great deal of attention[20] with mathematical models being formulated by, for example, Gordon, Roemer, and Horvath (1976) and by

[20]See Hardy (1961) for a comprehensive review.

Werner (1977). Gordon *et al.* (1976) postulate a controller which utilizes head core temperature, mean skin temperature, and mean skin heat flux as input signals to control metabolism, skin blood flow, and extremity muscle blood flow. In this model, the body is conceptualized as consisting of 14 major cylindrical and spherical angular segments which are differentiated by their thermophysical properties, anatomy, physiological characteristics, and control system characteristics. The model generates predictions about temperature changes in various parts of the body in response to different ambient temperatures as a function of time. These predictions may be tested against the actual changes occurring in these conditions. Thus, Gordon *et al.* (1976) placed their subjects in a room at an ambient temperature of 28°C for 30 min, then switched them to a room with an ambient temperature of only 4.7°C where they remained for 120 min. Changes occurring in metabolic response, total arm blood flow, cardiac output, leg and foot skin temperatures, arm and hand skin temperatures, and rectal, forehead, and thorax skin temperatures, were measured and compared with predicted temperatures. The results indicated the importance of feedforward heat flux signals as temperature regulators as compared with the rate of change of skin temperature. Other examples of attempts to explain physiological functioning in terms of servocontrol systems (chosen from an almost unlimited number of possibilities) include cardiovascular control models (e.g., Katona, Martin, & Felix, 1976; E. E. Smith, Guyton, Manning, & White, 1976), renal hypertension (Floyer, 1975), cerebral circulation (Bentsen, Larsen, & Lassen, 1975), posture and movement (Young, 1974), and muscle control (Hatze, 1977a, b, c; Hatze & Buys, 1977).

The servocontrol of muscle activity, on which a great deal of work has been performed, is of course of particular interest and importance in relation to biofeedback, especially in relation to the rehabilitation of physical function following cerebral insult. The progressive adjustment of muscle activity in reaching for objects, for example, is of particular importance in cerebral palsy and the feedback mechanisms involved have been discussed in some detail in relation to this problem by F. A. Harris (1969) and by Harrison (1976). The feedback control system is shown in Figure 10. The muscle consists of intrafusal fibers surrounded on each side by extrafusal fibers. The extrafusal fibers are innervated by stimulation arising from the alpha efferents which emanate from the alpha motoneurons located in the spinal cord, the strength of the muscle contraction being a function of the number of active alpha motoneurons. The intrafusal fibers (also called muscle spindles) are innervated by gamma efferents emanating from the gamma motoneurons, also located in the spinal cord, producing the stretch reflex in response to static and dynamic changes in muscle length resulting from activation by the alpha efferents. The important point to note in Figure 10, however, is the feedback loop from the gamma efferents via gamma afferents to the alpha motoneurons in the spinal cord. Thus, adjustment of muscle contraction is a function in part of the feedback information arising from the stretch reflex

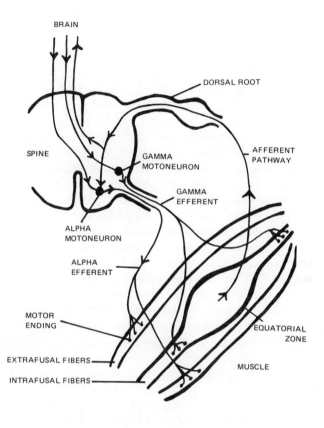

Figure 10. Schematic drawing of the efferent and afferent pathways that supply muscle fibers. (From Harrison, A. Components of neuromuscular control. In K. S. Holt (Ed.), *Movement and child development*. London: Spastics International Medical/Heinemann Medical, 1976, 36, Figure 1. Reprinted by permission of the author and the publisher.)

which influences the activity of the alpha motoneurons and helps to produce, maintain, and (where necessary) correct the degree of muscle contraction so that it is appropriate to the end result (such as reaching a target) required. Both F. A. Harris (1969) and A. Harrison (1976) consider that a fault in the feedback loop rather than a fault in the efferent activity of the alpha motoneurons is the critical defect in movement in cerebral palsy, and F. A. Harris (1969) has provided an account of the various therapeutic approaches which attempt to rectify the fault in the gamma loop.[21]

---

[21]It is not suggested that this loop is self-contained and unaffected by activity at higher levels of the nervous system.

This is a particularly striking and important example of the relevance of servosystems to biofeedback, but there are many other examples which could be cited to illustrate the point. Thus, feedback control models have been provided in respect of the triceps surae muscle (Inbar & Joseph, 1976), the elbow joint angle (Andreeva, Zhukova, & Chernov, 1975; Fel'dman, 1966; Hallett, Shahani, & Young, 1975a, b), thumb position (Marsden, Merton, & Morton, 1972, 1976), finger movement (Radonjic & Long, 1971), and jaw movement (Folkins & Abbs, 1975). Radonjic and Long (1971), for example, examined the pattern of innervation of groups of muscles in the wrist during finger movement. They recorded activity from six muscles in the wrist, using implanted electrodes, while various types of finger exercises were performed. Two basic patterns of wrist muscle activity were found, associated with closing and opening activities of the hand, and they concluded that the wrist muscles and the associated nervous activity constituted a typical positional control system, with information arising from the joint and muscle receptors providing feedback which is used to monitor the ongoing activity until the required result is achieved.

These studies deal with relatively discrete and limited activities. Other work has clearly demonstrated the role of feedback in much more complicated forms of behavior. Cappozzo, Figura, and Marchetti (1976), for example, made very careful measurements of the activity in a large number of muscles involved in level walking at natural speeds while simultaneously using filmed records and force-plate measurements to determine the mechanical forces involved. In this way, the velocities and accelerations of body segments; the muscular movements at the hip, knee, and ankle; the work done by muscular movements; the energy levels of each segment and of the whole body; and the lengths of muscles could all be assessed during walking. The results obtained were compared with those expected from a mechanical model of the body which they had constructed. Similar investigations have been carried out in respect not only of walking (Milner, Basmajian, & Quanbury, 1971), but also, for example, of bodily movements in relation to changes in the abdominal musculature (Carman, Blanton, & Biggs, 1972) and knee activity (Murphy, Blanton, & Biggs, 1971), soleus muscle activity during sudden unexpected falls (Greenwood & Hopkins, 1976a, b), efferent and afferent control of fast and slow arm movements (Pardew, 1976; Van der Staak, 1975), the feedback control of handwriting (K. U. Smith & Murphy, 1963), and the maintenance of upright posture (Litvinenkova & Hlavecka, 1973). Held and his colleagues (Held & Bossom, 1961; Held & Freedman, 1963; Held & Mikaelian, 1964; Held & Rekosh, 1963) have investigated the significance of movement-produced feedback in adaptation to distorted visual fields. These studies need not be described in detail here; they are mentioned so that the interested reader can pursue the literature on servocontrol of skilled behavior further. They clearly indicate the importance of feedback control in the maintenance and modification of ongoing behavior.

In more general terms, two important points need to be made about the operation and interaction of feedback control systems in the human organism.

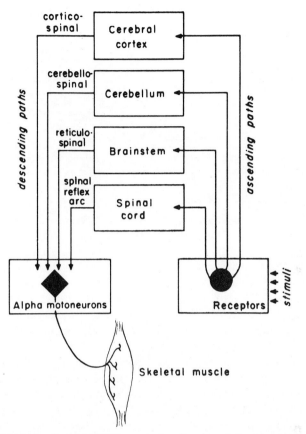

Figure 11. "Multiple-loop" model of CNS organization. Impulse activity, set up in afferent fibers as adequate stimuli impinge upon various sensory receptors, takes many parallel routes (each of which involves elements at different levels of the neuraxis) which ultimately lead back to a common target, the alpha motoneurons at the spinal cord level. The behavior which emerges will reflect which of the circuits has carried the major part of the impulse traffic; particular details may reflect modulatory influences exerted through the other circuits. (From Harris, F. A. Multiple-loop modulation of motor outflow: A physiological basis for facilitation techniques. *Journal of the American Physical Therapy Association*, 1971, *51*, 392, Figure 1. Reprinted by permission of the author and the publisher.).

The first is that control can be exercised at different levels of the nervous system; the second, that the control systems are best conceptualized as being hierarchical in nature.[22] Thus, local control may be exercised at the peripheral level without the higher nervous centers being involved. However, higher levels of control may intervene and override local control under certain circumstances. The number of levels of control which may be involved has been variously specified

[22]Ideas expressed by Hayes-Roth (1977) in her recent review of the evolution of cognitive structures and processes seem quite consonant with the ideas presented here of the hierarchical structure of feedback control and the notion of levels as well as with the concept of central command units.

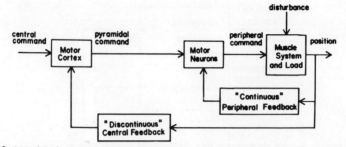

Figure 12. A model of voluntary control. (From Houk, J. C. On the significance of various command signals during voluntary control. *Brain Research,* 1972, *40,* 49, Figure 1. Reprinted by permission of the author and the publisher.)

by different authors. F. A. Harris (1971) has postulated four levels of control (as shown in Figure 11) operating at the spinal cord, brainstem, cerebellum, and cerebral cortex. Impulses may travel to each of these levels simultaneously but resulting efferent impulses may or may not emanate from each of these levels. It will be noted that feedback channels are not included in Harris's model, but, of course, he would incorporate such feedback into a complete system. Houk (1972) has identified three levels of control with two kinds of feedback, as shown in Figure 12. The levels of control involve "central commands" to the motor cortex, "pyramidal commands" to the motor neurons, and "peripheral commands" to the muscle system itself, while the two kinds of feedback involve continuous peripheral information fed from the muscle system to the motor neurons on the one hand, and discontinuous central feedback to the motor cortex on the other hand. The whole question of levels of control in the nervous system in relation to skilled movements has been discussed in great detail by Paillard (1960), who contents himself with identifying two levels: motor neurons in the medulla oblongata and spinal cord which exercise "direct" control over the peripheral organs, and neuronal groups in the cerebral cortex which control pyramidal efferent activity. In spite of these differences in detail, there is general agreement that levels of control exist and that the control is hierarchically organized (A. Harrison, 1976; Pew, 1966)[23].

The detailed working out of the essential components of these control systems has hardly begun and the complexity of the task is immense. That the hierarchical nature of the control systems must be recognized, however, is increasingly evident from recent reviews such as those by Beck (1976) and Broadbent (1977), the latter placing the question of control within a very broad framework indeed.

One final aspect of servocontrol systems remains to be mentioned. Lashley (1951) long ago drew attention to the difficulty, if not impossibility, of explaining serial behavior entirely in terms of feedback from lower to higher control

[23]See also K. U. Smith and Henry, 1967; and Tatton and Lee (1975) for examples of similar approaches to the hierarchical control of behavior.

centers via neural pathways because of the inevitable time lag involved in feedback information's reaching the highest control centers. This has led in recent years to the postulation of two alternative solutions to the problem. One relates to the automatic running off of skilled behaviors as long as error signals remain within certain predetermined levels; only when the error signal exceeds the preset criterion will corrective action at a higher level occur. The other postulates the development of what is termed "central motor program control" or "motor programming" in which a program is developed at the highest level and then runs off without further monitoring until it is complete, at which stage the state of the organism is assessed and corrective action taken if necessary. Such motor programming has been postulated by many workers[24] and experimental evidence has been gathered in support of the notion by Barr, Schultheis, and Robinson (1976) and by Rosenbaum (1977; Rosenbaum & Radford, 1977), among others. Some of the most compelling evidence relating to central programming mechanisms operating independently of peripheral feedback comes from the long series of studies by Laszlo and her colleagues, using the nerve compression block technique. Laszlo (1966), for example, showed that although loss of tactile information and passive and kinesthetic feedback interfered with fast tapping performance, feedback was not essential for fast tapping performance. In subsequent investigations, Laszlo (1967a, b) investigated in detail the relative importance of loss of kinesthetic, auditory, and visual feedback, alone and in combination, on fast tapping performance, and subsequently extended her investigations to the study of the acquisition of novel responses (Laszlo, 1968) and transfer from preferred to nonpreferred hand (Laszlo & Baguley, 1971; Laszlo, Baguley, & Bairstow, 1970). She developed the concept of a central motor program capable of controlling behavior directly, even in the absence of peripheral feedback (Laszlo, Shamoon, & Sanson-Fisher, 1969). The central motor program operates independently of error information and error correction procedures.

Thus, in summary, the importance of feedback information in the control of behavior can hardly be denied while it is necessary to recognize different levels of control, the hierarchical nature of feedback control, and the existence of high-level control which operates without direct reference to and, if necessary, in the absence of, feedback from lower control levels.

The Language of Biofeedback

It is now time to return to the question with which this chapter opened: Why is it that the therapist cannot tell the patient how to achieve increased control with biofeedback, and why is it that when control is achieved, the patient cannot tell

---

[24]See, for example, Keele (1968), McGuigan and Boness (1975), Paillard (1960), Perkel, Gerstein, Smith, and Tatton (1975), Schmidt (1975), A. A. Smith (1953), Summers, (1975), Voronin (1962).

the therapist how he did it? The answer lies in the nature of control and this in turn reflects on the meaningfulness of the attempts to determine the "mediators" of biofeedback control described in earlier sections of this chapter.

Let us suppose that two people express contrary opinions as to the height of a door. How may the dispute be resolved? The answer lies in the fact that there are agreed measurement procedures for determining the height of the door. Suppose, on the other hand, that two people claim to be suffering from tension headaches and one maintains that his tension headache is worse than the other person's. In the absence of some independent criterion of measurement of sever- ity of tension headache there is no way in which this difference of opinion can be resolved. Suppose now that the experimenter asks his subject: "How is your frontalis muscle activity today?" or the therapist asks his patient: "How is your tension headache today?" The answers given (if indeed any meaningful answer can be given at all) are likely to be couched in a vague and unhelpful set of terms. The point to be made is that there is no language of a communicable kind with which to describe the internal activities of the human organism comparable to the precision of the shared language which can be used to discuss matters such as the height or color of a door or other aspects of the physical world. At the very least, the "language" of the internal activities of the human organism is nonverbal. Thus, at a superficial level, it is not really surprising that neither the experimenter/therapist nor the subject/patient can readily describe what happens in successful biofeedback training. Consider as a parallel problem the task of teaching a young child how to urinate successfully from a standing or sitting position. It is well known that voluntary urination involves the following sequ- ence of events: steadying of the diaphragm, contraction of the lower abdominal muscles, relaxation of the pubococcygeus of the levator ani (all of which lead to a rapid lowering of the neck of the bladder), increase in abdominal pressure, contraction of the detrusor muscle, and as a consequence, urination. But no mother in her right mind, even if she were a physiologist specializing in bladder function and "aware" of the sequence of events necessary for successful urina- tion, would dream of placing her child on the toilet and proceed to instruct him verbally to "steady your diaphragm...good... now contract your lower ab- dominal muscles...good...now relax the pubococcygeus of your levator ani..." Yet apparently the specified aim of many biofeedback researchers and therapists is to achieve just this kind of "understanding" and "awareness" of what happens when increased voluntary control of a function with biofeedback training is undertaken.

Let us look again at the biofeedback training situation. The subject or patient is required to increase his voluntary control over some designated[25] func- tion and he is provided with a feedback display which reflects, either continu- ously or discontinuously, in binary or proportional form, changes in activity of

[25]It is assumed for the sake of the argument that the subject is fully informed, but it is equally applicable to situations in which the subject is not informed at all.

that function. The feedback display, however, is in an important respect the least important aspect of the whole procedure, although it is the one that has received the most attention. The reason for this is obvious: the display is intended to provide more detailed information about the function in question than is normally available to the subject. Thus, before training begins the subject may be quite unable to report anything about, for example, fluctuations in the activity of the frontalis muscle, but the display will provide him with more or less (depending on the nature of the display) accurate information about very small fluctuations in activity of the muscle. Clearly, however, it is not the aim of the experimenter or therapist to make the subject or patient permanently dependent on the availability of the display in order that increased voluntary control may be exercised. The aim of the procedure is to increase voluntary control of the function to the point at which it can be maintained when the feedback display is no longer present. The control must, therefore, in some sense, be "internalized." Put another way, the subject uses biofeedback to learn about the activity of the function in question so as to be able to exercise increased control over it on (hopefully) a permanent basis without the aid any longer of the external "crutch" (the display). But the crucial question still remains: What is the "language" that he has learned? *It is maintained here that the "language" that is learned relates not the activity of the function (e.g., muscle) itself but to the servocontrol system underlying the activity of the function.*

This point of view needs some further clarification. Consider a subject whose arm hangs loosely and relaxed by his side. The electrical activity of the muscle in such a relaxed state will not be zero but will take an average value resulting from random oscillations about the average value. But this activity is not "uncaused"; it is determined, within the framework adopted here, by the operation of the servocontrol system or systems pertinent to this particular function. This servosystem can be regarded as being constituted of a number of components, each of which may take any one of a range of values; the "resting state" is defined as a particular combination of individual component settings. Suppose now that a decision is reached to increase the tension in that particular muscle. This will be achieved by altering the setting of some (but not necessarily all) of the components of the servosystem so as to produce a new combination. Now, of course, the subject is not "aware" of the component parts of the servosystem, and the particular combination of components which produce particular states of muscle tension is not accessible to "awareness" either. Thus, if the servosystem develops a fault so that an inappropriate combination is set and the muscle malfunctions, there is no reason to suppose that the subject (or patient, as he may now turn out to be) will be able to describe what is wrong (except to say that he gets tension headaches which may be indexed by an increased level of frontalis muscle activity of which the patient is "unaware"). In providing a feedback display of the frontalis muscle activity, the therapist is able to provide the patient with a detailed account of small changes in that activity. But what the patient learns when he produces changes in the muscle activity which are reflected in the feedback display is not a greater "awareness" of his muscle activity. *What he learns is the "language" of the servocontrol system; that is, how to modify the relative settings of the components of the control system so as to produce the appropriate muscle activity in a specified situation.* The feedback display is merely a device to teach the patient about his control systems.

Let us now look briefly at the implications of this position for the attempts that have been reviewed earlier in this chapter to explain biofeedback in mediational terms. The somatic mediational model assumes that the subject learns to become more sensitive to or "aware of" the activity of his muscles (or heart rate or blood pressure, etc.). The cognitive mediational model assumes that voluntary control is increased because of "cognitive processes" which enable him to control his somatic processes. But if what is being acquired is "knowledge" of the servocontrol systems, then "awareness" becomes redundant (and indeed may even be harmful). We do not go around talking to ourselves about the need to increase (or decrease) our heart rate or breathing rate; and even if it is the case that engaging in mental arithmetic will raise our heart rate, is it patently undesirable that a patient with bradycardia should spend the rest of his life performing mental arithmetic so as to keep his heart rate elevated. Nor do we go around concentrating on sensations from our lower limbs in order to ensure that we "know" when our left leg has been successfully placed in front of our right leg, so that we can tell ourselves it is now time to advance the right leg in front of the left, in order to locomote successfully from point A to point B. Indeed, it is well known, and has been experimentally demonstrated, that the essence of skilled behavior resides precisely in the degree to which its execution is not open to awareness. Thus, in learning to drive a car, verbal exhortations to oneself may play an important role in the early states of learning, but learning is complete only when the verbal aspect drops out altogether[26]. And while it is quite possible to run down a steep set of stairs three at a time, disaster is likely to ensue if the person tries to give a detailed verbal description of how he is accomplishing the feat while actually performing it. The language of the control of internal functions is a nonverbal language; it is the language of the servocontrol systems. Not only is it not surprising that the subject cannot verbally describe how he achieves control, it is both unnecessary and probably highly undesirable that he should be able to do so.

With respect to the role of reinforcement, the position also becomes clear if it is accepted that what is learned in biofeedback training is the language of the servocontrol system. A simple example will suffice. Consider the bus driver who successfully maneuvers his bus around a tight corner, just missing a stationary vehicle by a matter of inches. It is absurd to argue that on the next occasion he

---

[26]Which is why a skilled driver is not necessarily a good instructor; teaching a person how to drive a car is a quite different skill from driving a car.

will also successfully manipulate his bus around the same corner, again just missing a parked car, because he was reinforced on the first occasion by not hitting the car. The manipulation of the bus around the corner, avoiding obstacles, involves the delicate coordination of many servocontrol systems with constant fine adjustments of the systems as a result of incoming information which changes its nature from second to second. The reinforcement "explanation" no more works in this case than it does in the case of a skilled pianist's successfully completing a concerto involving maybe 40,000–50,000 notes arrayed in complex sequences. To be sure, the bus driver drives his bus because he is genuinely reinforced (rewarded) by being paid at the end of the week; but he does not drive his bus skillfully because of reinforcement, but because of the proper coordination of his servocontrol systems.

It may be protested that an explanation in terms of servosystem control is no more satisfactory than an explanation in terms of reinforcement, somatic mediation, or cognitive mediation since in each case the "explanation" itself needs explaining. There are two answers to this objection. The first relates to the undoubted fact that the kind of model which is espoused does make a significant difference to how a particular problem in biofeedback will be approached. In the case of stuttering, for example, three main "explanations" have been advanced. The psychoanalytic or psychodynamic explanation of stuttering holds that stuttering is a symptom of an underlying conflict, the reinforcement explanation holds that stuttering is a function of the rewarding and aversive consequences of speech, and the servocontrol explanation of stuttering holds that stuttering arises as a result of a defect in the control system for speech form. In each case, the consequences for the approach to treatment are quite different. The psychodynamic view leads to the position that the underlying conflict rather than the stutter must be treated, the reinforcement view leads to the presentation of differential consequences for nonstuttered and stuttered speech, while the servocontrol view leads to attempts to eliminate the stuttering by postulating the nature of the defect in the servocontrol system and attempting to overcome the effects of the defective component. In relation to this example, it may be noted that it is possible to turn stuttering on and off at will instantaneously by preventing or not preventing the stutterer from hearing the sound of his own voice, a fact which it is impossible to explain in terms of the psychodynamic or reinforcement model of stuttering.

The second answer to the objection is that the postulation of servocontrol systems with specified function to explain behavior and variations in behavior of a quite specific kind is a commonplace in engineering. Perhaps the most clear-cut example that can be given relates to attempts to explain the regulation of body temperature, a function not without interest to biofeedback workers. It is not considered in the least strange to formulate such models and test them against empirical observations.

The task of the biofeedback research worker or therapist, then, is to attempt to formulate servocontrol systems for various functions, and particularly the components of those control systems, and in the case of abnormalities of function to formulate hypotheses as to the nature of the defect in the control system which may be responsible for the defective behavior. His task then becomes one of helping the subject or patient, with the aid of feedback, to learn the language of the servosystem so that the correct relative settings of the component parts of the system may be achieved in order that appropriate responding may be obtained in a given situation. Until the biofeedback worker begins to do this, satisfactory explanations of how functional control with biofeedback is achieved will not begin to be obtained.

References

Alexander, A. B. An experimental test of assumptions relating to the use of electromyographic biofeedback as a general relaxation training technique. *Psychophysiology*, 1975, *12*, 656–662. (1975/76:20)

Alexander, A. B., French, C. A., & Goodman, N. J. A comparison of auditory and visual feedback assisted muscular relaxation training. *Psychophysiology*, 1975, *12*, 119–123.

Alexander, A. B., White, P. D., & Wallace, H. M. Training and transfer of training effects in EMG biofeedback assisted muscular relaxation. *Psychophysiology*, 1977, *14*, 551–559.

Ancoli, S., & Green, K. F. Authoritarianism, introspection, and alpha wave biofeedback training. *Psychophysiology*, 1977, *14*, 40–44.

Andreeva, E. A., Zhukova, G. N., & Chernov, V. I. Control of slow changes in the elbow joint angle. *Automation and Remote Control USSR*, 1975, *36*, 445–451.

Bakal, D. A., & Kaganov, J. A. Muscle contraction and migraine headache: Psychophysiologic comparison. *Headache*, 1977, *17*, 208–214.

Barber, T. X. Implications for human capabilities and potentialities. In T. X. Barber, N. P. Spanos, & J. F. Chaves (Eds), *Hypnosis, imagination, and human potentialities*. New York: Pergamon, 1974, pp. 109–126. (1974:4)

Barr, C. C., Schultheis, L. W., & Robinson, D. A. Voluntary, non-visual control of the human vestibulo-ocular reflex. *Acta Otolaryngologica*, 1976, *81*, 365–375.

Basmajian, J. V. Facts vs. myths in EMG biofeedback. *Biofeedback and Self-Regulation*, 1976, *1*, 369–370.

Beatty, J. T. Effects of initial alpha wave abundance and operant training procedures on occipital alpha and beta activity. *Psychonomic Science*, 1971, *23*, 197–199. (1971:9)

Beck, H. Neuropsychological servosystems, consciousness, and the problem of embodiment. *Behavioral Science*, 1976, *21*, 139–160.

Bell, I. R., & Schwartz, G. E. Voluntary control and reactivity of human heart rate. *Psychophysiology*, 1975, *12*, 339–348. (1975/76:34)

Belmaker, R., Proctor, E., & Feather, B. W. Muscle tension in human operant heart-rate conditioning. *Conditional Reflex*, 1972, *7*, 97–106. (1973:6)

Bentsen, N., Larsen, B., & Lassen, N. A. Chronically impaired autoregulation of cerebral blood flow in long-term diabetics. *Stroke*, 1975, *6*, 497–502.

Bergman, J. S., & Johnson, H. J. The effects of instructional set and autonomic perception on cardiac control. *Psychophysiology*, 1971, *8*, 180–190. (1971:17)

Bergman, J. S., & Johnson, H. J. Sources of information which affect training and raising of heart rate. *Psychophysiology*, 1972, *9*, 30–39. (1972:16)

Bird, B. L., Newton, F. A., Sheer, D. E., & Ford, M. Biofeedback training of 40-Hz EEG in humans. *Biofeedback and Self-Regulation,* 1978, *3,* 1–11. (a)

Bird, B. L., Newton, F. A., Sheer, D. E., & Ford, M. Behavioral and electroencephalographic correlates of 40-Hz EEG biofeedback training in humans. *Biofeedback and Self-Regulation,* 1978, *3,* 13–28. (b)

Birk, L., Crider, A., Shapiro, D., & Tursky, B. Operant electrodermal conditioning under partial curarization. *Journal of Comparative and Physiological Psychology,* 1966, *62,* 165–166. (R:23)

Black, A. H. The operant conditioning of central nervous system electrical activity. In G. H. Bowers (Ed.), *The psychology of learning and motivation: Advances in research and theory.* New York: Academic, 1972. (1972:9)

Blanchard, E. B., Young, L. D., & McLeod, P. Awareness of heart activity and self-control of heart rate. *Psychophysiology,* 1972, *9,* 63–68.

Blanchard, E. B., Haynes, M. R., Kallman, M. D., & Harkey, L. A comparison of direct blood pressure feedback and electromyographic feedback on the blood pressure of normotensives. *Biofeedback and Self-Regulation,* 1976, *1,* 445–451.

Blankstein, K. R., & Egner, K. Relationship of the locus of control construct to the self-control of heart rate. *Journal of General Psychology,* 1977, *97,* 291–306.

Blizard, D. A., Cowings, P., & Miller, N. E. Visceral responses to opposite types of autogenic-training imagery. *Biological Psychology,* 1975, *3,* 49–55. (1975/76:14)

Boulougouris, J. C., Rabavilas, A. D., & Stefanis, C. Psychophysiological responses in obsessive-compulsive patients. *Behaviour Research and Therapy,* 1977, *15,* 221–230.

Brady, J. P., Luborsky, L., & Kron, R. E. Blood pressure reduction in patients with essential hypertension through metronome-conditioned relaxation: A preliminary report. *Behavior Therapy,* 1974, *5,* 203–209. (1974:21)

Braud, L. W., Lupin, M. N., & Braud, W. G. The use of electromyographic biofeedback in the control of hyperactivity. *Journal of Learning Disabilities,* 1975, *8,* 420–425.

Brener, J. Heart rate as an avoidance response. *Psychological Record,* 1966, *16,* 329–336.

Brener, J. M. A general model of voluntary control applied to the phenomena of learned cardiovascular control. In P. A. Obrist, A. H. Black, J. Brener, & L. V. Di Cara (Eds.), *Cardiovascular psychophysiology.* Chicago: Aldine–Atherton, 1975, pp. 365–391.

Brener, J., & Hothersall, D. Paced respiration and heart rate control. *Psychophysiology,* 1967, *4,* 1–6. (R:5)

Brener, J., & Jones, J. M. Interoceptive discrimination in intact humans: Detection of cardiac activity. *Physiology and Behavior,* 1974, *13,* 763–776. (1974:19)

Brener, J. P., Kleinman, R. A., & Goesling, W. J. The effects of different exposure to augmented sensory feedback on the control of heart rate. *Psychophysiology,* 1969, *5,* 510–516.

Broadbent, D. E. Levels, hierarchies, and the locus of control. *Quarterly Journal of Experimental Psychology,* 1977, *29,* 181–201.

Brolund, J. W., & Schallow, J. R. The effects of reward on occipital alpha facilitation by biofeedback. *Psychophysiology,* 1976, *13,* 236–241. (1976/77:32)

Brown, B. B. Recognition of aspects of consciousness through association with EEG alpha activity represented by a light signal. *Psychophysiology,* 1970, *6,* 442–452. (1970:15)

Brown, B. B. Awareness of EEG-subjective activity relationships detected within a closed feedback system. *Psychophysiology,* 1971, *7,* 451–464. (1971:8)

Brown, B. B. Critique of biofeedback concepts and methodologies. In J. I. Martin (Ed.), *Proceedings of the San Diego biomedical symposium* (Vol. 16). New York: Academic, 1977, pp. 187–192.

Brucker, B., Dworkin, B. R., Eisenberg, L., Miller, N. E., & Pickering, T. G. Learned voluntary control of diastolic pressure, and circulatory effects of attempted muscle contraction in severely paralysed patients. *Journal of Physiology,* 1975, *252,* 67–68.

Canter, A., Kondo, C. Y., & Knott, J. R. A comparison of EMG feedback and progressive muscle relaxation training in anxiety neurosis. *British Journal of Psychiatry*, 1975, *127*, 470–477. (1976/77:44)

Cappozzo, A., Figura, F., & Marchetti, M. The interplay of muscular and external forces in human ambulation. *Journal of Biomechanics*, 1976, *9*, 35–43.

Carlson, J. G. Locus of control and frontal electromyographic response training. *Biofeedback and Self-Regulation*, 1977, *2*, 259–271.

Carman, D. J., Blanton, P. L., & Biggs, N. L. Electromyographic study of the anterolateral abdominal musculature utilizing indwelling electrodes. *American Journal of Physical Medicine*, 1972, *51*, 113–129.

Carroll, D. Cardiac perception and cardiac control: A review. *Biofeedback and Self-Regulation*, 1977, *2*, 349–369.

Clark, R. E., & Forgione, A. G. Gingival and digital vasomotor response to thermal imagery in hypnosis. *Journal of Dental Research*, 1974. *53*, 792–796.

Cohen, M. J. The relation between heart rate and electromyographic activity in a discriminated escape avoidance paradigm. *Psychophysiology*, 1973, *10*, 8–20.

Coursey, R. D. Electromyograph feedback as a relaxation technique. *Journal of Consulting and Clinical Psychology*, 1975, *43*, 825–834. (1975/76:19)

Davidson, R. J., & Schwartz, G. E. Patterns of cerebral lateralization during cardiac biofeedback versus the self-regulation of emotion: Sex differences. *Psychophysiology*, 1976, *13*, 62–68.

Davidson, R. J., & Schwartz, G. E. Brain mechanisms subserving self-generated imagery: Electrophysiological specificity and patterning. *Psychophysiology*, 1977, *14*, 598–602.

Davidson, R. J., Schwartz, G. E., Pugash, E., & Bromfield, E. Sex differences in patterns of EEG asymmetry. *Biological Psychology*, 1976, *4*, 119–138.

Davidson, R. J., Schwartz, G. E., & Rothman, L. P. Attentional style and the self-regulation of mode-specific attention: An electroencephalographic study. *Journal of Abnormal Psychology*, 1976, *85*, 611–621.

Davis, M. H., Saunders, D. R., Creer, T. L., & Chai, H. Relaxation training facilitated by biofeedback apparatus as a supplemental treatment in bronchial asthma. *Journal of Psychosomatic Research*, 1973, *17*, 121–128. (1974:52)

DeGood, D. E., & Chisholm, R. C. Multiple response comparison of parietal EEG and frontalis EMG biofeedback. *Psychophysiology*, 1977, *14*, 258–265.

Diekhoff, G. M. Effects of feedback in a forced-choice GSR detection task. *Psychophysiology*, 1976, *13*, 22–26.

Diekhoff, G. M., Garland, J., Dansereau, D. F., & Walker, C. A. Muscle tension, skin conductance, and finger pulse volume: Asymmetries as a function of cognitive demands. *Acta Psychologica*, 1978, *42*, 83–93.

Dugan, M., & Sheridan, C. Effects of instructed imagery on temperature of hands. *Perceptual and Motor Skills*, 1976, *42*, 14.

Eason, R. G., & Sadler, R. Relationship between voluntary control of alpha activity level through auditory feedback and degree of eye convergence. *Bulletin of the Psychonomic Society*, 1977, *9*, 21–24.

Edelman, R. I. Effects of differential afferent feedback on instrumental GSR conditioning. *Journal of Psychology*, 1970, *74*, 3–14.

Edelman, R. I. Desensitization and physiological arousal. *Journal of Personality and Social Psychology*, 1971, *17*, 259–266.

Elder, S. T., & Eustis, N. K. Instrumental blood pressure conditioning in out-patient hypertensives. *Behavior Research and Therapy*, 1975, *13*, 185–188. (1975/76:46)

Engel, B. T. Operant conditioning of cardiac function: A status report. *Psychophysiology*, 1972, *9*, 161–177. (1972:13)

Engel, B. T. Operant conditioning of cardiac function: Some implications for psychosomatic medicine. *Behavior Therapy*, 1974, *5*, 302–303.

Engel, B. T., & Chism, R. A. Operant conditioning of heart rate speeding. *Psychophysiology*, 1967, *3*, 418–426.

Engel, B. T., & Hansen, S. P. Operant conditioning of heart rate slowing. *Psychophysiology*, 1966, *3*, 176–187. (R:3)

Epstein, L. H., & Abel, G. G. An analysis of biofeedback training effects for tension headache patients. *Behavior Therapy*, 1977, *8*, 37–47.

Epstein, L. H., & Blanchard, E. B. Biofeedback, self-control, and self-management. *Biofeedback and Self-Regulation*, 1977, *2*, 201–211.

Epstein, L. H., & Stein, D. B. Feedback-influenced heart rate discrimination. *Journal of Abnormal Psychology*, 1974, *83*, 585–588.

Epstein, L. H., & Webster, J. S. Instructional, pacing, and feedback control of respiratory behavior. *Perceptual and Motor Skills*, 1975, *41*, 895–900.

Epstein, L. H., Cinciripini, P. M., McCoy, J. F., & Marshall, W. R. Heart rate as a discriminative stimulus. *Psychophysiology*, 1977, *14*, 143–149.

Fel'dman, A. G. Functional tuning of the nervous system during control of movement or maintenance of a steady posture. III. Mechanographic analysis of the execution by man of the simplest motor tasks. *Biophysics*, 1966, *11*, 766–775.

Fender, D. H. Control mechanisms of the eye. *Scientific American*, 1964, *211*, 24–33.

Finley, W. W., Niman, C., Standley, J., & Ender, P. Frontal EMG-biofeedback training of athetoid cerebral palsy patients: A report of six cases. *Biofeedback and Self-Regulation*, 1976, *1*, 169–182.

Finley, W. W., Niman, C. A., Standley, J., & Wansley, R. A. Electrophysiologic behavior modification of frontal EMG in cerebral-palsied children. *Biofeedback and Self-Regulation*, 1977, *2*, 59–79.

Floyer, M. A. Renal control of interstitial space compliance: A physiological mechanism which may play a part in the etiology of hypertension. *Clinical Nephrology*, 1975, *4*, 152–156.

Folkins, J. W., & Abbs, J. H. Lip and jaw motor control during speech: Responses to resistive loading of the jaw. *Journal of Speech and Hearing Research*, 1975, *18*, 207–220.

Fowler, J. E., Budzynski, T. H., & VandenBergh, R. L. Effects of an EMG biofeedback relaxation program on the control of diabetes: A case study. *Biofeedback and Self-Regulation*, 1976, *1*, 105–112.

Frazier, T. W. Avoidance conditioning of heart rate in humans. *Psychophysiology*, 1966, *3*, 188–202.

Freedman, R., & Papsdorf, J. D. Biofeedback and progressive relaxation treatment of sleep-onset insomnia: A controlled, all-night investigation. *Biofeedback and Self-Regulation*, 1976, *1*, 253–271.

Gaarder, K. Control of states of consciousness. II. Attainment through external feedback augmenting control of psychophysiological variables. *Archives of General Psychiatry*, 1971, *25*, 436–441. (1971:3)

Gannon, L. The role of interoception in learned visceral control. *Biofeedback and Self-Regulation*, 1977, *2*, 337–347.

Gannon, L., & Sternbach, R. A. Alpha enhancement as a treatment for pain: A case study. *Journal of Behaviour Therapy and Experimental Psychiatry*, 1971, *2*, 209–213. (1971:38)

Gatchel, R. J. Frequency of feedback and learned heart rate control. *Journal of Experimental Psychology*, 1974, *103*, 274–283. (1975/76:39)

Gatchel, R. J. Change over training sessions of relationship between locus of control and voluntary heart rate control. *Perceptual and Motor Skills*, 1975, *40*, 424–426.

Gavalas, R. J. Operant reinforcement of a skeletally mediated autonomic response: Uncoupling of the two responses. *Psychonomic Science*, 1968, *11*, 195–196.

Gavalas-Medici, R. Uses and abuses of the mediation construct: A case of operant reinforcement of autonomic and neural responses. *Behaviorism*, 1972, *1*, 103–117.

Gellhorn, E. *Principles of autonomic-somatic interactions: Physiological basis and psychological and clinical implications.* Minneapolis: University of Minnesota Press, 1967.

Gellhorn, E., & Kiely, W. F. Mystical states of consciousness: Neurophysiological and clinical aspects. *Journal of Nervous and Mental Disease,* 1972, *154,* 339–405. (1973:43)

Goesling, W. J., May, C., Lavond, D., Barnes, T., & Carreira, C. Relationship between internal and external locus of control and the operant conditioning of alpha through biofeedback training. *Perceptual and Motor Skills,* 1974, *39,* 1339–1343.

Goldman, H., Kleinman, K. M., Snow, M. Y., Bidus, D. R., & Korol, B. Relationship between essential hypertension and cognitive functioning: Effects of biofeedback. *Psychophysiology,* 1975, *12,* 569–573. (1975/76:45)

Goldstein, I. B., Grinker, R. R., Heath, H. A., Oken, D., & Shipman, W. G. Study in psychophysiology of muscle tension. I. Response specificity. *Archives of General Psychiatry,* 1964, *11,* 322–330.

Good, R. Frontalis muscle tension and sleep latency. *Psychophysiology,* 1975, *12,* 465–467.

Goodkin, R. Case studies in behavioral research in rehabilitation. *Perceptual and Motor Skills,* 1966, *23,* 171–182.

Gordon, R. G., Roemer, R. B., & Horvath, S. M. A mathematical model of the human temperature regulatory system–Transient cold exposure response. *IEEE Transactions on Biomedical Engineering,* 1976, *BME-23,* 434–444.

Grace, W. J., & Graham, D. T. Relationship of specific attitudes and emotions to certain bodily diseases. *Psychosomatic Medicine,* 1952, *14,* 243–251.

Graham, D. T., Stern, J. A., & Winokur, G. Experimental investigation of the specificity of attitude hypothesis in psychosomatic disease. *Psychosomatic Medicine,* 1958, *20,* 446–457.

Graham, D. T., Kabler, J. D., & Graham, F. K. Physiological response to the suggestion of attitudes specific for hives and hypertension. *Psychosomatic Medicine,* 1962, *24,* 159–169. (R:69)

Greene, W. A., & Nielson, T. C. Operant GSR conditioning of high and low autonomic perceivers. *Psychonomic Science,* 1966, *6,* 359–360.

Greenwood, R., & Hopkins, A. Muscle responses during sudden falls in man. *Journal of Physiology,* 1976, *254,* 507–518. (a)

Greenwood, R., & Hopkins, A. Landing from an unexpected fall and a voluntary step. *Brain,* 1976, *99,* 375–386. (b)

Grings, W. W., & Schandler, S. L. Interaction of learned relaxation and aversion. *Psychophysiology,* 1977, *14,* 275–280.

Guitar, B. Reduction of stuttering frequency using electromyographic feedback of muscle action potentials, (Occasional Paper No. 2). Human Communications Laboratory, University of New South Wales, Australia, 1974.

Hallett, M., Shahani, B. T., & Young, R. R. EMG analysis of stereotyped voluntary movements in man. *Journal of Neurology, Neurosurgery and Psychiatry,* 1975, *38,* 1154–1162. (a)

Hallett, M., Shahani, B. T., & Young, R. R. EMG analysis of patients with cerebellar deficits. *Journal of Neurology, Neurosurgery, and Psychiatry,* 1975, *38,* 1163–1169. (b)

Hamano, K. Studies on self-regulation of internal activity: Preliminary report on transaction with interoceptive feedback in the discrimination of cardiac activity. *Japanese Psychological Research,* 1977, *19,* 143–148.

Hamano, K., & Okita, T. Some experiments on instrumental modification of autonomic responses. *Psychologia,* 1972, *15,* 101–109. (1972:17)

Hardy, J. D. Physiology of temperature regulation. *Physiological Review,* 1961, *41,* 521–607.

Harris, F. A. Control of gamma efferents through the reticular activating system. *American Journal of Occupational Therapy,* 1969, *23,* 1–12.

Harris, F. A. Multiple-loop modulation of motor outflow: A physiological basis for facilitation techniques. *Journal of the American Physical Therapy Association,* 1971, *51,* 391–397.

Harris, V. A., Katkin, E. S., Lick, J. R., & Habberfield, T. Paced respiration as a technique for the modification of autonomic response to stress. *Psychophysiology, 1976, 13,* 386–391. (1976/77:6)

Harrison, A. Components of neuromuscular control. In K. S. Holt (Ed.), *Movement and child development* (Clinics in Developmental Medicine, No. 55). London: Heinemann, 1976, pp. 34–50.

Harrison, R. S., & Raskin, D. C. The role of feedback in control of heart rate variability. *Psychophysiology, 1976, 13,* 135–139.

Hatze, H. A myocybernetic control model of skeletal muscle. *Biological Cybernetics, 1977, 25,* 103–119. (a)

Hatze, H. The relative contribution of motor unit recruitment and rate coding to the production of static isometric muscle force. (Special Report WISK 244). National Research Institute for Mathematical Sciences, CSIR, Pretoria, South Africa, 1977, p. 14. (b)

Hatze, H. A teleological explanation of Weber's law and the motor unit size law (Special Report WISK 248). National Research Institute for Mathematical Sciences CSIR, Pretoria, South Africa, 1977, p. 26. (c)

Hatze, H., & Buys, J. D. Energy-optimal controls in the mammalian neuromuscular system (Special Report WISK 243). National Research Institute for Mathematical Sciences, CSIR, Pretoria, South Africa, 1977, p. 31.

Hayes-Roth, B. Evolution of cognitive structures and processes. *Psychological Review, 1977, 84* 260–278.

Haynes, M. R., Blanchard, E. B., & Young, L. D. The effects of distribution of training on learning feedback-assisted cardiac acceleration. *Biofeedback and Self-Regulation, 1977, 2,* 427–434.

Haynes, S. N. Electromyographic biofeedback treatment of a woman with chronic dysphagia. *Biofeedback and Self-Regulation, 1976, 1,* 121–126.

Haynes, S. N., Moseley, D., & McGowan, W. T. Relaxation training and biofeedback in the reduction of frontalis muscle tension. *Psychophysiology, 1975, 12,* 547–552. (1975/76:17)

Hebert, R., & Lehmann, D. Theta bursts: An EEG pattern in normal subjects practising the transcendental meditation technique. *EEG and Clinical Neurophysiology, 1977, 42,* 397–405.

Held, R., & Bossom, J. Neonatal deprivation and adult rearrangement: Complementary techniques for analyzing plastic sensory-motor coordination. *Journal of Comparative and Physiological Psychology, 1961, 54,* 33–37.

Held, R., & Freedman, S. J. Plasticity in human sensorimotor control. *Science, 1963, 142,* 445–462.

Held, R., & Mikaelian, H. Motor-sensory feedback versus need in adaptation to rearrangement. *Perceptual and Motor Skills, 1964, 18,* 685–688.

Held, R., & Rekosh, J. Motor-sensory feedback and the geometry of visual space. *Science, 1963, 141,* 722–723.

Henson, D. E., & Rubin, H. B. Voluntary control of eroticism. *Journal of Applied Behavior Analysis, 1971, 4,* 37–44. (1971:39)

Hess, W. R. *On the relations between psychic and vegetative functions.* Zurich: Schwabe, 1925.

Honorton, C., Davidson, R., & Bindler, P. Feedback-augmented EEG alpha, shifts in subjective state, and ESP card-guessing performance. *Journal of the American Society for Psychical Research, 1971, 65,* 308–323.

Houk, J. C. On the significance of various command signals during voluntary control. *Brain Research, 1972, 40,* 49–53.

Ikeda, Y., & Hirai, H. Voluntary control of electrodermal activity in relation to imagery and internal perception scores. *Psychophysiology, 1976, 13,* 330–333.

Inbar, G. F., & Joseph, P. J. Analysis of a model of the triceps surae muscle reflex control system. *IEEE Transactions on Systems, Man and Cybernetics, 1976, SMC-6,* 25–33.

Jacobson, E. Variation of blood pressure with skeletal muscle tension and relaxation. *Annals of Internal Medicine, 1939, 12,* 1194–1212.

Jacobson, E. Variation of blood pressure with skeletal muscle tension and relaxation II. The heart beat. *Annals of Internal Medicine,* 1940, *13,* 1619–1625.

Jacobson, E. Electrophysiology of mental activities and introduction to the psychological process of thinking. In F. J. McGuigan & R. A. Schoonover (Eds.), *The psychophysiology of thinking.* New York: Academic, 1973, pp. 3–31.

Jacobson, G. R., Wilson, A., & La Rocca, L. Perceptual field dependence and biofeedback training (EEG alpha) among male alcoholics. In F. A. Seixas (Ed.), *Currents in alcoholism* (Vol. 2). New York: Grune & Stratton, 1977, pp. 197–206.

Johnson, H. J., & Schwartz, G. E. Suppression of GSR activity through operant reinforcement. *Journal of Experimental Psychology,* 1967, *75,* 307–312. (R:25)

Johnson, R. K., & Meyer, R. G. The locus of control construct in EEG alpha rhythm feedback. *Journal of Consulting and Clinical Psychology,* 1974, *42,* 913.

Johnston, D. Biofeedback, verbal instructions and the motor-skills analogy. In J. Beatty & H. Legewie (Eds.), *Biofeedback and behavior.* New York: Plenum, 1977, pp. 331 –342. (a)

Johnston, D. Feedback and instructional effects in the voluntary control of digital pulse amplitude. *Biological Psychology,* 1977, *5,* 159–171. (b)

Katona, P. G., Martin, P. J., & Felix, J. Neural control of heart rate: A conciliation of models. *IEEE Transactions on Biomedical Engineering,* 1976, *23,* 164–166.

Keele, S. W. Movement control in skilled motor performance. *Psychological Bulletin,* 1968, *70,* 387–403.

Kimmel, E., & Kimmel, H. D. A replication of operant conditioning of the GSR. *Journal of Experimental Psychology,* 1963, *65,* 212–213.

Kimmel, H. D. Instrumental conditioning of autonomically mediated responses in human beings. *American Psychologist,* 1974, *29,* 325–335. (1974:2)

Kimmel, H. D., & Gurucharri, F. W. Operant GSR conditioning with cool air reinforcement. *Pavlovian Journal of Biological Science,* 1975, *10,* 239–245.

Kleinman, K. M., Goldman, H., Snow, M. Y., & Korol, B. Relationship between essential hypertension and cognitive functioning. II. Effects of biofeedback training generalize to non-laboratory environment. *Psychophysiology,* 1977, *14,* 192–197.

Klinge, V. Effects of exteroceptive feedback and instructions on control of spontaneous galvanic skin response. *Psychophysiology,* 1972, *9,* 305–317. (1972:23)

Klinger, E., Gregoire, K. C., & Barta, S. G. Physiological correlates of mental activity: Eye movements, alpha, and heart rate during imagining, suppression, concentration, search, and choice. *Psychophysiology,* 1973, *10,* 471–477.

Kohlenberg, R. J. Operant conditioning of human anal sphincter pressure. *Journal of Applied Behavior Analysis,* 1973, *6,* 201–208.

Kondo, C. Y., Travis, T. A., & Knott, J. R. The effect of changes in motivation in alpha enhancement. *Psychophysiology,* 1975, *12,* 388–389.

Kotses, H., Glaus, K. D., Crawford, P. L., Edwards, J. E., & Scherr, M. S. Operant reduction of frontalis EMG activity in the treatment of asthma in children *Journal of Psychosomatic Research,* 1976, *20,* 453–459.

Lacey, J. I., Bateman, D. E., & VanLehn, R. Autonomic response specificity: An experimental study. *Psychosomatic Medicine,* 1953, *15,* 8–20.

Lacroix, J. M. Effects of biofeedback on the discrimination of electrodermal activity. *Biofeedback and Self-Regulation,* 1977, *2,* 393–406.

Lader, M. H., & Mathews, A. M. Electromyographic studies of tension. *Journal of Psychosomatic Research,* 1971, *15,* 479–486.

Lang, P. J. Learned control of human heart rate in a computer directed environment. In P. A. Obrist, A. H. Black, J. Brener, & L. V. DiCara (Eds.), *Cardiovascular psychophysiology.* Chicago: Aldine, 1974, pp. 392–405.

Lang, P. J. Acquisition of heart rate control: Method, theory, and clinical implications. In D. C.

Fowles (Ed.), *Clinical applications of psychophysiology*. New York: Columbia University Press, 1975, pp. 167–191.

Lang, P. J., & Twentyman, C. T. Learning to control heart rate: Binary vs. analog feedback. *Psychophysiology*, 1974, *11*, 616–629. (1974:16)

Lang, P. J., & Twentyman, C. T. Learning to control heart rate: Effects of varying incentive and criterion of success on task performance. *Psychophysiology*, 1976, *13*, 378–385. (1976/77:20)

Lapides, J., Sweet, R. B., & Lewis, L. W. Role of striated muscle in urination. *Journal of Urology*, 1957, *77*, 247–250. (R:30)

Lashley, K. S. The problem of serial order in behavior. In L. A. Jeffress (Ed.), *Cerebral mechanisms in behavior*. New York: Wiley, 1951, pp. 112–136.

Laszlo, J. I. The performance of a simple motor task with kinesthetic sense loss. *Quarterly Journal of Experimental Psychology*, 1966, *18*, 1–8.

Laszlo, J. I. Kinesthetic and exteroceptive information in the performance of motor skills. *Physiology and Behavior*, 1967, *2*, 359–365. (a)

Laszlo, J. I. Training of fast tapping with reduction of kinesthetic, tactile, visual and auditory sensations. *Quarterly Journal of Experimental Psychology*, 1967, *19*, 334–349. (b)

Laszlo, J. I. The role of visual learning and kinesthetic cues in learning a novel skill. *Australian Journal of Psychology*, 1968, *20*, 191–196.

Laszlo, J. I., & Baguley, R. A. Motor memory and bilateral transfer. *Journal of Motor Behavior*, 1971, *3*, 235–240.

Laszlo, J. I., Shamoon, J. S., & Sanson-Fisher, R. W. Reacquisition and transfer of motor skills with sensory feedback reduction. *Journal of Motor Behavior*, 1969, *1*, 195–209.

Laszlo, J. I., Baguley, R. A., & Bairstow, P. J. Bilateral transfer in tapping skill in the absence of peripheral information. *Journal of Motor Behavior*, 1970, *2*, 261–271.

Lavallée, Y-J., Lamontagne, Y., Pinard, G., Annable, L., & Tétreault, L. Effects of EMG feedback, diazepam and their combination on chronic anxiety. *Journal of Psychosomatic Research*, 1977, *21*, 65–71.

Lazarus, R. S. A cognitively oriented psychologist looks at biofeedback. *American Psychologist*, 1975, *30*, 553–561. (1975/76:1)

LeBoeuf, A. The effects of EMG feedback training on state anxiety in introverts and extroverts. *Journal of Clinical Psychology*, 1977, *33*, 251–253.

Leib, W., Tryon, W. W., & Stroebel, C. S. Alpha biofeedback: Fact or artifact? *Psychophysiology*, 1976, *13*, 541–545.

Lind, A. R., & McNicol, G. W. Circulatory responses to sustained hand-grip contractions performed during other exercise, both rhythmic and static. *Journal of Physiology*, 1967, *192*, 595–607.

Lind, A. R., Taylor, S. H., Humphreys, P. W., Kennelly, B. M., & Donald, K. W. The circulatory effects of sustained voluntary muscle contraction. *Clinical Science*, 1964, *27*, 229–244.

Litvinenkova, V., & Hlavecka, F. The visual feedback gain influence upon the regulation of the upright posture in man. *Aggressologie*, 1973, *14*, C:95–99.

Luborsky, L., Brady, J. P., McClintock, M., Kron, R. E., Bortnichak, E., & Levitz, L. Estimating one's own systolic blood pressure: Effects of feedback training. *Psychosomatic Medicine*, 1976, *38*, 426–438.

Lutzenberger, W., Birbaumer, N., & Steinmetz, P. Simultaneous biofeedback of heart rate and frontal EMG as a pretraining for the control of theta activity. *Biofeedback and Self-Regulation*, 1976, *1*, 395–410.

Lynch J. J., & Paskewitz, D. A. On the mechanisms of the feedback control of human brain wave activity. *Journal of Nervous and Mental Disease*, 1971, *153*, 205–217. (1971:12)

McCanne, T. R., & Sandman, C. A. The impact of two different reinforcers on conditioned operant heart rate acceleration and deceleration. *Biological Psychology*, 1975, *3*, 131–142.

McCanne, T. R., & Sandman, C. A. Proprioceptive awareness, information about response-reinforcement contingencies, and operant heart rate control. *Physiological Psychology*, 1976, *4*, 369–375.

McCutcheon, B. A., & Adams, H. E. The physiological basis of implosive therapy. *Behavior Research and Therapy*, 1975, *13*, 93–100.

McFarland, R. A. Heart rate perception and heart rate control. *Psychophysiology*, 1975, *12*, 402–405. (1975/76:35)

McFarland, R. A., & Campbell, C. Precise heart-rate control and heart-rate perception. *Perceptual and Motor Skills*, 1975, *41*, 730.

McGuigan, F. J., & Boness, D. J. What happens between an external stimulus and an overt response? A study of covert behavior. *Pavlovian Journal of Biological Science*, 1975, *10*, 112–119.

McKenzie, R. E., Ehrisman, W. J., Montgomery, P. S., & Barnes, R. H. The treatment of headache by means of electroencephalographic biofeedback. *Headache*, 1974, *13*, 164–172.

Magnusson, E. The effects of controlled muscle tension on performance and learning of heart-rate control. *Biological Psychology*, 1976, *4*, 81–92.

Malec, J. Sipprelle, C. N., & Behring, S. Biofeedback-assisted EMG reduction and subsequent self-disclosure. *Journal of Clinical Psychology*, 1978, *34*, 523–525.

Malmo, R. B., & Shagass, C. Physiologic studies of reaction to stress in anxiety and early schizophrenia. *Psychosomatic Medicine*, 1949, *11*, 9–24. (a)

Malmo, R. B., & Shagass, C. Physiologic study of symptom mechanisms in psychiatric patients under stress. *Psychosomatic Medicine*, 1949, *11*, 25–29. (b)

Malmo, R. B., & Shagass, C. Studies of blood pressure in psychiatric patients under stress. *Psychosomatic Medicine*, 1952, *14*, 82–93.

Malmo, R. B., Shagass, C., & Davis, F. H. Symptom specificity and bodily reactions during psychiatric interview. *Psychosomatic Medicine*, 1950, *12*, 362–376.

Malmo, R. B., Shagass, C., Belanger, D. J., & Smith, A. A. Motor control in psychiatric patients under experimental stress. *Journal of Abnormal and Social Psychology*, 1951, *46*, 539–547.

Malmo, R. B., Shagass, C., & Davis, J. F. Electromyographic studies of muscular tension in psychiatric patients under stress. *Journal of Clinical and Experimental Psychopathology*, 1951, *12*, 45–66.

Malmo, R. B., Wallerstein, H., & Shagass, C. Headache proneness and mechanisms of motor conflict in psychiatric patients. *Journal of Personality*, 1953, *22*, 163–187.

Mandler, G., Mandler, J. M., & Uviller, E. T. Autonomic feedback: The perception of autonomic activity. *Journal of Abnormal and Social Psychology*, 1958, *58*, 367–373.

Manuck, B. The voluntary control of heart rate under differential somatic restraint. *Biofeedback and Self-Regulation*, 1976, *1*, 273–284.

Marsden, C. D., Merton, P. A., & Morton, H. B. Servo action in human voluntary movement. *Nature*, 1972, *238*, 140–143.

Marsden, C. D., Merton, P. A., & Morton, H. B. Servo action in the human thumb. *Journal of Physiology*, 1976, *257*, 1–44.

Martin, R. B., & Dean, S. J. Instrumental modification of the GSR. *Psychophysiology*, 1971, *7*, 178–185.

Martin, R. B., Dean, S. J., & Shean, G. Selective attention and instrumental modification of the GSR. *Psychophysiology*, 1968, *4*, 460–467.

Martindale, C., & Armstrong, J. The relationship of creativity to cortical activation and its operant control. *Journal of Genetic Psychology*, 1974, *124*, 311–320.

Martindale, C., & Hines, D. Creativity and cortical activation during creative, intellectual and EEG feedback tasks. *Biological Psychology*, 1975, *3*, 91–100.

Mathews, A. M., & Gelder, M. G. Psychophysiological investigations of brief relaxation training. *Journal of Psychosomatic Research*, 1969, *13*, 1–12.

May, J. R. Psychophysiology of self-regulated phobic thoughts. *Behavior Therapy*, 1977, *8*, 150–159. (a)

May, J. R. A psychophysiological study of self and externally regulated phobic thoughts. *Behavior Therapy*, 1977, *8*, 849–861. (b)

May, J. R., & Johnson, H. J. Physiological activity to internally elicited arousal and inhibitory thoughts. *Journal of Abnormal Psychology,* 1973, *82,* 239–245.

Meichenbaum, D. Cognitive factors in biofeedback therapy. *Biofeedback and Self-Regulation,* 1976, *1,* 201–216. (1976/77:4)

Meyerson, L., Keer, N., & Michael, J. L. Behavior modification in rehabilitation. In S. W. Bijou & D. M. Baer (Eds.), *Child development: Readings in experimental analysis.* New York: Appleton–Century–Crofts, 1967, pp. 214–239.

Milner, M., Basmajian, J. V., & Quanbury, A. O. Multifactorial analysis of walking by electromyography and computer. *American Journal of Physical Medicine,* 1971, *50,* 235–258.

Molinari, H. H., Greenspan, J. D., & Kenshalo, D. R. The effects of rate of temperature change and adapting temperature on thermal sensitivity. *Sensory Processes,* 1977, *1,* 354–362.

Mulholland, T., & Eberlin, P. Effects of feedback contingencies on the control of occipital alpha. *Biofeedback and Self-Regulation,* 1977, *2,* 43–57.

Murphey, D. L., Blanton, P. L., & Biggs, N. L. Electromyographic investigation of flexion and hyperextension of the knee in normal adults. *American Journal of Physical Medicine,* 1971, *50,* 80–90.

Obrist, P. A. The cardiovascular-behavioral interaction as it appears today. *Psychophysiology,* 1976, *13,* 95–107.

Obrist, P. A., Webb, R. A., Sutterer, J. R., Howard, J. L. The cardiac-somatic relationship: Some reformulations. *Psychophysiology,* 1970, *6,* 569–587. (1970:30)

Obrist, P. A., Galosy, R. A., Lawler, J. E., Gaebelein, C. J., Howard, J. L., & Shanks, E. M. Operant conditioning of heart rate: Somatic correlates. *Psychophysiology,* 1975, *12,* 445–455.

Paillard, J. The patterning of skilled movements. In J. Field, H. W. Magoun, & V. E. Hall (Eds.), *Handbook of physiology* (Vol. 3, Sect. 1). Washington, D.C.: American Physiological Society, 1960, pp. 1679–1708.

Pardew, D. L. Efferent and afferent control of fast and slow arm movements. *Journal of Motor Behavior,* 1976, *8,* 59–67.

Pardine, P., & Napoli, A. Personality correlates of successful biofeedback training. *Perceptual and Motor Skills,* 1977, *45,* 1099–1103.

Passini, F. T., Watson, C. G., Dehnel, L., Herder, J., & Watkins, B. Alpha wave biofeedback training therapy in alcoholics. *Journal of Clinical Psychology,* 1977, *33,* 292–299.

Pearne, D. H., Ziegelbaum, S. D., & Peyser, W. P. Biofeedback-assisted EMG relaxation for urinary retention and maintenance: A case report. *Biofeedback and Self-Regulation,* 1977, *2,* 213–217.

Peper, E., & Mulholland, T. Methodological and theoretical problems in the voluntary control of electroencephalographic occipital alpha by the subject. *Kybernetik,* 1970, *7,* 10–13. (1970:16)

Perkel, D. H., Gerstein, G. L., Smith, M. S., & Tatton, W. G. Nerve-impulse patterns: A quantitative display technique for three neurons. *Brain Research,* 1975, *100,* 271–296.

Peters, J. E., & Gantt, W. H. Effect of graded degrees of muscular exertion on human heart rate and the role of muscular exertion in cardiac conditioned reflexes. *Journal of General Psychology,* 1953, *49,* 31–43.

Pew, R. W. Acquisition of hierarchical control over the temporal organization of a skill. *Journal of Experimental Psychology,* 1966, *71,* 764–771.

Philips, C. The modification of tension headache pain using EMG biofeedback. *Behavior Research and Therapy,* 1977, *15,* 119–129.

Pickering, T. Learned voluntary control of autonomic functions: Investigations of mechanisms and possible clinical applications. *British Heart Journal,* 1976, *38,* 320. (Abstract)

Plotkin, W. B. On the self-regulation of the occipital alpha rhythm: Control strategies, states of consciousness, and the role of physiological feedback. *Journal of Experimental Psychology: General,* 1976, *105,* 66–99.

Plotkin, W. B. Long-term eyes-closed alpha-enhancement training: Effects on alpha amplitudes and on experiential state. *Psychophysiology,* 1978, *15,* 40–52.

Plotkin, W. B., & Cohen, R. Occipital alpha and the attributes of the "alpha experience." *Psychophysiology,* 1976, *13*, 16–21. (1975/76:25)

Plotkin, W. B., Mazer, C., & Loewy, D. Alpha enhancement and the likelihood of an alpha experience. *Psychophysiology,* 1976, *13*, 466–471. (1976/77:31)

Pressner, J. A., & Savitsky, J. C. Effect of contingent and noncontingent feedback and subject expectancies on electroencephalogram biofeedback training. *Journal of Consulting and Clinical Psychology,* 1977, *45*, 713–714.

Radonjic, D., & Long, C. Kinesiology of the wrist. *American Journal of Physical Medicine,* 1971, *50*, 57–71.

Raskin, M., Johnson, G., & Rondestvedt, J. W. Chronic anxiety treated by feedback-induced muscle relaxation. *Archives of General Psychiatry,* 1973, *28*, 263–267. (1973:22)

Ray, W. J. The relationship of locus of control, self-report measures, and feedback to the voluntary control of heart rate. *Psychophysiology,* 1974, *11*, 527–534. (1974:14)

Ray, W. J., & Lamb, S. B. Locus of control and the voluntary control of heart rate. *Psychosomatic Medicine,* 1974, *36*, 180–182.

Reading, C., & Mohr, P. D. Biofeedback control of migraine: A pilot study. *British Journal of Social and Clinical Psychology,* 1976, *15*, 429–433.

Reeves, J. L. EMG-biofeedback reduction of tension headache: A cognitive skills training approach. *Biofeedback and Self-Regulation,* 1976, *1*, 217–225.

Regestein, Q. R., Pegram, V., Cook, B., & Bradley, D. Alpha rhythm percentage maintained during 4- and 12-hour feedback periods. *Psychosomatic Medicine,* 1973, *35*, 215–222. (1973:14)

Reinking, R. H., & Kohl, M. L. Effects of various forms of relaxation training on physiological and self-report measures of relaxation. *Journal of Consulting and Clinical Psychololgy,* 1975, *43*, 595–600. (1975/76:21)

Richardson, A. *Mental imagery.* London: Routledge & Kegan Paul, 1969.

Rosenbaum, D. A. Selective adaptation of "command neurons" in the human motor system. *Neuropsychologia,* 1977, *15*, 81–91.

Rosenbaum, D. A., & Radford, M. Sensory feedback does not cause selective adaptation of human "command neurons." *Perceptual and Motor Skills,* 1977, *44*, 447–451.

Rosenfeld, J. P., Rudell, A. P., & Fox, S. S. Operant control of neural events in humans. *Science,* 1969, *165*, 821–823. (R:42)

Rotter, J. B. Generalized expectancies of internal versus external control of reinforcement. *Psychological Monographs,* 1966, *80* (1, Whole No. 609), 28.

Sachs, D. A., Talley, E., & Boley, K. A comparison of feedback and reinforcement as modifiers of a functional motor response in a hemiparetic patient. *Journal of Behavior Therapy and Experimental Psychiatry,* 1976, *7*, 171–174. (1976/77:41)

Sadler, R. A., & Eason, R. G. Voluntary alpha control, visually evoked potentials, and peripheral physiological indicants of activation. *Perceptual and Motor Skills,* 1977, *44*, 491–496.

Schmidt, R. A. A schema theory of discrete motor skill learning. *Psychological Review,* 1975, *82*, 225–260.

Schneider, J. A. Finger temperature feedback procedures: Sympathetic inhibition training or placebo effect? *Psychotherapy,* 1976, *13*, 141–147.

Schwartz, G. E. Cardiac responses to self-induced thoughts. *Psychophysiology,* 1971, *8*, 462–467.

Schwartz, G. E. Toward a theory of voluntary control of response patterns in the cardiovascular system. In P. A. Obrist, A. H. Black, J. Brener, & L. V. DiCara, (Eds.), *Cardiovascular psychophysiology: Current issues in response mechanisms, biofeedback and methodology.* Chicago: Aldine, 1974, pp. 406–455.

Schwartz, G. E. Biofeedback, self-regulation, and the patterning of physiological processes. *American Scientist,* 1975, *63*, 314–324. (1975/76:2)

Schwartz, G. E. Self-regulation of response patterning: Implications for psychophysiological research and therapy. *Biofeedback and Self-Regulation,* 1976, *1*, 7–30.

Schwartz, G. E., & Higgins, J. D. Cardiac activity preparatory to overt and covert behavior. *Science*, 1971, *173*, 1144–1146.

Schwartz, G. E., Davidson, R. J., & Pugash, E. Voluntary control of patterns of EEG parietal asymmetry: Cognitive concomitants. *Psychophysiology*, 1976, *13*, 498--504. (1976/77:33)

Schwartz, G. E., Fair, P. L., Salt, P., Mandel, M. R., & Klerman, G. L. Facial expression and imagery in depression: An electromyographic study. *Psychosomatic Medicine*, 1976, *38*, 337–347.

Schwartz, G. E., Young, L. D., & Vogler, J. Heart rate regulation as skill learning: Strength–endurance versus cardiac reaction time. *Psychophysiology*, 1976, *13*, 472–478. (1976/77: 25)

Shapiro, D. A monologue on biofeedback and psychophysiology. *Psychophysiology*, 1977, *14*, 213–227.

Shapiro, D., & Schwartz, G. E. Biofeedback and visceral learning: Clinical applications. *Seminars in Psychiatry*, 1972, *4*, 171–184. (1972:35)

Shapiro, D., & Watanabe, T. Timing characteristics of operant electrodermal modification: Fixed-interval effects. *Japanese Psychological Research*, 1971, *13*, 123–130. (1972:24)

Shapiro, D., Crider, A. B., & Tursky, B. Differentiation of an autonomic response through operant reinforcement. *Psychonomic Science*, 1964, *1*, 147–148. (R:21)

Shearn, D. W. Operant conditioning of heart rate. *Science*, 1962, *137*, 530–531.

Shedivy, D. I., & Kleinman, K. M. Lack of correlation of frontalis EMG activity with other neck muscles and verbal ratings of tension or relaxation. *Psychophysiology*, 1977, *14*, 182–186.

Sherrington, C. S. *The integrative action of the nervous system*. New Haven: Yale University Press, 1906.

Silverstein, S. J., Nathan, P. E., & Taylor, H. A. Blood alcohol level estimation and controlled drinking by chronic alcoholics. *Behavior Therapy*, 1974, *5*, 1–15.

Sime, W. E., & DeGood, D. E. Effect of EMG biofeedback and progressive muscle relaxation training on awareness of frontalis muscle tension. *Psychophysiology*, 1977, *14*, 522–530.

Sittenfeld, P., Budzynski, T., & Stoyva, J. Differential shaping of EEG theta rhythms. *Biofeedback and Self-Regulation*, 1976, *1*, 31–46. (1976/77:35)

Smith, A. A. An electromyographic study of tension in interrupted and completed tasks. *Journal of Experimental Psychology*, 1953, *46*, 32–36.

Smith E. E., Guyton, A. C., Manning, R. D., & White, R. J. Integrated mechanisms of cardiovascular response and control during exercise in the normal human. *Progress in Cardiovascular Diseases*, 1976, *18*, 421–443.

Smith, K. U., & Henry, J. P. Cybernetic foundations for rehabilitation. *American Journal of Physical Medicine*, 1967, *46*, 379–467.

Smith, K. U., & Murphy, T. J. Sensory feedback mechanisms of handwriting motions and their neurogeometric bases. In V. Herrick (Ed.), *New horizons for research in handwriting*. Madison: University of Wisconsin Press, 1963, pp. 111–157.

Spilker, B., Kamiya, J., Callaway, E., & Yeager, C. L. Visual evoked responses in subjects trained to control alpha rhythms. *Psychophysiology*, 1969, *5*, 683–695.

Sroufe, L. A. Learned stabilization of cardiac rate with respiration experimentally controlled. *Journal of Experimental Psychology*, 1969, *81*, 391–393.

Sroufe, L. A. Effects of depth and rate of breathing on heart rate and heart rate variability. *Psychophysiology*, 1971, *8*, 648–655.

Stark, L. *Neurological control systems: Studies in bioengineering*. New York: Plenum, 1968.

Staudenmayer, H., & Kinsman, R. A. Awareness during electromyographic biofeedback: Of signal or process? *Biofeedback and Self-Regulation*, 1976, *1*, 191–199.

Steffen, J. J. Electromyographically induced relaxation in the treatment of chronic alcohol abuse. *Journal of Consulting and Clinical Psychology*, 1975, *43*, 275.

Stephens, J. H., Harris, A. H., Brady, J. V., & Shaffer, J. W. Psychological and physiological variables associated with large magnitude voluntary heart rate changes. *Psychophysiology*, 1975, *12*, 381–387. (1975/76:33)

Stern, G. S., & Berrenberg, J. L. Biofeedback training in frontalis muscle relaxation and enchance-ment of belief in personal control. *Biofeedback and Self-Regulation*, 1977, *2*, 173–182.

Stern, J. A., Winokur, G., Graham, D. T., & Graham, F. K. Alterations in physiological measures during experimentally induced attitudes. *Journal of Psychosomatic Research*, 1961; *5*, 73–82.

Stern, R. M., & Kaplan, B. E. Galvanic skin response: Voluntary control and externalization. *Journal of Psychosomatic Research*, 1967, *10*, 349–353.

Summers, J. J. The role of timing in motor program representation. *Journal of Motor Behavior*, 1975, *7*, 229–241.

Suter, S. Independent biofeedback self-regulation of EEG alpha and skin resistance. *Biofeedback and Self-Regulation*, 1977, *2*, 255–258.

Tatton, W. G., & Lee, R. G. Evidence for abnormal long-loop reflexes in rigid Parkinsonian patients. *Brain Research*, 1975, *100*, 671–676.

Townsend, R. E., House, J. F., & Addario, D. A comparison of biofeedback-mediated relaxation and group therapy in the treatment of chronic anxiety. *American Journal of Psychiatry*, 1975, *132*, 598–601. (1976/77:43)

Travis, T. A., Kondo, C. Y., & Knott, J. R. Personality variables and alpha enhancement: A correlative study. *British Journal of Psychiatry*, 1974, *124*, 542–544.

Travis, T. A., Kondo, C. Y., & Knott, J. R. Subjective aspects of alpha enhancement. *British Journal of Psychiatry*, 1975, *127*, 122–126. (1975/76:23)

Valle, R. S., & DeGood, D. E. Effects of state-trait anxiety on the ability to enhance and suppress EEG alpha. *Psychophysiology*, 1977, *14*, 1–7.

Valle, R. S., & Levine, J. M. Expectation effects in alpha wave control. *Psychophysiology*, 1975, *12*, 306–309. (1975/76:24)

Vandercar, D. H., Feldstein, M. A., & Solomon, H. Instrumental conditioning of human heart rate during free and controlled respiration. *Biological Psychology*, 1977, *5*, 221–231.

Van der Staak, C. Intra- and interhemispheric visual-motor control of human arm movements. *Neuropsychologia*, 1975, *13*, 439–448.

Vaughn, R., Pall, M. L., & Haynes, S. N., Frontalis EMG responses to stress in subjects with frequent muscle-contraction headaches. *Headache*, 1977, *16*, 313–317.

Vogt, A. T. Electromyograph responses and performance success estimates as a function of internal-external control. *Perceptual and Motor Skills*, 1975, *41*, 977–978.

Voronin, L. G. Some results of comparative-physiological investigations of higher nervous activity. *Psychological Bulletin*, 1962, *59*, 161–195.

Wagner, C., Bourgeois, A., Levenson, H., & Denton, J. Multidimensional locus of control and voluntary control of GSR. *Perceptual and Motor Skills*, 1974, *39*, 1142.

Walker, B. B., & Sandman, C. A. Physiological response patterns in ulcer patients: Phasic and tonic components of the electrogastrogram. *Psychophysiology*, 1977, *14*, 393–400.

Walsh, D. H. Interactive effects of alpha feedback and instructional set on subjective state. *Psychophysiology*, 1974, *11*, 428–435. (1974:30)

Weiss, T., & Engel, B. T. Operant conditioning of heart rate patients with premature ventricular contractions. *Psychosomatic Medicine*, 1971, *33*, 301–321. (1971:36)

Wells, D. T. Large magnitude voluntary heart rate changes. *Psychophysiology*, 1973, *10*, 260–269. (1973:3)

Werner, J. Mathematical treatment of structure and function of the human thermoregulatory system. *Biological Cybernetics*, 1977, *25*, 93–101.

Whitehead, W. E., Drescher, V. M., Heiman, P., & Blackwell, B. Relation of heart rate control to heartbeat perception. *Biofeedback and Self-Regulation*, 1977, *2*, 371–392.

Wickramasekera, I. E. Temperature feedback for the control of migraine. *Journal of Behavior Therapy and Experimental Psychiatry*, 1973, *4*, 343–345. (1974:42)

Wright, A., Carroll, D., & Newman, C. V. The effects of verbal feedback of elicited heart rate changes on subsequent voluntary control of heart rate. *Bulletin of the Psychonomic Society*, 1977, *10*, 209–210.

Yates, A. J. Psychological deficit. *Annual Review of Psychology*, 1966, *17*, 111–144.

Young, L. R. Role of the vestibular system in posture and movement. In V. B. Mountcastle (Ed.), *Medical physiology* (13th ed., Vol. 1). Saint Louis: C. V. Mosby, 1974, pp. 704–721.

Young, L. R., & Stark, L. Variable feedback experiments testing a sampled data model for eye-tracking movements. *IEEE Transactions*, 1963, *4*, 38–51.

CHAPTER 8

Biofeedback: Still "A Promise as Yet Unfulfilled"?

The Promise of Biofeedback: The Optimists and the Pessimists

The original enthusiasm generated by the development of biofeedback stemmed in part, as has already been pointed out, from the belief that it might provide a royal road to higher (or even mystical) states of awareness or consciousness. Just as it has been claimed that the mastery of transcendental meditation on a significant scale in any community leads to a drop in antisocial behaviors, so it was hoped by some that biofeedback training (particularly of that portion of the "mind" indexed by alpha or theta activity) might lead to a greater mastery of the complexities of living, even if only by way of a retreat (or advance!) into the higher reaches of consciousness.

This enthusiasm has shown little sign of waning, even among those biofeedback experts who are (or should be) most acquainted with the empirical literature which has been reviewed in this book. Thus, for example, Budzynski (1977), one of the pioneers of experimental research in biofeedback, can still refer, and not merely because he is writing in a magazine for popular consumption, to "tuning in on the twilight zone" (the title of his article) and maintain that the achievement of an optimal level of theta activity (where "optimal" means neither too much nor too little theta) is conducive to more efficient creative and cognitive activities, by which means such skills as language learning, problem solving, and the like will be facilitated. Again, the search for biofeedback correlates of extrasensory perception continues unabated. Triggered off by the studies of Honorton and his colleagues (Honorton & Carbone, 1971; Honorton, Davidson, & Bindler, 1971), the search has continued unabated up to the present time (e.g., Braud & Wood, 1977), even though the results obtained so far have been utterly trivial (see, for example, the recent study by Venturino, 1978, who also provides an excellent review of the literature).

Optimism about the clinical potential of biofeedback training also continues, as is evident from the ever-increasing reports of its use as a remedial tool for an ever-widening range of disorders. Letourneau (1976), to cite but one example, has suggested that biofeedback may be useful in a wide range of visual problems commonly found and treated by optometrists such as limitations of gaze, convergence insufficiency or excess, esotropia and exotropia (where the macula is intact), and ptosis (or blind eye). Many examples of new applications have been reported in various places in this book, additional to the well-known uses of biofeedback in the clinical area.

As recently as 1973, however, Blanchard and Young described the self-control of cardiac functioning as "a promise as yet unfulfilled" insofar as clinical applications of the voluntary control of heart rate and blood pressure were concerned. Only 1 year later, following a review of all the clinical applications they could find, they were forced by the evidence to conclude as follows:

> It would seem premature to hail biofeedback training as a panacea for psychosomatic and other disorders. The evidence is often interesting and highly provocative, but with the exception of a few areas . . . no definite conclusions can be made. Wholesale therapeutic application of biofeedback techniques cannot be supported by the available data. . . . It may be that clinicians and practitioners are seeking the "ultimate weapon" in the form of biofeedback training before there has been an adequate demonstration that the phenomena are reliable. . . . (Blanchard & Young, 1974, pp. 587–588)

Nor does the most recent review (by Blanchard & Epstein, 1977) arrive at substantially different conclusions. Many other similar reviews, which need not be detailed here, confirm the significant degree of reservation expressed by Blanchard as to the clinical usefulness of biofeedback.

It is difficult not to agree with these rather pessimistic evaluations but that does not necessarily mean that biofeedback is or should be regarded as a briefly blazing meteor in the sky, showering sparks as it passes, only to disappear into oblivion in a short while. It will be argued here that such a conclusion is both unnecessary and unjust, for the failure of clinical biofeedback to sustain its early promise stems largely from its abuse and misuse (not, of course, deliberately) in much the same way (as will be shown) that behavior therapy has been abused and misused. In order to sustain this argument, however, it is desirable first to look more closely at some of the evidence which leads to the superficial conclusion that biofeedback is not indeed the panacea it has occasionally been presented as being. The relevance of this evidence to the potential value of biofeedback will be examined by comparing it with evidence which indicates a high degree of promise for biofeedback as a clinical tool. Most (but not all) of the studies to be considered (some of which have already been described in detail in earlier chapters) are those in which biofeedback as a form of therapy is compared directly with alternative forms of therapy (thus, studies which compare the effects of different kinds of biofeedback will not be included here). The work with normal groups will be considered separately from that carried out on abnormal conditions. The longer-term effectiveness of biofeedback as judged from follow-up assessment will be reviewed, and certain other difficulties relating to the use of biofeedback in a therapeutic setting will also be mentioned.

Comparative Studies with Normal Subjects

There have been several studies with normal subjects in which the effects of biofeedback training in relaxation of a single muscle complex have been compared with more general relaxation training without feedback. In some cases, changes in subjectively estimated or test-measured anxiety and other adjustment variables have also been examined.

Coursey (1975) found that biofeedback training in reduction of frontalis muscle activity produced a significantly greater reduction in the activity of that muscle than did either general instructions to relax or "cognitive" instructions to relax. However, there was no concomitant differential change in relaxation as measured by various tests, nor was there any change in manifest anxiety although subjectively rated anxiety declined significantly in all three groups. Thus, no clear relationship was shown to exist between physiological muscle relaxation and other measures of relaxation and anxiety. Rather similar results were reported by Reinking and Kohl (1975), who also found that training in frontalis muscle reduction without feedback was superior to general relaxation training without feedback on the one hand, and simple instructions to relax (but without training or feedback being provided) on the other. However, this differential result was accompanied by an equal drop in self-rated anxiety in all of the treated groups (two other groups combined feedback training with relaxation training or monetary reinforcement for meeting a criterion). Ohno, Tanaka, Takeya, Matsubara, Kuriya, and Komemushi (1978) confirmed that feedback training in frontalis muscle reduction produced a greater effect than simple instructions to relax the forehead. On the other hand, while Haynes, Moseley, and McGowan (1975), also using the frontalis muscle, found feedback training to be superior to simple instructions to relax and to active relaxation training (involving alternately tensing and relaxing muscles), it was not superior to passive relaxation training. They did, however, find a low but significant correlation between manifest anxiety scores and baseline levels of frontalis activity, and highly anxious subjects were less successful in reducing frontalis muscle activity than nonanxious subjects. Schandler and Grings (1976) found that reductions in forearm muscle activity were paralleled by a reduction in anxiety differential scores. However, they also found that reduction in forearm muscle activity using tactile feedback was equalled by the reduction which occurred with relaxation training, and that both methods were superior to the use of visual feedback.

The evidence relating to the comparative effectiveness of biofeedback and relaxation training in the area of muscle activity is not, therefore, particularly impressive. The story is much the same in other areas of voluntary control, using normal subjects. Thus, Ohno, Tanaka, Takeya, and Ikemi (1977) found that better control of temperature was achieved with feedback than without feedback. On the other hand, Beatty (1972), in a study of the control of alpha and beta waves, could not differentiate between the effects of providing feedback only, information only, or a combination of feedback and information, although all three procedures produced better results than did the provision of no information, no feedback, or information and false feedback. White, Holmes, and Bennett (1977), in one of the few well-controlled studies of biofeedback involving large numbers of subjects, were able to show that instructions alone were as effective in raising or lowering heart rate as a combination of instructions and feedback.

Overall, therefore, comparative studies of biofeedback and other relaxation training procedures do not present a picture suggesting a clear-cut superiority for biofeedback over alternative approaches.

Comparative Studies with Abnormal Subjects

As pointed out earlier, it is not intended to review comprehensively all of the comparative studies that have been conducted. However, a representative selection of studies will be provided from a number of areas of abnormal functioning from which a clear picture of the current situation will emerge.

Anxiety

Gatchel, Hatch, Watson, Smith, and Gaas (1977) successfully trained subjects with speech anxiety to reduce their heart rate. Following this training, heart-rate increases during preparation and delivery of a speech were found to be smaller than was the case prior to training in heart-rate reduction. However, biofeedback (of heart rate), active muscle relaxation training (alternately tensing and relaxing), and a combination of biofeedback and muscle relaxation training were equally effective in reducing heart rate, while the combined method produced less heart-rate increase during posttraining speech preparation and delivery than did either technique alone. Furthermore, although the feedback, relaxation, and combined training groups did better than a false-feedback control group in heart-rate training, all four groups decreased significantly and to the same extent in anxiety, whether self-rated or as judged by independent observers. Thus, there was no evidence in this study to indicate a superiority of biofeedback over general muscle relaxation training in effecting a reduction in speech anxiety.

Results obtained with patients suffering from general or free-floating anxiety have been equivocal (and often involved serious confounding). Townsend, House, and Addario (1975) claimed that biofeedback training of frontalis muscle activity reduction was more beneficial than group therapy in reducing anxiety, but their feedback training was accompanied by deep muscle relaxation training, making it impossible to assess the relative contribution of each technique. Canter, Kondo, and Knott (1975) found that frontalis muscle activity reduction with feedback and progressive relaxation training were both effective in reducing anxiety in patients, with biofeedback generally superior in its effects to relaxation training; the differences, however, were not very great. Lavallée, Lamontagne, Pinard, Annable, and Tétreault (1977) compared the effects of combinations of feedback/no feedback and drug (diazepam)/placebo on outpatients with free-floating anxiety. At the end of treatment, feedback (frontalis muscle) alone and diazepam alone were equally effective in reducing frontalis muscle activity levels and even more effective in combination, the poorest results being obtained in the control condition (no feedback/no drug). However, various measures of level of anxiety were not predictive of the effects of treatment, and no differential changes in anxiety levels as a result of the treatments were found. Beiman, Israel, and Johnson (1978) reported that live (therapist present) progressive relaxation was more effective than taped relaxation, self-relaxation, or biofeedback training of frontalis muscle activity in reducing anxiety. Furthermore, no differential effects of any of the four techniques were found in a posttraining self-control assessment period, during which the subject attempted to relax as much as possible using whichever of the skills he had been taught. Once again, little relation between these results and subjective tension estimates was found.

Asthma

Several comparative studies dealing with asthma are tangentially relevant to the matter in hand without shedding much light on the relative effectiveness of biofeedback training. Alexander (1972; Alexander, Miklich, & Hershkoff, 1972) had provided evidence indicating that merely practicing relaxation would increase peak expiratory flow rates (PEFR) in asthmatic children more than just sitting quietly. Davis, Saunders, Creer, and Chai (1973) found relaxation training alone was as effective as relaxation training combined with frontalis muscle reduction biofeedback training in increasing PEFR in asthmatic children, both techniques producing better results than instructions to relax while reading. However, these differences had vanished 8 days after the end of treatment. Khan, Staerk, and Bonk (1973) claimed that direct feedback of forced expiratory volume under instructions to increase the volume (produce bronchodilation) followed by use of the training to reduce artificially induced bronchospasm produced a significant degree of clinical improvement (as indexed by hospital emergency visits, etc.) compared with a no-treatment control group. These results, however, were not successfully replicated in respect of clinical status in a later study by Khan (1977). Two carefully conducted studies by Kotses and his colleagues (Kotses, Glaus, Crawford, Edwards, & Scherr, 1976; Kotses, Glaus, Bricel, Edwards, & Crawford, 1978) have demonstrated convincingly that contingent frontalis muscle reduction training in asthmatic children produces greater increases in PEFR than does noncontingent frontalis training, contingent or non-contingent brachioradialis muscle reduction training, or no treatment at all. Kotses, in fact, concludes that frontalis muscle reduction training is a necessary and sufficient condition for increases in PEFR, a conclusion which may be overstated in the absence of concrete knowledge of the effects of general relaxation training (unless that training leads to a reduction in frontalis muscle activity). Nevertheless, the studies by Kotses certainly constitute positive evidence in favor of specific biofeedback training (although Kotses's method is clearly dependent on the generality assumption rather than the specificity assumption).

Hyperactivity

Braud (1978) compared the effectiveness of relaxation training, frontalis muscle activity reduction training, and no intervention on hyperactivity. The specific frontalis training produced a greater reduction in frontalis muscle activity than did the relaxation training, the latter being itself very successful. However, parental ratings of behavior in the home indicated that the biofeedback and relaxation training techniques were equally successful in reducing hyperactivity.

Hypertension

The most extensive comparative studies are those carried out by Patel (1975b, 1976; Patel & Carruthers, 1977; Patel & Datey, 1976; Patel & North, 1975). Unfortunately, all of the studies are confounded, since Patel invariably combined the use of biofeedback (usually auditory and of GSR responding) with relaxation training (and sometimes meditation as well). Although this combined method consistently produced greater decreases in diastolic blood pressure and/or systolic blood pressure than just resting (Patel, 1975b), attention (Patel, 1975c), no treatment (Patel & Datey, 1976), and instructions just to relax (Patel & North, 1975), as well as producing beneficial physiological changes such as reduced serum cholesterol levels (Patel, 1976; Patel & Carruthers, 1977), it is, of course, impossible to sort out the relative contribution of the feedback, relaxation, and meditation components of the combined treatment. Shoemaker and Tasto (1975) found that relaxation training was as effective as feedback of blood pressure in reducing blood pressure in hypertensives, both being superior to a no-treatment control group; if anything, the relaxation training appeared to have the edge over the biofeedback training. Similar results were obtained by Walsh, Dale, and Anderson (1977), who compared the (confounded) effects of audio/visual feedback of pulse wave velocity in combination with verbal feedback at the end of each trial and relaxation training. In phase 1 of training, both methods were equally effective; in phase 2, the addition of biofeedback to relaxation produced no additional effects. Friedman and Taub (1977) compared the use of hypnosis alone with feedback (a direct readout of diastolic blood pressure) alone, a combination of hypnosis and feedback, and no treatment. Hypnosis alone was reported by them to be more effective in reducing diastolic blood pressure than feedback alone or in combination with hypnosis (suggesting that the two techniques interfered with each other when used together). Feedback alone, in fact, proved no more helpful than no treatment in this study. Thus, no firm evidence has yet been produced to suggest that biofeedback is superior to alternative forms of treatment for hypertension.

Insomnia

Nor is the picture any more encouraging when comparative studies are considered in this area. Haynes, Sides, and Lockwood (1977) allocated patients suffering from insomnia to one of three treatment conditions: frontalis muscle reduction training with auditory feedback, general relaxation training, and instructions to relax (but no training in how to relax was given). Both the feedback and relaxation training groups achieved a marked reduction in the time to fall asleep after six ½-h treatment sessions but there was no differential effectiveness between the two techniques. Exactly the same results were reported by Freedman and Papsdorf (1976) after a similar length of training. Furthermore, no correlation was found in this study between frontalis muscle activity changes and changes in the amount of time to fall asleep, suggesting, of course, that the results produced in the feedback group were the result of the same factors operating in the relaxation group.

Migraine

Andreychuk and Skriver (1975) found that training in self-hypnosis (involving instruction in relaxation, use of visual imagery, presentation of reinforcers, and instructions on how to deal with pain) produced a significant reduction in severity and duration of headaches, but so also, and to an equal extent, did two forms of biofeedback training (hand temperature increases and alpha enhancement, both with auditory feedback). Improvement was correlated with hypnotizability, regardless of which treatment was involved. Mullinix, Norton, Hack, and Fishman (1978) have reported that migraine patients given true feedback for skin temperature changes succeeded in raising skin temperature more than patients given false feedback (although no quantitative data were provided). However, no difference in headache activity reduction was found between the two treatments. Both of these studies were poorly reported, which was not the case with the important study by Price and Tursky (1976). They recorded changes in both peripheral and cephalic vascular responses (blood volume) in migraine sufferers allocated to one of four treatment conditions: visual feedback of finger blood volume, false feedback of finger blood volume, relaxation instructions involving listening to a relaxation training tape, and neurtal instructions involving listening to a recording of instructions on how to grow plants. The first two groups were told to try to increase temperature in the left hand; in the two instructional groups, subjects were told that listening to the tape would help them increase temperature in the left hand. The results indicated that there was no difference between the effects of the two feedback (true and false) conditions and the relaxation condition.

Rehabilitation of Physical Function

Although this area has been one of the major successes of biofeedback, there are few comparative studies available even though the existence of standard therapy procedures constitutes a ready-made situation for the evaluation of the effectiveness of biofeedback compared with the more traditional techniques. Basmajian, Kukulka, Narayan, and Takebe (1975) compared the effects of traditional therapeutic exercises used with patients suffering from residual foot-drop following a cerebrovascular accident with the effects of such exercise supplemented by biofeedback training and found that biofeedback supplementation produced superior results in respect of range of movement and walking skill. It will be recalled that favorable results have been reported for large numbers of patients followed up over considerable periods of time in respect of the biofeedback treatment of the sequelae of cerebrovascular accidents and other disabilities (Basmajian, Regenos, & Baker, 1977; Brudny, Korein, Grynbaum, Friedmann, Weinstein, Sachs-Frankel, & Belandres, 1976). But these studies are not, of course, comparative in nature so that they do not really help to evaluate the relative efficacy of biofeedback training. The pioneering study by Jacobs and Felton (1969) is, however, very relevant. They were able to show that patients with trapezius muscle dysfunction as a result of accidents could not reduce the level of activity in the muscle until biofeedback of the activity was provided, following which they succeeded in reducing the activity not merely to the normal resting level, but below it, to the level achieved by normal subjects with training. This study is one of the few to provide strong evidence of the differential effectiveness of biofeedback training.

Tension Headaches

Not surprisingly, rather more comparative studies have been carried out in the area of tension headaches than in relation to any other disorder, without, however, producing any strong evidence that biofeedback is demonstrably superior to alternative techniques. The suggestion that biofeedback frontalis muscle reduction training might be a suitable form of treatment for tension headaches was originally made as a result of the uncontrolled study by Budzynski, Stoyva, and Adler (1970) and was well supported by the subsequent controlled study by Budzynski, Stoyva, Adler, and Mullaney (1973), who showed that relevant feedback produced a greater reduction in tension headaches than irrelevant feedback or no treatment. This finding has in fact been replicated several times since (e.g., Kondo & Canter, 1977; Philips, 1977). However, when biofeedback is compared with relaxation training (specific or general) without feedback, a very different picture emerges. In only one of these studies does biofeedback emerge as the more successful form of treatment for tension headaches. Hutchings and Reinking (1976) found that frontalis muscle relaxation training with feedback produced a faster decline in frontalis muscle activity and a greater decline in headache activity in tension headache patients than did relaxation training alone. Furthermore, the combined use of relaxation and biofeedback training was not superior to the use of biofeedback training alone. However, even in this study all three groups were equally low on frontalis muscle activity at the end of training. Two studies (Cox, Freundlich, & Meyer, 1975; Haynes, Griffin, Mooney, & Parise, 1975) found no difference between biofeedback training in reduction of frontalis muscle activity and general relaxation training in their effects on headache activity, although in each case these techniques were superior to no treatment or medication. McKenzie, Ehrisman, Montgomery, and Barnes (1974) found that training in alpha and beta enhancement produced marginally better results than general relaxation training, but the only difference was that the latter procedure took somewhat longer to produce favorable results. Sime and De Good (1977) reported no difference in effectiveness between frontalis muscle relaxation training with biofeedback and progressive relaxation training directed mostly, but not entirely, at the frontalis muscle. Chesney and Shelton (1976) compared the effects of muscle relaxation training, biofeedback training of frontalis muscle activity reduction, the combined use of the two techniques, and no treatment. Headache activity (as indicated by frequency, duration, and severity measures) was significantly reduced by relaxation training alone, and by the combination of relaxation and biofeedback training, while biofeedback training alone appeared to be less effective than either of the other two treatment approaches (although the differences were not large).

Torticollis

Cleeland (1973) found that feedback of spasm was less effective in the treatment of torticollis than was a combination of feedback and shock administered as soon as a spasm was detected and continued for the duration of the spasm (the shock was administered to the finger, not the muscle involved in the spasm).

As pointed out earlier, this brief survey of comparative studies of the effectiveness of biofeedback in the treatment of various disorders of behavior is incomplete, representing a broad selection from the evidence available. The conclusion to be drawn is irresistible: so far, no firm evidence of a convincing kind has been forthcoming to suggest that biofeedback training is significantly superior in its remedial effects to alternative (and less costly) methods. The significance of this conclusion will be considered later.

Long-Term Effectiveness of Biofeedback

Even if biofeedback has not been shown to be more effective than other treatment approaches, its long-term effectiveness may be considerable, thus justifying its use. Very little evidence is available concerning the comparative long-term effectiveness of biofeedback, but a good deal of scattered (and largely unsatisfactory) information is available in which patients have been followed up for varying periods of time. The following survey is again intended to be representative, rather than complete.

Anxiety

The successful use of frontalis muscle training in the reduction of anxiety by Lavallée et al. (1977) was not sustained at follow-up 6 months later. Indeed, the no-treatment group in that study manifested less anxiety at follow-up than any of the three treated groups. Similarly, Gatchel et al. (1977) reported that the reduction in heart rate produced in speech-anxiety subjects by biofeedback training was not maintained at follow-up (1–2 months) and none of the groups reported any differential benefits of training.

Asthma

Kahn et al. (1973) had found that biofeedback training in bronchodilation produced strikingly beneficial effects over a 1-year follow-up period (compared with a control condition) in reducing emergency hospital visits, amount of medication, and number of asthmatic attacks. However, these results were not confirmed in a subsequent study by Kahn (1977) in that both treated and untreated asthmatic children showed similar reductions over the follow-up period in frequency, duration, and severity of asthmatic attacks, as well as being fairly similar in frequency of emergencies and number of hospital visits.

Headaches

Follow-up studies in the case of tension headaches suggest that improvements may be maintained to a significant degree. However, the length of follow-up has, with two exceptions, been quite short and the number of cases too small to enable confident conclusions to be drawn. Budzynski et al. (1973) found end-of-training treatment differences were maintained at a 3-month follow-up while 15 months later four of the six biofeedback-treated patients were reported to be still in an improved state. The only other long-term follow-up is that by

Kondo and Canter (1977), which extended over 1 year and also found that end-of-treatment differences were maintained. Montgomery and Ehrisman (1976) followed up the patients studied by McKenzie *et al*. (1974) for an unstated period and claimed that end-of-treatment improvements were maintained, accompanied by an increased ability to relax. Follow-up was, however, by questionnaire and only 13 of the 22 patients treated responded. In four other studies, maintenance of end-of-training improvements have been reported as maintained over relatively short follow-up periods (Cox *et al.*, 1975, 4 months; Epstein & Abel, 1977, 3 months; Haynes *et al.*, 1975a, 5–7 months; Hutchings & Reinking, 1976, 1 month).

In two studies of migraine, maintained improvements have been reported after follow-up periods of 1–2 months (Reading & Mohr, 1976) and 6 months (Mitch, McGrady, & Iannone, 1976), although the latter study was very inadequately reported. Positive results have also been reported in two studies involving migraine and tension headache patients as well as patients with both types of headache. Adler and Adler (1976) reported on a 5-year follow-up of the first 58 patients they treated with temperature training (migraine, mixed tension headache and migraine, and cluster headache) or muscle relaxation with feedback (tension headache). They reported that at the time of follow-up 42% of the patients had no or very occasional headaches while a further 44% had reduced the frequency of headaches by 75–90%. More success was obtained with the "pure" tension headache and migraine patients than with mixed or cluster headache patients. However, not only do Adler and Adler (1976) attribute their success to the combined (i.e., confounded, as far as evaluation of biofeedback is concerned) use of psychotherapy and biofeedback training, but their report is seriously deficient in quantitative material relevant to their conclusions. Medina, Diamond, and Franklin (1976) claimed that the patients (migraine or migraine and tension headache) they treated with finger temperature increase and frontalis muscle activity reduction, and who were improved at the end of treatment, maintained that improvement at a follow-up assessment of at least 6 months. However, their study is so full of confounding that it is impossible to assess the claim. Philips (1977), who treated patients with tension headaches or mixed tension-migraine headaches, found complicated and not particularly impressive results at the end of treatment and at a short-term follow-up 6–8 weeks later. Thus headache intensity was reduced in the biofeedback group at the end of treatment and somewhat more so at follow-up. On the other hand, headache frequency was hardly affected. Medication was not reduced in the biofeedback group at the end of the treatment but had declined significantly at the time of follow-up.

Thus, in spite of the number of studies of tension headaches and migraine where a follow-up was carried out, the results can hardly be described as very impressive even if the possibility that relaxation training without feedback might produce equal or better results is ignored.

Hypertension

The work of Patel, to which reference has already been made, is notable for the fact that a follow-up period of 1 year has usually been employed (Patel, 1975a, a follow-up of the work reported in Patel, 1973; Patel, 1975b; Patel & North, 1975) with maintenance of improvements at end-of-treatment supported by quantitative data. Unfortunately, these sustained improvements cannot be attributed to the effects of biofeedback training alone since general relaxation training was incorporated into the treatment procedures as well. Friedman and Taub (1977, 1978) reported that the superiority of hypnosis over biofeedback at the end of training was maintained throughout a 6-month follow-up period. In a small-scale but carefully conducted study, Kristt and Engel (1975) found that five hypertensive patients were able to increase and decrease systolic blood pressure. A follow-up assessment at 1 month and again at 3 months indicated a drop in baseline systolic blood pressure levels while the ability to control pressure was retained. Walsh *et al.* (1977) found that control of blood pressure in hypertensives was maintained at follow-up 1 year later, although no difference was apparent between patients trained with biofeedback and patients given general relaxation training.

Temporomandibular Joint Dysfunction Syndrome

Carlsson and Gale (1977) reported that 5 of 11 patients treated with masseter muscle activity reduction biofeedback training were totally symptom free at follow-up periods ranging from 4 to 12 months. However, this favorable outcome must be tempered by two facts: little relationship was found between outcome and ability to relax the masseter muscle during training, and some of the patients for whom the treatment was not successful proved unusually good at relaxing the masseter muscle and also had relatively low initial muscle tension. Dohrmann and Laskin (1978) conducted a very careful study of the effects of biofeedback training (masseter muscle activity reduction) compared with no treatment. End-of-treatment differences were found in favor of biofeedback, but at a 6-month follow-up all of the patients in both groups (with one exception) were symptom free, while at a 12-month follow-up similar results were found, except that two of the treated patients had required further treatment.

Other Group Studies

Brief mention may be made of a few studies in other areas relating to the long-term effectiveness of biofeedback training. In two studies, Lamontagne and his colleagues (Lamontagne, Beauséjour, Annable, & Tétreault, 1977; Lamontagne, Hand, Annable, & Gagnon, 1975) compared the effects of various kinds of biofeedback training (alpha enhancement, frontalis reduction) with irrelevant feedback, no-feedback control, and no treatment in changing soft-drug usage of college students (it should be noted that the students were not aware that the effect of the training on drug usage was being measured). At 6-month follow-up some reduction in drug usage was found, but the differential effects of treatment were relatively very small. Marked improvement as a result of treatment, maintained at follow-up, has been reported by Ayer and Levin (1973), who used massed practice to eliminate tooth grinding (follow-up period: 1 month); by Cleeland (1973), who used a combination of feedback and shock to treat torticollis (follow-up period: 1–40 months); and by Weiss and Engel (1971), who found that acquired control of heart rate in four patients with premature ventricular contractions was maintained for up to 21 months after the end of treatment. Reeves and Mealiea (1975) used biofeedback-assisted relaxation training to eliminate a fear of flying in three male subjects who were all flying without anxiety 1 year after the end of treatment. A less satisfactory result was reported by Freedman and Papsdorf (1976); the favorable changes produced by both biofeedback and relaxation training in reducing sleep onset time in insomnia were not sustained over a follow-up period as short as 2 months.

Individual Case Studies

Quite a number of individual case studies involving follow-up have been reported. A selection of these is summarized in Table 1. A number of points

Table 1. Follow-up Results in Individual Case Studies

Study	Abnormality	Follow-up	Outcome
Braud et al. (1975)	Hyperactivity	7 months	Gains maintained
Carlsson & Gale (1976)	TMJ syndrome	1 year	Symptom-free
Carlsson et al. (1975)	TMJ syndrome	6 months	Symptom-free
Finley (1976)	Seizures	6 months	Improved
Gatchel (1977)	Fear of injections	6 months	Improved
Le Boeuf (1976)	Severe tremor	6 months	Gains maintained
Levee et al. (1976)	Facial tension (musician)	6 months	Reemployed
Peck (1977)	Blepharospasm	4 months	Gains maintained
Reavley (1975)	Writer's cramp	8 months	Gains maintained
Reeves (1976)	Tension headache	6 months	Gains maintained

should be noted. All the studies report gains following treatment and maintenance of those gains at follow-up. But, of course, case studies are not very likely to be published unless they do eventuate in success so they are not in any way representative of the outcome of case studies in general. The studies vary considerably in degree of sophistication and the extent to which they could be regarded as rigorous in relation to attribution of the results to the biofeedback procedures used. Thus, the study by Finley (1976; a follow-up to the investigation of the same case reported by Finley, Smith, & Etherton, 1975) is extremely sophisticated and painstaking in its attempt to elucidate the factors responsible for the improvement, while Peck's (1977) study of a case of blepharospasm is also highly sophisticated.

Large-Scale Follow-Up Studies

Impressive results have been reported from the area of rehabilitation of physical function, where careful long-term follow-up of patients has been instituted. Basmajian *et al.* (1977) have summarized the results of their biofeedback treatment of patients with foot-drop ($n = 39$), shoulder subluxation ($n = 13$), and impaired hand function (n not stated). Brudny *et al.* (1976) have detailed their results with patients suffering from peripheral nerve injuries, spinal cord lesions, hemiparesis, and kindred disorders over follow-up periods varying from 3 months to 3 years, while Korein and Brudny (1976) have reported very satisfactory results with torticollis and dystonia patients followed up for as long as 4 years. Engel, Nikoomanesh, and Schuster (1974) reported equal favorable results in the treatment of daily fecal incontinence with biofeedback in six patients followed up for periods ranging from 6 months to 5 years, while a brief subsequent report by Cerulli, Nikoomanesh, and Schuster (1976) confirms these findings for 40 patients followed up for periods ranging from 4 months to 8 years, with an average follow-up period of 20 months. The work of Sargent, Walters, and Green (1973) on the application of autogenic and temperature training to the treatment of migraine headaches produced a follow-up report which claimed that 81% of the original patients showed improvement when assessed about 6 months after the end of treatment. However, no details of any kind were given to substantiate this claim.

Other Problems with Biofeedback

The doubts which must naturally arise as to the claims made for the clinical usefulness of biofeedback compared with alternative approaches as a result of the review of comparative and follow-up studies just concluded must be serious enough. However, the tale of woe is still incomplete. Many of the methodological and theoretical problems arising in relation to biofeedback, both as a fundamental research and as a clinical tool, have been raised for consideration at various points in this book and need not be reviewed here (see, for example, the recent critical article by Brown, 1977). Two points, however, merit special attention as they cast even more fundamental doubt on what biofeedback is all about than any of the material considered thus far.

The first point relates to one of the most fundamental assumptions underlying much of the clinical biofeedback work, namely, the specificity assumption which was considered in some detail in Chapter 7. The problem has recently been vividly illustrated by the work of Bakal and Kaganov (1977). To understand the importance of their results, it is necessary to reiterate briefly some points made earlier. It has been assumed that tension headaches are associated with excessively high levels of activity in the frontalis (and possibly neck) muscles; migraine headaches, on the other hand, have been assumed to be associated with either excessive dilation of the superficial cranial arteries (if prodromal symptoms are absent) or excessive constriction of the arteries, followed by excessive dilation (if prodromal symptoms are present). It has further been assumed that the appropriate biofeedback treatment for tension headaches involves feedback training in the control of frontalis muscle activity and that if by exercising the acquired control the patient can maintain frontalis activity at a low (and hopefully normal) level he will be able to reduce the frequency, duration, and severity of his tension headaches. On the other hand, it has been assumed that the appropriate treatment for migraine headaches involves training in voluntary control of blood flow and volume either in the peripheries (in earlier studies) or in the cranial arteries themselves (in more recent studies) and, likewise that the acquired ability to control constriction and dilation will enable the patient to reduce the frequency, duration, and severity of his migraine headaches. It has further been assumed that frontalis muscle activity reduction training would be inappropriate in the treatment of migraine headaches, and that it would be inappropriate to train patients with tension headaches to control constriction and dilation of the temporal arteries.

Early clinical studies, reviewed elsewhere in this book, appeared to offer some support for these assumptions but the evidence was never very strong—basic data were not collected to test the assumptions, and as has been observed repeatedly, successful reduction of tension headache activity was often uncorrelated with changes in frontalis muscle activity. Thus, the fundamental rationale for the biofeedback treatment of tension headaches and migraine headaches (not infrequently acclaimed as the major success areas of biofeedback) remained in doubt. The recent study by Bakal and Kaganov (1977) has completely undermined all of the assumptions indicated above. They measured the frontalis muscle activity levels of migraine, tension headache, and combined tension-headache/migraine patients in the resting, nonheadache state and while actually suffering a headache, and measured the actual changes in frontalis muscle activity level which occurred when frontalis muscle activity reduction training with biofeedback was provided for ten patients from the migraine and ten patients from the tension headache groups. They found that migraine and tension headache patients did not differ in the frequency with which various locations in the head and neck were involved, or in the intensities of the pain reported from each of these locations. Furthermore, both groups reported similar symptoms (such as throbbing headache, visual disturbances) equally often, the migraine patients being differentiated from the tension headache patients only in terms of reporting more occurrences of nausea and vomiting. Even more strikingly, they reported that the migraine headache patients had significantly higher levels of frontalis muscle activity than did the tension headache patients, both in headache-free periods and while a headache was actually in progress, and there was no significant increase in frontalis muscle activity during headache periods compared with nonheadache periods. When five patients from each group were provided with frontalis muscle activity reduction training with feedback, both groups were equally successful at reducing the muscle activity and both groups showed an equally significant decrease in headache activity.

The most parsimonious interpretation of all of these findings would be that a single dimension of headache is involved, with migraine simply being a more severe form of headache than tension headache and therefore manifesting some new symptomatology (such as nausea and visual disturbances). If this is the case, it would be predicted that migraine patients would be older than tension headache patients (since the dimension is essentially one of duration of the disorder) and that most patients, if adequately interrogated, would report a sequence involving tension headache characteristics initially with the additional symptoms said to characterize migraine developing later. Other interpretations are, of course, not ruled out. (For example, there might be a general factor common to all patients, with group factors common only to migraine patients on the one hand and tension headache patients on the other; or patients developing headaches early in life might always begin with tension headaches and move on to migraine headaches if severity increases, whereas patients who develop headaches only late in life might always begin with migraine symptoms.) It cannot be denied, however, that the results obtained by Bakal and Kaganov (1977) undermine some of the basic assumptions underlying biofeedback training.[1]

The second point to be made is a much more general one, but it is important and has received no attention whatever in the biofeedback literature. It is apparent as a result of the most superficial observation that the human organism consists of a very large number of vital functions (heart rate, breathing, biochemical balances, and so on *ad infinitum*) which must be regarded as being

---

[1]Bakal and Kaganov (1977) also measured blood flow velocity from the right and left superficial arteries but, for reasons unstated but which may be related to difficulties of data interpretation, did not provide evidence from this source relating to the various assumptions which have been mentioned.

under the finest and most delicately adjustable control imaginable, a control, furthermore, which is exercised automatically and of which the organism is unaware unless something goes wrong. Moreover, all of these control systems operate simultaneously and continuously. Yet with one or two relatively minor exceptions (such as the simultaneous independent control of heart rate and blood pressure increases and decreases) no success has been achieved (indeed, has scarcely been attempted) in training subjects to control more than one function at a time. Furthermore, in the area in which it would have been expected that very fine control with feedback would have been possible—muscle control—the results have been (with one exception, to be discussed later) ludicrously in-adequate when compared with the degree of control already possible by most subjects. The point is worth pursuing in a little more detail. It will be recalled that Dewan (1967) successfully trained three subjects to transmit Morse code signals representing letters of the alphabet by varying the characteristics of alpha activ-ity. This was an interesting and sensible endeavor for we do not usually attempt to transmit Morse code in this way. Consider, however, the analogous endeavor using muscle activity control. Presumably, one could train subjects to tense and relax muscle activity and also hold the self-induced level of tension for varying periods of time so that particular combinations of tension level and duration defined dots, dashes, and intervals between letters and words. It might be quite difficult for subjects to achieve this, yet it would probably be possible to shape the development of the skill so that smaller and smaller levels of tension and duration would define letters and intervals, and messages could be transmitted with great speed. But what would such a demonstration mean? For it is already the case that Morse code can be transmitted at great speed for appropriately trained persons using a Morse key—and clearly this skill involves fine muscle control on the part of the transmitter—finer control than could probably be achieved by any biofeedback training. We are faced with the paradox that biofeedback workers are attempting to train subjects in the control of muscle activity when those subjects already possess a very high degree of such control. An important distinction is involved here between movement control and muscle control. In transmitting Morse code signals (or playing the piano, or indulging in any other form of skill) we are dealing with and measuring the end product— behavior. The behavior is, of course, the result of the skilled coordination of many muscle groups but interest lies in the end product, not the activity of the muscle groups *per se*—not, at least, unless the investigator is a physiologist. It can be argued that the biofeedback researcher or clinician should be interested in the behavior which is mediated via muscle activity, rather than in the muscle activity itself—and indeed this has sometimes been the case, as in the measure-ment of range of movement in the ankle joint when retraining paralyzed or spastic muscles in the rehabilitation of physical function following cerebrovas-cular accidents. There is an interesting side effect to this point. Ankle joint movement is clearly dependent on the integration of the activity of several muscle groups. Likewise, the primary function of the frontalis muscle is to enable one to raise one's eyebrows or to frown—the equivalent of ankle joint movement. Once this is remembered, it becomes less surprising to find the relative lack of correlation between frontalis muscle activity levels and tension headache levels, either before or after treatment. It may, in other words, be the case that frontalis muscle activity has no bearing whatever on the understanding or treatment of tension headaches. This would represent a somewhat extreme view, of course, because there is no doubt that excessive muscle activity will produce reports of tension and fatigue in that muscle—but whether tension headaches do in fact reflect or represent the effects of excessive muscular tension is an issue yet to be resolved.

The crucial point being made here is that there appears to be a massive discrepancy between the degree of voluntary control achieved in biofeedback experiments and the extraordinary degree of simultaneous multifunction control already possible in the human organism. Nor does this discrepancy appear explainable by reference to a distinction between voluntary and involuntary control even though much of the control referred to is apparently exercised automatically, involuntarily, and without direct awareness.

The Other Side of the Coin: Positive Aspects of Biofeedback

The gloomy picture presented thus far in this chapter of the current status of biofeedback is offset, in part at least, by evidence which when properly interpreted shows the way out of the present unsatisfactory position. First and foremost among this evidence are the results obtained in studies of the voluntary control of single motor units (SMUs; see Chapter 3). Here we encounter yet another paradox, for while it has been a struggle to demonstrate voluntary control of gross muscle activity using surface electrodes, quite remarkably precise control of SMU activity has been achieved with the use of implanted electrodes. It may well be the case, of course, that precise control of SMU activity is achieved because the technique significantly reduces noise levels, whereas in the case of gross muscle activity the noise level is very high. It is merely necessary to note here, however, the discrepancy in the degree of control achieved with SMU as compared with gross muscle activity.

A second area in which very precise control has been achieved is in the otherwise rather barren area of electrical activity of the brain. The outstanding studies carried out by Mulholland and his colleagues on the control of alpha (see Chapter 5 for a review) contrast markedly with the doubtful control achieved in the more traditional alpha studies. Similarly, the ingenious study by Dewan (1967) on the transmission of Morse code by variations in alpha enhancement indicate how precise control of internal activities may be trained.

Mention should perhaps also be made here of the sophisticated approaches to the use of biofeedback training in helping deaf children to speak with correct flow and intonation (see Chapter 6), of the studies involving the teaching of facial expressions of emotion to blind people (see Chapter 6), and of the impressive results of biofeedback training with disabled people, to name but a few instances. The point can be sustained: there are areas in which real advances have been made using biofeedback techniques—advances which could not have been made by the use of alternative approaches such as general relaxation training. There are other areas, among them some which have helped to make the inflated reputation which biofeedback holds (or held until recently), in which a close look shows that the claims made on behalf of biofeedback simply cannot be sustained. How may the paradox be explained?

Biofeedback: Blunderbuss or Precision Tool?

In order to account for this extraordinary situation, and hopefully to indicate how it may be resolved, it is necessary to draw a parallel between what has happened in biofeedback and what happened in behavior modification. The latter therapeutic approach arose in part as a reaction against the application of the medical model to the explanation and treatment of disorders of behavior.[2] In the medical model, by analogy with procedures that had worked well with physical disorders, the aim was to arrive at a diagnosis which hopefully would have implications for etiology, treatment, and prognosis. Behavior therapists rejected this model because it seemed inappropriate to the explanation and remediation of disorders of behavior which were not diseases of the mind by analogy with diseases of the body but rather failures to adjust to society and other individuals. One particular aspect of this new approach stressed the importance of investigating the problem of the presenting client on an individual experimental basis by trying not to arrive at a diagnosis but at a behavioral analysis of the client's situation in life and then attempting to resolve the problems so discovered by also using experimental techniques to change the behavior of the client. In a very real sense, then, the aim was a precise control of the behavior of the individual client. The approach involved the use of theoretical constructs, and hypotheses derived from those constructs, involving predictions about how behavior would change under specified circumstances. Thus, the validity of the approach was not a function primarily of whether the "patient got better, stayed the same, or got worse," but rather whether the behavior of the client changed in the way predicted from the theory in precisely defined experimental (or, later, real-life) situations. Unfortunately, this prescription proved difficult to follow so that, ironically, it was not long before the medical model was being used to test the

[2]For a fuller account of the development and background of behavior modification (therapy), see Yates (1970, pp. 3–23).

comparative effectiveness of various forms of behavior therapy when set against more traditional methods of treatment. Thus, in several studies groups of phobic patients matched carefully on possibly confounding variables were allocated to various treatment conditions (one or more variants of behavior therapy, perhaps group psychotherapy, or control no treatment) and the effects of these treatments were compared on various measures (changes in strength of phobia, work history, sexual satisfaction, and so on) during and at the end of treatment and at various follow-up points, the criteria for differential success usually being the percentage of patients showing improvement on various measures. Such procedures represented a full swing of the circle back to the use of the very approaches which had originally led to the development of behavior therapy and which were utterly unsuited to the determination of the validity of behavior therapy.

It is being argued here that precisely the same fate has befallen biofeedback, particularly in the evaluation of its clinical usefulness. The reason for the failure of biofeedback training to show any consistent superiority over other relaxation training techniques stems from its use as a blunderbuss rather than as a rapier or precision instrument. Where it has been used as a precision instrument it has achieved outstanding success, as in the training in voluntary control of single motor unit activity and the careful clinical investigations of the rehabilitation of physical function. It has, however, suffered the fate of so many new approaches in psychology during the course of this century: overenthusiastic adoption by clinicians eager to add a new technique to their clinical armamentarium long before the experimental foundations and theory have been adequately developed to enable its use as a precision instrument rather than as a crude new weapon. Thus, as the title of this chapter indicates, biofeedback does indeed still remain a promise as yet unfulfilled. To fulfill that promise it is essential that biofeedback be developed as a precision tool, a development which will happen only when clinical psychologists realize that they have a responsibility to future as well as present clients and ensure that knowledge is advanced and not merely applied.

References

Adler, C. S., & Adler, S. M. Biofeedback psychotherapy for the treatment of headaches: A 5-year follow-up. *Headache*, 1976, *16*, 189–191.

Alexander, A. B. Systematic relaxation and flow rates in asthmatic children: Relationship to emotional precipitants and anxiety. *Journal of Psychosomatic Research*, 1972, *16*, 405–410.

Alexander, A. B., Miklich, D. R., & Hershkoff, H. The immediate effects of systematic relaxation training on peak expiratory flow rates in asthmatic children. *Psychosomatic Medicine*, 1972, *34*, 388–394.

Andreychuk, T., & Skriver, C. Hypnosis and biofeedback in the treatment of migraine headache. *International Journal of Clinical and Experimental Hypnosis*, 1975, *23*, 172–183. (1975/76:12)

Ayer, W. A., & Levin, M. P. Elimination of tooth grinding habits by massed practice therapy. *Journal of Periodontology*, 1973, *44*, 569–571.

Bakal, D. A., & Kaganov, J. A. Muscle contraction and migraine headache: Psychophysiologic comparison. *Headache*, 1977, *17*, 208–214.

Basmajian, J. V., Kukulka, C. G., Narayan, M. G., & Takebe, K. Biofeedback treatment of foot-drop after stroke compared with standard rehabilitation technique: Effects on voluntary control and strength. *Archives of Physical Medicine and Rehabilitation*, 1975, *56*, 231–236. (1975/76:56)

Basmajian, J. V., Regenos, E. M., & Baker, M. P. Rehabilitating stroke patients with biofeedback. *Geriatrics*, 1977, *32*, 85–88.

Beatty, J. Similar effects of feedback signals and instructional information on EEG activity. *Physiology and Behavior*, 1972, *9*, 151–154. (1972:19)

Beiman, I., Israel, E., & Johnson, S. A. During training and posttraining effects of live and taped extended progressive relaxation, self-relaxation and electromyogram biofeedback. *Journal of Consulting and Clinical Psychology*, 1978, *46*, 314–321.

Blanchard, E. B., & Epstein, L. H. The clinical usefulness of biofeedback. In M. Hersen, R. M. Eisler, & P. M. Miller (Eds.), *Progress in behavior modification* (Vol. 4). New York: Academic, 1977, pp. 163–250.

Blanchard, E. B., & Young, L. D. Self-control of cardiac functioning: A promise as yet unfulfilled. *Psychological Bulletin*, 1973, *79*, 145–163. (1973:30)

Blanchard, E. B., & Young, L. D. Clinical applications of biofeedback training: A review of evidence. *Archives of General Psychiatry*, 1974, *30*, 573–589. (1974:1)

Braud, L. W. The effects of frontal EMG biofeedback and progressive relaxation upon hyperactivity and its behavioral concomitants. *Biofeedback and Self-Regulation*, 1978, *3*, 69–89.

Braud, W. G., & Wood, R. The influence of immediate feedback on free-response GESP performance during ganzfeld stimulation. *Journal of the American Society for Psychical Research*, 1977, *71*, 409–427.

Braud, L. W., Lupin, M. N., & Braud, W. G. The use of electromyographic biofeedback in the control of hyperactivity. *Journal of Learning Disabilities*, 1975, *8*, 420–425.

Brown, B. B. Critique of biofeedback concepts and methodologies. In J. I. Martin (Ed.), *Proceedings of the San Diego biomedical symposium* (Vol. 16). New York: Academic, 1977, pp. 187–192.

Brudny, J., Korein, J., Grynbaum, B. B., Friedmann, L. W., Weinstein, S., Sachs-Frankel, G., & Belandres, P. V. EMG feedback therapy: Review of treatment of 114 patients. *Archives of Physical Medicine and Rehabilitation*, 1976, *57*, 55–61. (1976/77:3)

Budzynski, T. Tuning in on the twilight zone. *Psychology Today*, 1977, *11*, 38–44.

Budzynski, T., Stoyva, J., & Adler, C. Feedback-induced muscle relaxation: Application to tension headache. *Journal of Behavior Therapy and Experimental Psychiatry*, 1970, *1*, 205–211. (1970:31)

Budzynski, T. H., Stoyva, J. M., Adler, C. S., & Mullaney, D. M. EMG biofeedback and tension headache: A controlled outcome study. *Psychosomatic Medicine*, 1973, *35*, 484–496. (1973:19)

Canter, A., Kondo, C. Y., & Knott, J. R. A comparison of EMG feedback and progressive muscle relaxation training in anxiety neurosis. *British Journal of Psychiatry*, 1975, *127*, 470–477. (1976/77:44)

Carlsson, S. G., & Gale, E. N. Biofeedback treatment for muscle pain associated with the temporomandibular joint. *Journal of Behavior Therapy and Experimental Psychiatry*, 1976, *7*, 383–385.

Carlsson, S. G., & Gale, E. N. Biofeedback in the treatment of long-term temporomandibular joint pain. *Biofeedback and Self-Regulation*, 1977, *2*, 161–171.

Carlsson, S. G., Gale, E. N., & Ohman, A. Treatment of temporomandibular joint syndrome with biofeedback training. *Journal of the American Dental Association*, 1975, *91*, 602–605.

Cerulli, M., Nikoomanesh, P., & Schuster, M. M. Progress in biofeedback treatment of fecal incontinence. *Gastroenterology*, 1976, *70*, 869.

Chesney, M. A., & Shelton, J. L. A comparison of muscle relaxation and electromyogram biofeedback treatments for muscle contraction headache. *Journal of Behavior Therapy and Experimental Psychiatry*, 1976, *7*, 221–225. (1976/77:13)

Cleeland, C. S. Behavior technics in the modification of spasmodic torticollis. *Neurology*, 1973, *23*, 1241–1247. (1973:23)

Coursey, R. D. Electromyograph feedback as a relaxation technique. *Journal of Consulting and Clinical Psychology*, 1975, *43*, 825–834. (1975/76:19)

Cox, D. J., Freundlich, A., & Meyer, R. G. Differential effectiveness of electromyograph feedback, verbal relaxation instructions, and medication placebo with tension headaches. *Journal of Consulting and Clinical Psychology*, 1975, *43*, 892–898. (1975/76:15)

Davis, M. H., Saunders, D. R., Creer, T. L., & Chai, H. Relaxation training by biofeedback apparatus as a supplemental treatment in bronchial asthma. *Journal of Psychosomatic Research*, 1973, *17*, 121–128. (1974:52)

Dewan, E. M. Occipital alpha rhythm, eye position, and lens accommodation. *Nature*, 1967, *214*, 975–977. (R:38)

Dohrmann, R. J., & Laskin, D. M. An evaluation of electromyographic biofeedback in the treatment of myofascial pain-dysfunction syndrome. *Journal of the American Dental Association*, 1978, *96*, 656–662.

Engel, B. T., Nikoomanesh, P., & Schuster, M. M. Operant conditioning of rectosphincteric responses in the treatment of fecal incontinence. *New England Journal of Medicine*, 1974, *290*, 646–649. (1974:38)

Epstein, L. H., & Abel, G. G. An analysis of biofeedback training effects for tension headache patients. *Behavior Therapy*, 1977, *8*, 37–47.

Finley, W. W. Effects of sham feedback following successful SMR training in an epileptic: Follow-up study. *Biofeedback and Self-Regulation*, 1976, *1*, 227–235.

Finley, W. W., Smith, H. A., & Etherton, M. D. Reduction of seizures and normalization of the EEG in a severe epileptic following sensorimotor biofeedback training: Preliminary study. *Biological Psychology*, 1975, *2*, 189–203. (1975/76:48)

Freedman, R., & Papsdorf, J. D. Biofeedback and progressive relaxation treatment of sleep-onset insomnia: A controlled, all-night investigation. *Biofeedback and Self-Regulation*, 1976, *1*, 253–271.

Friedman, H., & Taub, H. A. The use of hypnosis and biofeedback procedures for essential hypertension. *International Journal of Clinical and Experimental Hypnosis*, 1977, *25*, 335–347.

Friedman, H., & Taub, H. A. A six-month follow-up of the use of hypnosis and biofeedback procedures in essential hypertension. *American Journal of Clinical Hypnosis*, 1978, *20*, 184–188.

Gatchel, R. J. Therapeutic effectiveness of voluntary heart rate control in reducing anxiety. *Journal of Consulting and Clinical Psychology*, 1977, *45*, 689–691.

Gatchel, R. J., Hatch, J. P., Watson, P. J., Smith, D., & Gaas, E. Comparative effectiveness of voluntary heart rate control and muscular relaxation as active coping skills for reducing speech anxiety. *Journal of Consulting and Clinical Psychology*, 1977, *45*, 1093–1100.

Haynes, S. N., Griffin, P., Mooney, D., & Parise, M. Electromyographic biofeedback and relaxation instructions in the treatment of muscle contraction headaches. *Behavior Therapy*, 1975, *6*, 672–678. (1975/76:16)

Haynes, S. N., Moseley, D., & McGowan, W. T. Relaxation training and biofeedback in the reduction of frontalis muscle tension. *Psychophysiology*, 1975, *12*, 547–552. (1975/76:17)

Haynes, S. N., Sides, H., & Lockwood, G. Relaxation instructions and frontalis electromyographic feedback intervention with sleep-onset insomnia. *Behavior Therapy*, 1977, *8*, 644–652.

Honorton, C., & Carbone, M. A preliminary study of feedback-augmented EEG alpha activity and ESP card-guessing performance. *Journal of the American Society for Psychical Research*, 1971, *65*, 66–74.

Honorton, C., Davidson, R., & Bindler, P. Feedback-augmented EEG alpha, shifts in subjective state, and ESP card-guessing performance. *Journal of the American Society for Psychical Research,* 1971, *65,* 308–323.

Hutchings, D. F., & Reinking, R. H. Tension headaches: What form of therapy is most effective? *Biofeedback and Self-Regulation,* 1976, *1,* 183–190. (1976/77:12)

Jacobs, A., & Felton, G. S. Visual feedback of myoelectric output to facilitate muscle relaxation in normal persons and patients with neck injuries. *Archives of Physical Medicine and Rehabilitation,* 1969, *50,* 34–39.

Kahn, A. U. Effectiveness of biofeedback and counter-conditioning in the treatment of bronchial asthma. *Journal of Psychosomatic Research,* 1977, *21,* 97–104.

Kahn, A. U., Staerk, M., & Bonk, C. Role of counterconditioning in the treatment of asthma. *Journal of Asthma Research,* 1973, *11,* 57–62.

Kondo, C., & Canter, A. True and false electromyographic feedback: Effect on tension headache. *Journal of Abnormal Psychology,* 1977, *86,* 93–95.

Korein, J., & Brudny, J. Integrated EMG feedback in the management of spasmodic torticollis and focal dystonia: A prospective study of 80 patients. In M. D. Yahr (Ed.), *The basal ganglia.* New York: Raven Press, 1976, pp. 385–424.

Kotses, H., Glaus, K. D., Crawford, P. L., Edwards, J. E., & Scherr, M. S. Operant reduction of frontalis EMG activity in the treatment of asthma in children. *Journal of Psychosomatic Research,* 1976, *20,* 453–459.

Kotses, H., Glaus, K. D., Bricel, S. K., Edwards, J. E., & Crawford, P. L. Operant muscular relaxation and peak expiratory flow rate in asthmatic children. *Journal of Psychosomatic Research,* 1978, *22,* 17–23.

Kristt, D. A., & Engel, B. T. Learned control of blood pressure in patients with high blood pressure. *Circulation,* 1975, *51,* 370–378. (1975/76:43)

Lamontagne, Y., Hand, I., Annable, L., & Gagnon, M.-A. Physiological and psychological effects of alpha and EMG feedback training with college drug users: A pilot study. *Canadian Psychiatric Association Journal,* 1975, *20,* 337–349.

Lamontagne, Y., Beauséjour, R., Annable, L., & Tétreault, L. Alpha and EMG feedback training in the prevention of drug abuse. *Canadian Psychiatric Association Journal,* 1977, *22,* 301–310.

Lavallée, Y.-J., Lamontagne, Y., Pinard, G., Annable, L., & Tétreault, L. Effects of EMG feedback, diazepam and their combination on chronic anxiety. *Journal of Psychosomatic Research,* 1977, *21,* 65–71.

Le Boeuf, A. The treatment of a severe tremor by electromyogram feedback. *Journal of Behavior Therapy and Experimental Psychiatry,* 1976, *7,* 59–61.

Letourneau, J. E. Application of biofeedback and behavior modification techniques in visual training. *Journal of Optometry and Physiological Optics,* 1976, *53,* 187–190.

Levee, J. R., Cohen, M. J., & Rickles, W. H. Electromyographic biofeedback for relief of tension in the facial and throat muscles of a woodwind musician. *Biofeedback and Self-Regulation,* 1976, *1,* 113–120.

McKenzie, R. E., Ehrisman, W. J., Montgomery, P. S., & Barnes, R. H. The treatment of headache by means of electroencephalographic biofeedback. *Headache,* 1974, *13,* 164–172.

Medina, J. L., Diamond, S., & Franklin, M. A. Biofeedback therapy for migraine. *Headache,* 1976, *16,* 115–118.

Mitch, P. S., McGrady, A., & Iannone, A. Autogenic feedback training in migraine: A treatment report. *Headache,* 1976, *15,* 267–270.

Montgomery, P. S., & Ehrisman, W. J. Biofeedback-alleviated headaches: A follow-up. *Headache,* 1976, *16,* 64–65.

Mullinix, J. M., Norton, B. J., Hack, S., & Fishman, M. A. Skin temperature biofeedback and migraine. *Headache,* 1978, *17,* 242–244.

Ohno, Y., Tanaka, Y., Takeya, T., & Ikemi, Y. Modification of skin temperature by biofeedback procedures. *Journal of Behavior Therapy and Experimental Psychiatry,* 1977, *8,* 31–34.

Ohno, Y., Tanaka, Y., Takeya, T., Matsubara, H., Kuriya, N., & Komemushi, S. Biofeedback modification of frontal EMG in normal subjects. *Biofeedback and Self-Regulation*, 1978, *3*, 61–68.

Patel, C. H. Yoga and biofeedback in the management of hypertension. *Lancet*, 1973, *2*, 1053–1055. (1973:27)

Patel, C. Twelve-month follow-up of yoga and bio-feedback in the management of hypertension. Lancet, 1975, *1*, 62–64. (a) (1975/76: 8)

Patel, C. Yoga and biofeedback in the management of hypertension. *Journal of Psychosomatic Research*, 1975, *19*, 355–360. (b)

Patel, C. Yoga and biofeedback in the management of "stress" in hypertensive patients. *Clinical Science and Molecular Medicine*, 1975, *48*, 171–174. (c) (Suppl.)

Patel, C. Reduction of serum cholesterol and blood pressure in hypertensive patients by behavior modification. *Journal of the Royal College of General Practitioners: British Journal of General Practice*, 1976, *26*, 211–215.

Patel, C., & Carruthers, M. Coronary risk factor reduction through biofeedback-aided relaxation and meditation. *Journal of the Royal College of General Practitioners: British Journal of General Practice*, 1977, *27*, 401–405.

Patel, C., & Datey, K. K. Relaxation and biofeedback techniques in the management of hypertension. *Angiology*, 1976, *27*, 106–113.

Patel, C., & North, W. R. S. Randomized controlled trial of yoga and biofeedback in the management of hypertension. *Lancet*, 1975, *2*, 93–95.

Peck, D. F. The use of EMG feedback in the treatment of a severe case of blepharospasm. *Biofeedback and Self-Regulation*, 1977, *2*, 273–277.

Philips, C. The modification of tension headache pain using EMG biofeedback. *Behavior Research and Therapy*, 1977, *15*, 119–129.

Price, K. P., & Tursky, B. Vascular reactivity of migraineurs and nonmigraineurs: A comparison of responses to self-control procedures. *Headache*, 1976, *16*, 210–217.

Reading, C., & Mohr, P. D. Biofeedback control of migraine: A pilot study. *British Journal of Social and Clinical Psychology*, 1976, *15*, 429–433.

Reavley, W. The use of biofeedback in the treatment of writer's cramp. *Journal of Behavior Therapy and Experimental Psychiatry*, 1975, 6, 335–338.

Reeves, J. L. EMG-biofeedback reduction of tension headache: A cognitive skills training approach. *Biofeedback and Self-Regulation*, 1976, *1*, 217–225.

Reeves, J. L., & Mealiea, W. L. Biofeedback-assisted, cue-controlled relaxation for the treatment of flight phobias. *Journal of Behavior Therapy and Experimental Psychiatry*, 1975, *6*, 105–109.

Reinking, R. H., & Kohl, M. L. Effects of various forms of relaxation training on physiological and self-report measures of relaxation. *Journal of Consulting and Clinical Psychology*, 1975, *43*, 595–600. (1975/76:21)

Sargent, J. D., Walters, E. D., & Green, E. E. Psychosomatic self-regulation of migraine headaches. *Seminars in Psychiatry*, 1973, *5*, 415–428.

Schandler, S. L., & Grings, W. G. An examination of methods of producing relaxation during short-term laboratory sessions. *Behavior Research and Therapy*, 1976, *14*, 419–426. (1976/77:5)

Shoemaker, J. E., & Tasto, D. L. The effects of muscle relaxation on blood pressure of essential hypertensives. *Behavior Research and Therapy*, 1975, *13*, 29–43. (1975/76:42)

Sime, W. E., & DeGood, D. E. Effect of EMG biofeedback and progressive muscle relaxation training on awareness of frontalis muscle tension. *Psychophysiology*, 1977, *14*, 522–530.

Townsend, R. E., House, J. F., & Addario, D. A comparison of biofeedback-mediated relaxation and group therapy in the treatment of chronic anxiety. *American Journal of Psychiatry*, 1975, *132*, 598–601. (1976/77:43)

Venturino, M. An investigation of the relationship between EEG alpha activity and ESP performance. *Journal of the American Society for Psychical Research*, 1978, *72*, 141–152.

Walsh, P., Dale, A., & Anderson, D. E. Comparison of biofeedback pulse wave velocity and progressive relaxation in essential hypertensives. *Perceptual and Motor Skills,* 1977, *44,* 839– 843.

Weiss, T., & Engel, B. T. Operant conditioning of heart rate patients with premature ventricular contractions. *Psychosomatic Medicine,* 1971, *33,* 301–321. (1971:36)

White, T. W., Holmes, D. S., & Bennett, D. H. Effects of instructions, biofeedback, and cognitive activities on heart rate control. *Journal of Experimental Psychology (Human Learning and Memory),* 1977, *3,* 477–484.

Yates, A. J. *Behavior therapy.* New York: Wiley, 1970.

Index